The Green Guide

J.-P. Lescouret/PIX

French Riviera

Travel Publications

Hannay House, 39 Clarendon Road
Watford, Herts WD17 1JA, UK
☎ (01923) 205 240 - Fax (01923) 205 241
www.ViaMichelin.com
TheGreenGuide-uk@uk.michelin.com

Manufacture française des pneumatiques Michelin
Société en commandite par actions au capital de 304 000 000 EUR
Place des Carmes-Déchaux – 63 Clermont-Ferrand (France)
R.C.S. Clermont-Fd B 855 200 507

© Michelin et Cie, Propriétaires-éditeurs, 2001
Dépôt légal 2001 – ISBN 2-06-000092-0 – ISSN 0763-1383
Printed in France 11-01/4.3

Typesetting: Le Sanglier, Charleville-Mézières
Printing: Aubin, Ligugé
Binding: Aubin, Ligugé

Cover design: Carré Noir, Paris 17ᵉ arr.

THE GREEN GUIDE
Spirit of Discovery

Leisure time spent with The Green Guide is also a time for refreshing your spirit, enjoying yourself, and taking advantage of our selection of fine restaurants, hotels and other places for relaxing: immerse yourself in the local culture, discover new horizons, experience the local lifestyle. The Green Guide opens the door for you.

Each year our writers go touring: visiting the sights, devising the driving tours, identifying the highlights, selecting the most attractive hotels and restaurants, checking the routes for the maps and plans.

Each title is compiled with great care, giving you the benefit of regular revisions and Michelin's first-hand knowledge. The Green Guide responds to changing circumstances and takes account of its readers' suggestions; all comments are welcome.

Share with us our enthusiasm for travel, which has led us to discover over 60 destinations in France and other countries. Like us, let yourself be guided by the desire to explore, which is the best motive for travel: the spirit of discovery.

Contents

S. Sauvignier/MICHELIN

Green, the pines of Porquerolles

S. Sauvignier/MICHELIN

Red, the rose petals of Grasse

Sights

Yellow, this façade in Nice

Blue, the sea and sky at St-Jean-Cap-Ferrat

Maps and plans

Companion publications

Motorists who plan ahead will always have the appropriate maps at hand. Michelin products are complementary: for each of the sites listed in The Green Guide, map references are indicated which help you find your location on our range of maps. The image below shows the maps to use for each geographic area covered in this guide.

To travel the roads in this region, you may use any of the following:

• the **regional map** at a scale of 1:200 000 no 245, which covers the main roads and secondary roads, and includes useful indications for finding tourist attractions. This is a good map to choose for travelling in a wide area. At a quick glance, you can locate and identify the main sights to see. In addition to identifying the nature of the road ways, the map shows castles, churches and other religious edifices, scenic view points, megalithic monuments, swimming beaches on lakes and rivers, swimming pools, golf courses, race tracks, air fields, and more. You may also consult Michelin map no 84, La Côte d'Azur.

• the **detailed maps** are based on the regional map data, but with a reduced format (about half a region), which makes them easier to consult and fold. These maps are recommended for tourists who plan to stay within a limited area, without travelling far. For the Riviera, use maps 114 (Var) and 115 (Alpes-Maritmes).

• **departmental maps** (at a scale of 1:150 000, an enlargement of the 1:200 000 maps). These maps are very easy to read, and make it easy to travel on all of the roads in the following departments: Var (4083) and Alpes-Maritime (4006). They come with a complete index of place names and include a plan of the towns which serve as administrative seats (préfectures).

And remember to travel with the latest edition of the map of France no 989, which gives an overall view of the region of Provence, and the main access roads which connect it to the rest of France. The entire country is mapped at a 1:1 000 000 scale and clearly shows the main road network.

Michelin is pleased to offer a route-planning service on the Internet: **www.ViaMichelin.com.** Choose the shortest route, a route without tolls, or the Michelin recommended route to your destination; you can also access information about hotels and restaurants from The Red Guide, and tourist sites from The Green Guide.

There are a number of useful maps and plans in the guide, listed on the following page.

Bon voyage!

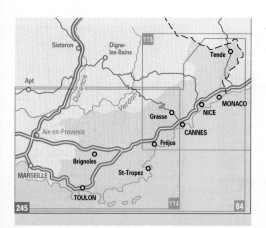

Thematic maps

Town plans

Monuments and sites

Local maps for touring

Key

Selected monuments and sights

⊚ ⇒ Tour - Departure point

Catholic church

Protestant church, other temple

Synagogue - Mosque

Building

Statue, small building

Calvary, wayside cross

Fountain

Rampart - Tower - Gate

Château, castle, historic house

Ruins

Dam

Factory, power plant

Fort

Cave

Prehistoric site

Viewing table

Viewpoint

Other place of interest

Special symbol

Beach

Sports and recreation

Racecourse

Skating rink

Outdoor, indoor swimming pool

Marina, sailing centre

Trail refuge hut

Cable cars, gondolas

Funicular, rack railway

Tourist train

Recreation area, park

Theme, amusement park

Wildlife park, zoo

Gardens, park, arboretum

Bird sanctuary, aviary

Walking tour, footpath

Of special interest to children

Abbreviations

A Agricultural office (Chambre d'agriculture)

C Chamber of Commerce (Chambre de commerce)

H Town hall (Hôtel de ville)

J Law courts (Palais de justice)

M Museum (Musée)

P Local authority offices (Préfecture, sous-préfecture)

POL. Police station (Police)

Police station (Gendarmerie)

T Theatre (Théatre)

U University (Université)

	Sight	Seaside resort	Winter sports resort	Spa
Highly recommended ★★★	★★★	⌂⌂⌂	✳✳✳	⧫⧫⧫
Recommended ★★	★★	⌂⌂	✳✳	⧫⧫
Interesting ★	★	⌂	✳	⧫

Additional symbols

🛈		Tourist information
═══	═══	Motorway or other primary route
➊	➊	Junction: complete, limited
⊨══⊨	══	Pedestrian street
⊥ = = = ⊥		Unsuitable for traffic, street subject to restrictions
⊔⊔⊔⊔	- - - -	Steps - Footpath
🚂	🚋	Train station - Auto-train station
🚌	S.N.C.F.	Coach (bus) station
┅┅┅		Tram
⌒		Metro, underground
P.R.		Park-and-Ride
♿		Access for the disabled
⊗		Post office
☎		Telephone
⬚		Covered market
⋅✕⋅		Barracks
△		Drawbridge
℧		Quarry
⚒		Mine
B	F	Car ferry (river or lake)
⛴		Ferry service: cars and passengers
⛵		Foot passengers only
③		Access route number common to Michelin maps and town plans
Bert (R.)...		Main shopping street
AZ B		Map co-ordinates

Hotels and restaurants

20 rooms: 38,57/57,17€	Number of rooms: price for one person/ double room
half-board or full board: 42,62€	Price per person, based on double occupancy
⊃ 6,85€	Price of breakfast; when not given, it is included in the price of the room (i.e., for bed-and-breakfasts)
120 sites: 12,18€	Number of camp sites and cost for 2 people with a car
12,18€ lunch- 16,74/38,05€	Restaurant: fixed-price menus served at lunch only- mini/maxi price fixed menu (lunch and dinner) or à la carte
rest. 16,74/38,05€	Lodging where meals are served mini/maxi price fixed menu or à la carte
meal 15,22€	"Family style" meal
reserv	Reservation recommended
⊘	No credit cards accepted
P	Reserved parking for hotel patrons

The prices correspond to the higher rates of the tourist season

Principal sights

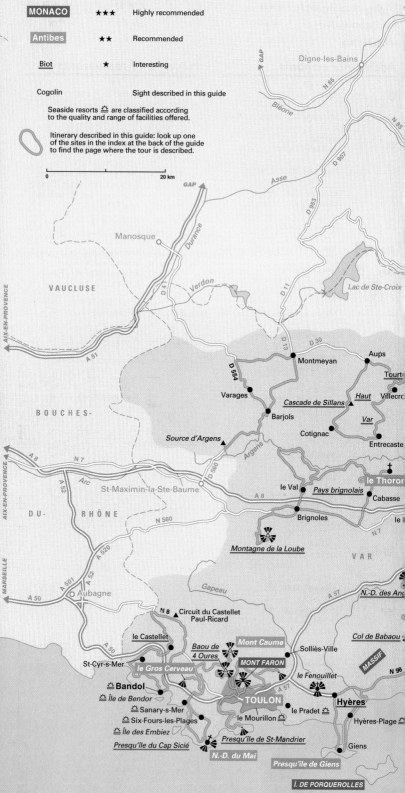

MONACO ★★★ Highly recommended

Antibes ★★ Recommended

Biot ★ Interesting

Cogolin Sight described in this guide

Seaside resorts ⚓ are classified according to the quality and range of facilities offered.

Itinerary described in this guide: look up one of the sites in the index at the back of the guide to find the page where the tour is described.

0   20 km

BRIANÇO

Digne-les-Bains

Bléone

Asse

GAP

N 85

N 85

D 907

D 953

Manosque

Durance

VAUCLUSE

Verdon

D 4

Lac de Ste-Croix

AIX-EN-PROVENCE

D 11

BOUCHES-

A 51

D 554

Montmeyan

Aups

Tourt

D 30

D 13

Varages

Cascade de Sillans

Haut

Villecro

Barjols

Var

Source d'Argens

Cotignac

Entrecaste

A 8

N 7

Argens

D 560

St-Maximin-la-Ste-Baume

le Val

Pays brignolais

le Thoror

†

Cabasse

DU-

RHÔNE

Arc

A 52

N 560

Brignoles

le

MARSEILLE

A 520

Montagne de la Loube

VAR

A 50

A 501

Gapeau

A 57

N.-D. des Ang

Aubagne

N 8

Circuit du Castellet
Paul-Ricard

Col de Babaou

le Castellet

Baou de
4 Oures

Mont Caume

Solliès-Ville

MASSIF

N 98

St-Cyr-s-Mer

le Gros Cerveau

MONT FARON

le Fenouillet

Bandol

Île de Bendor

TOULON

le Pradet

Hyères

Sanary-s-Mer

le Mourillon

Hyères-Plage

Six-Fours-les-Plages

Île des Embiez

Presqu'île de St-Mandrier

Giens

Presqu'île du Cap Sicié

N.-D. du Mai

Presqu'île de Giens

Î. DE PORQUEROLLES

ÎLES

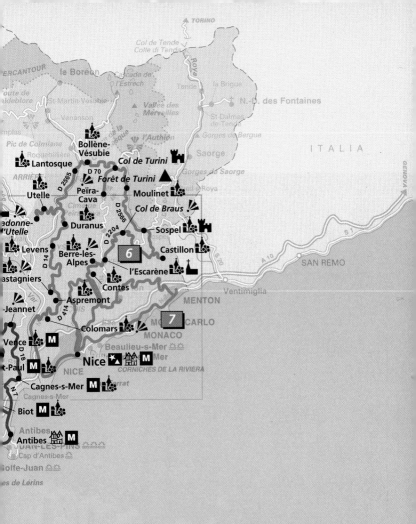

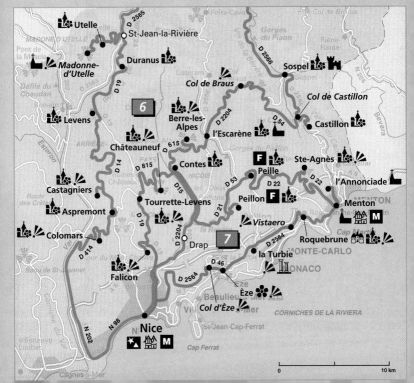

Nice by night

Practical
information

Planning your trip

Useful addresses

INTERNET

www.ambafrance-us.org
The French Embassy in the USA has a Website providing basic information (geography, demographics, history), a news digest and business-related information. It offers special pages for children, and pages devoted to culture, language study and travel, and you can reach other selected French sites (regions, cities, ministries) with a hypertext link.

www.franceguide.com
The French Government Tourist Office / Maison de la France site is packed with practical information and tips for those travelling to France. The home page has a number of links to more specific guidance, for American or Canadian travellers for example, or to the FGTO's London pages.

www.FranceKeys.com
This sight has plenty of practical information for visiting France. It covers all regions, with links to tourist offices and related sites. Very useful for planning the details of your tour across France!

www.fr-holidaystore.co.uk
The French Travel Centre in London has gone on-line with this service, providing information on all French regions, including updated special travel offers and details on available accommodation.

www.visiteurope.com
The European Travel Commission provides useful information on travelling to and around 27 European countries, and includes links to some commercial booking services (ie vehicle hire), rail schedules, weather reports and more.

FRENCH TOURIST OFFICES

For information, brochures, maps and assistance in planning a trip to France travellers should apply to the official French Tourist Office in their own country:

Australia – New Zealand
Sydney – BNP Building, 12 Castlereagh Street, Sydney, New South Wales 2000
☎ (02) 9231 5244 – Fax: (02) 9221 8682.

Canada
Montreal – 1981 Avenue McGill College, Suite 490, Montreal PQ H3A 2W9
☎ (514) 288-4264 – Fax: (514) 845 4868.
Toronto – 30 St Patrick's Street, Suite 700, Toronto, Ontario
☎ (416) 979 7587.

Eire
Dublin – 10 Suffolk Street, Dublin 2
☎ (01) 679 0813 – Fax: (01) 679 0814.

South Africa
P.O. Box 41022, Craig Hall 2024,
☎ (011) 880 8062.

United Kingdom
London – 178 Piccadilly, London WIV 0AL
☎ (0891) 244 123 – Fax: (0171) 493 6594.

United States
East Coast – New York – 444 Madison Avenue, 16th Floor, NY 10022-6903,
☎ (212) 838-7800 – Fax: (212) 838-7855.
Mid West – Chicago – 676 North Michigan Avenue, Suite 3360, Chicago, IL 60611-2819.
☎ (312) 751-7800 – Fax: (312) 337-6339.
West Coast – Los Angeles – 9454 Wilshire Boulevard, Suite 715, Beverly Hills, CA 90212-2967.
☎ (310) 271-6665 – Fax: (310) 276-2835.
Information can also be requested from **France on Call**,
☎ (202) 659-7779.

LOCAL TOURIST OFFICES

Visitors may also contact local tourist offices for more detailed information, to receive brochures and maps. The addresses and telephone numbers of tourist offices in the larger towns are listed after the symbol 🖻, in the *Admission times and charges* section at the end of the guide. Below, the addresses are given for local tourist offices of the *départements* and *régions* covered in this guide. The index lists the *département* after each town.

- **Comité Régional du Tourisme de Provence-Alpes-Côte d'Azur** – Espace Colbert, 14 Rue Sainte-Barbe 13001 Marseille ☎ 04 91 39 38 00.
- **Comité Régional du Tourisme Riviera-Côte d'Azur** – 55 Promenade des Anglais, BP 602, 06011 Nice Cedex 1 ☎ 04 93 37 78 78.
- **Comité Départemental du Tourisme du Var** – 1 Boulevard Foch, BP 99, 83003 Draguignan Cedex ☎ 04 94 68 58 33 and 5 Avenue Vauban, BP 5147, 83000 Toulon ☎ 04 94 09 00 69.
- **Office de Tourisme et des Congrès de la Principauté de Monaco** – 2A Boulevard des Moulins, 98000 Monaco ☎ 04 93 50 60 88.
- **Fédération Départementale des Offices de Tourisme et Syndicats d'Initiative des Alpes-Maritimes** – 2 Rue Deloye, 06000 Nice.
- **Parc Naturel National du Mercantour** – 23 Rue d'Italie, 06000 Nice ☎ 04 93 87 86 10.
- **Parc Naturel National de Port-Cros** – Castel Ste-Claire, Rue Ste-Claire, 83400 Hyères ☎ 04 94 65 32 98.
- **Fédération Nationale des Comités Départementaux de Tourisme**, 2 Rue Linois, 75015 Paris ☎ 01 45 75 62 16.

Tourist Information Centres – **The Red Guide France** gives the addresses and telephone numbers of the Tourist Information Centres *(Syndicats d'Initiative)* to be found in most large towns and many tourist resorts. They can supply large-scale town plans, timetables and information on local entertainment, accommodation, sports and sightseeing.

EMBASSIES AND CONSULATES IN France

Australia	Embassy	4 Rue Jean-Rey, 75015 Paris ☎ 01 40 59 33 00 – Fax: 01 40 59 33 10.
Canada	Embassy	35 Avenue Montaigne, 75008 Paris ☎ 01 44 43 29 00 – Fax: 01 44 43 29 99.
Eire	Embassy	4 Rue Rude, 75016 Paris ☎ 01 44 17 67 00 – Fax: 01 44 17 67 60.
New Zealand	Embassy	7 ter Rue Léonard-de-Vinci, 75016 Paris ☎ 01 45 01 43 43 – Fax: 01 45 01 43 44.
South Africa	Embassy	59 Quai d'Orsay, 75007 Paris ☎ 01 53 59 23 23 – Fax: 01 53 59 23 33
UK	Embassy	35 Rue du Faubourg St-Honoré, 75008 Paris ☎ 01 44 51 31 00 – Fax: 01 44 51 31 27.
	Consulate	16 Rue d'Anjou, 75008 Paris ☎ 01 44 51 31 01 (visas).
USA	Embassy	2 Avenue Gabriel, 75008 Paris ☎ 01 43 12 22 22 – Fax: 01 42 66 97 83.
	Consulate	2 Rue St-Florentin, 75001 Paris ☎ 01 42 96 14 88.
	Consulate	15 Avenue d'Alsace, 67082 Strasbourg ☎ 03 88 35 31 04 – Fax: 03 88 24 06 95.

Formalities

DOCUMENTS

Passport – Nationals of countries within the European Union entering France need only a national identity card. Nationals of other countries must be in possession of a valid national **passport**. In case of loss or theft, report to your embassy or consulate and the local police.

Visa – No **entry visa** is required for Canadian, US or Australian citizens travelling as tourists and staying less than 90 days, except for students planning to study in France. If you think you may need a visa, apply to your local French Consulate.
US citizens should obtain the booklet *Safe Trip Abroad*, which provides useful information on visa requirements, customs regulations, medical care etc for international travellers. Published by the Government Printing Office, it can be ordered by phone – ☎ (202) 512 1800 – or consulted on-line (www.access.gpo.gov). General passport information is available by phone toll-free from the Federal Information Center (item 5 on the automated menu), ☎ 800-688-9889. US passport application forms can be downloaded from http://travel.state.gov.

CUSTOMS

Apply to the Customs Office (UK) for a leaflet on customs regulations and the full range of duty-free allowances; available from HM Customs and Excise, Dorset House, Stamford Street, London SE1 9PS, ☎ 0171 928 3344. The US Customs Service offers a publication *Know Before You Go* for US citizens: for the office nearest you, consult the phone book, Federal Government, US Treasury (www.customs.ustreas.gov).
There are no customs formalities for holidaymakers bringing their caravans into France for a stay of less than six months. No customs document is necessary for pleasure boats and outboard motors for a stay of less than six months but the registration certificate should be kept on board.
Americans can bring home, tax-free, up to US$ 400 worth of goods (limited quantities of alcohol and tobacco products); Canadians up to CND$ 300; Australians up to AUS$ 400 and New Zealanders up to NZ$ 700.
Persons living in a member-state of the European Union are not restricted with regard to purchasing goods for private use, but the recommended allowances for alcoholic beverages and tobacco are as follows:

Spirits (whisky, gin, vodka etc)	10 litres	Cigarettes	800
Fortified wines (vermouth, ports etc)	20 litres	Cigarillos	400
Wine (not more than 60 sparkling)	90 litres	Cigars	200
Beer	110 litres	Smoking tobacco	1kg

Health

First aid, medical advice and chemists' night service rota are available from chemists/drugstores *(pharmacies)* identified by a neon sign in the shape of a green cross.
It is advisable to take out comprehensive insurance coverage as the recipient of medical treatment in French hospitals or clinics must pay the bill. Nationals of non-EU countries should check with their insurance companies about policy limitations. Reimbursement can then be negotiated with the insurance company according to the policy held.
All prescription drugs should be clearly labelled; it is recommended that you carry a copy of the prescription.
British and Irish citizens should apply to the Department of Health and Social Security for Form E 111, which entitles the holder to urgent treatment for accident or unexpected illness in EU countries. A refund of part of the costs of treatment can be obtained on application in person or by post to the local Social Security Offices *(Caisse Primaire d'Assurance Maladie)*.
The American Hospital of Paris is open 24hr for emergencies as well as consultations, with English-speaking staff, at 63 Boulevard Victor-Hugo, 92200 Neuilly sur Seine, ☎ 01 46 41 25 25. Accredited by major insurance companies.
The British Hospital is located just outside Paris in Levallois-Perret, at 3 Rue Barbès, ☎ 01 46 39 22 22.

Seasons

CLIMATE

The **tourist season** on the French Riviera lasts virtually all year round.

The **winter months** are characterised by a mild, sunny climate and are ideal for those who seek to avoid the peak influx of tourists.

Spring and **autumn** can sometimes bring heavy rainfalls and the infamous *mistral* wind, but neither overshadows the magnificent display of flora in full bloom at these times.

Summer is of course the best season for bathing and working up a suntan, not to mention taking part in the energetic nightlife. Traffic on the coast is, however, always very congested during this period; it can also be difficult to find accommodation so it is advisable to book well in advance.

Weather forecasts

Recorded report
– for the Alpes-Maritimes – ☎ 04 36 65 02 06
– for the Var – ☎ 04 36 65 02 83

Forecast of conditions at sea
– for the Alpes-Maritimes – ☎ 04 36 65 08 06
– for the Var – ☎ 04 36 68 08 83
– 5-day forecasts – ☎ 04 36 68 08 08.

Road conditions
– www.ViaMichelin.com (itineraries and updates)

Snowfall in winter sports stations (24 hour) – ☎ 04 42 66 64 28

5-day forecast
– for the mountains – ☎ 04 36 68 04 04
– snow and avalanche forecast – ☎ 04 36 68 10 20

General weather information – ☎ 05 45 55 91 09

5-day forecast – ☎ 04 36 85 01 01

WHAT TO PACK

As little as possible! Cleaning and laundry services are available everywhere. Most personal items can be replaced at reasonable cost. Try to pack everything into one suitcase and a tote bag. Porter help may be in short supply, and new purchases will add to the original weight. Take an extra tote bag for packing new purchases, shopping at the market, carrying a picnic, etc. Be sure luggage is clearly labelled and old travel tags removed. Do not pack medication in checked luggage, but keep it in your carry-on.

PUBLIC HOLIDAYS

Museums and other monuments may be closed or may vary their hours of admission on the following public holidays:

1	January	New Year's Day *(Jour de l'An)*
		Easter Day and Easter Monday *(Pâques)*
1	May	May Day *(Fête du Travail)*
8	May	VE Day *(Fête de la Libération)*
Thurs 40 days after Easter		Ascension Day *(Ascension)*
7th Sun-Mon after Easter		Whit Sunday and Monday *(Pentecôte)*
14	July	France's National Day *(Fête de la Bastille)*
15	August	Assumption *(Assomption)*
1	November	All Saint's Day *(Toussaint)*
11	November	Armistice Day *(Fête de la Victoire)*
25	December	Christmas Day *(Noël)*

National museums and art galleries are closed on Tuesdays; municipal museums are generally closed on Mondays. In addition to the usual school holidays at Christmas and in the spring and summer, there are long mid-term breaks (10 days to a fortnight) in February and early November.

TIME

France is 1hr ahead of Greenwich Mean Time (GMT). When it is **noon in France**, it is

3am	in Los Angeles
6am	in New York
11am	in Dublin
11am	in London
7pm	in Perth
9pm	in Sydney
11pm	in Auckland

In France "am" and "pm" are not used but the 24-hour clock is widely applied.

Budget

As a rule, prices for hotels and restaurants as well as for other goods and services are significantly less expensive in the French regions than in Paris.
Here are a few indicative prices (in euros; one euro = 6.55 French francs), based on surveys conducted by French authorities between 1999 and 2000.

Hotel rooms (based on double occupancy) in a city	Euros
1 star (French Tourist board standards)	27.44 – 53.36
2 star	53.36 – 76.22
3 star	76.23 – 121.97
4 star	137.21 – 228.69
4 star (luxury)	228.69 – 381.15

Food and entertainment	Euros
Movie ticket	7.62
River cruise	6.1 – 9.91
Dinner cruise	68.61 – 76.23
Expresso coffee	1.83
Café au lait	3.35
Soda (in a café)	3.35
Beer	3.05
Mineral water	3.05
Ice cream	4.88
Ham sandwich	3.20
Baguette of bread	0.69
Soda (1 litre in a shop)	2.13
Restaurant meal (3 courses, no wine)	22.87
Big Mac menu	5.34
French daily newspaper	0.91
Foreign newspaper	1.52 – 2.29
Compact disc	12.00 – 21.00
Telephone card – 50 units	7.47
Telephone card – 120 units	14.86
Cigarettes (pack of 20)	2.44 – 3.25

Public transportation	Euros
Bus, street car, metro	1.30
Book of ten tickets	9.30
Taxi (5km + tip)	9.91
TGV ticket Paris-Lyon 2nd class	60.98

The overall average yearly salary in France in 1999 was 141,970 French francs (21,643 €). The minimum wage per hour was 40.22 French francs (6.13 €).

Restaurants usually charge for meals in two ways: a *menu*, that is a fixed price menu with 2 to 3 courses, sometimes a small pitcher of wine, all for a set price, or *à la carte*, the more expensive way, with each course ordered separately.

Cafés have very different prices, depending on where they are located. The price of a drink or a coffee is cheaper if you stand at the counter *(comptoir)* than if you sit down *(salle)* and sometimes it is even more expensive if you sit outdoors *(terrace)*. In some big cities, prices go up after 10pm in the evening.

Discounts

Significant discounts are available for senior citizens, students, under 25-year-olds, teachers, and groups for public transportation, musuems and monuments and some leisure activities such as movies (at certain times of day). Bring student or senior cards with you, and bring along some extra passport-size photos for discount travel cards. The **International Student Travel Conference** (www.istc.org), global administrator of the International Student and Teacher Identity Cards, is an association of student travel organizations around the world. ISTC members collectively negotiate benefits with airlines, governments, and providers of other goods and services for the student and teacher community, both in their own country and around the world. The non-profit association sells international ID cards for students, youngsters under the age of 25 and teachers (who may get discounts on museum entrances, for example). The ISTC is also active in a network of international education and work exchange programmes. The coorporate headquarters address is Herengracht 479, 1017 BS Amsterdam, The Netherlands ☎ 31 20 421 28 00; Fax 31 20 421 28 10.
See the section below on travelling by rail in France for discounts on transportation.

Travellers with special needs

The sights described in this guide which are easily accessible to people of reduced mobility are indicated in the *Admission times and charges* by the symbol &.
Useful information on transportation, holidaymaking and sporting associations for the disabled is available from the *Comité National Français de Liaison pour la Réadaptation des Handicapés* (CNRH), 236bis Rue de Tolbiac, 75013 Paris. Call their international information number ☎ 01 53 80 66 44, or write to request a catalogue of publications. Web-surfers can find information for slow walkers, mature travellers and others with special needs at **www.access-able.com** and **www.handitel.org**. For information on museum access for the disabled contact La Direction, Les Musées de France, Service Accueil des Publics Spécifiques, 6 Rue des Pyramides, 75041 Paris Cedex 1, ☎ 01 40 15 35 88.
The Red Guide France and the **Michelin Camping Caravaning France** publications indicate hotels and camp sites with facilities suitable for the disabled.

Transport

Getting there and getting around

BY AIR

The French domestic network operates frequent services from Paris (Charles de Gaulle and Orly), covering the whole country. The main holiday destinations in the south of France are Nice, Marseille, Toulon and Monaco. Air France is the leading airline for domestic flights but there are a number of other regional companies such as Air Littoral. At the time of going to press, AOM and Air Liberté were going into liquidation and the name of their rescuer was not known. Direct flights from England can be booked on board EasyJet, British Airways and British Midland.
There are transfer buses to town terminals and to rail stations. **Roissy-Rail** and **Orly-Rail** operate fast rail links to the centre of Paris. There are also package tour flights with a rail or coach link-up. Air France sells tickets including a boat shuttle service that will take you directly to St-Tropez or St-Raphaël. Information, brochures and timetables are available from airlines and travel agents.

EasyJet 0289 448 4929 from England (bookings 08 706 000 000)
British Airways 0191 490 7901 from England (0825 825 400 from France)
British Midland 0133 285 4000 from England (01 41 91 87 04 from France)
Air France 0 820 820 820
Air Littoral 0 803 834 834
Aéroports de Paris 0 836 681 515
Aéroport de Nice-Côte d'Azur 04 93 21 30 30

BY SEA (from the UK or Ireland)

There are numerous **cross-Channel services** (passenger and car ferries, hovercraft) from the United Kingdom and Ireland, as well as the Shuttle rail service through the Channel Tunnel (**Le Shuttle-Eurotunnel**, ☎ 0990 353-535). To choose the most suitable route between your port of arrival and your destination use the Michelin Tourist and Motoring Atlas France, Michelin map 911 (which gives travel times and mileages) or Michelin maps from the 1:200,000 series (with the yellow cover). For details apply to travel agencies or to:

P & O Stena Line Ferries	Channel House, Channel View Road, Dover CT17 9JT, ☎ 0990 980 980 or 01304 863 000 (switchboard), **www.p-and-o.com**
Hoverspeed	International Hoverport, Marine Parade, Dover, Kent CT17 9TG, ☎ 0990 240 241, Fax 01304 240088, **www.hoverspeed.co.uk**
Brittany Ferries	Millbay Docks; Plymouth, Devon. PL1 3EW, ☎ 0990 360 360, **www.brittany-ferries.com**
Portsmouth Commercial Port (and ferry information)	George Byng Way, Portsmouth, Hampshire PO2 8SP, ☎ 01705 297391, Fax 01705 861165
Irish Ferries	50 West Norland Street, Dublin 2, ☎ (353) 16 610 511, **www.irishferries.com**
Seafrance	Eastern Docks, Dover, Kent, CT16 1JA, ☎ 01304 212696, Fax 01304 240033, **www.seafrance.fr**

BY RAIL

Eurostar runs via the Channel Tunnel between **London** (Waterloo) and **Paris** (Gare du Nord) in 3hr (bookings and information ☎ 0345 303 030 in the UK; ☎ 1-888-EUROSTAR in the US). In Paris it links to the high-speed rail network **(TGV)** which covers most of the country and which has recently been extended to the South of France *(see box below – for details call ☎ 0 836 676 869)*. The main towns served by the new TGV network are Lyon, Avignon, Valence, Montpellier, Aix-en-Provence, Marseille, Toulon and Nice. As far as the Riviera is concerned, there are 6-8 trains leaving daily from Paris-Gare de Lyon for Nice station, running roughly between 8am and 10.30pm (night train).

Eurailpass, Flexipass, and **Saverpass** are three of the travel passes which may be purchased by residents of countries outside the European Union. In the US, contact your travel agent or **Rail Europe** 2100 Central Avenue, Boulder, CO, 80301 ☎ 1-800-4-EURAIL or **Europrail International** ☎ 1 888 667 9731. If you are a European resident, you can buy an individual country pass, if you are not a resident of the country you are buying it for. In the UK, contact Europrail at 179 Piccadilly London W1V OBA ☎ 0990 848 848. Information on schedules can be obtained on websites for these agencies and the **SNCF**, respectively: **www.raileurop.com.us, www.eurail.on.ca, www.sncf.fr**. At the SNCF site, you can book ahead, pay with a credit card, and receive your ticket in the mail at home free of charge (7 days minimum before leaving in the case of foreign countries, 4 days for France).

There are numerous **discounts** available when you purchase your tickets in France, from 25-50% below the regular rate. These apply to passengers over 60 years of age (**Carte Senior**), young people aged between 12 and 26 (**Carte 12-25**) and passengers travelling with a child under 12 (**Carte Enfant +**). Cheaper tickets may also be purchased by groups of 2 to 9 people travelling together (**À Deux Découverte**). There are a limited number of discount seats available during peak travelling times, and the best discounts are available for travel during off-peak periods.

Tickets bought in France must be validated *(composter)* by using the orange automatic date-stamping machines at the platform entrance (failure to do so may result in a fine).

The French railway company SNCF operates a telephone information, reservation and prepayment service in English from 7am to 10pm (French time). In France call ☎ 08 36 35 35 39 (when calling from outside France, drop the initial 0).

TGV Méditerranée

In June 2001, the President of the Republic, Jacques Chirac, officially inaugurated France's southern high-speed rail link, bringing Provence within three hours of Paris and six of London. The smart, streamlined blue and silver train will now reach Marseille after a mere 177 minutes, leaving from Paris. The 12-year campaign to complete the route followed by the TGV Méditerranée was fraught with difficulties. Besides the opposition shown by local residents, there were a number of geographical, architectural and ecological constraints. Considerable care was taken to preserve the natural environment and to avoid disturbing protected species. Moreover, new bridges and viaducts had to be built with local stone in order to blend in with the surrounding landscape.

The new trains provide a far better service to passengers: more legroom, a central luggage rack, an area set aside for bicycles, facilities for changing babies and heating up bottles, telephone booths, electric plugs for laptop computers *(1st class)*, a wide range of light snacks or meals and even a free newspaper with your breakfast!

BY COACH

Regular coach services between **London** and **Paris**, connection for **Nice**:

Eurolines (London), 52 Grosvenor Gardens, Victoria, London SW1W 0AU,
☎ 0171 730 8235 Fax 0171 730 8721.

Eurolines (Paris), 28 Avenue du Général-de-Gaulle, 93541 Bagnolet, ☎ 01 49 72 51 51.
www.eurolines.fr

MOTORING

The area covered in this guide is easily reached by main motorways and national routes.
Michelin map 911 indicates the main itineraries as well as alternative routes for avoiding
heavy traffic during busy holiday periods, and gives estimated travel times. **Michelin map
914** is a detailed atlas of French motorways, indicating tolls, rest areas and services along
the route; it includes a table for calculating distances and times. The latest Michelin route-
planning service is available on Internet, **www.ViaMichelin.com**. Travellers can calculate a
precise route using such options as shortest route, route avoiding toll roads, Michelin-
recommended route and gain access to tourist information (hotels, restaurants,
attractions). The service is available on a pay-per-route basis or by subscription.
The roads are very busy during the holiday period (particularly weekends in July and
August) and, to avoid traffic congestion it is advisable to follow the recommended secondary routes (signposted as *Bison Futé – itinéraires bis*). The motorway network
includes rest areas *(aires d'autoroute)* and petrol stations, usually with restaurant and
shopping malls attached, about every 40km/25mi, so that long-distance drivers have
no excuse not to stop for a rest every now and then.

DOCUMENTS

Travellers from other European Union countries and North America can drive in France
with a valid national or home-state **driving licence**. An **international driving licence** is useful
because the information on it appears in nine languages (bear in mind that traffic officers are allowed to fine motorists). A permit is available from the National Automobile
Club, 1151 East Hillsdale Boulevard, Foster City, CA 94404 ☎ 650-294-7000 or
nationalautoclub.com; or contact your local branch of the American Automobile Association. For the vehicle, it is necessary to have the registration papers (logbook) and
a nationality plate of the approved size.
Certain motoring organisations (AAA, AA, RAC) offer accident **insurance** and **breakdown
service schemes** for members. Check with your current insurance company with regard
to coverage while abroad. If you plan to hire a car using your credit card, check with
the company, which may provide liability insurance automatically.

HIGHWAY CODE

The minimum driving age is 18. Traffic drives on the right. All passengers must wear **seat
belts**. Children under the age of 10 must ride in the back seat. Headlights must be switched
on in poor visibility and at night; use side-lights only when the vehicle is parked.
In the case of a **breakdown**, a red warning triangle or hazard warning lights are oblig-
atory. In the absence of stop signs at intersections, cars must **yield to the right**. Traffic
on main roads outside built-up areas (priority indicated by a yellow diamond sign) and
on roundabouts has right of way. Vehicles must stop when the lights turn red at road
junctions and may filter to the right only when indicated by an amber arrow.
The regulations on **drinking and driving** (limited to 0.50g/l) and **speeding** are strictly
enforced – usually by an on-the-spot fine and/or confiscation of the vehicle.

Speed limits – Although liable to modification, these are as follows:
– toll motorways *(autoroutes)* 130kph/80mph (110kph/68mph when raining);
– dual carriageways and motorways without tolls 110kph/68mph (100kph/62mph
when raining);
– other roads 90kph/56mph (80kph/50mph when raining) and in towns
50kph/31mph;
– outside lane on motorways during daylight, on level ground and with good visibility,
minimum of 80kph/50mph.

Parking regulations – In town there are zones where parking
is either restricted or subject to a fee; tickets should be
obtained from the ticket machines (*horodateurs* – small
change necessary) and displayed inside the windscreen
on the driver's side; failure to display may result in a fine,
or towing and impoundment.

Tolls – In France, most motorway sections are subject to a toll *(péage)*. You can pay in
cash or with a credit card (Visa, Mastercard).

CAR RENTAL

There are car rental agencies at airports, railway stations and in all large towns
throughout France. European cars have manual transmission; automatic cars are available in larger cities only if an advance reservation is made. Drivers must be over 21;
between ages 21-25, drivers are required to pay an extra daily fee of 50-100F; some

companies allow drivers under 23 only if the reservation has been made through a travel agent. It is relatively expensive to hire a car in France; Americans in particular will notice the difference and should make arrangements before leaving, take advantage of fly-drive offers, or seek advice from a travel agent, specifying requirements.

Central Reservation in France:

Avis: ☎08 20 05 05 05	**Europcar:** ☎08 25 358 358
Budget France: 08 00 10 00 01	**Hertz France:** ☎01 39 38 38 38
Century: 01 53 70 68 48	**Rent A Car:** 01 55 43 29 99
Prestige Limousines: 01 40 43 92 92	**Executive Car:** 42 65 54 20

Worldwide Motorhome Rentals offers fully equipped camper vans for rent. You can view them on the company's web pages **(mhrww.com)** or call (US toll-free) US ☎ 888- 519-8969; outside the US ☎ 530-389-8316 or Fax 530-389-8316.

Overseas Motorhome Tours Inc. organises escorted tours and individual rental of recreational vehicles: in the US ☎ 800-322-2127; outside the US ☎ 1-310-543-2590; Internet www.omtinc.com

Petrol – French service stations dispense: *sans plomb 98* (super unleaded 98), *sans plomb 95* (super unleaded 95), *diesel/gazole* (diesel) and *GPL* (LPG). Petrol, or gas for the Americans, is considerably more expensive in France than in the USA. Prices are listed on signboards on the motorways; it is usually cheaper to fill up after leaving the motorway; check the large hypermarkets on the outskirts of town.

Where to stay, Where to eat

Finding a Hotel

THE GREEN GUIDE is pleased to offer a new feature: lists of selected hotels and restaurants for this region. Turn to the pages bordered in blue for descriptions and prices of typical places to stay and eat with local flair. The key on page 9 explains the symbols and abbreviations used in these sections. Use the **Map of Places to stay** below to identify recommended places for overnight stops. For an even greater selection, use **The Red Guide France**, with its famously reliable star-rating system and hundreds of establishments all over France. Book ahead! The French Riviera is a very popular holiday destination.

For further assistance, **Loisirs Accueil** is a booking service that has offices in some French *départements* – contact tourist offices for further information.

A guide to good-value, family-run hotels, **Logis et Auberges de France**, is available from the French tourist office, as are lists of other kinds of accommodation such as hotel-châteaux, bed-and-breakfasts etc.

Relais et Châteaux provides information on booking in luxury hotels with character: 15 Rue Galvani, 75017 Paris, ☎ 08 25 323 232.

Economy Chain Hotels – If you need a place to stop en route, these can be useful, as they are inexpensive (200-300F for a double room) and generally located near the main road. While breakfast is available, there may not be a restaurant; rooms are small, with a television and bathroom. Central reservation numbers:
- **Akena** ☎ 01 69 84 85 17
- **B&B** ☎ 0 803 00 29 29
- **Etap Hôtel** ☎ 08 36 68 89 00
- **Mister Bed** ☎ 01 46 14 38 00
- **Villages Hôtel** ☎ 03 80 60 92 70

The hotels listed below are slightly more expensive (from 300F), and offer a few more amenities and services. Central reservation numbers:
- **Campanile** ☎ 01 53 74 60 00
- **Climat de France** ☎ 01 45 42 81 43
- **Ibis** ☎ 01 43 20 89 12

Renting a Cottage, Bed & Breakfast

The **Maison des Gîtes de France** is an information service on self-catering accommodation on the French Riviera (and the rest of France). *Gîtes* usually take the form of a cottage or apartment decorated in the local style where visitors can make themselves at home, or bed and breakfast accommodation *(chambres d'hôtes)* which consists of a room and breakfast at a reasonable price.

Contact the Gîtes de France office in Paris: 59 Rue St-Lazare, 75439 Paris Cedex 09, ☎ 01 49 70 75 75, or their representative in the UK, **Brittany Ferries**. You can also contact the local tourist offices which may have lists of available properties and local bed and breakfast establishments.

Hostels, Camping

To obtain an International Youth Hostel Federation card (there is no age requirement, "senior cards" are available too), you should contact the IYHF in your own country for information and membership applications (US ☎ 202 783 6161; UK ☎ 1727 855215;

Canada ☎ 613-273 7884; Australia ☎ 61-2-9565-1669). There is a new booking service on the internet (iyhf.org), which you may use to reserve rooms as far as 6 months in advance.

There are two main youth hostel associations *(Auberges de Jeunesse)* in France, the **Ligue Française pour les Auberges de la Jeunesse** (38 Boulevard Raspail, 75007 Paris, ☎ 01 45 48 69 84, Fax 01 45 44 57 47) and the **Fédération Unie des Auberges de Jeunesse** (27 Rue Pajol, 75018 Paris, ☎ 08 36 688 698).

There are numerous officially graded **camping sites** with varying standards of facilities on the French Riviera. The **Michelin Camping Caravaning France** guide lists a selection of camp sites. The area is very popular with campers in the summer months, so it is wise to reserve in advance.

Terrace of restaurant looking onto an old street of Cannes

Finding a Restaurant

Turn to the pages bordered in blue for descriptions and prices of selected restaurants in the different locations covered in this guide. The key on pages 8-9 explains the symbols and abbreviations used in these sections. Use **The Red Guide France**, with its famously reliable star-rating system and hundreds of establishments all over France, for an even greater choice. If you would like to experience a meal in a highly rated restaurant from The Red Guide, be sure to book ahead! In the countryside, restaurants usually serve lunch between noon and 2pm and dinner between 7.30pm and 10pm. It is not always easy to find an establishment open between lunch and dinner, as "round-the-clock" restaurants are still scarce in the provinces. However, a hungry traveller can usually get a sandwich in a café, and ordinary hot dishes may be available in a *brasserie*.

A typical French Menu

La Carte	The Menu
ENTRÉES	STARTERS
Crudités	Raw vegetable salad
Terrine de lapin	Rabbit terrine (pâté)
Frisée aux lardons	Curly lettuce with bacon bits
Escargots	Snails
Salade au crottin de Chavignol	Goat cheese on a bed of lettuce
PLATS (VIANDES)	MAIN COURSES (MEAT)
Bavette à l'échalotte	Sirloin with shallots
Faux filet au poivre	Sirloin with pepper sauce
Pavé de rumsteck	Thick rump steak
Côtes d'agneau	Lamb chops
Filet mignon de porc	Pork filet
Blanquette de veau	Veal in cream sauce
Nos viandes sont garnies	Our meat dishes are served with vegetables
PLATS (POISSONS, VOLAILLE)	MAIN COURSES (FISH, FOWL)
Filets de sole	Sole fillets
Dorade aux herbes	Sea bream with herbs
Saumon grillé	Grilled salmon
Truite meunière	Trout fried in butter
Magret de canard	Duck filets
Poulet rôti	Roast chicken
FROMAGE	CHEESE
DESSERTS	DESSERTS
Tarte aux pommes	Apple pie
Crème caramel	Cooled baked custard with caramel sauce
BOISSONS	BEVERAGES
Bière	Beer
Eau minérale (gazeuse)	(Sparkling) mineral water
Une carafe d'eau	Tap water (no charge)
Vin rouge, vin blanc, rosé	Red wine, white wine, rosé
Jus de fruit	Fruit juice
MENU ENFANT	CHILDREN'S MENU
Jambon	Ham
Steak haché	Ground beef
Frites	French fries

For information on local specialities, turn to page 82.

In French restaurants and cafés, a service charge is included. Tipping is not necessary, but French people often leave the small change from their bill on their table, or about 5% for the waiter in a nice restaurant.

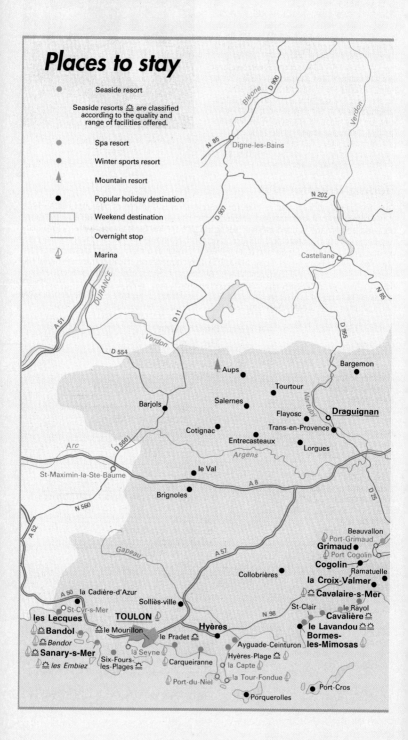

Places to stay

- Seaside resort

  Seaside resorts ⚓ are classified according to the quality and range of facilities offered.

- Spa resort
- Winter sports resort
- Mountain resort
- Popular holiday destination

  Weekend destination

  Overnight stop

⚓ Marina

Bléone

D 900

Verdon

N 85

Digne-les-Bains

D 907

N 202

DURANCE

A 51

Castellane

N 85

Verdon

D 11

D 965

D 554

Bargemon

Aups

Tourtour

Salernes

Barjols

Flayosc

Draguignan

Cotignac

Trans-en-Provence

Nartuby

Entrecasteaux

Lorgues

Arc

D 560

Argens

St-Maximin-la-Ste-Baume

le Val

A 8

D 25

Brignoles

N 560

A 52

Beauvallon

Port-Grimaud

Grimaud

Gapeau

A 57

Port Cogolin

Cogolin

Ramatuelle

Collobrières

la Croix-Valmer

la Cadière-d'Azur

A 50

Cavalaire-s-Mer

Solliès-ville

le Rayol

les Lecques

St-Cyr-s-Mer

St-Clair

Cavalière ⚓

TOULON

le Mourillon

Hyères

N 98

le Lavandou ⚓⚓

Bandol

le Pradet ⚓

Bormes-

Bendor

Ayguade-Ceinturon

les-Mimosas

Sanary-s-Mer

la Seyne

Hyères-Plage ⚓

Six-Fours-

Carqueiranne

la Capte ⚓

les Embiez

les-Plages ⚓

la Tour-Fondue ⚓

Port-du-Niel

Port-Cros

Porquerolles

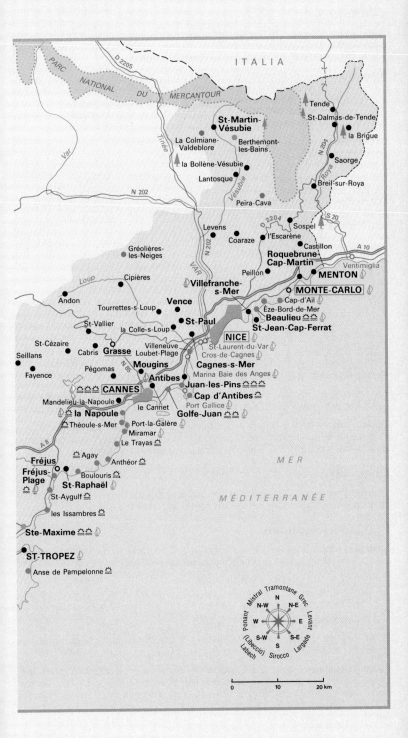

ITALIA

PARC NATIONAL DU MERCANTOUR

Tende
St-Dalmas-de-Tende
St-Martin-Vésubie
la Brigue
La Colmiane-Valdeblore
Berthemont-les-Bains
Saorge
la Bollène-Vésubie
Lantosque
Breil-sur-Roya
Peïra-Cava

Gréolières-les-Neiges
Levens
Coaraze
Sospel
l'Escarène
Castillon
Roquebrune Cap-Martin
Peillon
Cipières
Andon
Villefranche-s-Mer
MENTON
Ventimiglia
Tourrettes-s-Loup
Vence
MONTE-CARLO
Cap-d'Ail
Éze-Bord-de-Mer
St-Vallier
St-Paul
Beaulieu
la Colle-s-Loup
St-Jean-Cap-Ferrat
St-Cézaire
Cabris
Grasse
NICE
Villeneuve Loubet-Plage
St-Laurent-du-Var
Cros-de-Cagnes
Seillans
Pégomas
Mougins
Cagnes-s-Mer
Fayence
Antibes
Marina Baie des Anges
Juan-les-Pins
CANNES
Mandelieu-la-Napoule
le Cannet
Cap d'Antibes
Port Gallice
la Napoule
Golfe-Juan
Théoule-s-Mer
Port-la-Galère
Miramar
Le Trayas
Agay
Anthéor
Fréjus
Fréjus-Plage
Boulouris
St-Raphaël
St-Aygulf
les Issambres
Ste-Maxime
ST-TROPEZ
Anse de Pampelonne

MER MÉDITERRANÉE

Ponant Mistral Tramontane Grec Levant
N-W N N-E
W E
S-W S-E
(Libeccio) S Largade
Labech Sirocco

0   10   20 km

29

Basic information

Currency

There are no restrictions on the amount of currency visitors can take into France. Visitors carrying a lot of cash are advised to complete a currency declaration form on arrival, because there are restrictions on currency export.

Notes and coins – Until the introduction of the European currency unit (euro), the only unit of currency in France used to be the French franc. However, banknotes and coins belonging to the European single currency went into circulation in January 2002. Until the end of June 2002, franc notes and coins can be exchanged in banks. After that, they will only be accepted by the Banque de France.

Banks – Banks are open from 9am to noon and 2pm to 4pm and branches are closed either on Monday or Saturday. Banks close early on the day before a bank holiday. A passport is necessary as identification when cashing travellers cheques in banks. Commission charges vary and hotels usually charge more than banks for cashing cheques. One of the most economical ways to use your money in France is by using **ATM machines** to get cash directly from your bank account or to use your credit cards to get cash advances. Be sure to remember your PIN number, you will need it to use cash dispensers and to pay with your card in most shops, restaurants, etc. ATM code pads are numeric; use a telephone pad to translate a letter code into numbers. PIN numbers have 4 digits in France; inquire with the issuing company or bank if the code you usually use is longer. Visa is the most widely accepted credit card, followed by MasterCard; other cards (Diners Club, Plus, Cirrus) are also accepted in some cash machines. American Express is more often accepted in premium establishments. Most places post signs indicating the cards they accept; if you don't see such a sign, and want to pay with a card, ask before ordering or making a selection. Cards are widely accepted in shops, hypermarkets, hotels and restaurants, at tollbooths and in petrol stations. If your card is lost or stolen in France, call one of the following 24-hour hotlines:

American Express	☎ 01 47 77 70 00	**Visa**	☎ 08 36 69 08 80
Mastercard/Eurocard	☎ 01 45 67 84 84	**Diners Club**	☎ 01 49 06 17 50

You must report any loss or theft of credit cards or travellers' cheques to the local police who will issue you with a certificate (useful proof to show the issuing company).

Tipping – Since a service charge is automatically included in the price of meals and accommodation in France, any additional tipping is up to the visitor, generally small change, and generally not more than 5%. Taxi drivers and hairdressers are usually tipped 10-15%.

Electricity

The electric current is 220 volts. Circular two-pin plugs are the rule. Adapters should be bought before your leave home; they are on sale in most airports.

Post and telephone

Main post offices open Monday to Friday 8am to 7pm, Saturday 8am to noon. Smaller branch post offices generally close at lunchtime between noon and 2pm and at 4pm.

Postage via air mail:

  UK: letter (20g) 0.46€

  North America: letter (20g) 0.67€

  Australia and NZ: letter (20g) 0.79€

Stamps are also available from newsagents and *bureaux de tabac*. Stamp collectors should ask for *timbres de collection* in any post office.

Public Telephones – Most public phones in France use pre-paid phone cards *(télécartes)*, rather than coins. Some telephone booths accept credit cards (Visa, Mastercard/Eurocard). Phone cards (50 or 120 units) can be bought in post offices, branches of France Télécom, *bureaux de tabac* (cafés that sell cigarettes) and newsagents and can be used to make calls in France and abroad. Calls can be received at phone boxes where the blue bell sign is shown; the phone will not ring, so keep your eye on the little message screen.

National calls – French telephone numbers have 10 digits. Paris and Paris region numbers begin with 01; 02 in northwest France; 03 in northeast France; 04 in southeast France and Corsica; 05 in southwest France.

International calls – To call France from abroad, dial the country code (33) + 9-digit number (omit the initial 0). When calling abroad from France dial 00, then dial the country code followed by the area code and number of your correspondent.

International dialling codes (00 + code):

Australia	☎ 61
New Zealand	☎ 64
Canada	☎ 1
Eire	☎ 353
United Kingdom	☎ 44
United States	☎ 1

To use your **personal calling card** dial:

AT&T . . . ☎ 0-800 99 00 11	Sprint . . . . ☎ 0-800 99 00 87
MCI . . . . ☎ 0-800 99 00 19	Canada Direct . . . . ☎ 0-800 99 00 16

International Information, US/Canada: 00 33 12 11
International operator: 00 33 12 + country code

Emergency numbers:

Police:	17	**"SAMU"** (Paramedics):	15
Fire *(Pompiers)*:	18		

Local directory assistance: 12

Minitel – France Télécom operates a system offering directory enquiries (free of charge up to 3min), travel and entertainment reservations, and other services (cost per minute varies). These small computer-like terminals can be found in some post offices, hotels and France Télécom agencies and in many French homes. 3614 PAGES E is the code for **directory assistance in English** (turn on the unit, dial 3614, hit the *connexion* button when you get the tone, type in "PAGES E", and follow the instructions on the screen).

Cellular phones in France have numbers which begin with 06. Two-watt (lighter, shorter reach) and eight-watt models are on the market, using the Itinéris (France Télécom) or SFR network. *Mobicartes* are pre-paid phone cards that fit into mobile units. Cell phone rentals (delivery or airport pick-up provided):

Rent a Cell Express   ☎ 01 53 93 78 00, Fax 01 53 93 78 09
A.L.T. Rent A Phone   ☎ 01 48 00 06 06, E-mail altloc@jve.fr

Riviera Radio

Feeling pangs for your native language? Desperately seeking an English-speaking doctor or nanny? Looking for rented accommodation? Riviera Radio is the answer to all your problems. The only 100% English-speaking radio in the area, it broadcasts on FM *(106.5 in the Alpes-Maritimes, 106.3 in Monte-Carlo – ☎ 00 377 97 97 94 94 from France)* and covers the stretch of coastline running between St-Tropez and the Italian resort of San Remo. This Monaco-based radio station provides useful tips for tourists and residents alike and presents a great many regular programmes: business and financial news, local traffic and weather reports, guide to English-speaking films in VO, job offers, updated news bulletins in conjunction with the BBC World Service, calendar of major fairs and conferences etc. One of Riviera Radio's most popular features is their Saturday morning Community Chest *(10-11am)*, when listeners call in to buy or sell miscellaneous items, ranging from a luxury yacht or vintage car to a second-hand computer...

Conversion tables

Weights and measures

| 1 kilogram (kg) | 2.2 pounds (lb) | 2.2 pounds |
| 1 metric ton (tn) | 1.1 tons | 1.1 tons |

to convert kilograms to pounds, multiply by 2.2

| 1 litre (l) | 2.1 pints (pt) | 1.8 pints |
| 1 litre | 0.3 gallon (gal) | 0.2 gallon |

to convert litres to gallons, multiply by 0.26 (US) or 0.22 (UK)

| 1 hectare (ha) | 2.5 acres | 2.5 acres |
| 1 square kilometre (km²) | 0.4 square miles (sq mi) | 0.4 square miles |

to convert hectares to acres, multiply by 2.4

1centimetre (cm)	0.4 inches (in)	0.4 inches
1 metre (m)	3.3 feet (ft) - 39.4 inches - 1.1 yards (yd)	
1 kilometre (km)	0.6 miles (mi)	0.6 miles

to convert metres to feet, multiply by 3.28, kilometres to miles, multiply by 0.6

Clothing

Women	🇪🇺	🇺🇸	🇬🇧		🇪🇺	🇺🇸	🇬🇧	Men
	35	4	2½		40	7½	7	
	36	5	3½		41	8½	8	
	37	6	4½		42	9½	9	
Shoes	38	7	5½		43	10½	10	Shoes
	39	8	6½		44	11½	11	
	40	9	7½		45	12½	12	
	41	10	8½		46	13½	13	
	36	4	8		46	36	36	
	38	6	10		48	38	38	
Dresses &	40	8	12		50	40	40	Suits
Suits	42	12	14		52	42	42	
	44	14	16		54	44	44	
	46	16	18		56	46	48	
	36	08	30		37	14½	14,5	
	38	10	32		38	15	15	
Blouses &	40	12	14		39	15½	15½	Shirts
sweaters	42	14	36		40	15¾	15¾	
	44	16	38		41	16	16	
	46	18	40		42	16½	16½	

Sizes often vary depending on the designer. These equivalents are given for guidance only.

Speed

kph	10	30	50	70	80	90	100	110	120	130
mph	6	19	31	43	50	56	62	68	75	81

Temperature

Celsius (°C)	0°	5°	10°	15°	20°	25°	30°	40°	60°	80°	100°
Fahrenheit (°F)	32°	41°	50°	59°	68°	77°	86°	104°	140°	176°	212°

To convert Celsius into Fahrenheit, multiply °C by 9, divide by 5, and add 32.
To convert Fahrenheit into Celsius, subtract 32 from °F, multiply by 5, and divide by 9.

Shopping

Most of the larger shops are open Mondays to Saturdays from 9am to 6.30 or 7.30pm. Smaller, individual shops may close during the lunch hour. Food shops – grocers, wine merchants and bakeries – are generally open from 7am to 6.30 or 7.30pm; some open on Sunday mornings. Many food shops close between noon and 2pm and on Mondays. Bakery and pastry shops sometimes close on Wednesdays. Hypermarkets usually open until 9pm or later.

People travelling to the USA cannot import plant products or fresh food, including fruit, cheeses and nuts. It is acceptable to carry tinned products or preserves.

There is a Value Added Tax in France *(TVA)* of 19.6% on almost every purchase (some foods and books are subject to a lower rate). However, non-European visitors who spend more than 182.94€ in any one participating store can get the VAT amount refunded. Usually, you fill out a form at the store, showing your passport. Upon leaving the country, you submit all forms to customs for approval (they may want to see the goods, so if possible don't pack them in checked luggage). The refund is usually paid directly into your bank or credit card account, or it can be sent by mail. Big department stores that cater to tourists provide special services to help you; be sure to mention that you plan to seek a refund before you pay for goods (no refund is possible for tax on services). If you are visiting two or more countries within the European Union, you submit the forms only on departure from the last EU country. The refund is worthwhile for those visitors who would like to buy fashion wear, furniture or other fairly expensive items, but remember, the minimum amount must be spent in a single shop (though not necessarily on a single day).

Wildlife –
Parc National
du Mercantour

Mercantour National Park, the last of the French National State Parks, was created in 1979 and covers an area of 68 500ha/169 267 acres in the Alpes-Maritimes and Alpes-de-Haute-Provence *départements* (encompassing 22 and 6 *communes* from each respectively).

The park, which was once the French part of Italian royal hunting grounds and extended over both sides of the Alps prior to 1861, has been twinned since 1987 with the Italian Argentera Nature Park with which it shares a border along 33km/20.5mi. These two organisations are in charge of introducing and monitoring animal species in the whole of this protected region. In this way, ibexes which have wintered in the Argentera arrive to spend the summer months in the Mercantour, while wild sheep (mouflons) do the opposite.

The Mercantour is a high, mountainous park, with terraces from 500-3 143m/1 640-10 312ft in altitude, offering breathtaking views of natural amphitheatres, glacial valleys and deep gorges.

It contains a rich variety of flora; over 2 000 species have been counted there, including **Saxifraga florulenta** which was for a time the park's emblem. All levels of vegetation are present, from olive trees to rhododendrons and the gentians which make such a splendid display of colour in the spring.

Fauna includes some 6 300 chamois, nearly 300 ibexes and 1 250 moufflons which are well adapted to the Mediterranean climate. The wooded slopes at medium altitude are home to various deer and smaller mammals such as hares, ermines and marmots. Feathered members of this community include black grouse, ptarmigans and splendid examples of birds of prey such as the short-toed eagle *(circaëtus)* and the golden eagle.

The reintroduction of the bearded vulture was achieved successfully in the summer of 1993. There are now five birds in the park. For the first time in France since 1942, wolves have returned of their own accord to live in the park. They come from Italy where this protected species is now spreading.

The 600km/373mi of footpaths laid out within the park's boundaries enable tourists to discover the park on foot. These include the GR5 and the GR52A④, or the Mercantour panoramic footpath which crosses the Vallée des Merveilles, as well as footpaths at L'Authion, Le Boréon and Madone de Fenestre.

This guide describes the regions of the Vésubie and Merveilles valleys, the Authion Massif and Turini Forest.

Mountain bikes are not allowed in the central area of the park.

Marmot

Recreation

OFFSHORE

Boat trips

There are regular ferries to the Île de Bendor, Île des Embiez, Île d'Hyères and Île de Lérins, and also boat trips from the following resorts.

Port of embarkation	Destination
BANDOL	Les Embiez – Toulon via Cap Sicié
	Gare Maritime ☎ 04 94 32 51 41
	Cassis and the Calanque d'En-Vau via La Ciotat – Whole day to the Château d'If and Le Frioul
	– Underwater exploration with l'Aquascope (Cie Atlantide)
SANARY	Îles des Embiez – Toulon Anchorage and Cap Sicié
	Calanques de Cassis
Le LAVANDOU	Île du Levant
CAVALAIRE	Îles d'Hyères
St-TROPEZ	Îles d'Hyères (Cie MMG ☎ 04 94 96 51 00) – Ste-Maxime (shuttle) – St-Raphaël (in summer)
Ste-MAXIME	St-Tropez (shuttle) – Îles d'Hyères
CANNES	Îles de Lérins – excursion to St-Tropez and Monaco on a catamaran
JUAN LES PINS	Underwater viewing cruise off Cap d'Antibes (departure from Ponton Courbet)
NICE	Îles de Lérins – La Riviera
MENTON	St-Jean-Cap-Ferrat (and Villefranche Bay) – Monaco (with and without stopping)

Sailing

Most of the seaside resorts on the French Riviera, from Lecques to Menton, have well-equipped marinas, making this coast the best in France for sailing. Although nearly every port has moorings with good facilities, the enthusiasm for sailing is such that

Sailing into the blue

S. Sauvignier/MICHELIN

enormous marinas have been constructed with extensive services to satisfy even the most exacting yachtsman. Ports providing over 1 000 berths are Bandol, Toulon, Hyères (Port-St-Pierre), La Londe (Port Miramar), Le Lavandou, St-Raphaël (Ste-Lucia), Cannes (Pierre Canto and the Vieux Port), St-Laurent-du-Var and Antibes (Port-Vauban), which is the largest to date.

The marinas open to visiting crafts are marked on the Places to stay map on p 28.

There are sailing clubs which provide lessons in most resorts; during the summer it is possible to hire craft with or without a crew.

The services available in each port are listed in the *Guide du Plaisancier en Méditerranée*, published by Editions France Yachting Service.

Further information is available from each port authority and from the **Fédération Française de Voile**, 55 Avenue Kléber, 75084 Paris Cedex 16 ☎ 01 44 05 81 00.

Scuba diving

There are many clubs providing scuba diving lessons accompanied by instructors. The main centres are Bendor (Centre Padi is one of the largest in Europe), Le Pradet (Garonne beach), Giens (La Tour Fondue), Sanary, Cavalaire, Ramatuelle (L'Escalet), St-Tropez, Ste-Maxime, St-Raphaël, La Napoule, Cannes and Villefranche.

A brochure listing all the local clubs is available from **La Maison du Tourisme du Golfe de St-Tropez** in Gassin (☎ 04 94 43 42 10).

Excursions to explore the Mediterranean flora and fauna are provided by the Centre du Rayol-Canadel and the Parc National de Port-Cros.

Sailing the Mediterranean

Single-hulled sailboat

Offshore

Mediterranean "Pointu"

Recreational fishing boat

Catamaran

Cabin cruiser

Day cruiser

Yacht

R.Corbel/MICHELIN

35

The **Fédération Française d'Études et de Sports Sous-Marins** (24 Quai de Rive-Neuve, 13007 Marseille ☎ 04 91 33 99 31) is an umbrella organisation, comprising 100 local clubs, which publishes a comprehensive yearbook covering all underwater activities in France. Information also available from the **Comité Régional Côte d'Azur des Sports Sous-Marins**, Cap Blanc, Port de Bormes, 83230 Bormes-les-Mimosas ☎ 04 94 71 63 43.

Finest Underwater Landscapes – The coves of the Maures and the Esterel on the Var coast and the clear water round the Îles d'Hyères are invitations to discover the charm of the Mediterranean *(La Grande Bleue)* and of the silent underwater world. The volume of marine traffic over the centuries has turned the seabed into a museum of shipwrecks – about 100 ships and upwards of 20 aircraft have sunk along this coast. Most of them are lying in more than 20m/65ft of water, accessible only to experienced divers who are members of specialist clubs. Other wrecks, lying in shallower waters, can easily be visited by amateurs. Information about underwater centres near such wrecks is available from the Fédération des Sports Sous-marins in Marseille.

The wrecks of the Provençal coast and their history are described in *Naufrages en Provence* by J-P Joncheray.

Underwater fishing

The abundance of creeks along the coast should satisfy all demands. The sport is strictly regulated; the essential regional regulations are given below.

Underwater fishing is forbidden in certain areas of the coastline from early November to the beginning of March. It is essential to check with the local maritime authority – Toulon, 244 Avenue de l'Infanterie-de-Marine ☎ 04 94 46 92 00 and Nice, 22 Quai Lunel ☎ 04 92 00 41 50.

Some areas are out of bounds to fishing all the year round – south coast of St-Mandrier Peninsula, part of Porquerolles Island, Port-Cros Island and its neighbouring islets.

There are underwater nature reserves, marked by buoys, near Golfe-Juan, Beaulieu and Roquebrune-Cap-Martin. Villefranche anchorage is a protected area. Underwater anglers must comply with general fishing regulations and bear in mind that in the Mediterranean Sea

– it is illegal to catch or fish for grouper and oysters (for mother-of-pearl)
– it is illegal to fish for sea urchins from 1 May to 30 September
– it is illegal to pursue or catch marine mammals (dolphins, porpoises), even without intending to kill them
– the minimum size of catch is 12cm/4.72in (except for sardines, anchovies), 18cm/7.09in for crayfish.

Whatever the circumstances, it is illegal to be in possession of both diving equipment and an underwater gun.

Underwater safety – Enthusiasm for exploring the superb underwater landscape of the Riviera should not blind the occasional diver to the need to observe certain regulations
– never go diving alone, nor after eating a heavy meal, nor after drinking alcohol or fizzy drinks, nor when tired
– avoid shipping lanes and areas used by wind-surfers

Underwater exploration

– when signalling for help, make it known that it is a diving accident so that the rescuers can prepare a decompression chamber, which is the only effective aid in the case of diving accidents, even minor ones.

Sea fishing

In Sanary, in the Cogolin Marina and in Ste-Maxime there are organisations through which visitors may hire out boats and professional fishermen for sea fishing or join a sea fishing party (usually in summer from 6am to 10am).

Other Seaside Activities

The long stretches of the Var coast, consisting of beaches where the *mistral* blows, have become some of the most popular locations in the Mediterranean for those who enjoy riding the waves on a **sail-board** (wind-surfing) or a **funboard**; the shorter board used for the latter makes acrobatics possible. Almanarre beach on the west side of the Giens Peninsula has become a mecca for funboarders and played host to the World Championships. More technical skill is required on other beaches such as Six-Fours-les-Plages and the two sides of Cap Nègre.

Grégor/EXPLORER

For a different view of their favourite beaches, holidaymakers can fearlessly indulge in the joys of **parascending** – flying over the water below a parachute which is towed by a motorboat. The aim is to stay in the air for as along as possible and as high as possible. Instruction in this sport is available on nearly all the organised beaches, where there is enough wind.

Jet-skiing is practised on certain stretches of coast, which have been carefully chosen and are not accessible from the land. The sport provides a superb experience of moving alone at speed. It is, however, strictly regulated
– machines must be 150m/164yd apart;
– machines may operate only during the day;
– machines may operate between 300m/328yd outside the channels and up to 1 nautical mile
– in future pilots must hold a proficiency certificate.

Most of the large resorts offer jet-ski hire by the hour or the half day. It is also possible to hire sea canoes in Salins d'Hyères and certain resorts on the Var coast.

Motor vessels are forbidden within 300m/328yd of the shore (except in the access channels) and must not exceed 5 knots in certain restricted areas (Îles d'Hyères, Îles de Lérins and Villefranche anchorage). Elsewhere the top speed is 10 knots.

Coastal walks

Before the recent building boom the famous Customs Path ran all along the Riviera coast; some particularly picturesque sections still survive and have been developed by the Coast Conservancy *(Conservatoire du Littoral)*.

There are several signed country footpaths along the Var coast, of which about 10, from Bandol to St-Aygulph, are described in a topo-guide published by the **Fédération Française de la Randonnée Pédestre**.

INLAND

Rambling

A network of waymarked paths covers the region described in this guide.

GR (Grande Randonnée) paths, which are fully open only from the end of June to early October, are for experienced ramblers accustomed to mountain conditions.

– **GR 5**, the oldest and most majestic, which terminates in Nice after crossing Europe; the last section from Nice to St-Dalmas-Valdeblore passes through Aspremont, Levens, the Vésubie gorge and Madone d'Utelle.

– **GR 52**, from St-Dalmas-Valdeblore to Menton via Le Boréon, La Vallée des Merveilles, Turini Forest, Sospel and Val Rameh Tropical Garden

– **GR52A**, among the peaks in the eastern part of the Parc National du Mercantour beyond the Col de Tende

Other paths, open all year, for walkers of all levels of competence

– **GR 4**, from Grasse via Gréolières and Entrevaux to the Verdon Gorge

– **GR 51**, nicknamed "the Mediterranean balcony", from Castellar (east of Menton) to Col de la Cadière (Estérel) providing panoramic views of the coast from the first ridge

– **GR 510**, entirely in the Alpes-Maritimes region, from Breil-sur-Roya via Sospel, Villars-sur-Var, Puget-Rostand, Roquestéron, St-Auban and Escragnolles to St-Cézaire-sur-Siagne, discovering another valley dotted with hill villages at each stage of the 10-day ramble

– **GR 9**, from Signes through the Massif des Maures to St-Pons-les-Mûres

– **GR 99**, from Toulon through the Brignolais country to the Verdon Gorge

– **GR 90**, the shortest, from Le Lavandou through the Massif des Maures to Notre-Dame-des-Anges, where it meets the GR 9.

Various bodies organise rambles adapted to the competence of those taking part.

Week-long rambles in the Vallée des Merveilles are organised by **Destination Merveilles**, Le Grand Provence, 38 Rue Clément-Roassal, 06100 Nice ☎ 04 93 16 08 72.

Topo-guides for the **Grandes Randonnées** and **Petites Randonnées** are published by the Fédération Française de la Randonnée Pédestre – Comité National des Sentiers de Grande Randonnée, and are obtainable from the Centre d'Information, 64 Rue de Gergovie, 75014 Paris ☎ 01 45 45 31 02 (or order the catalogue of 170 publications by internet at the association's site - in French - www.ffrf.asso.fr).

Over the frontier

The old royal hunting ground of the Sardinian monarchy extended until the Second World War over the two slopes of the Mercantour and the Marguareis. Since then the Italian section has been administered as a nature reserve with an active policy for the conservation of species and habitats. Two large natural parks have been created – **Parco dell'Argentera**, the largest, and Alta Valle Pesio, further east. Together with the Parc du Mercantour they have conducted a campaign for the reintroduction of endangered species – the bearded vulture and the ibex. In the Parco dell'Argentera there are many "royal" botanical paths easily accessible to ramblers from the French side of the border by the frontier passes – Col de la Lombarde and Col de Tende. From the latter pass two paths *(each about 3hr)* follow the peaks towards Rocca dell'Abisso (2 755m/9 039ft – west) and Cima di Pepino (2 335m/7 661ft – east).

The **Alta Valle Pesio** park, in the Marguareis, is the wildest and least easy to reach from France. Ramblers should branch into the northeast route from Limone-Piemonte or go up the valley from Savone.

The Vermenagna Valley which extends from Col de Tende to the Cuneo Plain is still within the range of the Provençal culture; Provençal spectacles *(Roumiage de Provenço)* are held in the Grana Valley in July. Among the specialities of the district is a famous cheese, Castelmagno, and hand-made cutlery, such as the Vernantino pocket knife.

Parco Naturale Regionale dell'Argentera – Corso Dante Livio Bianco 5 – 12010 Valdieri (CN) ☎ 39 171 97 397

Parco Naturale Regionale Alta Valle Pesio e Tanaro – Via Sta Anne 34 – 12013 Chiusa Pesia (CN) ☎ 39 171 73 40 21

Tourist office in Limone-Piemonte – Via Roma (CN) ☎ 39 171 92 101.

Lac du Basto

Riding

Ligue Provence – Côte d'Azur de Tourisme Équestre – 19 Boulevard Victor-Hugo, 06130 Grasse ☎ 04 93 42 62 98

Comité Départemental d'Équitation de Randonnée des Alpes-Maritimes – Mas de la Jumenterie, Route de St-Cézaire, 06460 St-Vallier-de-Thiey ☎ 04 93 42 63 98 (Mr Desprey)

Comité Départemental du Tourisme Équestre du Var – Centre de Tourisme Équestre de l'Estérel, les 3 Fers, Domaine du Grenouillet, Agay 83700 St-Raphaël ☎ 04 94 82 75 28

Association Varoise de Développement du Tourisme de Randonnée (AVDTR) – 1 Boulevard Foch, 83000 Draguignan ☎ 04 94 68 97 66 – which publishes the brochure *Guide Annuaire de Cavalier Varois*.

Exploring the Border on Horseback – This is an unusual way of exploring the Massif du Mercantour. There is a waymarked route on the **Franco Italian Natural Spaces Equestrian Itinerary** *(Itinéraire Équestre des Espaces Naturels Franco-Italiens – Itinerario Equestre degli Soazi Naturali Franco-Italiani)* from St-Martin-Vésubie through the Italian parks – Argentera and Alta Valle Pesio – to Certosa di Pesio; there are 10 staging posts with facilities for riders and their mounts.
Practical information is available from the Parc du Mercantour and the Parco dell'Argentera information offices *(see Rambling)*.
The Parc du Mercantour publishes a brochure containing various bridle routes and staging posts in the Argentera and Mercantour highlands.

Winter sports

It is only a short distance (less than 2hr by car) from the coast to a range of winter sports stations:

La Colmiane-Valdeblore
Boréon-St-Martin-Vésubie
Peïra-Cava
L'Audibergue

La Gordolasque-Belvédère
Turini-Camp d'Argent
Gréolières-les-Neiges

There are off-piste runs near La Haute-Roya – La Brigue (alt 900m/2 953ft) and Tende-Val Casterino (alt 1 500m/4 921ft).
The proximity of the Italian ski resort, Limone-Piemonte, which can be reached by rail, means that many types of snow sport are available.

Mountaineering

There is a large variety of climbing in the highlands from the Pre-Alps of Nice via the steep faces of the *baous* in the Var Valley and the Rock in Roquebrune-sur-Argens to the rock faces of the Verdon Gorge.
Guided excursions in rock-climbing, mountaineering, rambling, downhill skiing and overland skiing are organised by:
– the **Club Alpin Français**, 25 Rue Victor-Clappier, 83000 Toulon
– the **Club Alpin Français**, 14 Avenue Mirabeau, 06000 Nice ☎ 04 93 62 59 99
– the **Association des Guides et Accompagnateurs des Alpes Méridionales**
Roquebillière ☎ 04 93 03 44 30
St-Martin-Vésubie ☎ 04 93 03 26 60
Tende ☎ 04 93 04 69 22 or 04 93 04 68 72
– **Bureau des Guides de la Côte d'Azur**
3 Rue de la Suisse, 06000 Nice ☎ 04 93 39 64 77
06450 St-Martin-Vésubie ☎ 04 93 03 26 60
– **Compagnie des Guides du Mercantour**
Place du Marché, 06450 St-Martin-Vésubie
Tende ☎ 04 93 04 77 85

Caving and Potholing

The Var has many sites of original configuration; the Siou Blanc Plateau is a catalogue of variants of chasms and potholes which the amateur can explore. Among these is the deepest pothole in the region (350m/1 148ft). The Grotte de Mouret, near Draguignan, is useful for practice.
In the Alpes-Maritimes, both the Pays Grassois and the Caussols Plateau offer many opportunities for seasoned cavers. The legendary Massif du Marguareis (northeast of Tende), the site of the exploits of the potholer Michel Siffre in the 1960s, is still a paradise for the experienced caver. This immense chalky plateau is peppered with sinkholes, with vertiginous rock faces overhanging the Italian slopes, and contains deep chasms (more than 900m/2 953ft).

Information available from
– **Comité Départemental de Spéléologie du Var**, l'Hélianthe, Rue Émile-Olivier, 83000 Toulon ☎ 04 94 31 29 43
– **Comité Départemental de Spéléologie des Alpes-Maritimes**, Boulevard Paul-Montal, bâtiment 5, l'Alsace, 06200 Nice ☎ 04 93 62 09 54
– Speleology divisions of the Club Alpin Français in Nice or Toulon.

Water Sports

Canoeing – Some of the rivers in the Alpes-Maritimes can be explored by canoe throughout the year but the best time is in spring. In any season beware of sudden floods caused by heavy rain upstream.

The most attractive stretches of river are to be found just inside the boundaries of the Mercantour or near St-Martin-Vésubie. Shooting rapids excursions through gorges accompanied by experts are organised by the Toulon division of the Club Alpin Français. Those offering the best services are awarded the title **Point-Canoë-Nature** by the Fédération Française de Canoë-Kayak; list available from the federation and on Minitel 3615 Canoë 24.

Fédération Française de Canoë-Kayak, 87 Quai de la Marne, 94340 Joinville-le-Pont ☎ 02 48 89 39 89.

Canyoning – The most attractive stretches of water provided by the Alpes-Maritimes for this activity, which combines rock-climbing, potholing and swimming in running water, are to be found within the Parc du Mercantour and in St-Martin-Vésubie. There are also two exceptional sites in the valley of the Haute-Roya near Saorge – La Maglia (through caves) and La Bendola (2 days in the water). Canyoning is strictly forbidden in the central part of the Parc du Mercantour.

Between St-Martin-Vésubie and its confluence with the Var, the River Vésubie offers a variety of canyons – Duranus, the agreeable site at L'Imberguet, La Bollène and Gourgas, which is technically demanding.

The Estéron, an eastern tributary of the Var, provides classic stretches in exceptional settings between Roquestéron and St-Auban.

The network of rivers in the Var provides many opportunities for canyoning, with 11 authorised sites of varying difficulty suitable to all levels of competence. The Destel Gorge, between Caramy and Carcès, the lower stretches of the Jabron (downstream of Trigance) and the Pennafort Gorge are suitable for beginners. Seillans-la-Cascade, the Nartuby and the Destéou in the Maures demand greater skill.

At all times of the year there is a risk of sudden increases in the volume of water following a storm upstream and the sudden release of retained water.

Canyoning trips with guides are organised by the Toulon branch of the Club Alpin Français.

Information is also available from the **Comité Départemental de Spéléologie du Var** (☎ 04 94 87 42 72).

Lakes – The largest lake in the Estérel, **Lac de St-Cassien** (430ha/1 062 acres), not only supplies electricity and water to the eastern Var and provides water for the fire-fighting aircraft but also has a nature reserve at the west end with a reed-bed where more than 150 species of over-wintering migrating seabirds have been recorded. There are facilities for wind-surfing and pedalo – tuition from the base and equipment for hire from the open-air cafés along the sometimes steep banks; motorised vessels are forbidden.

Centre Régional d'Entraînement et de Formation à l'Aviron – Lac de St-Cassien 83440 Montaurous ☎ 04 94 76 43 08

The **Lac de Carcès** (100ha/247 acres) is a reservoir formed by a dam and fed by the River Argens. There is a pleasant wooded road along the eastern bank; the opposite bank, more rural, is much used by fishermen. Canoeing in kayaks is permitted.

Game Fishing – Local and national fishing regulations apply to fishing in lakes (Carcès and St Cassien) and in rivers (Gapeau, Réal Martin, Argens, Roya, Bévéra etc). It is also advisable to join the Association de Pêche et de Pisciculture in the area in question by paying the annual fees appropriate to the form of fishing practised and then by buying a daily permit from an authorised vendor.

Trout fishing is permitted from the 2nd Saturday in March to the 3rd Sunday in September; pike fishing is allowed only between 31 January and 15 April. Fishing for common grayling in the Siagne is banned through the year.

Up-to-date information available from
– **Fédération Départementale du Var** ☎ 04 94 69 05 66
– **Fédération Départementale des Alpes-Maritimes** ☎ 04 93 72 06 04
– **Conseil Supérieur de la Pêche**, 134 Avenue Malakoff, 75016 Paris ☎ 01 45 01 20 20, which provides a leaflet *Pêche en France*.

Cycling and mountain biking

The diversity of terrain inland and the network of cycle tracks along the coast and in the massifs of the Estérel and the Maures are very popular with mountain bike enthusiasts. Many organisations, hotels and clubs in the region hire out this kind of bicycle and provide details of local cycle tracks. Lists of suppliers are also available from local tourist offices.

Main railway stations – Antibes, Bandol, Cagnes-sur-Mer, Cannes, Hyères, Juan-les-Pins, St-Raphaël – hire out various types of bicycle, which can be returned to a different station. The regulations concerning admission to the Parc du Mercantour apply also to cyclists;

details available from the Maisons du Parc and the headquarters (23 Rue d'Italie, Nice).
The **Comité Départemental du Tourisme du Var** distributes a leaflet describing more than
20 signed routes for cyclists; among the principal ones are
– Roof of the Var *(Toit du Var)* (70km/43mi)
– Bauxite Road *(Route de la Bauxite)* (80km/50mi)
– North face of the Maures *(l'Ubac des Maures)* (80km/50mi)
– Maures chestnut woods *(Châtaigneraies des Maures)* (90km/56mi)
One of the most famous mountain biking events in Europe is the Roc d'Azur at Rama-
tuelle with a height difference of nearly 200m/656ft (50km/31mi long) *(see Calendar of
events)*.
Comité Départemental de Cyclotourisme des Alpes-Maritimes, 22bis Rue Trachel, 06000 Nice
☎ 04 93 82 16 39 (Mr Rény Bernage)
Comité Départemental de Cyclotourisme du Var, Les Ibis, bâtiment A, Avenue de Bellegou,
83000 Toulon ☎ 04 94 46 00 25 (Mr J-Marc Pappon)
Fédération Française de Cyclotourisme, 8 Rue Jean-Marie-Jégo, 75013 Paris ☎ 01 45 80 30 21.

Aerial Sports

Hang-gliding, parachuting and ultra-light craft – There are about 20 suitable sites
for parachuting, hang-gliding *(vol libre)* and ultra-light craft *(planeur ultra léger moto-
risé)*. For a list of centres consult
– Minitel 3615 FFLV
– **Comité Départemental de Vol Libre Varois**, Domaine de la Limatte, 83870 Signes
☎ 04 94 90 86 13
– **Fédération Française de Vol Libre**, 4 Rue de Suisse, 06000 Nice ☎ 04 93 88 62 89
– **Fédération Française de Planeur Ultra-Léger Motorisé**, 96bis Rue Marc-Sangnier, 94700
Maisons-Alfort ☎ 05 49 81 74 43.

Gliding – The main gliding centre, which is run by the **Association Aéronautique Provence-
Côte d'Azur**, is near Fayence where aerological conditions are exceptional. It has become
the leading gliding centre in Europe and has contributed to the rapid development of
glider aerobatics. Each year champions from all over the world demonstrate their skill
at the *Open de France de Planeur*.
– **Association aéronautique Provence-Côte d'Azur**, 83440 Fayence ☎ 04 94 76 00 68.

Air trips – It is possible to fly over part of the Riviera such as St-Tropez Bay, the
Estérel, the Îles de Lérins, Monaco and the Verdon Gorge.
 For details of timetables and fares contact the following companies, all based at the
international airport of Cannes-Mandelieu, 06150 Cannes-la-Bocca
– **Compagnie Air Nice** ☎ 04 93 90 40 26, Cannes-Mandelieu Airport, 06150 Cannes la Bocca
– **Toulon-Hyères Airport** ☎ 04 94 22 81 60.
Short trips over the Riviera by **helicopter** are available from
– **Héli-Air-Monaco**, Monaco-Fontvieille heliport ☎ 00 377 92 05 00 50.

Unusual sites and themed itineraries

UNUSUAL VIEWS OF THE COTE D'AZUR

Riviera Caves – The limestone region of the Pays Grassois (especially the Caussols Plateau) boasts many interesting geological features dating from different periods – the caves (*grottes*) at St-Cézaire *(see GRASSE)*, the potholes within gigantic limestone crevices such as the Grotte des Audides *(see CABRIS)* or the original caves consisting of a succession of natural dams *(gours)* such as the Grotte de Baume Obscure *(see ST-VALLIER-DE-THIEY)*. The **Grottes de Villecroze** near Draguignan *(see VILLECROZE)* are formed of tufa.
Other caves, which are accessible with adequate equipment and some technical knowledge, belong in the caving category *(see above)*. People with no caving experience can receive an impression of the activity in the first section (about 12m/39ft) of the **Embut de Caussols** (*embut* is the Provençal word for swallowhole).

Military Fortifications of the Alpes-Maritimes – The strategic significance of the frontier zone in the southeast, identified by Vauban, was exploited from 1880 onwards by the system of defence begun by Sérés de Rivières. The project was completed and improved from 1929 by its integration into the Maginot Line which defended the eastern frontier from Dunkirk to Menton. The whole construction gives an interesting view of military architecture in the 19C and 20C. Some of the buildings have been disarmed, restored by associations and are accessible to visitors
– Fort de Ste-Agnès *(see MENTON)*
– Fort du Barbonnet *(see Forêt de TURINI)*
– Fort Suchet (19C), the only one that can be visited *(see Forêt de TURINI)*
– Fort St-Roch *(see SOSPEL)*.
Other less interesting forts make pleasant destinations for walks with fine views.
Visitors should bear in mind that, although the buildings of the Maginot Line appear to be in good condition, they may conceal indoor wells or dangerous passages. Some properties are private as they have been acquired by individuals.
In the highly strategic sector of L'Authion, near Col de Turini *(see Forêt de TURINI)*, several structures designed by Sérés de Rivières have survived and can be reached by the loop road encircling the massif:
– Fort des Mille-Fourches
– La Forca
– Redoute des 3 Communes (1897), the first building constructed of reinforced concrete.
From Mont Chauve d'Aspremont *(see NICE)* there is a brilliant view of the whole coast in ideal high-pressure conditions. On the summit (854m/2 802ft) is a Sérés de Rivières fort with a monumental south façade typical of the period; it is occupied by the Service des Télécommunications. Mont Chauve de Tourette is visible further north capped by a fort of similar period.
The section near Col de Tende, which was Italian from 1860 to 1947, is an impressive example of the Italian system of defence. The remarkable central fort is set on top of the *col* and approached by the narrow road which branches off by the entrance to the road tunnel; each of its façades has a different architectural style. The interior *(access difficult)* resembles a small town, self-sufficient in supplies.

On the Track of Macaron – The old track bed of one of the dismantled sections of the pine-cone train *(train des pignes)*, which linked Toulon to St-Raphaël from early in the 20C to 1950, is open to walkers. Although the track and stations have mostly disappeared owing to the effects of time and events, such as the Allied landings at the end of the Second World War, works of art and some stations (Carqueiranne) have survived. The tunnels are often used by walkers as short cuts, providing unusual and surprising glimpses of the Maures coast.

FOREST PARKS

All along the Alpes-Maritimes coast there are islands of greenery *(parcs forestiers départementaux)* provided for walkers of all ages
– **Parc de la Grande-Corniche** à Èze (access from Col d'Èze on the Grande Corniche)
– **Parc de Vaugrenier** (access by N 7 between Antibes and Marina Baie des Anges)
– **Parc de la Vallée de la Brague** (at the northern end of Biot village)
– **Parc du San Peyre** (from La Napoule towards A 8 motorway and a left turn onto Route du Cimetière), a former look-out post (alt 131m/430ft) which offers a superb panorama of Cannes Bay
– **Parc de la Pointe de l'Aiguille** (car park on N 98 at the edge of Théoule).

THEMED ITINERARIES

Route Historique des Hauts-Lieux de Provence – A circuit from St-Maximin-la-Ste-Baume via Draguignan and Les Arcs to Fréjus returning along the coast to Toulon, organised by an association at the Office de Tourisme, 83460 Les Arcs-sur-Argens ☎ 04 94 73 37 30.

Route des Côtes de Provence – *See p 64.*

DRIVING TOURS

For an overall impression of these various driving tours, consult the map on p 13.

1 Var Coastline and the Golden Islands

Round tour of 235km/146mi starting from Toulon

The city of Toulon should be visited in the local tradition, in other words at a leisurely pace, taking time to explore the intricate streets shaded by century-old plane trees. After dropping by the lively marché Lafayette and choosing a few fresh vegetables and mouthwatering sweetmeats, set out to discover "the most attractive anchorage" on the Riviera, passing by Pointe du Fort Balaguier and Cap Sicié. Nestling between land and sea, Sanary and Bandol, continued by the islands of Bendor and Embiez, will seduce you by their heavenly setting. Further on, the perched villages of Le Castellet, Beausset and Evenos compose the perfect picture of Provençal bliss. The anchorage may also be admired from atop Mont Faron. The bird sanctuary at La Londe will transport you to tropical climes. Treat yourself to a stay on the gorgeous islands of Port-Cros and Porquerolles; the underwater path offers incomparable views of the sea depths as well as local fauna and flora. A tour of the Mine de Cap-Garonne at Le Pradet is the perfect way to round off your outing.

2 Le Haut-Var

Round tour of 245km/153mi starting from Draguignan

This itinerary will take you across the upper stretches of the Var Valley, characterised by rolling wooded countryside dotted with old abbeys and remarkable sites: Tourtour nestling on the crest of a hill overlooking olive groves; Cotignac precariously perched on a cliff; Villecroze and Seillans enhanced by tufa concretions; Entrecasteaux, whose château is graced by gardens attributed to Le Nôtre. You may be surprised by the diversity of the villages and towns you will encounter. Some clearly enjoy perpetuating local tradition while others are resolutely turned towards the future. Do not fail to patronise the colourful markets offering truffles, goat's cheese or olives, depending on the season, and the restaurants, where you will be served tasty regional cuisine pleasantly seasoned with aromatic herbs.

3 Le Massif des Maures

Round tour of 275km/171mi starting from Fréjus

Far away from the coast and its bustling crowd, this tour will take you through refreshingly cool forests of cork oak and the pretty Gratteloup arboretum, where eucalyptus, chestnut, maple, cedar and juniper trees exude their intoxicating aroma. Visit the superb Domaine du Rayol, designed at the turn of the century and rediscover regional arts and crafts: cork industry in Gonfaron, *marrons glacés* in Collobrières, pipe-making and carpet weaving in Cogolin. The hill villages of Ramatuelle, Grimaud or Gassin command panoramic views of the coast, as do the Moulins de Paillas. Before having a swim in one of the many sheltered inlets, you may want to settle on the terrace of the Sénéquier tea room alongside the rich and famous or you may prefer to browse among the market stalls set up in the old port in the hope of chancing upon a fake Picasso...

4 Massif de l'Esterel and the Fayence region

Round tour of 285km/177mi starting from Cannes

Whatever the season, this itinerary will prove an enchanting experience on many counts: the rich, luxuriant vegetation, the chirping of the cicadas, the delicately fragrant mimosa blossom, the warm embrace of the sun and the reddish tinge of porphyry around the Esterel heights...Running between La Napoule and Agay, the Corniche d'Or offers stunning views of the sea, glimpsed through a kaleidoscope of blues, reds and greens. You will succumb to the charms of St-Raphaël, a lively seaside resort, and Fréjus with its prestigious military past, not to mention Fréjus-Plage, which boasts the longest sandy beach on the Riviera. Further inland, the Fayence area will introduce you to a host of perched villages huddled on mountain slopes, dominated by vestiges of their medieval citadels: Caillan, Fayence, Tourrettes, Seillan, Tanneron and Auribeau-sur-Siagne.

⑤ Fragrances and colours of the Pre-Alps

Round tour of 215km/134mi starting from Grasse

The Pre-Alps of Provence, extending to the foot of the Alpine range and cut across by steep ravines, offer a delightful combination of colours and fragrances, where the heady smells of olive and cypress tree vie with the more subtle scent of rose, jasmin, oleander and violet. Flowers have made the reputation of Grasse and your first stop in this city must be the International Museum of Perfume and the different *parfumeries* explaining the secrets of the trade. The entrance to the Gorges du Loup is the perfect place to stop and admire the hill village of Gourdon, jealously guarding its abyss, and the Caussols Plateau, a curiously barren stretch of land riddled with chasms. After observing fine concretions in the caves of St-Vallier and St-Cézaire, pursue your route to St-Paul-de-Vence, a typical medieval village known for its arts and crafts, and to the delightful hamlet of Tourrettes-sur-Loup, where terraced violet fields have been cultivated from generation to generation. The Baou of St-Jeannet dominating the Var River is a sheer rocky cliff popular among seasoned climbers. Lastly, the coastal road stretching between Cagnes-sur-Mer and Antibes offers pretty views of the Baie des Anges and provides access to a number of contemporary art museums.

⑥ L'arrière-pays Niçois

Round tour of 270km/168mi starting from Nice

This driving tour will provide you with a fascinating selection of natural sites and architectural riches: quaint perched villages, chapels decorated by famous painters or unknown artists from the Middle Ages, steep cliffs overlooking gorges echoing with the swirling of crystal clear waters and lush forests rustling with the sounds of local fauna. Running alongside the lower Var Valley, bordered to the west by the Baou of St Jeannet, you will start to approach the heights extending beyond Nice, dominated by Mont Chauve. After driving through Aspremont, Levens and Duranus, you will reach the breathtaking Vésubie Gorges. From there, brace yourself for the long series of steep hairpin bends leading up to the Madone d'Utelle sanctuary, a popular place of pilgrimage, and the nearby belvedere commanding a splendid panorama of the Alpes-Maritimes and Mediterranean Sea. Proceeding upstream along the Vésubie River in the direction of Col de Turini, you will come to Bollène-Vésubie, precariously nestling on the mountain slope. On reaching L'Authion, go round to Pointe des Trois-Communes to feast your eyes on the sweeping landscape. Continue towards the Gorges de Piaon. After the curious Notre-Dame-de-la-Menour Chapel with its two-storey Renaissance façade, you will come to Sospel, springing from its verdant setting, where tasty regional dishes may be sampled. You will drive through several passes before rejoining Lucéram Valley, famed for its Christmas festivities attended by local shepherds. Finally, three belvederes, each home to a small village, Berre, Falicon and Tourrettes, will complete this charming tour of the Nice hinterland.

⑦ The Corniches of the Riviera

Round tour of 250km/155.5mi starting from Nice

If you have seen Hitchcock's thriller *To Catch a Thief*, set at the heart of the Riviera, then you will know that it is advisable to hug the road winding its way between Nice and Monte-Carlo as closely as possible. This route, which features a series of vertiginous belvederes, goes past some of the prettiest spots of the Côte d'Azur. Set out from Villefranche, famous not only for its Chapelle St-Pierre decorated by Jean Cocteau, but also for its pretty anchorage and succulent seafood dishes. Follow the Grande Corniche up to Roquebrune, with occasional forays downhill to Beaulieu (Villa Kérylos), St-Jean-Cap-Ferrat (Fondation Île de France) and Èze, clinging to its rocky spur, where a tour of artists' workshops can be pleasantly rounded off by a visit to the Jardin Exotique. Enjoy the view from the Vistaero before descending towards Roquebrune with its medieval castle and venerable olive tree believed to be over one thousand years old. After Menton, the road will take you through the perched villages of Ste-Agnès, Peille and Peillon, where the steep alleyways *(calades)* lead to chapels adorned with fine frescoes.

FOR CHILDREN AND THEIR ESCORTS

For a change from the beach, on cloudy days or when the *mistral* is blowing, there are many attractions all along the Riviera – leisure pools, animal parks and miniature collections.

Leisure Pools

- **Parc Nautique Niagara**, Route du Canadel, 83310 La Môle ☎ 04 94 49 58 87
- **Aquasplash**, RN7, 06600 Antibes ☎ 04 93 33 49 49
- **Aquatica**, RN98, 83600 Fréjus ☎ 04 53 58 58
- **Aqualand**, 559 Chemin Départemental, 83270 St-Cyr-sur-Mer ☎ 04 94 32 09 09

Animal Parks

- Sanary-Bandol – Zoo
- Toulon – Zoo du Mont-Faron
- La Londe-les-Maures – Jardin d'Oiseaux Tropicaux *(see HYÈRES)*
- Gonfaron – Village des Tortues *(see Massif des MAURES)*
- Fréjus – Zoo
- Antibes – La Jungle des Papillons, La Petite Ferme, le Golf Adventureland and Marineland
- St-Jean-Cap-Ferrat – Chimpanzee shows at the Zoo
- Monaco – Jardin Animalier

Specialist Fairs in the Var

2 February	Grimaud	Candlemas Fair
14 April	Six-Fours-les-Plages	Plant Fair
Ascension Day	Grimaud	Wool Fair
8 June	Les Issambres	St Médard's Fair
24 June	Le Beausset	Leatherwork Fair
First Sunday in July	Trigance	Craft Fair
2-10 July	Draguignan	Olive Fair
24 July	La Verdière	Dog Fair
26 July	St-Tropez	St Anne's Fair
Mid-August	Seillans	Decorated Earthenware Fair
17-18 August	Barjols	Leatherwork Fair
28 August	La Garde-Freinet	Pottery Market
First weekend in September	Le Val	Sausage Fair
2 September	La Garde	Garlic and Livestock Fair
8-9 September	Cogolin	Provençal Fair
19 September	Lorgues	St Ferréol's Fair
29 September	Many villages	Michaelmas fairs
6 October	Fréjus	Garlic Fair
Monday after 11 November	Collobrières	St Martin's Fair
Third Sunday in November	Taradeau	New Wine *(vin nouveau)* Fair
30 November	Ramatuelle	St Andrew's Fair

Santon Fairs in the Var

Clay figurines *(santons)* became popular in Provence at the time of the French Revolution, when many churches were officially closed. A craftsman in Marseilles decided to market these figurines so that people could set up nativity scenes at home. The term derives from the Provençal word *santoun*, meaning "little saint". Originally, these statuettes were confined to religious or biblical themes but over the years they came to represent traditional aspects of the region (local arts and crafts, folklore, animals, etc).

Carqueiranne	Second weekend in December
La Celle	Last weekend in November
Draguignan	One week before Christmas in Bon-Pasteur Chapel
Entrecasteaux	First fortnight in December
Fréjus	The week before Christmas
La Garde	The week before Christmas
Hyères	Mid-July
Ollioules	December at the Vieux-Moulin
Puget-Ville	Second week in December
Signes	First fortnight in November
Solliès-Ville	Second fortnight in December at Moulin d'Oli
La Valette	Second fortnight in December at Moulin d'Ardouvin

Great Sporting Events on the Riviera

End of January	Monte-Carlo Automobile Rally
Second or third weekend in April	Sailing competitions in St-Tropez
Ascension weekend	Grand Prix Automobile de Formula 1 in Monaco
Last weekend in May	Truck driving Grand Prix (with trailer-handling displays) at Le Castellet circuit
Third weekend in September	Bol d'Or (Golden Bowl for motorcycles) at Le Castellet circuit
First weekend in October	La Nioulargue (sailing regatta) in St-Tropez
Weekend in mid-Ocotber in Ramatuelle	Roc'Azur (motorcross – championnat de VTT)

Scenic rail journeys

The single-track main railway line between Nice and Cuneo in Italy crosses the old county of Nice passing through Peille, L'Escarène, Sospel, Breil-sur-Roya, Fontan-Saorge, St-Dalmas-de-Tende, Tende, Vievola and finally Limone in Italy. The track was built from 1920 onwards and incorporates some spectacular engineering feats as it twists and turns through the tortuous mountain landscapes, sometimes even spiralling to change level. The train affords wonderful views that are not always visible from the road, particularly between L'Escarène and Sospel and between Breil and Tende along the rugged gorges of the River Roya. The line is 119km/74mi long; over a stretch of 85km/53mi it rises from sea-level to 1 279m/4 196ft at the entrance to the tunnel bored through Col de Tende. The French section of the line suffered extensive damage during the Second World War and repair work was not completed until 1980. On the Italian side of the border, the line descends less steeply down to Cuneo through the charming Vermegnagna Valley.

The frequent service enables skiers to reach the Massif du Mercantour and spend the day skiing in the Italian winter sports resort of Limone-Piemonte.

There are at least four daily return services to and from Nice-Ville station. In Breil-sur-Roya the line rejoins the main line running between Ventimiglia and Cuneo, which has better interconnections with the Italian train network; for timetable information ☎ 04 93 87 50 50.

Provençal Railway

The famous pine-cone train *(Train des Pignes)* is named after the pine cones which were used as fuel to stoke the engines. It runs between Nice and Digne-les-Bains (150km/93mi) passing through Puget-Théniers, Entrevaux, Annot, St-André-les-Alpes. The single track was constructed from 1890 to 1911 and comprises 60 remarkable feats of engineering – metal bridges, viaducts, tunnels (one of which is 3.5km/2.3mi long). It is a relic of a vast regional network which early in the 20C served the whole inland area from Toulon to Draguignan. The journey, 2hr by train, 3hr by omnibus, passes through five valleys, offering fine views of the landscape and perched villages which are often difficult to reach by car.

All year round it is possible to take the train to Lac de Castillon, the Verdon Gorges and the winter sports stations in the Alpes-Maritimes *département*. From Plan-du-Var there is a service to the walking country in the Vésubie Valley. In summer the **Alpazur** service runs from Nice as far as Grenoble and there is a tourist steam train on the Puget-Théniers section. There are wayside halts at which walkers can leave or rejoin the train at the beginning and end of a day's rambling.

The violent storms in autumn 1994 caused serious damage to some sections of the line so it is advisable to check the availability of trains with the **Chemins de Fer de Provence**, 4 Rue Alfred-Binet, 06000 Nice ☎ 04 93 82 10 17.

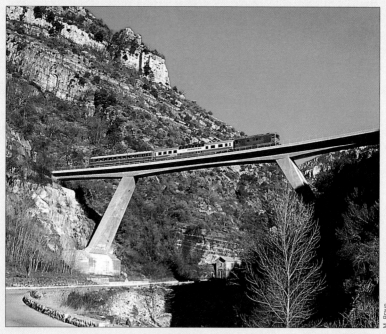

Scarassoui Viaduct, Nice-Cuneo railway

Crafts and souvenirs

In high season many villages and resorts organise courses focusing on local arts and crafts – painting on porcelain in Le Cannet, weaving and woodwork in the Cannes district and regional cuisine in St-Martin-Vésubie.
The names of the appropriate bodies are available from the Comités Départementaux de Tourisme in Toulon and in Nice.

Crystallised fruit

PROVENCAL MARKETS

Provençal markets, fragrant with thyme, tarragon, lavender and garlic, are part of the traditional image of the South of France.
As a rule, during the summer season, stalls selling fruit and vegetables and craftwork can be found under the plane trees of even the smallest village.
The most picturesque and lively markets of the Var and the days on which they are held are listed below.

Aups	Wednesdays, Saturdays
Bargemon	Thursdays
Le Beausset	Fridays (fair)
Bormes-les-Mimosas	Wednesdays
Brignoles	Saturdays
Callas	Tuesdays, Saturdays
Cogolin	Wednesdays, Saturdays (fair)
La Croix-Valmer	Sundays
Draguignan	Wednesdays, Saturdays
Fayence	Tuesdays, Thursdays (fair)
Fréjus	Wednesdays, Saturdays (fair)
La Garde	Tuesdays, Saturdays (fair)
Grimaud	Thursdays (fair)
Hyères	Tuesdays, Thursdays (fair)
Le Lavandou	Thursdays
Lorgues	Tuesdays
Le Luc	Fridays
Ramatuelle	Thursdays, Sundays (fair)
St-Tropez	Tuesdays, Saturdays (fair)
Ste-Maxime	Thursdays (fair)
Toulon	daily
Tourtour	Tuesdays, Saturdays
Trans-en-Provence	Sundays
Villecroze	Thursdays (fair)

A list of traditional craft markets, where the products of the Var region are sold, is published annually by the **Chambre des Métiers**, BP 69 – 83402 Hyères Cedex ☎ 04 94 21 00 57.

WINE TASTING AND REGIONAL PRODUCE

The main areas where craftwork and local produce can be bought by visitors from the producers are shown on the map – Spécialités et Vignobles *(see p 64)*.

Further information on specialist products

Sweets – Confiserie des Gorges du Loup, Le Pont-du-Loup, 06140 Tourrettes-sur-Loup ☎ 04 93 59 32 91.

Marrons glacés and preserved chestnuts – Nouvelle Confiserie Azuréenne, Boulevard Koenig, Collobrières ☎ 04 94 48 07 20.

Glassware – Verrerie de Biot in Biot where it is possible to watch master glassblowers at work.

Leather – The *sandale tropézienne* is the same model that has been made by the same company since 1927 *(see SAINT-TROPEZ p 285)*.

Wine Cooperative Cellars – The **Côte de Provence wine road** winds its way through the vineyards; the wine cellars which are open for tasting are advertised on the roadside signs.
There are three vineyards on Île de Porquerolles producing an AOC *(Appellation d'Origine Contrôlée)* Côte de Provence wine. All offer wine tasting sessions:
– Domaine de l'Île, the oldest
– Domaine Perzinsky
– Domaine Courtade

Another wine road *(Route du Vin)* advertises the wines of Bandol.
Information from the **Syndicat des Domaines en Appellation Bandol Contrôlée**, Les Domaines du Bandol, Allée Viven, 83150 Bandol ☎ 04 94 29 45 03.
Vin de Bellet is produced on the hillsides behind Nice round St-Romain-de-Bellet; it is on sale in the cellars which are open to the public; further information from the Nice tourist office.

Summer Aïoli Festivals in the Var
(see p 82)

8-11 July	Châteauvieux
8 August	Mazaugues
9 August	Entrecasteaux (one of the largest)
12 to 15 August	La Motte-du-Var
12 to 15 August	La Celle
12 to 16 August	Collobrières
14 to 16 August	Ampus
20 to 22 August	Solliès-Ville
26 to 28 August	Fayence

(Admission by reserving and paying the entrance fee at the local tourist office).

Spotlight on the Riviera

Because of the high number and diversity of its natural sites and the quality of the light, the whole of the Riviera seems to have been predestined to become a backdrop for all the varied scenarios of film-makers. Here are the main locations which have featured in the history of the cinema.

The steep inlets of the south coast of the Île de Porquerolles enabled Jean-Paul Belmondo to demonstrate his skills in *Pierrot le Fou*. Several districts of Hyères can be spotted in *Le Passager de la Pluie* by René Clément, starring Marlène Jobert, as well as in *Vivement Dimanche!* by François Truffaut.

Roger Vadim launched both Brigitte Bardot and **St-Tropez** with his provocative *And God Created Woman* (1956). The resort is renowned in the world of the cinema and has provided the setting for many location shots – *The Collector* (1967) by Eric Rohmer, *La Cage aux Folles* (1978) by Édouard Molinaro and, of course, the celebrated comic series *Le Gendarme de St-Tropez* by Jean Girault with Louis de Funès, six episodes of which were filmed between 1964 and 1982.

The old port in Cannes still contains the galleon *Neptune* on which Roman Polansk's *Pirates* was set in 1986; admirers of *Mélodie en Sous-Sol* by Henri Verneuil will be nostalgic at the sight of the Palm Beach Casino.

The **Studios de la Victorine** in **Nice** have been closely involved in the development of cinema on the Riviera *(see NICE)*. In 1929 *À Propos de Nice* by **Jean Vigo** focused on the contrast between holidaymakers loafing around on the beach and the working-class districts.

La Nuit Américaine directed by François Truffaut, partly filmed at the Studios de la Victorine, used several locations on the coast – the Atlantic Hotel in Nice, the Vésubie Valley and the Nice hinterland.

The location shots for *Les Visiteurs du Soir* were filmed in Tourrettes-sur-Loup by Marcel Carné in 1942. Villefranche-sur-Mer and its picturesque *Rue Obscure* were used by Jean Cocteau in *The Testament of Orpheus* (1960). The medieval setting of **Sospel** was ideal for cloak-and-dagger scenes in *The Man in the Iron Mask* (1962) by Henri Decoin with Jean Marais and, more recently, in *Un sac de Billes* by Jacques Doillon.

Beginning with the 1913 silent comedy, *Max in Monaco*, featuring Max Linder, the principality has been popular with film-makers looking for exotic locations. The jet set clientele of the Monte-Carlo Casino has inspired several directors, namely Ernst Lubitsch who made *Monte-Carlo* with Jeanette MacDonald in 1930.

The impressive drops of the Grande Corniche provided a marvellous backdrop for *To Catch a Thief* (1955), a thriller by Alfred Hitchcock with Cary Grant and Grace Kelly; this film also provides an unintended record of the urban development of the Principality. The comic adventures of the *Love Bug* throughout the world had to include an episode in Monaco – *Herbie Goes to Monte Carlo* (1977) by Vincent McEveety, with Dean Jones.

The film *Le Fils Préféré* by Nicole Garcia (1994) with Gerard Lanvin makes use of the natural setting of Nice, Menton and Grasse.

Provençal Cinema – Local writers – Jean Aicard, Marcel Pagnol etc – and famous southern comedians are among those involved in the cinema who have drawn on local tradition. The location shots for *La Femme du Boulanger* (1938) by Pagnol were filmed in Le Castellet.

Together with Pagnol, film-maker André Hugon, who made the first French talking film, and who was fond of the Mediterranean coast, portrayed typical Provençal characters – *Maurin des Maures* (1932), *L'Illustre Maurin* and *Gaspard de Besse*.

The colourful pre-war setting of **Toulon** has made a contribution to Provençal cinema – *César* (1936) by Marcel Pagnol with the local film actor **Raimu** *(see COGOLIN)*, *L'Étrange Monsieur Victor* (1937) by Jean Grémillon, also with Raimu, and *Fleur d'Amour* (1927) by Maurice Vandal, which portrays the formerly "hot" district of "Chicago". Other works made in the Var – *Les Démons de l'Aube* (1945) by Yves Allégret about the Provençal landings and *En Haut des Marches* (1982) by Paul Vecchiali with Danielle Darrieux, the behind-the-scenes story of historical events in Toulon.

BOOKS

Voices in the Garden, by Dirk Bogarde (first published by Chatto & Windus in 1981, reprinted by Triad Paperbacks in 1982). The British actor, who resided in Grasse for many years during the latter part of his life, wrote this fascinating novel about a middle-aged couple living on the Riviera, whose life is irrevocably changed after meeting a young English tourist and his girlfriend and offering them hospitality in their sumptuous villa. The book was brilliantly adapted to the screen with Anouk Aimée starring in the lead role.

Tender is the Night, by F Scott Fitzgerald (first published in 1934, reprinted by Scribner, NY, in 1995) is a classic story of Americans adrift on the French Riviera. Inspired by the Boston art collectors Gerald and Sara Murphy, as well as by his own wife, Zelda, Fitzgerald's book describes the slow demise of Dick Diver, a psychiatrist who marries his patient Nicole. The wealthy couple pay a steep emotional price to support many friends and hangers-on, revealing the human frailties of both privileged and ordinary people.

The Garden of Eden, by Fitzgerald's contemporary, Ernest Hemingway, was unfinished by the author when he died, and first published in 1986 (Scribner). Some readers find the novel disturbingly unlike his other works, and others find it richer for its "imperfections". The story unfolds on the Riviera and involves a young writer, his glamorous wife, and the pressures of a destructive love triangle.

The Rock Pool (Cyril Connolly, reprinted in 1996 by Persea Books) is the author's only novel. The Englishman examined the decadent side of the expatriate community in Juan-les-Pins and Antibes; it was published in Paris in 1936 after British publishers rejected it on grounds of obscenity.

Maigret on the Riviera (Harcourt, Brace 1988) may be the perfect beach book, by Georges Simenon and starring, of course, Inspector Jules Maigret. Only mildly distracted by the balmy weather and lush vegetation, the famous, pipe-smoking detective must discover how an inoffensive, down-at-the-heels Australian came to be murdered in this idyllic setting.

Bonjour Tristesse (Hello Sadness), by Françoise Sagan, has become a classic of French literature. The French version is suitable for readers with an intermediate language level and high school students. First published in 1954, it has been read and loved by many young people in France since then. The heroine, Cécile, is a precocious 17-year-old (the author's age when she wrote the story), who grapples with her widowed father's second marriage and her own coming-of-age on the Esterel Coast.

Artists and their Museums on the Riviera (Barbara Freed, Alan Halpern; Harry Abrams, 1998) is a useful paperback guide for exploring the art museums in the region. It places the artists and their work in context.

Art-Sites France: Contemporary Art & Architecture Handbook (Sidra Stich; Artsites Press, San Fransisco, 1999). This new series is invaluable for those interested in contemporary artwork. The book covers the whole of France with detailed descriptions of galleries, museums, film and video centres, specialised bookstores, sculpture parks and many architectural sites. This well-organised, well-written book (available in paperback) includes useful maps.

France on the Brink is a new publication (Little, Brown, 1999), by Jonathan Fenby, a reporter who has been writing on France for 30 years. This masterful study covers politics, regional diversity, economics and just about every possible aspect of French life from both historical and contemporary perspectives.

France in the New Century is a new book by an expert on things continental, John Ardagh (Viking, 1999). The author has chronicled events and cultural changes in France for more than 20 years. The book offers excellent explanations of how the country's regions, cities and *départements* are run, and paints a portrait of the nation from the Mitterand years up to the present.

The French, by Theodore Zeldin (Kodansha International, reprinted 1996) was first published in 1984. Readers continue to admire its jocular (yet thoughtful) portrayal of the present-day Gauls, packed with funny advice on how to laugh at their jokes, love their grandmothers and more; it includes cartoons, interviews, charts and footnotes.

VIRTUAL RIVIERA

Here are a few selected websites devoted to the Côte d'Azur.

www.beyond.fr
"Beyond the French Riviera" is a site in English with lots of links, information on places, sports, history, accommodation and more; practical and comprehensive.

www.provenceweb.fr
"Provence on the Web" includes an on-line magazine with featured villages, upcoming events, recipes, and touring suggestions (thematic tours, bike tours...) for surfers.

www.monaco.mc
"Welcome to Monaco" brings the ancient principality up to date – but gives plenty of pages over to dynastic history (no gossip); Grand Prix updates; information for tourists and business travellers.

Calendar of events

Battle of flowers in Nice

51

Vallauris .... Pottery Festival

Entrecasteaux .... Chamber Music Festival: ☎ 04 94 04 44 83

Menton .... Chamber Music Festival (about 13 concerts are held in front of the Church of St-Michel)

Abbaye du Thoronet .... Poetry Festival

Ramatuelle .... Theatre Festival ☎ 04 94 79 20 50

Grasse .... Jasmine Festival

Fréjus .... Grape Festival

Roquebrune-Cap-Martin ..... Passion Procession through the old village streets (4pm to 6pm)

Bendor .... Fishermen's Festival

Cannes .... Royal Regattas

Peille .... Folk Festival *Festin des Baguettes* in honour of a young dowser-shepherd, who during a drought found water with a divining rod made from an olive branch

Monaco .... Vintage Car Rally

Gonfaron .... Chestnut Festival

Ollioules .... Olive Festival

Collobrières .... Chestnut Festival

Entrecasteaux .... Flower Show

La Garde-Freinet .... Chestnut Festival

Monaco .... Monaco's National Day

Cannes .... International Dance Festival

Bandol .... Wine Festival

Lucéram .... The Shepherds' Christmas Offering and Provençal Mass

Le Trayas on the Esterel coast

Introduction

Landscapes

This guide describes the Riviera from Les Lecques to Menton and the mountainous hinterland which comprises the Provençal Tableland, the Pre-Alps of Grasse and the high country north of Nice. This area is located within the larger administrative region known as Provence-Alpes-Côte d'Azur (PACA); the *départements* within the guide's boundaries are Alpes-Maritimes (06) and Var (83). There are 22 *Régions* in France, which encompass 96 *départements* (exclusive of overseas territories). The smallest administrative unit in France is the *commune* (they number 36 394), which is governed by the elected members of the municipal counsel and the mayor, or *maire*, who carries out the town's business in the town hall *(mairie)*. The town offices are generally centrally located, and play an important role in daily life; these offices often handle tourist affairs as well.

Monaco is a small principality on the Riviera, surrounded by the Alpes-Maritimes.

Adjacent regions described in the Michelin Green Guides are *Provence* and *French Alps*, both available in English.

CONTRASTS

This is a country of contrasts:

...in coastline – The Riviera extends from Les Lecques to Menton and is extremely varied *(see The Coast below)*. The little sheltered inlets between the porphyry promontories of the Esterel differ markedly from the great sweeping bays with flat shores which gently punctuate the coastline; while elsewhere on the coast, mountains plunge steeply into the sea, sheer as a wall, as at Cap Sicié.

...in relief – A countryside just as varied lies inland. The fertile plains and foothills of Provence are typically Mediterranean in their vegetation but among them are barren, rugged heights like those to the north of Toulon.

Then follow the mountain masses of the Maures and the Esterel which rise to no more than 800m/2 600ft: the first is crisscrossed by many valleys and ravines and covered with fine forests of cork oak and chestnut; the second massif is dominated by the outline of Mont Vinaigre and the peaks of Pic de l'Ours and Pic du Cap Roux. The country behind Cannes and Nice is one of undulating hills stretching to the Pre-Alps of Grasse, where gorges have been cut into the plateaux and the mountain chains are split by rifts *(clues)*, particularly in Haute-Provence.

Lastly, behind the Riviera the peaks of the Pre-Alps of Nice rise to more than 2 000m/6 560ft, while further to the north and northeast the true Alpine heights tower on the Italian border.

...in climate – There is a winter warmth on the Nice coast (the average temperatures for January in Nice are max 13°C/55°F; min 4°C/39°F) and, less than 2 hours away by car, the icy air of the ski slopes; the summer heat of the coast and the exhilarating coolness of the mountain resorts; the cold *mistral* wind and the burning *sirocco*; long days of drought, dried-up rivers and, suddenly, tremendous downpours and overflowing torrents.

...in vegetation – The forest of Turini, with its centuries-old beeches and firs, is like that of a northern land; the woods of the Maures and the Esterel are typically southern with their cork oaks and pines, periodically ravaged by forest fires. The wild scrub and underbrush of the *maquis* is far from the orderly rows of the orange and lemon groves; the lavender and thyme growing wild from the vast cultivated fields of flowers; the palm trees, agaves and cacti of the coast from the firs and larches of the highlands.

...in activity – The coast attracts all the activity of the area: the busiest roads, the most important towns and the varied and the best equipped resorts are concentrated there. Inland, however, there is peace and quiet, even complete solitude; sleepy little towns and old villages, perched like eagles' nests high up on the hillsides but now almost deserted *(see HILL VILLAGES)*.

...in economy – Nice is the coast's tourist capital; Monte-Carlo, a great gambling city. The busy flower trade and the production of perfume exist side by side with the new research centres dealing with oceanography and data processing.

Land of the Sun – Such a multiplicity of impressions has one common factor – the Mediterranean climate. In the Land of the Sun, the sun shines continually (2 725 hours annually in Nice compared with 1 465 hours in London).

Except in high summer, outlines are sharpened and natural features acquire an architectural aspect in the clear air. The shining blue of the sea and sky blends with the green of the forest, the silver-grey of the olive trees, the red porphyry rock and the white limestone.

TERRAIN

Provence was formed from two mountain systems: one very old – the Maures and the Esterel – the other much younger – the Provençal ranges of Pyrenean and the Pre-Alps of Alpine origin.

The Maures – This crystalline mountain mass spreads from the River Gapeau in the west to the Argens Valley in the east, from the sea in the south to a long depression in the north, beyond which are the limestone Pre-Alps. Long low parallel ranges, covered with fine forests which have not escaped the forest fires, make up the Maures Massif; the highest point is La Sauvette (779m/ 556ft).

The Esterel – The Esterel, separated from the Maures by the lower Argens Valley, has also been eroded by time and is, therefore, also of low altitude, its highest peak being Mont Vinaigre at 618m/2 027ft. The deep ravines cut into its sides and its jagged crests dispel any impression of mere hills.
The Esterel, like the Maures, was once entirely covered with forests of pine and cork oak but these have been ravaged periodically by forest fires.
Quantities of shrubs and bushes grow beneath the trees: tree heathers, arbutus, lentisks and lavender, while scrub *(maquis)* covers the open ground. In spring the red and white flowers of the cistus, yellow mimosa and broom and white heather and myrtle form a brilliant floral patchwork.

Provençal Ranges – These short limestone chains, arid and rugged, rise to heights of 400-1 150m/1 200-3 500ft. Of Pyrenean origin with a highly complex structure, they do not have the continuity of those of Alpine origin such as the Southern Pre-Alps. The most southerly peaks, just north of Toulon are the Gros Cerveau (429m/1 407ft), which is bisected by the Ollioules gorges, Mont Faron (542m/1 778ft), which dominates the town, and Le Coudon; Montagne de la Loube rises 28km/17mi to the north. Between the ranges are fertile valleys where the traditional crops of cereals, vines and olives are cultivated.

Maritime Alps and Mercantour – Away to the northeast the horizon is dominated by a vast mountainous mass (altitude: 1 500-2 900m/4 922-9 515ft), which is dissected by the upper valleys of the Var, Tinée, Vésubie and Roya. On the Italian border these mountains meet the great crystalline massif, Le Mercantour, the peaks of which exceed 3 000m/9 843ft.

Pre-Alps – This region contains a large part of the Southern Pre-Alps. Between the River Verdon and River Var the **Pre-Alps of Grasse** are formed by a series of parallel east-west chains, with altitudes varying between 1 100-1 600m/3 609-5 249ft which are frequently indented by wild and narrow rifts *(clues)*.
The **Nice Pre-Alps** rise from the coast in tiers to a height of 1 000m/3 281ft, affording a wide variety of scenery inland from Nice and Menton. These ranges, which are Alpine in origin, run north-south before changing direction abruptly to finish up parallel with the coast.

Provençal Tableland – From Canjuers plateau to the Vence pass, the Pre-Alps are rimmed with a tableland of undulating limestone plateaux, similar to the *causses*, into which water infiltrates, penetrating through rifts to feed resurgent streams like the Siagne. The River Loup has carved out a very picturesque gorge.
Below lies a **depression** or "lowland" where the towns of Vence, Grasse and Draguignan are situated. Beyond the River Argens, the depression extends east down the river to Fréjus and west towards Brignoles; the main axis, however, is southwest to Toulon to the northern slopes of the Maures and Le Luc basin.

RIVERS

Mediterranean rivers are really torrents and their volume, which varies considerably from a mere trickle to a gushing flood, is governed by melting snow, rainfall and evaporation, depending on the season.
The lack of rain and the intense evaporation of the summer months reduce the rivers to little dribbles of water along their stony beds.
In spring and autumn the rains fall suddenly and violently and even the smallest streams are immediately filled with rushing water; little brooks, trickling through the undergrowth, soon turn into torrents and their raging waters advance at the frightening speed of a galloping horse.
The flow of the Argens varies from 3-600m³/60-132 000gal a second and that of the Var from 17-5 000m³/3 790 to over a million gallons. At the height of its spate the Var is more than half a mile wide and the stain of its muddy waters can be seen in the sea as far away as Villefranche on the far side of Nice.
The water level in rivers in limestone regions is always very uneven. The rains seep into the ground through numerous fissures to reappear often a considerable distance away as large springs gushing out from the sides of valleys. Some of the springs rise in riverbeds, such as the gushers *(foux)*, which cause the River Argens to flood. Most of the rivers with torrential rates of flow transport material but the River Argens is the only one to have built up an alluvial plain comparable to those of the Languedoc coast. All the torrential rivers have created beautiful valleys, deep gorges (the Loup and the Siagne gorges) or rifts (*clues* – the Clue de Gréolières), which are among the attractions of inland Provence.

CAVES AND CHASMS

In contrast to the deeply dissected green valleys, such as the gorges of the Loup and the Siagne, the Caussols plateau *(see ST-VALLIER-DE-THIEY)* rolls away to the far horizon, stony and deserted, a typical karst relief. The dryness of the soil is due to the calcareous nature of the rock which absorbs rain like a sponge.

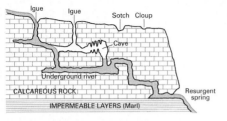

Development of a resurgent spring

Water infiltration – Rainwater, charged with carbonic acid, dissolves the carbonate of lime to be found in the limestone. Depressions, which are usually circular in shape and small in size and are known as **cloups** or **sotchs**, are then formed. The dissolution of the limestone rocks, containing especially salt or gypsum, produces a rich soil particularly suitable for growing crops; when the *cloups* increase in size they form large, closed depressions know as **dolines**. Where rainwater infiltrates deeply through the countless fissures in the plateau, the hollowing out and dissolution of the calcareous layer produces wells or natural chasms which are called **avens**. Little by little the chasms grow, lengthen and branch off, communicating with each other and enlarging into caves.

Underground rivers – The infiltrating waters finally produce underground galleries and collect to form a more or less swiftly-flowing river. The river widens its course and often changes level, to fall in cascades. Where the rivers run slowly they form lakes, above natural dams, known as **gours**, which are raised layer by layer by deposits of carbonate of lime. The dissolution of the limestone also continues above the water-level in these subterranean galleries: blocks of stone fall from the roof and domes form, the upper parts pointing towards the surface of the earth. When the roof of the dome wears thin it may cave in, disclosing the cavity from above and opening the chasm.

THE COAST

The mainly rocky coastline reflects the different types of mountain and plateau to be found inland emerging as cliffs and rocks where they meet the sea.

The Toulon Coast – This highly indented section of the coast provides well-sheltered harbours; Bandol and Sanary bays and the outstanding Toulon anchorage. The stretches of almost vertical cliffs are interrupted by some fine beaches.

The Maures Coast – Between Hyères and St-Raphaël, the Maures Massif meets the sea and the coastal scenery offers charming sites and enchanting views.
The Giens peninsula, formerly an island, is now joined to the mainland by two sandy isthmuses. Nearby are the Hyères islands, densely covered with vegetation, and the Fréjus plain, once a wide bay but now filled by alluvial deposits brought down by the Argens. Characteristic also of this particular section of the coast are great promontories such as Cap Bénat and the St-Tropez peninsula, narrow tongues of land such as Cap Nègre and Cap des Sardinaux and wide bays like the Bormes anchorage and the gulf of St-Tropez.

The Esterel Coast – The porphyry rocks of the Esterel Massif, steep and rugged, make a striking contrast with the blue of the sea. Along this stretch of coast the mountains thrust great promontories into the sea, between inlets *(calanques)* and small bays. Offshore, the surface of the sea is scattered with thousands of rocks and small, green moss-covered islets, while submerged reefs can be seen beneath the clear water. The Corniche d'Or *(see Massif de l'ESTEREL)* is reputed internationally for its breathtaking scenery, superb viewpoints and various resorts.

The Antibes Coast – The vista changes once again between Cannes and Nice. The shore is no longer eaten away by the sea; it is flat and opens into wide bays. It is a smooth, unbroken coast on which the Cap d'Antibes peninsula is the sole promontory.

The Riviera Proper – From Nice to Menton the Alps plunge abruptly into the sea. Here the coastline forms a natural terrace, facing the Mediterranean but isolated from its hinterland. Cap Ferrat and Cap Martin are the two main promontories along this stretch of coast. The term Riviera, which has already passed into the language of geography, is applied to this type of coast line. A triple roadway has been cut over the steep slopes, lined with villas and terraced gardens.

THE MEDITERRANEAN SEA

The Mediterranean is Europe's bluest sea. The shade – cobalt blue to artists – comes from the clarity of the water. Visitors soon realise that the colour often changes depending on the nature of the sky, the light, the seabed and the depth of water so that at times the "blue Mediterranean" is opal or a warm grey.

Roquebrune – Cap Martin

The water – The temperature of the water, governed on the surface by the sun's heat, is constant (13ºC/55.4ºF) from 200-4 000m/650-13 000ft downwards, whereas in the Atlantic it drops from 14-2ºC/57.2-35ºF. This is an important factor in the climate, for the sea cools the air in summer and warms it in winter. Rapid evaporation makes the water noticeably more salty than that of the Atlantic. The waves are small, short and choppy; storms come and go quickly.

The tides – Tides are almost non-existent (about 25cm/10in). Sometimes when the wind is very strong the tide may reach as much as 1m/3ft. These figures are markedly different from the tides of the Atlantic or from the tides of 13-15m/40-50ft round Mont-St-Michel off the Normandy coast. This relative tidal stability has resulted in the Mediterranean being chosen as the base level for all French altitudes.
The Provençal coastline drops sharply into water that becomes relatively deep a short distance from the shore. Between Nice and Cap Ferrat soundings indicate a depth of 1 000m/3 280ft about half a mile out.

THE SEASONS

A superb climate – Crowds come flocking in summer and the tourist season lasts almost the whole year.
The Côte d'Azur is one of the most inviting names in the world! Properly speaking, the name Riviera applies to the French coast between Nice and Menton and to the Italian coast between Ventimiglia and Genoa. English visitors, at first for the sake of health but later more and more in search of pleasure, were attracted to the Riviera (especially Nice) in the 18C. The Côte d'Azur (Les Lecques to Menton) has become widely known as the French Riviera.

Winter – The proverbial mildness of the French Riviera is due to a number of factors: a low latitude, the presence of the sea which moderates temperature variations, a wholly southern aspect, and the screen of hills and mountains which protects it from cold winds. The average temperature for January in Nice is 8ºC/16ºF. The unfavourable winds blow from the east and from the southeast bringing rain. Fog and sea-mists are rare except on the coast in the height of summer, harsh winters with ice and snow are practically unknown.
The thermometer may rise to 22ºC/72ºF but at sunset and during the night the temperature drops suddenly and considerably. There is little rainfall: it is the dew that keeps the vegetation fresh. The hinterland is cold and often snow-covered but the air is limpid and the sun brilliant – an ideal climate for winter sports.

Spring – Short but violent showers are characteristic of springtime on the Riviera. This is when the flowers are at their best and a joy to look at. The only drawback is the *mistral*, which blows most frequently at this season, especially west of Toulon. The mountains, however, act as a buffer and the wind is never as intense as it can be in western Provence and the Rhône Valley.
The Romans made a dreaded god of this fearsome wind. It comes from the northwest in cold gusts; after several days – three, six or nine – this powerful blast of clean air has purified everything and the wind-swept sky is bluer than ever.

Summer – The coast offers an unchanging blue and an average temperature of 22ºC/72ºF throughout July and August. The heat, however, is bearable because it is tempered by the fresh breeze that blows during the daytime. This is not the season for flowers: overwhelmed by drought the vegetation seems to sleep. When the hot breath of the *sirocco* comes out of the south everyone grumbles.

The hinterland offers a wide variety of places to stay at varying altitudes up to 1 800m/5 905ft; the higher one climbs the more vital the air.

Autumn – Autumn is the season for violent storms after which the sun reappears, brilliant and warm. In the whole year, there is an average of only 86 days of rain in Nice (150 in London), but the quantity of water which falls is higher (863mm/34in in Nice against under 609mm/24in in London). There are plenty of perfect days during the Mediterranean autumn.

Flora and Fauna

Plants and trees do not grow in the same way on the Riviera as they do further north. New shoots appear, as they do elsewhere, in the spring but a second growth begins in the autumn and continues throughout most of the winter. The dormant period is during the summer when the hot, dry climate favours only those plants that are especially adapted to resist drought. These have long tap roots, glossy leaves which reduce transpiration, bulbs acting as reservoirs of moisture and perfumes which they release to form a kind of protective vapour.

Olive tree

TREES

Olive Trees – 2 500 years ago, the Greeks brought olive trees to Provence where they grow equally well in limestone or sandy soils. The olive has been called the immortal tree for, grafted or wild, it will always grow from the same stock. Those grown from cuttings die relatively young, at about 300 years old. Along the coast, the trees reach gigantic dimensions, attaining 20m/65ft in height, their domes of silver foliage 20m/65ft in circumference and trunks 4m/13ft round the base. The olive tree, which has more than 60 varieties, is found up to an altitude of 600m/2 000ft and marks the limit of the Mediterranean climate. It grows mainly on valley floors and on hillsides. The trees begin to bear fruit between their sixth and twelfth year and are in full yield at 20 or 25. The olives are harvested every two years. Olive groves are numerous in the areas around Draguignan, Sospel and at Breil, in the Roya Valley.

Oak Trees – The oaks native to the Mediterranean region are evergreen. The **durmast oak** grows in the scrub *(garrigue)*. The **holm oak** grows in chalky soil at altitudes below 800m/2 500ft. As scrub-oak, it is a characteristic feature of the *garrigue* (rocky, limestone moors). In its fully developed state it is a tree with a short thick-set trunk covered in grey-black bark and with a dense, rounded crown. The **cork oak** is distinguished by its large dark-coloured acorns and its rough bark. Every eight to twelve years the thick cork bark is stripped off, exposing a reddish brown trunk.

Umbrella pine

Aleppo pine

Pine Trees – The three types of pine to be found in the Mediterranean region have unmistakable silhouettes.

The **maritime pine**, which grows only on limestone soil, has dark, blue-tinged green needles and deep red bark.

The **umbrella pine** is typically Mediterranean and owes its name to its easily recognisable outline. It is often found growing alone.

The **Aleppo pine** is a Mediterranean species that thrives on chalky soil along the coast; it has a twisted, grey trunk and lighter, less dense, foliage.

Other Provençal Trees – The smooth-trunked **plane tree** and the **lotus tree** shade the courtyards, streets and squares and also line the roads.

The dark silhouette of the coniferous, evergreen **cypress** is a common feature of the countryside; planted in rows, the pyramidal cypress forms an effective windbreak.

The common **almond tree**, a member of the Rosaceae, is widespread in Provence and blossoms early. The robust **chestnut** flourishes in the Maures Massif. Certain mountain species of **fir** and **larch** are to be found in the Alps; the forest of Turini is a fine fir-growing region.

Almond tree

Exotic Trees – In parks and gardens and along the roads stand magnificent **eucalyptus trees**. This hardy specimen is particularly suited to the climate. In winter another Australian import, **mimosa**, covers the slopes of the Tanneron Massif with a yellow mantle.

The greatest concentration of **palm trees** is to be found in the Hyères district. The two types most common to the Riviera are the date palm with its smooth, tall trunk sweeping upwards and the Canary palm which is much shorter and has a rough scaly trunk.

Orange and **lemon groves** flourish on the coastal stretches between Cannes and Antibes, and Monaco and Menton.

BUSHES AND SHRUBS

The **kermes oak** is a bushy evergreen shrub, which rarely grows more than 1m/3ft in height. Its name comes from the kermes, an insect half-way between a cochineal fly and a flea, which lives throughout its existence attached to the stems of the oak.

The **lentisk** is an evergreen shrub with paired leaves on either side of the main stem and no terminal leaf. The fruit is a small globular berry, which turns from red to black when it is mature.

The **pistachio** is a deciduous shrub which can grow to a height of 4-5m/13-16ft. The leaves grow in groups of five to eleven, one of which is terminal. The fruit is a very small berry, red at first, ripening to brown.

The Mediterranean **thistle** is a perennial, which attains a height of 1m/3ft. The irregular pointed leaves are bright green on top and covered with white down on the underside.

The Garrigue – Some of the limestone areas are so stony (Vence pass road and D 955 from Draguignan to Montferrat) that even thorns (kermes oak, gorse and thistle) and aromatic plants (thyme, lavender and rosemary) can survive only here and there in between the bare rocks; this is the *garrigue*.

The Maquis – Scrub *(maquis)* thrives on sandy soil and forms a thick carpet of greenery, which is often impenetrable. In May and June when the cistus is in flower it is a marvellous spectacle, especially in the coverts of the Esterel.

Mediterranean thistle

SUCCULENTS

Some varieties of succulents are African in character: Barbary figs, agaves, cacti and aloes grow in open ground. Ficoids with large pink and white flowers cling to old walls.

Barbary fig   Aloe

The **aloe** has thick and fleshy leaves, from which a bitter juice is extracted for medicinal use.

The **Barbary fig** is an unusual plant from Central America, which grows in arid soil in hot climates; its broad, thick, fleshy leaves bristle with spines. The Moroccans call it the Christian fig; it is also known as the "prickly pear".

For a wider knowledge of exotic flora, take a stroll in
Jardin Exotique in Monaco
Jardin de la Villa Thuret in Cap d'Antibes (see ANTIBES)
Several botanic gardens in Menton
Domaine du Rayol (including Val Rameh) (see CAVALAIRE)
Jardin Olbius Riquier in Hyères

FOREST FIRES

From time immemorial the scourge of the Provençal woodland, especially in the Maures and the Esterel, has been the forest fire, which causes more damage than deforestation by man, now carefully monitored, and destruction by goats which live on the tender young shoots. During the summer the dried-up plants of the underbrush, pine needles, resins exuded by leaves and twigs are highly combustible and sometimes catch fire spontaneously. Once started, a fire may spread to the pines with disastrous results in a strong wind. Great walls of flame, sometimes 10km/6mi in length and 30m/1 00ft high, spread at speeds of 5-6km/2-3mi per hour. When the fire has passed, nothing remains standing except the blackened skeletons of trees while a thick layer of white ash covers the ground.

The Riviera Corniches between Nice and Menton, the slopes of Mont Férion in the Nice Hinterland and the region from Grasse to Mandelieu still bear the scars of the particularly severe forest fires that raged during summer 1986, and it will be many years before regeneration of their natural habitat is complete.

Preventive measures include the removal of undergrowth near residential areas, creation of fire-breaks and the appointment of fire-watchers and patrols. Active intervention is provided by the fire brigade and the airborne water carriers based in Marignane. In the event of a major fire risk, the ALARME plan enables access roads to private homes to be cleared for firefighters and limits the movements of walkers. For information on the closures in forests, there is a recorded message service (☎ 04 94 47 35 45) for the use of ramblers.

MEDITERRANEAN MARINE LIFE

Life in the Mediterranean Sea resembles a house full of animal tenants with astonishing characteristics living one above the other. During an underwater dive, the following species may be observed.

Brown grouper – Depending on its age and size, the grouper is first female, then male. It changes sex at about nine years old when it weighs 10kg/22lb. Since the fish can live for about 50 years, it spends most of its life as a male. The young female grouper lives on rocky seabeds in shallow water (less than 10m/33ft deep) which makes it an easy prey for underwater hunters and other predators. As it reaches adulthood it makes its home in holes in the rocks at a depth of at least 50m/164ft where it lives as a formidable carnivore at the extremity of the marine food chain. It may eventually reach a length of 1.20m/4ft and weigh 30-40kg/66-88lb. This fish, which had become very rare in the Mediterranean, has benefited from a 5-year moratorium prohibiting the catching of groupers.

A project currently under way, led by the Parc Naturel de Port-Cros, is designed to protect the grouper within an area around the island.

Jellyfish – Jellyfish, which appear seasonally in coastal waters, sometimes cause problems for holidaymakers. The most common species, pelagia, can sting with its mouth, tentacles and umbrella. The poison, which is intended to immobilise prey, is powerful enough to cause redness and burning of the skin. The population of **pelagia** follows a 12-year cycle, depending on climatic conditions, and their arrival is usually preceded by a very dry spring. Another species of jellyfish, the Portugese Man-of-War has long tentacles (up to 10m/33ft), which are invisible to swimmers and have a very powerful sting. They are fortunately rare in the Mediterranean.

Posidonia – This flowering plant, which has bunches of long dark-green leaves, plays an essential role in the Mediterranean environment. Its rhizomes grow slowly, thus allowing it to fix the sediments from the coast and create a habitat rich in oxygen and favourable to many animal species. When the posidonia dies, these animal species either die out or migrate.

Brown grouper

A dive into the colourful world of the posidonia provides the possibility of seeing many amazing species. The **sea cucumber**, also known as holothurian, is the dustbin of the sandy seabed and lives only in the posidonia. The **sea-slug**, found all over the Mediterranean, is a white mollusc with brown spots which contrasts with the red sponges. The **striped weever fish** lives on the seabed near the posidonia, buried in the sand with just its head visible. It has a very poisonous dorsal fin, the sting of which can be serious. The **sea-horse** likes to hide near its relative, the **pipefish**, whose amazing threadlike form, with trumpet-shaped mouth, mimics the leaves of the posidonia among which it lives. In the last few decades harbour works and construction along the coast have caused much sedimentation and the resultant pollution is endangering the fragile habitat. Since 1989 one of the six varieties of tropical algae already identified in the Mediterranean, the non-toxic **taxifolia**, has spread rapidly along the French Riviera. It is feared that the spread of this alga may be harmful to the posidonia, although it seems to thrive in areas which are very acid and where the posidonia does not grow.

The Three Musketeers of the "Silent World"

In August 1937, two young divers with homemade equipment based on recycled tubes, attempted to beat a harpooning record. In the absence of any substantial booty, J-Y Cousteau and P Taillez found that their dive in the midst of shoals of grouper and bass revealed the potential of underwater exploration. A third leading harpoonist, J Dumas, soon joined them and the hunt for pictures superseded the hunt for sea bass. In the autumn of 1943, Dumas, experimenting with an aqualung, dived to a depth of 62m/203ft and was affected by nitrogen narcosis (rapture of the deep). After the Second World War the underwater explorers' odyssey was immortalised on film and their craft, *Calypso*, was seen all round the world.

Agriculture and crafts

FLOWERS AND EARLY VEGETABLES

Cut Flowers – Alphonse Karr *(See ST-RAPHAËL)*, a political refugee living in Nice before the annexation, is generally credited with having founded the flower trade. With the help of an associate, Karr began large-scale cultivation and had the idea of sending bunches of fresh violets and small packets of mixed seeds to Paris. From this modest start the trade in cut flowers and mimosa has developed considerably owing to irrigation and hothouses.

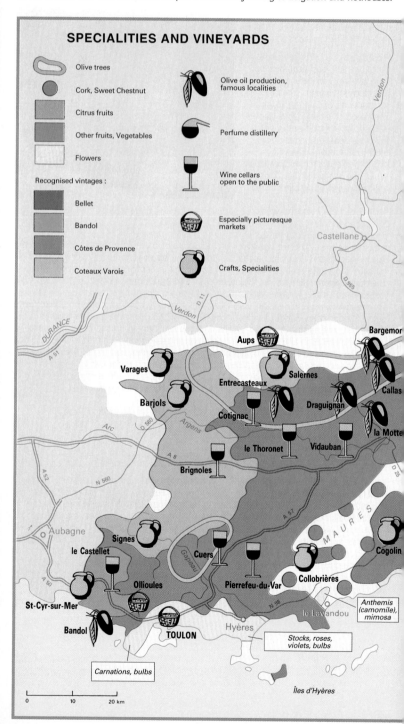

SPECIALITIES AND VINEYARDS

Olive trees

Cork, Sweet Chestnut

Citrus fruits

Other fruits, Vegetables

Flowers

Recognised vintages :

Bellet

Bandol

Côtes de Provence

Coteaux Varois

Olive oil production, famous localities

Perfume distillery

Wine cellars open to the public

Especially picturesque markets

Crafts, Specialities

Flowers and Scented Plants of the Grasse Region – The two main flower crops of this area are roses and jasmine. The May tea-rose is the same as that grown in the east but the Mediterranean variety has a fine scent. Jasmine is of the large flowered variety which has been grafted on to jasmine officinalis. It is a particularly costly and delicate plant which flowers from the end of July to the first winter frosts.

The orange blossom used for perfume is obtained from the bitter fruit tree, known as the Seville orange *(bigaradier)*. Orange-flower water is made from direct distillation. The cherry laurel, eucalyptus and cypress are distilled both for essence and for toilet water. Mimosa is used for the production of essence by extraction. Sweet

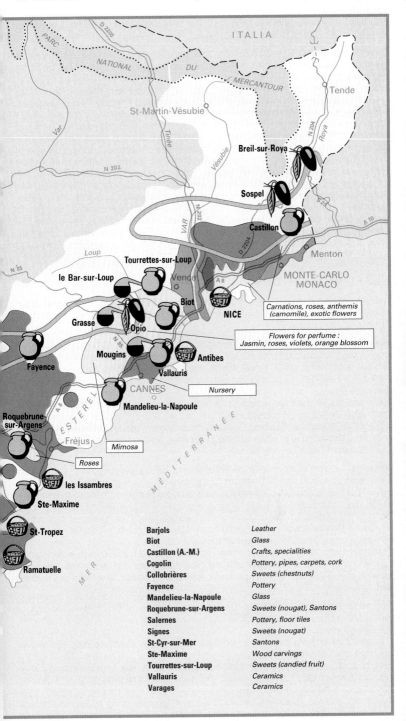

Barjols	*Leather*
Biot	*Glass*
Castillon (A.-M.)	*Crafts, specialities*
Cogolin	*Pottery, pipes, carpets, cork*
Collobrières	*Sweets (chestnuts)*
Fayence	*Pottery*
Mandelieu-la-Napoule	*Glass*
Roquebrune-sur-Argens	*Sweets (nougat), Santons*
Salernes	*Pottery, floor tiles*
Signes	*Sweets (nougat)*
St-Cyr-sur-Mer	*Santons*
Ste-Maxime	*Wood carvings*
Tourrettes-sur-Loup	*Sweets (candied fruit)*
Vallauris	*Ceramics*
Varages	*Ceramics*

basil, clary (sage), tarragon, melissa or balm mint, verbena, mignonette, peppermint and geranium all yield products used in perfumery, confectionery and pharmacy. Scented plants include wild lavender, aspic, thyme, rosemary, sage etc.

Le Bar-sur-Loup, Golfe-Juan, Le Cannet and Vallauris as well as Seillans (Var *département*), are major centres for the production of natural aromatic raw materials, although Grasse is number one in this domain.

This luxury industry, which caters mostly for the export market, is supplemented by the synthetic perfume industry. The French perfume industry's exports exceed 1 000 million francs ($184 500 000), the most important customers being the United States, Japan, Germany and the United Kingdom.

Early Vegetables – After North Africa, Spain and Italy, the region of Toulon and Hyères provides the earliest vegetables and fruit. The Var is noted for the cherries of Solliès-Pont and the peaches from around Fréjus.

Olive Trees and Oils – Traditionally, the northernmost place where olive trees (symbol of Southern agriculture) are grown, is also the limit of the Midi or South of France.

Production of olive oil in the region accounts for more than two-thirds of that of the whole country, and is spread throughout the Var, around Draguignan and Brignoles, and in the Bévéra and Roya valleys. Following the frosts of 1956, when nearly a quarter of the olive trees died, the olive groves have been replanted progressively with two more hardy species: the **aglandau** and the **verdale**. There are many other varieties, with flavours which vary according to the soil and the date of harvest. Traditionally, several varieties are grown in one olive grove. Harvest is from the end of August, depending on the area; table olives are picked by hand, while those destined for miling are shaken off the tree and collected in nets. Around Nice, shaking *(gaulage)* is always used. Olives from Nyons *(tanches)* are the only ones to be designated AOC (*Appellation d'origine contrôlée* – of guaranteed quality). The **belgentiéroise** olive, harvested at the end of August, can be eaten within the month; the **grossane**, is a fleshy black, salted olive, the **salonenque** is a green variety also known as *olive des Baux*. The **cailletier**, or little Nice olive, is stored in brine for six months before being eaten. All of these can be eaten as an apéritif or made into oil.

CRAFT WORKSHOPS

Numbers of craftsmen have moved into the old inland villages, which they have often restored with care, and are producing traditional objects made by the old methods or highly original creations.

Biot – The production of large earthenware jars in Biot *(see p 104)* goes back to the days of the Phoenicians. In the Middle Ages Biot was an important centre for ceramics and it was not until the 19C that it was eclipsed by Vallauris. There are several modern workshops specialising in traditional earthenware jars, pottery, ornamental stoneware and metalwork.

Since the 1960s Biot has owed its growing international reputation to its glass craftsmen. By visiting a glass workshop one can see how the various pieces are made using early techniques. Exhibits include carafes, bottles, glasses, small oil lamps and traditional Provençal jugs with long spouts *(calères, ponons)* for drinking without touching the vessel with one's lips.

Vallauris – Ceramics from Vallauris enjoy a worldwide reputation. In 1947 Picasso came to work in a studio in the town and attracted a crowd of followers. Nowadays it is difficult to distinguish between the mass-produced pot and the hand-made article in the shop windows.

Many of the potters – whether they use old methods (wood firing) or new techniques – produce attractive work: glazed kitchenware (tureens, bowls, jugs), handsome stoneware, various glazed or unglazed articles and clay pipes.

Besides pottery, many other interesting activities have been introduced, including the production of hand-crafted puppets, handsome furniture and decorative sculpture made from olive wood, colourful painted chests and cupboards, fine hand-woven linen and furnishings.

Tourrettes-sur-Loup – Tourrettes has been revived by its craftsmen. It was an important weaving town in the Middle Ages and renewed its connection with this craft after the Second World War.

It has become a centre for hand-woven fabrics. The weavers produce very high quality goods in small quantities.

Several of the workshops in the winding streets offer a very varied range of cloth: reproductions of old Provençal fabrics, shot material for the high fashion market or furnishings, hand-woven ties *(see p 326)*.

Tourrettes also houses potters (making earthenware sheep using a Mexican process, engraving in vivid enamels), painters and sculptors in olive wood.

Historical table and notes

Events in italics indicate milestones in history.

BC

1000 | The Ligurians occupy the Mediterranean seaboard.

600 | Foundation of Massalia (Marseille) by the Phocaeans. They bring olive, fig, nut, cherry trees, the cultivated vine; they substitute money for barter.

5-4C | The Greek settlers in Marseille introduce trading posts: Hyères, St-Tropez, Antibes, Nice and Monaco. The Celts invade Provence, mingling with the Ligurians.

Gallo-Roman Provence

122 | The Romans defeat the Celts.

102 | Marius defeats the Teutons from Germania near Aix.

58-51 | *Conquest of Gaul by Julius Caesar.*

49 | Julius Caesar founds Fréjus.

6 | Building of the Alpine Trophy at La Turbie

AD

1, 2 and 3C | Roman civilization in evidence in some coastal towns (Fréjus, Cimiez, Antibes); the Via Aurelia (Ventimiglia-Brignoles-Aix) is the country's main highway.

313 | *Constantine grants Christians freedom of worship by the Edict of Milan.*

4, 5C | Christianity takes root in the coastal towns, then inland.

5, 6C | Vandals, Visigoths, Burgundians, Ostrogoths and Franks invade Provence in turn.

496 | *Clovis, King of the Franks, defeats the Alemanni from Germania at Tolbiac.*

8C | The Saracens sack the seaboard in the first half of the century.

800 | *Charlemagne is crowned Emperor of the West.*

Provence up to the "Reunion"

843 | *Treaty of Verdun* regulates the division of Charlemagne's Empire between the three sons of Louis the Debonair. Provence is restored to Lothair (one of Charlemagne's grandsons) at the same time as Burgundy and Lorraine.

855 | Provence is made a kingdom by Lothair for his son, Charles.

884 | The Saracens capture the Maures and for a century terrorise the land.

962 | *Restoration of the Western Empire as the Holy Roman Empire under Otto I.*

10, 11C | Provence, after passing from hand to hand, is finally made part of the Holy Roman Empire. Despite this, the counts of Provence enjoy effective independence. The towns are freed and proclaim their autonomy.

12C | The County of Provence passes to the counts of Toulouse, then to the counts of Barcelona. The counts maintain an elaborate court at Aix.

1226 | *Accession of St Louis.*

1246 | Charles of Anjou, brother of St Louis, marries the daughter of the Count of Barcelona and becomes Count of Provence.

1254 | Landing of St Louis at Hyères on return from the seventh Crusade.

1308 | Overlordship of Monaco is bought from the Genoese by a member of the Grimaldi family.

1343-82 | Queen Jeanne becomes Countess of Provence. Plague decimates the population.

1388 | Nice hands itself over to the Count of Savoy.

1419 | Nice is officially ceded to the Duke of Savoy.

1434 | René of Anjou, "Good King René", becomes Count of Provence.

1481 | Charles of Maine, nephew of René of Anjou, bequeaths Provence (except Nice, which belongs to Savoy) to Louis XI.

1486 | Reunion of Provence with France ratified by the "Estates" of Provence (assembly of representatives of the three orders); Provence attached to the Kingdom "as one principal to another".

Provence after the "Reunion"

1501 | Establishment of Parliament at Aix (Parliament of Provence), sovereign court of justice, which later claims certain political prerogatives.

1515 | *Accession of François I.*

1524 | Provence is invaded by the Imperialists, commanded by the High Constable of Bourbon.

1536	Invasion of Provence by Emperor Charles V.
1539	Edict of Villers-Cotterêts decrees French as the language for all administrative laws in Provence.
1543	Nice besieged by French and Turkish troops. Catherine Ségurane instrumental in causing the Turks to withdraw.
1562-98	*Wars of Religion*. Promulgation of the Edict of Nantes.
1622	Louis XIII visits Provence.
1643-1715	*Reign of Louis XIV*.
1691	Nice taken by the French.
1696	France returns Nice to Savoy.
1707	Invasion of Provence by Prince Eugene of Savoy.
1718	County of Nice becomes part of the newly created Kingdom of Sardinia.
1720	The great plague decimates the population of Provence.
1746	Austro-Sardinian offensive is broken at Antibes. Austrian War of Succession.
1787	Reunion of the "Estates" of Provence.
1789	*The French Revolution*.

Revolution-Empire

1790	Provence divided into three *départements*: Bouches-du-Rhône, Var, Basses-Alpes.
1793	Siege of Toulon, in which Bonaparte distinguishes himself. Nice is reunited with France.
1799	On 9 October, Bonaparte lands at St-Raphaël on his return from Egypt.
1804	*Coronation of Napoleon*.
1814	*Abdication of Napoleon at Fontainebleau, 6 April.* Embarkation of Napoleon at St-Raphaël, 28 April, for the Island of Elba. The County of Nice is restored to the King of Sardinia.
1815	Landing of Napoleon at Golfe-Juan, 1 March. *Battle of Waterloo, 18 June.*

19th Century

1830	*Accession of Louis-Philippe*.
1832	The Duchess of Berry lands at Marseille, hoping to raise Provence in favour of a legitimist restoration.
1852-1870	*Reign of Napoleon III*.
1860	County of Nice restored to France.
1878	Opening of the Monte-Carlo Casino. Development of the winter tourist season of the Riviera.
late 19C	St-Tropez School of Painting.

20th Century

1914-18	Many village populations depleted by First World War.
1940	The Italians occupy Menton.
1942	The Germans invade the Free Zone. The scuttling of the French Fleet in Toulon harbour.
1944	Liberation of Provence.
1946	First International Film Festival in Cannes.
Since 1946	Development of summer tourist trade on the Riviera. Harnessing of the River Durance and River Verdon.
1947	Upper valley of the Roya incorporated into France.
1970	International technopole opened at Sophia Antipolis near Valbonne reflects increasing emphasis on development of the region into a hi-tech industrial belt.
1980	The Provençal Motorway (A8) links the Rhône and Italian networks.
1989	Law passed to strengthen measures against forest fires which pose an increasing threat to the region.
1989	The **TGV** (*train à grande vitesse* – high speed train) arrives on the Riviera.
August 1994	Celebration of the 50th anniversary of the Liberation of Provence.
1996	A high speed boat service (NGV) between Nice and Corsica.
June 2001	The TGV Méditerranée is inaugurated, bringing down the Paris-Marseille trip to three hours.

ALLIED LANDING IN PROVENCE (1944)

Operation "Dragon" – This was the aftermath of operation "Overlord" which had liberated Normandy three months earlier. At a critical moment in the battle of Normandy the Allies landed on the coast of Provence fortified by the Germans under the name "Südwall" with the American 7th Army under **General Patch**, of which the French Ist Army (composed mostly of African soldiers) formed the principal part.

"Nancy a le torticolis" (Nancy has a stiff neck) – This laconic message, broadcast on the BBC in the evening of 14 August announcing the landings in Provence, raised the hopes of the Resistance groups which had been on alert since the projected landings reported on 6 June 1944. Between June and August, the dropping of arms by parachute was stepped up, notably in the *pouvadous* (dry and stony moors); these arms were destined for the Maquis (Resistance) in the Maures, the Alps, Bessillon and Ste-Baume. In the early hours of 15 August, airborne Anglo-American troops were dropped around Le Muy to take control of the strategic communications route, RN 7. The village of **La Motte** became the first Provençal village to be liberated. At the same time, French commandos from Africa landed on the left wing at Cap Nègre, and on the right wing at Esquillon Point, while American Special Forces attacked the Îles d'Hyères. Thus protected, the main army, assembled on the 2 000 ships, including 250 battleships, landed at 8am on the beaches of Cavalaire, St-Tropez, Le Dramont and the Esterel. Despite a rapid advance, the two sectors were still separated at the end of the day by pockets of German resistance at St-Raphaël and Fréjus which fell only the following day. On 16 August the B Army under General De Lattre landed at Cavalaire Bay and in the gulf of St-Tropez and, having relieved the Americans, attacked the defences of Toulon. General Montsabert outflanked the town to the north to fall on Marseille. After the fall of Hyères and Solliès, Toulon was reached on 23 August but fighting continued until 28 August with the surrender of the St-Mandrier peninsula. On the same day, after five days of fighting, Marseille was liberated.

To the east, the Americans of the First Special Force advanced to the Alpes-Maritimes to back up the Resistance forces and drive the Germans back into the Italian Alps: Nice fell on 30 August and Menton on 6 September. In the hinterland, the Massif de l'Authion, transformed into an entrenched camp by the Germans, was the site of hard fighting for 8 months. L'Authion was overcome on 13 April 1945, Saorge on 18 April but Tende was liberated only on 5 May, three days before the general armistice! Provence had been liberated in less than 15 days. The Allies pursued the Germans, who retreated up the Rhône Valley; the 1st French Army under De Lattre de Tassigny effected a link-up with the 2nd Amoured Division under Leclerc in Côte d'Or south of Châtillon-sur-Seine.

Architecture and art

ABC OF ARCHITECTURE

Roman Era

LA TURBIE – The Alpine Trophy (1stC BC)

This monument was erected in homage to Augustus' victory in the Alps. Damaged and despoiled over the years, it was finally restored by the architect Formigé in the 1930s.

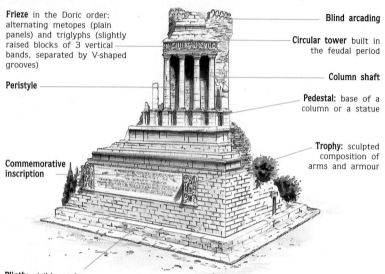

Frieze in the Doric order: alternating metopes (plain panels) and triglyphs (slightly raised blocks of 3 vertical bands, separated by V-shaped grooves)

Peristyle

Commemorative inscription

Plinth: visible projecting base of the wall.

Blind arcading

Circular tower built in the feudal period

Column shaft

Pedestal: base of a column or a statue

Trophy: sculpted composition of arms and armour

Early Christian Era

FRÉJUS – Interior of the baptistery (5C)

This is one of the few edifices from the Early Christian Era visible in the region. Some parts date from the Roman Era. An early 20C restoration restored the building to its former appearance.

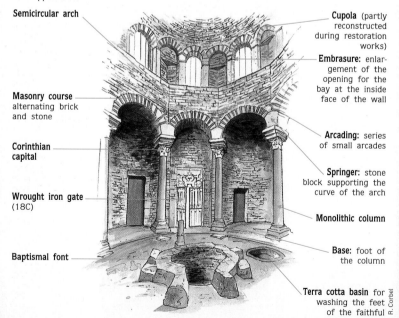

Semicircular arch

Masonry course alternating brick and stone

Corinthian capital

Wrought iron gate (18C)

Baptismal font

Cupola (partly reconstructed during restoration works)

Embrasure: enlargement of the opening for the bay at the inside face of the wall

Arcading: series of small arcades

Springer: stone block supporting the curve of the arch

Monolithic column

Base: foot of the column

Terra cotta basin for washing the feet of the faithful

R. Corbel

Religious architecture

LE THORONET – Ground plan of the abbey church (11C)

Because it did not serve a parish, the church in Thoronet does not have a central doorway. The rounded east end is typical of the region of Provence, in contrast to the flat chevet usually preferred by the Cistercian order.

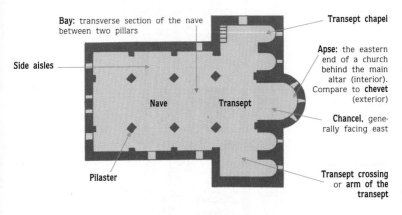

Bay: transverse section of the nave between two pillars

Transept chapel

Side aisles

Apse: the eastern end of a church behind the main altar (interior). Compare to **chevet** (exterior)

Nave   Transept

Chancel, generally facing east

Pilaster

Transept crossing or **arm of the transept**

Cross-section of a Romanesque Provençal church

The right and left-hand sides of the drawing show two main variations of this type of church.

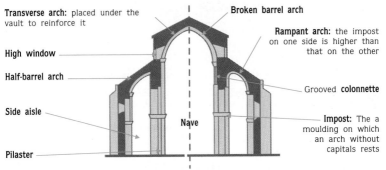

Transverse arch: placed under the vault to reinforce it

Broken barrel arch

Rampant arch: the impost on one side is higher than that on the other

High window

Half-barrel arch

Grooved **colonnette**

Side aisle

Pilaster

Nave

Impost: The a moulding on which an arch without capitals rests

GRASSE – Doorway of the Chapelle de l'Oratoire (14C)

The Gothic doorway and windows of this chapel were recovered from the old Franciscan church. In 1851, they were moved to this chapel, set on a hill in the old town centre.

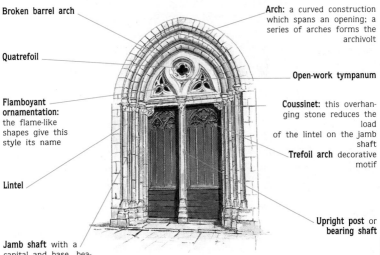

Broken barrel arch

Arch: a curved construction which spans an opening; a series of arches forms the archivolt

Quatrefoil

Open-work tympanum

Flamboyant ornamentation: the flame-like shapes give this style its name

Coussinet: this overhanging stone reduces the load of the lintel on the jamb shaft

Trefoil arch decorative motif

Lintel

Upright post or **bearing shaft**

Jamb shaft with a capital and base, bearing the arch above

R. Corbel

71

NICE – Cathédrale Sainte-Réparate (17C)

Sainte-Réparate was originally a chapel, built in the 13C. The current Baroque façade and ground plan are the work of the local architect Jean-André Guilbert.

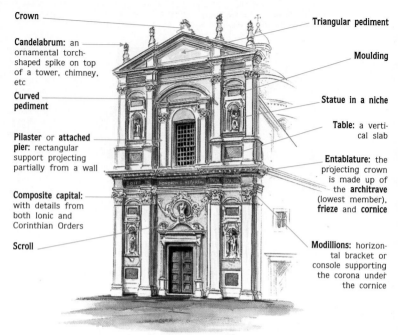

Crown

Candelabrum: an ornamental torch-shaped spike on top of a tower, chimney, etc

Curved pediment

Pilaster or attached pier: rectangular support projecting partially from a wall

Composite capital: with details from both Ionic and Corinthian Orders

Scroll

Triangular pediment

Moulding

Statue in a niche

Table: a vertical slab

Entablature: the projecting crown is made up of the architrave (lowest member), frieze and cornice

Modillions: horizontal bracket or console supporting the corona under the cornice

LES ARCS – Altar screen of the Sainte-Roseline chapel (early 16C)

Baroque altar screens in Nice and the surrounding region are mostly made of coloured marbles and stucco; gilded wood is more common on the other side of the Var.

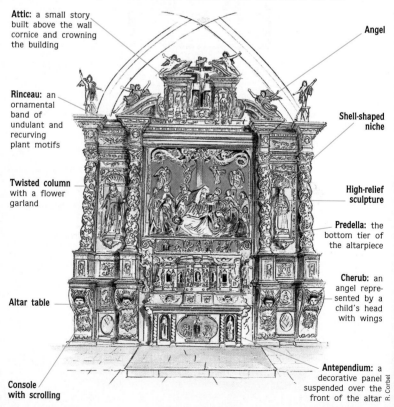

Attic: a small story built above the wall cornice and crowning the building

Rinceau: an ornamental band of undulant and recurving plant motifs

Twisted column with a flower garland

Altar table

Console with scrolling

Angel

Shell-shaped niche

High-relief sculpture

Predella: the bottom tier of the altarpiece

Cherub: an angel represented by a child's head with wings

Antependium: a decorative panel suspended over the front of the altar

R. Corbel

72

SAINT-TROPEZ – Houses on the harbour

The houses typically found in a village on the Riviera, known in France as the Côte d'Azur, are narrow and high, packed together along the waterfront or the winding streets of a hillside town; they are enlivened by colourful façades.

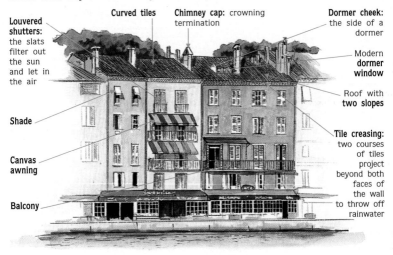

Louvered shutters: the slats filter out the sun and let in the air

Curved tiles

Chimney cap: crowning termination

Dormer cheek: the side of a dormer

Modern **dormer window**

Roof with **two slopes**

Shade

Canvas awning

Balcony

Tile creasing: two courses of tiles project beyond both faces of the wall to throw off rainwater

LE VIEUX-CANNET – Campanile

Campaniles appeared in the 16C, atop bell towers or belfries. Of various sizes, some are quite elaborate.

Metal frame withstands wind

Masonry course: the height of the regular rows is variable

Ressaut (projecting part)

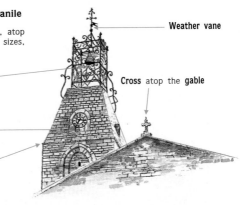

Weather vane

Cross atop the **gable**

LORGUES – Fontaine de la Noix (1771)

Each town or village has one or more fountains, whether a simple spigot or a sculpted, dated monument.

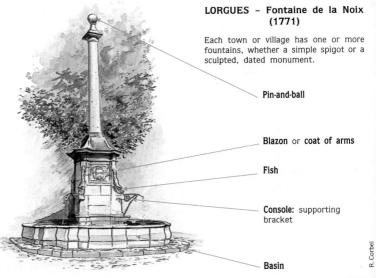

Pin-and-ball

Blazon or **coat of arms**

Fish

Console: supporting bracket

Basin

R. Corbel

73

HYÈRES – Villa Tunisienne (1884)

Seaside architecture of the 19C was inspired by Moorish culture. Chapoulart, the architect who designed the Villa Mauresque in Hyères, built this variation on the theme for himself, with a patio. Previously, it was also known as the "Algerian Villa".

Crenellations: made of crenels (notches) and merlons

Rosette: round pattern with a floral motif

Projecting pointed arch

Denticulated merlons

Interlace

Ceramic ornamentation

Multifoil arch

Meshrebeeya: lattice screen

Fore part of the building, projecting from the façade and as high as the main building

Balustrade: railing with balusters

MONTE-CARLO – Game room in the casino (late 19C)

Monte-Carlo grew up around the casino, which typifies the eclectic style of seaside architecture at the end of the 19C. The luxurious decoration inside echoes the elaborate ornamentation on the outside.

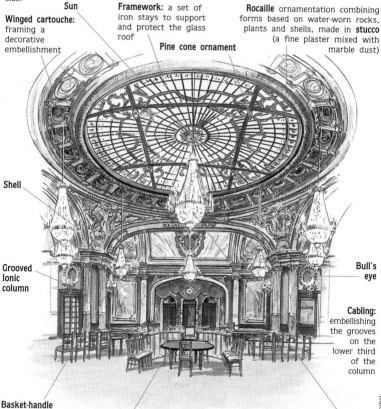

Sun

Winged cartouche: framing a decorative embellishment

Framework: a set of iron stays to support and protect the glass roof

Pine cone ornament

Rocaille ornamentation combining forms based on water-worn rocks, plants and shells, made in **stucco** (a fine plaster mixed with marble dust)

Shell

Grooved Ionic column

Bull's eye

Cabling: embellishing the grooves on the lower third of the column

Basket-handle arch

Gaming tables

Chandelier

R. Corbel

74

ANTIBES – Fort Carré (16C)

The ramparts of Antibes were demolished in 1895. All that remains is this fort, completed in 1585; the bastion design is a precursor of the star bastion defensive system developed by Vauban in the century following.

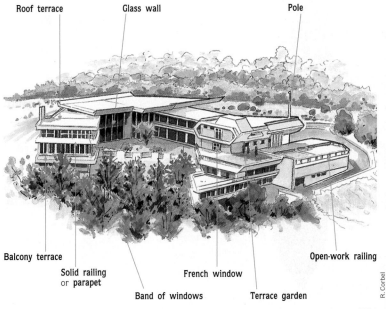

Straight stair: a steep stairway built against a fortification

Old St-Laurent tower (first fort)

Governor's lodge

Bastion: pentagonal projection from the fortified wall

Chapel

Second **fortified wall**

Sentry box

Watchpath

Curtain wall between two bastions

Cavalier: raised portion of the fortress for commanding adjacent defences or for the placement of weapons

Cannon carriage fitting

Batter slope: the inclined plane on the outer surface of the wall

Contemporary architecture

SOPHIA ANTIPOLIS – Commercial building (1978)

The buildings in the Valbonne business park were constructed beginning in 1970. They have been designed to fit into the natural shape of the landscape. Some are equipped to use solar energy.

Roof terrace   **Glass wall**   **Pole**

Balcony terrace

Solid railing or parapet

Band of windows

French window

Terrace garden

Open-work railing

R. Corbel

History of architecture

Compared with Provence, which is rich in monuments of all sorts, the Riviera has less to offer. Here, however, the sightseer will discover art in its earliest forms side by side with its most modern expressions. Right up until the 19C the art of the region remained highly conservative. When the Romanesque and Gothic styles were flourishing elsewhere in France, the Riviera remained untouched.

Gallo-Roman Antiquities – Provence and particularly the Riviera have been thriving areas since Roman times. As later generations took the materials used by the Romans for the construction of their own new buildings, only a few fragments of the ancient civilization have survived. In the districts of Fayence, Fréjus and St-Raphaël, Roman works are still being used to carry water.

The Roman ruins at Cimiez *(see NICE)* are extensive. At Fréjus *(see FRÉJUS)*, as well as the arena, there are traces of the harbour installations. The Alpine Trophy at La Turbie *(see LA TURBIE)* is of special interest; it is one of the few such Roman trophies still in existence. Buildings from the Merovingian and Carolingian periods include the baptistry at Fréjus and the chapels of Notre-Dame-de-Pépiole and La Trinité at St-Honorat de Lérins.

Regulations concerning underwater archeological finds:
All cultural goods from the sea (amphorae etc) found on public property belong to the State. Therefore anyone diving who finds any archeological remains must leave them in place and untouched.
In the event of objects being brought up by chance (in nets, for example), it is forbidden to dispose of them and the find should be reported to the nearest Affaires Maritimes within 48 hours. Offenders are dealt with in the High Courts.
Lastly, a small consolation, divers who have declared a find of a wreck or archeological remains could benefit from a reward fixed by the government.

Amphorae

From ancient times, the Provençal coasts have been visited by numerous merchants ships often of imposing size (more than 30m/8ft long) and heavily laden (up to 8 000 amphorae). The problems of manœuvring these heavy boats with oar, sail and a lack of knowledge of the reefs led to innumerable shipwrecks. The wrecks salvaged with their cargoes of amphorae bear witness to the busy commercial exchanges between areas of production and the consumers in urban centres. Navigation took place between April and September when the weather conditions were most favourable. Foodstuffs such as wine, oil and fish were also transported. The cargo on these boats was arranged at right angles to the keel; the pointed ends of the amphorae were wedged in place by the branches of trees, and the empty spaces between their necks were filled with the next row, thus assuring that the whole cargo was stable. Some holds contained up to four levels of amphorae.

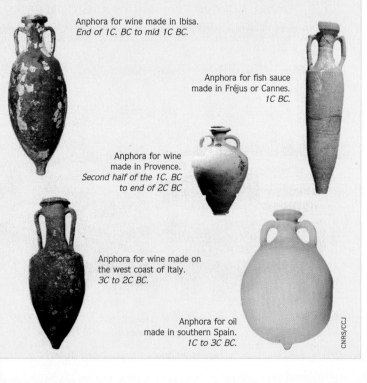

Anphora for wine made in Ibisa.
End of 1C. BC to mid 1C BC.

Anphora for fish sauce made in Fréjus or Cannes.
1C BC.

Anphora for wine made in Provence.
Second half of the 1C. BC to end of 2C BC

Anphora for wine made on the west coast of Italy.
3C to 2C BC.

Anphora for oil made in southern Spain.
1C to 3C BC.

CNRS/CCJ

Romanesque Period – In the 12C an architectural renaissance in Provence blossomed in the building of numerous churches. The Romanesque style here is more eclectic than innovative, resulting not in large buildings, such as those in Burgundy, but rather in unpretentious churches, remarkable for the bonding of their evenly cut stones with fine mortar work.

The churches are plain outside, their façades being often poor in style; the only break in the flatness of the sides comes from powerful buttresses. The square belfry and the east end are sometimes decorated with applied blind arcades, known as **Lombard bands**, evidence of northern Italian influence.

On entering, the visitor is struck by the simplicity and austerity of the interior which often consists of a single nave and a shallow transept. If aisles form part of the plan, the apse ends in a semicircle flanked by two apsidal chapels.

The interesting abbey of Le Thoronet *(See Le THORONET)* contains a church of the Cistercian Order with the wide transept and bare appearance characteristic of the churches built by the Benedictines. In contrast, however, the roof of broken barrel vaulting and the semicircular apse show the influence of local craftsmen.

Gothic to Baroque – There are few Gothic buildings in the region. Provençal Gothic is a transitional style which depends heavily on Romanesque traditions. The style is represented in the powerful groined vaulting at Fréjus and Grasse. The cloisters at Fréjus are remarkable.

In the 15C, Good King René brought numerous Italian craftsmen to Provence, but, though Provençal painting was influenced by the Renaissance, architecture remained unaffected.

Classical buildings, however, abound (17C and 18C). Design lost its original style and became more severe and majestic. In the towns the wealthier citizens built town houses. The development of Baroque is to be seen in ecclesiastical buildings in the County of Nice at Sospel, Menton, Monaco, La Turbie and Nice. Façades are adorned with pediments, niches and statues; inside, the architectural lines are often concealed by highly ornate altarpieces, panelling and baldaquins.

Modern Period – The 19C showed little originality and Baroque continued to be favoured for new constructions and restorations. The Romanesque-Byzantine style was employed in the church of Notre-Dame-de-la-Victoire-de-Lépante, St-Raphaël, the neo-Gothic on the west front of the church at Cimiez and neo-Romanesque for Monaco's cathedral. Slightly later, the Casino in Monte-Carlo and the Hôtel Negresco in Nice were designed in an ostentatious style borrowed from the Belle Epoque (c 1900).

Examples of 20C works include the church of Ste-Jeanne-d'Arc in Nice, the country church of St-Martin-de-Peille and the Chapelle Matisse at Vence. The Fondation Maeght in St-Paul, the Musée Marc-Chagall in Nice, and the striking property development at the Baie des Anges Marina in Villeneuve-Loubet or Port-Grimaud are other fine examples of modern architecture.

Pierre Puget (1620-94)

This native of Marseille was one of the greatest French sculptors of the 17C. He began by carving the prows of ships and later developed huge carved poops. During a journey in Italy he developed his talents by working as a pupil of Pietro da Cortona.

After the fall of Fouquet, his patron, he established himself away from Versailles and was appointed director of Toulon harbour by Colbert, who thought well of him. Jealousy and conspiracy soon brought him into disgrace, so he threw himself into the embellishment of Toulon. His best-known works are the atlantes supporting the balcony of Toulon Town Hall and the *Milo of Croton*, which is exhibited in the Louvre in Paris. His Baroque style could express power, movement and pathos.

Painting

Primitives – From the middle of the 15C to the middle of the 16C a school of painting, at first purely Gothic then influenced by the Italian Renaissance, flourished in the County of Nice. It is best-known through the works of **Louis Bréa** and **Durandi**. It is said of Bréa that he was a "Provençal Fra Angelico", praise justified by the sincerity and sobriety of his brushwork and his gift for stressing the humanity of his subjects. However, his simplicity is a far cry from the mysticism of Fra Angelico, and his colours and dull tones lack the sparkle of the great Italian genius. These Provençal artists worked mainly for the Penitent brotherhoods, which explains why their paintings are scattered in many churches and pilgrim chapels. They can be seen in Nice (where Brea's brother Antoine and nephew François are represented), Gréolières, Antibes, Fréjus, Grasse and Monaco.

During the same period, the humblest churches of the County of Nice were decorated with the most striking mural paintings. These are to be seen at Coaraze, Venanson, Lucéram, Saorge and Notre-Dame-des-Fontaines where Renaissance Primitive **Giovanni Canavesio**, working beside **Jean Baleison**, created Gothic-inspired works of exceptional quality.

B. Kaufmann/MICHELIN

History of architecture

P. Ricou

Ste-Jeanne d'Arc. (1934). Nice

P. Ricou

Château Smith. Nice

P. Ricou

Baroque house (1890). Nice

J.L. Gallo/MICHELIN

Jardin Japonais. Monte-Carlo

J. Guillard/SCOPE

Hôtel de l'Ermitage. Monte-Carlo

J.L. Gallo/MICHELIN

Russian Orthodox Cathedral. Nice

The Classical Period – The 17C and 18C were marked by the fine pictures of the Parrocles, the Van Loos, Joseph Vernet and Hubert Robert. It is **Fragonard**, however, who is the pride of Provence. Rakish scenes were his favourites; he painted them with great enthusiasm and exquisite style. He often used as background to his jubilant party scenes, the landscapes flooded with light and the gardens full of flowers seen round his native town of Grasse.

Modern Painting – At the end of the 19C numerous artists, representing the main trends in modern painting, were fascinated by the radiant light of the Mediterranean South of France.

Impressionism – The Impressionists sought to portray the subtle effects of light on Mediterranean landscapes. Berthe Morisot lived in Nice, Monet in Antibes and **Renoir** in Cagnes where he spent his last years, painting flowers and fruits, landscapes and people of the South.

Impressionism gave birth to a new school, **Pointillism**, a method of painting created by **Seurat**, which consisted of dividing shades into tiny dots of pure colour distributed so as to intensify the effect of light.

Paul Signac, Seurat's disciple, established himself in St-Tropez in 1898 and many of his friends followed him, namely Manguin, Bonnard and Matisse.

St Martin by Louis Bréa

P. et G. Leclerc. Nice

Fauvism – Matisse and Dufy, who had settled in Nice, reacted against Impressionism and, through the use of pure and brilliant colours, juxtaposed in simplified forms and perspectives, tried to express not just the fleeting sensation evoked by the spectacle of nature but the very thoughts and emotions of the artist.

Contemporary Movements – **Picasso**, co-founder with Braque of Cubism – an art concerned above all with form – was in his turn seduced by the Riviera, and lived in Vallauris in 1946, then in Cannes and finally in Mougins.

Braque spent his last years painting in Le Cannet while **Fernand Léger**, another Cubist painter, lived in Biot.

Dunoyer de Segonzac was untiring in his portrayal of St-Tropez.

Chagall found the light and flowers of Vence a marvellous stimulus to his multi-coloured dreams.

Other artists, such as **Kandinsky** in La Napoule, **Cocteau** in Menton, **Van Dongen** in Cannes, **Magnelli** in Grasse and **Nicolas de Staël** in Antibes, although not spending much time in the region, nevertheless marked their stay in an unforgettable manner.

At the same time in Nice in the 1960s a group of artists including **Arman**, **César**, Dufrêne, Hains, **Klein**, Raysse, Rotella, Spoerri, Tinguely and Villeglé for-

L'Estaque by Georges Braque

Musée de l'Annonciade. St-Tropez, © ADAGP, Paris 2001

med the **Nouveau Réalisme** joined later by Niki de Saint Phalle, Deschamps and Christo. They were reacting against Abstraction, which was the prevailing artistic trend after the war, and experimented with new approaches to reality making use of objects found in the modern industrial and consumer world. Alongside these innovators were the members of the **Nice School**, who each sought his own vision (**Ben**, Bernar Venet, Sacha Sosno); and **Bernard Pagès** and **Claude Viallat**, who, closely linked to the theories of Conceptual Art, led to the creation of the Support-Surface in the 1970s *(for more on contemporary movements see* NICE Musée d'Art Moderne et d'Art Contemporain p 249).

Perched villages

Many old villages may be seen perched like an eagle's nest on a hilltop or set on the flank of a hill; some are practically deserted, while others have been restored. For centuries the peasants built their villages in this way, at a distance from their lands and water supplies, and surrounded them with ramparts.

This was a wise precaution in the days of the great Germanic invasions, the Moslem pirates, and the attacks by the mercenaries of the Middle Ages and the Renaissance. The coming of security, better communications and the development of farming techniques in the 19C ended this isolation. Villages began to expand in the plains, sometimes doubling in size, and country dwellers were able to live on the land they cultivated and build their house there. Gourdon, Èze, Utelle, Peille and many other villages *(see map below)* still bear witness to the ancient Provençal way of life.

These secluded villages are picturesque to visit. Built with stones from the hillsides, they seem to blend in with the countryside. The winding streets and alleyways *(calades)*, which are steeply sloped and only to be traversed on foot, are paved with flagstones or cobbles, intersected by tortuous stairways and crossed overhead by vaults and arches. Sometimes arcades follow one another at ground level, affording the passerby shelter from the sun and rain.

The houses, roofed with curved clay tiles, have high narrow fronts, worn by the centuries. They buttress each other and surround the church or château, which dominates the village. Old nail-studded doors, wrought-iron hinges and bronze knockers still adorn the more prosperous residences.

Sometimes the little townships, which have attracted many craftsmen, are still enclosed by ramparts and one enters by a fortified gate.

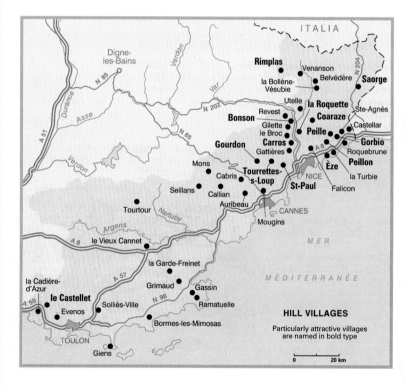

HILL VILLAGES

Particularly attractive villages are named in bold type

Life on the Riviera

ON THE COAST

The Riviera has attracted man since the earliest times and strongholds have been built on isolated hills; the curious village of Èze is the best example.

Since the great expansion of the tourist trade, life on the Riviera has been dominated by a beach and holiday atmosphere nearly all year round. Local life is gradually being overshadowed by the great influx of visitors.

A Holiday Destination – Visitors seeking fashionable and elegant resorts can choose between the bustle of Cannes and Monte-Carlo or the quieter and more discreet setting of Hyères, Beaulieu, Menton, Cap Ferrat or Cap Martin. Those longing for the appeal of a big city with all its amusements will undoubtedly turn to Nice. Lively St-Tropez will attract a large number of summer visitors; the seeker of solitude will find isolated inlets and localities; and a full range of hotels will cater for every budget.

The region features charming country houses, built in Provençal rustic style, with pink or ochre-coloured façades, overhanging red-tiled roofs and arbours covered with wistaria and climbing plants. There are also beautiful gardens in which great earthenware jars, which once contained olive oil or wine, are now purely decorative. Magnificent parks offer fine views from their terraces, and everyone can enjoy the light and colour in a charming and relaxed atmosphere.

Numerous constructions are invading the coast and one can see here and there towns built over water, such as the lake town of Port-Grimaud, the Cogolin Marina and the marine city of Port-la-Galère.

Ambitious building projects, some of which are totally out of proportion, have sprung up on all sides; a great number of private properties have appeared at the water's edge, although the public has right of access all along the coast.

Ports and Fishing – The naval port of Toulon is in a league of its own on the popular recreational coast. Cannes, Monaco and Menton are long-established pleasure boat ports: beautiful yachts with gleaming steelwork lie at anchor in the bay or are moored to the quays.

Fishing on the Riviera is confined to the coast and, as the catch is insufficient for the area, it has to be supplemented by shipments from the Atlantic.

There are no large fishing ports but numerous little harbours along the coast – Bandol, St-Tropez, St-Raphaël, Villefranche-sur-Mer, for example, are adapting to the demands of tourists and equipping themselves with moorings for pleasure boats.

For some years now the Nice region has made efforts to modernise the fishing industry and increase the number of boats in use. This has been achieved through the use of very large running nets known as *lamparos* and *seinches* and the construction of fish canneries.

The Markets – Most of the coastal towns have their own flower and fish markets where, to the colourful banks of flowers and stalls of gleaming fish, are added the noisy bustle and the warmth of the local accents of buyers and sellers, creating a truly meridional scene.

INLAND

The interior reveals the last vestiges of what was once a rough and precarious way of life. Valley sides and hill slopes were terraced with stone walls retaining small strips of soil growing cereals or two or three rows of vines and a few olive and almond trees. The *garrigue*, where small flocks of sheep and goats were put to graze, formed a sharp contrast with the fertile valleys and irrigated plains of the lowlands and the coast, where cereals, early vegetables and flowers were harvested and vines and fruit trees flourished. The lonely villages clinging to solitary ridges *(details above)* and small farms lying abandoned among their terraced walls bore no resemblance to the market towns of the plains, spread along the main roads, or to the farms *(mas)* scattered in the midst of large cultivated areas.

The centre of the village is the little square *(cours)* shaded by plane trees round a small fountain. This is where the cafés are to be found, always full in this region where people love social life, conversation and politics and where much of the day is spent away from the houses, which are left with the shutters closed to keep out the heat and insects.

THE GAME OF BOULES

This, the most popular game of the region, is played with ironclad balls. Matches are between teams of three players *(triplettes)* or four *(quadrettes)*. The *pointeurs* (attackers) must roll their balls as close as possible to a small ball *(cochonnet)*, acting as a jack, which is set at the limit of the pitch. The *tireurs* (defenders) must knock away the balls of their opponents by striking them with their own and the best players can do this so that their ball takes the exact place of the one knocked

Pétanque in St-Tropez

away. Over short distances, in which it is forbidden to move the feet, the play is *à la pétanque*. Over long distances (10m/30ft or more), where the players throw their balls after making three hopping steps, the play is *à la longue*. The intense concentration of the players, often mirrored in their facial expressions, and the passionate disputes which break out when judging the distance between balls make this a fascinating game to watch.

Food and wine on the Riviera

The main features of Provençal cooking are garlic and frying in oil (preferably olive oil). Garlic has inspired many poets who have written of the "Provençal truffle", the "divine condiment", "man's friend". Olive oil is used wherever butter would be used further north. "A fish lives in water and dies in oil" according to a local proverb.

Bouillabaisse – Here we salute the most celebrated of Provençal dishes. The classic *bouillabaisse* must consist of the "three fishes": scorpion fish *(rascasse)*, red gurnet and conger eel. Several other kinds of fish and shellfish are usually added – it is essential that the fish be freshly caught and cooked in good quality olive oil. The seasoning is just as important: salt, pepper, onion, tomato, saffron, garlic, thyme, bay leaves, sage, fennel and orange peel. Sometimes a glass of white wine or brandy gives the final flavour to the broth, which is poured onto thick slices of bread.

Aïoli – *Aïoli* is another Provençal speciality and is a mayonnaise made with olive oil, strongly flavoured with crushed garlic. Comparing the northern variety of mayonnaise with *aïoli*, Mistral dismissed it as insipid "jam". *Aïoli* is served with *hors-d'œuvres*, or with *bourride* (a soup of angler fish, bass and whiting etc), or many other dishes.

Fish – One of the Mediterranean's tastiest fish is the red mullet *(rouget)*, which the famous chef, Brillat-Savarin, called the "woodcock of the sea" probably because gourmets cook it without first scaling or cleaning it. The *loup* (local name for bass) grilled with fennel or vine shoots, is another delicious dish. *Brandade de morue* is a purée of pounded cod mixed with olive oil, some garlic cloves and truffle slices.

Aromatic herbs – Considered with garlic and olive oil to be one of the basics of Southern cooking, aromatic herbs, cultivated or growing naturally on sunny hillsides, perfume gardens and markets and enhance local cuisine. Known as *herbes de Provence*, the mixture includes **savory** *(sarriette)*, used to flavour goats' and ewes' milk cheeses; **thyme** *(thym)* cooked with most vegetables and also grilled meat; **basil** *(basilic)*, **sage** *(sauge)*, **wild thyme** *(serpolet)*, **rosemary** *(romarin)* which is good for the digestion, **tarragon** *(estragon)*, **juniper** *(genièvre)* used to flavour game, **marjoram** *(marjolaine)* and **fennel** *(fenouil)*. It is used in many dishes and can, according to taste, be a main constituent or just a trace.

Thirteen desserts – Provençal tradition presents diners at Christmas with 13 desserts (representing Christ and the 12 Apostles): raisins, dried figs, walnuts, hazelnuts, almonds, raisins on the vine, apples, pears, black nougat (made with honey), *fougasse* (sort of brioche), prunes stuffed with almond paste, melons stored in straw and dry cakes flavoured with orange blossom.

At Epiphany, a **galette des rois** is served in the form of a brioche crown filled with almond paste and sprinkled with sugar and candied fruits, containing a china figure.

Wines – Vines have been cultivated in Provence since Antiquity.

The **rosé wines**, their glowing colour achieved by a special process from black grapes, are gaining increasingly widespread popularity: pleasant and fruity to the palate, they go well with any dish.

The **white wines** are generally dry in character but have a good bouquet and are an excellent accompaniment to shellfish and Mediterranean fish.

There is a wide variety of full-flavoured **red wines**: full-bodied or subtle and delicate depending on whether they come from Bandol or the southern slopes of the Maures or, on the other hand, from the Argens Valley or St-Tropez.

The most popular wines are from the region of Bandol, Ollioules, Pierrefeu, Cuers, Taradeau and La Croix-Valmer, from the Niçois area and particularly the wines of Bellet, La Gaude, St-Jeannet and Menton *(see Practical information: Wine tasting)*.

SPECIALITIES FROM NICE

Niçois cuisine, a lively expression of the character of Nice, is inspired by the cooking of Provence and of Liguria in Italy as it is the meeting point of the two traditions. The narrow streets of Old Nice, clustered at the foot of the castle hill, overflow with opportunities to try the best-known specialities as well as seasonal variations.

Ch. Sappa/CEDRI

Two well-known examples of the cooking of Nice are an **onion tart** *(pissaladière)*, garnished with a thick anchovy sauce *(pissala)* and black Nice olives, and **salade niçoise**, a tasty combination of local tomatoes, cut into four, lettuce leaves, beans, radishes, peppers, onions, hard-boiled eggs and Nice olives, garnished with anchovy fillets and basil leaves and moistened with olive oil.

For a snack to be eaten in the street there is a large chickpea flour pancake *(socca)*, divided into portions and accompanied by a small glass of local wine *(pointu)*; it is sold in and around place St-François.

At lunchtime recharge the batteries for more sightseeing with a round sandwich (**pan bagnat** – soaked bread) containing tomatoes, lettuce, onions, anchovies and olives, moistened with olive oil and flavoured with garlic.

Teatime hunger *(merenda)* can be appeased with fried slices of a thick chickpea pancake *(panisses)*.

Salad or soup or omelette may accompany a marinade of young fish **(poutina)** which are caught with the permission of the local authorities between Antibes and Menton in February. During the rest of the year gourmets may console themselves with a **fish soup** *(soupe aux poissons de roche)* made with little crabs *(favouilles)*.

The evening menu may be enlivened by a slice of **sucking pig** *(porchetta)* stuffed with herbs and its own offal, served with a mixed salad *(salade de mesclun* in the local dialect) composed of 14 types of young salad plants picked in the area.

The dishes on offer in the tiny restaurants in the villages inland include – stuffed courgette flowers *(fleurs de courgette farcies)*; a vegetable stew *(ratatouille)* made of tomatoes, aubergines, peppers and courgettes gently cooked in oil; shell-shaped pasta *(gnocchi)* made of wheat and potato flour and served with a thick sauce *(daube)*; deep-fried pastry parcels *(barbajouan* – Uncle John) filled with rice, squash, garlic, onion and cheese; a stockfish dish known as **estocaficada** *(see below)*.

The convivial family dish, known as **pistou**, is a vegetable soup to which is added an unctuous concoction of basil, garlic, tomatoes and unstinted olive oil.

For dessert there is a sweet tart **(tourte de blea)** garnished with chopped chard leaves, pine kernels and currants.

Halfway through Lent the pastry cooks' windows display small sweet pastry cushions known as **ganses**. A cake flavoured with orange flower water *(fougasse)* is sold all year round; in Monaco it is decorated with aniseed in the national colours of red and white. One may resist the torpor of midday by sitting in the shade with a glass of crushed ice flavoured with mint *(gratta queca)*.

Estocaficada – This is the local version of the stockfish of Marseille, known for short by old hands as "estocafic". As it takes a whole day to prepare, it has become a dish for special occasions. To fillets of stockfish (dried cod), flaked with a fork and lightly browned, are added peeled and de-seeded tomatoes, the tripes of the stockfish cut into strips, chopped olives and bouquets of herbs including fennel, marjoram, parsely, thyme, bay and savory. The dish is braised for three to four hours, generously laced with brandy *(la brande)*. When the liquor has reduced to a level which only the vigilance of the cook can determine, a good measure of stock is added to the pot.

At a family gathering this imposing dish is accompanied by a full-bodied wine from Le Bellet.

The French Riviera, one of the most famous holiday destinations in the world, has a reputation largely founded on the growth in popularity of winter "Grand Tourism". Nowadays, the crowds of royalty, the flashy, stucco-laden palaces and the enormous luxury yachts are no longer the main attraction; the compelling charm of the region lies in the wide variety of its attributes: hot sun and warm sea; red cliffs and golden beaches; peaceful villages and throbbing nightclubs; world-famous festivals and rich museums; traditional celebrations, markets and locally grown produce; architectural treasures set against a magnificent backdrop of mountains.

A few reasons for visiting the French Riviera

– **Tour of the modern art museums**. This can be undertaken at any time during the year, but some museums are shut in November and December.

– **Monte-Carlo Motor Rally.** *End of January.*
This is undoubtedly the supreme championship in the world line-up of rallies.

– **Nice Carnival.** *Fortnight around Shrove Tuesday.*
One of the most long-standing traditions of the Nice region, dating from the 13C. There are light shows, parades of decorated floats, balls, carnivals and a battle of flowers.

– **Cannes International Film Festival.** *May.*
Essential date in the diaries of all the big names in the world of cinema since 1946. New films, famous actors, "rising stars" and fans.

– **Monaco Formula I Motor Grand Prix.** *Weekend after Ascension.*
Breathtaking spectacle of racing cars hurtling round a wildly twisting track laid out through the town centre.

Curiosities of the Riviera

– **Exotic places**
Villa Grecque Kérylos in Beaulieu-sur-Mer
Mosquée Soudanaise and Pagode Boudhique in Fréjus
Conservatoire Botanique du Rayol in Rayol-Canadel
Églises Russes in Nice, Cannes and Menton
Jardin Japonais in Monte-Carlo

– **Experiencing nature**
Sentier Sous-marin in Port-Cros
Jardin Sous-marin in Rayol
Killer whales at Marineland in Antibes
Vallée des Merveilles and rock carvings
Village des Tortues in Gonfaron

– **Museums and special collections**
Musée des Amoureux de Peynet in Antibes
Prison du Masque de Fer on Île Ste-Marguerite
Changing of the guard in Monaco
Noël des Bergers in Lucéram

Peillon

Sights

ANTIBES★★

Population 72 412
Michelin map 84 fold 9, 115 folds 35 and 40 or 245 fold 37

The highly popular resort town of Antibes, built between the bays of La Salis and St-Roch, lies on the west of the Baie des Anges, facing Nice. It boasts its own harbour, **Port Vauban**, and the Cap d'Antibes *(see CAP d'ANTIBES below)* nearby is a pleasant place to explore.

The Antibes region is one of Europe's main centres for the commercial production of flowers. About 800 firms keep some 300ha/50 acres under glass frames or green-houses. Roses take first place, followed by carnations, anemones and tulips. Evergreens and spring vegetables are also cultivated.

HISTORICAL NOTES

Greek Antipolis – From the 4C BC the Greeks of Massalia set up a chain of trading posts with the Ligurian tribes along the coast. A new city sprang up opposite Nice; Antipolis, the Greek name for Antibes, may have meant "the town opposite" although this derivation is disputed. Antipolis was contained between the present Cours Masséna and the sea, the Greeks holding only the area commanded by their ships, their ware-houses and their ramparts. The prevailing atmosphere was one of mutual mistrust; the Ligurians never actually entered the town, which featured only one gate opposite the present town hall; all transactions took place outside the town walls.

The Greeks were succeeded by the Romans, and subsequently by the Barbarians, whose invasions gradually undermined the city's prosperity.

Antibes, frontier outpost – The kings of France realised the key military role that Antibes could play, above all from the end of the 14C when the town stood on the Franco-Savoyard frontier. It became the property of the Grimaldis in 1386 and was later purchased by Henri IV (1589-1610).

Each reign brought improvements or enlargements to its fortifications until the work was completed by Vauban in the 17C. Only the Fort Carré and the seafront remain.

Bonaparte at Antibes – In 1794 Bonaparte, charged with defending the coast, set-tled his family in Antibes. He was a general but his pay seldom arrived on the appointed day. Times were hard. Mme Lætitia, his mother, did the household laundry herself in a nearby stream. His sisters made furtive expeditions to the artichoke and fig planta-tions and were chased away by the landowner but the future princesses were fleet of foot and escaped. After the fall of Robespierre, Bonaparte was imprisoned for some time in Fort Carré.

Notable inhabitants – **General Championnet**, born in Valence, died in Antibes in 1800, from the cholera which was ravaging his army; this selfless leader, who performed admirably in the German and Italian campaigns, was barely 38. He asked to be buried in the moat of Fort Carré. His bust stands in Cours Masséna.

Old town, Antibes

Maréchal Reille (1775-1860) was born in Antibes. Aide-de-camp to Masséna, Reille distinguished himself in all of Napoleon's campaigns. Later, rallying to the monarchy, he was made a marshal by Louis-Philippe and died a senator under the Second Empire.
Nicolas de Staël (1914-55) painted his last canvases in Antibes, before taking his own life. A young glamorous American couple, **Sara** and **Gerald Murphy**, fell in love with Antibes in the mid-1920s, and their villa became a favoured holiday haunt for their many American friends, including the **Fitzgeralds** and **Hemingways**.

★STROLLING THROUGH THE OLD CITY *1hr 45min*

Avenue de Verdun – This road, skirting St-Roch Bay, commands a good **view** of the marina and the 16C **Fort Carré** ⊘ perched on its rock, with Cagnes and the heights of Nice in the background to the right.

Port Vauban – As well as being a marina – one of the largest in the Mediterranean – this port is also used by luxury cruise ships. The famous French novelist Maupassant had his yacht *Bel Ami* moored here in the 19C.

Enter by the old sea gate (V) *and follow Montée des Saleurs as far as the Promenade Amiral-de-Grasse.*

Promenade Amiral-de-Grasse – This road, once the seafront promenade, runs along the vestiges of 17C ramparts facing the sea, below the old cathedral and castle (Musée Picasso). It gives a fine **view**★ of the coastline stretching towards Nice with the Alps rising in the background, snow-covered for most of the year.

Place du Safranier – This square is the heart of the free commune known as "Le Safranier", set up in the wake of the Second World War. The Greek writer Nikos Kazantzakis, author of Zorba the Greek (written in Antibes), lived at 8 Rue du Bas-Castellet. The plaque adorning the front door encapsulates his philosophy: "I fear nothing. I expect nothing. I am a free man".

Turn back and take Rue de la Touraque straight ahead.

Old streets – To the left and right are picturesque side streets, bright with flowers in season and barely a stone's throw from the sea.

Take Cours Masséna, which serves as the market place, and turn right on Rue de l'Orme, then on Rue du Bateau.

Église de l'Immaculée-Conception – Of the original Romanesque church, which served as a cathedral in the Middle Ages, only the east end remains. The belfry is a converted 12C watchtower. The west front (carved **door panels** – 1710) is in the 17C Classical style. The art treasures feature a wooden Crucifix (1447) in the choir, a former pagan stone altar in the south apsidal chapel, a 1515 **altarpiece** by Louis Bréa in the south transept – the centre panel has been touched up but the 13 surrounding panels and the predella are treated like miniatures – and a 16C **Recumbent Christ** carved in lime wood.

Take Rue de l'Horloge (right), Rue du Revely (left) and Rue Aubernon (right) for a picturesque route heading back to the port.

SIGHTS

Château Grimaldi (Musée Picasso) ⊘ – The original castle was built in the 12C on a terrace overlooking the sea on the foundations of a Roman camp situated on the Antipolis acropolis. It was reconstructed in the 16C but the square Roman tower, the battlement walk and pairs of windows remain from the original structure. The castle, which was the bishops' residence in the Middle Ages, was home to the Grimaldi family until the 17C.

★ **Donation Picasso** – *On the first floor of the museum.* Soon after his arrival on the Riviera in the autumn of 1946, **Pablo Picasso** (1881-1973), who had part of the castle at his disposal, started work on some large-scale paintings. His output was remarkable; the majority of the paintings, lithographs and drawings on view in the castle were the result of one season's work. The original supports used by the artist, consisting of fibro-cement and plywood, testify to the shortages of the post war period.

La Joie de Vivre, a huge work in fibro-cement, is a smiling pastoral composition of a plant-woman dancing among exuberant goats and satyrs. Preliminary sketches and drawings are also on show.

His other **paintings** are mainly joyful works bursting with imagination, inspired by the marine and mythological life of the Mediterranean (fish, sea urchins, fishermen, centaurs...): *Ulysses and the Sirens, The Oak Tree* and an imposing triptych – *Satyr, Faun and Centaur with Trident*. Two still-life paintings of exceptional quality – *Fish* and *Watermelon* – illustrate strict geometrical design.

The showcases hold an impressive collection of Picasso's **ceramics**. His great powers of imagination and ingenuity are revealed in the variety of decoration and the beauty and originality of form, often quite humorous. In the case of some pieces, decoration and form combine to suggest a silhouette: woman, owl, bull, goat... These were created at Vallauris between 1948 and 1949.

ANTIBES

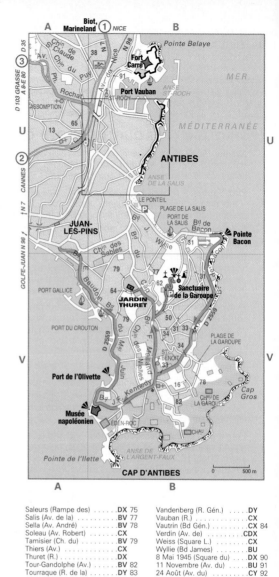

The prints and drawings of the Vollard Collection, which are grouped around monumental statues, date from the 1930s.

On the second floor, works by Nicolas de Staël are on display in Picasso's old studio. Note in particular *Still Life with Chandelier*, *Fort Carré* and the gigantic canvas entitled *Grand Concert*. The pieces by Nicolas de Staël are the result of a winter which he spent in Antibes.

The stairwell presents a display taken from the museum's collection of modern art: works by Arp, Magnelli, Ernst.

Inner courtyard – In the courtyard there is a composition by the sculptor Arman depicting guitars, reminiscent of a painting by Picasso, *À ma Jolie*. In the chapel hangs the **Deposition from the Cross**★ (1539) by Antoine Aundi, which contains the earliest known view of Antibes.

Terrace –In the terrace garden, fragrant with aromatic plants, are displayed seven statues by Germaine Richier and works by Miró, Pagès, Amado Spoerri and Poirier.

Archeological Collection – The Musée Picasso boasts Roman pottery, friezes, funerary urns and stelae, many of which carry inscriptions, displayed both inside the museum and outside on the terrace.

★ **Musée Peynet et de la Caricature** ⊙ – Located in an old 19C school are several hundred works (lithographs, stage sets, ink drawings, watercolours, sculptures, greeting cards, dolls...) by **Raymond Peynet** (1908-1999). The famous cartoonist, who

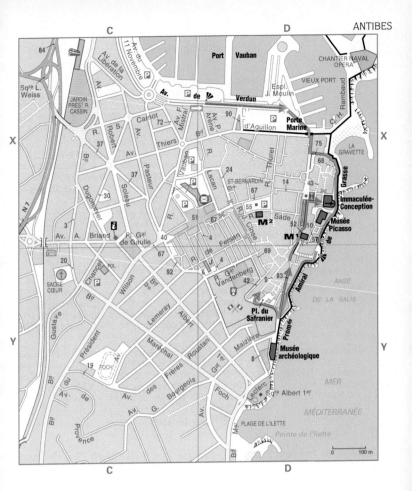

moved to Antibes in 1950, is known for his two young lovers, *Les Amoureux*, whose adventures were published in magazines such as *Paris Match, Marie-Claire, Elle and others*. The subjects illustrated include the seasons, city life, music etc.

For Carré – Built atop an isolated outcrop in 1550, the central St-Laurent tower was consolidated by four surrounding citadels 15 years later, named respectively, "Antibes", "Nice", "France" and "Corse". Thanks to the fortification work carried out by Vauban, this stronghold braved many an assault during its existence, yielding only to the Duke of Epernay and Napoleon's enemies.

Musée Archéologique ⊘ – The Bastion St-André, part of Vauban's fortifications, presents a **collection of archeological artefacts** illustrating 4 000 years of history. The back of a large vaulted room, built on a reservoir, houses a bread oven and, to the right, the reconstruction of a Roman ship used for transporting amphorae.
Some of the particularly interesting exhibits include a copy of the Mask of Silenus in bronze (the handle of a vase; the original is in the Musée Archéologique in Nice) and an ornamented lead sarcophagus. Local excavations are continually adding to the exhibits of pottery (Massaliote, Greek and Roman amphorae) as well as objects salvaged from shipwrecks from the Middle Ages to the 18C.

Musée de la Tour des Arts et Traditions Populaires ⊘ – *In Cours Masséna.*
This **Museum of Folk Arts and Tradition** is located in the Tour de l'Orme and contains a fine selection of local costumes, everyday objects and traditional furniture dating mostly from the 18C and 19C. Note also the water skis belonging to **Léo Roman** who launched this sport in Juan-les-Pins in 1921.

Eating out

MODERATE

La Croustille – *4 Cours Masséna* – ☎ *04 93 34 84 83* – *Closed during Nov school holidays, 20-26 Dec and Tue* – *7.62/15.24€*. Settle on the charming terrace of this creperie-salad bar in old Antibes and soak up the lively, colourful atmosphere of the local market. The cosy interior is decorated with family photographs and models of sailing boats. Warm, hospitable welcome at highly reasonable prices.

Le Troppo – *2 Boulevard du Maréchal-Leclerc* – ☎ *04 93 34 00 21* – *Closed 15 Nov-15 Dec, Mon evening and Tue off season.* – *12.20/20.58€*. A stone's throw from the Archeological Museum, this restaurant is a kaleidoscope of warm, earthy hues that harmonise well with its Provençal backdrop. Pancakes or more elaborate cuisine can be served in the cool interior or outside, on the sun drenched terrace. Excellent service.

L'Oursin – *16 Rue de la République* – ☎ *04 93 34 13 46* – *Closed 18 Feb-1 Mar, 17-31 May, 18-29 Nov, Sun evening and Mon* – *16.01€*. The tempting displays of oysters laid out on the terrace of this quaint, old-fashioned restaurant are the perfect excuse to enter and sample their deliciously fresh fish and seafood dishes. A great favourite among locals.

MID-RANGE

Restaurant Chez Olive – *2 Boulevard du Maréchal-Leclerc* – ☎ *04 93 34 42 32* – *Closed 15-30 Oct, Sun evening and Mon in winter* – *21/25€*. Conveniently located near the Archeological Museum, Chez Olive offers regional cuisine and a congenial welcome in a pretty Provençal decor enhanced with flowered tablecloths and the works of local artists.

Chez les Poissonniers – *16 Cours Masséna, (Provençal market)* – ☎ *04 93 34 23 10* – *Closed Mon* – *21.02/52.55€*. This fish restaurant set up in an old house on the market square is known for the freshness of its produce. The dining rooms are on the small side. Sit down for an apéritif at the bar, where the "catch of the day" is chalked up on a slate. Considerate service.

Where to stay

MID-RANGE

Relais du Postillon – *8 Rue Championnet* – ☎ *04 93 34 20 77* – *15 rooms: 41.92/72.87€* – ☖ *6.56€* – *Restaurant 30/48€*. Small, tastefully appointed rooms in a spruce, neat setting are the hallmark of this hotel located in the old quarter of Antibes. Tuck into a hearty meal on the terrace or in the dining room, decorated with pretty Provençal tablecloths, before setting out to discover the pedestrian district.

Le Ponteil – *11 Impasse Jean-Mensier* – ☎ *04 93 34 67 92* – *Closed 8 Jan-6 Feb and 15 Nov-27 Dec* – *14 rooms: 47.26/77.75€* – ☖ *6.86€*. Unassuming bed and breakfast with a homely atmosphere within walking distance of the beaches. Quiet, welcoming rooms. Leafy garden bursting with colour. Restaurant open to residents only.

Bleu Marine – *2.5km/1.5mi Chemin des 4 Chemins* – ☎ *04 93 74 84 84* – *18 rooms: 50.31/57.93€* – ☖ *5.79€*. Situated in the vicinity of the hospital, this hotel offers medium-sized, well-kept rooms with all modern conveniences. The ones on the upper floors command pretty views of the coastline.

Chambre d'Hôte La Bastide du Bosquet – *14 Chemin des Sables, (Domaine des Mûriers)* – *06160 Cap-Antibes* – ☎ *04 93 67 32 29* – *sylvie.tossel@wanadoo.fr* – *Closed mid-Nov-20 Dec* – ✉ – *3 rooms: 62/84€*. Attractive 18C country house at the heart of a residential area that will guarantee you a peaceful stay (three nights minimum). Cool, pleasing rooms of different sizes with colourful Provençal furnishings. The garden and terrace are great assets in high season.

Ireland on the Riviera

The Hop Store Irish Pub – *38 Boulevard Aguillon* – *06160 Cap-Antibes* – ☎ *04 93 34 15 33* – *Sun-Thu 3pm-1.30am, Fri-Sat until 2am*. Once used for storing salt, these impressive vaulted cellars have now been converted into an Irish pub. Located near one of the coast's largest marinas, it is a popular meeting place with the English-speaking community.

Transport

Buses – *Sillager-STGA* – *Place Guynemer* – ☎ *04 93 34 37 60*. There are 15 bus lines. The most convenient ones are 1A and 3A (going towards Juan-les-Pins), 2A (going towards Cap d'Antibes), 10A (going towards Biot), 2VB (going towards Sophia-Antipolis and Valbonne) and 5V (going towards Vallauris).

Shopping

Most of the shops are located in Rue de la République and Rue James-Close.

Market – Along Cours Masséna every morning (except Mon in low season).

Having a Dip

Swimming pool – The fabulous pool belonging to the Cap Eden Rock Hotel is also open to non-residents. Admission: 30.49€. Pool mattress: 22.87€.

Beaches – The long beach of Antibes extends way beyond Fort Carré. Four other, smaller beaches are covered in fine sand: the Gravette (south of the old port), the Îlette, the Salis and the Garoupe.

EXCURSIONS

★ **Marineland** ⊘ – *4km/2.5mi north towards Nice.* This marine zoo, the first in Europe, consists of many large pools containing **killer whales** (large voracious cetaceans that are even known to attack other whales), dolphins, elephant seals, seals alongside maned and Californian sea lions. The dolphins and killer whales give regular acrobatic displays. In a penguin enclosure *(manchotière)*, about 20 king penguins have been reared. The spectacular show **"Sharks"** takes visitors down a 30m/98ft tunnel with a view of a dozen grey sharks and tiger sharks swimming in a vast tank. The zoo has been successful in breeding from many species which rarely reproduce in captivity; killer whales, maned sea lions and king penguins. Among other activities intended to protect the marine environment, specialists from Marineland offer a veterinary service to marine mammals in the Mediterranean.

Marineland also houses a small museum containing a fine collection of models, marine instruments and other items.

Parc Aqua-Splash ⊘ – *Entrance via Marineland.* This water leisure park offers an impressive range of water games: a swimming pool with waves, water chutes, giant pool.

Jungle des Papillons ⊘ – *Entrance via the Marineland car park. To get the best out of this butterfly centre, visitors are advised to wear brightly coloured clothes and a lemon-flavoured perfume, which will attract the butterflies towards them, and to choose a bright sunny day for their visit.*

This charming tropical hothouse welcomes 15 species of diurnal butterfly from all over the world and a large number of chrysalises, since the average life span of a butterfly is three weeks. The more adventurous visitors can get a few cheap thrills by observing the huge insects, iguanas and crocodiles. The centre also hosts regular exhibitions on themes from the animal kingdom.

⌂ A DRIVING TOUR OF CAP D'ANTIBES *10km/6mi – allow 2hr*

Cap d'Antibes – Strictly speaking the name Cap d'Antibes refers only to the southernmost tip of land but it has come to mean the whole peninsula, which is an enchanting garden dotted with sumptuous hotels and villas catering for both summer and winter visitors.

EDEN-ROC, an Edwardian Paradise

This majestic palace surrounded by an estate (8ha/20 acres) is set on a promontory of Cap d'Antibes. Famous for its quaint huts *(cabanes)* and its private beach, it has become an essential port of call for film stars visiting the Riviera. For a century it was also a favoured holiday destination among crowned heads from all over the world. A wonderful party given by Russian princes in spring 1870 launched the Grand Hôtel du Cap. After a slack period, during which Stephen Liégeard compared the hotel to Sleeping Beauty's castle, the Grand Hôtel was resuscitated at the instigation of the American Gordon Bennett. In 1914 an annexe, the Eden Roc together with its private beach, was built, foreshadowing the popularity of the Riviera as a summer resort. Since then, it has known unflagging success, with a varied and cosmopolitain clientele featuring celebrities such as General Eisenhower, who used it as his winter quarters, the painters Picasso and Chagall, who worked here, and a number of rich eccentrics like the oil magnate Gulbenkian *(Mister 5%)*.The swimming pool is open to non-residents.

Pointe Bacon – This point gives a **view★** of Antibes and Fort Carré, sweeping across the Baie des Anges opposite Nice and the surrounding countryside to Cap Ferrat and even Cap Martin near the Italian frontier.

Sanctuaire de la Garoupe ⊘ – Outside this church are two 17C wrought-iron grilles. Inside, two adjoining chapels, communicating by wide arches, form two aisles.

The widest aisle is ornamented with a fresco by J Clergues. It also contains an interesting **collection of votive offerings**; the oldest dates back to 1779.

On either side of the altarpiece over the high altar are: on the left the **Sebastopol icon**, a magnificent Russo-Byzantine work, believed to date from the 14C, and on the right the *plachzanitza* of the Woronzoffs, a splendid painted silk, also brought back at the time of the siege of Sebastopol.

In the second aisle, decorated with frescoes by Édouard Colin, are some 60 naval votive offerings and maritime souvenirs as well as a gilded wood statue of **Notre-Dame-de-Bon-Port** (Our Lady of Safe Homecoming), patron saint of sailors. Every year on the first or second Sunday in July the statue of Our Lady, taken to the old cathedral in Antibes on the previous Thursday, is brought back in procession to La Garoupe by the seamen. Beside the sanctuary stands the curious Oratoire de Ste-Hélène, first patron of Antibes, who has been worshipped here since the 5C AD in what was originally a pagan shrine.

Phare de la Garoupe ⊘ – The **lighthouse**, one of the most powerful on the Mediterranean coast, with a luminous intensity of 2 300 000 candelas, has a beam which nominally carries 52km/32mi out to sea and 100km/33 000ft up to aircraft. The radio beam has a range of 185km/100 nautical miles.

★ **Jardin Thuret** ⊘ – These **botanical gardens** covering 4ha/10 acres carry the name of the scientist Gustave Thuret, who created them in 1857. He sought to acclimatise plants and trees from hot countries, successfully spreading the different species throughout the region: the first eucalyptuses, from Australia, were planted here. Bequeathed to the state, these gardens are currently administered by the National Institute of Agronomic Research.

They contain a magnificent collection of 3 000 rare plant and tree species: palm trees, mimosas, eucalyptuses, cypresses...

Villa Thuret, the gardens' botanical centre, contains offices and research laboratories.

Musée Napoléonien ⊘ – The former Le Grillon battery has been converted into a museum devoted to Napoleon's reign. At the entrance stand two replicas of a magnificent Louis XIV bronze cannon. Also on display are **Napoleon's bust** sculpted by Canova in 1810, model soldiers and officers of the Great Army, Napoleon's autograph and imperial proclamations.

From the roof, there is a fine **view★** over the wooded headland to the Îles de Lérins and to the distant Alps.

Port de l'Olivette – From this harbour, there is a **view** over Golfe Juan, the heights of Super-Cannes, Pointe de la Croisette and the Îles de Lérins. The coast road, Avenue du Maréchal-Juin, follows the seashore to Juan-les-Pins and overlooks **Port Crouton** and **Port Gallice**.

Les ARCS

Population 5 334
Michelin map 84 fold 7, 114 fold 23 or 245 fold 35

The town, nestling in the heart of vineyards that produce excellent wines, vies with Brignoles *(See BRIGNOLES)* for the title of capital of the Côtes de Provence area. It is dominated by the ruins of Villeneuve Castle, where St Roseline was born, and which is the starting point for the Provence wine circuit.

A WALK IN THE OLD VILLAGE

Le Parage – *From Place de l'Église take Rue de la Paix leading up to the keep.*
Around the ruins of the medieval castle are the stepped streets and alleys of the old town winding between and beneath the houses. In the Middle Ages, from the keep, a watch was kept to ward off Saracen invasions.

Church – It attracts many visitors to its **mechanical crib** *(left on entering)*: the backdrop is the old village of Les Arcs. The side chapels are painted with frescoes: *(left)* the miracle of St Roseline's roses by Baboulaine; *(right)* a **polyptych★** in 16 sections by Louis Bréa (1501) of the Virgin and Child surrounded by Provençal saints.

EXCURSION

★ **Chapelle Ste-Roseline** – *4km/2.5mi east of Les Arcs by D91.*
In the quiet countryside and vineyards around Les Arcs stands the chapel of Ste-Roseline, part of the old abbey of La Celle-Roubaud, founded in the 11C. In the 13C it became a charter house and flourished during the priorate of **Roseline de Villeneuve** from 1300 to 1328. The 12C cloisters and the Provençal-style Romanesque chapel are all that remain.

★ **Interior** ⊘ – On the right of the nave lies the shrine of St Roseline, whose corpse is amazingly well-preserved. Pilgrimages take place five times a year, the most popular being on Trinity Sunday and the first Sunday in August. A Renaissance chancel grille surmounted by a polychrome statue of St Catherine of Alexandria divides the nave; on the high altar stands a superb early 16C Baroque altarpiece depicting the Descent from the Cross; the delicately carved choir stalls date from the 17C. The altar at the far end of the nave bears a Renaissance altarpiece showing the Nativity; on the left of the chancel hangs a precious 15C predella. Contemporary works of art include a large mosaic by Chagall (south aisle) inspired by the legend of St Roseline; a bronze low relief illustrating St Roseline and the miracle of the roses and a lectern in the shape of a bush by Alberto Giacometti's brother, a stained-glass window in iridescent colours (rose petals) by Bazaine and others by Ubac.

LUXURIOUS AND UNIQUE

Logis du Guetteur – *Medieval village* – ☎ *04 94 99 51 10 – Closed 15 Jan-2 Mar – 13 rooms: 103.67/190.56€ – ☲ 10.37€ – Restaurant 27/59€*. In an 11C fort at the heart of the village, this hotel-restaurant has used its superb vaulted stone cellars as a setting for its lounges and dining rooms. There are a few air-conditioned rooms housed in the outbuildings. Outdoor pool.

Shopping

Château Ste-Roseline – *Sauteirane district (next to the Chapelle Ste-Roseline)* - ☎ *04 94 99 50 30*. Tasting sessions and wine sales. Groups of 15 or more visitors can be shown round the vineyards and the wine storehouses.

AUPS

Population 1 903
Michelin map 84 fold 6, 114 fold 21 or 245 fold 34

From the foot of the Espiguières hills, Aups overlooks the Uchane plain, a fertile area of gently rounded hillocks, which is bordered to the northwest by the steep highlands of Haute-Provence. To the south, the Massif des Maures dominates the horizon. Aups is renowned for its honey.
Ramparts and a ruined castle evoke the past. The huge main square planted with magnificent plane trees, the many fountains and the picturesque old streets add to the charm of this delightful old town; there is a fine wrought-iron belfry in Rue de l'Horloge.

VISITING AUPS

Collégiale St-Pancrace – The collegiate church of St Pancras is 15C Provençal Gothic with a Renaissance doorway; the simple nave ends in a square apse. The church treasury houses some interesting 15C-18C gold- and silver-plate.

Musée Simon-Ségal ⊘ – *Rue du Maréchal-Joffre*. This museum of modern art contains 280 pictures, of which 175 are attributed to the Paris School, on display in the former Ursuline Convent's chapel.

DRIVING TOUR

★ **Le Haut Var** – *53km/33mi – about 5hr. From Aups take D 77 east.*
The road winds along the steep slopes of the Espiguières hills. Soon after Château de la Beaume bear left on D 51 towards Tourtour.

Black Gold of the Haut-Var

The truffle (called *rabasse* in Provence) is a fungus which grows on the secretions which seep out of diseased oak trees. There are two categories of truffle: the white, which are not particularly tasty, and the black, which ripen in the autumn and are recognisable by their distinctive smell. They are harvested from November to February by dogs or by sows that take two years to train. The largest truffle market in the Var takes place in Aups every Thursday during the gathering season. The uninitiated may be surprised by the unusual air of excitement which pervades transactions. Traditionally, the town of Aups hosts a large truffle fair on the fourth Sunday in January. In this truffle-producing region many restaurants offer dishes cooked with truffles – spinach or salad or eggs for example.

Shopping

Specialities – Here the famous truffle reigns supreme and can be found in many dishes, notably salads, omelettes and spinach. There is a truffle fair on the last Sunday in August. The area is also known for its production of honey and especially the delicious goat's cheese made in the Upper Var Valley.

Moulin à Huile Gervasoni – *Montée des Moulins* – ☎ *04 94 70 04 66 – Open Jul-Aug: 9.30am-0.30pm, 2-7pm; Apr-Sep 10am-noon, 2.30-7pm.* This 18C olive mill still manufactures and sells olive oil, alongside many other regional produce.

Mamie Martin – *10 Rue de l'Hôpital-Vieux* – ☎ *04 94 70 10 78.* Beautifully hand crafted traditional santons that have become collector's pieces.

Market – Wednesdays and Saturdays on Place Frédéric-Mistral. Truffle market on Thursday *(Nov to mid-Mar)*.

Sports

Office du tourisme de Sillans – ☎ *04 94 04 78 05.* Canoeing along the water-falls, hiking and riding in the lush countryside around Sillans.

★**Tourtour** – *See TOURTOUR.*

Villecroze – *See VILLECROZE.*

Salernes – *5km/3mi southwest of Villecroze.* Facilities. An agricultural and industrial centre, Salernes is known for the manufacture of floor tiles and pottery. The distinctive russet-coloured Provençal tiles known as *tomettes* can be seen adorning a great many local houses. Traditionally of hexagonal shape, they are made with local clay, featuring a high iron content, and their warm hues blend in harmoniously with the earthy landscape, echoing the reddish-pink roofs that charaterises most Mediterranean *mas*.

The church, set among 17C houses, boasts a belfry at both ends. Fountains abound and trees shade the main square.

D 31 follows the Bresque Valley south.

Entrecasteaux – *See ENTRE-CASTEAUX.*

From Entrecasteaux take D 31 south; turn right onto D 50.

Cotignac – *See COTIGNAC.*

Take D 22 north. There is a good view back over the site of Cotignac. Further on to the right the Cascade de Sillans can be glimpsed through the trees.

★ **Cascade de Sillans** – *30min on foot there and back. Before entering the village turn right onto a path (sign; car park).*
▮ In a sylvan setting the Bresque cascades over a 42m/138ft drop. Water sports enthusiasts may go canyoning on the waterfalls and there are also rambling and riding facilities in the lush countryside around Sillans. Tourists interested in finding out details about these sports should apply to the **tourist office** ⊙.

Old town, Aups

J.-L. Gallo/MICHELIN

Sillans-la-Cascade – An attractive, once fortified village on the Bresque, with a few picturesque streets near the post office, which boasts a pinnacle turret.
Continue on D 22 to return to Aups.

BANDOL ⚑⚑

Population 7 905
Michelin map 84 fold 14, 114 fold 44 or 245 folds 45 and 46

Bandol is a pleasant resort lying inside a pretty bay, sheltered from the north winds by high wooded slopes. It has always been a popular holiday destination among artists and literary celebrities such as Katherine Mansfield, Thomas Mann, or the great French actors Raimu and Fernandel.

A WHIFF OF SEA AIR

A charming marina – Enjoy the bracing sea air of this little port, squeezed in between **Allée Jean-Moulin**★ and Allée Alfred-Vivien, both charmingly bordered with pine trees, palms and brightly coloured flower beds.

Chemin de la Corniche skirts the little peninsula with Bendor Island lying off shore, affording a fine view of the coast from Cap de l'Aigle to Cap Sicié.

This seaside resort has three sandy beaches: the east-facing Lido, the well-sheltered Rènecros facing west and the Casino facing due south. The rest of the coast offers smaller beaches alternating with rocky areas.

Beyond the villas scattered in groves of pine and mimosa behind the seafront are fields of flowers and vineyards which produce Bandol, the best-known of the Côtes-de-Provence wines.

Côtes-de-Provence Wine

Wines from Provence have always been a great favourite in France, relished by both locals and foreign visitors. These vineyards cover five different *appellation d'origine contrôlée* (AOC) areas and therefore feature a variety of soils and micro-climates. The dry, aromatic white wines from the coastal region and the lively rosés are best enjoyed young. However, the full-bodied reds, in particular those produced on the sun-blessed terraces around Bandol, are definitely for laying down: made with the *mourvèdre* grape, they are high in tannin and their subtle flavour combining pepper, cinnamon, vanilla and black cherries are the perfect complement to venison or red meat. Provençal dialect is still spoken on some of the estates and it has given rise to some curious descriptions of the bunches of grapes: *ginou d'agasso* (magpie's knee) or *pecoui-touar* (twisted tail)!

Jardin Exotique et Zoo de Sanary-Bandol ⊘ – *3km/2mi north; 500m/550yd after passing over the motorway (A50), turn right (sign "Zoo-Jardin Exotique")*. In these shaded gardens cacti and tropical plants are grown to remarkable sizes. Among hundreds of rare plants, animals from all over the world can be seen – monkeys (marmosets, Capuchin monkeys, gibbons and their offspring) and also coatis, lemurs, fennecs, kinkajous, peccaries, deer, ponies, miniature goats and llamas. Our feathered friends have not been forgotten either as you can observe the noisy, colourful world of parrots, peacocks, pink flamingoes and cranes.

⚑ **Île de Bendor** – The **boat trip** ⊘ to the island makes a pleasant summer excursion. The island is an attractive tourist centre offering fine beaches, a harbour, a Provençal village with craft shops and a conference centre that organises lectures. The **Espace Culturel Paul-Ricard**, open to young painters and sculptors, offers art lessons.

The curious **Exposition des Vins et Spiritueux** ⊘, set up in a large hall decorated with frescoes, covers the production of wine, aperitifs and liqueurs in 51 different countries; 8 000 bottles are on display as well as a collection of glasses and decanters.

DRIVING TOURS

★**Perched Villages of Pays de Bandol** – *Round trip of 55km/29mi – allow 3hr. From Bandol take D 559 northeast; turn left on D 559ᴮ towards Le Beausset and pass under the railway bridge. In Le Beausset turn right on N 8 towards Toulon. After 1km/0.6mi turn right.*

The narrow road wends its way through olive groves, orchards and vineyards dotted with clumps of broom and cypress trees.

Chapelle Notre-Dame-du-Beausset-Vieux ⊘ – *Leave the car below the chapel.* The **chapel** has been restored by volunteer workers. It is a stark Provençal Romanesque structure with barrel vaulting in the nave and oven vaulting in the apse. The Virgin and Child in the choir comes from Pierre Puget's studio. In the left niche a group of 400-year-old **santons** illustrates the Flight to Egypt. Some of the votive offerings *(side aisle)* date back to the 18C.

From the terrace above the chapel a **sweeping panorama**★ takes in Le Castellet, Ste-Baume, Gros Cerveau and the coast from Bandol westwards to La Ciotat.

Return to N 8; and continue north towards Aubagne.

Eating out

MID-RANGE

L'Oasis – *15 Rue des Écoles* – ☎ *04 94 29 41 69* – *Closed Dec and Sun evening off season.* – *17.53/40.40€*. Delightful dining room painted in warm Mediterranean tones. The smallish but impeccably kept rooms are being renovated one by one. In summer, enjoy the charming terrace looking out onto the garden.

La Réserve – *Route de Sanary* – ☎ *04 94 29 30 00* – *Closed 6 Jan-22 Feb, 28 Oct-29 Nov, Sun evening and Mon Oct to Easter- 30.49/62.50€*. This ochre manor house lying at the water's edge just outside Bandol offers both regional and traditional cuisine served in a dining room with bay windows opening directly onto the sea. Relax on the terrace or the wooden landing stage in the evening. A few rooms are available for weary travellers.

Restaurant La Farigoule – *2 Place du Jeu-de-Paume – 83330 Le Castellet* – ☎ *04 94 32 64 58 – Closed 20 Nov-10 Dec, Tue and Wed off season.* – *Reservation required in summer – 17/29€*. Nestling in the heart of the village, this restaurant boasts a fine dining room with a colourful Provençal decor and a host of mementoes surrounding the open fireplace where tasty grilled meat is prepared. Shaded terrace graced by a century-old plane tree.

Castel Lumière – *1 Rue Portail – 83330 Le Castellet* – ☎ *04 94 32 62 20* – *Closed 7 Jan-9 Feb, Sun evening and Mon except public holidays* – *28.20/42.69€*. This restaurant is set up in the house where the Frères Lumière once lived, right in the medieval quarter. The long dining hall affords a panoramic view of the surrounding vineyards. The upstairs rooms are light and cool.

E. Baret

Bandol port

Where to stay

MID-RANGE

Golf Hôtel – *On Rénecros Beach by Boulevard Louis-Lumière* – ☎ *04 94 29 45 83 – Closed late Oct-7 Apr – 23 rooms: 64.03/99.09€* – ⌂ *6.86€ – Restaurant 16/16€*. A seaside hotel, complete with deckchairs and beach restaurant during the summer season. Most of the homey rooms give onto the sea; some are fronted by a small balcony. Dinner is served only in July and August (special menus for children).

Chambre d'Hôte Les Cancades – *1195 Chemin de la Fontaine de Cinq-Sous – 83330 Le Beausset – 3km/2mi E of Le Castellet, take Chemin de la Fontaine de Cinq-Sous which is just across from the Casino supermarket* – ☎ *04 94 98 76 93 – charlotte.zerbib@wanadoo.fr –* ✉ *– 4 rooms: 53.36/60.98€*. A steep, narrow path leads to the wooded, residential area where the owner of this hotel, a retired architect, has set up his charming Provençal *mas*. The fine, handsomely furnished rooms, the suite, the park, the swimming pool and the summer kitchen are all blissfully quiet and relaxing.

LUXURY

Hôtel La Ker-Mocotte – *103 Rue Raimu* – ☎ *04 94 29 46 53* – *www.ker-mocotte.com* – *Closed 15 Nov to Mar* – 🅿 – *20 rooms: 50/146€* – *Restaurant 23€*. This imposing villa, once the property of the actor Raimu, overlooks Réne-cros Bay and provides direct access to the beach. A selection of early film posters pay homage to the French entertainer. The quiet rooms are decorated strictly in Provençal style and the dining room opens onto the Mediterranean.

Hôtel Delos – *Île de Bendor* – *Access by boat* – ☎ *04 94 29 11 60* – *Closed Jan and Feb* – *55 rooms: 91.47/205.81€* – ☒ *11.43€* – *Restaurant 29/53€*. Attractive location on the Île de Bendor, half-way between sea and port. Pretty views can be had from all the comfortable rooms arranged in two stone cottages. However, the ones in the main building feature fine antiques. Lovely pool.

On the town

Tchin Tchin – *11 Allée Jean-Moulin* – ☎ *04 94 29 41 04* – *Daily 10am-1.30pm, 6pm-4am*. This prestigious bar saw its golden age in the 1970s, when it attracted many celebrities from the entertainment world, namely Jacques Brel and Richard Antony, who coined the title of the club. Single, unaccompanied clients get special treatment: each woman is given a rose and each man a cigar...

Shopping

Le Tonneau de Bacchus – *296 Avenue du 11-Novembre* – ☎ *04 94 29 01 01* – *letonneaubacchus.com* – *open Jul-Aug daily 9.30am-12.30am, 4-8pm; the rest of the year daily except Mon and Sun afternoons*. This cellar offers a wide selection of wines from France and especially the Bandol area. The cellarmen is extremely knowledgeable about wine and he will be delighted to introduce you to his vintage bottles. All year round, Le Tonneau de Bacchus organises oenology courses and thematic evenings. Fine gastronomic specialities from Provence are also on sale.

Domaine de Souviou – *83330 Le Beausset* – ☎ *04 94 90 57 63*. Sale of wine and olive oil.

Leisure activities

Var Voltige – *3250 Route des Hauts-du-Camp* – *83330 Le Castellet* – ☎ *04 94 90 62 44* – *Wed-Sun from 9am (during the day)*. This club organises maiden flights specialised in hair-raising aerobatics. 45.73€ per person. Several other clubs nearby also organise maiden flights in planes or helicopters.

Aquascope – *Tours (30min) leaving from the landing-stage on Quai d'Honneur* – ☎ *04 94 32 51 41 (high season)*. *10am-noon, 2-7pm. 9,91€ (child 4,57€)*.Boat with transparent hull for underwater observation of marine flora and fauna.

Casino – *2 Place Lucien-Artaud* – ☎ *04 94 29 31 31*. *Daily noon-10pm*.

Boat trips – ☎ *04 94 32 51 41*. There are many boat rides leaving for the Embiez Islands, Toulon via Cap Sicié, Cassis and its inlets, and the Frioul Islands.

Circuit du Castellet Paul-Ricard ⊘ – *8km/5mi north of Beausset by N8*. This track, built in 1970 on 1 000ha/2 471 acres of desolate scrubland, has become an essential feature in the lifes of Formula 1 and Formula 3 racing drivers. The track (5.8km/3.5mi long) was officially opened on the occasion of the first Grand Prix de France, won by Jacky Stewart. Since then, many international drivers, such as Alain Prost in 1976, have attended the driving school on the circuit. Developments to comply with new regulations and the building of an airfield at Le Castellet have permitted a far greater variety of track events as well as air shows. Meetings popular among the general public include the **Grand Prix Historique de Provence** and the **Deux Tours d'Horloge** (shows and races for vintage cars). Every year in May a colourful truck show, the **Grand Prix International de Camions** provides an opportunity to see stunts, early models and a *concours d'élégance* – a competition where first prize goes to the most creatively decorated juggernaut!

On leaving the circuit, turn left on RN 8 towards Aubagne. At the Camp-du-Castellet crossroads, turn left and left again on D 26 towards Le Beausset. 3km/2mi before the hill to Le Beausset, turn right on D 226 towards Le Castellet.

★ **Le Castellet** – Nestled on a woody hill dominating the vineyards, this remarkable stronghold, formerly owned by the lords of Les Baux and subsequently by King René, has well-preserved ramparts, a carefully restored 12C church and a castle, parts of which date back to the 11C. From beyond the gate on Place de la Mairie

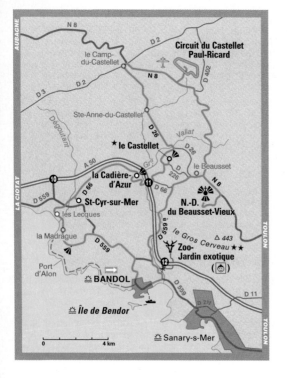

there is an attractive **view** inland towards Ste-Baume. Many houses were originally built in the 17C and 18C. There are art and craft workshops – painting, pottery, hollow-ware, weaving and leatherwork. Because of its charm, this perched village has often been used as a setting for films.

Leave Le Castellet going downhill towards D 66.

La Cadière-d'Azur – This very old hill town, which had 4 000 citizens at the Revolution, produces Bandol wine. Some of its former defences are still standing. The 13C Peï Gate, in front of the town hall leads to a maze of picturesque old streets. From the eastern end of the village there is a fine **view★** inland over Le Castellet to Ste-Baume.

Follow D 66 to Les Lecques.

Les Lecques – *See Les LECQUES.*

From Les Lecques the road south via La Madrague affords fine **views** of the coast and hinterland before joining D 559 which returns to Bandol.

BARJOLS

Population 2 414
Michelin map 84 fold 5, 114 fold 19 or 245 fold 33

The small town lies in a natural amphitheatre in lush countryside fed by many springs and streams. Barjols contributes to traditional Provençal life by making tambourines and flutes *(galoubets)* and holding an unusual festival.

Festival of St Marcel – *See Calendar of events.* Since time immemorial the people of Barjols have slaughtered an ox every year to celebrate their survival during a siege. In 1350 a group of pious citizens, rescuing the relics of St Marcel (a 5C bishop) from the abandoned abbey near Montmeyan, fell in with the other celebrants and religious and secular festivities were thus combined.

St Marcel was adopted as the patron saint of Barjols and each year in January his bust is dutifully carried in procession throughout the town. Sometimes the ox is adorned with trappings and blessed by the priest in front of St Marcel's statue. While it is being led round the town on its way to the abattoir, the people sing compline and light bonfires. On the following day, after High Mass, the statue, escorted by the clergy and the band, joins the float bearing the ox on a spit and proceeds to the main square where the ox is roasted whole, while people celebrate in true Provençal style with flutes, tambourines, music and dancing. On the third day the roast ox is distributed to the crowd.

STROLLING THROUGH BARJOLS

The old town contains 12 wash-houses and 30 **fountains**. The most remarkable fountain, near the town hall, is a limestone-encrusted mushroom-shaped one, known locally as the "Champignon". A magnificent plane tree (circumference 12m/39ft), said to be the largest in Provence, dominates the town hall square.

In the lower town, the Pontevès House, named after an old Provençal family from a nearby village, is enhanced by a Renaissance doorway.

Clinging to the hillside, north of the church, lies **Réal★**, the town's oldest quarter. Inhabited since the 12C, it has been occupied for the most part by tanners as water is essential tool of their trade; three levels of partially troglodyte (16C-17C)

"The Mushroom", Barjols

E. Baret

soaking and rinsing basins were uncovered in the 1980s. Nearby, beneath a vault, the entire text of the Déclaration des Droits de l'Homme et du Citoyen, has been carved on glazed stelae.

Church – The original Romanesque structure was rebuilt in the 16C with a fine Gothic nave. The organ loft, choir panelling and carved misericords are 17C. To the right of the entrance, behind a beautiful 12C font, is the original carved tympanum depicting Christ the King with angels and the symbols of the Evangelists.

EXCURSIONS

Source d'Argens – *15km/10mi to the southwest. From Barjols take D 560.*

Vallon de Font-Taillade – The road plunges into a green valley of fields and meadows and follows a winding stream. On the slopes vineyards alternate with pines and holm oaks.

500m/547yd after Brue-Auriac a narrow path to the left leads to a chapel.

Chapelle Notre-Dame – Next to a graveyard stands an abandoned Romanesque **chapel** built from the local red stone. Its pleasant façade, pierced by an oculus and a bay and topped by a wall-belfry with twin windows, is obscured by undergrowth.

Return to D 560 and turn left. Park the car after 3km/2mi, in front of the bridge.

Source d'Argens – ◪ On the right of the road a path leads through the bushes straight to the spring which is one of the sources of the River Argens.

DRIVING TOURS

Plateaux du Haut-Var – *52km/32mi – half a day.*

Varages – This pleasant village shaded by plane trees once vied with Moustiers in the production of faience. The decorative patterns here are often similar to those found in Moustiers – the craftsmen would sometimes work in several ceramicist centres – and the production of faience continues today in two factories in Varages, which export much of their production. A fair dedicated to faience, *Terre et Feu* (earth and fire), takes place each summer alongside an exhibition of works.

Church ⊙ – Built in the 17C in the Provençal Gothic style, the church has a fine bell-tower covered in glazed multicoloured tiles. Inside, the altar of St Claude, patron saint of faience-makers, is decorated with medallions and crosses made locally.

Musée des Faïences ⊙ – *On Place de la Libération.* This museum, housed in the Maison Gassendi, contains a complete retrospective of the history of faience in Varages from the end of the 17C, displayed on two levels. In the many glass cases the different techniques used by local dynasties such as the Armand, Clerissy and Niel families, are explained: hand decoration, decoration with stamps and enamelling techniques. On the first floor, there is a remarkable 19C **faience fountain** attributed to Mazières.
The factory **"Manufacture des Lauriers"** has perpetuated these traditions and produces many Provençal items. A workshop nearby, the **Atelier de Faïence** ⊙, exhibits its products and it is possible to watch the decorators at work.
To the north of Varages, D 554 runs between hills planted with vines and olive groves interspersed with holm oaks and pines.

La Verdière – This village, on the slopes of a hill, is dominated by its church and castle. The fortress, built in the 10C by the Castellane family, was acquired in the 17C through a marriage by the rich Forbin d'Oppède family. The castle today, in a dilapidated condition, shows the results of efforts by Louis-Roch de Forbin to make the building more comfortable in the 18C.

East of La Verdière take D 30 towards Montmeyan.

The road crosses a barren limestone plateau covered with sparse vegetation typical of such an area. Juniper, holm oaks and hawthorn bushes thrive here, as do Scots pine trees, indicating that we have reached the northern edge of the region. This forest of stunted trees is scattered with piles of stones, the remains of attempts to clear and acclimatise the land during the rural expansion of the 19C.

Montmeyan – This medieval village, perched on a hill, dominates the mouth of the Verdon Gorge. There is a fine **view★** from the southern entrance to the village over the rocky ridge of the Castellane Pre-Alps to the east. After passing the Tour Charlemagne, vestiges of the 14C castle, there is a panoramic viewpoint overlooking the *causse*, a barren limestone plateau with occasional bursts of colour provided by holm oaks alongside clumps of broom and hawthorn blossom.

Take D 13 south from Montmeyan to Tavernes.

Tavernes – This is a pleasant village, set in the midst of olive groves and vineyards, in an attractive dip surrounded by hills: there is a square belfry with an 18C wrought-iron campanile on top, and the remains of medieval walls. At the top of the village sits Notre-Dame-de-Bellevue, a chapel dedicated to Our Lady of Bellevue.

D 554, which takes you back to Barjols, crosses then runs along a charming brook called the Ruisseau des Écrevisses.

Provençal Bell-Towers in the Var	
Les Arcs	Tour de l'Horloge (18C)
Aups	Tours de l'Horloge (Clock tower)
Carces	Bell-tower crowning a fortified gateway (17C)
Carmoules	Belfry (17C)
Cotignac	Bell-tower (16C)
Flassans	Bell-tower (18C)
Salernes	Steeple (18C)
Tavernes	Finely carved bell-tower (18C)

Le BAR-SUR-LOUP

Population 2 465
Michelin map 84 fold 9, 115 fold 24 or 245 fold 37

Nestled between the River Loup and its tributaries, Le Bar enjoys a privileged **site**★ on a hillside surrounded by terraces planted with orange trees and beds of jasmine and violets. There is a perfume factory on the edge of the village. From the church square (Place de l'Église) there is an oblique **view**★ up the Gorges du Loup and eastwards over the hills to Vence.

Admiral de Grasse – Le Bar was part of the estate belonging to the counts of Grasse and Admiral François de Grasse (1722-88) lived in the castle during his youth. He embarked on a distinguished career and fought valiantly in the American War of Independence. He was rewarded by a grateful Congress with four artillery pieces taken from the English forces. The brave admiral was taken prisoner on his ship (1782) after a tough battle lasting for 10 hours.

VISITING THE TOWN

The narrow streets of the old town wind round the massive 16C castle with its four corner towers and ruined keep.

Église St-Jacques ⏱ – Embedded in the stonework at the foot of the church's bell-tower is a Roman tombstone. The magnificently carved **panels** of the Gothic door are attributed to the sculptor Jacques Bellot, who was responsible for the choir stalls in Vence. A fine **altarpiece** by Louis Bréa consisting of 14 scenes in three tiers painted on a gold background (high altar) depicts the Apostle James the Greater (St Jacques le Majeur) and the Virgin and Child surrounded by 12 saints; the pediment

> ### FINE DINING
>
> **La Jarrerie** – 8 Avenue Amiral-de-Grasse – ☎ 04 93 42 92 92 – Closed 2-31 Jan, Mon Oct-Apr, Wed for lunch May-Sep and Tue – 22.11/38.11€. Housed in a wing of a former 17C monastery, this restaurant provides first-rate cuisine in a majestic setting: visible beams, huge fireplace, stone masonry... Large reception hall. The pleasantly shaded terrace is a delight in summer.

is adorned with the Trinity and the symbols of the Evangelists.
Under the gallery is the **Dance of Death**★, a curious 15C painting on wood, naive in technique; it includes a poem in Provençal. The composition illustrates a legend: the Count of Le Bar gave a ball during Lent and his guests were struck dead in the middle of the revels. The Dance of Death was painted to record the divine punishment. Death, in the guise of an archer, strikes down the dancers with his arrows and their souls, escaping from their bodies through the mouths as tiny naked figures, are weighed in the balance by St Michael, at the feet of Christ, and are flung headlong into the gaping jaws of a monster representing the entrance to Hell.

BEAULIEU-SUR-MER ⌂⌂

Population 3 675
Michelin map 84 folds 10 and 19, 115 fold 27 or 245 fold 38
Local map see Corniches de la RIVIERA

This fashionable resort lies close under a ring of hills which protect it against the north winds and make it one of the warmest spots on the Riviera – an asset especially in winter. The town is also an oasis of peace and quiet. For the tourist, the charm of Beaulieu is centred chiefly round the **Baie des Fourmis**★ and Boulevard Alsace-Lorraine, lined with attractive gardens.
In 1891 this small harbour was discovered by the American press tycoon **Gordon Bennett**, who immediately fell in love with it. He offered to finance the building of a pier but the proud local fishermen declined his offer. However, the winding corniche road linking Beaulieu to Villefranche was his doing and it still bears his name.

WALKS

★★ **Sentier du Plateau St-Michel** – 1hr 45min on foot there and back – stiff climb.
🚶 Starting north of Boulevard Édouard-VII. The path leads up the Riviera escarpment to the plateau (viewing-table), affording wonderful views from Cap d'Ail to the Esterel.

★ **Promenade Maurice-Rouvier** – 1hr on foot there and back.
🚶 This remarkable promenade runs parallel to the shore from Beaulieu to St-Jean-Cap-Ferrat. On one side are fine white villas in beautiful gardens and on the other the sea with distant views of the Riviera and peninsular point of St-Hospice.

Eating out

MODERATE

Le Petit Paris – *Boulevard Marinoni* – ☎ *04 93 01 69 91* – *14.64/19.82€*. Rattan chairs, white tablecloths and advertising posters are the main features of this brasserie-type restaurant. Simple, traditional fare served in the dining room or on the mezzanine.

MID-RANGE

Le Marco Polo – *On the marina* – ☎ *04 93 01 06 50* – *Closed 25 Nov-16 Dec, Tue evening and Wed except Jul-Aug* – *22.11€*. Whether they are served on the radiant verandah or the terrace facing the marina and its luxury yachts, the dishes here all pay tribute to the Mediterranean, centring on fish, seafood and pasta. Attractive, reasonably priced menus.

Where to stay

MID-RANGE

Le Havre Bleu – *Boulevard Maréchal-Joffre* – ☎ *04 93 01 01 40* – *22 rooms: 45.73/53.36€* – ⌷ *6.10€*. A blue and white house off the main road provides simple accommodation at affordable prices. The bedrooms, which are gradually being refurbished, are quieter when they give onto the back of the building.

Le Sélect – *1 Rue André-Cane* – ☎ *04 93 01 05 42* – *Closed 15 Nov-15 Dec* – ⌷ – *19 rooms: 48.78/53.36€* – ⌷ *4.27€*. Housed in a handsome residence, this hotel with Provençal decor offers recently renovated rooms with large, comfortable beds and fully equipped bathrooms. In summer, visitors can settle on the square opposite to have breakfast.

Stones, sea and sun

Small stony beaches well sheltered from the northerly winds, enjoying a southern exposure. They are located on either side of the marina: Baie des Fourmis beach and Petite Afrique au Nord beach.

A TOUCH OF ANCIENT GREECE

★★**Villa Grecque Kérylos** ⊘ – This faithful reconstruction of a sumptuous Greek villa of ancient times was conceived by the archeologist Théodore Reinach, and built in 1902 by the architect Pontremoli. It was bequeathed to the Institut de France in 1928. On a **site**★ reminiscent of the Aegean, the villa stands in a pleasant garden above the sea looking out over the Baie des Fourmis, Cap Ferrat, Èze and Cap d'Ail.

Precious materials such as Carrara marble, alabaster and rare and exotic woods were used on the interior. The frescoes are reproductions or variations on originals. The furniture, made of wood inlaid with ivory, bronze and leather, is modelled on examples seen on vases and in mosaics. Some of the pieces are originals: mosaics, amphorae, vases, lamps, statuettes. Although the villa is well-equipped with modern conveniences, these are all extremely well concealed.

BIOT★

Population 7 385
Michelin map 84 fold 9, 115 fold 25 or 245 fold 37

Biot (the final "t" is voiced) is a picturesque village on rising ground some 4km/2.5mi inland. Cut flowers – roses, carnations, mimosa and anemones – are grown here for market. Since 1960 its name has been closely linked to that of Fernand Léger.

2 500 years of history – There is evidence of settlement by the Celto-Ligurians, Greeks and Romans from finds made in the area and in the La Brague plain. In 1209 the Templars took over from the local lords and unified the village. In 1312 the deeds passed to the Hospitallers of St John of Jerusalem and order reigned. In the 14C Biot suffered from the Black Death and warring factions; the decline was reversed only following an edict promulgated in 1470 by Good King René allowing 40 families from Oneglia and Porto Maurizio (now Imperia on the Ligurian coast) to settle in the village.

Crafts – Biot has long been known for its pottery as the area is rich in clay, sand, manganese and volcanic tufa (stone used for ovens). Amphorae from Biot were very popular until the mid-18C and were exported through the ports of Antibes and Marseille. It has now diversified and has developed into an important craft centre.

DISCOVERING BIOT

Old village – The evening is the best time to appreciate the authentic charm of the picturesque streets, starting from the tourist office *(syndicat d'initiative)* and following the arrows, through the town gates, Porte des Migraniers (Grenadiers) and Porte des Tines (both 16C), and emerging into the beautiful **Place des Arcades** with its rounded and pointed arches.

Church – It overlooks Place des Arcades and its multicoloured pavement. Rebuilt in 15C it was decorated with murals which the bishop of Grasse considered undecorous and had painted over.

On the west wall is the **altarpiece★** of the Virgin of the Rosary in red and gold attributed to Louis Bréa: on the central panel a Virgin of Pity covers the Child Jesus, clerics and laymen with her cloak and stands against a blue-green sky, holding a rosary in her hands. A graceful Mary Magdalene is depicted twisting a strand of golden hair between her fingers.

On the right at the far end of the church there is another altarpiece attributed to Canavesio who married a local girl: an **Ecce Homo** with two cherubs and the instruments of the Passion; above the Flagellation, Christ Reviled and the Resurrection.

SIGHTS

★★ **Musée National Fernand-Léger**
Ⓥ – *Southeast of the village, just off D 4 (signposted).* Built in 1960 by **Andreï Svetchine**, a local architect, the museum, which contains 348 works by Léger (1881-1955), and the gardens were given to the French nation by Mme Nadia Léger and Georges Bauquier.

The façade is decorated by a vast **mosaic** (500m^2/5 382sq ft) celebrating sports, designed for the Hanover Stadium. On the left is a monumental ceramic: *Children's Playground* and two large bronzes *Women with Parrot* and *Walking Flower*.

Birds on a Yellow Background
Musée Fernand Léger, Biot

Displayed in the entrance hall, lit by a stained-glass window, is a large tapestry in beige and grey: *The Bathers.*

The ground-floor gallery presents original ceramics produced between 1950 and 1955 in the Brice workshop in Biot and **paintings** reflecting the artist's evolution from 1905 to his death.

SERVICE WITH A SMILE

Le Café de la Poste – *24 Rue St-Sébastien –* ☎ *04 93 65 19 32 – Closed 15 Jan-15 Feb – 12.20/25.92€.* The new decor of this bistro-type restaurant features a pretty wooden counter, a huge fresco on painted ceramics and a collection of humorous paintings. Good service. Traditional cuisine served by friendly, thoughtful staff.

Shopping

Verrerie de Biot – *Chemin des Combes, at the foot of the village, along D 4.* ☎ *04 93 65 03 00.* ♿ *Apr-Oct 9.30am-7pm (Jul-Aug 9.30am-8pm), Sun and public holidays 10am-1pm, 3-7pm; Nov-Mar 9.30am-6pm, Sun and public holidays 10.30am-1pm, 2.30-6.30pm. Closed 25 Dec. 3€. Five-day introductory course on glass-blowing techniques: 228,67€.*This small factory founded in Biot in 1956 features several workshops that demonstrate the successive stages of the art of glass blowing, characterised by a bubbly texture peculiar to the Biot production. The different shops sell all kinds of glassware: vases, glasses, bottles, small oil lamps, jugs etc.

A Story of Success

The architect Andreï Svetchine was the son of a Russian general; he was born in Nice, where he grew up and attended the Academy of Decorative Arts. He soon demonstrated remarkable skills as an architect and was to design some of the most prestigious private residences and museums on the Riviera, notably the Fernand Léger Museum in Biot. In early 1960s, the painter Marc Chagall asked him to build a house and adjoining studio. The result, "La Colline", was a splendid construction in white Provençal stone arranged in rectangular shapes. He also undertook to refurbish La Colombe d'Or, the famous hotel in St-Paul-de-Vence that caters to an exclusive internationale clientele. In 1984, towards the end of his life, he supervised the challenging task of restoring St-Nicolas, the superb Russian Orthodox Cathedral in Nice.

Portrait of the Uncle (1905) and *My Mother's Garden* are Impressionist in style while Cézanne's influence is evident in *Study of a Woman in Blue* (1912) and *14 July*. Between the two World Wars the artist experimented with contrasting primary colours (unusual *Gioconda with Keys* – 1930) and geometrical compositions (*The Great Tug* – 1923). In *Study of Adam and Eve* (c 1934), the artist shows a total disregard for facial features – which was to become the rule – and the characters become secondary to the general composition.

At a later stage (1942) Léger gave equal importance to colour and line *(Divers)* used at random within a strict composition.

After 1945 the artist painted large canvases praising the virtues of hard work and industrial civilization – *Builders*, 1950, marks a significant achievement in style and inspiration – relaxation and *joie de vivre (Campers)*. *The Great Parade* (1954) pays homage to the fabulous world of the circus. A staircase lit through a stained-glass window leads to the graphic arts room on the ground floor, in which drawings and gouaches reflecting the artist's various phases of development are on display.

Outside, this wing features huge mosaic works (including one of 300m²/3 230sq ft) executed in 1990 after original designs by the artist. On the west front is a design planned for the Triennale de Milan; another version of *Les Oiseaux sur Fond Jaune* adorns the east façade.

Verrerie de Biot ⊙ – *At the foot of the village, on D 4 going southeast, near the museum.* The glassworks were opened in 1956 and produce a great variety of household articles that are in great demand: bottles, vases, glasses, oil lamps, jugs etc. Visitors can watch the different stages of glass blowing – in this case the famous **bubble-flecked glass** in bright colours (emerald, turquoise) that has earned the town its reputation. There are several shops where you can buy most of the pieces made on the premises. This bubble glass has a highly distinctive appearance and can be seen in many local hotels and restaurants.

For those interested in modern art

Antibes: Musée Picasso

Biot: Musée Fernand-Léger

Cagnes-sur-Mer: Musée Renoir and Musée d'Art Moderne Méditerranéen

Menton: Musée du Palais Canolès, the Salle des Mariages in the town hall and the Musée Jean-Cocteau

Nice: Musée Marc-Chagall, Musée des Beaux-Arts, Musée Matisse and the Musée d'Art Moderne et Contemporain

St-Paul: Fondation Maeght

St-Tropez: Musée de l'Annonciade

Vallauris: Musée National "La Guerre et la Paix" and the donation Magnelli

Vence: Chapelle du Rosaire (Chapelle Matisse)

Villefranche: Chapelle St-Pierre (Chapelle Jean-Cocteau)

Where to see the works of the great masters:

Chagall: Musée National du Message Biblique in Nice

Cocteau: Chapelle St-Pierre in Villefranche-sur-Mer, Musée Jean-Cocteau and the Salle des Mariages in the Menton town hall, Chapelle Notre-Dame-de-Jérusalem in Fréjus

Dufy: Musée des Beaux-Arts in Nice

Léger: Musée National Fernand-Léger in Biot

Matisse: Musée Matisse in Nice and the Chapelle du Rosaire in Vence

Picasso: Musée Picasso in Antibes and Musée National "La Guerre et la Paix" in Vallauris

Renoir: Musée Renoir in Cagnes-sur-Mer

Musée de Biot ⊙ – *Entrance from the Tourist Information Centre.* This museum of local history and ceramics is situated in the ruined Chapelle des Pénitents-Blancs, topped by a three-sided pinnacle, and retraces the main events in Biot's history. It was under the Phoceans that the production of ceramic jars originated in Biot. They were made with local clay extracted from nearby quarries. In the Middle Ages the town was famed for its large jars used for keeping and carrying oil. Today a few workshops have maintained the tradition, branching out into pottery, ornamental stoneware and silver plate. A collection of 19C domestic water cisterns in yellow enamel streaked with green and brown, jars bearing the stamps of former craftsmen and a reconstructed local kitchen are of great interest.

Bonsaï Arboretum ⊙ – *Chemin du Val de Pôme, 100m/109yd south of the Musée Fernand Léger.* This sloping garden (53 000m²/32 300sq ft), displays a large collection of bonsai trees against the backdrop of a reconstructed Japanese garden, as well as other tropical plants in nearby greenhouses.

BORMES-LES-MIMOSAS★

Population 6 324
Michelin map 84 fold 16, 114 fold 48 or 245 fold 48
Local map see Massif des MAURES

Bormes-les-Mimosas stands in an agreeable **setting**★, near the sea, on a steep slope at the entrance to the Forêt du Dom. It is an attractive place to stay with its colourful profusion of mimosa, oleander, camomile and eucalyptus. The road from Le Lavandou affords the best view of the town.
Bormes has 17km/10.5mi of beach, and 850 pleasure boats can berth at the marina. Two inhabitants of Bormes played an important part in the wars of independence in Latin America in the 19C. **Hippolyte Mourdeille** (1758-1807) lost his life chasing the Spaniards out of Montevideo and **Hippolyte Bouchard** (1780-1837) organised the Argentinian navy. Bormes honours their achievements by celebrating Argentina's National Independence Day on 9 July.

A PICTURESQUE WALK

★**Old streets** – Below the church the streets of old Bormes are typical of a Provençal village. Several covered passageways run between the lanes, providing shade for passers-by. Many steep alleyways tumble down from the castle: the steepest of these, known as "neck-breaker" *(Rompi-Cuo)*, is laid with smooth paving stones separated by a central drain.

Place St-François – A statue commemorating Francesco di Paola, who is said to have saved Bormes from the plague in 1481, stands in front of the massive 16C Chapelle St-François surrounded by dark cypress trees. Among the exotic plants in the neighbouring graveyard with its 18C tombs is a monument to the painter Jean-Charles Cazin, who was particularly attached to the place.

Terrace – Fronting the chapel, it affords a good **view** of Bormes anchorage and Cap Bénat. The round tower to be seen in the distance is the base of an old mill.

Église St-Trophyme – The robust three-aisled church near the town hall was built in the 18C in the Romanesque style. The façade bears a sundial with the Latin inscription: *Ab Hora Diei ad Horam Dei* (from daily time to divine time). The interior is decorated with 14 oil paintings by Alain Nonn (1980) depicting the Way of the Cross. Six reliquary-busts crowning the pillars date from the 18C.

Château – The signs *"Parcours Fleuri"* near the church lead to a flower-lined walk round the castle, which has been partially restored to provide a dwelling. Beyond the castle the terrace provides a fine **view**★ over Bormes, the anchorage, Cap Bénat and the islands of Port-Cros and Le Levant.

A TOUCH OF LOCAL HISTORY

Musée "Arts et Histoire" ⊙ – *65 Rue Carnot.* This museum presents the history of Bormes, Fort Brégançon and the Chartreuse de la Verne. It also retraces the lives of Bouchard and Mourdeille *(see above).*
A century of regional painting, including the works of **Jean-Charles Cazin** (1841-1901), a landscape painter and decorator, are also on show.

EXCURSION

Cap de Brégançon – *Not open to the public.* On the eastern edge of Hyères harbour a fortress sits on a rocky promontory. The **Fort de Brégançon** is built on a small island linked to the shore of Cap Bénat by a footbridge. It was neglected from the

Eating out

MODERATE

La Ferme des Janets – *378 Chemin des Janets – Route d'Hyères –* ☎ *04 94 71 45 11 – Closed 2 Jan-11 Feb, Mon evening, Tue evening, Thu evening and Wed Nov to late Mar – 12.20€ lunch – 18.29/33.54€.* A footpath wending its way past vineyards, cork oak trees, cypresses and oleanders leads to a charming *mas* where chickens and ducks are raised. After a hearty meal of traditional country food, relax on the leafy terrace or indulge in a game of *boules* with the owner.

MID-RANGE

Lou Portaou – *Rue Cubert-des-Poètes –* ☎ *04 94 64 86 37 – Closed 15 Nov-20 Dec, Sun for lunch, Wed for lunch 1 Jul-12 Sep and Tue off season. – Reservation required – 27.44€.* Set up in a 12C watchtower overlooking the village, this restaurant exudes an unpretentious atmosphere, enhanced by stone walls and antique furniture. Local cuisine is served in the dining room or on the terrace.

Where to stay

MID-RANGE

Le Grand Hôtel – *167 Route du Baguier – Exit N of Bormes, towards Collobrières –* ☎ *04 94 71 23 72 – www.augrandhotel.com – Closed 15 Nov-15 Dec –* ▯ *– 50 rooms: 42.69/60.98€ –* ☕ *6.10€ – Restaurant 15€.* For a whiff of Victoriana, check in at this grand hotel built in 1903 on the slope of the hill, dominating the town centre. Large, soundproofed rooms, most of which have a balcony giving onto the sea.

Hôtel Les Palmiers – *Chemin du Petit-Fort – 8km/5mi S of Bormes –* ☎ *04 94 64 81 94 – Closed 15 Nov-31 Jan – 22 rooms: 76.22/121.96€ –* ☕ *9.15€ – Restaurant 24/37€.* Lying in a residential district half-way between the beach and Brégançon Fort, this hotel is a haven of peace. Most of the rooms boast a large balcony. The dining room opens out onto a flowered terrace where meals are served in high season. Half-board only in summer.

Shopping

Markets – Tuesdays at Pin-de-Bormes, Wednesdays in the old village, Saturdays at La Favière (in summer).

beginning of the 18C but the young General Bonaparte began its restoration, which was completed between the two World Wars. The oldest parts of the building date from the 16C. The drawbridge and the two crenellated towers can be seen from the beach beside the walls. In 1968 it officially became the summer retreat of the French President of the Republic. Georges Pompidou was said to be particularly fond of the place and Jacques Chirac can sometimes be seen relaxing among the mimosa trees.

BREIL-SUR-ROYA

Population 2 058
Michelin map 84 fold 20, 115 fold 18 or 245 fold 26
Local map see NICE

Breil lies astride the River Roya – its waters are contained by a small dam – near the Italian border below the summit of l'Arpette (1 610m/5 282ft) on the main road from Ventimiglia to Turin via the Col de Tende (pass).

Several small industries – leather, olives, dairy farming – sustain the town, which is known for fishing and water sports (canoeing competitions).

"A Stacada" – This unusual and highly colourful event takes place every four years *(last edition in 1998)* to commemorate the abolition of the *droit du seigneur* brought about by the rebellion of the Breil inhabitants who had been subjugated by a local tyrant. Some of the villagers, adorned with rich medieval costumes, parade through town, stopping along the way to re-enact scenes from this historical event. The unexpected arrival of the lord allows the inhabitants to demand reparation. After many races between the lord's Turkish guard and the nobles, the latter are finally captured and put in chains *(a stacada)*.

Breil-sur-Roya

THE OLD VILLAGE

Situated on the east bank, it consists of picturesque streets where traces of the ramparts and gateways can be seen among the old buildings. The Renaissance Chapelle Ste-Catherine with its doorway flanked by two Corinthian pillars stands south of the parish church.

Santa-Maria-in-Albis – The vast 18C church with its carved doors (1719) and Baroque interior on a Greek cross plan, is adorned with an ornate 17C **organ loft** of carved and gilded wood (gallery) and an early **altarpiece** (1500) to the left of the chancel: St Peter as Pope with the triple crown between St Paul and St Jerome and above St Catherine and St Bartholomew on either side of The Transfiguration.

SIGHT

Écomusée du Haut-Pays ⊘ – *Closed for renovation work.* This museum is located in an old engine shed where the border station of Breil once stood. It presents an interesting account of the history of public transportation in the Nice hinterland since the

Eating out

MID-RANGE

Le Roya – *Place Brancion* – ☎ *04 93 04 47 38 – Closed Mon* – ✍ – *19.51/33.54€.* Has visiting the chapel made you hungry? Sit down in the vaulted dining room of this rustic restaurant adorned with early presses. Traditional French cuisine in a convivial setting.

Where to stay

MODERATE

Le Roya – *Place Brancion* – ☎ *04 93 04 48 10 – 13 rooms: 41.16/48.78€* – ☐ *5.34€ – Restaurant 20€.* This hotel erected on the left bank of the Roya stands out because of its brightly coloured façade. Simple, unadorned rooms and roomy bathrooms await you here. We recommend the rooms giving onto the mountain or the river.

MID-RANGE

Castel du Roy – *Route de Tende,: 1km/0.6mi* – ☎ *04 93 04 43 66 – Closed 2 Nov-31 Mar – 19 rooms: 64.03/68.60€* – ☐ *6.10€ – Restaurant 20/35€.* Set in a carefully tended park running along the banks of the Roya, this homely hotel is beautifully quiet. It is the perfect starting-point for many excursions: to the nearby mountains, the Vallée des Merveilles or the Parc du Mercantour. Have a dip in the swimming pool to recover from the day's exertions.

Transport

Access by train – The Italian and French rail links from Nice and Vintimille towards Cuneo and Turin pass by the stations of Breil (Roya-Bévéra), Sospel and Tende. A charming, delightful trip.

Leisure activities

Mme Carduner – ☎ *04 93 04 43 65.* Lace-making courses.

Rando Nature – ☎ *04 93 04 47 64.* Canoeing.

Roya Évasion – *1 Rue Pasteur* – ☎ *04 93 04 91 46 – www.royaevasion.com* – Roya Évasion organises a great many sporting activities: canoeing, rafting, rambling, mountain biking etc. Equipment for hire.

beginning of the century. The display includes a tram dating from 1900, similar to those running between Menton and Sospel, and a 141 R steam train. A separate exhibition covers the theme of agricultural and hydraulic activity in the region.

BRIGNOLES

Population 12 487
Michelin map 84 fold 15, 114 folds 20, 32, 33 and 34 or 245 fold 47
Local map see Excursions below

The narrow twisting streets of old Brignoles terrace the northern side of a low hill crowned by the venerable crenellated castle of the counts of Provence. The new town is developing in the plain. All around, green rolling countryside stretches over the broad Carami Valley.

This rich market town produces peaches, honey, olives and oil, and the exhibition-fair which is held annually in the first fortnight in April has made the town the wine capital of the Var and of Provence. The marble quarries situated at Candelon *(southeast of the town)* were once renowned.

Brignoles plums – Brignoles plums were famous throughout the kingdom until the 16C. As sugar-plums, they were a delicious addition to the sweetmeat dishes of the time: the Duke of Guise was nibbling one a few minutes before he was assassinated at Blois. All the plum trees used to belong to a local lord but during the League in the 16C, the people of Brignoles ransacked his lands and destroyed 180 000 trees. Since then "Brignoles plums" have actually been grown around Digne.

DISCOVERING OLD BRIGNOLES

South of Place Carami, picturesque old streets lead to the church of St-Sauveur and to the castle of the counts of Provence. Walk along the covered Rue du Grand-Escalier, Rue du St-Esprit and Rue des Lanciers, in which there is a **Romanesque house** with twin windows.

Église St-Sauveur – This church boasts a fine exterior Romanesque doorway (12C) framed by Ionic columns. The simple interior consists of a nave in Provençal Gothic style. The 15C low-relief sculptures in gilded wood, depicting the sacrifice of Abraham and the distribution of manna, frame the high altar. The south chapel contains a **Descent from the Cross** by Barthélemy Parrocel, who died at Brignoles in 1660 and whose descendants were also painters. The door to the sacristy is 16C.

Brignoles Church (detail)

Musée du Pays Brignolais Ⓥ – This regional museum is housed in a building which dates in part from the 12C, formerly the castle of the counts of Provence. The chief exhibit is the **La Gayole tombstone**★ (late 2C-early 3C) illustrating the transition from pagan to Christian iconography (bust of Apollo, the Sun God on the left).

Also on the ground floor are a reproduction of an 18C Provençal kitchen and an exhibition on the local mining of bauxite, with a reconstruction of a mine gallery. On display is a cement boat by Joseph Lambot, who invented reinforced concrete. There is some fine 17C woodwork in the castle chapel, as well as a beautiful 11C black **Virgin and Child** in carved wood. Barthélemy and Joseph Parrocel and Montenard (1849-1926) are represented in the gallery of religious and pagan art upstairs. An exhibition on local customs includes a **crib**, created in 1952 in the Provençal tradition.

BRIGNOLES

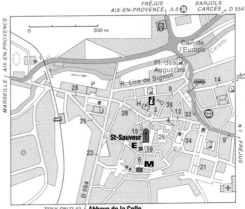

EXCURSION

Abbaye de la Celle Ⓥ – In the 13C the Benedictine convent attracted the daughters of the Provençal nobility, but by the 16C standards had fallen so low that the nuns were distinguished from other women only by their dress and the number of their lovers. Efforts at reform failed and the convent was closed in 1660 on the orders of Mazarin.

The 17C Prioress' house has been converted into a country hotel. The cloisters, chapterhouse and refectory can be visited. The austere Romanesque abbey church is now the parish church, containing a 15C Crucifixion, executed with striking realism.

Eating out

MODERATE

La Remise – *4 Avenue de la Libération – 83890 Besse-sur-Issole – 15km/9mi –SE of Brignoles on N 7 towards Le Luc and right on D 13 –* ☎ *04 94 59 66 93 – Closed Sun evening and Mon – 11.89/19.06€.* Small, unpretentious establishment discreetly located at the entrance to the village. The white walls are sparsely decorated with a few paintings and photographs. The kitchen, which can be glimpsed from the dining room, serves simple fare with a Mediterranean touch.

MID-RANGE

Le Bistrot du Boucher – *5 Rue Louis-Maître –* ☎ *04 94 69 17 22 – Closed Mon evening, Tue evening and Sun –* 🚭 *– 9.91€ lunch – 18.29/27.44€.* Amusing restaurant housed on the former premises of a butcher's shop, where the owners have kept the original decor. The dining room, repainted in Provençal shades, naturally serves meat grilled before your eyes in an open fireplace.

Where to stay

MID-RANGE

La Cordeline – *14 Rue des Cordeliers –* ☎ *04 94 59 18 66 – lacordeline@ifrance.com – Closed Jan-Feb – 5 rooms: 60.98/91.47€ – Meal 23€.* Handsome 17C mansion providing accommodation in tastefully furnished rooms, complete with fully equipped bathroom and small salon. Delightful terrace with arbour for basking in the sun. A haven of tranquillity at the heart of the town.

Chambre d'Hôte Château de Vins – *83170 Vins-sur-Caramy – 9/5km/5.5mi from Brignoles on D 24, Route du Thoronet –* ☎ *04 94 72 50 40 – chateau.de.vins@free.fr – Closed Nov to Apr –* 🚭 *– 5 rooms: 61/68.60€.* Listed 16C building with four turrets whose austere yet imposing rooms carry the names of famous musicians. Cultural events, concerts, music lessons and exhibitions will liven up your stay in this hotel, recently renovated by its dedicated and impassioned landlord.

Shopping

Farming Fair – This fair-exhibition launched in 1921 is dedicated to wines from Provence and the Var region, as well as honey, olives, olive oil and other typical produce. It is held for ten days during the month of April.

Specialities – The local delicacies are jams and sweets made with plums, to be found in many local stores.

DRIVING TOURS

★ ① **Brignoles Country** *56km/35mi – allow 3hr – see local map below.* Leave Brignoles to the north on D 554.

The dark green of the pines in this undulating countryside contrasts with the varied colours of mixed farming, dominated by vineyards, and with earth stained red by bauxite; until the 1970s the mining of bauxite was the main local industry.

Le Val – The village lies beside the Roman Via Aurelia and was once enclosed by ramparts. Its narrow houses cluster around an elaborate 18C wrought-iron campanile. Skilled development of the site has preserved its Provençal character.
On the way into the village stands the **Hôtel des Vins**, whose façade proudly bears a fresco painted by one of Dali's pupils. The Romanesque church still has some beautiful 18C frescoes as well as some 16C polychrome statues.
The old communal oven (12C) houses the **Musée du Santon** ⏱. Displayed in glass cases in the long vaulted bakehouse is a miscellaneous collection of Provençal *santons* as well as cribs from Venice, Israel, Latin America and Africa. The oven contains a large crib of Neapolitan origin.
In the Penitents' Chapel (16C) is the **Musée d'Art Sacré** ⏱ which contains a sizeable collection of commemorative plaques dating from the 17C onwards, statues and richly embroidered pastoral robes.
On the eastern edge of the village there is a picturesque old wash-house framed by lovely columns. A little further on is the **Musée de la Figurine Historique** ⏱. On the ground floor of this museum are antique toys, some dating from 1850, while old figurines and some antique military uniforms are displayed on the first floor. Remarkable dioramas of the Napoleonic period can be seen alongside old sheets of paper soldiers.

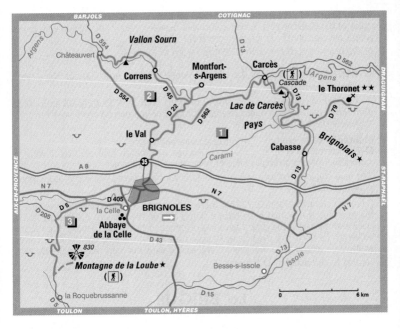

Go to Carcès on D 562, 17km/10.5mi northeast.

Vineyards alternate with lavender fields and pine plantations.

Carcès – Tall narrow houses crowned by flat roofs cover the hillside below the Gros Bessillon. The town produces oil and honey and has extensive wine cellars. The colourful glazed tiles adorning the roofs of Carcès afford protection against the strong *mistral* winds in winter.

2km/1mi south of Carcès *(heading towards Cabasse)*, the tree-lined D 13 comes to a **waterfall** where the river drops 7m/22ft in several tiers (🚶 waymarked footpath).

Lac de Carcès – The pine-clad shores of this lake are a favourite haunt of fishermen. The reservoir, retained by the beaten earth dam, supplies Toulon and other coastal towns. There is a fine **view** from the southern end of the lake.

Continue on D 13. Leaving behind the lake, turn left onto D 79 for the Abbaye du Thoronet.

★★ **Abbaye du Thoronet** – *See Abbaye du THORONET.*

Return to D 13 and turn left towards Cabasse along the Issole Valley.

Cabasse – The village on the Côtes de Provence wine road has a shady square around a mossy fountain. The green valley site has seen many generations of human habitation as the nearby dolmens, standing stones and Gallo-Roman ruins prove. The 16C **Église St-Pons** ⊘ has two aisles and a 16C doorway although the tympanum was carved in 1900. In the fifth bay an altarpiece of the Rosary is made up of several small paintings. Most noteworthy is the **high altar★** of carved and gilded wood in Spanish Renaissance style (1543). The altarpiece depicting the Virgin and Child with St Michael and St Pontius is crowned by an elegant canopy. In the side aisle the ribbed vaulting is supported on pendants representing faces with grotesque or gentle expressions. There are also Gallo-Roman remains: cippi, ruined sarcophagi, capitals. Milestones stand near a 2C funerary inscription set in the outside wall. *Enquire at the café on the church square.*

Proceed along D 13 then turn right onto N 7, which leads back to Brignoles.

② **Vallon Sourn**

Round tour 39km/25mi – about 1hr – see local map

From Brignoles take D 554 north. In Le Val turn right onto D 562 and then left onto D 22.

Montfort-sur-Argens – The ramparts and ruins of a forbidding feudal castle mark this former Templar commandery, which now produces excellent grapes and peaches. Two square towers remain, with mullioned windows, as well as a fine 15C spiral staircase.

Return to the crossroads and turn right onto D 45, following the Argens upstream.

Correns – This riverside village with its fountains beneath the towering Gros Bessillon is known for its white wine. The castle keep has interesting gargoyles.

Vallon Sourn – In Provençal *sourn* means sombre, used here to describe the upper valley of the River Argens, which is enclosed between steep cliffs riddled with caves where people sought refuge during the Wars of Religion.

In Châteauvert turn left onto D 554 to return to Brignoles.

★ **③** Montagne de La Loube *14km/10mi southwest – about 3hr – see local map opposite*

From Brignoles take D 554 south. Turn right onto D 405; turn left onto D 5. 1km/0.6mi before La Roquebrussanne, turn left onto a narrow road closed to traffic where there is room to park.

★ **Montagne de la Loube** – *2hr on foot there and back.*

⊠ The narrow road up this mountain *(closed to vehicles)* bordered by flowers in springtime, passes strangely shaped rocks resembling animals and human beings.

The final stage of the ascent is a rock climb (not dangerous) near the telecommunications mast.

From the summit (830m/2 723ft), there is an interesting **panorama★**. In the valleys the farmland is hemmed in by barren ridges and on the hillsides the bauxite mines ccast red gashes in the green covering of pine and holm oak. Beyond the Carami Valley to the north are the hills of Haute Provence; to the east are the Alps; to the south the mountains round Toulon, and to the west the long ridge of Ste-Baume.

Return to Brignoles by D 5 and N 7.

La BRIGUE

Population 595
Michelin map 84 folds 10 and 20, 115 fold 9 or 245 fold 26
Local map see NICE

Among the vineyards in the beautiful Levense Valley, tributary of the Roya, near a Romanesque bridge, stands the charming village of La Brigue. Its old green schist houses, below the ruins of the castle and tower of the Lascaris, local rulers from the 14C to 18C, give some idea of its age.

A WALK ROUND THE VILLAGE

Old village – Some of the houses are built over arcades; on some of the others the lintels are carved, often with a heraldic device. The square commands a fine **view** of Mont Bégo.

To the right of the parish church stand two Penitents' Chapels: the 18C **Chapelle de l'Assomption** ⊙, with its Baroque façade and graceful Genoese bell-tower; and to the left the **Chapelle de l'Annonciation** ⊙, also Baroque on a hexagonal plan. The latter houses the church treasure and a collection of ecclesiastical ornaments. *Both chapels are open to the public by appointment only.*

★ **Collégiale St-Martin** ⊙ – This parish church has a fine late-15C square Romanesque bell-tower; Lombard bands decorate the gable end and the side aisles.

The doorway, framed in the Antique style (1576) with an older (1501) green schist lintel, opens onto a sumptuously decorated gilded nave in the Italian tradition. The 17C organ in the gallery was repaired in the 19C by the same Italians who worked at Saorge. The white marble font is crowned by a painted and gilded conical baldaquin.

The church contains a remarkable collection of **Primitive paintings from the Nice School★**. Chapels along the

south aisle contain a Crucifixion with saints and donors comparable with Louis Bréa's in Cimiez; an altarpiece of St Martha recounting on the predella the local legend of her arrival at Marseille on a boat, here pictured as a sailing ship; the Sufferings of St Elmo, revealing a cruel realism unusual in the gentle Bréa; also by Bréa the fine altarpiece of the **Adoration of the Child**; and, finally, by the same school, the central panel of a triptych representing the Assumption.

On the north side, the first chapel contains a triptych of the Italian Fuzeri of **Our Lady of the Snows** (1507) with its 18C Baroque frame.

EXCURSION

★★ Chapelle Notre-Dame-des-Fontaines ☉ – *4km/2.5mi east on D 43.* Set alone in the Mont Noir Valley, not far from the fascinating Mont Bégo, and overlooking one of the region's many mountain streams, the chapel of Notre-Dame-des-Fontaines is a pilgrimage centre on the site of a former sanctuary dedicated to water.

It was built at two different periods: the chancel is 12C and the nave 14C; the latter was raised in the 18C in order to add seven clerestory windows. Although the exterior is plain and simple, the interior turns out to be unexpectedly ornate as the walls are covered with delightful **frescoes★★★**.

Jesus questioned by Pilate by J Canavesio

These are undoubtedly the most striking feature of the church. The chancel panels (badly damaged) were discovered in c 1950 under a coat of wash. They were painted in c 1451 by **Jean Baleison**, master of the Gothic style in this region of the Alps. These frescoes, peopled with delicate dancing figures, depict the Four Evangelists (on the vault), the Resurrection of Christ and the Virgin's Assumption (on the walls).

The nave, however, was decorated by the Renaissance Primitive **Giovanni Canavesio** (1420-early 16C), whose exuberant artistic style, always Gothic-inspired, asserts itself with a more lively brush and a better sense of perspective.

According to the theme and nature of the frescoes, it would seem that Canavesio painted those on the triumphal arch (scenes of the life of the Virgin and Jesus' Childhood) at the same time as Baleison painted those in the chancel.

The frescoes behind the façade and on the sides are dated 12 October 1492 (Latin inscription). They illustrate the Last Judgement and the Passion *(see plan above).* The compositions, often somewhat elaborate, seem by specific details

---

Painted Chapels of the Nice Hinterland

Scattered in the valleys of the Roya, the Paillon and the Basse-Tinée, many medieval chapels contain superb frescoes designed to teach the Scriptures:

– Coaraze, St-Sébastien;
– Lucéram, Notre-Dame-de-Bon-Cœur and St-Grat;
– Peillon, Pénitent Chapel;
– St-Dalmas-Valdeblore Church;
– Saorge, Notre-Dame del Poggio (private chapel);
– Venanson, St-Sébastien.

As well as these remarkable Gothic paintings, there are several modern successors worthy of note: Matisse in Vence, Cocteau in Villefranche and Tobiasse in Le Cannet. The frescoes of the chapels and parish churches of the Tinée Valley north of the Alpes-Maritimes are described in the Michelin Green Guide *French Alps.*

to want to reveal different levels of interpretation as well as the theories expounded at that time. For example Simon Peter is depicted brandishing a dagger during the Last Supper and a sword during the Arrest of Christ; in the Garden of Gethsemane he sleeps lying down and not seated and is found warming his feet during the Denial; in the Washing of the Feet, his feet float on top of the water before Jesus washes them. These irregularities may, perhaps, reveal the first hints of the Pre-Reformation, criticising the Papacy as avid of political and temporal (the dagger) power, attached to physical comfort and unconcerned with purity (symbolised by water).

Yet in this same scene (Washing of the Feet) Judas is the only one to remove his sandals, as if desirous to have his sins washed away; moreover, he is shown barefoot when overcome with remorse. His depiction hanged and disembowelled – the same scene uniting both versions of his death – with double internal organs (two hearts, two livers, two intestines), may perhaps symbolise his dual destiny of traitor, essential to the message discussed in the Scriptures, and the Repentant Sinner.

CABRIS★

Population 1 472
Michelin map 84 fold 8, 115 southwest of fold 24 or 245 fold 36

This charming village occupies a magnificent **site**★ on the edge of the Provençal plateau, looking out over the Grasse countryside to the sea (20km/12mi). Its name recalls the Marquise de Cabris, Mirabeau's sister, a restless character. The village and its neighbourhood have long been a favourite haunt of writers and artists.

A FORTIFIED VILLAGE

Church – The 17C church contains a painted wooden pulpit and a fine rustic altarpiece under the gallery. Behind the altar hangs a copy of a Murillo painting.

Castle ruins – From the defensive wall and terrace, there is a superb **view**★★: southeast to Mougins and the hills running down to Le Cannet, out to sea over La Napoule Bay to the Îles de Lérins, south beyond Peymeinade and over the brow of the Tanneron to the Esterel, swinging westwards to the Lac de St-Cassien with the Massif des Maures in the distance.

Bed & Breakfast

Chambre d'Hôte Mme Faraut – *14 Rue de l'Agachon* – ☎ *04 93 60 52 36* – *Closed 15 Oct-1 Apr* – ⌷ – *5 rooms: 46/52€.* Nestled in the old quarter, this hotel fronted by a yellow façade offers simply decorated rooms painted in white. Pretty views of St-Cassien Lake and the Esterel Massif from the lounge and some of the bedrooms. Peace and quiet guaranteed.

Chambre d'Hôte Villa Loubéa – *970 Chemin Daou Riba* – *06530 Spéracèdes* – *3km/2mi S of Cabris* – ☎ *04 93 60 63 80* – *Open Oct to Apr* – ⌷ – *5 rooms: 76.22€* – *Meal 38€.* From its privileged location on a small hillside surrounded by pine trees, this villa commands breathtaking views of the coastline, stretching from Cap Martin to Saint-Tropez. The tastefully decorated rooms all look out onto the sea. Charming terraced garden.

EXCURSION

Grotte des Audides ⊙ – *On leaving Cabris, take D 4 towards St-Vallier-de-Thiey for 4km/2.5mi. The entrance to the cave is located below the level of the road to the left coming from Cabris. It is advisable to wear waterproof shoes.*

This cave, discovered in 1988 and explored to a depth of 186m/610ft, is a chasm in which concretion is still taking place, which has given rise to a small underground river. Visitors take a narrow staircase *(275 steps)* down to a depth of 60m/197ft, where a permanent flow of air keeps the air fresh. All the way down there are beautiful concretions to be admired: "giant medusas" and stalagmites in the process of being formed.

The site encompasses six caves of the chasm type, many of which were inhabited during prehistoric times.

Outside in a park are reconstructed scenes of life in prehistoric times, as well as exhibits dug up during the excavation and exploration of the caves: carved tools, fossils and various bone fragments, testifying to these early settlements. Other geological exhibits include strange limestone shapes, some containing giant grooves eroded by water.

CAGNES-SUR-MER ★

Population 43 942
Michelin map 84 folds 9 and 18, 115 folds 25 and 26 or 245 fold 37

Cagnes-sur-Mer is set in a landscape of hills covered with olive and orange trees and cultivated flowers (carnations, roses, mimosa). The town comprises: Haut-de-Cagnes, crowned by a medieval castle, Cagnes-Ville, the modern residential and commercial quarter and Cros-de-Cagnes, an unusual fishing village and beach.

The picturesque upper town has become home to many painters who come each year in great numbers, attracted by the beautiful setting and the incomparable light.

A large racecourse, serving the whole of the Riviera, has a varied programme throughout the season from December to March and in August and September each year.

The Grimaldis of Cagnes – The history of Cagnes is that of its castle. This was originally a fortress built by Rainier Grimaldi, Lord of Monaco and Admiral of France, after he became Lord of Cagnes in 1309. A branch of the Grimaldi family *(see MONACO)* remained in possession of Cagnes up to the French Revolution.

Rainier's castle was converted in 1620 by Henri Grimaldi into a finely decorated château. Entirely loyal to the king of France, he persuaded his cousin, Honoré II of Monaco, to renounce Spanish protection and to place himself under French protection, invoking the *Treaty of Péronne* (1641). Heaped with honours and riches by Louis XIII and Richelieu, Henri led a life of luxury at Cagnes. This was the zenith of the family's power. When the Revolution broke out, the reigning Grimaldi was driven out by the inhabitants and sought refuge in Nice.

★ A MAZE OF ALLEYWAYS

★ **Haut-de-Cagnes** – *It is advisable to walk up to Haut-de-Cagnes along Montée de la Bourgade.* This quaint old town circled by ramparts and dominated by its medieval castle is a joy to visit. Its steep paved streets and vaulted passageways feature many 15C and 17C houses (Renaissance houses with arcades near the castle). The **Porte de Nice** near the church tower dates back to the 13C.

Église St-Pierre ⊙ – The door to the church opens onto the gallery. The early Gothic nave contains the Grimaldi tombs. The larger nave added in the 18C houses an altarpiece of the 18C Spanish School portraying St Peter receiving the keys to Paradise and an 18C statue of the Virgin and Child *(south side of chancel)*.

SIGHTS

★ **Château-Musée** ⊙ – A double staircase and a Louis XIII doorway give access to this imposing castle crowned with machicolations.

Ground floor – The Renaissance **patio**★★ has an agreeable freshness and elegance in sharp contrast to the feudal castle's austere façades. Two storeys of marble columned galleries decorated with arabesques surround the courtyard where thick foliage adds a note of greenery. Eight low vaulted medieval rooms open onto the patio galleries: Rooms 1 and 2 (fine Renaissance fireplace) present medieval history; Room 6 contains Roman sculpture dating from the 2C discovered in Cagnes. Rooms 3, 4 and 5 form a **Museum of the Olive Tree**: its history and cultivation, the use of its wood, pressing and olive oil.

★ **Suzy Solidor Bequest** – *First floor.* The former boudoir of the Marquise of Grimaldi houses 40 paintings donated by the famous singer: portraits of her attributed to famous contemporary artists. The ceiling of the adjoining oratory is decorated with Louis XIII style plasterwork *(gypseries)*. An antiphonary dates from 1757. Receptions were once held in these 17C rooms. The ceiling of the banqueting hall represents the **Fall of Phaeton**★; this *trompe-l'œil* was painted between 1621 and 1624 by the Genoese, Carlone, and conveys an extraordinary illusion of perspective. Once he had finished, the artist could not bring himself to leave it: "My beautiful Fall," he sighed, "I shall never see you again." As it happened, he died only six weeks after he left Cagnes.

Musée d'Art Moderne Méditerranéen – The museum, which pays tribute to contemporary Mediterranean art is housed in the banqueting hall on the first floor and in the apartments on the second floor. The rich collection of works by 20C painters who were either born on the shores of the Mediterranean or came to live there, such as Dufy and Vasarely, is shown in rotation or in temporary exhibitions.

Tower – From the top of the tower there is a fine **view**★ over the roofs of Old Cagnes to the sea, from Cap Ferrat to Cap d'Antibes and the Alps.

Musée Renoir ⊙ – This memorial museum is located at Les Collettes, where Pierre-Auguste Renoir (1841-1919) spent the last 12 years of his life. The artist's house and two studios *(first floor)* have been preserved just as they were.

Ten of his **canvases** are exhibited on the ground floor; they belong to his last, especially sensual period; a shimmering palette expressing the beauty of nature with lovely rounded female forms (second version of his *Bathers*, 1901-02). It is also at Cagnes that he attempted sculpture and a few masterpieces are on display. Right in front of the house stands **Venus Victrix**★; the large bronze statue overlooks the lovely garden, landscaped with olive, orange and lemon trees.

117

CAGNES-SUR-MER/VILLENEUVE-LOUBET

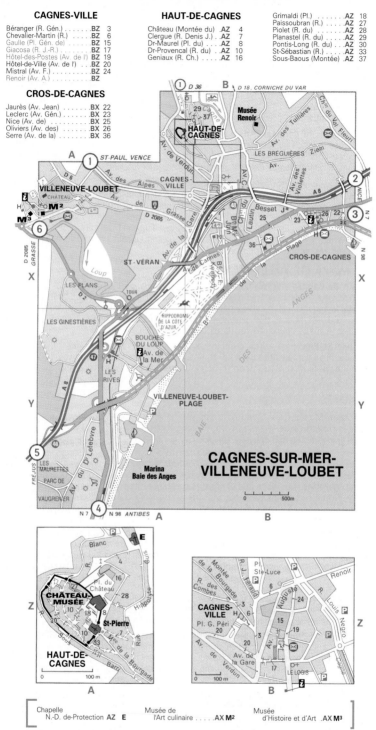

CAGNES-SUR-MER-VILLENEUVE-LOUBET

Chapelle N.-D. de-Protection **AZ E**   Musée de l'Art culinaire . . . . .**AX M²**   Musée d'Histoire et d'Art .**AX M³**

Chapelle Notre-Dame-de-Protection ⓥ – *Access on foot up Montée du Château.* The Italianate porch and bell-tower of this chapel inspired Renoir. The apse is decorated with rather stilted 16C **frescoes**: on the dome the Evangelists, Isaiah, the Sibyl; on the walls, scenes from the childhood of Christ and from the life of the Virgin; in the centre Our Lady of Protection as a Virgin of Mercy. A 17C altarpiece of the Virgin of the Rosary is in the north chapel.

Eating out

MODERATE

Le Vertigo – *12 Place du Château – Le Haut-de-Cagnes –* ☎ *04 92 02 00 00 – Closed Nov to Jan – 12.50/26€*. On a square pleasantly shaded by acacia trees, this pub offers a wide choice of beers from all over the world, alongside freshly prepared salads and delicious homemade ice cream. Pretty setting in ochre hues.

La Goutte d'Eau – *108 Montée de la Bourgade, Le Haut-de-Cagnes –* ☎ *04 93 20 81 23 – Closed 10 days in Oct and Mon – 13.42/19.06€*. After climbing the steep, cobbled alleys, you will reach this small restaurant serving simple fare, where the owner-chef also waits on customers. The sunblessed terrace welcomes you in the holiday season.

Where to stay

MODERATE

Hôtel Chantilly – *31 Rue Minoterie –* ☎ *04 93 20 25 50 – 20 rooms: 39.64/54.88€ –* ☕ *5.34€*. This hotel housed in a villa located behind the famous racecourse offers a modicum of comfort at extremely reasonable prices. Clean rooms in a verdant setting and a relaxed, family atmosphere are the key words at the Hôtel Chantilly, which succeeds in attracting a regular clientele throughout the year.

Hôtel Le Mas d'Azur – *42 Avenue de Nice –* ☎ *04 93 20 19 19 – Closed 15 Nov-15 Dec –* ▣ *– 15 rooms: 44.21/53.36€ –* ☕ *5.34€*. Just off a main road, in a building believed to be 18C, this hotel has small, tidy rooms with excellent soundproofing. Lush, flowery setting and lovely terrace for enjoying breakfast in the shade of pine trees.

MID-RANGE

Les Jardins Fragonard – *12 Rue Fragonard –* ☎ *04 93 20 97 12 –* ✒ *– 3 rooms: 68.60€ – Meal 17€*. A peaceful park planted with Mediterranean species forms the heavenly backdrop to this 1925 villa. The large rooms, renovated in the Provençal spirit with rattan furniture, all have new bathrooms. Start the day with a scrumptious breakfast out on the terrace.

LUXURY

Villa Estelle – *5 Montée de la Bourgade –* ☎ *04 92 02 89 83 –* ✒ *– 7 rooms: 144.83/182.94€ –* ☕ *15.24€ – Meal 30€*. Villa Estelle is fit for royalty. The splendid terrace with its red clay tiling overlooks the town and, in the background, the sweeping coastline. The luxurious interior and tasteful ornamentation, including many paintings and works of art, ensure that your stay here will be a resounding success.

A Day at the Races

Hippodrome de la Côte d'Azur – ☎ *04 92 02 44 44*. This famous racecourse is the backdrop to many equestrian events between December and March, as well as in July and August.

Guided Tours of the City

The tourist office organises tours of the small fisherman's village in Cros-de-Cagnes (Thu at 9am by appointment two days in advance) and the picturesque cobbled district of Haut-de-Cagnes (Sat at 11am, Sun at 4pm). Apply for details of rates.

DRIVING TOURS

★The Baous and the Corniche du Var

Round tour of 32km/20mi – about 1hr 15min (excluding the ascent of the Baou of St-Jeannet).

From Cagnes take Avenue Auguste-Renoir and D 18 north to La Gaude.

The road runs past elegant residential properties, olive groves, market gardens and flower fields, with **views** of Vence, the hills and La Gaude.

La Gaude – From the ridge above the River Cagne, La Gaude, which earned its living from vineyards and flower cultivation, now houses research centres in the fields of data processing, agronomy and horticulture. The 14C castle in the St-Jeannet district is thought to have been built by the Templars. At the crossroads in Peyron continue north on D 18 through orchards and vineyards.

St-Jeannet – The charming village occupies a remarkable **position**★ on a scree terrace at the foot of the Baou of St-Jeannet, among orange groves, flower fields and vineyards producing good quality wine. Behind the church on the left a sign "Panorama" points to a terrace offering a **view**★ of the peaks *(baous)*, the coast and the Var Valley.

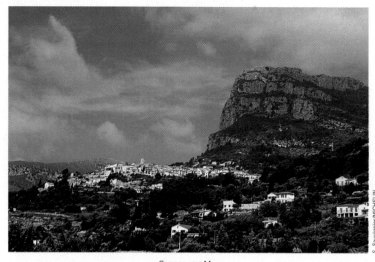

S. Sandmeier/MICHELIN

Cagnes-sur-Mer

★★ **Baou de St-Jeannet** – *2hr on foot three and back. The signposted path starts from Place Ste-Barbe by Auberge St-Jeannet.*
Also known as the Baou des Blancs, this sheer cliff 400m/1 312ft high dominates the village. From the top *(viewing table)* a huge **panorama**★★ extends from the Esterel to the French and Italian Alps.
Return to D 18 towards La Gaude. Turn left onto D 118.

Centre d'Études et de Recherches IBM – The huge buildings on the left of this IBM Research and Study Centre, consisting of two opposing Y-shapes raised on concrete pillars to accommodate the uneven ground, were designed by Breuer and are a good example of architecture harmonising with its natural surroundings.

★ **Corniche du Var** – This scenic road follows the ridge or clings to the hillside on the west bank of the Var with a clear view of the river valley and the Nice hinterland. The steep slopes of the valley are covered with the flower fields and olive groves.

St-Laurent-du-Var – Until the County of Nice passed to France in 1860, the Var formed the frontier with the Kingdom of Sardinia. Passengers usually forded the river, often on another man's back. The first permanent bridge was built downstream in 1864. Near the mouth of the River Var, a vast lake, protected by a dyke, has been developed into a yachting harbour (over 1 000 moorings).
Return to Cagnes by N 7.

Renoir at Les Collettes

Pierre-Auguste Renoir, the painter, was born in Limoges but, as a young man, he went to Paris where his talents soon developed under the influence of the Impressionists and the world of art. From 1882 he made several visits to Provence, particularly in the company of Cézanne, and learned to appreciate the Mediterranean light and landscape. In 1900, as he was suffering from rhumatism, his doctor advised him to try a change of climate and he spent some time near Grasse with his wife and younger son Jean, who later became a film director.

Once his reputation was universally established, he settled permanently in the South of France and in 1907 he bought the property of Les Collettes in Cagnes-sur-Mer, attracted by the view of the sea and the old village. Four of his paintings were inspired by the surrounding countryside. In 1913, at the suggestion of his friend Vollard, he took up sculpture with a pupil of Maillol called Guino and built a studio in the garden of Les Collettes where he worked. Under his directions, Guino created a little Venus and then the famous *Venus Victrix*, which is displayed in the garden of the museum.

Renoir's last years were saddened by the death of his wife, his sons being wounded in the First World War and the inexorable progress of his illness, which confined him to a wheelchair; he managed to paint despite the arthritis which paralysed his right hand. As his physical capacity diminished, he stated that "he was beginning to know how to paint". In August 1919, in addition to having received many honours and having his work hung in the major museums of the world, he was officially accepted by the Louvre where several of his works are displayed. On 2 December 1919, just before his death, he was still at work, painting a bouquet of anemones.

CANNES ✿✿✿

Population 67 304
Michelin map 84 fold 9, 115 folds 38 and 39 or 245 fold 37
Local map see Massif de l'ESTEREL

Cannes stands on the shores of La Napoule Bay, a superb anchorage dominated by the Esterel heights. The town owes its popularity to the beauty of its **setting★★**, its mild climate and magnificent festivals. From its early fame as the winter salon of the world's aristocracy, it has developed into an important resort and conference centre.

HISTORICAL NOTES

Cannes, the coastal watchtower – By the 10C, following the earlier Ligurian oppidum of Ægitna and the Roman settlements (42BC), a small cluster of dwellings, constructed by Genoese families, stood at the foot of the rock known today as Mont Chevalier or Le Suquet. The place was called Canoïs, cane harbour, after the reeds (cannes) that thrived in the surrounding marshes. In 1131, the Count of Provence, Raymond Bérenger II, gave the settlement to the abbots of Lérins. They built a tower and fortifications to protect the fishermen against possible attacks from the Saracens. As soon as the first enemy ships loomed on the horizon, the Lérins watchers gave the alarm. The defences were directed by the religious orders – first the Templars, then the Knights of Malta. The Fathers of Mercy dealt with the ransoming of prisoners.

Birds on a Yellow Background
Musée Fernand Léger, Biot

Lord Brougham and the origin of the resort (1834) – Cannes' riches and renown are due to the misfortunes of a Lord Chancellor of England (1830-34), Lord Brougham (politician, famous orator; he designed the four-wheeled one-horse carriage, which bears his name, the brougham), who was on his way to Nice in 1834. Cholera in Provence prevented the wealthy traveller from crossing the *cordon sanitaire* to Nice; he returned to Cannes. The place, then a small fishing village, pleased him so much that he built himself a house there. For the next 34 years, right up to the time of his death (d 1868), Lord Brougham exchanged the winter fogs of London for the Mediterranean sunshine. His example was soon followed by the English aristocracy of the time and the town's population of 4 000 grew rapidly.

Two famous French writers dearly loved Cannes: Prosper Mérimée died there in 1870; Guy de Maupassant anchored his yacht in the bay between 1884 and 1888 and wrote his enthusiastic impressions of the town in his story *Sur l'Eau* (On the Water). **Frédéric Mistral**, the Provençal poet, celebrated Cannes and there is scarcely a famous person in art or literature who has not visited Cannes.

Cannes Festivals – The festivals hosted by the city of Cannes are world famous. The **International Film Festival** is the most glittering artistic gathering on the Riviera *(see box)*. Other popular events include the prestigious regattas, the International Record and Music Market (MIDEM), which takes place in January, and the International Market for Television Programmes held in April and May.

★★ ① SEAFRONT *by car: 30min*

★★ **Boulevard de la Croisette** – Local residents enjoy strolling here in winter. This elegant promenade, bordered by palm trees and gardens, overlooks a fine sandy beach. Luxury hotels and elegant boutiques line the front and the side streets as far as Rue d'Antibes. The chic crowd meets here, in the galleries and antique shops, the cinemas, nightclubs, cafés and bars. At the top end of La Croisette, east of the port, stands the new **Festival and Conference Centre**, which includes the municipal casino, designed by P Braslawsky, F Druet and Sir Hubert Bennet. Its ultra-modern facilities comprise a 2 400-seat auditorium, Debussy Theatre (1 000 seats), broadcasting studios, meeting rooms overlooking terraces, press offices...

Dominating the bay is an open-air theatre (Théâtre de la Mer) seating 1 200. To the east of the conference centre lies the verdant Esplanade Président-Georges-Pompidou, affording lovely views of La Napoule Bay.

Between the conference centre and the gardens lies the **Allée des Stars**, an avenue consisting of 200 tiles where handprints of the great movie stars who attended the Film Festival have been set in the concrete.

D. Faure/SCOPE

La Croisette, Cannes

Further east on the opposite side of the road, beyond the sumptuous Majestic Hotel, is a private 19C mansion, **La Malmaison** ⊙, once part of the Grand Hotel; it now houses the municipal cultural service and art exhibitions. Nearby stands the Hôtel Noga-Hilton, incorporating the façade of the former Palais des Festivals, which was pulled down in 1988 after serving as the venue for the Cannes Film Festival for 40 years.

Further on beyond the rose gardens is Port-Canto, a sports and cultural centre and marina able to accommodate 650 boats. From the promenade there are fine views of La Napoule Bay and the Esterel heights.

★ **Pointe de la Croisette** – Proceed east along Boulevard de la Croisette to Pointe de la Croisette. The spit of land owes its name to a small cross which used to stand there. It offers splendid views of Cannes, La Napoule Bay and the Esterel, particularly at sunset. In addition to the beautiful gardens, modern tourist developments have provided artificial beaches and the Palm Beach and Mouré Rouge marinas. Beyond Palm Beach (summer casino) round the point, a **view**★ of Golfe-Juan and Cap d'Antibes opens up. Boulevard Gazagnaire follows the seafront and Avenue Maréchal-Juin, continued by the Rue d'Antibes, leads back into town.

Quartier de la Californie – This district to the east of the old town consists of luxurious villas, the majority dating from the 19C, set in magnificent gardens. There are stunning examples of extravagant architecture with exotic, quirky features: pagodas and Moorish minarets, façades surmounted by turrets and colonial villas, bow-windows and moucharaby etc. All are private residences and the outside view is often obscured by thick foliage.

The Stuff of Dreams

A number of exceptional residences have contributed to the history of Cannes.

Avenue Roi Albert Ier: **Villa Kazbeck**, known for the lavish parties thrown by the Grand Duc de Russie and **Villa Champfleuri**, famous for its exotic gardens which can be seen in the film *Macao, Enfer du Jeu* by J Delannoy.

Avenue Jean-de-Noailles: **Villa Marie-Thérèse** and **Villa Béatrice** (1881), formerly Rothschild properties, built in the Classical style, which now house the Médiathèque de Cannes.

Avenue Maréchal-Juin (eastern edge of town): **Château Scott**, an amazing combination of styles, dominated by Flamboyant Gothic; *Le Mystere de la Chambre Jaune* by M L'Herbier was filmed here in 1930.

Avenue Victoria (in Cannet): **Villa Yakimour** *(see LE CANNET).*

② OLD CANNES AND THE HARBOUR – *1hr 30min*

The harbour – Boulevard J.-Hibert runs parallel with Midi beach round the point to the harbour with its rows of fishing boats and luxury yachts. Larger cruise liners and merchant ships anchor further out. The west side of the harbour is lined with shops and restaurants. In the northeast corner is the **shipping terminal** (note the large frieze running along the top) and embarkation quay for trips to the Îles de Lérins.

Allées de la Liberté – Beneath the plane trees, an early morning flower market is held, overlooking the harbour where pleasure craft and fishing boats are moored.

Take Rue Félix-Faure and Rue Rouguière to Rue Meynadier.

Rue Meynadier – Formerly the main street linking the new town to Le Suquet, it is bordered by a variety of shops and some fine 18C doorways.

Go to Le Suquet via Rue Louis-Blanc, Rue Félix-Faure and Rue Mont-Chevalier.

Le Suquet – The old town, built on the site of the former Canoïs castrum on the slopes of Mont Chevalier, is known locally as Le Suquet. Rue Perrissol leads to Place de la Castre surrounded by a defensive wall and dominated by the church of Notre-Dame-d'Espérance, built in the 16C and 17C in the Provençal Gothic style.

The old bell-tower leads to a long tree-lined terrace offering a fine **view** of the town and harbour and Île Ste-Marguerite.

Eating out

MODERATE

Côte d'Azur – *3 Rue J.-Daumos* – ☎ *04 93 38 60 02* – *Closed evenings and Sun* – *13€*. Modest restaurant with a friendly ambience and cosy setting consisting of period furniture and miscellaneous posters. The traditional cooking attracts a great many locals. Low prices guaranteed.

Aux Bons Enfants – *80 Rue Meynadier* – *Closed 4 Aug-3 Sep, 22 Dec-2 Jan, Sat evening Oct to Apr and Sun* – ⌷ – *14.79€*. Simplicity, generosity and congeniality are the hallmarks of this informal establishment where customers are required to pay for their meal in cash. Tasty Mediterranean dishes. No telephone.

Le Comptoir des Vins – *13 Boulevard de la République* – ☎ *04 93 68 13 26* – *www.comptoirdesvins.com* – *Closed Feb, Mon evening, Tue evening, Wed evening, Sun and public holidays* – *16.77€*. This handsomely stocked off-licence shop leads to a colourful dining area where light snacks can be served, washed down with a glass of wine.

MID-RANGE

Le Caveau 30 – *45 Rue F.-Faure* – ☎ *04 93 39 06 33* – *18.60/26.22€*. Large restaurant comprising two dining rooms done up in the style of a 1930 brasserie. The terrace gives onto a shaded square popular among *boules* players. Fish and seafood are the specialities of the house.

Au Poisson Grillé – *8 Quai St-Pierre* – *Vieux Port* – ☎ *04 93 39 44 68* – *18.75€*. Appropriately located in the old port, this fish restaurant was opened back in 1949. It serves grilled fish alongside many other Mediterranean dishes, in a warm setting of varnished wood evoking the interior of a luxury cabin. Attentive service at highly affordable prices.

Fred L'Écailler – *7 Place de l'Étang* – ☎ *04 93 43 15 85* – *www. fredlecailler/voila.fr* – *14.48€ lunch* – *23.63€*. A large neon sign marks the entrance to this rustic-style restaurant whose walls are draped with fishing nets. The tiny square affords a glimpse of village life with its bustling activity and daily games of *pétanque*. Fine selection of freshly caught fish.

CANNES

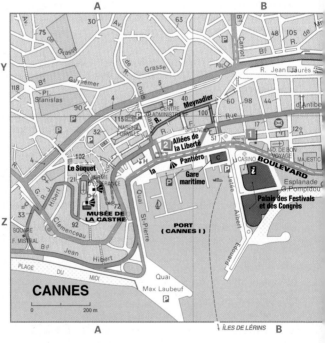

CANNES

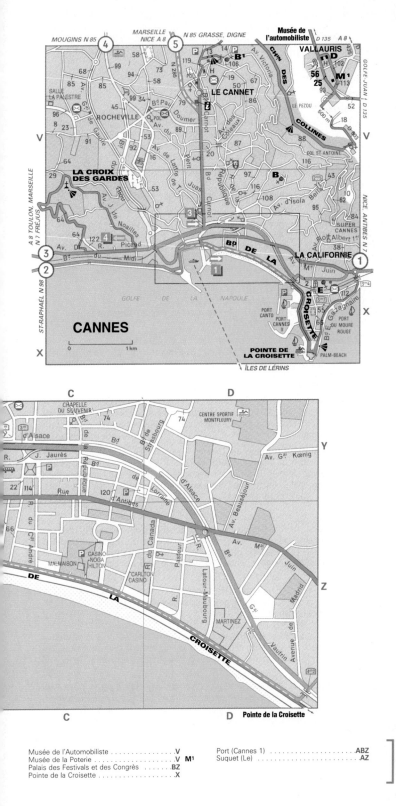

CANNES

MARSEILLE
NICE A 8

N 85 GRASSE, DIGNE

Musée de
l'automobiliste

MOUGINS N 85

VALLAURIS

LE CANNET

ROCHEVILLE

LA CROIX
DES GARDES

LA CALIFORNIE

SUPER
CANNES

GOLFE DE LA NAPOULE

PORT
CANTO

PORT
CANNES II

POINTE DE
LA CROISETTE

PALM-BEACH

ÎLES DE LÉRINS

CHAPELLE
DU SOUVENIR

CENTRE SPORTIF
MONTFLEURY

CASINO
NOGA
HILTON

CARLTON
CASINO

MARTINEZ

CROISETTE

Pointe de la Croisette

Bistrot des Artisans – *67 Boulevard de la République* – ☎ *04 93 68 33 88 – Closed 15 Jul-15 Aug and Sun – 25.15€*. Treat yourself to hearty, lovingly prepared meals served in a curious setting combining naive wall paintings with old tools and implements, workmen's helmets and crudely fashioned furniture.

Where to stay

MODERATE

Le Chanteclair – *12 Rue Forville* – ☎ *04 93 39 68 88 – Closed Nov-15 Dec – ✍ – 15 rooms: 36.59/41.16€ – ⌂ 3.81€*. After walking through a building, you will discover this friendly hotel laid out on several floors, offering a selection of variously priced rooms depending on the level of comfort. Pleasant inner courtyard where breakfast is served in summer.

Beverly – *14 Rue Hoche* – ☎ *04 93 39 10 66 – Closed 15-31 Dec – 19 rooms: 36.59/56.41€ – ⌂ 6.86€*. In a lively shopping street, a tall façade fronts a number of tiny, functional rooms that are gradually being refurbished. Reasonable rates for the area.

Hôtel National – *9 Rue du Maréchal-Joffre* – ☎ *04 93 39 91 92 – hotelnationalcannes@wanadoo.fr – 17 rooms: 38.11/53.36€*. The main advantage of this hotel is its location near the Conference Centre (Palais des Festivals) and the sea. The bedrooms designed in white and grey with tiled bathrooms are on the small side but they are clean and carefully maintained.

MID-RANGE

Hôtel Lutetia – *6 Rue Michel-Ange* – ☎ *04 93 39 35 74 – 8 rooms: 49.55/53.36€ – ⌂ 5.34€*. This friendly hotel in a quiet street at night offers simple, homely accommodation.

Hôtel Albert 1 – *68 Avenue de Grasse* – ☎ *04 93 39 24 04 – Closed 20 Nov-20 Dec – 11 rooms: 50.31/56.41€ – ⌂ 5.49€*. In a quiet, residential area tucked away from the town centre, this villa houses a small, family business that will give you a warm welcome indeed. Have breakfast on the shaded terrace enhanced by the intoxicating aroma of pink oleander.

Hôtel Appia – *6 Rue Marceau* – ☎ *04 93 06 59 59 – 30 rooms: 50.31/68.60€ – ⌂ 5.79€*. Practicality takes precedence over comfort in this downtown hotel where the well-kept, smallish rooms are both air-conditioned and soundproofed. Pristine bathrooms.

Les Charmettes – *17 Avenue de Grasse* – ☎ *04 93 39 17 13 – hotelcharmcan@aol.com – 11 rooms: 54.88/64.03€ – ⌂ 5.79€*. Perched on the heights overlooking Cannes, this hotel is decorated in pastel hues and furnished with white rattan chairs. Each room has a summer balcony or terrace that turn breakfast into a magic experience.

LUXURY

Villa L'Églantier – *14 Rue Campestra* – ☎ *04 93 68 22 43 – www.bnbnet.com – ✍ – 4 rooms: 94.52€*. Impressive white villa dating from 1920, surrounded by palm trees and other exotic species, dominating the city of Cannes. The large, peaceful rooms are all extended by a terrace or a balcony.

On the town

The best way to get to know this glamorous city is to frequent its luxury hotel bars: order a cocktail on the terrace belonging to the Carlton, on the beach of the Majestic or in the piano-bar of the Martinez...
The more energetic will be able to indulge in sailing, deep-sea diving or water-skiing. If you want to get away from the madding crowd, sail out to the îles de Lérins, where shaded paths bordered by eucalyptus and pine trees will provide peace and quiet.

Casino Carlton Club – *58 Boulevard de la Croisette* – ☎ *04 92 99 51 00 – Daily 11am-4am (slot machines); 8pm-4am (games)*. This casino, laid out on the seventh floor of the famous Carlton Hotel, offers traditional slot machines and other arcade games. Restaurant and terrace commanding nice views of the sea.

Cat Corner – *22 Rue Macé* – ☎ *04 93 39 31 31 – Daily from 10pm*. Trendy nightclub with an extravagant clientele known for its wild, electrifying evenings. Great atmosphere.

L'Amiral – *73 Boulevard de la Croisette* – ☎ *04 92 98 73 00 – hotel.martinez.com – Daily 10am-2am*. Attached to the Martinez Hotel, this bar is by far the most popular meeting place along the coast. It owes its reputation to the head barman and to Jimmy, the American piano player. Live music every evening from 8pm.

Pavillon Croisette – *42 Boulevard de la Croisette* – ☎ *04 92 59 06 90 / 04 93 38 58 68* – *May-Nov: daily 9am-2am; Dec-Apr: noon to midnight.* The Pavillon Croisette could easily rival any of London's most exclusive clubs with its choice of over 300 types of alcohol and 150 cigar sizes! Musical performances nightly.

Festival Palace

Palais des Festivals et des Congrès – *Esplanade Georges-Pompidou – La Croisette* – ☎ *04 93 39 01 01 – cannes-on-line.com – Daily 9am-7pm.* Opened in 1982, it covers an area of 60 000 m²/72 000sq yd, laid out over 8 levels. The **Grand Auditorium** (seating capacity of 2 300) and the **Théâtre Debussy** (1 000 seats and near perfect acoustics) are fitted with interpreting facilities. There are also 26 small auditoriums for meetings and press conferences, crowned by the Salon des Ambassadeurs (1 200 m²/1 435sq yd, standing capacity of 3 000), a reception area affording stunning views of Cannes.

Water-skiing

Ponton Majestic Ski Nautique – *Boulevard de la Croisette* – ☎ *04 92 98 77 47 / 06 11 50 77 53* – *Apr-Oct: daily 8am until dark.* Get away from the crowded beaches and the burning sand and try your hand at water-skiing or parascending!

Rendez-vous for football fans

Taverne Lucullus – *4 Place du Marché-Forville* – ☎ *04 93 39 32 74* – *Tue-Sun 5am-3pm.* Leave all the glitz behind and discover the hidden side of Cannes. Situated on the market place, this small, congenial café is dedicated to soccer and its fans. Note the dozens of scarves and pennants decorating the walls.

Shopping

Market – Marché de Forville: daily except Mondays in low season; fine stalls displaying fresh regional produce.

Allées de la Liberté – Flower market every morning. Very popular flea market on Saturdays.

Shopping streets – Rue Meynadier: tempting window displays of food and craftwork in a lively pedestrian area. Rue d'Antibes: luxury clothes and luggage.

Cannolive – *16 et 20 Rue Vénizelos* – ☎ *04 93 39 08 19 – Mon-Sat 8am-noon, 2.15-7pm.* This shop boasts an incredible choice of Provençal products to take back home: household linen, crockery, *santons*, soap, and even Lérina liqueur from the nearby islands for those who get seasick!

Boutique du Festival – *On the ground floor of the Palais du Festival.* A treasure trove of collectabilia for film buffs...

Leisure activities

Ponton Majestic Ski Nautique – *Boulevard de la Croisette* – ☎ *04 92 98 77 47 / 06 11 50 77 53 – Apr-Oct daily 8am until dusk.* If you want to get away from the bustling crowds, why not try your hand at water-skiing or parascending?

Beaches – Not all the beaches on the Croisette charge a fee (details of prices are listed at the top of the steps), or belong to a hotel (located opposite). There are also three free beaches, one of which is located behind the Palais du Festival. The other public beaches lie west of the old port, on Boulevard Jean-Hibert and Boulevard du Midi, at Port Canto and on Boulevard Gazagnaire beyond La Pointe.

Trans Côte d'Azur – *Quai Laubeuf* – ☎ *04 92 98 71 30 – Feb-Oct daily 8.30am-noon, 1.30-6pm (Jul-Aug 8am-7pm). Closed Nov, Dec and Jan. 8.38€ (child 5.34€).* Boat trips.

Calendar of events

International Film Festival – 10 days in May.

MIDEM – January. International market for recording and musical publishing.

MIPTV – April-May. International market for television programmes.

In summer there are many **classical concerts** on the esplanade fronting the Église du Suquet.

Cannes Film Festival

In 1939, Jean Zay, the French Minister of Fine Arts, founded the International Film Festival at Cannes, whose location was chosen on account of its sunny climate. The inauguration, planned for 1 September, was cancelled when the declaration of war broke out two days later. The real launch of the festival took place on 20 September 1946 in the former Casino Municipal near the Old Port; the festival returned to this site 40 years later at the time of the inauguration of the Nouveau Palais des Festivals in 1983. In 1949 the festival moved to the Palais de la Croisette (demolished in 1990).

In spite of its suspension in 1948 and 1950 for financial reasons and an interruption in May 1968, the fame of the festival has grown over the years, with a star-studded jury presided over by celebrities such as Jules Romains, Marcel Pagnol, Jean Cocteau, and, more recently, David Cronenberg and Liv Ulman. As it became a forum for international cinema, the Festival brought together an impressive number of participants and works. In 1994, 2 000 professionals (buyers and sellers) were present for screenings.

During the 10 days of the event, several competitions take place: the *Selection Officielle* (competing for the prestigious **Palme d'Or**); *Hors-Compétition* (not in competition); *Semaine de la Critique* (critics' picks); *Quinzaine des Réalisateurs* (film directors' programme); *Caméra d'Or* (first films); *Un Certain Regard* (independent productions). The great media interest in the various ceremonies of the festival offers a unique springboard to all films, whether mainstream or fringe, and confirms its role in uncovering talent in the so-called seventh art.

Carole Bouquet and Michel Blanc arriving at the Cannes Film Festival

SIGHTS

★ **Musée de la Castre** ⊘ – The old Cannes Castle, built in the 11C and 12C by the Lérins monks to watch over the harbour, houses substantial collections of archeology and ethnography brought back from the five continents and bequeathed by two learned travellers in the 19C.

The small Cistercian Chapelle Ste-Anne at the entrance holds temporary exhibits. The rooms that follow are concerned with religion and mythology (works from the Fontainebleau School) as well as paintings of Provence and Cannes by 19C and 20C artists.

Room 4 looks out onto the inner courtyard; here stands the 12C square watchtower (22m/72ft), **Tour du Suquet**, where temporary photographic exhibitions are held. From the top there is an extensive **view**★ of La Croisette, La Napoule Bay, the Îles de Lérins, the Esterel heights and the hills to the north of Cannes (raised relief model).

The extensive archeological collection displays objects from the Mediterranean Basin and the Middle East (Iran, Lebanon, Syria, Cyprus, Egypt, Etruria, Rome...) as well as Primitive art from Africa, Oceania, the Americas and Asia. Contemporary works of art are also on display.

Follow Rue J.-Hibert and Rue J-Dollfus to reach square Frédéric-Mistral where a statue of the "immortal bard of Provence" was erected in 1930 to commemorate the centenary of his birth.

Chapelle Bellini ⊙ – *From the Cannes-Nice motorway, take the first exit to the left towards Vallauris, turn right onto Avenue de Vallauris. At no 67, turn right onto Avenue Poralto, then left onto Allée de la Villa-Fiorentina.*

This chapel was included in the grounds of the sumptuous Tuscan palace "Villa Fiorentina" built at the end of the 19C for the Balkan nobility.

This religious building, in elaborate Baroque style, proudly sports the coat of arms of Count Vitali on its west face. The interior retains several works by the last owner, the Cannes painter Bellini (1904-89) who had his studio here.

Église Orthodoxe St-Michel-Archange ⊙ – *30 Boulevard Alexandre-III.* Since Empress Maria Alexandrovna, wife of Czar Alexandre III, had taken to spending the winter months in Cannes, it was necessary to build a church large enough to accommodate her court. The construction of the church was supervised by the Cannes architect Nouveau and its inauguration took place in November 1894. The richly ornamented interior contains some remarkable icons (one of which represents **St Michael the great captain**) and banners received from the Russian imperial family. The spire with its onion-shaped dome is of a later date than the main building.

The church's choral group is particularly renowned for its interpretations of the liturgy. The crypt *(closed to the public)* contains the bodies of members of the imperial family who died in exile and of the white Russian general Youdenitch who took part in the siege of Petrograd in 1919.

Opposite the church, and slightly to its right, in Alexandra Square, is the **Chapelle Tripet-Skryptine**, a neo-Byzantine building which was the first Russian Orthodox church in Cannes.

DRIVING TOURS

③ Le Cannet

See plan of Cannes. Leave Cannes by Boulevard Carnot

There is no break between Cannes and Le Cannet which is reached by Boulevard Carnot.

Admirably sheltered from the wind by a circle of wooded hills, Le Cannet, at an altitude of 110m/361ft, complements the climate of Cannes. This bustling resort has been popular with many artists; the actress Rachel, the painter Renoir and the playwright Victorien Sardou. The artist **Pierre Bonnard** (1867-1947) stayed here and spent the last years of his life painting views of Le Cannet from Villa **Le Bosquet** (Avenue Victoria).

Le Vieux Cannet – The old town is reached by Rue St-Sauveur *(mostly pedestrian)* which features 18C houses with unusual façades as well as pleasant small squares shaded by plane trees and linked by alleyways. At no 19, where a side road goes up to the left, a blank façade has been covered with a mural by Peynet representing *Les Amoureux* (the lovers). Further on the left is the little 15C **Chapelle St-Sauveur** sheltering behind a large lime tree, with a pediment decorated with polychrome mosaics. The **Musée Tobiasse** ⊙ inside the chapel is a museum exhibiting mosaics, wooden panels adorned with figures (to be read from right to left) and objects made by the artist. The interior is lit thanks to five stained-glass windows of vivid design by Tobiasse.

Place Bellevue overlooks the square tower of Ste-Philomène Church and offers a superb view of Cannes and the Îles de Lérins. The old Calvys tower (12C) still stands nearby, as well as the taller Danys Tower (14C). Both towers have fine façades topped with machicolations. There is an amusing fresco dedicated to the founding families of Le Cannet on one wall. The Jardins de Tivoli can be reached from the Hôtel de Ville via the pedestrian Rue Cavasse, passing some luxurious 1900 villas.

★**Chemin des Collines** – This is a particularly attractive road along the flanks of the hills above Cannes. There are many fine views over the built-up area, the gulf of La Napoule and the Îles de Lérins to reconcile the driver to the winding road.

Continue to the east, to the Col de St-Antoine.

It is possible to return to Cannes by Avenue Victoria.

On the left in Avenue Victoria, at the top of a magnificent avenue of populars, sits the **Villa Yakimour** *(private property, no visiting).* This Oriental residence was given by the Aga Khan to his wife Yvette Labrousse (Yakimour is derived from their initials and *amour*).

To continue to Vallauris, over the Col de St-Antoine, turn left onto D 803.

Vallauris – *See VALLAURIS*

Golfe-Juan – *2km/1.2mi southeast of Vallauris by D 135. See GOLFE-JUAN.*
On returning towards Cannes on N 7, the road skirts round the hills of Super-Cannes while on the horizon can be seen the Îles de Lérins and the red barrier of the Massif de l'Esterel; the **view**★ is at its best at sunset.

Return to Cannes along the seafront.

★4 La Croix des Gardes

Round tour of 8km/5mi (steep climb) plus 15min on foot there and back. Leave Cannes on Avenue Dr-Picaud. At the traffic lights near the Sol-Hôtel turn right on Boulevard Leader. 100m/110yd beyond the entrance to the Pavillon de la Croix des Gardes, turn right onto Avenue J-de-Noailles and leave the car 100m/110yd further on in the car park provided.

Take a footpath on the right which leads to the top of the hill (alt 164m/538ft), where there is a large cross 12m/39ft high. This strategically placed feature, which has given its name to the hill, has been a permanent lookout post since the 16C. From the foot of the cross there is a marvellous **panorama★** over Cannes and its setting, the Îles de Lérins, the Esterel and, in clear weather, the St-Tropez peninsula.

Continue along Avenue J.-de-Noailles to return to Cannes.

★★★Tour of the Massif de l'Esterel – *96km/60mi – half a day.* We recommend that the round tour be made in the direction in which it is described, from Cannes to St-Raphaël by the inland route and from St-Raphaël to Cannes by the coast road *(see Massif de l'ESTEREL* 4 *and* 1 *respectively).* Tours of the interior of the massif can be made using a local map – *see Massif de l'ESTEREL.*

★★Îles de Lérins – *See Îles de LÉRINS. Allow half a day's walk.*

The attraction of the French Riviera for the Russian aristocracy gave rise to a large number of Russian Orthodox churches
In Cannes – St-Michel-Archange (1894)
In Menton – the Russian sanatorium chapel (1908)
In Nice – the church in Rue Longchamp (1858), which is the oldest, and St-Nicholas (1912), the most recent and most magnificent.

CAP FERRAT★★

Population 1 895
Michelin map 84 folds 10 and 19, 115 fold 27 or 245 fold 38
Local map see Corniches de la RIVIERA

Cap Ferrat, originally the southernmost tip, has now given its name to the whole peninsula, which protects the Villefranche-sur-Mer anchorage and Baie des Fourmis towards Beaulieu. Elegant houses shelter discreetly in the dense vegetation, which tends to conceal views of the shore except from the streets of St-Jean, the lighthouse or St-Hospice Point.

A HEAVENLY SETTING

★★Villa Ephrussi-de-Rothschild

The foundation, which was bequeathed to the Institut de France on behalf of the Academy of Fine Arts in 1934 by the Baroness Ephrussi de Rothschild, boasts an incomparable **setting★★★** in magnificent gardens on the narrow neck of the peninsula and enjoys a fine view of the Villefranche and Beaulieu anchorages. Inside is a museum exhibiting more than 5 000 works of art.

Villa Île-de-France, St-Jean-Cap-Ferrat

ST-JEAN-CAP-FERRAT

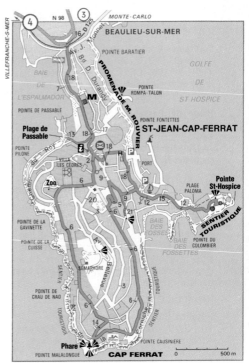

Villa Ephrussi-de-Rotschild . . . . . **M**

★★ **Musée Île-de-France** ⊙ – The villa which houses this museum was built in the Italianiate style soon after 1900 to hold the furniture and works of art that the Baroness collected throughout her life. Her favourite period was the 18C. Pink marble columns from a palace in Verona surround a covered patio in which pieces of medieval and Renaissance furniture stand on an 18C Savonnerie carpet and a mosaic floor; the walls are hung with 16C and 17C Flemish tapestries. It is decorated with a collection of medieval and Renaissance works of art: a late-15C altarpiece depicting St Bridget of Ireland; a Carpaccio painting depicting a Venetian *condottiere*.

The adjoining rooms and galleries display works of art from various periods: 18C furniture (some items belonged to Marie-Antoinette), Savonnerie carpets, Beauvais, Aubusson and Gobelins tapestries, canvases by Boucher, Coypel, Fragonard, Lancret, Hubert Robert, terracottas by Clodion and candelabra by Thomire. The private apartments of Madame Ephrussi, which can be visited, include her bedroom, bathroom, boudoir and the Sèvres dining room.

On the first floor, the outstanding presentation of porcelain from Vincennes, Sèvres and Dresden adds to the dazzling effect of the whole collection. The curious monkey room ("Salon des Singes") evokes the theme of animals which was so dear to Baroness Ephrussi; note the unusual monkey orchestra in Meissen porcelain. Two Chinese lacquer panels open into the gallery of Far Eastern art, arranged in Gothic decor and including lacquerwork from Coromandel, Chinese vases and carpets and a series of Mandarin costumes in an adjoining room. The Impressionists' Gallery contains landscapes by Monet, Renoir and Sisley.

★★ **Gardens** – Magnificent grounds (7ha/17 acres) surround the villa. The French garden abounds in Mediterranean flora and terminates in a stepped cascade spilling into a rockery by a Temple of Love copied from Versailles. Broad steps lead down among the arums, papyrus, pomegranates and daturas of the Spanish garden, which is followed by the Florentine garden with its graceful marble statue. Fountains, columns, gargoyles and sculptures, both medieval and Renaissance, ornament the Stone Garden. A delightful Japanese garden contrasts with the unusual plants in the tropical garden. The Baroness Ephrussi was very partial to roses, many varieties of which can be seen in the rose garden.

★★ DRIVING TOURS

Cap-Ferrat Peninsula – *10km/6mi – about 3hr*

Plage de Passable – This gently sloping shingle beach faces Villefranche anchorage.

Zoo ⊙ 🖼 – A dried-out lake in grounds that once belonged to Leopold II of Belgium has been converted into a **tropical garden** in which a 3ha/7-acre zoo has been set up. It contains 350 species of animals and exotic birds. Several times a day a troop of chimpanzees perform in front of an enthusiastic audience.

Eating out

MID-RANGE

Capitaine Cook – *Avenue Jean-Mermoz – 06230 St-Jean-Cap-Ferrat – ☎ 04 93 76 02 66 – Closed 15 Nov-26 Dec, Thu for lunch and Wed – 19.82/24.39€.* Lying half-way between Paloma beach and the marina, this neat, tidy restaurant, where diners sit side by side, serves traditional cuisine with a strong emphasis on fish and seafood.

Plage de Passable – *Chemin de Passable – 06230 St-Jean-Cap-Ferrat – ☎ 04 93 76 06 17 – jcv7@wanadoo.fr – Closed mid-Oct to Mar – 20/50€.* Beach restaurant located in Villefranche anchorage on the way to St-Jean-Cap-Ferrat Peninsula offering salads, pizzas, pasta and seafood. Enchanting spot sheltered by umbrella pines and palm trees.

Where to stay

MODERATE

Hôtel Frégate – *Avenue Denis-Séméria – 06230 St-Jean-Cap-Ferrat – ☎ 04 93 76 04 51 – Closed 15 Dec-5 Jan – 10 rooms: 38.11/68.60€ – ☒ 5.34€ – Restaurant 18/21€.* Unpretentious establishment in a lively shopping street, recently renovated by its current owners. Some of the small but well-kept rooms have a balcony. Conveniently located 100yards from the beach and the town centre.

MID-RANGE

Hôtel La Bastide – *3 Avenue Albert-1 – 06230 St-Jean-Cap-Ferrat – ☎ 04 93 76 06 78 – ▣ – 14 rooms: 45.73/60.98€ – ☒ 4.57€ – Restaurant 26€.* Although this small hotel may not have all the latest comforts, its rooms command pretty views of the bay and, in the far distance, Cap d'Ail; only one has a private terrace. Home cooking in the restaurant.

LUXURY

Hôtel Brise Marine – *Avenue Jean-Mermoz – 06230 St-Jean-Cap-Ferrat – ☎ 04 93 76 04 36 – Closed Nov to Jan – 16 rooms: 123.48€ – ☒ 9.15€.* Located in a quiet street, this charming house with a welcoming façade is reached through lush, blossoming grounds. Superb views of the bay and Cap Ferrat. It is advisable to book the rooms in the villa, more comfortable than those in the annexe.

Phare – The beam of this **lighthouse** is visible from a distance of 46km/30mi. The top *(164 steps)* commands a **panorama★★** from Bordighera Point in Italy to the Esterel heights including the Alps and Pre-Alps. The Sun Beach swimming pool has been hollowed out of the rocks nearby.

★**St-Jean-Cap-Ferrat** – Once a fishing village, St-Jean is now a quiet resort, its old houses looking down on the harbour of pleasure craft.
The stepped street to the south of Boulevard de la Libération leads to a **viewpoint★** from which Èze, the Tête de Chien, Mont Agel and the Alps on the Italian border can be seen.

Pointe St-Hospice – A pleasant stroll up between the private houses, past an 18C prison tower, leads to a 19C chapel, which replaces an old oratory dedicated to St Hospice, a hermit from Nice. From the chapel there is a good **view★** of the coast and inland from Beaulieu to Cap Martin.

WALKS

From St-Jean, visitors can take pleasant walks, mostly in the shade.

★**Promenade Maurice-Rouvier** – *1hr there and back on foot, leaving from the port of St-Jean.* Starting at the northern end of Plage de St-Jean, the walk follows the coast towards Beaulieu, offering pretty views of Èze and the Tête de Chien.

★**Sentier Touristique de la Pointe St-Hospice** – *1hr there and back on foot. Take Avenue Jean-Mermoz to the Paloma-Beach restaurant and go down the steps on the left.* The path winds along the shore past Paloma Beach with a view of Èze, Monaco and Cap Martin. Once round the Pointe St-Hospice, it skirts the Pointe du Colombier and leads along the shoreline of the Baie des Fossettes before leading back to Avenue Jean-Mermoz.

Long before it became the mecca of the sun-worshipping 20C tourist, the Riviera was popular among foreigners as a winter resort.

Lord Brougham, the Lord Chancellor of England, was accustomed to winter in Nice but in 1834 he was forced by an outbreak of cholera in Provence to stay in Cannes; he liked it so well that he built a house, where he stayed every winter until his death in 1868.

Other famous Englishmen who made a home on the Riviera were the writers, Somerset Maugham in Cap Ferrat, Graham Greene in Antibes and the film actor/writer, Sir Dirk Bogarde, who was President of the Cannes Film Festival in 1984, when he lived near Grasse.

Another foreign colony was the Russian nobility, who until the Revolution in 1917, were regularly joined by the Imperial Court. Their legacy is a number of beautiful Russian Orthodox churches in Cannes, Nice and Menton.

The benefit of the dry climate attracted many patients suffering from tuberculosis, including Katharine Mansfield, a New Zealand writer, who settled in Menton.

The Americans began to make a mark in the 1920s – Douglas Fairbanks and Mary Pickford from the film world, Ernest Hemingway and Scott Fitzgerald, the writers, and other young Americans with money. They introduced jazz, the music of Cole Porter and sunbathing. There was more jazz at the end of the Second World War stimulated by the US Naval base; the Juan-les-Pins Jazz Festival dates from this period.

In the 1930s many German artists in exile settled in Sanary-sur-Mer. Other communities of artists have been established in Vallauris, where Picasso revived the traditional craft of pottery and which now hosts a bi-annual International Festival of Ceramic Art (July to mid-October), and in St-Paul-de-Vence, where James Baldwin, the American author lived for many years.

Monaco, where fortunes have been lost and won on the gaming tables, still attracts a significant number of wealthy tax exiles.

... The diffused magic of the hot, sweet south had withdrawn into them – the soft-pawed night and the ghostly wash of the Mediterranean far below... a sea as mysteriously coloured as agates and cornelians of childhood, green as green milk blue as laundry water, wine dark.

Tender is the Night
F Scott Fitzgerald

COARAZE★

Population 654
Michelin map 84 fold 19, 115 folds 16 and 17 or 245 south of fold 25
Local map see NICE

Coaraze is situated at an altitude of 640m/2 100ft on the **Col St-Roch** road (altitude of pass: 990m/3 248ft), also called the Route du Soleil ("Sunshine Road"), which links the upper basins of the two Paillon rivers. The name of the village is derived from "coa" and "raza" (*queue rasée* – bobbed tail) and has been given different interpretations.

The villagers, of a naturally lively disposition, make a point of celebrating several festivals every year, namely the Fête de St-Jean *(end of June)*, the Fête de Ste-Catherine *(end of August)*, the Olive Festival *(15 August)* and the Chestnut Festival *(end of October)*.

A MEDIEVAL HAMLET

Craftsmen have taken up residence in this nicely restored village with its picturesque **old streets★**, long vaulted passageways and pretty little squares adorned with fountains. From the terraced gardens, flanked by cypress trees, there is a lovely view down into the valley and north to the upper slopes of Rocca Seira. The square is decorated with sundials designed by Cocteau, Goetz and Ponce de Léon.

Church – The old cemetery, with above-ground tombs set atop the impenetrable bedrock, leads to the church.

The interior is Baroque. At the far end hangs an early painting of St Sebastian pierced by arrows.

> ### SUNSHINE INN
>
> **L'Auberge du Soleil** – *Village Centre* – ☎ *04 93 79 08 11 – Closed Nov-15 Feb* – *8 rooms: 53.36/80.80€ –* ⌷ *7.62€ – Restaurant 22€.* Fine 1863 mansion shrouded in silence, accessible only on foot. The hotel's interior decoration achieves an artful combination of antique and modern and the cosy dining room is fitted with a large terrace opening out onto the valley.

Take D 15 north and turn left almost immediately onto a narrow road.

Chapelle Notre-Dame-de-la-Pitié ⊘ – The "blue chapel" was decorated in 1962 with blue monochrome scenes illustrating the life of Christ. Behind the altar a glass panel enhances a metal Pietà. The terrace affords a lovely view of the village.

Take D 15 heading south and after 2km/1mi turn right towards La Gardiola.

Chapelle St-Sébastien ⊘ – Nestled in the lush countryside, this chapel is dedicated to St Sebastian, who protected his disciples by warding off epidemics of the plague. It is decorated with elegant 1530 frescoes (restored in the 19C) depicting the saint pierced by arrows and surrounded by his archers, in a style reminiscent of Il Perugino. The soft hues and delicate contours are inspired by the Renaissance period.

▨ **Ramblers** will find a brochure of local footpaths in the Tourist office.

COGOLIN

Population 9 079
Michelin map 84 fold 17, 114 fold 36 or 245 fold 48
Local map see Massif des MAURES

This typical Provençal village with trading and industrial interests lies along the foot of a slope overlooked by an ancient tower and a ruined mill.

Many of the villagers are employed in the manufacture of carpets, pipes and bottle corks, and in the collection of reeds and canes from the marshes suitable for use in clarinets, fishing rods, furniture etc. It is also a wine-growing centre.

There is a lively market every Wednesday and Saturday morning.

A TOUCH OF MEDIEVAL CHARM

At the top of the village, behind the Hôtel de Ville, the many alleyways joined by vaulted passages have retained their medieval character. There is an original fountain on Place Dolet, and, in **Rue Nationale**, fine Renaissance doorways in green serpentine stone, some of which date back to the 12C; the bourgeois building at no 46 is know as Château Sellier. On the crest of the hill stands the **clock tower** (14C), all that remains of the fortified castle *(access at the end of Rue Nationale, via Montée de l'Horloge).* Coming back down to the left, the **Chapelle Ste-Croix** on Place Bellevue is decorated with contemporary art.

Église St-Sauveur – Parts of the church date from the 11C and a fine Renaissance serpentine gateway remains. Inside, a side chapel houses a fine altarpiece by Hurlupin (1540) depicting St Antony accompanied by St Eligius and St Pons, alongside a beautiful 17C Baroque bust.

CENTRE FOR ARTS AND CRAFTS

Cogolin pipes – *42/58 Avenue Georges-Clémenceau*. Briar roots from the nearby Maures Forest provide the raw material for the manufacture of pipes. In Avenue Clémenceau many **workshops (Fabrique de Pipes)** , including the Maison Courrieu, more than 200 years old, are open to visitors and show manufacturing techniques as well as beautiful collections of the finished product.

Pipes from Cogolin

Manufacture de Tapis de Cogolin – *10 Boulevard Louis-Blanc (off Avenue Georges-Clemenceau)*. In the early 1920s, some Armenian refugee weavers settled in Cogolin, and the **carpet factory** was established in 1928, with the transfer of some high warp looms from Aubusson. Two techniques are currently used; hand weaving on request (using low warp looms – **la basse lisse**), and hand tufting, the technology of which permits very intricate decoration. The tour ends with the workshops where furnishing fabrics and carpets are made, including knotted deep pile wool carpets in the Aubusson style.

Espace Raimu ◷ – *Avenue Georges-Clemenceau*. Located on the ground floor of the local cinema, this centre pays homage (posters, photographs, memorabilia) to the French actor Jules Auguste César Muraire (1883-1946), better known as **Raimu**. Raimu is best-known to English-speaking audiences for his performance as César in Marcel Pagnol's trilogy *Marius*, *Fanny*, *César* and for his role in *La Femme du Boulanger*, also by Pagnol.

MARINES DE COGOLIN

5km/3mi northeast by N 98 and D 98A

Near Cogolin is a fine sandy beach and a marina (22ha/54 acres) with more than 1 500 moorings. The four basins are surrounded by a residential complex built in a striking architectural style. There are regular boat shuttle services to the ports nearby.

A PLACE TO ROOST

Le Coq'Hôtel – *Place de la Mairie* – ☎ *04 94 54 63 14 – Closed 1-15 Jan* – 🅿 *– 25 rooms: 57.93/73.18€ –* ⌂ *6.40€ – Restaurant 21€*. The hotel's mascot is the cock, whose emblem can be found on the pretty façade, decorated with blue shutters, or perched inside the lounge. Gay, lively colours adorn the rooms, whose furniture covers a variety of styles. Many of the bathrooms have a definite Seventies' touch.

Shopping

Établissements Rigotti – *Zone Industrielle – 5 Rue François-Arago* – ☎ *04 94 54 62 05 – 8am-noon, 1.30-5.30pm.*

This workshop (guided tours available) manufactures and sells reeds and other spare parts for musical instruments.

Market – Wednesdays, Saturdays.

COTIGNAC

Population 2 026
Michelin map 84 folds 5 and 6, 114 fold 21 or 245 fold 34

★The site – This village seems to flow down from a cliff (80m/262ft high) of vary-ing colours, shaped by the course of the Cassole and riddled with caves. Some of the chasms are more than 50m/164ft deep. On top of the cliff sit two 14C towers, the remains of Castellane Castle. There is a good view of the site from D 22 com-ing from Sillans.

Cotignac is famed for its production of wine, olive oil and honey, which you can buy at the colourful market on Cours Gambetta *(Tuesday mornings)*. The local *crois-sants* made with **pignon nuts** are simply delicious!

Nuts about them!

Pine nuts, also called pignons, are delicately flavoured seeds taken from the cones of the stone pine. Their presence in Provençal cooking is by no means recent as the Romans are believed to have used them to make wine and mustard. Today pine nuts are a common feature of Mediterranean cuisine. In savoury dishes, they add texture to green vegetables and a lend crunchy consistency to stuffings. They are also used in pastries, preferably toasted, notably in the delicious almond tarts known as *amandines*.

A MAZE OF ROOFS

Old village – Several fountains and elm and plane trees add to the charm of the old streets with their 16C and 17C doorways. From Place de la Mairie, the bell-tower leads to the 16C Romanesque church, the front of which was rebuilt in the 18C.

A path goes up from the church to a two-storey cave which gives a good **view** of the village and its surroundings. At the foot of the rock lies an open-air theatre where concerts and stage productions are performed during the summer season *(see Calendar of events)*.

Chapelle Notre-Dame-des-Grâces – *1km/0.6mi south on D 13 and a side road to the right (45min on foot there and back).*

The chapel, surmounting Mont Verdaille, is associated with an appearance of the Virgin in the 16C, which is depicted in a painting above the altar. In 1660 young Louis XIV came here on a pilgrimage with his mother Anne of Austria, an event commemorated by a black marble tablet on a pillar.

From the esplanade around the church, there is a pleasant **panorama** of Carcès, the Argens Valley and the Brignoles region to the south.

DRAGUIGNAN

Population 32 829
Michelin map 84 fold 7, 114 fold 23 or 245 fold 35

Draguignan, situated between the Haut-Var and the Haute-Provence plateau, developed from a Roman fort built on an isolated knoll where the clock tower now stands. On 8 September, a pilgrimage is made to the Notre-Dame-du-Peuple church, built in the 16C, in honour of the Holy Virgin, who spared the city the ravages of the black plague.

Place du Marché hosts a lively, colourful market on Wednesday and Saturday mornings, when the otherwise peaceful streets are streaming with people from the surrounding wine-growing district.

From the Middle Ages to the present – In the 13C the town grew at the foot of the hill, and a defensive wall with three gates, two of which remain (Porte des Portaiguières and Porte Romaine), and a keep (on the bluff) were built. Louis XIV ordered the keep to be razed in retribution for the conflict between local factions in 1649.

In 1797 the town became the administrative centre (Préfecture) of the Var by order of Napoleon; in 1974 Toulon took over. In the 19C barons Azémar and Haussmann, both prefects of the Var, laid out tree-lined walks and straight boulevards to the west and south of the town.

An American Cemetery, to the east of the town, and a memorial to the Liberation on the corner of Avenue Lazare-Carnot and Avenue Patrick-Rosso, recall the fierce fighting that took place in the region in August 1944, notably around Le Muy, where 9 000 British and American soldiers were parachuted or landed from gliders on the morning of 15 August. The town has been home to an artillery school since 1976.

St Hermentaire and the dragon – The name Draguignan is derived from Draconio, from the Latin *draco* meaning dragon.

Legend has it that, in the 5C, pilgrims on their way from Ampus to the renowned Lérins Abbey via Lentier encountered a dragon roaming the marshes, now meadows watered by the Nartuby. The terrified pilgrims appealed for the help of the hermit Hermentaire, who lived in the area. He slayed the dragon and built a chapel dedicated to St Michael the Archangel.

The existing church of **St-Michel**, north of Place du Marché, contains an 18C statue of St Hermentaire in gilded wood.

A PROSPEROUS PROVENÇAL CITY

To the east of Boulevard de la Liberté, between two of the original gateways – **Porte des Portaiguières**, pierced in a 15C square tower, and **Porte Romaine** (14C) – an intricate maze of charming streets lined with ornate doorways and houses at odd angles constitutes the old town (pedestrian precinct). The market place is set with fountains and shaded by plane trees. The vast façade of an old 13C synagogue in Rue de la Juiverie and the old mansion at no 42 are worthy of interest.

Tour de l'Horloge ⊘ – The **clock tower** replaces the keep, which was pulled down in 1660. It has four flanking turrets and an ornate wrought-iron campanile. The **view** from the top encompasses the town and the Nartuby Valley; on the horizon stretch the Maures mountains.

Cimetière Américain et Mémorial du Rhône ⊘ – *Leave Draguignan by Boulevard J-Kennedy.*

Clock tower, Draguignan

In the landscaped cemetery (5ha/12 acres) are the graves of 861 American soldiers belonging to General Patch's 7th Army who fell in Provence during the campaign launched on 15 August 1944 in support of the Normandy landings. At the foot of the memorial a bronze relief map traces the troop movements. The names of the fallen are inscribed on the supporting wall. The chapel is decorated inside with mosaics by the American Austin Purves.

Chapelle Notre-Dame-du-Peuple – A chapel was built in the 16C in Flamboyant Gothic style and subsequently enlarged (west front in 19C). It is dedicated to the Virgin who saved the town from the plague *(pilgrimage, 8 September)* and contains many votive offerings. On the north wall is the central panel of a 16C altarpiece of the Nice School representing the Virgin saying her rosary.

Eating out

MODERATE

L'Accomedia – *13 Rue des Endronnes – 83300 Draguignan –* ☎ *04 94 50 72 72 – Closed Feb, 15 days in Aug, Mon evening and Sun – 12.96/25.15€.* This Italian restaurant is situated right opposite the local theatre and it is embellished with a fresco evoking the Carnival. In a light, modern setting, typical Mediterranean specialities are prepared and attractively served by friendly, smiling staff.

MID-RANGE

Restaurant du Parc – *21 Boulevard de la Liberté – 83300 Draguignan –* ☎ *04 94 50 66 44 – 15.50€ lunch – 16.50/30.50€.* At the height of summer, the sturdy boughs of a century-old plane tree provide a welcome patch of shade to diners seated on the terrace of this restaurant specialised in Provençal cooking made with choice ingredients. The dining room features a simple decor with rustic-style furnishings.

Where to stay

MID-RANGE

Hôtel Les Oliviers – *83300 Draguignan – 4km/2.5mi W of Draguignan by D 557 (Route de Flaysoc) –* ☎ *04 94 68 25 74 – Closed 5-20 Jan – 12 rooms: 42.69/53.36€ –* ☞ *5.34€.* Roadside hotel conveniently situated on the way to Flayosc. Fortunately, there is very little traffic at night. The rooms, all on the ground floor, are light and neatly arranged.

Chambre d'Hôte St-Amour – *986 Route de la Motte – 83720 Trans-en-Provence – 5km/3mi S of Draguignan, Route du Muy –* ☎ *04 94 70 88 92 –* ⌷ *– 3 rooms: 64€.* A large, rambling park and a curious swimming-pool are the backdrop to this old stone house offering a self-contained flat and several rooms, each decorated in a distinctive style (Africa, Provence). The nearby house also provides accommodation in the form of a pretty studio.

SIGHTS

Musée Municipal ⊙ – The museum, an old Ursuline convent built in the 17C and remodelled in the 18C by the Bishop of Fréjus for use as his summer residence, displays some interesting and rare items, as well as antique furniture, sculpture, ceramics from France (Vallauris, Moustiers, Sèvres) and the Far East, most of which come from the old Château de Valbelle at Tourves.

One gallery presents three paintings by Ziem (1821-1911), including two of Venice, *The Deliverance of St Peter* by J-B Van Loo, a suit of parade armour made between 1570 and 1575 for François de Montmorency, and a graceful composition sculpted by Camille Claudel (1903).

The next room, devoted to French and Dutch 17C painting, displays a Rembrandt *(Child Blowing Bubbles)*, a small Frans Hals *(Kitchen Interior)* and a *Head of Christ* by P de Champaigne.

Also on display are a bust of the Count of Valbelle, Marquis of Tourves, by Houdon and 17C-18C paintings: pastels by the Boucher School, two canvases by Teniers the Younger, a charming *Portrait of a Young Girl* by Greuze and *St Peter's Basilica* by Panini.

The final room is devoted to archeology and displays items discovered during the excavation of Gallo-Roman sites of St-Hermentaire and medieval ones of the town.

★ **Musée des Arts et Traditions Populaires de Moyenne Provence** ⊙ – The traditional activities of the region encompassing the Provençal tableland, the Haut-Pays Varois, the Maures and the Esterel are exhibited in this museum. It was essentially an agricultural region where cereals (primary crop), vineyards (in Provence since Antiquity), olive trees and cork (cork-maker's workshop) were cultivated. Other

DRAGUIGNAN

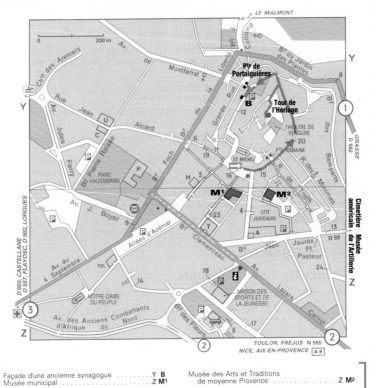

Façade d'une ancienne synagogue ....**Y B**
Musée municipal ....**Z M¹**

Musée des Arts et Traditions
  de moyenne Provence ....**Z M²**

activities included bee-keeping, sheep-raising, hunting, arts and crafts (floor tiles from Salernes, glassworks from the area around Fayence to Fréjus) and the raising of silkworms. Everyday life is evoked with displays of religious objects, domestic furnishings and crockery, costumes...

At the junction of Allées d'Azémar, shaded by six lines of hundred-year-old plane trees, and Boulevard Clemenceau stands a bronze bust of Clemenceau by Rodin.

Musée de l'Artillerie ⊙ – *3km/2mi east of Draguignan by Boulevard J.-Kennedy and D 59; at the artillery school's main entrance, in a military zone.*
The artillery school (f 1791) was transferred to Draguignan in 1976; it merged in 1983 with the anti-aircraft school from Nîmes.
The museum, which the school uses for military instruction, presents the evolution of weaponry and military strategy from ancient times up to the contemporary period.
The ground floor contains displays of heavy arms. Old-fashioned small arms are represented by various types of gun – coastal guns, naval guns, drill guns, siege guns, field guns – and rockets. The display of modern artillery comprises field weapons, trench equipment, fortifications, mountain weapons, anti-tank weapons and anti-aircraft defence equipment. A life-size diorama illustrates the use of the French 75mm guns during the First World War and the crucial role played by the artillery in the Battle of Garigliano during the 1944 Italian campaign.
The mezzanine has been laid out as a military camp at the time of the Second Empire. A series of tents house a display on the evolution of small arms, running from the invention of the cannon up to the Gulf War.

EXCURSIONS

Pays Dracénois

★ **Malmont Viewpoint (Table d'Orientation du Malmont)** – *6km/4mi – about 45min. From Draguignan take Boulevard Joseph-Collomp north. After 6km/4mi, the road reaches a pass. Turn left onto a narrow road which leads to a viewing table 300m/330yd away.* An extensive **view**★ covers Mont Vinaigre in the Esterel range, Agay anchorage, the Argens Valley, the Maures heights and Toulon.

Trans-en-Provence – *5km/3mi from Draguignan. Leave Draguignan by ② on the plan and then take N555.*
Up to the Second World War, this lively village was renowned for its silk spinning, an industry fuelled by the 20 odd mills spanning the River Nartuby.
The town hall, built in 1779, with its lovely Louis XV **façade★** decorated in *trompe-l'œil*, is a rare example of 18C civic architecture.
There is a fine reredos in St-Victor (14C church).

Gorges and Waterfalls of the Nartuby – A path leads from Place de la Mairie in front of the town hall to the bridges. This outstanding **site★** is best viewed from between Pont Vieux and Pont Bertrand.

Puit Aérien – *Chemin du Cassivet.* This "aerial well" was an original design by the Belgian engineer Knapper, who built it in 1930. The well, which has never been used locally, works by recovering moisture during the night in order to water crops. It was originally intended for the African continent.

Flayosc – *7km/4.5mi – about 45min. From Draguignan take D 557, ③ on the plan, going west.*
This typical Var village, overlooking a smiling countryside of vineyards, meadows and orchards, has retained its 14C fortified gates. The typically Provençal **Place de la Reinesse** has plane trees, a mossy fountain and a small wash-house; the Romanesque **church** has a massive square bell-tower. The terrace commands a sweeping **view** of the countryside and the Massif des Maures.

★Chapelle Ste-Roseline – *See Les ARCS: Excursion. 10km/7mi from Draguignan. Leave the town to the south on N 555 and turn right onto D 91.*

DRIVING TOURS

★Gorges de Châteaudouble

41km/26mi – about 1hr. From Draguignan take D 955, ④ on the plan.

Pierre de la Fée – This "fairy's stone" is a fine dolmen of which the table, 6m/19.5ft long, 4.50m/14.5ft wide and weighing 40t, rests on three raised stones more than 2m/6ft high.

★Gorges de Châteaudouble – The deep, green, serpentine gorge was hollowed out by the Nartuby, a tributary of the River Argens.

Before reaching Montferrat, return to Le Plan and turn right onto D 51.

The road goes through the old village of Châteaudouble.

★Châteaudouble – This village occupies an exceptional site on the top of a cliff over-hanging the gorges of the Nartuby by 100m/330ft. Its medieval charm can be seen by following the many passages interspersed with little squares adorned with fountains. Notre-Dame-de-l'Assomption, a 16C church flanked by a Romanesque bell-tower boasts a fine studded portal. The Saracen Tower offers a superb **view★** over the whole village and the rough outlines of the gorges.
From the gorges, several steep paths lead to the prehistoric **caves** of Mouret, Chèvres and Chauves-Souris.

From Châteaudouble drive north towards Ampus.

The D 51 crosses a plateau through the Bois des Prannes.

Ampus – The village church is a well restored Romanesque building. At the back of the church, a path marked by modern Stations of the Cross (1968) leads to a rocky outcrop.
Return to Draguignan on D 49 which affords a good **view** of the town.

Îles des EMBIEZ ⌂

Michelin map 84 fold 14, 114 fold 44 or 245 fold 46
Local map see SANARY-SUR-MER: Excursions

The Embiez archipelago lies off Port du Brusc on rich fishing banks, which are the delight of the amateur angler. It consists of five islands: the biggest one (95ha/235 acres), officially called **Île de la Tour Fondue**, is commonly known as Les Embiez. The second largest one, **Grand Gaou**, with its public park, is linked to the mainland by a footbridge. The **Île du Grand Rouveau** has an automatically-manned lighthouse. **Petit Rouveau** is a bird sanctuary devoted to the reproduction of several species, namely gulls. The smallest isle, **Petit Gaou**, serves as a car park on the road from Le Brusc.

A HAVEN OF PEACE

Ile des Embiez ⌚ boasts a remarkable variety of natural features: fine gravel beaches, rugged coastline with many coves, salt marshes, umbrella pine woods and vineyards yielding a popular rosé wine.

Y. Arthus-Bertrand/ALTITUDE

Île des Embiez

There is a busy modern **marina** overlooked by the ruins of the medieval Château de Sabran, with houses built in the Provençal style. Those keen on diving will enjoy the waters teeming with an exceptional variety of fauna; those interested in Mediterranean wildlife can obtain information from the **Centre de Plongée des Embiez** ⊘. For the less adventurous there is the small train which tours the island as well as a chance to view the underwater world from on board the **Aquascope** ⊘.

★ **Institut Océanographique Paul-Ricard**· ⊘ – The old naval gun site on St-Pierre promontory houses an oceanographic institute devoted to the Mediterranean Sea. The **Observatoire** is fitted with high-tech laboratories where research is carried out on marine biology, fish farming and sea pollution in conjuction with Elf-Aquitaine and the state body **IFREMER** *(see below)*.

A **museum** on the ground floor displays the main Mediterranean types of environment and the species which thrive on them, including an extensive collection of molluscs, stuffed fish and fossils.

About 30 large seawater **aquariums** *(first floor)* provide a natural

> ### The Deep End
>
> **Aquascope** – ♿ *Jul-Aug 9am-6.30pm; Apr-Jun and Sep 2-5pm; Jan and Mar Sat-Sun and public holidays. Tours (30min). 11.43€ (child 7.62€).* ☎ *04 94 34 17 85.* An unusual way to observe underwater life through the transparent hull of a boat.
>
> **Centre de Plongée des Embiez** – ☎ *04 94 34 12 78 or 06 07 58 65 96.* This diving centre will introduce you to the intricacies of marine fauna and flora thanks to its many courses and maiden outings.

setting for some 100 species of Mediterranean aquatic animals, some in gorgeous colours: gorgonias, hermit crabs, grouper, blue lobsters, spider crabs, octopi, sting rays, scorpion fish, little eels.

A Maritime Vocation

The French Institute for Research and Exploitation of the Sea **(IFREMER)** was founded by the French State in June 1984. Its purpose is to ensure better knowledge and assessment of maritime resources, to protect and restore the marine environment, to encourage scientific or economic research in this field and to disseminate international oceanographic information. To do so, it has considerable means at its disposal: a substantial budget, several teams of engineers, seamen and researchers, and 72 laboratories located both in France and overseas. Lastly, it contributes to implementing agreements and conventions for worldwide cooperation on all matters relating to the sea.

ENTRECASTEAUX

Population 863
Michelin Map 245 fold 34 or 114 fold 21

Built on the slopes of a hill overlooking the banks of the River Bresque, this village prides itself on its public gardens attributed to Le Nôtre. It is a pleasure to wander through the old Provençal streets under an old fortified church with a buttress spanning a road. The main avenue, shaded by hundred-year-old plane trees, is a very lively thoroughfare. Decorative carpets are produced here, as well as olive oil.

A WHIFF OF PROVENCE

Lou Picatéou – *Place du Souvenir* – ☎ *04 94 04 47 97 – Closed 15 Dec-15 Feb, Wed evening Oct to Dec and Thu except Jul-Aug – 11.90€ lunch – 14.96/22.13€*. Lying the foot of the castle, this small restaurant with colourful walls, wooden beams and strong Provençal overtones proposes two menus to customers. Summer terrace shaded by the trees growing on the square.

Shopping

Market on Friday mornings.

Calendar

Local patron saints – Sainte-Anne is celebrated on 26 July and Saint-Sauveur during the first weekend in August.

Flea market – The third Sunday in July (until midnight).

Pesto soup banquet – Mid-August.

Flower Festival – Dried flowers fair around mid-October.

Chamber Music Festival – Early September.

OLD VILLAGE

Château ⊘ – This austere 17C building dominates the valley of the Bresque, a tributary of the Argens. Its high façade is topped by a double row of tiles and wrought-iron balustrades. The château was the stronghold of the Castellane, followed by the Grignan (who received the Countess de Sévigné) before passing to the Bruni family. This family included **Admiral Bruni d'Entrecasteaux** who died at sea in 1793 during an expedition to find the explorer La Pérouse who had disappeared five years earlier. A group of islands in New Guinea have been named after him.
After a long period of neglect, the château was restored by the British painter Ian McGarvie-Munn who turned part of it into a museum before his death in 1981. The tour now includes the former castle kitchen and outbuildings in the basement, the guard-rooms and the salons on the ground floor.

Massif de l'ESTEREL★★★

Michelin map 84 fold 8, 115 folds 33 and 34 or 245 folds 36 and 37

The Esterel between St-Raphaël and La Napoule is an area of breathtaking natural beauty. One of the loveliest parts of Provence, it was opened to large-scale tourism by the Touring Club's creation in 1903 of the scenic tourist road known as the **Corniche d'Or** (Golden Scenic Route).

The contrast between the bustling life along the coast and the seclusion of the roads inland is striking – the latter will appeal to tourists who prefer to stray from the beaten track for the pleasure of exploring on their own.

GEOGRAPHICAL NOTES

The massif – The Esterel, which is as old as its neighbour the Maures from which it is separated by the Argens Valley, has been worn down by erosion so that its highest point, Mont Vinaigre, is now a mere 618m/2 027ft. However, in this mountain mass, the deep ravines and broken skyline dispel any impression of this being mere hills.

The Esterel is made up of volcanic rocks (porphyry), which were forced up during the Hercynian foldings, thus distinguishing it from the Maures. These hard porphyry rocks, which give the range its characteristic profile, its harsh relief and vivid colouring, appear in full beauty in the red tints of the Cap Roux range. Agay is where the blue porphyry is found from which the Romans made the column shafts for their monuments in Provence; elsewhere the colours are green, yellow, purple or grey.

The jagged relief extends down to the waterline: the mountains thrust promontories into the sea; the sea cuts deep into the mountains. On the mainland rugged points alternate with tiny bays, narrow strands and small shaded beaches or creeks hemmed in between vertical walls; offshore are thousands of rocks and islets coloured green with lichen, while underwater there are reefs which can be clearly seen.

The fiery red of the rocks forms a strong contrast with the deep blue of the sea.

Fragile flora – Up to the First World War, the Esterel, like the Maures, was carpeted with thick pine and cork-oak forests. Following the repeated outbreaks of forest fires which ravaged most of the Esterel in 1943, 1964, 1985 and 1986, the forest has survived only in a few places. Reafforestation involves a considerable amount of work. Over the past century, scrubland (maquis), which was unknown in 1903, has taken over more than 60% of the Esterel area. The maritime pine, currently plagued by a disease stunting its growth, accounts for more than half of the coniferous trees. L'Office National des Forêts has undertaken much replanting, introducing new species (coniferous and broad-leaved) and cutting back shoots of cork-oak. By 1993 the forest was made up of more than half maquis, 18 % cork-oak and 13 % maritime pine. Other species present in smaller numbers are the Aleppo pine, umbrella pine and holm oak. The Massif de l'Esterel also boasts fine shrubby vegetation which holds down the soil and slows down erosion: heather, arbutus, lentisk, cistus, gorse and lavender. In spring and early autumn their flowers provide a glorious multicoloured and fragrant display.

Diverse fauna – The heart of the massif is home to many herds of wild boar, as well as partridge, pheasant and hares. Roedeer have been succesfully reintroduced into the area.

HISTORICAL NOTES

Via Aurelia – The Esterel was bordered to the north by the Via Aurelia (Aurelian Way) constructed during the reign of Aurelius. It ran from Rome to Arles, via Genoa, Cimiez, Antibes, Fréjus and Aix, and was one of the most important roads under the Empire.

Mediterranean Pine Trees

Maritime Pine – This is the original species of the Mediterranean coast, growing thickly in the past. In spite of its highly combustible nature, it had the advantage of being able to regenerate speedily after fires. However, in the past 25 years, it has been attacked by another enemy – a parasite, the Matsucocus Feytaudi, has brought about its downfall by preventing it from reaching maturity. This explains its often bare appearance. It still accounts for 60% of the species in coastal forests.

Umbrella Pine – On account of its attractive appearance, which blends in wonderfully with the Mediterranean setting, this tree is a great favourite for replanting the maquis scrubland. The mushroom-shaped foliage casts a welcome ring of shade.

Aleppo Pine – More common inland, this tree is known to grow on dry soil up to an altitude of 500m/1 640ft. The tree, which can be seen on land left fallow or on isolated south-facing slopes, is easily identifiable thanks to its red-brown bark and the curve of its trunk.

Scots Pine – This variety thrives on the plateaux of the Haut-Var and the north of the Alpes-Maritimes. Together with the fir it forms magnificent forests.

Massif de l'ESTEREL

The roadway, paved and cambered and more than 2.5m/8ft wide, was laid upon a cement base, as is N 7, which follows much the same route. In the local dialect it is still called *lou camin aurélian*. Taking the shortest route, it made use of many bridges and other civil engineering works. At the end of each Roman mile (1 478m/1 617yd) distances would be indicated by a tall milestone – one of these can be seen in the museum at St-Raphaël (Musée Archéologique). As the road approached the towns, it had raised pavements for pedestrians, which also served as mounting blocks. Stage posts, equipped with hostelries, horses and workshops, minimised delays to the imperial post.

PRACTICAL INFORMATION
About visiting the massif

– Roads marked as "RF" on the map below *(see p 62)* are open to traffic under certain conditions: speed limited to 40kph/25m, no vehicles weighing over 3.5t and no traffic between 9pm and 6am. The roads marked in a red dotted line are closed to public traffic and offenders may be liable to heavy fines. Pedestrian access is however possible.
– During periods of high fire risk, the ALARME plan is put into action and some public roads may be closed to vehicles. Ramblers are strongly advised to avoid such areas for safety reasons.
– Camping is prohibited throughout the massif and within 200m/656ft of any of the forests.
– When walking in the massif, respect plants and wild animals, do not litter the grounds, stay on the paths and keep dogs under control. Mountain bikers must not stray from the signposted paths and tracks laid out in the forests.
– For up-to-date information concerning the massif, call ☎ 04 98 10 55 41.

Esterel Gap – The road skirting the north side of the Esterel, which for many years was the only land route to Italy, was rife with highwaymen; "to survive the Esterel Gap" became a local saying. The most dangerous spot was to the west of Mont Vinaigre; in those days the coach road left N 7 at the Carrefour du Logis-de-Paris and ran nearer the foothills past the forester's lodge (Maison Forestière du Malpey) at Le Malpey (Evil Mountain).
In 1787 the naturalist Saussure showed real courage in exploring the region on foot. Until the end of the 19C the massif remained the refuge of convicts escaping from Toulon.

STAYING IN THE ESTEREL

⌂ **Boulouris** – This small resort, where villas are dotted among pines in beautiful gardens, has several little beaches and a pleasure boat harbour.

⌂ **Agay** – The resort borders a deep anchorage, the best in the Esterel, used in earlier times by the Ligurians, the Greeks and the Romans. Roman *amphorae*, believed to have come from a ship that sunk some 2 000 years ago, have been found in these waters. The French aviator and novelist **Antoine de Saint-Exupery** spent many a summer in Agay. In 1932 he married a local girl whose brother, Pierre d'Agay, was a well-known figure in the area.

Antoine de St-Exupéry

Born in Lyon in 1900, Antoine de St-Exupéry attended the Jesuits College and completed his education in Fribourg, Switzerland. Interested in flying from an early age, he joined the French Army Air Force in 1921 but resigned five years later to become a civilian pilot. He soon turned to literature and began writing in 1928. His second novel *Vol de Nuit* was awarded a prize by the French Academy in 1931. However, the book for which he will always be fondly remembered is *Le Petit Prince* (1943), a charming fable for children. In the Second World War, he served as an instructor and would carry out reconnaissance flights over the South of France. On 31 July 1944, he set out for the Alps on one of these assignments and never returned. A few days later, he was officially reported missing. His body was never recovered from the ocean waters.

Le Dramont and Île d'Or, Esterel Coast

The bay is overlooked by the **Rastel d'Agay**, its slopes resplendent in red porphyry, and is lined by a large, sunny beach, which extends eastwards as far as the small jetty, and beyond by a more popular shady beach.

Anthéor – The resort of Anthéor is dominated by the three peaks of the Cap Roux range.

Just before the Pointe de l'Observatoire, there is a **view** inland of the red rocks of St-Barthélemy and Cap Roux. The road to the summit of Cap Roux is described under 4 below.

Le Trayas – The resort is divided into two parts: one terraced on wooded slopes, the other by the seashore. The creeks and inlets which mark the coast include many small beaches, the largest of which lies at the end of Figueirette Bay. This bay was once a thriving centre for tunny fishing in the 17C, when nets were cast offshore and left floating for four months. To watch the nets, a tower was built on the shore.

Miramar – This elegant resort, with its private harbour, lies in Figueirette Bay.

La Galère – The resort is built on wooded terraces on the slopes of the Esterel where it forms the western limit of La Napoule Bay. Below the road, the seaside development of **Port-la-Galère** *(private port)*, an astonishing design by the architect Jacques Couelle, seems to merge into its rocky environment. The fronts of the houses are strangely hollowed to give the effect of a honeycomb.

Théoule-sur-Mer – This resort, which is sheltered by the Théoule promontory, has three small beaches. The crenellated building on the shore, now a château, used to be a soap factory in the 18C.

Eating out

MID-RANGE

Le Marco Polo – *Avenue de Lérins – 06590 Théoule-sur-Mer –* ☎ *04 93 49 96 59 – Closed mid-Nov to mid-Dec , closed for lunch service 1-15 Nov and mid-Dec to mid-Apr – 24.39€.* Ideally located at the water's edge, this hotel boasts a giant aquarium. The dining room, furnished with rattan tables and chairs, serves salads for lunch and more elaborate dishes in the evening. The terrace commands a nice panorama of Cannes Bay. Informal service.

Riding excursions

Les Trois Fers – *6001 Domaine des Lacs du Dramont – 83700 St-Raphaël –* ☎ *06 85 42 51 50 – saintraphael.com/cheval – Open all year, book in adavance.* Horse lovers will appreciate the riding excursions that will take them through some of the prettiest spots in the Esterel Massif. Lovely views of the sea and île d'Or can be had on reaching Cap Dramont.

EXCURSIONS

★★★① Corniche de l'Esterel

40km/25mi – about 5hr – see local map p 148

★**St-Raphaël** – *See ST-RAPHAËL.*

From St-Raphaël take N 98, ① on the plan.

The road skirts the marina. On the seafront stands a memorial to the campaigns of the French Army in Africa.

After driving through Boulouris, proceed along N 98.

Plage du Dramont – A stele erected to the right of the road commemorates the landing of the US Army, 36th Division, on 15 August 1944. The beach is bordered by Dramont Forest which covers the headland.
Running alongside the lovely Camp-Long beach, the road leads to the resorts of Agay and Anthéor, situated on either side of the Rade d'Agay. Shortly before reaching the Pointe de l'Observatoire, enjoy the **view** to the left, encompassing the red rocks of St-Barthélemy and Cap Roux.

★**Pointe de l'Observatoire** – The ruins of a blockhouse command a stunning **view★** of blood-red porphyry rocks standing out against the cobalt blue of the sea. From this point can be seen the Anthéor, Cap Roux and Esquillon Points and La Napoule Bay further north along the coast. The magnificent red rocks of the Esterel drop sheer into the sea.

Drive through Le Trayas. On a bend near the Hôtel Tour de L'Esquillon, pull off the road into the car park. A path (sign) leads up to Pointe de l'Esquillon.

★★**Pointe de l'Esquillon** – *15min there and back on foot.*
🚶 A beautiful **panorama★★** *(viewing table)* of the Esterel heights, the coast, Cap Roux, the Îles de Lérins and Cap d'Antibes.
After La Galère, the road skirts Pointe de l'Aiguille, opening up a **view★** of La Napoule Bay, Cannes, the Îles de Lérins and Cap d'Antibes. On reaching La Napoule *(see La NAPOULE)*, N 98 crosses the River Siagne and then follows the curve of the bay up to Cannes *(see CANNES)*.

The Kingdom of Auguste I

Off Dramont beach is a small island of red porphyry, l'**Île d'Or**, marked by a strange tower which appears to grow out of the rock. This rock, less than 1ha/2.5 acres in area, has an unusual history which has contributed to the many myths associated with the Riviera. When it was put up for auction by the Domaines in 1897, a Parisian doctor bid for it. Doctor Auguste Lutaud transformed the island into the realm of the operetta and built a four-storey tower in medieval style out of the red stone of the Esterel. Thus the building merged both with its foundations and with the backdrop of the Esterel.
The eccentric proprietor proclaimed himself King Auguste I of the Île d'Or. He became the darling of fashionable society on the coast and organised lavish receptions. Many celebrities of the Belle Époque attended these parties, namely General Galliéni and Jean Aicard, a member of the French Academy. The monarch died in 1925 and is buried in his kingdom. Since then the island, which has remained private property, has changed hands several times.
The cartoonist Hergé, who created Tintin, used the island as a backdrop to his album *L'Île Noire*.

B. Kaufmann/MICHELIN

★ ② VIA AURELIA

46km/29mi – about 6hr – see local map p 149

Cannes – *See CANNES.*

From Cannes take N 7, ③ on the town plan.

For most of the way this route runs through Esterel Forest. After passing through the industrial zone of La Bocca, the road crosses the alluvial plain of the River Siagne.

Turn left onto the road leading to Cannes-Mandelieu airport, then right.

Ermitage de St-Cassien – The 14C chapel set on a low rise in an oak plantation with a few cypress trees standing guard makes a charming picture. Tradition says it was once the site of a Roman temple; it is now a place of pilgrimage.

Return to N 7.

Mandelieu-la-Napoule – *See MANDELIEU-LA-NAPOULE.*

N 7 runs along the valley hollowed out between the Esterel and Tanneron Massifs.

Auberge des Adrets – This inn was the favourite haunt of the highwayman **Gaspard de Besse** whose exploits in the 18C have remained legendary. After attacking and plundering the coaches and horsemen passing within their reach, Gaspard and his band would take refuge in a cave on the side of Mont Vinaigre. The brigand chief had a soft spot for sartorial elegance: he sported a splendid red costume studded with precious stones and fine silver buttons and buckles. For many years the mounted constabulary were at his heels. He was eventually arrested in an inn near Toulon and was broken on the wheel in 1781 at the age of 25. His head was nailed to a tree on the road which had been the scene of his many escapades.

At the crossroads, Carrefour du Logis-de-Paris, the road skirts the foot of Mont Vinaigre, the highest peak in the Esterel (618m/2 027ft).

At the Carrefour du Testannier, turn left onto a road marked "Forêt Domaniale de l'Esterel". At the Le Malpey forester's lodge, follow signs to Mont Vinaigre.

★★ Mont Vinaigre – *30min there and back on foot.*

▲ A path leads to the top which offers a splendid **panorama★★★** on all sides: on the coast Cap d'Antibes, Pointe de la Croisette, Cannes and La Napoule Bay, Pic de l'Ours with its tower and TV mast, Pic du Cap Roux and Fréjus Bay, inland the Massif des Maures and the Argens Valley, and the limestone hills of Provence. On a clear day you can see as far as the Alps and Ste-Baume.

Return to N 7.

At the bend, there is a **view** on the right towards Fayence; then the road follows the the Moure Valley. The original Via Aurelia, however, followed the line of the forest road on the opposite bank.

★ Fréjus – *See FRÉJUS.*

Return to St-Raphaël by Boulevard S.-Decuers.

★ St-Raphaël – *See ST-RAPHAËL.*

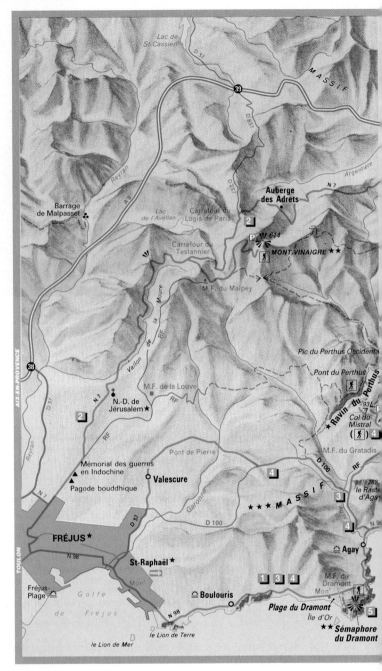

★★ 3 PIC DE L'OURS

57km/35.5mi along steep, narrow roads that are not always surfaced – allow one day
From St-Raphaël take N 98 heading southeast. Leaving Agay, take the Valescure road
and bear right towards Pic de l'Ours. After Gratadis forester's lodge (Maison Forestière
du Gratadis), bear right and, having forded the River Agay, leave the Plateau d'Anthéor
on the right and bear left towards Pic de l'Ours (Moutrefrey crossroads).

The road climbs to the summit past evergreen oaks, barren land and red rocks,
with the Mal Infernet ravine in the distance. Winding round the north side of St-
Pilon and Cap Roux, the road reaches Col de l'Évêque and then Col des Lentisques
(one-way traffic between the two passes: take the road to the east of the peak on
the outward journey, and the interior road on the way back), with frequent **glimpses**
of the sea to the right.

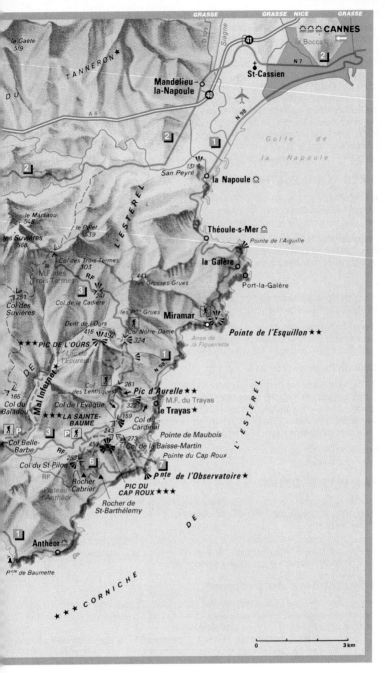

★★ Pic d'Aurelle – *1hr there and back on foot by a marked path starting from Col des Lentisques.*

🚶 The Aurelle is one of the major peaks in the coastal chain of the Esterel. From the top (323m/1 060ft) a fine **panorama★★** takes in the area running from Cap d'Antibes to the Pointe de l'Observatoire.

The stretch between Col des Lentisques and Col Notre-Dame is one of the most beautiful drives in the Esterel. Immediately overlooking the coast, the road offers breathtaking **bird's-eye views★** of the Corniche de l'Esterel cliff road and splendid perspectives of the shore facing Cap d'Antibes. From Col Notre-Dame (323m/1 060ft), a remarkable **panorama** extends over Cannes, the Îles de Lérins and La Napoule Bay.

★★★ Pic de l'Ours – *1hr 30min on foot there and back. Car park at Col Notre-Dame.*

◪ The series of hairpin bends by which the road *(private vehicles prohibited)* reaches the summit affords constantly changing views of the wooded ranges of the Esterel and the deeply indented coastline. The remarkable **panorama**★★★ from the summit (496m/1 627ft) where there is a television transmitting station, includes the coast – from the Maures to the Alps – the Esterel range, dominated by Mont Vinaigre and the Var countryside.

From Col Notre-Dame, drive to Col des Trois Termes.

From Col Notre-Dame, the road *(surfaced for 5km/3mi)* clings to the peaks of the Petites Grues and the Grosses Grues before reaching Col de la Cadière where the **view**★ opens to the north towards La Napoule and the Massif du Tanneron. At Col des Trois Termes, take the track on the right (almost hairpin back on yourself) to join N 7.

Return to St-Raphaël on N 7 or by returning along the route described above.

★ 4 ROUTE DU PERTHUS

20km/12mi – 3 hr – map p 149. Leave St-Raphaël by N 98 south, as far as the Gratadis Masion Forestière, then turn left towards the Belle-Barbe Pass. Parking at the pass. Beyond the parking area, no private cars are allowed.

★ **Ravin du Mal Infernet** *– 2hr on foot there and back.*

◪ Follow the footpath which leads into the wooded ravine of Mal Infernet, a majestic setting overlooked by many jagged rocks. The path goes as far as the Lac de l'Écureuil. This lake contains a fine variety of fish: roach, tench, carp, perch and trout.

It is possible to continue on foot as far as Col Notre-Dame by skirting Pic de l'Ours and Dent de l'Ours to the north.

Return to Col de Belle-Barbe. Take the road heading northwest towards the Roussivau forester's lodge (Maison Forestière de Roussivau). Leave the car in the Col du Mistral car park and take the left-hand path.

★ **Ravin du Perthus** *– 1hr 30min on foot.*

◪ The road skirts the Perthus summits to the south. At Pont du Perthus a marked footpath leads off into the pretty Perthus ravine. It offers a nice setting for some easy rambles before heading off towards the foothills of Mont Vinaigre. To the right stands **Pic du Perthus** (266m/887ft), with its scarlet porphyry rocks towering above the southern limit of Esterel Forest.

Return to the car park at Col du Mistral and head towards Valescure on the Roussivau forest road.

RAMBLERS' DELIGHT

The following excursions are a wonderful opportunity for to stretch your legs after a long ride in the car and you will be delighted to discover the magnificent views of the landscape.

Immediately after the Dramont camp site, turn right. 100m/110yd further on, leave the car and take a left-hand path leading up to the signal station. 1hr there and back on foot; the path is paved and signposted.

★★ 5 Sémaphore du Dramont

Immediately after the Dramont camp site, turn right. 100m/110yd further on, leave the car and take a left-hand path leading up to the signal station. 1hr there and back on foot; the path is paved and signposted.

◪ From below the signal station there is a **panorama**★★: to the southwest of the Maures, the two porphyry rocks guarding the entrance to the gulf of Fréjus (the Sea Lion – *Lion de Mer* – and the Land Lion – *Lion de Terre*), and Île d'Or with its tower. On the horizon to the north lies Mont Vinaigre; behind the Rastel d'Agay peak in the foreground, can be seen the rocks of the Cap Roux range and lower down, on the right, the Agay anchorage. Walk back down along the signposted path leading to the little port; the attractive glimpses of clear water inlets will be a strong temptation for nature lovers.

★★ 6 Pic du Cap-Roux

2hr on foot there and back from the Sainte-Baume parking area. You can reach the parking are from St-Raphaëm by taking tour 3 *by N 98 and the forest road.*

◪ The footpath leads to the Cap-Roux pass. From the summit (452m/1 483ft), there is a superb **sweeping panorama**★★★ *(viewing table)*. If you continue on to the Col de l'Evêque, you can see as far as the Lérins islands, before continuing on to the Sainte-Baume spring, where the waters are sure to refresh you!

★★ 7 La Sainte-Baume

5hr 30min on foot there and back from the Sainte-Baume parking area.
🚶 This longer and steeper version of the previous walk leads to the Col du Saint-Pilon (view over the Cap du dramont). As you progress through meadows of wild rosemary, the view from the high road unfolds: to the right, Cabrier Rock, below, St Barthélemy's Rock. The path follows the coastline, partly on a paved road, and then on to a sloping trail that will get your muscles working. You come to a railway tunnel and then reach the Col de la Baisse-Martin, and then the Col du Cardinal. Then comes the reward: it's all downhill from here, and at the bottom is the heavenly spring.

ÈZE★★

Population 2 509
Michelin map 84 folds 10 and 19, 115 fold 27 or 245 fold 38
Local map see Corniches de la RIVIERA

A quaint, isolated hamlet dominating the Riviera coastline, Èze is the perfect example of a perched village *(see Introduction p 80)*. Like an eagle's nest, it clings to its rocky outcrop, towering 427m/1 410ft above the sea. Legend claims that it was founded by the Saracens but in fact it was a Celto-Ligurian settlement, which subsequently came under the rule of the Phœnicians, Romans and Saracens, rising to the status of a county in the 16C.

Each year this charming place and its stunning **site★★** welcome a great many foreign visitors and tourism has come to replace the area's former industries, the cultivation of tangerines and carnations. The German philosopher **Frédéric Nietzsche** was particularly fond of Èze and spent many summers here; the road leading down to the beach still carries his name *(see below)*.

Eating out

MID-RANGE

Bistrot Loumiri – *Avenue du Jardin-Exotique* – ☎ *04 93 41 16 42* – *Closed Feb school holiday, Wed evening and Mon* – *Reservation required* – *19.82/23.63€*. At the bottom of Èze Village, this bistro-type restaurant is known for its simple but tasty Provençal food and its low prices. Try the chef's special, chalked up on a slate. Aimed at passing trade, and tourists who have come to admire the majestic setting.

L'Oliveto – *Place du Général-de-Gaulle* – ☎ *04 92 41 50 40* – *19.82/25.92€*. Housed in a building on the main square, this upstairs restaurant provides two venues: a large traditional dining hall and a smaller area whose light, fresh atmosphere recalls a winter garden. In either case, the menu is a vibrant homage to nearby Italy.

Where to stay

MODERATE

Hôtel Hermitage du Col d'Eze – *2,5km/1.5mi by D 46 and Grande Corniche* – ☎ *04 93 41 00 68* – *Closed 1 Dec-1 Feb, Fri for lunch, Mon and Thu* – 🅿 – *14 rooms: 38.11/51.83€* – 🍽 *4.57€* – *Meal 29€*. Peace and quiet are guaranteed in this hotel with its splendid terraces and overflow pool. One side of the building gives onto the sea while the other affords nice views of the mountains. Try to book one of the more recent rooms; they are smaller but more attractive.

MID-RANGE

Auberge des Deux Corniches – *Route du Col Èze* – *1km/0.6mi on D 46* – ☎ *04 93 41 19 54* – *Closed 10 Nov-1 Feb* – *7 rooms: 45.73/51.83€* – 🍽 *5.34€*. Modest inn on the road leading up to Èze, fronted by a large terrace and shaded by a cluster of trees. The renovated rooms are unsophisticated but carefully kept and some afford pretty views of the sea and the rocky outcrop serving as a backdrop to the village.

Fragrances

Parfumerie Fragonard ⊘ – ♿ *Guided tours (30min) Feb-Oct 8.30am-6.30pm; Nov-Jan 8.30am-noon, 2-6pm. No charge.* ☎ *04 93 36 44 65*. This annexe of the Grasse perfumery displays the various stages in the manufacturing process of essential oils and cosmetics.

Parfumerie Galimard – *Place du Général-de-Gaulle* – ☎ *04 93 41 10 70* - *www.galimard.com - Open daily. No charge*.

Exotic garden, Èze

D. Pazery/MICHELIN

★A MAZE OF VAULTED PASSAGEWAYS

A 14C double gateway with crenellations and a sentry walk leads into the steep narrow streets, sometimes stepped and sometimes running beneath the tastefully restored houses converted into smart boutiques and artists' studios. At every corner there are flowers, shrubs, fountains and breathtaking views of the sea and mountains.

Church – The church was rebuilt in the 18C with a Classical façade and a two-storey tower. The Baroque interior contains a fine statue of the Assumption (18C) attributed to Muerto and an emblazoned 15C font.

Chapelle des Pénitents-Blancs ⊙ – The simple 14C chapel is decorated with enamelled panels illustrating the life and death of Christ and his mother.

To the left on entering is a Crucifixion, an early example of the Nice School; on the high altar an unusual Catalan crucifix, dating from 1258, in which Christ is pictured smiling; on the right a 16C hexagonal ciborium in mahogany; on the left a 14C statue, the Madonna of the Forest, so called because the child she is holding has a pine cone in his hand. A 16C wooden crucifix hangs on a pilaster in the gallery.

SIGHTS

Jardin Exotique ⊙ – Many varieties of succulents and cacti flourish in the gardens crowned by the remains of a 14C château dismantled on the orders of Louis XIV in 1706. The terrace commands a splendid **panorama★★★** of the Riviera and on a clear day one can even make out Corsica in the far distance!.

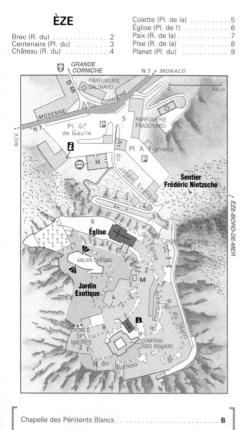

Astrorama ⊘ – *Take D 46 until you reach Col d'Èze (see map p 267)*. This observatory will allow you to gaze at shooting stars through a telescope on a fine summer's evening.

★ **Sentier Frédéric-Nietzsche** – *About 2hr on foot there and back*. Nietzsche thought out the third part of his masterpiece *Thus Spoke Zarathustra* on the picturesque mule path which winds down towards the Corniche Inférieure. It leads through pine woods and olive groves to the seaside resort of Èze-Bord-de-Mer.

FAYENCE

Population 4 253
Michelin map 84 folds 7 and 8, 114 folds 11 and 24 or 245 fold 36

Fayence lies on the edge of the Provençal tableland (view of the Signal de Lachens beacon – alt 1 715m/6 626ft), opposite its twin village, Tourrettes, on the road from Draguignan to Grasse, overlooking an important gliding field. It enjoys a privileged location, half-way between the mountains and the sea, surrounded by picturesque villages and only 10km/6mi from the Lac de St-Cassien. Potters, stone and wood carvers, weavers, painters and coppersmiths ply their trade here. Do not miss the lively markets held on Place de l'Église Tuesdays, Thursdays and Saturdays.

STROLLING IN FAYENCE

Old town – Below the church, steep streets lined by handsome doorways of houses and a 17C gateway lead to the town gates. The Porte Sarrasine is still crowned by machicolations.

Church – This church was built in the mid 18C, replacing the smaller, older church unable to accommodate a growing congregation. The interior is very Classical with tall pillars supporting a gallery round the nave. The high altar, Baroque in style, is the work of the Provençal marble mason Dominique Fossatti (1757). In the nave's south aisle, a 16C gilded altarpiece represents scenes of the Passion and the Glorification of Christ; Christ in Agony is in the centre with a giant St Christopher carrying the Infant Jesus below.

From the terrace, to the right of the church, the **view**★ extends beyond the gliding field to the Maures and Esterel heights.

> **LUXURIOUS MILL**
>
> **Moulin de la Camandoule** – *83440 Fayence – 2km/1.2mi W of Fayence by D 19 Route de Seillans and a country lane* – ☎ *04 94 76 00 84 – 11 rooms: 80.04/ 151.69€ – ⊑ 10.67€ – Restaurant 27/49€*. An old olive mill at the foot of the village has been converted into a quaint Provençal stopping-place decorated in warm, southern colours. The grounds are home to a pool, a Gallo-Roman aqueduct and a terrace. Half board in summer only.

Panorama de l'Ancien Château – *Follow the signs from the church*. The view is to the north to the Provençal tableland, the Pre-Alps of Castellane and Grasse.

DRIVING TOURS

Col du Bel-Homme *64km/40mi – about 4hr*

From Fayence take D 563 south.

Almost immediately on the right, then the left, is the turning *(signpost)* to Notre-Dame-des-Cyprès, nestled in the vineyards.

Notre-Dame-des-Cyprès ⊘ – In a setting of tall cypress trees, the Romanesque chapel (12C) looks out over Fayence and Tourrettes. The oven-vaulted apse contains a 16C altarpiece set in a Baroque frame: scenes from the life of the Virgin painted on wood in a naive style flank a painted wooden statue.

Return to D 563 which skirts Fayence airport and turn right onto D 562 which crosses several streams as it winds among the trees.

To the north the villages of Fayence, Tourrettes and Montauroux are strung out along the ridge.

At Les 4 Chemins turn right onto D 25, heading towards Callas.

Callas – Grouped round the castle ruins against a hillside of olive, oak and pine trees, Callas is still a typical village of the Haut-Var with its 17C belfry, its porches and its dovecote... The Romanesque **church** ⊘, heavily restored in the 19C, displays a 17C altarpiece above nine hooded penitents on their knees.

From the terrace the **view** south takes in the Maures and Esterel heights.

Continue along D 25 which goes over Col de Boussague and winds up a pleasant valley to Bargemon.

Bargemon – An old stronghold at the foot of the Provençal Tableland, Bargemon still recalls its past in its old streets, its broken ramparts, ruined castle and 12C fortified gateways (in particular the so-called "Roman" gate, place de la Mairie). Large shaded squares and many fountains add to its charm while the presence of mimosa and orange trees indicate a mild climate. The markets on Place St-Étienne *(Thursday mornings)* are a wonderful showcase for the delicious local produce. The 15C **church** ⓧ near the town gateway was incorporated into the town's fortifications. Its square bell-tower is 17C. It has a fine flamboyant **doorway**. Pierre Puget is the putative artist of the angel heads on the high altar. Note the striking 16C triptych portraying St Antoine between St Raphaël and St Honorat.

The village is dominated by the spire of the **Chapelle Notre-Dame-de-Montaigu**, which houses three fine altarpieces resting on wreathed columns. It has been a place of pilgrimage since the 17C when a miraculous statue of the Virgin was brought here from Belgium by a monk who was a native of the village (the statuette, carved in olive wood, is shown only on Easter Monday).

From Bargemon take D 25 west.

The road climbs steeply offering fine views of Bargemon and its surroundings. This was once the path used by shepherds to lead their sheep and goats up to the summer pastures.

★ **Col du Bel-Homme** – Alt 951m/3 210ft. A path on the left leads to the top. From the viewing table a **panorama**★ extends south to the coast, northeast to Grasse, north to the Canjuers Plateau and the mountains around Castellane.

Return to Bargemon and take D 19 towards Fayence.

The road climbs above the town before turning eastwards through pine trees, evergreen holm oaks and broom. On the southern horizon rise the Maures and Esterel heights.

★ **Seillans** – *See SEILLANS.*

Notre-Dame-de-l'Ormeau – *See SEILLANS.*

Return to Fayence on D 19 with open views of the countryside.

Lac de St-Cassien – *Round tour of 29km/18mi – allow 2hr.*

From Fayence take the road to Tourrettes.

Tourrettes – The castle *(not open to the public)*, modelled on the St Petersburg Cadet School, was built around 1830 by Alexandre Fabre, a native of Tourrettes. Its curious silhouette can be spotted from afar.

Turn left onto D 19, D 562 and D 56 to reach Callian.

Callian – Streets lined with old houses wind round the castle on a delightful **site**. A fountain plays under the trees of the main square, from where **views** look southwest over the local flower fields to the Lac de St-Cassien beneath the Tanneron heights. The Esterel and Maures Massifs dominate the horizon to the south.

North of the village take D 37 towards Montauroux.

The road offers pleasant views of Callian and Montauroux.

Montauroux – Many craftsmen have settled in the village. There are 17C and 18C houses in Rue de la Rouguière, and the **view** from the square takes in the Lac de St-Cassien, the Tanneron heights, with a glimpse of the Maures and the Esterel. The **Chapelle St-Barthélemy**, built in the 17C by the Pénitents Blancs, features a great many painted panels depicting the Apostles, musical instruments etc. It was recently restored at the instigation of the famous French designer Christian Dior. The local church presents paintings from the 17C.

Continue on D 37 crossing D 562.

Lac de St-Cassien – Nestled at the foot of the Tanneron *(see Massif du TANNERON)*, the lake is prettily set in lush countryside. From the Pré-Claou bridge, there is a **view** of the whole lake which mainly supplies water for irrigation purposes. Its wooded slopes and waters teeming with fish attract hunters and anglers alike. Water sports are allowed on the lake *(no motor boats)* and there are areas set aside for swimming.

Return to Fayence by D 37; turn left onto D 562 and right onto D 19.

FRÉJUS★

Population of conurbation 83 840
Michelin map 84 fold 8, 114 fold 25, 115 fold 33 or 245 fold 36
Local maps see Massif de l'ESTEREL and Massif des MAURES

Fréjus lies between the Maures and the Esterel, in the alluvial plain of the Lower Argens, where vineyards and fruit orchards flourish. The town itself is built on a rocky plateau whose slopes descend gently towards the sea about a mile away. Fréjus attracts lovers of the past; its Roman ruins, although unspectacular, are among the most varied in France and its cathedral close is of great architectural interest. The construction of Port-Fréjus along the coast has given a boost to the local tourist industry.

HISTORICAL NOTES

Birth and heyday (1C BC) – Fréjus takes its name from **Forum Julii**, a village founded by Julius Caesar in 49 BC, a trading and staging post on the great coastal road which was to become known as the **Via Aurelia**.

Octavian, the future Emperor Augustus, turned the market town into an important naval base (39 BC), where he built and trained the fast, manoeuvrable light galleys which were later to win the battle of Actium (31 BC) against the heavy ships of Cleopatra and Antony.

In the town then called Colonia Octavanorum, Augustus established a large colony of his veterans (soldiers who had finished their military duties and to whom a sum of money and some land were given, along with the full rights of a Roman citizen). The city expanded (construction of the Platform or military headquarters and the Butte St-Antoine) until it numbered 40 000 inhabitants. It was exceedingly prosperous.

Fréjus 2 000 years ago – *See plan below*. Ramparts surrounded it, pierced by four gateways corresponding to the two broad streets, quartering the town, in the tradition of Roman settlements. Soldiers, sailors and citizens enjoyed the arenas, amphitheatre and baths free of charge.

An aqueduct 40km/25mi long brought fresh water from the Siagnole near Mons *(see MONS)* as far as the water tower from which it was piped to the fountains and public buildings.

Among the naval bases of the Roman world only Fréjus and Ostia, in Italy, offer sufficient remains to be reconstructed: from the eastern end of the Esplanade Paul-Vernet (Roman forum), one can look down on the plain where the port lay 2 000 years ago and, with the aid of the vestiges still standing, one can easily conjure up its shape, size and facilities.

The port, originally created by dredging and deepening a lagoon, was reconstructed during the reign of Augustus.

The harbour of some 22ha/54 acres, a considerable area for those times, included over 2km/1mi of quays, of which traces still remain.

It was linked with the sea by means of a canal, protected from the *mistral* by a wall, and approximately 30m/98ft wide and 500m/1 640ft long – the shore line has receded since Roman times. The entrance was guarded by two large symmetrical towers, of which one, bearing Augustus' Lantern, still rises high above the plain at the end of the south quay. An iron chain, which lay on the bottom all day, was stretched between the towers at night.

A strong outward current, obtained by a secondary canal from the Argens, prevented the harbour from silting up.

A large tower, boatyards, baths and buildings – the harbour-master's office, a health control office and laundry – completed the installations, together with the *palaestra* (sports ground) and hospital, of which traces are to be found at the Villeneuve farm, southwest of the town.

Decline – During the long years of Roman peace, the military aspect of the port declined and in the late 2C AD the fleet was moved away but the port remained a lively commercial centre until the 4C. Under Constantine an archbishopric was established. The harbour and canal, however, were neglected and began to silt up. At the beginning of the 10C the town was destroyed by the Saracens. In 990 under Bishop Riculphe, the city rose again on a much smaller scale; the medieval town walls *(see plan below)* followed the line of Rue Jean-Jaurès and Rue Grisolle. Henri II turned Fréjus into a large naval base.

Finally, under the Revolution, the whole port was sold as a national estate and was filled in by its new owner.

★AN EARLY ROMAN SETTLEMENT

The Roman ruins are scattered over a large area; allow 1hr 30min to 2hr. Go to Place Agricola and leave the car on the car park.

Porte des Gaules – The old gateway through the Roman ramparts is half-moon shaped. Of the two towers that once flanked it, only one remains. The Roman city covered about 40ha/99 acres.

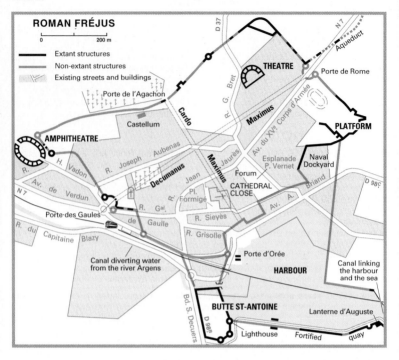

ROMAN FRÉJUS

0	200 m

▬▬▬ Extant structures

▬▬▬ Non-extant structures

▨ Existing streets and buildings

THEATRE

Porte de Rome

Aqueduct

D 37

N 7

Porte de l'Agachon

Castellum

Cardo

R. G. Bret

Maximus

Av. du XVᵉ Corps d'Armée

PLATFORM

AMPHITHEATRE

R. H. Vadon

R. Joseph Aubenas

Decumanus

R. Jean

Maximus

R. Jaurès

Forum

Esplanade P. Vernet

Naval Dockyard

Av. de Verdun

N 7

Pl. Formigé

CATHEDRAL CLOSE

Briand

D 98ᶜ

Porte des Gaules

R. Gal.

de Gaulle

R. Sieyès

Av. A.

R. du Capitaine Blazy

R. Grisolle

Porte d'Orée

Canal diverting water from the river Argens

HARBOUR

Canal linking the harbour and the sea

Bd. S. Decuers

BUTTE ST-ANTOINE

Lanterne d'Auguste

Lighthouse   Fortified   quay

★ **Arènes** ⊙ – Built outside the city in the 2C, the amphitheatre is 114m/124yd long by 82m/93yd wide (Nîmes 143yd by 109yd; Arles 149yd by 117yd), and could accommodate approximately 10 000 spectators. Half the amphitheatre lies against the flank of the hill crowned by ramparts.

Destined primarily for the pleasure of soldiers and veterans, it was clearly built with an eye to austerity and economy. In this respect it differs from the amphitheatres erected in Arles and Nîmes, intended for a far more sophisticated audience. Bull-fights and other spectacles are held here in summer.

On the esplanade stands *Le Gisant*, a sculpture commemorating the Malpasset disaster, which claimed more than 400 lives. Two columns discovered on a Roman wreck in the gulf of St-Tropez, erected at the junction of N 7 and D 37, can be seen to the southwest from the lawn surrounding the arena.

In summer a little train **(Petit Train du Soleil)** ⊙ provides a tour of the site starting from the Esplanade.

Take Rue Joseph-Aubenas, then Avenue du Théâtre Romain. A detour via Rue Gustave-Bret will lead you to the medieval ramparts.

Theatre – This theatre is far smaller than the amphitheatre; it consists of only the radial walls on which the arches supporting the tiers of seats once rested. It measures 84m/92yd by 60m/66yd.

Inside, the orchestra pit is clearly visible, together with the stage foundations and the slot into which the curtain was lowered.

Aqueduct – *Avenue du Quinzième-Corps-d'Armée.* Only pillars and ruined arcades remain of the aqueduct that reached the city level with the ramparts. The water was then channelled beneath the northern parapet walk as far as the water tower *(castellum)* from which the distribution conduits started. Some interesting remains can be seen in Avenue du Quinzième-Corps-d'Armée.

Platform – Still known as the eastern citadel, this area shows traces of a Roman platform which served as the military headquarters *(praetorium)*: offices, store-rooms, lodgings and baths. To the south lay the naval dockyard.

Harbour – The Porte d'Orée consists of a fine archway, most likely the remains of a chamber formerly attached to the harbour baths.

Butte St-Antoine – This mound formed a western citadel serving as a counterpart to the platform. Boulevard S.-Decuers skirts the western wall; the eastern wall would have overlooked the harbour; a few towers remain on the southern front, one of which may have been a lighthouse.

Nearby stood the military laundry where the soldiers' uniforms were cleaned by a process using fuller's earth and sulphur vapour.

Augustus' Lantern – *Follow the signed path skirting the south face of the Butte St-Antoine*. Beside the base of a tower the path turns right onto the southern quay; part of the defence wall still has survived.

At the far end of the quay a tower marked the entrance to the harbour and the beginning of the canal leading out to sea. Although the tower was a ruin by the Middle Ages a construction known as Augustus' Lantern was erected on it to act as a landmark for sailors entering the harbour. The wall marking the line of the sea canal stretches away to the southeast.

Eating out

MODERATE

Les Micocouliers – *34 Place Paul-Albert Février* – ☎ *04 94 52 16 52* – *Closed 20 Dec-10 Jan and evenings Nov to Mar* – *14.50/22.50€*. This restaurant set up on the square opposite the cathedral close (cloisters, cathedral, former bishop's palace, baptistry) has a most appealing summer terrace. Inside, the brightly coloured tablecloths and rustic-style decoration blend in well with the owner's Provençal cooking.

MID-RANGE

Le Poivrier – *52 Place Paul-Albert Février* – ☎ *04 94 52 28 50* – *Closed Mon Sep to May and Sun* – *10.52€ lunch* – *19.06/25.15€*. The tasty homemade cuisine is a mix of Mediterranean tradition and a pinch of exotica, served in a small, vaulted cellar going back to Roman times. In summer, have your meals out on the terrace on Place Paul-Albert Février or on the patio shaded by reed screening.

Where to stay

MID-RANGE

Hôtel L'Aréna – *145 Boulevard du Général-de-Gaulle* – ☎ *04 94 17 09 40* – *Closed 5-30 Nov* – *36 rooms: 83.85/114.34€* – ☑ *7.62€* – *Restaurant 22/40€*. A former staging post with a colourful front provides pleasant accommodation in carefully kept rooms arranged in the Provençal style. Relax sipping your cocktail on the terrace or reclining by the pool.

On the town

La Playa – *Boulevard de la Libération* – ☎ *04 94 52 22 98* – *Jul-Aug: nightly from 11pm; Sep-Jun: Thu-Sat from 11pm*. This nightclub is one of the most fashionable in the area and its tremendous success is continued throughout the year. On Thursdays, the *dînette* formula, alternating buffet food with dancing, is a great favourite among locals.

Souvenir figurines

Forum Julii – *Place de la Mairie* – ☎ *04 94 17 03 00* – *Jul-Aug: Tue-Sat 9am-noon and 3-7pm, Sun-Mon 9am-noon; Sep-Jun: closed Sun and Mon*. A boutique selling the region's famous clay figurines *(santons)* offers a broad choice covering local arts and crafts, religious history and Mediterranean life: the Three Wise Kings, the Holy family, shepherds and their flock, the fishmonger, grinder, drum player, etc.

Time for refreshments

Cave des Cariatides – *53 Rue Sieyès* – ☎ *04 94 53 99 67* – *Jul-Aug: Tue-Sat 8am-7.30pm, Sun 8am-12.30pm, Mon 2-7pm; Sep-Jun: daily 8am-12.30pm, 2-7pm*. This wine cellar was named after the two stone atlantes flanking the 17C door and supporting the portico of the house formerly belonging to Abbot Sieyes. He was responsible for the coup of 18 Brumaire in 1799.

La Maison de la Bière – *Boulevard de la Libération* – ☎ *04 94 51 21 86* – *Jul-Aug: daily 8am-4am; Oct and Mar-Jun: daily 8am-1am; Nov-Feb: Tue-Thu and Sun 8am-8pm, Fri-Sat until 1am*. A selection of 250 different beers are available to clients in this bar, together with over 30 brands of whisky. Wide choice of cocktails and ice-cream flavours too. You can sip your drink on the terrace facing out to sea.

Las Veglaces – Chez Angelo – *493 Boulevard de la Libération* – ☎ *04 94 51 29 74* – *Jul-Aug: daily 10am-4am; Sep-Jun: Wed-Mon 10am-11pm*. The delicious ice-cream made by Angelo comes in a variety of unusual flavours such as liquorice, treets or frozen yogurt. After tucking into a pot of ice-cream, walk down to no 473 of the same street and you will discover another facet of Angelo's personality – that of a dedicated guitar player!

Witches Pub – *93 Boulevard Séverin-Decuers* – ☎ *04 94 53 89 58* – *Mon-Sat 6pm-1am.* Typical Anglo-Saxon pub, complete with its hushed, cosy ambience, its dartboard, billiards table and beer or cider drinkers grouped around wooden casks. It is a pity that the pub should be so far from the beach, in a remote area away from the bustling town centre.

Transport

Parking – The town centre has several car parks. You need to pay to get into the ones on Place Agricola and Place Paul-Vernet. However, the one at Porte d'Orée is free (access via Avenue Aristide-Briant).

Buses – *Information and tickets on Place Paul-Vernet* – ☎ *04 94 53 78 46.* The 12 lines of Esterel Bus serve the town of Fréjus and the surrounding area (St-Tropez, Roquebrune, St-Aygulf, etc.).

Sightseeing

Small tourist train – ☎ *04 93 41 31 09* – *Jun-Sep 10am-noon, 2-8pm.* In summer, this charming little train will take you on a tour of the city, starting out from the Esplanade des Arènes.

Shopping

Cave Coopérative La Fréjusienne – *168 Rue Henri-Vadon* – ☎ *04 94 51 01 81* – *Closed Sun and at lunch.* Tasting sessions and sale of Côtes-de-Provence and Pays du Var wines.

Markets – Wednesdays and Saturdays in the old quarter. Tuesdays and Fridays on Place de la Poste in St-Aygulf.

Leisure activities

CIP Port Fréjus – *Aire de Carénage* – *Port Fréjus Est* – ☎ *04 94 52 34 99* – *Jun-Sep: daily 9am-noon, 2-7pm; Oct-May: daily 9am-noon, 2-5pm.* A deep-sea diving centre for both beginners and experienced swimmers will take you round the celebrated shipwrecks dotted along the Var coastline. An unusual outing indeed!

Aquatica – *RN 98* – *Le Capou* – ☎ *04 94 51 82 51* – *parc-aquatica.com* – *Early Jun to mid-Sep: daily 10am-6pm; Jul-Aug: daily 10am-7pm.* Water sports enthusiasts will love this theme park, with its amazing waterslides "Twin-Twister" and "White Hole", its swimming-pool with waves (the biggest in Europe) and its dodgem games with large rubber rings. Visitors in search of peace and quiet can play miniature golf or have a meal at the restaurant.

Marina – *Harbour authority* – ☎ *04 94 82 63 00.* The 220m/722ft pier can accommodate more than 750 boats.

Base Nature – *Boulevard de la Mer* – ☎ *04 94 51 91 10* – *Mon-Fri 8.30am-10;30pm, 1.30-15.15pm; Sat-Sun 3* . This nature park welcomes ramblers, cyclists (80ha/198 acres) as well as bathers over a 2km/1.2 stretch of beach. Additional activities include sand-yachting, flying kites, playing *boules* and roller-skating.

Les Ailes de l'Argens – *Quartier de la Plaine* – ☎ *04 94 17 09 33* – *Daily Jun-Sep 8am-9pm; Oct-May 8am-7pm.* This club organises maiden flights in micro-lite aircraft.

Luna Park – *RN 98* – ☎ *04 94 51 00 31.* Treat your children to some of the 40 attractions in this amusement park. Free car park. No charge.

A WALK THROUGH THE OLD CITY *45min on foot*

Starting from Place Formigé, walk north towards Rue Jean-Jaurès.

Rue de Fleury crosses the cathedral close; at the end *(n° 92 right)* there is a handsome doorway in green serpentine from the Maures.
In Rue Jean-Jaurès *(left)* the old 18C town hall *(n° 112)* features an unusual façade embellished with a curved balcony and a loggia supported on columns. The street follows the line of the medieval ramparts.
The doorway *(n° 53 Rue Sieyès)* framed by two 17C stone atlantes is all that remains of the former mansion of Abbé Sieyès.
Rue Grisolle follows the line of the medieval enclosure; there is a handsome round tower *(n° 71)* and a medieval façade *(n° 84 right).*
The picturesque **Passage du Portalet** *(at the end of the street)* connects a string of little old squares.

From Place Paul-Vernet return to Place Formigé.

★★ CATHEDRAL CLOSE ⏱ *allow 45min*

This fortified unit comprised the cathedral *(right)*, the cloisters *(opposite, no access)* and annexes, the baptistery *(left)* and the bishop's palace.

From Place Formigé go down a few steps beneath the cathedral porch until you come to the stairway into the cloisters.

Portal – Under an ogee arch are two **panels★** carved in the 16C to illustrate scenes from the life of the Virgin, St Peter and St Paul, portraits and military motifs.

★★ **Baptistery** – *Guided tours only.* This baptistery, one of the oldest buildings in France, is thought to date back to the 5C. Separated from the cathedral by the porch, it has a square external appearance with sides about 11m/36ft long. The octagonal-shaped interior features alternate curved and rectangular niches separated by black granite columns. These are topped by capitals of marble taken from Fréjus' ancient forum. Excavations have uncovered the original white marble pavement and the piscina.

A wrought-iron grille, given by Cardinal de Fleury, tutor and minister to Louis XV, who was at one time Bishop of Fréjus, leads to the baptistery. Formerly the two doors on either side of the grille were used: by the lower door the candidates for baptism entered and, after being baptised by the bishop, left by the upper, triumphal door as new Christians. Clad in a white tunic, they then went to the cathedral, attended full Mass for the first time and received their first Communion. Baptism was often administered to adults. It is believed that the bishop originally washed the feet of candidates in an earthenware basin *(dolium)* found in the ground. Then immersion took place in the octagonal font set up in the centre of the baptistery. A curtain, fixed to columns, surrounded the font. Unction was then administered on the head with holy oil.

Cloisters and garden

★ **Cathedral** – The cathedral is dedicated to Our Lady (south aisle) and to St Stephen (north aisle), and is an early example of Gothic art in Provence. Some parts of the building may date back to an earlier basilica.

The porch supporting the 16C belfry was erected 200 years later. Over the apse rises the battlemented tower which once defended the episcopal palace. In the 12C the north aisle was heavily restored and covered by a semicircular vault while in the 13C the nave was roofed with pointed vaulting resting on massive square pillars.

The lovely **choir stalls** date from the 15C and the high altar of white marble from the 18C. There are also two 14C tombs; the **altarpiece of St Margaret** above the sacristy door is attributed to the Nice artist **Jacques Durandi**, and at the end of the aisle, near the tombs of the bishops of Camelin (17C), is a remarkable Renaissance crucifix in wood.

★★ **Cloisters** – The 12C-13C cloisters were intended for the chapter canons and comprised two storeys; only one upper gallery remains. The ground level clerestory is formed by a series of twin columns of white marble with varied capitals. The groined

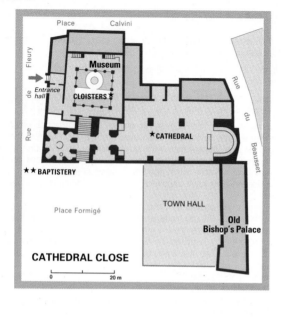

vaults which once covered the galleries were replaced by a pinewood ceiling with exposed beams, decorated in the 15C with curious little **painted panels★** of animals, chimerae, grotesques and characters from the Apocalypse. On the first floor the columns are finer and the arches round; on the ground floor the arches are pointed – such variations are often found in the architecture of Provence. In the garth there is a well. The west gallery is flanked by a once fortified building, where the monks lodged.

Archeological Museum – *First floor*. This museum presents a fine collection of Gallo-Roman antiquities recovered from the Fréjus excavations. Particularly outstanding are a rare Roman mosaic with floral motifs and geometrical designs found undamaged, a two-headed Hermes in marble (uncovered in 1970), a head of Jupiter (1C BC) and several statues in marble and bronze.

STAYING IN FREJUS

Port-Fréjus

In 1989, after 10 years' work, Fréjus paid tribute to its long-standing maritime traditions by opening a yachting harbour. The complex, whose architecture was inspired by the work of the Italian architect Palladio, recalls the town's Roman origins and offers a full range of services and accommodation. The different areas are joined by gangways which are the scene in summer of much colourful and lively activity. In the shelter of a breakwater (220m/240yd long) there are berths for more than 750 boats. Work presently underway, together with access to a future canal, will provide an additional 1 000 moorings.

⚓ **Fréjus-Plage** – The magnificent beach of fine sand that extends this new area runs several miles to the west of St-Raphaël. Beside the sea stands a memorial recalling the sacrifice of Senegalese infantrymen (L'Armée Noire).

★ **Parc Zoologique** ⊙ – *5km/3mi. From Fréjus take Avenue de Verdun (N 7) west. Turn right onto D 4. After 3km/2mi bear right onto a narrow road which crosses the motorway.*
📷 The Zoological Park covers about 20ha/49 acres in the foothills of the Esterel Massif. Visitors may walk or drive beneath the umbrella pines, cork-oaks and olive trees to observe a great variety of birds (pink flamingoes, vultures and parrots) and many wild animals (African elephants, zebras, primates such as lemurs etc). Animal training shows.

UNUSUAL OUTINGS

Souvenirs of the Navy

In 1910 Fréjus resumed an active military role with the creation of the first air and sea base in France, where Roland Garros became famous. At the beginning of the First World War this became a centre for colonial troups from Africa and Asia who established a rest and recreation base here. Fréjus thus became the principal naval base in France. The different cultures represented in the armies at that time have left a legacy of exotic buildings.
On 23 September 1913 the pilot **Roland Garros** took off from the naval air base at Fréjus in a Morane-Saulnier seaplane to make the first air crossing of the Mediterranean between Fréjus and Bizerte in just over 8 hours.

Mosquée de Missiri – *Leave Fréjus by Avenue de Verdun, then proceed towards Fayence on D 4. After 3km/2mi turn left. The mosque is currently undergoing restoration.*

In a pine wood *(left)* stands a large ochre Sudanese mosque, built in the 1920s by Senegalese soldiers from the naval camp. It is a concrete replica of the celebrated Missiri de Djenné mosque in Mali and consists of a central courtyard with a first-floor gallery around which one can walk, despite the rather dilapidated appearance of the building. Two false termite mounds have been raised nearby to create an impression of Africa.

Continue in the same direction. 1km/0.6mi after D 4 joins motorway A 8, past the bridge, on the right.

Musée des Troupes de Marine ⊘ – This museum is attractively housed in a modern building and contains fine collections of objects and documents arranged in chronological order to retrace the history of the Marine Corps which, since 1622, have played a decisive role both overseas and in world wars. The expeditions during the great colonial period from the Second Empire (1852-70) to 1914 (Africa, Indochina, Madagascar) are recreated using a collection of pieces of equipment, arms, pennants and local crafts, as well as many illustrations (watercolours, drawings, photographs). There are many personal belongings of General Galliéni, including his study in Indochina and the car which he used in Madagascar from 1900 to 1905. On the first floor a table in rare wood inlaid with mother-of-pearl features a map of Hanoi in 1906 as well as the famous "zinc palm" from Djibouti.

In the crypt are buried unknown marines from the Infantry Division who fell when fighting the Bavarians at Bazeilles (Ardennes) in 1870.

Take Avenue du Quinzième-Corps and then Avenue du Général-Callies towards Nice. Turn right after the roundabout. Leave car in the car park midway between the two monuments. Leave the car in the car park and continue on foot.

Mémorial des Guerres en Indochine ⊘ – At the foot of a hill this imposing circular necropolis symbolically faces the sea.

Since 1987, the remains of 24 000 soldiers and civilians who died in active service in former Indochina have been repatriated and gathered here. The bodies of soldiers are housed in a vast colombarium while unidentified casualties lie in an ossuary in the crypt. In the historical room, in front of the necropolis, the events and battles in the history of Indochina are displayed. Illuminated maps and models are used to describe the geographical locations of these events.

Pagode Bouddhique Hông Hiên ⊘ – This Buddhist pagoda stands in the centre of an Asian garden. The pagoda was built in 1917 by Vietnamese soldiers who had come to fight in France, then restored and extended during the 1970s. Traditional Vietnamese architecture was the inspiration for the building and the statues in the park are arranged in accordance with Buddhist tradition. The grounds surrounding the pagoda are planted with exotic flowers, including some superb lotus, and contains impressive representations of sacred animals and guardian spirits (dragons, white elephants...).

Missiri Mosque, Fréjus

E. Baret/MICHELIN

161

EXCURSIONS

5km/3mi south of Fréjus on N 98.

St-Aygulf – The resort of St-Aygulf is shaded by pines, cork and holm oaks; from the beach of fine sand, ringed with rocks, there is an attractive view of Fréjus Bay and Les Issambres.

Beyond St-Aygulf extends a beautiful **panorama** of the plain of the Lower Argens which separates the Maures from the Esterel. The magnificent rocks of Roquebrune Mountain stand out from the Maures Massif while in the Esterel chain, behind the Dramont semaphore, one can make out the summit of Cap Roux.

To the left the road runs alongside the **Aquatica** ⊘ water sports park *(see above)*, before leading into Fréjus.

Chapelle Notre-Dame-de-Jérusalem ⊘ – This tiny chapel, situated in the Tour de Mare district near N 7, was the last building to be designed by Jean Cocteau. He had finalised the layout and the interior decor as early as 1961 but the chapel remained unfinished until after the poet's death in 1963. It was completed in 1965, thanks to Édouard Dermit.

Remains of Malpasset Dam – *From Fréjus follow signs to "Nice par l'autoroute A 8". At the last roundabout before the motorway sliproad, take D 37 signposted "Barrage de Malpasset" for 5km/3mi. Park the car under the motorway viaduct; 1hr on foot there and back.*

🚶 The footpath leading off from the barrier goes up the Reyran Valley through sparse *garrigue* vegetation and huge scattered blocks of concrete, which were torn off the dam.

The dam is an arch dam, built in 1954 with a capacity of 49 million m^3/1 730 million cu ft. It was intended to relieve the scarce water supplies in the Var coastal region during the summer months. On the evening of 2 December 1959 the torrential rains of previous weeks reached the danger limit of the dam and caused the abutments of the arch to collapse. Within 20 minutes, a 55m/180ft high wave had surged through Fréjus, claiming 400 victims.

The footpath carries on down to the bottom of the valley, leading to the foot of the dam. From here, the size of the breach in the dam's arch makes a striking impression. The turbine is still in the middle of it.

Another viewpoint can be found by going up a footpath which forks to the left of the first one; a little lookout point overlooks the remains of the dam and the west side of the valley.

Étangs de Villepey – *5km/3mi. From Fréjus take N 98 west towards St-Tropez. Compulsory parking on the premises (fee charged at the entrance).*

These pools are fed by both sea water and by freshwater streams. The Coastal Authorities (Conservatoire du Littoral) are in the process of developing the area as a reserve. A great variety of vegetation is visible: reed-beds in the centre, umbrella pine groves in the south and brackish stretches along N 98. In this protected environment more than 200 species of birds, mostly migrants, are thriving. Spring is the best time to see pink flamingoes, grey herons and egrets. Among the nesting birds are several pairs of bee-eaters.

Bagnols-en-Forêt – *29km/17mi N. Leave Fréjus by D4 travelling towards Fayence.* Beyond the Pic de la Gardette, this charming hilltop village appears before your eyes as you round a bend. The main square is shaded by plane trees and the steep streets, some of them covered, give this town a special feeling of authenticity. Abandoned by the inhabitants in the 14C, it was empty until 1447 when a group of Italian immigrants from Liguria. Once the town was busy with the manufacture of millstones for making oil, but today it is better knows as a departure point for discovering the **forêt domaniale de Saint-Paul★**. There are many inviting paths under the cork-oak trees.

★Rocher de Roquebrune – *Round tour of 29km/18mi – allow 1hr 30min. From Fréjus take Avenue de Verdun, then N 7 west. After about 10km/6mi – turn left onto D 7 to Roquebrune-sur-Argens. For a description of the tour see ROQUE-BRUNE-SUR-ARGENS.*

La GARDE-FREINET

Population 1 619
Michelin map 84 fold 17, 114 fold 36 or 245 fold 48
Local map see Massif des MAURES

In the heart of the Maures Massif, between the Argens Valley and St-Tropez Bay, lies La Garde-Freinet (once called Le Fraxinet). It is a flourishing craft centre. Local wares are displayed in the disused **Chapelle St-Éloi** ⊘ at the entrance to the village. In season the tourist office maintains an information post here.

From the surrounding forests of cork-oaks and chestnut trees comes the raw material for the manufacture of bottle corks and the production of sweet chestnuts sold under the name *Marrons de Luc*. In the autumn, **chestnut festivals** are organised to celebrate the harvest. Local markets are held on Wednesdays and Sundays.

A SARACEN STRONGHOLD

Owing to its strategic location La Garde-Freinet suffered over a century of occupation by the Saracens. In local tradition the name Saracen is applied collectively to the Moors, Arabs, Turks and Berbers who harassed the country from the 8C to the 18C.

After being defeated by Charles Martel at Poitiers in 732l, the Arabs drifted down into Provence. Although driven back several times, they managed to hold on to the region around La Garde-Freinet. On the height which dominates the present village they built a fortress from which they used to descend to pillage inland Provence. It was only in 973 that Count William, the Liberator, managed to expel them.

In contrast to the damage they caused, the Saracens taught the Provençal people about medicine, how to use the bark of the cork-oak and how to extract resin from pine trees. They also introduced the flat house tile and the tambourine.

EXCURSIONS

Ruins of Fort Freinet – *1km/0.6mi – plus 45min on foot there and back. Take GR 9 on the south side of the village. Leave the car in the parking area levelled out at a bend in the road and follow the signs painted on a rock.*
There is a good view of the Le Luc Plain and the first Alpine foothills.

⬛ *A path leads first to a mission cross (Croix des Maures) and then climbs quite steeply to the fortress ruins.*

The ruins of the feudal castle attributed to the Saracens blended in for many years with the rocky site. Excavation work carried out has resulted in the discovery and uncovering of the foundations of a 15C fortified village. From the summit, the **panorama**★ extends out to sea and a long way inland.

Take the path running along the moat, leading back to the village. Or go back to the car park and follow the forest track for 5km/3mi until you reach the sign for Roches Blanches.

★ **Panorama des Roches Blanches** – At this spot, known as White Rocks *(for access, walk round the barrier)*, there is a view in all directions: *(left)* Garde-Freinet Forest and the valley of the River Argens, *(right)* over the slopes of the north Maures and *(east)* the bay of St-Tropez.

GOURDON★

Population 379
Michelin map 84 fold 8, 115 fold 24 or 245 fold 37

Gourdon "the Saracen" was built on a remarkable **site**★★ on a rocky spur *(see Perched Villages in the Introduction p 80)* more than 500m/1 640ft above the River Loup. The old houses have been restored and converted into boutiques and workshops.

AN OUTSTANDING VIEWPOINT

★★ **Panorama** – There is a magnificent panorama from the small church square with a 50km/30mi radius covering the coast from the mouth of the Var to Cap Roux and from the Esterel Massif inland to Pic de Courmettes, beneath which the Loup,

Gardens and parc of the château

163

THE OLD OVEN

Au Vieux Four – *Rue Basse (in the village)* – ☎ *04 93 09 68 60 – Closed 5-19 Jun, 5 Nov-7 Jan and Sat –* ✍ *– Reservation recommended- 14.94/16.46€.* This is the perfect stopping-place to round off your visit of the village. The young couple who run the place prepare delicious Provençal food and grilled meat in an open fireplace before your eyes. Simple, refreshing decoration and reasonable prices.

PROVENCE À LA CARTE

Taverne Provençale – *Place de l'Église* – ☎ *04 93 09 68 22 – Closed 3-28 Jan, 12 Nov-17 Dec and Wed except Jul-Sep – 16.77/25.15€.* Settle on the terrace and admire the superb views of the heights beyond Nice, as well as those of the Mediterranean. This Provençal bistro serves French cuisine according to tradition: trout, coq au vin, guinea fowl with mushrooms...

La Source Parfumée – ☎ *04 93 09 20 00.* ♿ The former distillery and blossoming fields may be visited by appointment.

a lively mountain stream, emerges from the upper gorge and winds its way to the coast.

Château ⊙ – The old fortress of Gourdon, built in the 13C on the foundations of an old Saracen fortress and restored in the 17C, contains architectural features of the Saracens (vaulted rooms), of the Tuscans of the 14C and of the Renaissance (doorway at the far end on the main courtyard).

Musée Historique – The Museum of History occupies the castle's ground floor. The entrance hall contains a fine collection of arms and armour. The imposing fireplace in the dining room is 14C and the furniture 17C.

In the drawing room the furniture is 16C; there is an Aubusson tapestry, a secretaire which belonged to Marie-Antoinette, a *Self-Portrait* by Rembrandt and a fine 1500 painting from the Cologne School: **St Ursula**.

The chapel contains a 16C triptych, a *Descent from the Cross* from Rubens' studio, a *Golgotha* by the Flemish School and a polychrome wood sculpture of St Sebastian by El Greco.

The guard-room contains a collection of 16C and 17C oriental arms.

In Henry IV's Tower, the documents on show bear the Royal Seal; an opening in the floor reveals the former dungeon.

★**Musée de Peinture Naïve** – Seven rooms on the second floor are hung with an exceptional collection of Naive paintings covering the period 1925-70, including a Douanier-Rousseau (portrait). Also represented are the French artists Séraphine, Bauchant, Vivin, Lefranc, Caillaud, Fous, Rimbert, Bombois and Lagru, the Croat artist Rabuzin, Kovacic and Vecenaj (all from the Hlebine School, Croatia); the American O'Brady; the Belfian Greff and the Spaniard Vivancos.

Gardens – The terraced gardens were designed by Le Nôtre and laid out on three levels. They have now been made into a botanical centre, preserving typical flora of the Pre-Alps. From the upper terrace the **view**★★ is similar to that described from the church square.

GRASSE★

Population 43 874
Michelin map 84 fold 8, 115 fold 14 or 245 fold 37

Grasse enjoys a privileged location, nestled at the foot of the high limestone plateaux overlooking the fragrant plains that have brought it fame and riches. There are broad views from the modern town with its terraced houses and split-level gardens, while below in the old Provençal town narrow alleys are linked by steep ramps or steps that wind between houses four, or even five, storeys tall.

HISTORICAL NOTES

A Small Republic (12C) – In the Middle Ages, Grasse was a tiny republic, administered by a council whose members called themselves "Consuls by the Grace of God". This regime was based on the Italian model and had diplomatic relations with Pisa and Genoa. By way of Cannes, it exported soap, oil and tanned skins to these cities; in exchange it received raw hides and arms. Raymond Bérenger, Count of Provence, put an end to this independent existence in 1227.

A Great Provençal Poet – Bellaud de la Bellaudière (1532-88), a soldier-poet, was born and died in Grasse although he lived mainly in Aix, Marseille and Avignon. His work, inspired by Rabelais and Petrarch, is both tender and vigorous and briefly revived the Provençal language in literature between the troubadours (12C) and Mistral (19C).

Jean-Honoré Fragonard, Child of Grasse (1732-1806) – Fragonard's father, a tanner and glove-maker, tried to make his son a lawyer's clerk rather than an artisan, but the young man was possessed by the urge to draw and left for Paris. He painted with Chardin and then Boucher. Winner of the Prix de Rome by the age of 20, he achieved great renown but the Revolution deprived him of his fashionable clientele and dictated a more severe style of painting.

Despite the protection of the artist David, Fragonard preferred to leave Paris and seek refuge in Grasse with his friend Maubert. Fragonard had brought with him five of his finest canvases, painted for Mme du Barry, who on a capricious whim had refused them. He sold them to his host for a minute sum.

Over the years the painter grew bored with Grasse and returned to Paris, where he led a frugal, if carefree, existence.

One hot afternoon in August 1806 this elderly artist entered a café and ordered an ice-cream before succumbing to a stroke.

An 18C Winter Resort – During the winter of 1807-08 the gay and impetuous Princess Pauline Bonaparte, separated from her husband, Prince Borghese, and on bad terms with her brother, the emperor, came to Grasse to seek relief from family worries and regain her strength in a warm climate. Every day she was carried in a sedan chair to a grove of holm oaks, which she particularly liked and which is now known as her garden: "Jardin de la Princesse Pauline". Later, Queen Victoria spent several winters in Grasse at the Grand Hotel and at the Rothschild property.

Napoleon's Passage (2 March 1815) – After the cool welcome he received in Cannes, the Emperor decided to take the Alpine road (Route des Alpes) via Grenoble and advanced on Grasse, but perhaps because of fear of a hostile demonstration from the populace, the Emperor skirted the town on what is now known as Boulevard du Jeu-de-Ballon. The "Plateau Napoléon" carries his name although he is believed to have camped there for barely one hour.

A KALEIDOSCOPE OF FRAGRANCES

The Perfume Industry – Grasse had long specialised in leather work and glove making when perfumed gloves came into fashion in the 16C. This was the beginning of the perfume industry. The great *parfumeries* were born in the 18C and 19C and still enjoy an international reputation.

There are three manufacturing processes: distillation, *enfleurage* and extraction. **Distillation** is the oldest process. Flowers and water are brought to boiling point in a still. The water and essence are condensed in a "florentine" flask where they separate owing to the difference in density and to their insolubility.

In the 18C **enfleurage** was invented. It uses the property that animal fats have of absorbing the scent of flowers. Fresh flowers are repeatedly laid on different layers of animal fat; washing with alcohol separates the perfume from the fats; a pomade is obtained. Few firms use the process nowadays, as it is labour-intensive.

The latest process is **extraction** by which the flowers yield their perfume in its most concentrated form. The flowers are brought into contact with a solvent which is then evaporated. A concretion *(concrète)* is thus obtained, consisting of perfume and wax. One tonne of Grasse jasmine blossoms yields 3kg/6.6lb of concretion. The wax is removed using alcohol and the 40% which remains is called absolute *(absolue de concrète)*.

The essences produced in Grasse, which are the base material of the perfume industry, are used locally or sent to Paris where the great perfume houses blend them according to secret formulas to produce the fascinating creations for which France is famous throughout the world.

The Grasse perfume industry has now diversified and has started the production of food flavourings.

★ **Musée International de la Parfumerie** ⊘ – This museum is devoted to one of the most famous activities in Grasse. It occupies three buildings of different periods: a mansion with a neo-Classical façade from the time of Napoleon III and two late-19C buildings. The exhibits cover more than 3 000 years in the history of perfume-making throughout the world.

The ground floor, set up like a perfume factory, presents the different techniques used to make perfume from the extraction of the sweet-smelling raw materials to the end product, with machines and explanatory panels. On the mezzanine is the research laboratory. Exhibited on the first floor are different kinds of perfume vessels (flasks, scent bottles...), boxes, chests, and posters which indicate man's

Eating out

MID-RANGE

Le Gazan – *3 Rue Gazan – Closed 15 Dec-5 Jan, Mon evening, Tue evening, Wed evening, Thu evening off season. and Sun –* ☎ *04 93 36 22 88 – 14.48€ lunch – 18.29/44.21€.* Two delightful dining rooms with rustic furniture, linked by a spiral staircase, provide the setting for a succulent meal seasoned with local olive oil and aromatic herbs. Warm, friendly welcome and good service in this restaurant in the old quarter of Grasse.

Arnaud – *10 Place Foux –* ☎ *04 93 36 44 88 – Closed 7-15 Jan, Nov school holidays and Sun – 20.58€.* Treat yourself to the speciality of the house - the homemade ravioli and *gnocchi* lovingly prepared by the owner's mother. Meals are served in a small vaulted cellar, on the noisy side when the restaurant is crowded. Reasonably priced lunches.

Where to stay

MODERATE

Pension Ste-Thérèse – *39 Avenue Y.-E.-Baudoin –* ☎ *04 93 36 10 29 –* 🅿 *– Restaurant for hotel patrons only – 31 rooms: 25.92/41.16€ –* ☕ *4.57€ – Restaurant 12€.* A humble establishment overlooking the city of Grasse. Peace and quiet are guaranteed in the sparsely decorated rooms, which exude old-fashioned charm. Some command pretty views of the coastline. Provençal fabric adds a lively touch to the dining room.

MID-RANGE

Hôtel Victoria – *7 Avenue Riou-Blanquet –* ☎ *04 93 40 30 30 – hotel.le.victoria@wanadoo.fr – Closed 3 Jan-6 Feb –* 🅿 *– 49 rooms: 46/75€ –* ☕ *6.50€ – Restaurant 18/23€.* Handsome turn-of-the-century residence commanding outstanding views of both Grasse and the sea beyond. Large comfortable rooms, pleasant lounges, a panoramic terrace, a brightly coloured dining hall and outdoor pool all make for an extremely pleasant stay. Themed evenings and other events can be organised.

Chambre d'Hôte Mas de Clairefontaine – *3196 Route de Draguignan – 06530 Le Tignet – 10km/6mi SE of Grasse on Route de Draguignan –* ☎ *04 93 66 39 69 – www.masdeclairefontaine.online.fr –* ✉ *– 3 rooms: 68.60/76.22€.* A stone cottage surrounded by a terraced garden dotted with umbrella pines and reeds is the charming backcloth to your stay at Mas de Clairefontaine. The rooms are tastefully appointed and the service of excellent standard. The terrace, shaded by a century-old oak tree, is the perfect place to relax after a tiring excursion!

Transports

Parking – ☎ *04 92 60 91 17.* There are 5 car parks in the town centre (1hr costs 1.22€). Season tickets are available (3 days, 1 week, 1 month).

Buses – *Bus station at the Notre-Dame-des-Fleurs car park -* ☎ *04 93 36 37 37.* The city is served by 12 lines.

Small tourist train – ♿ *Apr to end of Sep guided tours with commentary (45min) 10am-6pm (Apr to mid-Jun daily except Sun).* The train leaves from Cours Honoré-Cresp, stops on the heights of Grasse and ends its trip at Parc de la Princesse-Pauline. 4.57€.

Aromas Galore

Usine Fragonard – *20 Boulevard Fragonard –* ☎ *04 93 36 44 65. Feb-Oct guided tours (30min) 9am-6.30pm; Nov-Jan 9am-noon, 2-6pm. No charge.* Introductory course on "The Essence of Aromas" (Absolus Aromatiques) on request.

Fragonard-La Fabrique des Fleurs – *Carrefour des Quatre-Chemins – Route de Cannes –* ☎ *04 93 77 94 30.* Same times as above.

Parfumerie Molinard – *60 Boulevard Victor-Hugo –* ☎ *04 93 36 01 62. Guided tours May-Sep 9am-6pm; Oct-Apr 9am-0.30pm, 2-6pm. No charge. There are courses on how to create perfumes: 250F.* Visitors are explained the successive stages in the making of a perfume.

Usine Galimard – *73 Route de Cannes (going towards Mouans-Sartoux) –* ☎ *04 93 09 20 00 – www.galimard.com – Guided tours Apr-Oct 9am-6.30pm; Nov-Mar 9am-noon, 2-6pm. No charge.*

Galimard-Studio des Fragrances – *5 Route de Pégomas –* ☎ *04 93 09 20 00 - www.galimard.com – Course (2hr) on perfume-making. Daily by appointment 33.54€.*

It's a Gamble

Casino – *Boulevard du Jeu-de-Ballon –* ☎ *04 93 36 91 00.* Come here to indulge in a spot of gambling (roulette, blackjack etc). The café is open from 8.30pm to 2am. There are musical evenings at weekends. Package formulas available (casino, dinner and transport).

involvement with perfume, and other fragrance-related products (toiletries, cosmetics...) through the ages; famous names are evoked: Guerlain, Patou, Lanvin, Chanel... Note the travel accessories belonging to Marie-Antoinette.

A greenhouse on the terrace contains many different local and tropical plants used in the manufacture of perfume.

Perfumeries ⓥ – Usine Fragonard *(20 Boulevard Fragonard)* and Fragonard-La Fabrique des Fleurs *(Carrefour des Quatre Chemins, Route de Cannes)*; Usine Galimard *(73 Route de Cannes)* and Galimard-Studio des Fragrances *(5 Route de Pégomas)*; Molinard *(60 Boulevard Victor-Hugo)*. These three perfume factories are open to the public and give a general idea of the manufacturing process. In spring and summer, Fragonard and Molinard will take you round their lovely **flower fields**. The Domaine de Manon allows access to its rose garden *(May-June)* and jasmine fields *(July-November). See above for admission times.*

Old town

★ STROLLING THROUGH THE OLD TOWN *allow 2hr*

Leave the car in the car park on Cours Honoré-Cresp and take Rue Jean-Ossola, continued by Rue Marcel-Journet. Turn right into Rue Gazan and walk on until you reach Place du Puy.

Cathedral Notre-Dame-du-Puy – The cathedral dates back to the late 10C-11C but was restored and remodelled in the 17C; the double staircase at the entrance, with its wide stone handrail, and the two crypts were added on in the 18C. Note the panels of the main door (1721) in the façade, adorned with horizontal bands and arcading. The high narrow nave, with heavy pointed rib-vaulting, marks the beginning of the Gothic style in Provence; together with the robust round pillars it gives a grandiose air to the whole building. The organ (1855) is by Junk of Toulouse. In the south aisle there are three **paintings**★ by Rubens *(The Crown of Thorns, Crucifixion* and *St Helen in Exaltation of the Holy Cross)* executed in Rome in 1601 and offered to the town in the 19C by a generous patron; a fine **triptych** attributed to Louis Bréa depicting St Honoratus between St Clement and St Lambert; the *Mystic Marriage of St Catherine* by Sébastien Bourdon (17C); finally, **The Washing of the Feet**, one of the few religious canvases to be painted by Fragonard.

Place du 24-Août – From the far side of the square, the chevet and bell-tower of the cathedral can be seen to good effect. There is also a fine **view** eastwards over the Grasse countryside. Close at hand is the Clock Tower (Tour de l'Horloge).

Return to Place du Petit-Puy.

Tour de Guet – The town hall, formerly the Bishop's Palace, boasts a massive square watchtower in red tufa stone, dating from the 12C and bearing an inscription in memory of the poet Bellaud de la Bellaudière.

Place aux Aires – At the centre stands an elegant three-tiered **fountain**. The old houses bordering the square are built over uneven arcades. **Hôtel Isnard** on the north side, a town house built in 1781, has a fine door and an attractive wrought-iron balcony at first-floor level. Every morning there is a lively, colourful **flower and vegetable market** in progress beneath the aged lotus trees.

Rue Amiral-de-Grasse – Fontmichel House (no 18) was built in the 17C.

★ **Place du Cours** – This fine terraced promenade offers a charming **view★** over the cultivated and wooded countryside, which rolls gently towards the sea; the huge **fountain** dates from the Revolution; a monument to Fragonard stands in the small square where Promenade and Boulevard du Jeu-de-Ballon meet.

Jardin de la Princesse Pauline – *Access via Avenue Thiers, Boulevard Alice-de-Rothschild and Boulevard de la Reine-Jeanne.*
There is a good **panorama★** of Grasse, the Massif du Tanneron, the Esterel and the coast from the viewing table in Princess Pauline's garden.

Parc Communal de la Corniche – *Access as above; then turn a sharp left on Boulevard Bellevue and then right on Boulevard du Président-Kennedy; 30min on foot there and back.*
🔼 At the bend, a path to the right *(sign)* leads to the edge of the steep Pre-Alps of Grasse.
From the lookout point, the **view★★** extends from the Baou of St-Jeannet and from the Tanneron mountains to the peaks of the Esterel; on the horizon can also be seen the bays of La Napoule and Juan and the Îles de Lérins.

SIGHTS

★ **Musée d'Art et d'Histoire de Provence** ⊙ – The museum is in an 18C mansion erected by Louise de Mirabeau, sister of the tribune Mirabeau, when she married the Marquis de Cabris. The mansion, called "Petit Trianon", was planned and decorated by the Marquise with a view to entertaining on a grand scale, but all she ever experienced there were days troubled by court actions and family scenes.

A "nose" at work

B. Kaufmann/MICHELIN

This museum provides a remarkable compendium of the art and history of eastern Provence.

Ground floor – Pottery (18C-19C) from Apt and Le Castellet is displayed in the entrance hall. Some rooms are decorated in the style of Louis XIV and Louis XV. There are two rooms devoted to paintings: one to 19C Provençal artists (Chabaud, Camoin) and the other to reconstructed scenes of life in Grasse in the 18C and 19C.

Basement – On view are the reconstructed kitchen of the Cabris Mansion, fine pieces of Moustiers faience and ceramics from Biot and Vallauris. One room contains Provençal cribs and *santons*, and cherubs which once adorned altarpieces. Another features the Gallo-Roman period: pediment from a 4C funerary monument, lamps, flasks, jars. The archeological section evokes the daily life of local people from Prehistoric times to the late Middle Ages; the display includes objects used during burial rites and in peasant life from day to day. The exhibits were unearthed in local excavations.

Villa-Musée Fragonard ⊙ – In this elegant country house Fragonard took refuge during the Revolution, when it belonged to Maubert, a local glove-maker and perfumer. It now belongs to the municipality and serves as a cultural centre and museum devoted to a whole family of artists. A fine park surrounds it.
One of the ground-floor rooms contains copies (originals in the Frick Collection in New York City) of the panels painted by Fragonard between 1771 and 1772 and originally commissioned by the Duchesse du Barry. The stairwell is decorated with Republican and Masonic allegories executed in *trompe-l'œil* and monochrome by the artist's son, **Alexandre-Évariste Fragonard** (1780-1850) at the age of 14.
Upstairs the **Fragonard Room★** displays a broad spectrum of his works: original drawings and etchings, sketches, paintings – two self-portraits, *Landscape with Washerwomen, The White Bull* and *The Three Graces*. In a room on the left works by

GRASSE

Alexandre-Évariste are displayed, including *Reading the Bible* after Greuze. Another gallery is devoted to a grandson, **Théophile Fragonard** (1806-76): *Embarkation for Cythera* and *Visiting the Sick*. There are also canvases by Marguerite Gérard (1761-1837), Fragonard's pupil and sister-in-law *(Portrait of a Girl)*.

Musée de la Marine ⊘ – Housed in five vaulted rooms in the Hôtel Pontevès-Morel, the Marine Museum retraces the distinguished career of **Admiral de Grasse**, who was born at Bar-sur-Loup *(See BAR-SUR-LOUP)*, and his involvement in the American War of Independence. Among the 29 models of ships are 18C sailing ships, a Maltese galley, the flagship *La Ville de Paris* (Washington and Lafayette came on board on 17 September 1781), and the cruiser *De Grasse*, decommissioned in 1974.

Musée Provençal du Costume et du Bijou ⊘ – These private collections housed in an annexe of the Fragonard perfumery focus on women's clothing during the 18C. Peasants' robes, weavers' skirts and middle-class finery are on show alongside a series of crosses and curious ornaments made out of sea fossils (étoiles de Digne). A fine, interesting presentation in which all the exhibits are genuine, except for the aprons. A shop selling charming accessories rounds off the tour.

DRIVING TOURS

★★Préalpes de Grasse *Round tour of 104km/65mi – about 5hr*

From Grasse take Boulevard Georges-Clémenceau and turn left onto D 11.

After crossing the Plateau Napoléon, the road rises towards Cabris offering fine **views** of the Grasse countryside.

★**Cabris** – *See CABRIS.*

Bypass Spéracèdes by turning right onto D 513 at the beginning of the village.

From Tignet, there is a beautiful **view** of Cabris and Grasse. D 13 runs through magnificent sloping olive groves, passing the La Graou prehistoric tumulus.

St-Cézaire-sur-Siagne – From its site dominating the steep Siagne Valley, the walls and towers of this interesting village testify to its feudal past. Standing in its own churchyard is a pleasant Romanesque chapel which shelters the Gallo-Roman tomb of Julia Sempronia. From the church a marked path leads to a **viewpoint** *(viewing table)*.

Return to the village and turn left.

9 Puits de la Vierge – The road makes a detour past a group of nine wells, believed to be of Roman origin.

From St-Cézaire take D 5, turn right onto D 613 which leads to the St-Cézaire Caves.

★**Grottes de St-Cézaire** ⊙ – The caves, hollowed out of the limestone, remain at a constant temperature of 14°C/57°F. Both the stalactites, which have great musical resonance, and the stalagmites are remarkable for the variety of their shapes – toadstools, flowers, animals – and their reddish colour, which is ascribed to the presence of iron oxide in the rock. There are also beautiful rock crystallisations. The caves, which comprise several chambers with evocative names such as "Hall of Draperies", "Organ Chamber", "Fairies' Alcove" and "Great Hall", are connected by narrow passages, one of which arrives suddenly at the edge of an abyss, 40m/130ft below ground level.

Return to the crossroads on D 5.

Col de la Lèque – *5km/3mi – about 15min.* To the right of the road leading up to the pass, near Puades, there is a group of tumuli. From the pass and on the return journey there are successive **views**★ of the Siagne Gorges and the village of St-Cézaire huddled in its mountainous amphitheatre on the bluff.

Continue towards St-Cézaire-sur-Siagne and turn right onto D 105.

Gorges de la Siagne – The road runs up through the rich vegetation in the deep gorge which the waters of the Siagne have worn in the limestone.
After crossing the Siagne (from the bridge, **view** up and down the gorge), turn right onto D 656, a very steep and narrow road.
After meandering steeply above the gorge, the road broadens out into a colourful rock circus before entering a wooded valley which brings it to the plateau. Turn left onto D 56 following the hillside. Fig and olive trees grow on the terraces which are retained by low drystone walls.

At the crossroads, drive to Mons or turn left onto D 56. Cross the Siagnole.

Sources de la Siagnole – *30min on foot there and back.*
◪ On the right beyond the bridge a path leads to a very pleasant spot where several Vauclusian springs rise to form the River Siagnole.

Roche Taillée – There is a sign to indicate the remains of a Roman aqueduct *(on the left of the road)* which carried water from around the Mons area to Fréjus on the coast and is still in use. **View**★ eastwards towards Grasse.

Turn right onto D 37 and then right again onto D 563 to reach Mons.

The road is cut into the hillside high above the Siagnole Gorges. Once over the Col d'Avaye, the road offers a magnificent **view**★★ reaching as far as the Esterel.

★**Mons** – *See MONS.*
The mountainous and wooded environs of Mons give way to a barren landscape with outcrops of white rock. At Col de Valferrière (alt 1 169m/3 835ft) turn right onto N 85, the Route Napoléon.

★★Plateau de Grasse *round tour of 38km/24mi*

From Grasse take D 2085, ① on the town plan, going northeast.

The northeastern suburb of Grasse comprises attractive villas scattered among olive, cypress and orange trees.

Magagnosc – *900m/984yd – after the town signpost and immediately past the restaurant "La Petite Auberge" turn right at the sign "Église St-Laurent".*
There are two churches. **St-Laurent**, in Tuscan style, is adorned with some fine stained glass and a copy of a Byzantine fresco by the contemporary painter Robert Savary, who also decorated the walls and ceiling of **St-Michel**, the Romanesque chapel of the White Penitents.
From the churchyard there is a **view★** of the sea near Cannes and the Esterel Massif.

Return to D 2085 and at Pré-du-Lac take the first road, D 203, to Châteauneuf-de-Grasse.

Châteauneuf-de-Grasse – This elegant village perched on a promontory exudes a whiff of Provençal atmosphere with its lovely old houses grouped together on the overhang. The narrow stepped streets and the vaulted passageways are dominated by the wrought-iron campanile of the church. The interior features a lovely 18C altarpiece.

From the town head east towards Opio – a good view of the plain. At the cross-roads turn left onto D 3 and continue as far as Pré-du-Lac, turn right onto D 2210.

The picturesque **site★** of Bar-sur-Loup comes into view.

Bar-sur-Loup – *See BAR-SUR-LOUP.*
Return to Grasse via Opio, then on D 7.

GRIMAUD★

Population 3 780
Michelin map 245 fold 48, 84 fold 17 or 114 fold 50

This large perched village owes its name to the **Grimaldi family**, who once owned it. In the 10C Gibelin de Grimaldi received the fief from the Count of Provence in recognition of his help in expelling the Saracens from Provence.
Isolated from the summer bustle of the coast, the village has retained its Provençal character with its small shaded squares and fountains and its winding alleyways enlivened by the many craftsmen. *In summer, leave the car in the car park near the graveyard.*

OLD VILLAGE

Walk towards the centre of the village from the car park and take one of the lanes which leads onto Place Neuve with its remarkable monumental fountain. Rue des Templiers has fine basalt arcades and serpentine doorways, for example on the Maison des Templiers; this leads to St-Michel, a church built in the form of a cross in Romanesque style, dating from the 11C.

Château – The castle, built at the beginning of the 11C, originally consisted of three enclosures surrounded by four three-storey towers. The imposing ruins of this great building were left after the demolition ordered by Mazarin in 1655.

S. Sauvignier/MICHELIN

Port-Grimaud

From the upper covered way there are fine **views**★ of the Maures and the Golfe de St-Tropez. The castle hosts live performances on summer evenings.

On the hill in the graveyard beyond there is a charming windmill, and from there a fine **view**★ of the Golfe.

EXCURSIONS

Chapelle Notre-Dame-de-la-Queste – *3km/1.8mi towards Port-Grimaud.* This chapel, built by the monks of the abbey of St-Victor in Marseille, houses a remarkable Baroque altarpiece (1677) in gilded wood illustrated with scenes from the life of the Virgin. There is a pilgrimage here on 15 August.

★ **Port-Grimaud** – *Access: follow the signs for Port-Grimaud (Nord) – and not Port-Grimaud (Sud) – to the visitors' car park. Only residents are allowed to drive into town.* Port-Grimaud, which was designed by the architect **François Spoerry**, has a unique charm but remains as controversial as Marina Baie des Anges *(See VILLENEUVE-LOUBET)*. It looks like a Mediterranean fishing village on the north shore of St-Tropez Bay; in fact it is a modern complex of luxury housing with a fully-equipped marina and a fine beach; it provides facilities for a wide range of leisure activities.

It is pleasant to stroll through this lively village, past the coloured houses with their *trompe-l'œil* façades, covered with Roman tiles, linked by canals, narrow alleys, tiny shaded squares and neat little bridges. Public transport is available in passenger barges *(coches d'eau)* which ply the lagoon.

The **Église St-François-d'Assise** is an ecumenical church dedicated to St Francis of Assisi; it was conceived as part of the overall plan and is resolutely modern although inspired by the Provençal Romanesque style. The interior is plain; no ceiling conceals the wooden roof beams. The stained glass is by Vasarély. The tower affords a pretty **view**★ of Port-Grimaud, St-Tropez Bay and the Maures Massif.

HYÈRES★

Population 51 417
Michelin map 84 fold 16, 114 folds 46 and 47 or 245 fold 47
Local map see Massif des MAURES

Hyères, lying in a pleasantly sheltered site, is the southernmost Riviera resort; it is also the oldest as it became popular at the turn of the 20C, when it was patronised by wealthy aristocrats. The old quarters cling to the southern slope of the Castéou hillside (204m/670ft) and overlook the modern town and the anchorage enclosed by Cap Bénat and the Giens Peninsula. The new harbour is used by pleasure boats and the ferries commuting between the mainland and the Îles d'Hyères. The modern town's most outstanding features are its wide avenues flanked by magnificent palm trees.

Early history – Excavations on the coast at L'Almanarre reveal that Greeks from Marseille set up a trading station called **Olbia**, which was succeeded by a Roman town – Pomponiana – and a nunnery, called St-Pierre-d'Almanarre during the medieval period.

In the early Middle Ages the inhabitants moved further up the hill to where the lords of Fos had built a castle. Agriculture and particularly the salt marshes brought Hyères success and the port of L'Aygade (subsequently silted up) was a base for Crusaders; **St Louis** disembarked there in 1254 on returning from the Seventh Crusade. Soon afterwards the town passed to the counts of Provence. In 1620 the castle was demolished by Louis XIII and Hyères declined in favour of Toulon.

Modern revival – The town became well known in the 18C and 19C, particularly among the English, as an inland resort; 20C tourism has led to the development of the beaches.

Hyères is a lively town throughout the year and not solely dependent on tourism. The surrounding plain is extensively cultivated to produce early fruit (strawberries, peaches) and vegetables; great vineyards thrive on rich soil. The town also exports potted palms and ornamental plants.

STAYING IN HYÈRES

L'Almanarre – Long sandy beach near the site of the Greek town of Olbia *(see above). Take the salt road (Route du Sel; accessible only in summer) down the western side of the peninsula.*

This picturesque route passes a vast salt-marsh (400ha/988 acres) and then the Étang des Pesquiers, home of many waterbirds.

A Touch of Exoticism

Hyères is famous for palm trees. The cultivation of palms began to expand in 1867 and reached its peak in the 1930s. There are no less than 10 varieties named Hyères palms. The renown of these trees has brought about their export as far as Saudi Arabia. In Hyères itself, strollers can enjoy the exotic charm of the palms in Avenue Godillot, one of the most attractive roads in France, and in three public gardens: the Casino gardens, Roy gardens and Denis gardens. In the fine Olbius-Risquier gardens there is a complete range of existing species.

Hyères-Plage – A small forest of umbrella pines shelters this village. Boats leave from the port for the Îles d'Hyères.

Ayguade-le Ceinturon – This is the old port of Hyères, where St Louis disembarked on his return from the Seventh Crusade. It is now a pleasant seaside resort.
Continue via **Berriau-Plage** to **Port-Pothuau**, a picturesque little fishing port.

Marais salants – The Hyères region became famous for its two salt-marshes: the **Salins des Pesquiers** on the Giens tombolo and the **Vieux Salins**. In the salt tables, vast rectangles of 2-4ha/5-10 acres, the sea water deposits its salt. The constant dry wind speeds evaporation while concentration is aided by mechanical gyrating movements. The "harvest" or collection of the salt takes place in the last week of August (according to tradition between harvest and grape-picking).
The operation involves first lifting the salt crust which has formed on the salt tables – this is the job of the *détoureur*. This crust or *sel gris* (grey salt) is set aside to be sprinkled on snow-covered roads. The white salt, washed and fit for consumption, is collected and piled into immense white mountains *(camelles)*, which signal the presence of salt-marshes from afar. The production of salt began in 1848 and ended in 1996.

★Jardins Olbius-Riquier ⊙ ▣ – The gardens are very extensive (6.5ha/16 acres) and grow a rich variety of tropical plants, particularly palms and cacti, in the open. In the **greenhouse** the more fragile species of tropical and equatorial plants can be seen together with a few rare animals.
The gardens include a small zoo in a special enclosure, and the lake is home to water birds.

Parc St-Bernard (Jardin de Noailles) – *From Cours de Strasbourg drive north, take Avenue Paul-Long following the signs "Montée de Noailles" on the left.* The park encloses the castle ruins and boasts a remarkably wide range of Mediterranean flora. The terraces command a picturesque **view★**: from the old town and the Collégiale St-Paul, over Pic des Oiseaux and Costebelle Hill to the peninsula and the islands; to the east is the outline of the Massif des Maures.

Parc du Château Ste-Claire ⊙ – A fine villa built in 1850 by Colonel Voutier, the man who discovered the Venus de Milo, sits in the middle of this park filled with exotic plants. The château currently houses the administrative offices of the Parc National de Port-Cros.

★A STROLL THROUGH THE OLD STREETS *1hr 15min*

Leave from Place Georges-Clémenceau.

Porte Massillon – The gate leads onto Rue Massillon, a bustling shopping street, once the main street of the old town; note the many Renaissance doorways.

Almanarre Funboard Festival

Almanarre beach stretches (6km/3.7mi) along the salt-marshes of the Étang des Pesquiers, facing the Golfe de Giens. On windless days it is popular with families on holiday but, when the *mistral* starts to blow, it becomes a mecca for "funboarding". The beach offers ideal conditions because it is protected by the slight tombolo to the east, the low-lying land to the west and by Cap de Carqueiranne from the heavy swell out at sea.
Almanarre is known as the top windsurfing location on the Riviera. In 1966 it was chosen as the venue for the European Championships for production boards and funboarding.
The beach also attracts many spectators who come to marvel at the spectacular acrobatics, particularly "jibes" – amazing somersaults in the air which have become the symbol of funboarding.
There are schools all along the beach offering windsurfing lessons for beginners and for more seasoned adepts.

View of the old town

Place Massillon – In the square, where the daily market is held, stands the 12C tower, **Tour St-Blaise**, last remnant of a Knights Templar commandery. To the left is Rue Rabaton where the great preacher, Massillon (1663-1742) was born (no 7).

Place St-Paul – From this terrace square, once the site of the cloisters of the Collégiale St-Paul, there is a good **panorama★** *(viewing table)*.

Old streets – Porte St-Paul (gateway) near the collegiate church is incorporated into a handsome **Renaissance house** with a turret at one corner. Pass beneath and follow Rue St-Paul to Rue Ste-Claire where Porte des Princes stands framing the chevet and bell-tower of the Collégiale St-Paul.
Retrace your steps to Rue de Paradis where there is a fine **Romanesque house** (no 6) which has been restored (twin windows with slender columns).
Return through Porte St-Paul and take picturesque Rue Barbacane to Rue St-Esprit which runs onto Rue Bourgneuf. Continue to Place de la République with its shaded plane trees.

Château Ruins – *Same route as for Parc St-Bernard but go round the right-hand side of the park to the car park. Take the well-trodden path up the hill (45min on foot there and back). The ruins can also be reached by car along Montée de Noailles (car park).*
The Château d'Hyères passed from the lords of Fos to the counts of Provence, who rebuilt it in the 13C. The ruins are quite extensive, particularly the towers and crenellated keep which dominate the town.

Seaside Architecture, a Victorian Legacy

The development of winter tourism in Hyères dates back to the mid-19C, with the mass visits of the English, including many celebrities: Queen Victoria, the novelist RL Stevenson, and some great French figures: Victor Hugo, Michelet and Maupassant. The resort is therefore endowed with the luxury hotels that needed to meet the requirements of these wealthy visitors: Hôtel des Palmiers, Grand Hôtel des Îles d'Or and the extension of the venerable Park Hôtel where the young Bonaparte stayed.
Alexis Godillot, supplier to the armies of the Second Empire and owner of a quarter of the town, decided to launch his own resort by rechristening it "Hyères-les-Palmiers", and by entrusting the architect Chapoulard with the building of various follies in composite style which can still be seen in many streets, namely Avenue Riondet.
There are other buildings, in the most electic styles, throughout the residential districts: the Villa Tunisienne, Avenue Beauregard, built by Chapoulard around 1870; the Villa Thosolan, Avenue du XVᵉ Corps; the Villa Roux, Rue de Verdun; the Villa Mauresque and the Collège Anglo-Français. On Boulevard Chateaubriand and Boulevard d'Orient, you can admire the Villa Léon-Antoinette, La Favorite and Villa Ker-André.

HYÈRES
GIENS

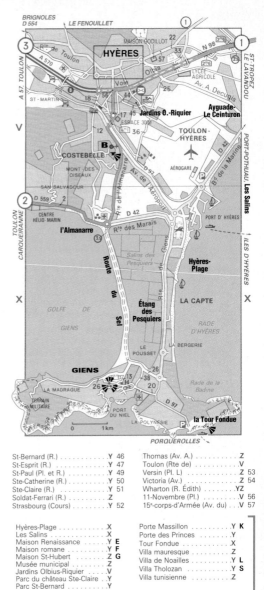

HYÈRES

Eating out

MODERATE

Les Santonniers – *18 Rue Jean-Jaurès, (town centre) – 83320 Carqueiranne – ☎ 04 94 58 62 33 – Closed 5-19 Jan, Wed except Jul-Aug and Thu Sep-May – 14.48€.* Set up in a local building in the town centre, this homey restaurant decorated in Provençal tradition has two undeniable assets: a lovely terrace sheltered from the beating sun by a plane tree and a menu offering extremely attractive prices. Two reasons to give in to temptation...

MID-RANGE

Colombe – *83400 Hyères – 2,5km/1.5mi W of Hyères by Route de Toulon – ☎ 04 94 35 35 16 – Closed Sun evening Sep-Jun and Mon – 22.11/29.73€.* Carefully prepared local cuisine is served in the Provençal dining room or out on the spacious sun-drenched terrace of this restaurant, which is fronted by a tidy, squeaky clean façade.

Where to stay

MID-RANGE

Hôtel Port Hélène – *D 559 – At L'Almanarre – 83400 Hyères – ☎ 04 94 57 72 01 – www.hotel-port-helene.fr – 12 rooms: 51.07€ – ⌂ 5.34€.* A friendly atmosphere awaits you at this cute hotel fronted by a pink façade, lost among umbrella pines and palm trees. The rooms are extremely well kept and give onto balconies offering views of the sea. Good service and very reasonable prices for the area.

Chambre d'Hôte L'Aumônerie – *620 Avenue de Fontbrun – 83320 Carqueiranne – ☎ 04 94 58 53 56 – www.bbfrance.com/menard.html – ⊠ – Reservation recommended – 4 rooms: 53.35/91.46€.* Away from the bustling crowd, this pink house, which once belonged to a navy chaplain, is set against a leafy backdrop of maritime pines. The sparsely appointed rooms are blissfully quiet. There is a private path leading directly to the beach.

Hôtel La Rose des Mers – *3 Allée E.-Gérard – 83400 Hyères – 5km/3mi SE of Hyères – ☎ 04 94 58 02 73 – Closed 5 Nov-14 Mar – 20 rooms: 54.88/74.70€ – ⌂ 6.86€.* This small, welcoming hotel at the water's edge has tidy rooms with white shutters that look out to sea and the Hyères Islands. Beach mattresses are supplied free of charge.

Transport

Parking – No charge for parking in the harbour or on Place Louis-Versin. Underground car parks (fee) can be found outside the Casino, in the Olbia shopping mall and in the Denis Gardens on Place du Maréchel-Joffre. During the day, you need to pay to park on the pavement in the town centre.

Buses – *Bus station on Place Joffre – ☎ 04 94 12 55 00.* Bus no 39 crosses the city via Carqueiranne and Le Pradet. Another line will take you to the tip of the Giens Peninsula, linking up with boat trips headed for the îles d'Or.

Shopping

Markets – Tuesdays and Thursdays from May to September on Place de la République. Saturdays along Avenue Gambetta.

Shopping streets – Rue Massillon, walking up towards the old quarter. The Briand pedestrian district. Avenue du Général-de-Gaulle and Avenue des Îles-d'Or.

Wine – There are 8 wine cellars in and around Hyères. For details apply to the tourist office.

Living it up

Casino – *Casino des Palmiers – Avenue Ambroise-Thomas – ☎ 04 94 12 80 80.* Fruit machines, roulette, blackjack... Restaurant and nightclub.

Hippodrome – *☎ 04 94 58 14 45.*

Karting – *Speedkart Hyères – 1714 Avenue de l'Aéroport – ☎ 04 94 38 76 99.*

Hyères-Port Saint-Pierre – *☎ 04 94 12 54 40 (Hyères), 04 94 58 02 30 (La Capte, 125 moorings), 04 94 66 33 98 (l'Ayguade, 500 moorings).* Four basins able to accommodate 1 350 moorings, 120 of which are for temporary stays.

From the top *(viewing table)* a vast **panorama**★ of the coast and the interior can be seen.

St-Louis – This former church of the Franciscan convent has three elegant doors beneath round arches, a rose window and a corniche. It brings to mind the Italian Romanesque style. The nave, with its thick-ribbed pointed vaulting, ends in a square apse, as do the side aisles. The whole ensemble is an example of the transition from Romanesque to Provençal Gothic.

SIGHTS

Villa de Noailles ⊙ – *Access by Rue St-Bernard or Montée de Noailles.* In 1923 the Noailles, a rich couple of patrons, commissioned a winter villa from the Belgian architect Mallet-Stevens, which was to be as open to the sunlight as possible. The villa (1 600 m²/1 914sq yd), which features a covered swimming pool and 60 or so rooms, was one of the first modern homes on the Riviera. All the famous artists of the 1920s (Picasso, Dali...) attended the extravagant parties given at the villa. The American photographer Man Ray shot some sequences of a Surrealist film here and Buñuel set *L'Âge d'or* in the villa.

After a long period of neglect, the first stage of restoration in 1986 has meant that temporary exhibitions can be held on the first floor. Note the curious Cubist garden designed by Gabriel Guévrékian.

Musée Municipal ⊙ – The Greek and Roman archeological specimens displayed in this museum come from excavations conducted at Olbia.

Collections of minerals, fossils, shells, fish and birds. Gallery of local artists. Louis XV and Louis XVI furniture.

Ancienne Collégiale St-Paul ⊙ – The oldest parts of the former collegiate church go back to the 12C; the bell-tower is pure Romanesque. A fine Renaissance door and monumental stairway give access.

The narthex, which is probably the nave of the original structure, to which a ceiling has been added, is covered with votive offerings (some dating from the 17C). To the left of the entrance is a large crib of Provençal santons with the medieval town as a backdrop. The Gothic nave, set at right angles to the original church, has Flamboyant Gothic side chapels. Altarpieces adorned with wreathed columns, reliquaries and gilded wooden statues date from the 17C.

TOURING THE COAST

★★Giens Peninsula

Double Tombolo – The Gien peninsula is a rare natural phenomenon: the former island of Giens is linked to the mainland by two coastal bars (each 4km/2.5mi long). In similar cases, such as Quiberon, a single tombolo (sandbar) has formed, joining the island to the coast. At Giens, a curious combination of circumstances – the mouths of two rivers, the Gapeau and the Roubaud, one on each side of Giens, coupled with strong currents at sea – has given rise to a double tombolo on the rocky seabed.

The parallel bars enclose a lagoon that provides an ideal habitat for birds. Pink flamingoes and avocets are common here. The best time to see flamingoes is in mid-September when up to 1 500 birds migrate here. The flora is interesting and unusual: glasswort, sea rocket, white mignonette and thorny rushes.

A project aimed at replanting posidonia is under way in the gulf of Giens; this will slow down the erosion of the seabed and encourage the revival of species which live in it. In fact the underwater life concentrated in this area is dependent on this plant. With its disappearance, caused by man, the sand is no longer protected and the beaches are washed away by the sea. For three decades the west tombolo has been

The western tombolo at Giens, under the protection of the Conservatoire du Littoral, is subject to strict regulations:
– Road traffic is permitted from Easter to All Saints' Day on the tombolo road, with no parking en route; the road is closed the rest of the year.
– Parking is allowed only in the two car parks at each end of the western tombolo.
– To reach the beaches, use only the marked paths, without walking on the dunes or vegetation, and avoiding the marked protected zones.
– Drying sails or any canvas on the vegetation is not allowed.

eroded by wind and by equinoctial storms which attack the sea walls, sweep away the beach and cover parts of the road with sand. A project by the Conservatoire du Littoral is currently in progress to preserve this site.

Giens – The village, in the middle of a former island, is a small seaside resort. The castle ruins form a mound from which there is a magnificent **panorama**★★ *(viewing table)*. The poet St-John Perse stayed here and lies at rest in the cemetery.

To the south is the little port of Niel, surrounded by a lovely pine wood.

Drive east from the village to the Tour Fondue.

Tour Fondue – Boats sail from here to the Île de Porquerolles. The name comes from the fort built under Richelieu to control the narrows of La Petite Passe, which was also protected by forts on the small islands of Grand and Petit Ribaud *(private property)*. There is a beautiful view of the islands and the Giens Peninsula.

Tour of the peninsula on foot – *18km/11mi – allow 5hr.*

🚶 The route, which is partly signed, links the port of La Madrague to Badine beach. Take D 97 along the eastern side of the peninsula – fine views of the Hyères plain and the Maures. Continue to Hyères-Plage via La Bergerie and La Capte set in pine woods.

EXCURSIONS

★**Chapelle Notre-Dame-de-Consolation** – There has been a sanctuary on the top of Costebelle hill since the 11C. The present chapel was built in 1955. There is a huge coloured sculpture of Our Lady against the cross which forms the bell-tower's vertical axis. A series of sculpted groups depicting the main events in the Virgin's life are picked out in cement and stone on the principal front between the windows. The stark architecture of the interior is enhanced by the Apostle sculptures in the apse and the shimmering play of colours from the huge blue and gold **stained-glass windows★** designed by Gabriel Loire to illustrate the cult of Mary and the history of the sanctuary.

The neighbouring promenade *(viewing table)* gives a **view★** of the Hyères *(left)* and Toulon *(right)* anchorages.

★Sommet du Fenouillet

4km/2.5mi – plus 30min on foot there and back

From Hyères take Avenue de Toulon then turn right onto a signed road to Le Fenouillet.

From the neo-Gothic **chapel** there is a marked path to Le Fenouillet, the highest point of the Maurettes (291m/955ft) with a very good **panorama★**, particularly of the Hyères and Toulon harbours and the surrounding mountains.

Jardin d'Oiseaux Tropicaux ⊘

East by N 98 through La Londe-les-Maures towards St-Raphaël

📷 A signposted trail through this **exotic bird sanctuary**, shaded by eucalyptus and pine trees, leads past large aviaries containing, one after another, many species of parrot, toucan and hornbill, large birds such as the hooded cassowary and emus all the way from Australia. Various types of wader complete this interesting visit.

Tour Foudue, Gien Peninsula

Îles d'HYÈRES★★★

Michelin map 84 folds 16 and 17, 114 folds 47 and 48, 49 or 245 folds 47 and 48
Local map see Massif des MAURES

These well-known islands, which separated from the Massif des Maures in a relatively recent geological age, lie close to the south entrance to Hyères harbour. They are also known as the **Îles d'Or** (Golden Islands), a name given to them during the Renaissance, no doubt due to the fact that in certain lights their mica shale rocks cast golden reflections. The short sea crossing and the variety of walks on the islands – on the coast or inland – provide unforgettable memories.

FROM PIRATES TO LIBERATORS

A land of asylum – In the 5C the monks of Lérins arrived, succeeding the Ligurians, the Greeks and the Romans as the islands' overlords. In the following centuries they were repeatedly attacked by pirates until François I raised the islands of Port-Cros and Levant to the status of the marquisate of the Îles d'Or provided that the marquis keep them under cultivation and protect them from pirates. Despite exemption from taxes, the islands lacked manpower until a right of asylum was established under which criminals were granted immunity so long as they remained on the islands. This idea had unfortunate consequences; jailbirds swarmed to the islands, where they turned to piracy, being so bold as to attempt the capture of one of the king's ships from Toulon. Only in the reign of Louis XIV did the last of these dubious characters leave the area.

A British coup – In 1793, after the capture of Toulon by the Revolutionaries *(see TOULON)*, British and Spanish squadrons anchored off the Îles d'Hyères. The commander of Fort Ste-Agathe at Porquerolles, forgotten on his island by the French authorities, had only the vaguest idea of what was happening on the mainland. The British admiral invited him on board his flagship and the commander went unsuspectingly. While the whisky was circulating, British sailors landed, surprised the garrison and tried to blow up the fort. The ships then raised anchor taking with them, as prisoner, the crestfallen commander.

Allied landing (August 1944) – During the night of 14 to 15 August, American troops landed on the islands of Port-Cros and Levant and silenced German batteries which threatened Allied shipping.

TOURING THE ISLANDS

★★★Île de Porquerolles

Porquerolles, the largest and most westerly of the Hyères Islands, measures 7km/4mi long by 3km/2mi wide, and was called Protè (First) by the Greek settlers who came to live along its shores. The north coast is well supplied with sandy beaches bordered by pine trees, heather, arbutus and scented myrtle; the south coast is steep and rugged with one or two inlets that are easily accessible. There are few inhabitants inland, only vineyards, pine and eucalyptus woods and thick Mediterranean vegetation.

The major part of the island has been acquired by the State to protect the natural heritage. In 1979, the **Conservatoire Botanique National Méditerranéen** ⊘ was set up to preserve the area and to protect the Mediterranean fauna and flora thriving in the basin.

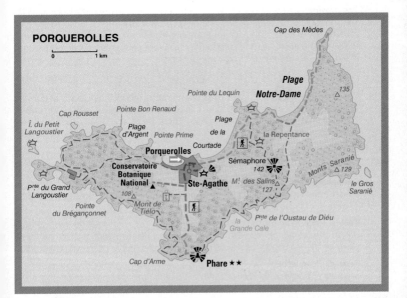

PORQUEROLLES
0   1 km

Cap des Mèdes
Pointe du Lequin
Plage Notre-Dame   135
Cap Rousset   Pointe Bon Renaud
Î. du Petit Langoustier   Plage d'Argent   Plage de la   la Repentance
    Pointe Prime   Courtade
Porquerolles   Sémaphore   Monts Saranié   129
Conservatoire Botanique National   **Ste-Agathe**   142
    M! des Salins   le Gros Saranié
P!!e du Grand Langoustier   108   127
Pointe du Brégançonnet   Mont de Tiélo
    la Grande Cale   Pnte de l'Oustau de Diéu
Cap d'Arme   **Phare ★★**

Access

– From La Tour Fondue (Giens Peninsula) (TLV, Transports Littoral Varois); in season there is a tour of the three islands (Trois Îles), starting from La Tour Fondue, which includes a visit of 1-2hr to each island;
– From Hyères (TLV, ☎ 04 94 57 44 07), 1hr crossing to Port-Cros and 1hr 30min crossing to Île du Levant;
– From Le Lavandou, Cavalaire (☎ 04 94 71 01 02 Vedettes des Îles d'Or) direct to Porquerolles or Port-Cros; the Île du Levant is accessible only on a round tour including Port-Cros. *Apr-Oct daily, Nov-Mar Thu, Sat and Sun.*

Before leaving

During periods of major fire risk, the ALARME plan comes into force (announced before embarkation); it means that access is limited to the beaches, the coastal path and the villages. Bicycles are not allowed on Port-Cros.

Île de Porquerolles

The best way to tour the island is by bicycle. Bikes can be hired near the port and in the vicinity of the town hall. There are many places for refreshment – in the road leading from the town hall, which is lined with restaurants, and in several more peaceful spots, such as at the foot of Ste-Agathe Fort.
As watering-places are rare, especially in high season, it is advisable to obtain supplies at the fountain in Place d'Armes before setting off round the island.

Île de Port-Cros (National Park)

Port-Cros, Îles d'Hyeres

The whole of the island of Port-Cros, both land and sea, is a nature reserve to which strict regulations apply:
– road traffic is prohibited on the island;
– smoking is not allowed outside the village and no plants of any kind should be removed;
– animals are permitted but must be kept on a leash;
– harpooning is forbidden throughout the Parc National de Port-Cros; line fishing is forbidden within a radius of 50m/164ft from the island's coast;
– drinking water should be carried since supplies are very rare on Port-Cros and there is no public watering-place; there are, however, several shops selling drinks in the village.
In season there is an information centre in the first building to the left of the landing-stages (☎ 04 94 05 90 17).
Trips in a glass-bottomed boat are available.

Île du Levant

The accessible areas of the island are in the west and north; in the north a channel is reserved for water sports and an area is set aside for windsurfing. Apart from the cafés on the landing-stage, the only restaurants are at Héliopolis, above the port. The mainl beaches, reached by the coast path on each side of the landing-stages, are for the exclusive use of nudists.

Diving

The great depths and the lack of strong currents around the islands and in the Baie de Carqueiranne provide ideal conditions for diving as well as for underwater photography of the many wrecks. There are several diving clubs in Hyères and La Londe; *Sun Plongée* in Port-Cros and *Porquerolles Plongée* in Porquerolles.

Water sports

Aquascope – *83400 Port-Cros* – ☎ *04 94 05 92 22.* Guided tours (30min) in a boat specially designed to observe underwater life. Departures every 40min. 11,43€ (2-10 year-olds 7,62€). 10 seats.

TMV – *Port de la Tour-Fondue – 83400 Giens* – ☎ *04 94 58 95 14 – Jul-Aug departures at 10am. 15.55€.* This boat and its transparent hull afford lovely views of the sea depths as well as marine flora and fauna. Each trip lasts 40min.

Tour of Porquerolles – A boat race takes place every Whit Sunday, starting from the port with a view to sailing round the island in the least possible time.

La Palud Cove, Port-Cros Island

B. Kaufmann/MICHELIN

An unusual destiny – For 60 years this island was the private property of a single family. In 1911, a Belgian engineer, F-Joseph Fournier, having made his fortune in Mexico, decided to give Porquerolles as a wedding gift to his young bride. Once settled on the island with his family and an army of gardeners, he attempted to recreate the atmosphere of a south American hacienda by importing exotic plants. He began with the cultivation of several exotic fruits then unknown in France, pineapples and kumquats. Along the walks are South American plants such as the bellombra with its massive roots. Also witness to this replanting, the 180 ha/445 acres of vines originally planted have been reduced to half the quantity but continue to produce a reputable rosé. This was the first vineyard to gain the AOC Côtes de Provence *appellation*.

The village – The small village of Porquerolles, which lies at the end of a minute anchorage now used as a harbour for pleasure boats, has given its name to the whole island. The village was built by the military in the mid-19C and consists of a main square, a humble church with an unusual Stations of the Cross carved by a soldier with his penknife, and a few fishermen's cottages.
To this nucleus, which resembles a North African colonial settlement rather than a Provençal village, hotels and private houses have been added.

Fort Ste-Agathe ⊘ – This fort is the first building one sees before landing on the island. Dominating a mound that overlooks the port, the fort occupies an enviable strategic position. Its walls in the shape of a trapezium are surmounted by a massive corner tower, all that remains of the original structure built by François I in 1532. The English ruined and subsequently burnt the fort in 1793 and reconstruction began in 1810 with buildings adapted to meet new military requirements. The round tower is constructed on a massive scale: walls 4m/13ft thick, 20m/66ft in diameter and 15m/49ft high. The Parc de Port-Cros has organised exhibitions in the tower's various rooms on underwater archeology, artefacts, and on the history of the islands and Hyères harbour. The great circular room has a 6m/20ft-high ceiling and fine wooden beams. From the terrace on top of the tower, with its five embrasures for large-bore cannon, there is a magnificent **view**★ over most of the island: La Courtade beach, Notre-Dame beach, the Sémaphore peak (summit 142m/466ft) to the east and, to the west, wooded hills obscuring the beaches.

Walks

★★ **Lighthouse Walk** – *1hr 30min on foot there and back.*
🚶 This walk to the lighthouse *(phare)* is a "must" even for tourists with only a few hours to spend on the island. The **lighthouse** ⊘, which stands on the most southerly point of the island some 96m/307ft up, has a beam which carries 54km/34mi. There is a **panorama**★★ extending over most of the island: the Langoustier hills, Fort Ste-Agathe, the signal station and the cliffs on the south coast, the Hyères anchorage and the Maures Massif.

★★ **Beach Walk** – *2hr on foot there and back.*

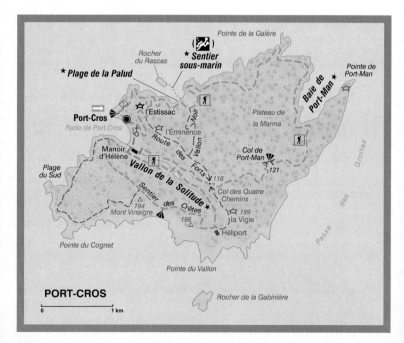

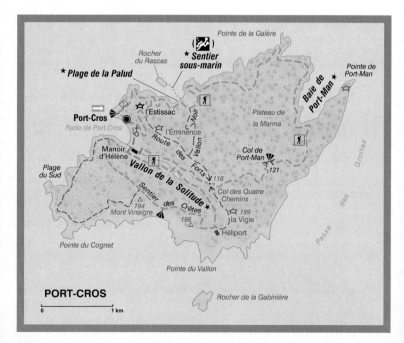 This pleasant walk along sandy paths continually in the shade of the pine trees, starts from Fort Ste-Agathe *(bear left)* and skirts the Plage de la Courtade.

After Pointe du Lequin the path dips towards the sea, revealing the **Plage Notre-Dame**, a beautiful sandy beach bordered by pine trees.

The **signal station** *(sémaphore)*, Plage d'Argent, **Pointe du Grand Langoustier** and **Cap des Mèdes** all make excellent walks.

A **boat** ⊙ with underwater viewing facilities makes cruises off shore.

★★★ Île-de Port-Cros

Port-Cros, which was the Mèse – Middle Island – to the Greeks, owes its present name to the hollowed out *(creux)* shape of its small harbour. A few fishermen's cottages, a bunch of shops and a small church adorn the area around the bay, which is commanded by Fort du Moulin (also known as the "Château").

Port-Cros Island is hillier and more rugged and rises higher above the sea than its neighbours; its lush vegetation is unrivalled – it is a true Garden of Eden and a peaceful place in which to stay. The island is 4km/2.5mi long by 2.5km/1.5mi wide and its highest point, Mont Vinaigre, reaches 194m/679ft. Port-Cros, together with Île de Bagaud and the neighbouring islets, Rascas and La Gabinière and an area extending 600m/656yd around the coastline, has been designated a **Parc National** ⊙. The park covers 700ha/2.69sq mi on land and 1 800ha/7sq mi at sea and forms a unique protected site for Mediterranean flora and fauna.

The principal walks are signed at the quayside; possible variations are shown by a broken line in red on the plan.

★ **Plage de la Palud** – *1hr 15min on foot there and back along a marked path.*

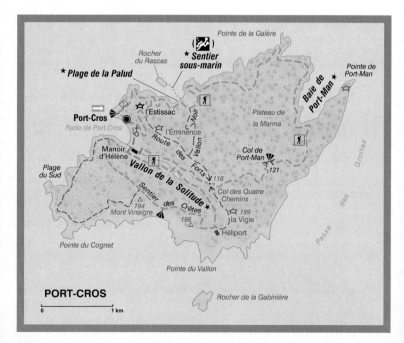 Climb up to the castle for a view of the neighbouring Île de Bagaud. A **botanical path** planted with Mediterranean specimens winds its way round **Fort de l'Estissac** ⊙, built under Richelieu, which houses exhibitions on the marine environment and the relation between man and the sea, and which follows the curve of the bay before reaching the beach.

★ **Underwater path** ⊙ – *A preliminary visit to the Parc office in the port is strongly recommended and, in the case of a solitary dive (diver providing his own mask, breathing apparatus and palms), a plastic aquaguide which fastens on to the wrist will help you to identify marine flora and fauna.*

In the section between the little island of Rascas and La Palud beach in an area signposted by yellow buoys, an underwater observation point, no deeper than 10m/33ft, has been set up.

PORT-CROS

Here anyone who can swim – diving is not necessary – can observe a great variety of typical Mediterranean species that live at this depth. Numbered buoys mark the best viewpoints: the highest numbered signposts indicate the best positions. Among other flora and fauna, the principal stages in the development of posidonia, and the types of animal that thrive on it, can be studied.

Return to the village passing between the forts of L'Éminence and L'Estissac.

★ **Vallon de la Solitude** – *2hr on foot there and back along marked paths.*

▮ This is the ideal walk for visitors spending half a day on the island. At the beginning of the valley stands the Manoir d'Hélène – a manor house converted into a hotel – so called after the heroine in Melchior de Vogüé's novel *Jean d'Agrève* which is set on Port-Cros. The path is in deep shade for almost all its length.

Once within sight of Fort de la Vigie start back along the cliff walk (Route des Crêtes), which affords **views** of the sea. At Mont Vinaigre bear right into the Vallon de la Fausse Monnaie (Valley of False Currency).

★ **Port-Man** – *Round tour of 10km/6mi – 4hr there and back on foot; marked paths.*

▮ This pleasant excursion is made along a shaded and nearly level path from which, at the end of the Col de Port-Man, there is a pretty **view** of the Île du Levant, the coast and the Maures. It ends in the **Baie de Port-Man**, a wonderful green amphitheatre or bay, which is well sheltered from the north winds. Return via Pointe de la Galère, Plateau de la Marma and Plage de la Palud.

Other Walks – These include Plage de la Palud by way of the Route des Forts and the Vallon Noir; the beach and the awesome cliffs along the south shore; Pointe de Port-Man.

There are other opportunities to discover the underwater world: a boat with underwater window sails around Porquerolles in the high season.

Île du Levant ⊙ *local map see Massif des MAURES*

The island consists of a rocky spine 8km/5mi long but only 1 200m/1 300yd wide rimmed by prodigious vertical cliffs inaccessible except at two points: the Avis and Estable *calanques.* The disembarkation point on the island is the Aiguade landing-stage from which a path leads up to Héliopolis.

When the Lérins monks inhabited the islands, the Île du Levant was the abbey's garden and granary. The majority of the island (80%) is occupied by the Marine Nationale. *Access is forbidden.*

Héliopolis – In the western part of the island, the village of Héliopolis and the Grottes area attract a considerable number of nudists each summer. This part of the island *(private property)* was one of the first places where, in 1931, the nudist principles of the doctors Durville were put into practice.

In season local clubs organise diving activities which are open to the general public *(see Practical information).*

JUAN-LES-PINS ✿✿✿

Michelin map 84 fold 9, 115 folds 39 and 40 or 245 fold 37

This elegant winter and summer resort lies at the end of a magnificent bay, well protected by the luxurious Cap d'Antibes and Pointe de la Croisette.

Juan-les-Pins beach

The "swing" era – The thriving musical night-life of Juan-les-Pins began during the 1920s, with the arrival of the first American tourists. They revolutionised the atmosphere of the resort with their exuberance: they sunbathed on the beaches, they water-skied and they listened to strange music called jazz. A magnate named Frank Gould founded the first summer casino and the young jet set whiled away the nights dancing to the lively music of Cole Porter, in the company of Douglas Fairbanks, Mary Pickford and Mistinguette.

At the end of the Second World War, soon after the Liberation, the music started again thanks to a clientele from the US Navy based on the Riviera. In 1951 Sydney Bechet was married here in an atmosphere which recalled New Orleans carnivals. From then on each summer Juan-les-Pins was transformed into the European jazz capital by Sydney Bechet and Claude Luter. After Bechet's death in 1959 the first jazz festival was born; its success was assured by the presence of Louis Armstrong, Count Basie, Duke Ellington, Dizzy Gillespie and Miles Davis.

Jazz is now inseparable from the name of Juan-les-Pins.

The summer season is marked by many events including the famous **World Jazz Festival** hosted by the Palais des Congrès.

PARADISE ON EARTH

The exotic pine trees and the heavenly sand beaches make this resort one of the most attractive on the French Riviera. The Promenade au Soleil running between the landing-stage and the Casino is strongly reminiscent of the star-studded Croisette in Cannes. **Port-Gallice**, located to the east, is a pretty harbour for pleasure boats. In the evening, activity centres on the numerous restaurants, open-air cafés and nightclubs round the casino, where baccarat and roulette can be played.

Beaches – A pine wood grows right down to the gently sloping beach of Juan-les-Pins, a superb stretch of fine sand some 2km/1.2mi long, which is sheltered from the winds. There are several private and public beaches all around, dotted between the ports of Golfe-Juan and Juan-les-Pins.

EXCURSIONS

✿✿ **Golfe-Juan** – This popular resort at the foot of the Vallauris hills, clad with orange trees and mimosa, boasts a 1km/1 094yd beach of fine sand extending in a shallow curve. It overlooks a good anchorage protected by Cap d'Antibes and the Îles de Lérins. **Napoleon** landed here in March 1815 *(see Route NAPOLEON)* after escaping from Elba with 1 100 men in the brigantine *Inconstant* and other ships. A mosaic on the quay commemorates the event. When land was sighted, Napoleon summoned the lookout and rewarded him with all the money he had in his pockets.

Eating out

Le Capitole – *26 Avenue Amiral-Courbet* – ☎ *04 93 61 22 44* – *alainfont@free.com* – *Closed 15 Nov-15 Dec, Mon evening and Tue off season.* – *16.01€.* Of the former grocery shop, only the original shelves remain. The premises are now occupied by a large, smart restaurant serving traditional fare.

L'Amiral – *7 Avenue Amiral-Courbet* – ☎ *04 93 67 34 61* – *Closed Nov and Mon* – *15.24€ lunch* – *21.34/29.73€.* Small family business providing highly acceptable local cuisine on prettily laid tables in a modern, smiling setting. Friendly welcome and service. If you like *couscous*, the day to go is Thursday but you must book first!

Bijou Plage – *Boulevard Guillaumont* – ☎ *04 93 61 39 07* – *25.15/42.69€.* During the summer season, locals and tourists alike flock to this beach restaurant on the road to Golfe-Juan. The menu pays tribute to *bouillabaisse* and other fish dishes. Its low prices, private beach and water sports facilities are additional incentives.

Nounou – *On the beach* – *06220 Golfe-Juan* – ☎ *04 93 63 71 73* – *Closed 10 Nov-25 Dec, Sun evening and Mon except Jul-Aug* – *29.73/53.36€.* Settle on the terrace overlooking the beautiful sandy beach, or inside one of the dining rooms, and order a Provençal speciality or a fish dish. Choosing the menu tends to be more judicious than eating *à la carte*.

Where to stay

Hôtel Les Charmettes – *25 Vieux Chemin de la Colle* – ☎ *04 93 61 47 41* – *Closed Nov school holidays* – 🅿 – *17 rooms: 43.45/52.59€* – ⌷ *5.03€.* If you shy away from the throng and from loud, blaring night spots, this is definitely the place for you. The simple, narrow rooms are well kept and the pretty terrace ablaze with mimosa is sheltered by reed screening.

Hôtel Cécil – *Rue Jonnard* – ☎ *04 93 61 05 12* – *http://sites.netscape.net/hotelcecilfrance* – *Closed 3 Nov-15 Jan* – *21 rooms, half-board: 47.26€.* A handsome residence built in accordance with local tradition was converted into a hotel in 1920. The smallish, impeccably kept rooms are laid out over three floors. Dinner is served out on the terrace in high season. Conveniently situated in the town centre, yet not far from the coast.

Hôtel La Marjolaine – *15 Avenue du Docteur-Fabre* – ☎ *04 93 61 06 60* – *Closed 15 days in Mar and Nov* – 📷 🅿 – *17 rooms: 51.83/60.98€* – ⌷ *5.34€.* This turn-of-the-century manor is charmingly set among flowers and provides quality accommodation: rooms with visible beams decorated in warm, generous hues. The most appealing one is called "Manoir" and it is appointed with antique Provençal furniture.

Hôtel Ste-Valérie – *Rue de l'Oratoire* – ☎ *04 93 61 07 15* – *Closed 1 Oct-8 Apr* – *30 rooms: 91.47/146.35€* – ⌷ *9.15€* – *Restaurant 21/60.88€.* Just off a quiet street, this hotel has carefully kept rooms with terraces or balconies giving onto its pretty garden, where breakfast is served on warm days. Outdoor pool shared with the Christie annexe. Peaceful ambience guaranteed.

On the town

Pam Pam – *137 Boulevard du Président-Wilson* – ☎ *04 93 61 11 05* – *Apr to mid-Nov: 2-5pm.* Diners come from afar to relish the famous *accras* *(cod fritters served between 6pm and 9pm), to sip an exotic punch or to watch the Brazilian girls gyrate to the strains of a live orchestra in a Polynesian setting. One of Juan-les-Pins' hottest night spots.

Le Crystal – *Avenue Gallice* – *06160 Juan-les-Pins* – ☎ *04 93 61 02 51* – *Jul-Aug: daily 8.15am-4am; Sep-Jun: Sun-Thu 8.15am-midnight, Fri-Sat until 2am.* When it first opened in 1936, this family brasserie was housed in a small hut on a plot of land with palm trees where sheep would come to graze. The owner still remembers those early days. Today Le Crystal is hemmed in between the Casino and a host of other bars and discotheques. A must for any self-respecting night clubber...

Leisure activities

Visiobulle – *Leaves from the Embarcadère Courbet, opposite the Maison du tourisme* – ☎ *04 93 34 09 96* – *29 Mar-30 Sep and Nov 1. Booking recommended in Jul and Aug.* This boat offering views of the fascinating sea depths takes its passengers right up to the tip of Cap d'Antibes, which cannot be reached by land.

Parc Exflora – *N°7 between Juan-les-Pins and Golfe-Juan. No charge. Car park.* A walk through this park will introduce you to a wide variety of landscapes: Mediterranean and Provençal flora, antique parks, Islamic gardens...

General Cambronne was the first to land and, in spite of the opposition of the local authorities, tricolour cockades were distributed and soon sported by all. Napoleon's proclamation including his famous remark "Victory will sweep the land; the eagle with the tricolour will fly from steeple to steeple until he reaches the towers of Notre-Dame" was first posted here. The Emperor rested at a nearby inn while attempts were made to win over the Antibes garrison. As the move proved unsuccessful, he gave orders to march on Cannes.

⌂ **Cap d'Antibes** – *10km/7.1mi. Allow 2hr. See ANTIBES: Driving tours.*

★★★ **Massif de l'Esterel** – *96km/60mi. Allow half a day. See Massif de L'ESTEREL.*

★ **Massif du Tanneron** – *56km/34.5mi. Allow 1hr 30min. See Massif du TANNERON.*

Le LAVANDOU ⌂⌂

Population 5 449
Michelin map 84 folds 16 and 17, 114 fold 48 or 245 fold 48
Local map see Massif des MAURES

This charming resort in the shelter of Cap Bénat has so far preserved its Provençal character; its name recalls the lavender fields flanking the banks of the Batailler. It remains active as a **fishing port** as well as offering moorings for pleasure-craft. It is also a departure point for boat rides to the Îles d'Hyères.

The main square, **Place Ernest-Reyer**, is laid out like a garden and commands a pretty **view** of the Îles du Levant and Port-Cros; a broad beach curves south towards the port of Bormes-les-Mimosas with the wooded slopes of Cap Bénat in the background. The **Boulevard de-Lattre-de-Tassigny** is a pleasant promenade running alongside the beach; **view** of the port and the coast eastwards to Cap Lardier.

There are lively, colourful markets on Place du Marché and along Avenue du Président-Vincent-Auriol on Thursdays and in Cavalière on Mondays *(June to September).*

Yachting harbour

Eating out

MODERATE

Chez Zète – *41 Avenue du Général-de-Gaulle* – ☎ *04 94 71 09 11* – *Closed Dec and Mon* – *13.57/19.67€.* In Le Lavandou's main shopping street, this family business has become a huge success and continues to draw large crowds all year round. Its main assets? Succulent Provençal cooking, an unpretentious setting and a shaded terrace giving onto the back of the house.

Hélios Plage – *In Aiguebelle* – *Avenue du Général-Bouvet, then take the footbridge* – ☎ *04 94 71 49 79* – *Closed mid-Nov-1 Apr and evenings* – *13.72/22.87€.* If you want to lounge around on the sand and enjoy views of the Levant Island, sit down in this charming cabin with white wainscoting and choose between a salad, the chef's special or a tasty dish of pasta...before succumbing to a well-deserved sieste!

MID-RANGE

L'Auberge Provençale – *11 Rue Patron-Ravello* – ☎ *04 94 71 00 44* – *provençale.au berge@wanadoo.fr* – *Closed 10 Jan-1 Feb, 15 Nov-15 Dec,* – *17.99/27.44€.* A pedestrian street leads to this inn, entirely dedicated to Provence and its traditions: Mediterranean recipes and colourful tablecloths in a typical setting featuring a huge olive press screw.

Krill – *Rue Patron-Ravello* – ☎ *04 94 71 06 43* – *Closed 1 Nov-20 Dec and Mon* – *22.11/25.15€.* Located in a pedestrian street in the town centre, this restaurant is fronted by a colourful façade. Settle on the pretty terrace or in the air-conditioned dining room to sample simple food made with market produce. Special menu for children.

Where to stay

MID-RANGE

Roc Hôtel – *In St-Clair – 2km/1.2mi from Le Lavandou* – ☎ *04 94 01 33 66* – *Closed 21 Oct-29 Mar* – *25 rooms: 77.75/120.43€* – ☐ *6.86€.* An ochre building houses this hotel lying on a handsome sandy beach. Most of the light, modern rooms have balconies giving onto the sea. Breakfast is served on the terrace during the summer season.

Hôtel Les Alcyons – *In Aiguebelle – 4,5km/3mi from Lavandou* – ☎ *04 94 05 84 18* – *Closed 16 Oct-7 Apr* – *24 rooms: 79.27/88.42€* – ☐ *5.79€.* At the foot of the Maures Massif, barely twenty minutes from the beach, this congenial establishment is an opportunity to combine the pleasures of swimming with those of rambling across the countryside. Each of the rooms, appointed with rattan furniture, has a balcony and air-conditioning.

On the town

Le Bora Bora – *Boulevard Maréchal de-Lattre-de-Tassigny* – ☎ *04 94 71 05 54* – *Oct-Mar: daily 7.30am-9pm; Apr-Sep: daily 7.30-3am.* Bar lizards can choose among the one hundred different cocktails prepared in this bar, served in coconut shells or large Thai seashells, which you can buy and take home in memory of your trip. During the summer season, a live orchestra performs tunes from Latin America and the East Indies.

Outdoor theatre

Théâtre de Verdure-Cinéma Plein Air – *Avenue du Grand-Jardin* – ☎ *04 94 00 41 71* – *Jul-Aug: See the programme for events.* This outdoor theatre puts on plays and organises concerts of classical music and contemporary pop.

Sailing club

École de Voile de Cavalière – *Avenue du Cap-Nègre* – ☎ *04 94 05 86 78* – *Apr-Oct: daily 9am-6pm.* This club gives sailing lessons and rents various sailing boats (catamaran, dinghy, optimist) as well as windsurfing boards. On the same beach, bathers may try their hand at windsurfing, water-skiing, parascending or a sea version of dodgem cars in which contestants wear large rubber rings!

Boat trips

Hoëdic – *Port du Lavandou* – ☎ *04 94 71 69 89 ou 06 09 37 30 62* – *bateauhœdic@clubinternet.fr* – *Jun-Sep.* Give in to temptation and embark on a one-day cruise on the *Hoëdic*, a handsome sailing boat built 50 years ago. When you have finished swimming, diving and paddling around in a canoe, come back on board to tuck into the delicious cold buffet and soak up the sun on the deck.

Seascope – *Gare Maritime –* ☎ *04 94 71 01 02 – Open all year.* The Seascope's transparent hull affords wonderful views of the sea depths, marine flora and many Mediterranean fish species, notably mullet, bass and bream.

Vedettes Îles d'Or – *Gare Maritime –* ☎ *04 94 71 01 02 – Daily service.* This is the landing-stage for boats leaving for the islands of Levant, Port-Cros and Porquerolles. The first island, partly occupied by the French army, is a popular destination among nudists.

Fruit of the vine

Domaine de l'Anglade – *Avenue Vincent-Auriol –* ☎ *04 94 71 10 89 – Jul-Aug: daily 9am-12.30pm, 4.30-7pm. Sep-Jun: Tue-Sat 9am-noon, 5-7pm.* This attractive vineyard, located in the town of Le Lavandou, produces red, white and rosé wine, wine for apéritifs (orange and lemon-flavoured) and vinegar. Tasting sessions and shop on the premises.

Bathers' paradise

Small beach train – ☎ *04 94 12 55 12 – Jun-Sep.* Tour (50min) of Le Lavandou Port up to Pramousquier including access to the 12 beaches of the resort: 1st departure at 9.40am, last departure at 7.30pm. Nightly tours (30min) are also available.

CIP Lavandou – *Le Lavandou Port – Car Park –* ☎ *04 94 15 13 09.* Diving club.

Lavandou Scuba Diving School – *New Port – underneath the restaurant Le Barracuda –* ☎ *04 94 71 83 65.* Lessons for both beginners and experienced divers and various other services (hire of equipment, tours of shipwrecks, exploring sites around Port-Cros etc).

BEACHES

All the beaches at Le Lavandou are sandy ones; they are placed under constant surveillance and are equipped with emergency signals. Standards of comfort, hygiene and sporting facilities vary from one beach to the other. Adventurous tourists can take up windsurfing in Saint-Clair and canoeing in La Fossette. But for those who prefer to take it easy, there is nude sunbathing on Plage du Rossignol and a nudist beach in Le Layet.

BOAT TRIPS ⊘

★★★**Îles d'Hyères** – *Allow one day. For maps and description see Îles d'HYÈRES.*

The Song of Summer

The image of the Mediterranean is invariably associated with the song of the cicada, which forms an unbreakable trio with the game of bowls *(pétanque)* and a siesta under the pine trees. The song of the cicada is stimulated by a combination of particular conditions – the temperature must be at least 25°C

in the shade and there should not be too much noise. A tiny change – such as a cloud passing in front of the sun or the wind rustling in the trees – is enough to upset the insect. Only the male cicada sings, since the noise is a mating call to females. The dawn serenade is produced when the insect contracts two rigid plates on its abdomen, cymbals, which vibrate at 500 times a second. The sound is amplified by a ventral cavity full of air which acts as a resonance chamber. When the female has located the sound using ears on her abdomen, she joins her suitor in the tree. There are nearly 15 different varieties of cicada in France, of which the most common is the *cacau gris (cicada orni),* an emblem of Provence.

J. Ch. Gérard/PHOTONONSTOP

Îles de LÉRINS★★

Michelin map 84 fold 9 or 115 fold 39 or 245 fold 37

The interest and attraction of an excursion to the Îles de Lérins lie in the enjoyment of the outing both at sea and on the islands themselves, in the fine panorama of the coast from Cap Roux to Cap d'Antibes and in the visits to the fortress on Ste-Marguerite and the keep of the old fortified monastery on St-Honorat.

In season there are **son et lumière** performances *(information at the tourist office in Cannes).*

★★ÎLE SAINTE-MARGUERITE

The higher and the larger of the two islands, Ste-Marguerite, is separated from the mainland by a shallow channel 1 100m/1 200yd wide. The island, which lies east-west and is 3km/2mi long and 900m/1 000yd wide, belongs to the State except for the Domaine du Grand Jardin in the south. Pleasant walks have been laid out in the pine and eucalyptus woods.

The island in Antiquity – The Îles de Lérins were mentioned by the ancient historians. The larger was called Lero, a name, according to Strabo, which commemorates a Ligurian hero to whom a temple was dedicated. Pliny, on the other hand, talks of a Roman port and town.

Recent excavations near Fort Royal have uncovered a number of houses, wall paintings, mosaics and ceramics dating from between the 3C BC and 1C AD. Various wrecks and port substructures found to the west of the island prove that Roman ships called in at Lero.

The riddle of the "Iron Mask" – In 1687 the fortress of Ste-Marguerite, a state prison, received the famous "Man in the Iron Mask", a character who, according to Voltaire, wore a mask with a chinpiece which had steel springs. His identity has never been established with certainty. He is said to have been: an illegitimate brother of Louis XIV, a secretary of the Duke of Mantua who had tricked the "Sun King", a black sheep of the nobility, an accomplice of Madame La Brinvilliers the poisoner etc.

According to another version: Anne of Austria's doctor, having performed an autopsy on Louis XIII, expressed misgivings about the king's ability to father a child. His son-in-law, who inherited the papers, is said to have let out this state secret and he, therefore, may have been the prisoner on Ste-Marguerite.

An even more interesting theory maintains that a lady companion to the Man in the Iron Mask gave birth to a son who was immediately taken away to Corsica. Entrusted (*remis de bonne part* in French – *di buona parte* in Italian) to reliable foster parents, this nameless child is said to have been called "Buonaparte" and to have been the great-grandfather of Napoleon.

The most recent theory is that the man was a black page given to Queen Maria Theresa by the Duke of Beaufort in 1661. The Queen allegedly had an affair with her page and gave birth to a daughter, Marie-Anne, who, like Sister Louis-Marie-Thérèse, became a nun in 1695, better known as the "Moresse de Moret".

M de Saint-Mars, charged with guarding the Man in the Iron Mask and bored to tears on Ste-Marguerite, managed to obtain the post of Governor of the Bastille in 1698. His prisoner went with him and died there in 1703.

A LUSH SETTING *2hr*

Botanical nature trail ⏱ – Most of the island is covered with trees: tall eucalyptus and various species of pine protect a dense undergrowth of tree-heathers, arbutus, mastic trees, cistus, thyme and rosemary.

🄺 Many broad paths flanked by explanatory panels on Mediterranean flora cut through the forest to provide charming **walks**. Starting from the landward side of the fort, the Eucalyptus Walk – the trees are huge – leads to the Domaine du Grand Jardin; the Allée Ste-Marguerite returns to the landing-stage. The cliffs are mostly fairly steep making it difficult to reach the shore. There is a path right round the edge of the island *(about 2hr walk).*

Fort Royal ⏱ – The fortress was built by Richelieu and reinforced by Vauban in 1712. Its main entrance on the west side is monumental. A small **aquarium** *(left)* contains Mediterranean specimens.

In the building beyond, Maréchal Bazaine was imprisoned from 1873 until August 1874 – when he escaped to Spain (official reports do not reveal how). From the terrace there is an extensive **view★** of the nearby coast.

Pass behind Bazaine's quarters to reach the prisons and old castle; the latter currently houses a Marine Museum (Musée de la Mer).

Prisons – The entrance hall gives access to the museum *(right)* and the prisons *(left)*. Until the 19C the corridor leading to the cells used to open directly onto the courtyard.

On the right is the cell of the Man in the Iron Mask. The cells opposite were occupied by six Protestant pastors imprisoned after the Revocation of the Edict of Nantes (1685); they have been converted into a Huguenot memorial with documents on the Protestants, the Wars of Religion, the Edict of Nantes and its Revocation.

Musée de la Mer – The castle's ground floor was built onto the original Roman vaulted rooms. The Marine Museum exhibits archeological finds excavated in the fort and offshore (1C BC Roman galley, 10C Saracen ship). There is an attractive display of artefacts salvaged from wrecked ships: a fine collection of Roman amphorae, glass and ceramics and Arab ceramics with elaborate decorative motifs. Pleasure boating and regattas are the themes evoked in the other rooms.

★★ ÎLE SAINT-HONORAT

St-Honorat (1.5km/1mi long by 400m/437yd wide) has a less hospitable coastline than Ste-Marguerite, from which it is separated by a narrow strait known as the Plateau du Milieu. The island is the private property of the monastery but walking and bathing are nonetheless permitted.

Some of the land is cultivated by the monks, who make a liqueur called Lerina, but the rest is covered by a fine forest of umbrella and sea pines, eucalyptus and a few cypress trees.

At the end of the 4C, **St Honoratus** settled on Lerina, the smaller of the two islands; his retreat soon became known and his disciples hastened to join him. Resigned to not living as a solitary, the saint founded a monastery which was to become one of the most famous and powerful in all Christendom. Pilgrims came in crowds to walk round the island barefoot – a Pope on a visit followed this ancient tradition in all humility. Many of the faithful from France and Italy were buried in the monastery which governed 60 dependent priories. In 660 St Aigulf founded the Benedictine Order in the monastery. Raids by Saracens and Genoese pirates, government by commendation, attacks by the Spaniards and the arrival of military garrisons were not favourable to monastic life so that by 1788 only four monks remained and the monastery was closed. During the Revolution it was confiscated and sold.

In 1859 the monastery once more became a place of worship and in 1869 it was taken over by Cistercians from Sénanque Abbey.

LANDMARKS 2hr

★★ **Island tour** – ▮ Starting from the landing-stage, an attractive shaded path skirts the edge of the island. Occasionally veering inland, it offers many different views of the island, its crops, its trees and wooded walks; Île Ste-Marguerite and the coast on the mainland are also visible.

DINING OUT

L'Escale – *06400 Ste-Marguerite (Island)* – ☎ *04 93 43 49 25 – Closed Dec and evenings Sep-Jun – 25.92€*. Cannes Bay, Cap d'Antibes and the Alpine range in the distance are the views glimpsed from this enchanting restaurant and its long terrace running alongside the beach. Choose between the buffet and seafood platter.

CISTERCIAN SOUVENIRS

Boutique de l'Abbaye de Lérins – *Île Saint-Honorat – 06400 St-Honorat (island)* – ☎ *04 92 99 54 00 – Daily 10.10am-12h15pm, 2-5pm*. This shop attached to the Cistercian abbey sells wine, honey, lavandin *(see p 83)* and naturally the famous liquor Lérina, whose ingredients include 45 different aromatic herbs.

Transport

To the île Ste-Marguerite – *Compagnie Esterel Chanteclair* – ☎ *04 93 39 11 82*. Regular shuttle service leaving from Cannes *(harbour station)*. 8.38€.

To the île St-Honorat – *Société Planaria* – ☎ *04 92 98 71 38*. Shuttle service leaving from Cannes *(harbour station)* every hour 8am-noon, 2-4.30pm (5.30pm May-Sep). 7.62€ there and back (child 4.57€).

On the islands

On the île Ste-Marguerite – No hotels, only restaurants and cafés. Visitors will find many watering places on the island but in high season they are nonetheless advised to bring food and water supplies with them for the day.

On the île St-Honorat – The whole island is occupied by a Cistercian monastery and does therefore not have any restaurants (sale of sandwiches at the landing-stage between April and October. There are few watering places and moreover water may be rationed in summer. Bicycles are forbidden on the island. Tourists are expected to dress decently.

★ **Ancien Monastère Fortifié** ⊙ – The remarkable high "keep" or "castle" of this old fortified monastery is set on a spit of land projecting into the sea from the southern coastline. It was built in 1073 by Aldebert, Abbot of Lérins, on Roman foundations, to protect the monks from Saracen pirates.

The gate is over 4m/13ft above ground level and access to it was by a ladder which has now been replaced by a stone stairway. Facing the entrance, a staircase leads to a barrel-vaulted storeroom. On the left, a few steps lead up to the first floor.

The **cloisters** with pointed arches and the 14C and 17C vaulting (one of the columns is a Roman milestone) enclose a square courtyard covering a rainwater tank paved with marble. The upper gallery, with small columns of white marble, goes to the chapel of the Ste-Croix (Holy Cross), a high room with Gothic arches still called the "Holy of Holies" owing to the many relics it contained.

From the platform with its 15C battlements and crenellations at the top of the old keep, the **view★★** extends over the Îles de Lérins and the coastline from the Esterel to Cap d'Antibes, with the often snow-capped peaks of the Alps in the far distance.

Monastère Moderne ⊙ – *Only the museum and church are open to the public.* The early buildings occupied by the monks, parts of which date from the 11C and 12C, have been incorporated into the "new" 19C monastery.

Museum – Situated on the left of the cloisters, it groups Roman and Christian lapidary fragments found on the island, together with documents on the monastery's history and influence. There is also a panel from an altarpiece (St Benedict, St Peter, St John the Baptist), believed to be by Louis Bréa.

Church – The abbey church was built in the 19C in the neo-Romanesque style. In the north transept is an 11C Chapel of the Dead.

Chapels – Seven chapels scattered about the island completed the monastery; they were intended for anchorites, monks who prayed in the privacy of their retreat. Two have retained their former appearance.

La Trinité – Situated at the eastern tip of the island, it pre-dates the 11C. It is built on a trefoil plan with an oval cupola resting on pendentives. The Byzantine influence leads some experts to date it around the 5C.

St-Sauveur – The chapel located in the northwest corner of the island is as old as La Trinité but built to an octagonal plan. It was restored in the 17C and once again more recently.

The balls of fibre which roll on the beaches and catch on the vegetation of the dunes are in fact the dry remains of posidonia. This marine plant forms "meadows" on the seabed and is an essential producer of oxygen.

LEVENS

Population 3 700
Michelin map 84 fold 19, 115 fold 16 or 245 fold 25
Local map see NICE

The medieval village (alt 600m/1 968ft) has given refuge to the coastal population over the centuries. With its modern facilities it is a pleasant place for a holiday.

THE OLD VILLAGE

Place de la Mairie opens into an attractive public garden, its shaded terraces overlooking the valley; nearby stands the curved façade of the Baroque Chapelle des Pénitents-Blancs. In Rue du Docteur-Faraud, the Chapelle des Pénitents-Noirs presents a fine collection of works of art, many of which are displayed in the crypt.

In Rue Masséna stands the house, dated 1722, of the Masséna family; some amusing **frescoes** on the life of Marshal Masséna, executed by the painter Dussour in 1958 in the style of strip cartoons, are to be found at the town hall **(mairie)** ⊙. At the end of the street, you walk past the surviving ramparts and the **Maison du Portal** *(temporary exhibitions)* before reaching Place de la Liberté. A vaulted passageway leads to the church, which was been heavily restored both inside and outside.

Take the path on the left and climb up towards the swimming pool.

Local specialities

Les Santons – *Village* – ☎ 04 93 79 72 47 – *Closed 3 Jan-9 Feb, 25 Jun-4 Jul, 1-10 Oct, Wed and evenings except Sat – Reservation required –* 16.77/29.73€. Stop for a break on this pretty terrace in a restaurant ideally located in a perched village overlooking the Vésubie Gorges. The owner will be happy to introduce you to the gastronomic subtleties of local cuisine at reasonable prices.

★ **View** – From near the 1914-18 War Memorial and further as the outer boulevard loops back to the village, the view extends over the junction of the Var and the Vésubie in its setting of high mountains from the Cheiron to Le Mercantour.

OUTINGS

Duranus – *8.5km/5mi – allow 30min. From Levens take D 19 north.*
The road overlooks the deep Gorges de la Vésubie *(See Vallée de la VÉSUBIE)* from a great height, and affords a glimpse of the chapel of Madone d'Utelle *(left)* high up in the mountains.
Duranus, a pretty village set in the midst of orchards and vineyards, was founded in 17C by the people of Rocca-Sparviero, a ruined village at Col St-Michel.
Although Queen Jeanne was in fact childless, the legend recounts that she cast a spell on the local population because she was tricked by villagers into eating her own children at a banquet.

★★ **Saut des Français** – At the northern end of Duranus is the Frenchmen's Leap, marked by a viewpoint. It commemorates Republican soldiers who were hurled over the edge in 1793 by bands of guerillas from the Vésubie Valley. The view is almost lost in the dizzy vertical drop to the bottom of the gorges, with Utelle and its chapel dominating the scene.

LORGUES

Population 7 319
Michelin map 84 fold 6, 114 fold 22 or 245 fold 35

Lorgues spreads up a slope towards wooded hilltops. The ground is well suited to the cultivation of vines and olives. Oil, both from olives and grape seeds, is produced in large quantities here.
It is a small, pleasant town where the main square is one of the most beautiful in the whole region. The splendid plane trees gracing this market square and other narrow streets were originally planted in 1835. Markets are held in Lorgues on Tuesdays.

VISITING THE OLD QUARTER

A touch of medieval charm – The fortified gateways are 12C. The streets of the town, which radiate from a central square, are dotted with charming fountains. A stroll along any of them reveals many interesting old houses with their attractive façades, lintels, wrought-iron work and stairways.

Collégiale St-Martin – The 18C church was built by Bishop Fleury of Fréjus, who later became a cardinal and a minister to Louis XV. It is unusually large with a dressed stone façade. The high altar in multicoloured marble is decorated with angels' heads. The Virgin and Child is attributed to Pierre Puget. The church features a fine organ and a carved pulpit.

EXCURSIONS

Ermitage de St-Ferréol – *1km/0.6mi. Follow the signs to the northeast of the town.* The chapel stands on a low wooded hill; note the traces of a Roman settlement.

SWEET OR SAVOURY?

Sucrés-Salés – *7 Avenue Allongue –* ☎ *04 94 67 63 80 – Closed Sun for lunch and Mon –* 🗇 *– 9.15/15.24€.* Beyond the curious façade decorated with children's drawings lies a treasure trove of delicacies, both sweet and savoury. The owner is renowned for his delicious homemade production of chocolate (not in summer), honey, jam, together with olive oil, foie gras and *rillettes* available for sale. Besides the shop, there is also a small delicatessen where gastronomic specialities can be relished in the dining room or on the tiny terrace.

Le Chrissandier – *18 Cours de la République –* ☎ *04 94 67 67 15 – Closed Jan and Wed off season. – 10.67€ lunch – 14.48/38.11€.* Nestled in the old medieval quarter, this recently decorated rustic-style restaurant attracts a regular clientele at lunchtime and caters for tourists in the evening. The menu changes every day as it is dictated by the availability of fresh market produce.

Wine

Around a dozen wine-growing estates are located in the vicinity of Lorgues. All of these organise tastings and sales of Côtes-de-Provence and other wines coming from the Var and Argens regions. Some vineyards can be visited. Other estates provide bed-and-breakfast accommodation. For details apply to the local tourist office.

Riding clubs

Appaloosa Ranch – *28 Hameau de Chateaurenard –* ☎ *04 94 73 74 92.* Pony-trekking.
Le Jas de Barna – *La Colle district in Villecroze –* ☎ *04 94 70 76 43.*
These two riding clubs will delight horse lovers.

Chapelle Notre-Dame-de-Benva ⏱ – *3km/2mi northwest (D 50) on the Entre-casteaux road*. The chapel of Our Lady of Benva (corruption of Provençal *ben vai*: good journey) stands on a hillside. Its porch is built astride the old Entrecasteaux road so that passers-by should notice it. Both the porch and the interior are decorated with 15C frescoes in the Naïve tradition.

Monastère Orthodoxe St-Michel ⏱ – *8km/5mi north by D 10. – 10km/6mi by D 77*. These stone buildings of Byzantine inspiration were once home to an Orthodox community founded under the authority of the Patriarch of Antioch. The crypt, refectory and church are adorned with frescoes in the Romanesque and Byzantine styles. The only part open to the public is the wooden chapel, a miniature replica of Souzdal Cathedral in Russia.

Taradeau – *9km/6mi – southeast on D 10*.
A "Saracen" tower and a ruined Romanesque chapel crown the bluff dominating the village, which is a wine-producing centre.
Take D 73 north uphill.

Turn right into a stony path marked Table d'Orientation 800m" *(viewing table)* and park the car. From the top there is a vast **panorama**★ over Lorgues, Les Arcs, the Provençal tableland and the Grasse Pre-Alps, the Esterel and the Maures.

★★**Abbaye du Thoronet** – *13km/8mi southwest. From Lorgues take D 562 towards Carcès. Bear left onto D 17 and turn right onto D 79. See Abbaye du THORONET.*

Vallée du LOUP★★

Michelin map 84 folds 8 and 9, 115 folds 24 and 25 or 245 fold 37

The Loup rises at an altitude of 1 300m/4 250ft in the Pre-Alps of Grasse (north face of the Audibergue Mountain). For almost all of its short journey to the Mediterranean, the river has cut a valley gorge through the mountains – and this ranks among the most beautiful natural sights of Haute-Provence. The approach roads to the gorges pass through a picturesque region where there are many perched villages.

DRIVING TOURS

★★**Gorges du Loup** *56km/35mi – about 1 day leaving from Vence*

★**Vence** – *See VENCE.*
From Vence take D 2210 northwest; after 2km/1.2mi bear right onto a road signposted "Galerie Beaubourg–Château-Notre-Dame-des-Fleurs".

Château Notre-Dame-des-Fleurs – *See VENCE: Excursions.*
The road is bordered by pleasant houses nestled among the olive trees. There is a view back over the hills round Vence.

★**Tourrettes-sur-Loup** – *See TOURRETTES-SUR-LOUP.*
The road loops round the attractive village of Tourrettes-sur-Loup before passing the limestone fissures of the Loup Valley. The perched village of Bar-sur-Loup comes into sight, followed by the tiny hamlet of Gourdon clinging to its promontory.

Pont-du-Loup – The Draguignan-Nice railway line, which crossed the entrance to the Gorges du Loup was blown up by the Germans in 1944; the viaduct ruins are still visible.
The area has a good reputation for the fruit jellies *(pâte de fruits)* and delicately scented jams (roses, violets etc) it produces.
Outside the village turn right onto D 6.
The road runs through the splendid **Gorges du Loup**★★, cut vertically through the Grasse mountains, with huge, gaping holes, smooth and round, hollowed out of their sides. Just before the second tunnel, in a semicircular hollow, the **Cascade de Courmes**★ spills down onto a mossy bed (40m/130ft).
Only when the site is open in season leave the car beyond the third tunnel.

Further on, amid lush vegetation, a huge megalith marks the entrance to the **Saut du Loup** ⏱, an enormous cauldron shaped by marine and glacial erosion in the Tertiary and Quaternary eras, in which the waters of the Loup swirl furiously in spring. The waterfall known as **Cascades des Demoiselles** gushes down through a strange setting of mosses and vegetation petrified by the spray, which has a high lime carbonate content.
Just before the bridge, **Pont de Bramafan**, turn sharp left onto D 3. As the road rises to Caussols Plateau, the vegetation grows sparser but as far as Gourdon there are continual **views**★ down into the depths of the gorges with a particularly breathtaking **view**★★ where an overhang has been built out from a sharp right-hand turn *(signpost)*. Beyond the end of the gorges the view widens out southwards towards the coast.

★**Gourdon** – *See GOURDON.*
Interesting drive downhill from Caussols plateau along D 3. In Le-Pré-du-Lac turn left onto D 2085.

THE NATURAL CHOICE

Auberge de Courmes – *3 Rue des Platanes – 06620 Courmes – ☎ 04 93 77 64 70 – Closed 5-29 Jan, Sun evening and Mon – 5 rooms: 41€ – ☑ 6€ – Restaurant 17.53/20.58€.* This local inn on the square of a tiny hamlet dominating the Loup Gorges offers 5 small rooms and a welcoming dining area. Outstanding views of the mountains, facilities for hiking and rambling, and a peaceful atmosphere will guarantee a most enjoyable stay.

Chambre d'Hôte La Cascade – *635 Chemin de la Cascade – 06620 Courmes – ☎ 04 93 09 65 85 – lacascade@wanadoo.fr – 6 rooms: 41.16/44.21€ – Meal 12€.* The sign marking this guest house illustrates the nearby waterfall of Courmes. The original building, now enlarged and restored, contains clean, tidy rooms. Particularly suitable for nature lovers and overworked city executives.

St-Pons – The small village lies on a slope where olives, vines and jasmine grow.

After Le Collet bear left onto D 7 and drive down a wooded valley which becomes more and more enclosed until it joins the lower Loup Valley, where there is a good **view** of the river and of the precipitous Pre-Alps of Grasse in the background.

After a *corniche* section (cut into the rock face with good views), the road descends to the valley floor to cross the river.

La Colle-sur-Loup – The name comes from the Latin word *collis*, meaning hill or mound. A picturesque village in the plain where fruit and flowers are cultivated. The main street features a series of antique shops selling typical Provençal furniture. The church has a Renaissance door and a square bell-tower.

★★ **St-Paul** – *See ST-PAUL.*

Beyond St-Paul the **view** extends to the foothills of the Pre-Alps of Grasse.

Return to Vence by D 2 and D 236.

Courmes waterfall

Haute Vallée du Loup

47km/29mi – about 1hr 30min leaving from Vence.

Leave Vence by D 2 going northwest. From Vence to Coursegoules the route is described in reverse order under Route des Crêtes above.

From Coursegoules return to D 2 going west.

The road descends a green valley and suddenly emerges into the **upper Loup Valley★**, a beautiful stretch of country with superb views both before and after Gréolières.

Gréolières – This is a perched village at the southern foot of Mont Cheiron; to the north are the extensive ruins of Haut-Gréolières; to the south are the remains of an important stronghold.

The **church**, which has only one aisle, has a Romanesque façade and a squat bell-tower. On the left (on entering) stands a 15C silver-gilt processional cross and a fragment of a 16C retable of John the Baptist; opposite stands a 14C wooden statue of the Virgin and Child; the finest work (high on the right) is the **retable of St Stephen★** by an unknown artist with Christ and his Apostles on the predella (15C).

West of Gréolières the road climbs above the village and then snakes westward along the side of the gorge passing in and out of brief tunnels and beneath huge rock spurs of fantastic shape and size. More than 400m/1 312ft below flows the River Loup.

★**Clue de Gréolières** – The rift was formed by a tributary of the Loup; its bare slopes are pitted with giant holes and spiked with curious dolomitic rocks.
The road emerges from the rift onto a broad alluvial plateau, Plan-du-Peyron.

In Plan-du-Peyron turn right onto D 802.

As the road climbs the south face of Mont Cheiron, there are interesting **views** to the west and north.

Gréolières-les-Neiges – Alt 1 450m/4 757ft. The resort, which lies on the north face of Mont Cheiron, is the most southerly of the Alpine ski stations; it is well equipped, easily accessible and attracts large crowds of local skiers.

Drive back via Col de Vence (see VENCE: Excursions) or via the Gorges du Loup.

Le LUC

Population 7 282
Michelin map 84 fold 16, 114 fold 54 or 245 fold 47
Local map see Massif des MAURES

This important farming centre lying on the former Via Aurelia is a collection point for harvests among the vine and olive growers of the Var Plain and acts as the crossroads of the central Var region.
The marine engineer **Jean-Baptiste Lebas** (1797-1873), born in Le Luc, was in charge of transporting the famous obelisk from Luxor to Place de la Concorde in Paris. The main events of his life are chronicled in the Musée du Centre-Var.

THE OLD VILLAGE

An imposing belfry – Le Luc lies in the shade of a 16C hexagonal tower some 27m/89ft high. This tower, built in the style of Italian campaniles, is used as a bell-tower. An identification table on the main buildings provides a detailed description of the village.

View from the Oppidum de Fouirette – *45min on foot. Walk towards the Vergeiras district, then follow a signposted path leading to the top of the hill (300m/984ft high).*
There is a wonderful **view★** over the Maures Plain, from Gonfaron to Rocher de Roquebrune.

SIGHTS

Musée Historique du Centre-Var ⊙ – This museum about local history is housed in the 17C Chapelle Ste-Anne and displays collections of historical artefacts uncovered during excavations carried out in the area: fossils (dinosaur eggs), a carved Roman sarcophagus, medieval sculptures, minerals from the Maures Massif and ancient weapons. There is also a historical display on Le Luc.

Musée Régional du Timbre ⊙ – This regional museum devoted to the history of **postage stamps and philately** is housed in the Château de Vintimille, a striking 18C building. The clear and spacious display follows the different stages in the traditional (that is using copper-plate engraving) manufacture of postage stamps. A reconstruction of the studio of Albert Decaris, the designer and engraver of many stamps, both French and foreign, provides a fitting backdrop for these processes. Numerous examples of philatelic counterfeiting and non-French stamps round off the exhibition. A wide range of literature *(documentation)* on philately is available for visitors to consult.

Campaniles in the Var

Les Arcs	Tour de l'Horloge (18C)
Aups	Tour de l'Horloge
Carcès	Campanile atop a fortified gate (18C)
Carnoules	Belfry (17C)
Cotignac	Campanile (16C)
Draguignan	Tower (17C)
Flassans	Atop the belfry (18C)
Le Luc	Tower (16C)
St-Tropez	Campanile (19C)
Salernes	Belfry (18C)
Tavernes	Campanile (18C)
Toulon	Arsenal tower (18C)

Clock tower, Toulon Arsenal

J.-L. Gallo/MICHELIN

LUCÉRAM★

Population 1 035
Michelin map 84 fold 19, 115 fold 17 or 245 fold 25
Local map see NICE

The village stands on a steep rock between two ravines in a wooded region beneath the mountain peak, Cime du Gros Braus; it was also defended by ramparts including the 13C tower which dominates the town. Lucéram not only boasts a remarkable **setting★★** but is exceptionally rich in works of art.

★ **Noël des bergers** – Each year shepherds from the neighbouring mountains make their offering of lambs and fruit to the church to the strains of fife and tambourine music.

★THE GOTHIC TOUCH

On Place Adrien-Barralis, follow the arrows pointing to the church (église).

A maze of stepped streets and vaulted alleyways make up the medieval town. Note the Ionic columns framing a 14C doorway to the right and the many Gothic houses all along the route. From the church terrace one can look down over Lucéram, its tower and crenellated walls, and beyond the hills behind Nice to the sea.

Eglise Ste-Marguerite ⊙ – The interior of the simple 15C church was remodelled in the 18C with elaborate plasterwork.

★★ **Altarpieces** – These form the most complete group attributed to the Nice School and they are among the best presented in the County of Nice. In the south transept is the remarkable **altarpiece of St Antony** framed in Flamboyant Gothic panelling with decorative motifs, sometimes against a gilded chequered backdrop.

Behind the high altar, the outstanding **altarpiece of St Margaret**, which is divided into 10 panels, is by Louis Bréa: around the central figure are Mary Magdalene (bottom left) and St Michael (top left).

Lucéram

Three fine altarpieces by the Bréa School are placed in the nave.

★**Treasury** – It comprises some remarkable pieces: a chased silver statuette of St Margaret (1500), a finely engraved 14C reliquary, a statue-reliquary of St Rosalie from Sicily, two candlesticks and an alabaster Virgin (16C).

Additional works – On the left of the entrance stands an unusual Baroque Pietà in painted wood and to the left of the chancel another one in plaster on cloth dating from the 13C. Old processional lanterns in wrought iron are displayed.

CHAPELS

Chapelle St-Grat ◷ – *1km/0.6mi to the south on D 2566.*
This chapel is decorated with frescoes attributed to Jean Baleison. Parts of the vaults show the four Evangelists writing; beneath a triple Gothic canopy are the Virgin and Child who is holding a dove, St Grat bearing the head of John the Baptist and St Sebastian in elegant attire with an arrow in his hand.

Chapelle Notre-Dame-de-Bon-Cœur ◷ – *2km/1.3mi northwest on D 2566, then 15min on foot there and back. Park the car on the open space and take the path on the left past a ruined house to the chapel.*
The frescoes, attributed to Baleison, are interesting despite some unfortunate repainting. In the porch: Good and Bad Prayer and St Sebastian; in the chapel: the Adoration of the Shepherds, the Adoration of the Magi and scenes illustrating the life of the Virgin.

MANDELIEU-LA-NAPOULE★

Michelin map 84 fold 8, 114 fold 26, 115 folds 34-35 or 245 fold 37
Local map see Massif de l'ESTEREL

Lying at the foot of the Esterel and Tanneron Massifs, Mandelieu is a charming locality extending right to the shores of the Mediterranean. In the Middle Ages, it was a small fishing harbour called Epulia but today it is famed throughout the region for its lovely mimosa trees. The pretty bay and the River Siagne, bordered by lush plains and beaches further downstream, make this town a highly popular resort, both in summer and winter.
During the 19C, Mandelieu was frequented by many wealthy foreigners: the Grand Duke of Russia, the American sculptor Henry Clews turned the château into a home for visiting artists and English aristocrats introduced canoeing along the Siagne.
There are local markets held on Place de la Casinca in Mandelieu *(Wednesdays)*, and in La Napoule, on Place St-Fainéant *(Thursdays)* and Place Jeanne-d'Arc *(Saturdays)*.

A PRIVILEGED SETTING

Three heavenly beaches run along the bay, offering impressive views of the area *(Victoria and Sweet are private beaches)*. The extensive marina can accommodate 1 300 pleasure craft.

Eating out

MID-RANGE

Bistrot du Port – *Port* – ☎ *04 93 49 80 60* – *Closed mid-Nov to mid-Dec and Wed Sep to Jun* – *19.82/25.61€.* The quiet pedestrian quays of the marina are the setting for this restaurant, complete with terrace and verandah. The dining room with its wooden furnishings evokes the interior of a luxury yacht. The perfect place to order fresh pasta, homemade pizza or, in the afternoon, a sundae or a cocktail.

Restaurant de Plage la Voile d'Azur – *Avenue du Général-de-Gaulle – 2km/1mi by N 98 along the coast, towards Cannes* – ☎ *04 93 49 20 44 – 22.87€.* Beach restaurant commanding a sweeping panorama of the whole coastline. Its attractive terrace is fought over as soon as the sun makes an appearance. Interesting choice of salads and grilled fish dishes.

Where to stay

MODERATE

Corniche d'Or – *Place de la Fontaine – 06210 La Napoule* – ☎ *04 93 49 92 51 – Closed 16 Oct-24 Apr* – ⊟ – *12 rooms: 28.20/46.50€* – ☕ *4.88€.* On a tiny square near the station, this modest hotel has simple rooms, many of which have a small balcony. Two, however, have a large terrace.

MID-RANGE

Hôtel Villa Parisiana – *Rue Argentière* – ☎ *04 93 49 93 02 – Closed 19 Nov-3 Dec – 13 rooms: 41.16/59.46€* – ☕ *5.34€.* This Edwardian villa located in a residential area houses a congenial, family-style hotel with a treillised terrace. Most of the rooms have balconies; ask for one that has been renovated. The inadequate soundproofing sometimes reveals the presence of the nearby railway.

Casino

Royal Hôtel Casino – *605 Avenue du Général-de-Gaulle* – ☎ *04 92 97 70 00* – *royal.hotel.casino.com* – *Bar Blue-wave: 9am-2am. Piano bar: 7.30pm-10.30pm. Bar dancing: 10.30pm-3am (closed Sun off season).* Luxury establishment with a terrace and pool giving onto Cannes Bay. The hotel also features a casino, two restaurants, a newly opened nightclub and a piano bar with live musical performances every evening.

Sport

Golf Club de Cannes Mandelieu – *Route du Golf.* ☎ *04 92 97 32 00.* This golf course founded by the Grand Duke of Russia in 1891 is one of the oldest in France. Located at the heart of town, its design is similar to that of St-Andrews, the prestigious golf course in Scotland.

Guy Durante Organisation – *Avenue du Général-de-Gaulle-Plage de Robinson* – ☎ *04 93 49 44 19 ou 06 80 64 03 50 – Mid-May to mid-Oct: daily.* This is the landing-stage used for water sports such as wake-board, water-skiing and parascending.

Sant'Estello Country Club – *3300 Avenue Paul-Ricard* – ☎ *04 93 49 44 00* – *Daily, also open nights in Jul-Aug.* This tennis club set up on the handsome Sant'Estello estate is comprised of ten courts, including four clay courts, which remain open all year round.

Family recreation

Domaine de Barbossi – *3300 Avenue Paul-Ricard* – ☎ *04 93 49 64 74 – School holidays: daily 10am-noon, 2-8.30pm; rest of the year: Wed, Sat, Sun 10am-noon and 1.30pm-7pm.* A perfect outing for the whole family. Besides the tennis club, there are facilities for mountain cycling, trampoline jumping, miniature golf, pony riding, alongside several playing areas for children.Red wine and rosé wine, produced and bottled on the estate, are available for sale.

Panoramic tour – *Leave from the post office by Rue des Hautes-Roches, then 45min on foot there and back along a signposted route.*
▣ This pleasant walk winding its way up Colline de San Peyré affords fantastic **views**★ over the Tanneron, La Napoule Bay, Cannes and Cap d'Antibes.

SIGHT

Château-Musée ⊙ – *In La Napoule.* Only two towers remain of the original 14C stronghold converted by Henry Clews and his wife, who was an architect. Located in an outstanding **site**★ at the foot of the Esterel corniche, the château offers a curious blend of Romanesque and Gothic styles enhanced by Oriental-like decoration. The public can visit the beautiful grounds, the salons, the cloisters and Henry Clews' studio. The walls are used as a backdrop for his extraordinary sculptures, combining grace, wit, realism and irony.

Massif des MAURES★★★

Michelin map 84 folds 7, 16 to 18, 114 folds 34 to 37
or 245 folds 47 to 49

The wooded Massif des Maures extends eastwards from Hyères to St-Raphaël, between the sea to the Gapeau and Argens river valleys. The coast is continuously indented, providing delightful viewpoints and beauty spots which can be seen from the magnificent tourist road, particularly the section from Le Lavandou to La Croix-Valmer known as the **Corniche des Maures**. The interior is broken up by shaded valleys and wild ravines.

GEOGRAPHICAL NOTES

The Maures, composed for the most part of crystalline schists (gneiss and mica-schists), are, with the Esterel range, the oldest geological area in Provence. The Hercynian folding pushed up a vast continent, Tyrrhenia, which included Corsica and Sardinia.

Successive thrusts originating from the Pyrenees and the Alps broke up this mass, forming the western basin of the Mediterranean and reshaping the Maures into four parallel lines of relief.

The Îles d'Hyères mark the southern chain, which is partially submerged; the second chain along the coast reaches its highest point at Les Pradels (528m/1 725ft); the two inland chains, La Verne and La Sauvette, are separated by the River Grimaud and River Collobrières. La Sauvette, the most northerly chain, includes the highest peaks, Notre-Dame-des-Anges (780m/2 559ft) and La Sauvette (779m/2 556ft), and ends in Roque-brune Mountain overlooking the lower Argens Valley.

The coastline juts out in the blunt promontories of Cap Bénat and St-Tropez Peninsula, the pointed headlands of Cap Nègre and Cap des Sardinaux and retreats into the Bormes anchorage, and the bays of Cavalaire and St-Tropez.

The pines along the coast, and the cork-oaks, holm oaks, arbutus, cistus and chestnuts inland, which form the main vegetation of the Maures, are sometimes devastated by raging forest fires. The massif's principal industry, the manufacture of bottle corks, derives from the cork-oaks that are carefully cultivated.

HISTORICAL NOTES

Maouro, a Provençal word that refers to dark forests, has become *Maures* in French and is used to describe this densely wooded mountain range.

On the other hand, tradition sees in the name an allusion to the Moorish pirates from Spain, who ravaged the coast in the 8C and established themselves in the following century on the slopes around the Grimaud plain; but these pirates were really Saracens. Driven out in 973, they continued to raid the coast up to the 18C and set up a reign of terror. To defend themselves, the inhabitants withdrew from the shore, going up into the hills from where they could watch the horizon.

It was the 20C vogue for sea-bathing, limited at first to an aristocratic clientele, which brought this magnificent coast back to life and ended the economic isolation of the region. On 15 August 1944 the Allied and French Armies landed on the Maures beaches to liberate the south of France.

Gonfaron tortoises

Hermann's Tortoise

This tortoise, the only species native to France, appeared in Mediterranean Europe about one million years ago. It lives in the scrub *(maquis)* which provides all its food – oak leaves, fruit and molluscs. After hibernating in a tree stump until about June, the female lays her eggs in a nest which she immediately abandons. If they survive the first two months of life and predatory badgers, the baby tortoises can look forward to a life of 60 to 100 years. Hermann's tortoise has already disappeared from mainland Spain, the Balearic Islands and part of the Balkans, because of natural predators as well as fire (which is the greatest threat); it is now falling victim to alterations in its habitat caused by man and unregulated collecting. The tortoises now survive only in Corsica and in the Massif des Maures, where a tortoise village has been established to protect the species.

Massif des Maures coast

★★ CORNICHE DES MAURES

From Le Lavandou to St-Tropez

⌂⌂ **Le Lavandou** – *See Le LAVANDOU*.
From Le Lavandou the road runs along the wooded coastline, which is bright and colourful with flowers in season.

St-Clair – The small resort of St-Clair, a short distance from the main road, has a large and beautiful beach.

Aiguebelle – Pleasant, peaceful seaside resort.

⌂ **Cavalière** – Cavalière has a fine beach, sheltered from the *mistral*. The view extends over Cap Nègre and the Bormes anchorage as far as the Île du Levant and Port-Cros.

Pramousquier – A modest resort with a sheltered beach of fine sand.
The road leaves the shore and meanders up among pine trees and gardens.

⌂ **Le Rayol-Canadel-sur-Mer** – Canadel, lying at the base of the last foothills of the Pradels range and flanked by superb pine woods, possesses one of the most sheltered beaches on the Maures coast.

⌂ **Cavalaire-sur-Mer** – A perfect holiday destination for the family. Fine 4km/2.5mi sandy beach and marina with room for 1 000 moorings. *See CAVALAIRE*.

La Croix-Valmer – The village is a climatic resort and a spa. The local wine is well considered among Côtes de Provence.
The site of La Croix village is said to be where Constantine had his vision while on his way to Rome to claim the Empire. According to tradition he saw a cross in the sky with the words "*In hoc signo vinces*" (in this sign you will conquer), a prediction of his forthcoming victory which was shared by Christianity; after the battle Constantine converted to Christianity. A stone cross erected on the

J. Guillard/SCOPE

pass commemorates the legend and gives the village its name. An alternative tradition relates that Constantine's vision of his victory over Maxentius occurred at the Milvian Bridge outside Rome.

Col de Collebasse – Alt 129m/43ft. *8km/5mi from La Croix-Valmer along the very winding D 93*. There is a superb **view★** of the Pampelonne bight, Cavalaire Bay and the Îles d'Hyères.

Drive back to St-Tropez on D 93.

★★ **St-Tropez** – *See St-Tropez.*

★★ From St-Tropez to Fréjus

On the opposite side of the peninsula, the Massif des Maures slopes gently down towards the Mediterranean. On the sunny coast running along N 98, these smiling seaside resorts boast fine beaches, with clusters of rocks breaking the clear surface.

Beauvallon – Beauvallon is a beautifully located resort on the north shores of St-Tropez Bay shaded by pine and cork-oak woods.

⌂⌂ **Ste-Maxime** – *See STE-MAXIME.*
The road, which skirts the coast closely as far as St-Aygulf, circles Cap Sardinaux.

La Nartelle – The beach of what is now the resort of La Nartelle was one of the landing points for the Allied forces in August 1944.
The coastline between La Nartelle and St-Aygulf is broken up into several inlets *(calanques)* with small beaches and rocks emerging from the sea.

⌂ **Les Issambres** – This pretty resort is associated with Val d'Esquières, San Peïre and Les Calanques and forms a rapidly expanding holiday centre. Houses of various sizes, some built in the Provençal style, have been discreetly sited in the hills. Les Issambres probably takes its name from "Sinus Sambracitanus", the Roman name for St-Tropez Bay.

General advice about visiting the Massifs

Roads belonging to the DFCI (Défense Forestière Contre l'Incendie – forest fire-fighters) are closed to public traffic. They count as private roads; an open barrier does not indicate that access is permitted. Parking in front of these barriers is prohibited and cars should be parked well to the side of narrow roads to allow the passage of emergency vehicles. Pedestrian access is always possible.

During periods of high fire risk, the ALARME plan is put into action and certain public roads (classed as major fire risks) may be closed to vehicles. Offenders are liable for heavy fines. Walkers are strongly advised to avoid such areas for reasons of safety.

Camping is prohibited in the massif and within 200m/656ft of any of the forests. While walking in the massif, respect plants and wild animals and do not touch them, stay on the paths and keep dogs under control. Do not pick fruit, in particular chestnuts, as you may be requested to pay a fine.

Eating out

MODERATE

Maures – *19 Boulevard Lazare-Carnot – 83610 Collobrières – ☎ 04 94 48 07 10 – 8.38€ lunch – 15.24€*. This village inn enjoys a well-deserved reputation among its regular clientele on account of the excellent quality/price ratio and the warm welcome it extends. In summer meals are served on the terrace beneath the plane trees.

MID-RANGE

Alizés – *Promenade de la Mer – 83240 Cavalaire-sur-Mer – ☎ 04 94 64 09 32 – 16.77/28.97€*. A lively atmosphere and the undeniable charisma of the owners are the main assets of this modern-style hotel offering pretty views of the sea. Family cooking with an emphasis on fish and homemade desserts. Some of the recently refurbished rooms are extended by a balcony.

Chante-Mer – *Village – 83380 Les Issambres – ☎ 04 94 96 93 23 – Closed 15 Dec-31 Jan, Sun evening Sep to Easter, Tue for lunch Easter to Sep and Mon – 19.51/32.78€*. The running of this restaurant is, quite literally, a family business: the father busies himself in the kitchen while his wife and two daughters wait on customers. Settle on the terrace or inside the small, neat dining room and treat your tastebuds to a delicious experience... at no great expense.

Where to stay

MODERATE

Chambre d'Hôte Le Mas des Oliviers – *83390 Puget-Ville – 2.5km by N 97 Route de Cuers – ☎ 04 94 48 30 89 – sapori@club-internet.fr – Closed late Oct to late Mar – ⌷ – 3 rooms: 48.78/56.41€ – Meal 18€*. Charming Provençal *mas* lost among vineyards and olive groves. Large, carefully kept rooms decorated in the Mediterranean style. Horse riding and cycling facilities available nearby.

MID-RANGE

Chambre d'Hôte L'Amandari – *Vallat Emponse – 83120 Plan-de-la-Tour – ☎ 04 94 43 79 20 – ⌷ – 6 rooms: 60.88/91.32€ – ⌷ 6.86€ – Meal 21.31€*. This former sheep barn tucked away by a river exudes a peaceful, friendly atmosphere. The small rooms, each with their own personal touch, give onto a patio. The swimming pool, terrace and leafy grounds are a good excuse to opt for the farniente life.

Golfe Bleu – *Route de La Croix-Valmer – 83240 Cavalaire-sur-Mer – 1km/0.6mi from the wayside cross on D 559 Route de La Croix-Valmer – ☎ 04 94 64 07 56 – Closed 2 Nov-31 Jan – 15 rooms: 60.98/68.60€ – ⌷ 5.95€ – Restaurant 14€*. Neat, homey establishment away from the town centre. The rooms are soundproofed and air-conditioned. The sparsely decorated restaurant opens out onto a small terrace.

Sport and recreation centre

Smash Club – *Avenue du Golf – 83980 Cavalière – ☎ 04 95 05 84 31 – smash-club.fr.st – Jul-Aug: daily 8am-2am. Apr-Jun and Sep-Oct: daily 9am-9pm. Nov-Mar: daily 2.30-7pm*. Do not fail to visit this sports centre catering for all tastes: six tennis courts, golf links, a weights room, an archery gallery, a sauna, mountain bikes for rental... Tennis tournaments and badminton, beach-volley, football and *boules* competitions are organised during the summer season. The latest novelty is the "Indiana Jones itinerary".

DRIVING TOURS

① In Maures Country

70km/44mi leaving from Hyères – allow one day

Leave Hyères to the northeast on N 98.

After crossing the Gapeau, the road runs past the salt-marshes across the Hyères plain with views of Cap Bénat and the Île du Port-Cros.

After the glassworks, turn right onto D 559. After Le Lavandou it follows the coast up to Canadel-sur-Mer. Turn left onto D 27.

★★ **Col du Canadel** – Alt 267m/876ft. Suddenly the sea comes into view; there is a superb **panorama**★★ of Canadel, Pramousquier beach, Cap Nègre, the Bormes anchorage, Cap Bénat and beyond, on the horizon, the Île de Porquerolles.

Leave the car in the car park on the col. Take the forest track on the right to the Col de Caguo-Ven (closed to cars).

This is a picturesque route with magnificent **views**★ of the Maures Massif and, to the south, the coast and the Îles d'Hyères.

The forest track along a ridge, bordered with chestnuts and mimosas, is shared with GR 51 to Col de Barral. Vieux-Sauvaire is reached after one hour's walk *(restaurant open here in season)* after which the path goes back down to Col de Barral (372m/1 220ft). There are fine views from the ridge which the path follows for 5km/3mi to the Pierre d'Avenon.

Continue along D 27 then turn left onto N 98, heading towards La Môle. Proceed straight on until you reach Dom Forest.

★ **Forêt Domaniale du Dom** – This state forest, composed mainly of pines, cork-oaks and chestnuts, spreads over the Les Pradels and La Verne ranges, which are separated by the steep-sided Môle Valley. **Jean Aicard** (1848-1921), poet and novelist, set his work *Maurin des Maures* in this area.

1km/0.5mi before the pass, stop by the Maison Forestière de Gratteloup.

Arboretum de Gratteloup – *Leave the car in the car park beside N 98.* This arboretum, created in 1935, consists of various areas covering almost 3ha/7 acres. The first, and oldest, part contains mostly Mediterranean species (cypress, pines, juniper, yoke elms and hop hornbeams); more varied species grow in other areas: red cedar, eucalyptus, maple, alder and birch. Lastly, an area is devoted specifically to the development of the chestnut tree.

At Col de Gratteloup, take D 41 heading for Bormes-les-Mimosas.

★ **Pierre d'Avenon** – Alt 443m/1 450ft. From the top of this huge mound of giant boulders the circular **view**★ encompasses the whole Maures coastline from Cap Lardier to Hyères with the portuary facilities of Le Lavandou and Bormes in the foreground.

🚶 *From here it is a 45min walk to Col de Caguo-Ven.*

Col de Caguo-Ven – Alt 237m/778ft. From the pass, there is a **view** of the Hyères and Bormes anchorages and the Île de Porquerolles.

At the pass, take the forest lane heading east towards Col de Barral and Col du Canadel. Go back to Hyères via Le Pin, then take D 559.

★★② Pass Road

109km/67mi leaving from Le Lavandou – allow one day

This beautiful circular tour, along very hilly but unfrequented roads, goes over at least seven passes *(cols)* and penetrates deep into the heart of the massif.

⌂⌂ **Le Lavandou** – *See Le LAVANDOU.*

From Le Lavandou take D 559 west and when you reach Le Pin turn right onto D 41.

The road winds uphill among cypresses, eucalyptus and mimosa alongside white, pink and red oleanders. Fine **view** ahead of Bormes and its castle.

★ **Bormes-les-Mimosas** – *See BORMES-LES-MIMOSAS.*

Continue on D 41 to Col de Caguo-Ven. Continue downhill to Col de Gratteloup (alt 199m/656ft).

The road passes over wooded slopes of cork-oak and chestnut – deep valleys *(east)* and glimpses of the sea and the mountains round Toulon *(west)*.

Continue along D 41.

★ **Col de Babaou** – Alt 415m/1 362ft. There is an attractive **panorama**★ from the pass of the Hyères anchorage, the Giens Peninsula and the Îles d'Hyères. Beyond the pass rise the tallest of the Maures summits, their slopes wooded by magnificent chestnuts and cork-oaks. The road descends to the Réal Collobrier Valley which widens to form the Collobrières Basin.

Turn right onto D 14.

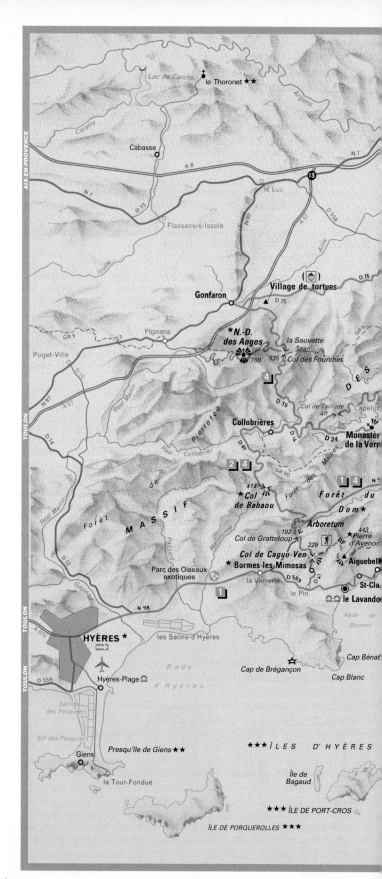

le Thoronet ★★

Lac de Carcès

Argens

Caramy

AIX-EN-PROVENCE

Cabasse

A 8

N 7

N 7

13

D 13

le Luc

D 558

Flassans-s-Issole

Issole

Aille

A 57

D 75

Village de tortues

D 75

Gonfaron

Pignans

★N.-D. des Anges

la Sauvette
780

GR 9

780

535

Col des Fourchés

DES

Puget-Ville

D 12

Real Martin

4

D 39

Col de Taillude
411

Capelu

Collobrières

TOULON

N 97

A 57

D 74

Pierrefeu

Real

Collobrier

D 14

D 24

Monastèr
de la Verr

GR 90

2 4

414

★Col
de Babaou

GR 90

Forêt des Maures

1 4

N

Forêt du
Dom ★

Real Martin

D 12

Forêt

de

MASSIF

pascal

Maravenne

192

Arboretum

443
★Pierre
d'Avenor

Col de Gratteloup

229

Aiguebell

Parc des Oiseaux
exotiques

Col de Cagyo-Ven
★ Bormes-les-Mimosas

D 559

D 41

Gapeau

1

la Verrerie

le Pin

St-Cla

☆☆ le Lavando

N 98

Rade de
Bormes

HYÈRES ★

les Salins-d'Hyères

TOULON

A 570

Cap Bénat

D 559

Hyères-Plage ☆

Rade

Cap de Brégançon

Cap Blanc

d'Hyères

Salins
des Pesquiers

Etg des Pesquiers

Presqu'île de Giens ★★

★★★ ÎLES D'HYÈRES

Giens

la Tour-Fondue

Île de
Bagaud

★★★ ÎLE DE PORT-CROS

ÎLE DE PORQUEROLLES ★★★

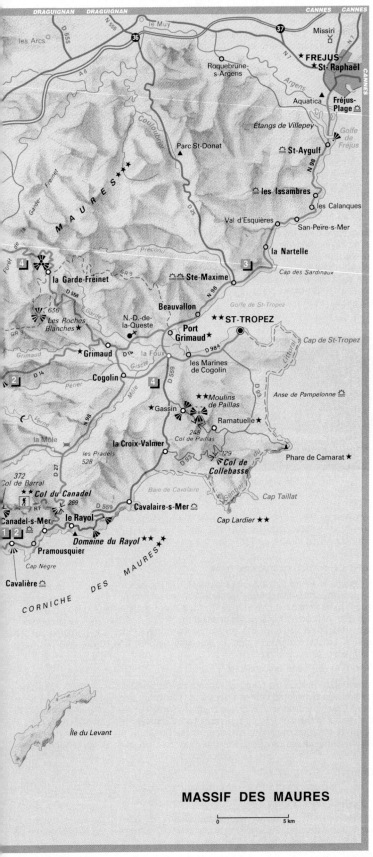

MASSIF DES MAURES

0   5 km

205

Collobrières – The picturesque houses of the well-shaded town look down on the river swirling underneath an old humpback bridge. The local forests provide the raw material for bottle corks and the vineyards the grapes for rosé wine.

This is definitely a place to visit for those with a sweet tooth. Indeed, the local specialities are *marrons glacés* and other delicacies made with chestnuts (jam). The *confiserie* (confectionery) is open to the public.

Continue east on D 14. After 6km/4mi turn right.

A narrow road leads to the ruins of the former Carthusian monastery of La Verne, in its majestic forest setting.

Monastère de la Verne – The monastery was founded in 1170 on an isolated sitea on a wooded slope in the Maures, off the beaten track near a spring. It was rebuilt several times and survived until the Revolution, when the monks abandoned it. Since 1983 it has been occupied by the religious Order of Bethlehem.

The buildings are of brown Maures schist but are distinguished by the use of serpentine (bluish-green polished stone) for the door frames, arcades, vaulting and additional ornamentation.

E. Baret/MICHELIN

A quiet retreat

Porch – The huge doorway is built of serpentine stone; two ringed columns flank the door, surmounted by a triangular pediment resting on two pilasters; a statue of the Virgin and Child stands in a recess.

Guesthouse – A path on the right of the porch leads to the guesthouse. Beyond the reception room is a large courtyard with a fountain at the centre, bordered by the buildings where guests were received. On the left is the bakery. Opposite is a Classical façade with a Regency panelled door. A porch on the left of this door opens into a passage which leads to the scullery and the 12C **kitchen** with rib vaulting.

Leave the building by the same route.

A wooden staircase in the courtyard this side of the porch leads to the kitchen and the remains of the **little cloisters**: six barrel-vaulted serpentine bays. The monks' refectory is used for exhibitions. The ruins of the Romanesque chapel open off the little cloisters (handsome Renaissance door on the site of the chancel). The **great cloisters** have depressed vaulting and serpentine decoration; they are bordered by the monks' cells – four rooms and an adjoining garden. One of the cells has been restored.

Return to D 14 and proceed east.

After Col de Taillude the road looks across La Verne Valley to the ruins of the charter house crowning the opposite slope and then, after passing high above the hamlet of Capelude, makes its way into the upper valley of the Le Périer stream. From the centre of the valley there is a **vista** of the Grimaud Plain and St-Tropez Bay. Abruptly the road turns into the valley of the Giscle (or the Grimaud rivulet) from where Grimaud can be spotted in the distance overlooked by its beautiful castle ruins.

★**Grimaud** – *See GRIMAUD.*

From Grimaud take D 558 south, crossing the Grimaud Plain.

Cogolin – *See COGOLIN.*

N 98 follows theMôle Valley upstream. 8km/5.1mi from Cogolin, just before La Môle, the winding D 27 strays from the valley to cut across the coastal range. Go back to Le Lavandou by the coast road.

Cork-oak

The cork-oak is an evergreen that requires heat and humidity. It grows near the sea up to a height of 500m/1 640ft and has proved to be particularly resilient in the case of fire. It is easy to spot on account of its large blackish acorns and heavily scored bark. Gathering the bark *(démasclage)* takes place for the first time when the tree is 25 years old; this is known as the male bark. Subsequent harvests, which take place in July and August when the sap is rising, occur every 9 or 10 years, which is the time it takes for a new layer of cork to form; this is known as the female bark, which is highly prized by industry (manufacture of chipboard at Le Muy) and craftsmen

(boards, ornamental objects and materials for ceramicists). The greater part of the production is exported, particularly to Sardinia.

By the mid-1960s the Maures area was producing 5 000t of cork every year, supplying 100 or so local firms. In 1994 the foresters of the Var *département* produced 500t of cork but the local firms had disappeared. The Cork Museum in Gonfaron pays homage to these regional traditions.

③ From St-Tropez to St-Raphaël

39km/24mi – half a day not including tours of St-Tropez and St-Raphaël

★★ St-Tropez – *See ST-TROPEZ.*

Leave St-Tropez to the southwest on D 98ᴬ.

The road skirts the southern shore of the bay looking across to the opposite coast. *After 4km/2.5mi turn right.*

★ Port-Grimaud – *See GRIMAUD.*

Return to N 98 which skirts the north shore of the bay, overlooking St-Tropez. Follow N 98 up to St-Aygulf.

⌂ St-Aygulf – *See FRÉJUS.*

On the left the road follows the nautical theme park **Aquatica** before entering the city of Fréjus. Beyond St-Aygulf the view sweeps over the lower Argens Plain. The splendid rocks of the Montagnes de Roquebrune stand out from the Maures Massif. Turning towards the Esterel range, you can see the Dramont Signal with the peak of Cap Roux looming in the background.

★ Fréjus – *See FRÉJUS.*

From Fréjus take Boulevard S.-Decuers south.

⌂ Fréjus-Plage – *See FRÉJUS: Port-Fréjus.*

Take N 98 by the sea to reach St-Raphaël.

★④ CREST ROAD

Round tour starting from St-Tropez

120km/74.5mi – allow one day not including tour of St-Tropez

This excursion passes through wooded countryside and affords some fine views. Quiet roads lead to the lower slopes of the twin peaks of Notre-Dame-des-Anges and La Sauvette.

Leave St-Tropez to the southwest on D 98ᴬ.

The road skirts the southern shore of the bay of St-Tropez.

At La Foux turn left onto N 98 heading for Cogolin.

Cogolin – *See COGOLIN.*

Continue west on N 98 up the Môle Valley.

Shortly before the village of La Môle stands a château *(right)* flanked by two round towers with pepper-pot roofs. It was here that **Antoine de Saint-Exupéry** (1900-44), aviator and writer, spent some of his childhood years *(see p 144)*. Vineyards give way to forest-covered slopes belonging to **Dom Forest★**.

Continue along N 98. At Col de Gratteloup turn right onto D 41, proceeding up to Collobrières, then after La Rivière turn right onto D 14. 3km/2mi east of Collobrières turn left onto D 39.

The road winds through wooded countryside overlooking a steep-sided stream and affords the occasional glimpse of La Sauvette peak to the right. Shortly before Col des Fourches the road to the left leads to the Notre-Dame-des-Anges Hermitage, pinpointed by the television relay mast.

★ **Ermitage Notre-Dame-des-Anges** ⊘ – The **priory** near the summit (780m/2 559ft) stands in an attractive **setting★** amid schist rocks where only trees such as the chestnut thrive. The Merovingian foundation may well have superseded an earlier pagan place of worship. Remodelled in the 19C, the buildings included accommodation for pilgrims and a chapel, the walls of which are covered with votive offerings.
Beyond the screen of trees surrounding the chapel there is a remarkable **view★** *(north)* of the Argens depression backed by the Alps; *(west)* Ste-Baume; *(south)* over the Maures heights to the sea, the Hyères islands, the Giens Peninsula and Toulon; and even Corsica on a clear day.

Return to Col des Fourches and turn left towards Gonfaron.

The road passes by La Sauvette (779m/2 556ft), the highest point in the Maures Massif, before descending to Le Luc Plain.

Gonfaron – This village, set against the backdrop of the Massif des Maures, is still an active centre of cork manufacturing. At the north edge of the village rises an isolated hill, crowned by a chapel dedicated to St Quinis.

The Legend of the Flying Donkey

In the 17C, during a procession in honour of St Quinis, a householder in Gonfaron refused to sweep the area in front of his house and suggested that the statue of the saint should fly over the rubbish. Some time later the same man and his donkey had reached the top of a hill when the animal slipped and they both tumbled into the ravine below.
The locals saw the saint's hand in this misfortune and the legend is told in respect of this hill which rises from the Luc Plain.

Écomusée du Liège ⊘ – The traditions of the cork industry in the Maures region are preserved through these reconstructions and displays of tools.

Village de Tortues de Gonfaron ⊘ – *In Gonfaron turn right onto D 75. The best times to visit are during the morning (11am) and in the late afternoon (4pm).*
📷 The village is a breeding centre for the Hermann tortoise species *(Testudo Hermanni Hermanni)*, a one-million-year-old herbivore threatened with extinction. The village is also home to France's freshwater turtle and the common or European tortoise *(Testudo Graeca)*.
The visit includes the nesting house *(écloserie)*, the nursery for the under five years, the *terrarium* for the hibernation of the young, the various enclosed areas set up according to age or species and the infirmary. Courtship occurs in April, May and September, egg-laying from mid-May to mid-June, and hatching in early September.

Continue on D 75; at the crossroads turn right onto D 558 towards La Garde-Freinet.

The road climbs to La Garde-Freinet, which is dominated by the castle ruins.

La Garde-Freinet – *See La GARDE-FREINET.*

Take D 558 south.

Still descending, the road passes cork-oak and chestnut-covered slopes and affords glimpses of the bay and peninsula of St-Tropez.

★ **Grimaud** – *See GRIMAUD.*

Return to St-Tropez by D 14 and D 98 at La Foux.

MENTON★★

Population 28 812
Michelin map 84 folds 10 and 20, 115 fold 28 or 245 fold 39
Local maps see Excursions below, NICE and Corniches de la RIVIERA

View of Menton by night

Menton claims to be the warmest resort on the Riviera and it is a pleasant place to spend a winter holiday. Winter, however, is hardly mentioned here where the sun reigns supreme, and long sandy beaches, two marinas and festivities and cultural activities welcome the summer visitor. The town is backed by terraced slopes planted with citrus fruits and olives. The climate is particularly suitable for flowers and tropical plants; lemon trees, which die if the temperature falls below -3°C/26°F, thrive throughout the year, providing the famous Menton lemons much sought after by connoisseurs. The picturesque old town standing out against a mountainous backdrop occupies a magnificent **site★★**.

Early history – Evidence of a human settlement in the Paleolithic Era from excavations near the Italian frontier is displayed in the Musée d'Anthropologie Préhistorique in Monaco and in the Musée de Préhistoire in Menton but little is known about the town's origins. The name Menton was first mentioned in 1261. In 1346 the town was bought by the Grimaldis of Monaco although it remained under the Bishop of Ventimiglia. Together with Monaco it oscillated between the protection of France and Sardinia until it was permanently attached to France in 1860.

Modern town – In the late 19C and early 20C Menton shared in the popularity of the Riviera with the European aristocracy. Wealthy, famous personalities from all over the world came to live here, including several writers – the New Zealander Katherine Mansfield (1888-1929), the Spaniard Blasco Ibáñez (1867-1928) and Ferdinand Bac (1859-1952), a French essayist and painter. 20C tourism brought new blood and light industry grew up in the Carei Valley, while the residential district spread west to Roquebrune-Cap-Martin and east to the Italian frontier. The old town and vast green spaces have been preserved.

"Artium Civitas" – This inscription on the front of the town hall declared Menton's ambition to be a city of the arts. The aim is to offer a variety of cultural activities. Art exhibitions are held throughout the year at the Palais de l'Europe.
The **Chamber Music Festival** enjoys an international reputation and its guest artists are world-famous. A prize for the best short story is awarded each year by the Katherine Mansfield Foundation. Shrove Tuesday brings the annual **Lemon Festival** and there are flower carnivals throughout the summer. Festivals are also held by night in the Pian Gardens *(access from Promenade de la Mer)*.

Fête du Citron – The mild climate and the fertile citrus fruit orchards around Menton have given birth to a local lemon festival, which has been held in the Biovès Gardens since 1929. The event calls for more than 100t of citrus fruit – oranges, grapefruit and kumquats as well as lemons – which are used to cover decorative metal frames erected in the gardens to illustrate a different theme each year (Tintin in 1998, Lucky Luke in 1999). The festival closes with a procession of floats decorated with citrus fruit.

★★ A VISIT TO THE OLD TOWN *allow 2hr*

Rue St-Michel – This pedestrian street linking the old and new towns is bordered by a great many boutiques interspersed with orange trees. Below on the left, **Place aux Herbes** with its coloured paving stones, colonnade and fountain is a pleasant spot within sight of the sea; nearby the covered market is a lively meeting-place offering delicious local produce. Note the splendid Belle Époque façades: former Hôtel d'Orient *(1 Rue de la République)*; Winter-Palace *(20 Avenue Riviera)*; Riviera-Palace *(28 Avenue Riviera)*; covered market *(Quai de Monléon)*.

Rue Longue – The steps up to St-Michel are cut across by Rue Longue, once the main street of the town and formerly called Via Julia Augusta, which becomes Rue des Logettes and joins Rue St-Michel.

★★ **Parvis St-Michel** – *Access by the Chanoine-Gouget ramps.* At the top of the steps is a charming square in the Italian style, overlooking the sea and the coast, where the concerts of the Chamber Music Festival are held during August. The square is paved with a handsome mosaic depicting the Grimaldi arms in grey and white, framed by typical old houses and the façades of two churches.

★ **Façade of the Chapelle de la Conception** – On leaving the church climb a few steps on the left to admire this chapel of the White Penitents (1685, restored in the 19C), with its garlands of flowers and basket-handled pediment surmounted by statues of the three theological virtues.

Basilique St-Michel-Archange ⊘ – This is the largest and finest Baroque church in the region. Its two-tier **façade** in yellow and pale green reflects a variety of architectural motifs. The tower (15C) on the left, which belonged to an earlier building, was crowned with an octagonal campanile with a glazed tile roof in the 17C, and the great Genoese-style campanile (53m/174ft) on the right was added in the 18C. Above each of the three doors is a niche; the central one houses a statue of St Michael, with St Maurice on the left and St Roch on the right. The ornate interior was inspired by the church of the Annunziata in Genoa, giving rise to the basilica plan with false transept and shallow chevet and barrel vaulting; it also resembles St-Véran at Utelle. Local artists such as Puppo and Vento contributed to the decoration of the side chapels, which commemorate various local celebrities.

In the first north side chapel is the fine Baroque **altarpiece** by Puppo, *Le Pape urbain VIII intercédant auprès de l'Enfant Jésus pour les âmes du purgatoire* (Pope Urban VIII interceding with the infant Jesus for the souls in Purgatory), framed by gilt columns wreathed with vine leaves; in front stands a marble altar under a crown-shaped canopy. Next door is a Crucifixion by Ferrari and an unusual 17C Virgin and Child. The third chapel contains an Assumption by Puppo embellished with angels, drapes and scrolls.

The choir contains the huge 17C **organ casing**; above the handsome 18C choir stalls is the **altarpiece of St Michael** (1569) by Manchello: the saint is flanked by Peter bearing papal insignia and John the Baptist; the upper sections show a fine Pietà. The exuberant Baroque high altar is crowned by St Michael slaying the Devil. The next side chapel is devoted to the Princes of Monaco: a late-17C painting shows St Devota, patron of the Principality, in front of the rock of Monaco. Another Ferrari, the *Adoration of the Shepherds*, hangs in the first south side chapel and in the last chapel is an altarpiece by JA Vento: *The Rest during the Flight into Egypt*. The baptistery (1806) is adorned with a dome in *trompe-l'œil*. Damask hangings from Genoa, the colour of amaranth (crimson), decorate the choir and the central nave. They were presented by Prince Honoré III of Monaco on the occasion of his wedding in this church in 1757.

Climb the steps into the quaint Rue du Vieux-Château, which leads to the cemetery.

Cimetière du Vieux-Château – This international cemetery, laid out in the last century on the site of the former medieval castle, consists of terraces one above the other which can be seen clearly from the port. Each level contains tombs associated with a different religion or nationality. The cemetery is the most striking souvenir of the time when Menton used to welcome rich summer residents from all over the world. Among the celebrities from this era whose fame still endures are several great Russian princes (Troubetzkoy, Volkonsky and Ouroussof), the uncle and aunt (Delano) of the American president Roosevelt, Webb Ellis who is credited with inventing the game of Rugby football and the Danish architect Georg Tersling, who designed many palaces and houses on the Riviera at the turn of the century.

From the southern corner of the English graveyard there is a beautiful **view**★ of the old town, the sea and the coast from Mortola Point in Italy to Cap Martin.

Return to Parvis St-Michel by Montée du Souvenir, bordered by fragrant oleanders.

★★ STAYING IN MENTON

Start from the Casino Municipal.

The Seafront and Beaches

★★ **Promenade du Soleil** – The promenade with its broad terraces facing out to sea follows the shore beneath the old town with the Alps in the background.

Plage des Sablettes – *Sea scooters and windsurfing boards forbidden.* This gravel beach is dominated by Promenade de la Mer and **Quai Bonaparte**. From the top, there is a nice view of the old quarter. A huge flight of steps leads up to the church of St-Michel between tall narrow houses.

Old port – The harbour is used by local fishermen and tourists alike. It is flanked by **Quai Napoléon-III**, which follows the jetty sheltering the harbour and ending in a lighthouse, and **Jetée Impératrice-Eugénie**. The far end of the port, home to Volti's sculpture of Saint Michael, commands nice **views★** of old Menton, fronted by a row of arcades; in the distance you can admire the mountains inland and the stretch between Cap Martin and Bordighera (Cap Mortola blots out Vintimiglia). There are facilities for **boat trips** ⓥ.

Garavan – Once a cluster of elegant mansions set apart from Menton, Garavan has now become a luxurious residential suburb of the town, running between Promenade de la Mer and Boulevard de Garavan, in a splendid setting. The marina can accommodate boats up to 40m/132ft. The pretty 17C Baroque **Chapelle St-Jacques** houses a municipal gallery displaying contemporary art exhibitions.

★ GARDENS

The choice of tropical species and the unusual layout of these gardens reflect the fertile imagination of the foreign residents who have come here to stay over the past century. The best time of year to visit all these gardens is around June, when the trees, bushes and flower beds are ablaze with colour.

★ **Jardin du Val Rameh** ⓥ – *From Promenade de la Mer take Chemin de St-Jacques.* These grounds were arranged around the Val Rameh Villa by the English in the 1930s and then taken over by the Musée d'Histoire Naturelle of Paris; the terraced garden features over 700 species of Mediterranean, tropical and sub-tropical flora. All these plants have grown accustomed to the Menton climate and flourish abundantly. Exotic species are dotted amid the citrus trees: passiflora, guava, avocado etc. The terraces afford a magnificent view of the old town and the sea.

Jardin des Colombières ⓥ – *From Promenade de la Mer take Avenue Blasco-Ibañez. Private property; guided tours by appointment only.* This garden, designed by Ferdinand Bac (1859-1952), a humorous author, architect and landscape gardener, forms a homogenous architectural ensemble.

Jardin des Romanciers, Garavan

J.-L. Gallo/MICHELIN

Jardin des Romanciers ⓥ – This unusual residence, known as the Villa Fontana Rosa, stands out because of its porch adorned with ceramics paying homage to leading names in Spanish literature. It was built in 1924 by the Spanish novelist **Blasco Ibañez**. Only the garden is open to visitors. It consists of a harmonious row of pergolas and structures, interspersed with ponds and embellished with ceramics of Spanish design.

Eating out

MODERATE

Oh ! Matelot – *Rue Loredan-Larchey* – ☎ *04 93 28 45 40* – *Closed Jan, Nov, Sun and evenings except Jun to Sep* – *9.15/15.24€*. Children love this restaurant, where the nautical setting is made up of miniature lighthouses and other marine curiosities. Parents appreciate the buffet formula and the homey cooking at afford-able prices. Board games available to all. Clowns, puppets and magicians can be hired if required. Have tea on the terrace shaded by fragrant orange blossom.

Au Pistou – *9 Quai Gordon-Bennett* – ☎ *04 93 57 45 89* – *Closed 20 Nov-18 Dec and Mon* – *13.42€*. A family business situated beneath the arcades at the far end of the port, with the senior member bringing in the day's catch every morning! ★Unusual summer terrace.

Le Darkoum – *23 Rue St-Michel* – ☎ *04 93 35 44 88* – *Closed mid-May to mid-Jun, Tue off season. and Mon- 15/21€*. For a whiff of Morocco, come to Le Darkoum, where you will be treated like a friend of the family and served *couscous, tajines,* or *briouates*★ in a typically Oriental setting enhanced with glazed earthenware tiling. Small terrace giving onto the street.

MID-RANGE

A Braijade Méridiounale – *66 Rue Longue* – ☎ *04 93 35 65 65* – *Closed 10 Nov-10 Dec and Wed Sep-Jun* – *20.12/43.45€*. Discreetly located in an alley of the old quarter, this homely restaurant provides Provençal dishes and grilled meat at very reasonable rates. Pretty dining room with visible stonework, beams and a fireplace.

Where to stay

MID-RANGE

Le Globe – *21 Avenue de Verdun* – ☎ *04 92 10 59 70* – *Closed 15 Nov-15 Dec* – ▣ – *23 rooms: 45.73/60.98€* – *Restaurant 46€*. Homey establishment enjoying a privileged location on a luxuriant avenue just opposite the Palais de l'Europe and within walking distance of the Casino. Cosy, tidy rooms. The ter-race extending the bar has recently been refurbished.

Hôtel de Londres – *15 Avenue Carnot* – ☎ *04 93 35 74 62* – *hotel-de-lon-dres@wanadoo.fr* – *Closed 20 Oct-27 Dec* – *27 rooms: 53.36/76.22€* – *Restau-rant 21€*. This recently renovated hotel near the coast features efficiently soundproofed rooms of varying sizes, appointed with either rustic or modern furniture. Pleasant terrace set back from the street.

Dauphin – *28 Avenue du Général-de-Gaulle* – ☎ *04 93 35 76 37* – *Closed 20 Oct-20 Dec* – *28 rooms: 57.17/77.75€* – ⌷ *6.10€* – *Restaurant 13/17€*. This hotel is a haven for musicians as it features two recording studios and air-con-ditioned, soundproofed rooms for the other residents! Musical events and evenings can be organised. The rooms afford pretty views of the sea.

Orly – *27 Porte de France* – ☎ *04 93 35 60 81* – *Closed 15 Nov-27 Dec* – *29 rooms: 58.69/96.04€* – ⌷ *6.10€* – *Restaurant 17/28€*. Seaside hotel facing the exclusive Garavan beach providing simple rooms; the ones giving onto the back are quieter. Traditional fare served on the terrace or inside the sober din-ing room fronted by huge bay windows.

Theatre and arts

Palais de l'Europe – *8 Avenue Boyer, BP 239* – ☎ *04 92 41 76 50* – *villede-menton.com* – *Gallery open daily except Tue 10am-noon, 2-6pm. Tickets at the tourist office: Mon-Fri 10am-noon,2-5pm*. Handsome auditorium with a seating capacity of 730, where ballets, plays, operas, operettas and classical music con-certs are organised. The premises are also home to a modern art gallery used as a venue for temporary exhibitions free of charge for the public.

Treats for all

L'Arche des Confitures – *2 Rue du Vieux-Collège* – ☎ *04 93 57 20 29* – *Mon-Sat 9.30am-noon, 3-7pm, Sun 10am-noon, 3-6pm*. Who could resist the impres-sive range of mouthwatering jams made on the premises of this family business, alongside different types of honey, vinegar, confit and mustard? If you wish to, you may also visit the kitchens.

Mini Pub (American Bar) – *51 Quai Bonaparte* – ☎ *04 93 35 79 86* – *minipub@libr-ertysurf.fr* – *Wed, Thu, Sun, Mon 6pm-3am, Fri-Sat until 4am*. Trendy establish-ment for all ages that attracts a local clientele as well as passing trade

Transport

Buses – *Bus station on Avenue de Sospel* – ☎ *04 93 35 93 60. Autocars Breuleux, Rue Masséna.* ☎ *04 93 35 73 51*. The town of Menton and its outskirts are served by 9 bus lines. Single tickets and one-day passes available from bus drivers. The "3 Villages Pass" will enable you to visit Gorbio, Ste-Agnès and Castellar at reduced rates within one month of purchase.

Sightseeing

Small tourist train – Departures from Promenade du Soleil, near the citadel. Guided tours with commentary *(30min)* 10am-noon, 2.15-7pm (5pm Christmas to Easter). In high season there are nightly tours *(8.30-11pm)* to see the city of Menton illuminated.

Shopping

Lemons – Many shops in Menton pay tribute to this sunny fruit by selling a wide range of produce made or flavoured with lemons: tarts and pies, gingerbread, almond paste, boiled sweets, wine, vinegar, jam, soaps, candles, perfume...

Marchés – Daily in the morning. Covered market on Quai de Monléon. Careï market at the top of the Biovès Gardens, beneath the railway bridge.

Taking it easy

Koaland – *Avenue de la Madone* – ☎ *04 92 10 00 40. Daily except Tues 10am-noon, 3pm-midnight (2-7pm in winter)*. Leisure park for children and the younger generation. Miniature golf course.

ULM Club – *Promenade de la Mer* – ☎ *06 15 96 35 04* – *May-Sep daily 8am-9pm; Oct-Apr daily 9am-5pm (by appointment)*. This club organises maiden flights (22.87€ and 47.73€) and introductory courses for flying seaplanes (30.49€ and 53.36€).

Compagnie Navigation et Tourisme – *Quai Napoléon III* – ☎ *04 93 35 51 72*. Mid-Apr to mid-Oct boat trips with commentary going direct to Monaco Tue, Wed and Fri at 10am (10.67€); to the French Riviera (1hr 45min) Mon and Sat at 2.30pm (13.72€); to the Italian Riviera (1hr 45min) Tue, Thu and Sun at 2.30pm (13.72€).

Calendar of festivities

Lemon Festival – Two weeks in February-March. Book at least 2 months in advance for this popular event attracts a great many people.

Orchid Fair – Takes place during the Lemon Festival.

Chamber Music Festival – In August on the esplanade fronting the Église St-Michel. This prestigious event is attended by many talented soloists and conductors enjoying a worldwide reputation.

Jardin Biovès – These beautiful gardens in the town centre are bordered by palms and lemon trees, planted with flowers and ornamented by fountains and statues (*Goddess of the Golden Fruit* by Volti). The grounds follow the loops of the River Careï and open up a **view** of the mountains rising beyond the town.

Jardin de Maria-Serena ⊘ – *Promenade Reine-Astrid*. This garden could be said to have the most temperate climate in France, since the temperature never falls below 5°C. It is known for its extensive collection of palm trees.

Oliveraie du Pian – *Boulevard de Garavan*. This olive grove is planted with more than 500 olive trees over 100 years old.

Serre de la Madone et Clos du Peyronnet – Serre de la Madone has some plants unique to this garden and Clos du Peyronnet specialises in plants from South Africa. Although they are private properties and usually closed to the public, it is occasionally possible to visit them during events organised by the **Maison du Patrimoine** ⊘, which can provide information on the relevant dates.

SIGHTS

★ **Musée des Beaux-Arts (Palais Carnolès)** ⊘ – *Avenue Carnot*. This former summer residence of the princes of Monaco was built in the 17C in the spirit of the Grand Trianon, according to plans by Robert de Cotte and Gabriel. After heavy remodelling in the 19C, it had the honour of welcoming celebrities such as Elisabeth-Louise, the last queen of Prussia, and Prince Metternich. It then fell into the hands of the American Allis, a celebrated ichthyologist, on whose intructions the building was restored by the Danish architect Georg Tersling and decorated with frescoes on antique themes by Matthiessen, a German artist. The original stuccowork and gilding have survived in the Grand Salon de Musique Antoine I and the Salon Bleu.

Upstairs – The first floor is dedicated to the collection of early art. The beautiful 13C *Virgin and Child* is a Tuscan work by the Master of the Maddalena. The following galleries illustrate religious themes from different countries – *Virgin and Child with St Francis* by Louis Bréa, *Virgin and Child* by Leonardo da Vinci and *Holy Family* by Bernardino Luini. In another room hangs a *Portrait of Urban of Bologna* by Bernardino Orsi. The works of various European schools of the 16C, the 17C and the 18C include *St Benedict with the young St Maurus and St Placidus* by Philippe de Champaigne as well as works by Magnasco, Weenix, Bruyn the Elder and Verbugh. Note the modern works by Suzanne Valadon, Kisling and Camoin.

Ground floor – A collection of contemporary and modern work is housed on the ground floor. The museum displays in rotation works from the Wakefield Mori Collection (Picabia, Forain, Dufy etc), contributions from various Biennales de Peinture (up to 1980) and gifts from artists (Gleizes, Desnoyers, Delvaux, Sutherland).

Jardin d'agrumes – A vast **garden of citrus fruit trees** (grapefruit, mandarin, kumquat, orange and lemon) and avocado trees contains a number of sculptures. Space in the central alleyway, around the Palais Carnolès, is devoted to Magda Frank; in the first lateral alleyway note busts of Prince Rainier II of Monaco, Princess Grace, Katherine Mansfield and other famous names of the 20C. The other alleyways are decorated with works by Lazareff, Sigaldi and Gleb.

Musée Jean-Cocteau ⊘ – This museum is housed in a 17C bastion built by Honoré II of Monaco. Cocteau, the "Prince of the Poets", worked there from 1957 onwards. It was his initiative that led to the bastion being converted into a museum and it was he who oversaw the restoration. The remaining parts of the original building include a large vaulted salon and two small annexe rooms, one of which still contains an oven. The guard-rooms and the munitions store now contain the museum.

Outside, the artist has designed pebble mosaics in traditional Menton style on several themes – Orpheus, the Faun of youth, a lass of Menton and the fisherman. The floor of the entrance is decorated with the Mediterranean emblem, the lizard, made of small grey and white pebbles. On the wall hangs an Aubusson tapestry, **Judith and Holophernes**, which Matisse described as the "only truly contemporary tapestry". The wrought-iron display cases were designed by Cocteau especially for his museum; they contain zoomorphic ceramic vases. The tapestry hanging above the stairs, *l'Âge du Verseau*, was woven in the Gobelins workshops. The first floor gallery houses a series of pastels entitled *Gli Innamorati* (1961), and a large portrait of the poet by Marc Avoy depicting Cocteau leaving the body of a faun.

Hôtel de Ville ⊘ – The town hall is a handsome building inspired by the 17C Italian style. The **hall★** where marriages are celebrated owes its decoration to Jean Cocteau. On the wall at the back, the angler, who has a fish as an eye, is wearing a typical Menton fisherman's hat; the girl opposite him is sporting a traditional hat from Nice. The walls depict Orpheus and Eurydice on one side and a fictitious marriage on the other. On the ceiling, Poetry is depicted astride Pegasus, Science is juggling with the planets, and Love is no longer blind.

In the entrance there are two Mariannes (the French Republic, represented by a woman wearing the liberty cap), drawn by Cocteau, engraved onto two large mirrors. The furniture was chosen by Cocteau himself: candelabra in the form of palm trees; Spanish style chairs; and a panther skin leading to the marriage table.

Musée de Préhistoire Régionale ⊘ – This museum was opened at the beginning of the century in a building specially designed by the architect Adrien Rey. It houses collections from local prehistoric sites, the oldest of which come from excavations carried out by Bonfils (a 19C naturalist from Menton) in the Grimaldi caves

On the ground floor reconstructions of everyday life illustrate the evolution of prehistoric man in the Alpes-Maritimes and Liguria from 1 000 000 BC to 1 500 BC: the taming of fire, the awakenings of artistic expression (30 000 years ago), the early stages of agriculture (5 000 BC) and metallurgy on Mont Bégo (1 800 BC). A film room and an interactive question-and-answer terminal enable visitors to test their knowledge.

Katherine Mansfield (1888-1923)

This writer from New Zealand spent a year in Menton from spring 1920. Her delicate health caused her to choose Garavan and she moved into the Villa Isola-Bella *(now in Avenue Katherine-Mansfield)*. In this peaceful haven she wrote five of her best works including *The Stranger, The Chambermaid, The Girl*. Writing in her diary, she said: "The house faces the sea; on the right is the old town with its little port and pepper plants growing on a tiny quay... This old town... is the loveliest place I have ever set eyes on."

MENTON

Bosano (R. Lt) . . . . Y 5
Boyer (Av.) . . . . Z 6
Carnot (Av.) . . . . Z 10
Ciapetta (R.) . . . . Z 12
Félix-Faure (Av.) . . . . Z
Gallieni (R. Gén.) . . . . Z 18

Guyau (R.) . . . . Y 19
Herbes (Pl. aux) . . . . Y 20
Laurenti (Av.) . . . . Y 21
Logettes (R. des) . . . . Z 22
Longue (R.) . . . . Y 24
Monléon (Q. de) . . . . Z 27
Partouneaux (R.) . . . . Z 30

République (R. de la) . . . . . . Z 33
St-Michel (R.) . . . . Z
St-Roch (Pl. R.) . . . . Z 35
Trenca (R.) . . . . Z 37
Verdun (Av. de) . . . . Z 40
Vieux-Château (R. du) . . . . . Y 42
Villarey (R.) . . . . Z 44

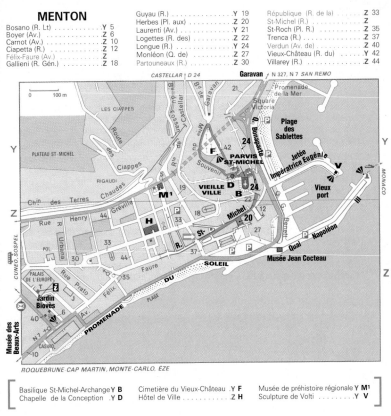

Basilique St-Michel-Archange **Y B**   Cimetière du Vieux-Château . **Y F**   Musée de préhistoire regionale **Y M¹**
Chapelle de la Conception . **Y D**   Hôtel de Ville . . . . **Z H**   Sculpture de Volti . . . . **Y V**

The basement contains displays on the history of Menton and popular art and traditions. There are the reconstructions of the interiors of Menton houses during the last century; a kitchen and a bedroom. Two more rooms display traditional objects associated with the cultivation and harvesting of lemons and olives. A gallery of posters commemorates the golden age of Menton's popularity as a winter resort from 1870 to 1914.

Église Orthodoxe Russe ◷ – *Rue Morillot; access via Avenue Carnot*. The Russian Orthodox Church (1892) was designed by Georg Tersling, a Danish architect. Although its small size would be more appropriate to a chapel, the interior is lavishly decorated with murals by Prince Gagarin and many icons. The present congregation gathers elderly people of Russian origin but in the 19C a sizeable Russian colony would spend the winter months on the Riviera. In 1880 they decided to found a rest home, La Maison Russe, so that patients with tuberculosis could benefit from the mild climate of Menton. The home, which stands near the church, was particularly helpful to soldiers who had contracted tuberculosis in Manchuria during the Russo-Japanese War (1905).

EXCURSIONS

★ **Roquebrune-Cap-Martin** – *See ROQUEBRUNE-CAP-MARTIN*.

★ **Gorbio** –*9km/5.5mi. From Roquebrune-Cap-Martin take D 23 north to Gorbio, a narrow winding road where passing is often difficult*.
The Gorbio Valley, with its flowers, its olives and pines and its luxury residences, contrasts with the stark appearance of the village, perched on its wild and rocky **site★**. Near the entrance to the narrow cobbled lanes stands the old Malaussène fountain. The elm tree in the square was planted in 1713. For the feast of Corpus Christi, the villagers organise a very attractive parade, known as the **procession des limaces**, in which everyone carries a snail shell filled with olive oil and lit by a little wick. Rue Garibaldi leads round the church to a fine **viewpoint** looking across to Bordighera Point.

L'Annonciade – *6km/4mi. From Menton take Avenue de Verdun (Z 40) running into Avenue de Sospel, D 2566 going north*.
Ignore a left-hand turning to L'Annonciade and continue on under the Provençal motorway. After two hairpin bends D 2566 bears right to Sospel; bear left and go under the motorway again and continue to the Auberge des Santons where the path to the monastery begins.

The 17C **chapel** ⊙ has been a centre for pilgrimages to the Virgin since the 11C. From the terrace (225m/738ft) there is a **panorama★** of the coast from Bordighera Point to Cap Martin and of the mountains ringing Menton.

Return by a winding road which leads back to Avenue de Sospel in Menton.

★**Ste-Agnès** – *13km/8mi – about 45min. From Menton take Avenue Carnot north, turn right onto Cours René-Coty, Avenue des Alliés and Rue des Castagnins, D 22. The road is uphill all the way with views of the Gorbio Valley. Bear right at Col St-Sébastien (alt 600m/1 969ft) which gives a particularly picturesque **view★** of Ste-Agnès. The **site★** is exceptional. Located barely 3km/2mi from the sea, yet at an altitude of 780m/2 559ft, the village (the highest on the coast) is perched like an eagle's nest at the foot of a grey limestone cliff which lights up in superb shades of pink at sunset.

The picturesque cobblestone streets of the village, lined with craft shops, include Rue Longue and the vaulted Rue des Comtes-Léotardi.
A rocky track leads from behind the graveyard to a viewing table in the ruins of the castle. There is a marvellous **panorama★★**.

Fort Maginot de Ste-Agnès ⊙ – *At the entrance to the village, turn towards the parking Sud, and park the car on the left near the entrance to the fort.*
This imposing building, camouflaged by the overhanging rocks surrounding it, was built between 1931 and 1938 as part of the reinforcement of the Alpine Maginot Line. Its firing slots, equipped with 81mm mortars and 75/135mm guns faced southeast over Menton Bay to protect its approaches. The barracks, deep in the cliff, still house an electric generator, a neutralisation room and the kitchens. The tour of the

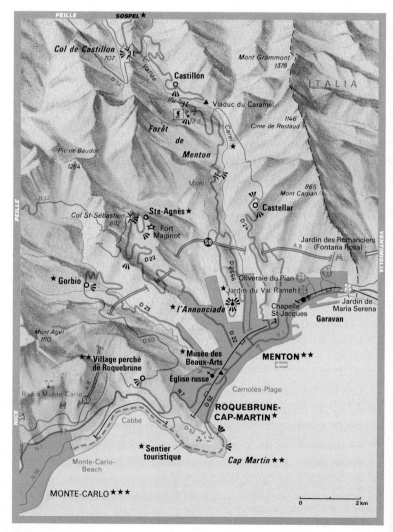

fort gives an insight into life in such strongholds during the Second World War. Outside, set slightly downhill, a platform overlooking the intricacies of the Provençal motorway affords a marvellous **view**★★ of the coast from Bordighera in Italy to Cap Martin and Mont Agel to the southwest.

Castellar – *13km/8mi – about 45min. From Menton take Route de Castellar, north on the plan.*
Castellar is an attractive hilltop village and a good centre for walking. Its parallel streets are linked by covered alleys. From the terrace on Place Clémenceau, there is a good **view** of the sea and the surrounding heights.
On the return drive, follow the same route for 2.5km/1.5mi, then turn right on the winding "Chemin du Mont-Gros". Admire the fine views.
After the cemetery, follow the winding road which leads to D 2566.

PASS ROAD

Col de Castillon Road *21km/13mi – about 1hr 30min*

Leave Menton by Avenue de Verdun running into Avenue de Sospel.

The road riding over Col de Castillon – also called Col de la Garde – makes its way through a break in the ridge of hills running parallel to the coast and dividing the Menton district from the Sospel Basin. From the pass the River Careï flows south to the Mediterranean, and the River Merlanson north to join the River Bévera.
After passing under the motorway, D 2566 climbs, twisting and turning as it goes, up the beautiful **Vallée du Careï**★ beneath the bare ridges of the Franco-Italian border to the east. The lemon groves give way to olive and pine trees.
After leaving the hamlet of Monti, the road skirts Menton Forest, offering fine views. The tortuous little road which leads directly to the village of Castellar *(see above)* leads off from the start of a bend at the bottom of a dip.

Forêt de Menton – A variety of trees contributes to the beauty of the forest. To the left of the forest refuge *(M. F. on the local map)* a path (🚶 *1hr on foot there and back)* leads to a **view**★ *(viewing table)* of the coast. The road soon passes the **Caramel Viaduct**, formerly used by the tramway running between Menton and Sospel.

Castillon – On the right lies the new village of Castillon, a model of rural planning, built halfway up the hillside in the Provençal style. The village was reconstructed twice: after the earthquake of 1887 and after the bombardments of 1944. Its main district *(car park nearby)*, overlooking the village, is occupied for the most part by craftsmen. From the summit, the **view** opens out onto the Careï Valley and the Mediterranean Sea.
After the village, the road to the Sospel Valley leads off to the left, plunging in and out of tunnels following the tracks of the old tramway. The road leading off to the right soon brings you to the pass.

Col de Castillon – Alt 707m/2 320ft. The **view** to the north takes in the Bévera Valley with the Peïra-Cava and Aution peaks in the distance. To the left D 54 takes a picturesque route to Col St-Jean.
From here the road drops gradually down into the Merlanson Valley. The forest is gradually replaced by olive groves and terraced vineyards. First the stronghold on Mont Barbonnet looms into sight, followed by the town of Sospel and the surrounding heights.

Vallée des MERVEILLES★★

Michelin map 84 folds 9, 10, 19 and 20,
115 folds 7 and 8 or 245 folds 25 and 26

To the west of Tende, around **Mont Bégo** (alt 2 872m/9 423ft), lies a region of glacial lakes and valleys, rocky cirques and moraines, formed during the Quaternary Era, cut off by the scarce roads and the harsh mountain climate. The Minière, Casterino and Fontanalbe Valleys are clothed with larch woods but the Vallée des Merveilles, which lies between the Grand Capelet and Mont Bégo, has only a thin carpet of vegetation which is covered in flowers in summer. The peaks, valleys and lakes make a magnificent spectacle.
The region, which is part of the **Parc National du Mercantour** is famous for the thousands of rock engravings which have been discovered there, most of which are carved on huge slabs of schist or polished sandstone, known as *chiappes*. It is reached along a tributary valley of the Roya.
The whole of the site known as the Vallée des Merveilles consists of five distinct regions around Mont Bégo.

– the Vallée des Merveilles itself, which is the largest area and contains more than half the carvings;
– the Vallée de Fontanalbe, which is narrower and contains about 40% of the carvings;
– the Valmasque, Valaurette and Sabion areas which contain only a few scattered carvings.

Hiking in the Vallée des Merveilles

It is important to bear in mind that these sites are at high altitude (between 1 600-2 500m/5 429-8 202ft) and that certain preparations are advisable – good physical stamina, mountain boots or shoes and warm clothing providing protection from cold and rain. As storms are frequent and sometimes very violent, it is wise to listen to the weather forecast. To study the route in advance see Map 1/25 000 – Vallée de la Roya – published by the Conseil Général des Alpes-Maritimes.

Guided tours ⊙ organised by the guides of the Vallée des Merveilles, are the best way of seeing those engravings which are rarely visible or difficult of access. In the high season, apply to the office in Casterino; otherwise apply to the guides office in Tende.

The Fontanalbe area may be visited without a guide from the Baisse de Valmasque up to the Fontanalbe mountain refuge using the authorised path. The Arpette area cannot be visited without a guide.

The regulations appropriate to open-air sites apply within the boundaries of the Vallée des Merveilles – no domestic animals, no fires, no camping or bivouacing within an hour of the park boundaries and no disposing of waste within the boundaries.

Visitors must not stray from the waymarked paths unless accompanied by an official guide.

Refreshments and accommodation are available from the two **refuges** ⊙. it is however wise to book in advance during the summer season by contacting the refuge directly.

The local map shows the routes available within the approved boundaries.

Regulations at the Sites

Although the Bronze Age rock engravings are protected for most of the year by a covering of snow *(from mid-October to late June)*, in recent years they have suffered considerable damage, inflicted intentionally or unintentionally by human visitors. To prevent such defacement the trustees and the officers of the Parc National du Mercantour have limited public access to the Arpette and Fontanalbe sectors only.

Visitors may enter these two areas only if they are accompanied by seasoned guides *(apply to the Guides Office in Tende)* who are on duty at these two sites daily throughout the summer season *(2 or 3 tours, each lasting 3hr)*.

The main regulations are symbolised by the signs shown below. Violations of these regulations, detected by the official park guides, are punishable by heavy fines.

Contacts

Destination Merveilles – *10 Rue des Mesures – 06270 Villeneuve-Loubet –* ☎ *04 93 73 09 07 - www.destination-merveilles.com* - Organises various outings and hiking tours in the Vallée des Merveilles.

Association des Guides, Accompagnateurs et Amis des Alpes Méridionales *– Bureau de la Haute Vésubie – 06450 St-Martin-Vésubie –* ☎ *and fax 04 93 03 26 60*. This organisation stages events and supplies qualified guides for visits to the Vallée des Merveilles.

THE ENGRAVINGS

The name Bégo is derived from an Indo-European root which means the sacred mountain *(Be)* inhabited by the bull-god *(Go)*. The region of Mont Bégo is an **open-air museum** ⊙ comprising over 30 000 engravings. Although they were discovered and identified at the end of the 17C, it was not until 1897 that they were studied systematically by the British scholar Clarence Bicknell. In 1947, when the region became part of France, more intensive research was carried out by a team working under Henry de Lumley, which spent 30 years recording every engraving within a wide area (12ha/30 acres). The engravings are cut into the rock face worn smooth by glacial erosion 15 000 years ago. The linear engravings date from the Gallo-Roman period through the Middle Ages to the present. The engravings which are of most interest to the archeologists are even earlier – the majority date back to the early Bronze Age (c 1800 BC to 1500 BC). A stippling technique was used: the contours and surfaces were obtained by the juxtaposition of tiny dots (between 1 and 5mm/up to 0.2in across) punched in the rock face with flint or quartz tools.

Magic mountain – The engravings reveal the preoccupations of the Ligurian people who lived in the lower valleys and made pilgrimages to Mont Bégo, to which they ascribed divine power – both protective, owing to the many streams which rise there, and awesome, owing to the sudden violent storms which rage there.

The engravings exhibit five themes – horns, arms or tools, anthropomorphs, geometric figures and other unidentified images. Here as elswhere, the mountain cult was linked to that of the bull; drawings of horns and bovine creatures feature in half the engravings. Ploughs and harrows harnessed to animals suggest that agriculture was practised; some crisscross patterns may represent parcels of land. There are many representations of weapons that reflect those excavated on contemporary archeological sites. Human figures are, however, not very numerous; the best-known have been given names – **Christ**, the **Wizard**, the **Chieftain**, the **Dancer**; others, of a more enigmatic nature, are open to interpretation such the **Tree of Life** at Fontanalbe *(guided tour only)*.

| Do not stray from signposted paths without an official guide | Do not touch the engravings | Do not tread on the engravings | Do not damage or deface the engravings |

ACCESS ROUTES

– either by N 204 up the Roya Valley to St-Dalmas-de-Tende, by D 91 to Casterino village and by one of two footpaths:

– from Lac des Mesches to the Arpette area and the Refuge des Merveilles *(3hr walk)*

– from the Casterino refuge to the Fontanalbe refuge and the Fontanalbe district *(2hr 30min walk)*

– or from Belvédère up the Gordalasque Valley to St-Grat *(see Vallée de la VÉSUBIE)* and the footpath to Pas de l'Arpette.

The two most popular excursions from St-Dalmas-de-Tende are described below.

WALKING TOURS ⊘

Vallée des Merveilles – *10km/6mi north of St-Dalmas-de-Tende by D 91; leave the car at Lac des Mesches.*

Take the signposted footpath *(3hr on foot)* to the Refuge des Merveilles and then to Lac Long, the starting point for a guided tour of the Arpette area. It is possible to spend the night at the refuge (reservation necessary).

The following morning, walk up the Vallée des Merveilles as far as the Baisse de Valmasque *(about 2hr 30min)* and then return by the same route to reach the car park in the late afternoon.

The Wizard and the Mont des Merveilles

B. Kaufmann/MICHELIN

Fontanalbe – *12km/8mi north of St-Dalmas-de-Tende by D 91; park the car in Casterino. Allow one whole day.*

South of Casterino by the information panel *(sign: Fontanalbe)* take the wooded track west and continue to the refuge *(about 1hr)*. Bear left of the refuge building and continue to Lac Vert *(about 45min)*. For a guided tour of the engravings continue along the side of the lake to the guides' hut at **Lacs Jumeaux**.

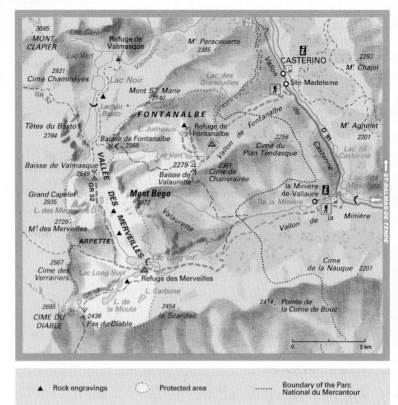

▲ Rock engravings   ⋯ Protected area   ⋯⋯⋯ Boundary of the Parc
                                                            National du Mercantour

By staying overnight at the Fontanalbe refuge *(reservation necessary)* it is possible
to climb the foothills of Mont Bégo as far as the Baisse de Fontanalbe
(alt 2 568m/8 423ft) – fine views of the three lakes in the Valmasque Valley. It is
possible to continue towards the Valmasque Refuge or to return to Casterino by
the outward route.

MONACO★★★

Population 29 876
Michelin map 84 folds 19 and 20, 115 folds 27 and 28 or 245 fold 38
Local map see Corniches de la RIVIERA

The Principality of Monaco, a sovereign state of only 197ha/487 acres, consists of: Monaco, the old town; Monte-Carlo, the new town; La Condamine, linking them together; the industrial district of Fontvieille. Several million tourists flood into the Principality each year. The glamour of Monaco is embodied not least by its royal family: Prince Rainier, who lost his wife Princess Grace, the former Hollywood actress, in a tragic car accident in 1982 after 26 years of marriage. Their three children are Prince Albert and Princesses Caroline and Stephanie.

Native Monégasque citizens (4 500 in 1990) are exempt from taxes and military service.

The Grimaldi family – Monaco, which was inhabited in prehistoric times and later became a Greek settlement and a Roman port, first takes its real place in history with the Grimaldi dynasty. There are numerous branches of the family in France, at Cagnes and Beuil, and in Italy, at Genoa and Naples. During the conflict that broke out between the Guelphs and the Ghibellines, François Grimaldi was expelled from Genoa and, disguised as a monk together with his men, captured Monaco in 1297; hence the two armed monks on the Grimaldi coat of arms.

One Grimaldi bought the domain of Monaco from the Genoese in 1308 and, since then, the name and the Grimaldi coat of arms have always been carried by the heirs to the title, whether these come from the House of Goyon-Matignon (1731-1949) or, as in the case of the present Prince of Monaco, Rainier III, from the House of Polignac.

A turbulent history – The history of Monaco has been fraught with family and political dramas. In the 16C Jean II was killed by his brother Lucien, who in turn was assassinated by his nephew; in 1604 Honoré I was thrown into the sea by his subjects. Monaco was subjected to foreign occupation: by the Spaniards from 1524 to 1641 (it was from the king of Spain that the Grimaldis received the title of Prince); by the French from 1641 to 1814; by the kingdom of Sardinia from 1815 to 1861; by the French again, when Menton and Roquebrune, which belonged to the Principality, were bought in 1861 by Napoleon III, at the time of the annexation of Nice.

Birth of Monte-Carlo – The first casino was an unremarkable establishment in Monaco itself, set up in 1856 by the Prince, who was short of funds. Only in 1862 did the casino move to its own premises in Monte-Carlo where it remained in humble isolation for several years. The arrival of **François Blanc**, director of the casino in Bad Homburg, brought success. Within a few years the casino became fashionable and the surrounding land was covered with luxurious houses, most of them the property of the casino company, La Société des Bains de Mer. The gaming tables in Monte-Carlo became the most famous and most popular in Europe.

A thriving economy – To accommodate the influx of visitors attracted by the gambling tables and tax concessions, Monaco began to put up buildings at a furious pace. Once all the available space had been occupied the shoreline was extended into the sea, providing 22% more land.

Tourism remains the main activity. Without neglecting the traditional visitor, Monaco has sought to capture the business traveller and the conference trade. The hotel complex at Les Spélugues, built on piles below the Casino, includes a conference centre fitted with the latest equipment capable of seating 1 100 people. Monaco now has facilities rivalling those of Cannes and Nice. At Fontvieille light industry is being encouraged: clothing, printing, pharmaceutical products, plastics, precision engineering, perfumery, food processing. Around 40 international banking institutions count Monaco as a front-runner in the financial world. The media are represented by Radio Monte-Carlo and Télé Monte-Carlo. The Société des Bains de Mer, owner of the Casino and the Hôtel de Paris, is the largest private employer in Monaco.

Original and revolutionary town-planning – The first large-scale town-planning projects that accompanied the economic explosion of the mid-1960s were hampered by the cramped nature of the territory.

During the first period, until the end of the 1970s, the solution favoured was to build upwards. A dozen high-rise buildings, more than 30 storeys high, were erected, adding an "American" touch to the landscape.

Since the 1980s a new urban plan has been developed to satisfy the growing residential and service requirements: the future of property in Monaco would seem to lie underground.

All the new access roads are now linked to the French network by deep tunnels. Connections between districts are facilitated by groups of automatic lifts or escalators. Behind the façade of some of Monaco's luxury hotels are access ramps to large public car parks hollowed out of the rock.

In the Fontvieille district, a bus station has been built 10m/33 ft below sea-level and a peninsula (22ha/54 acres in area) has been reclaimed from the sea in 10 years.

Eating out

MODERATE

Le Jazz – *3 Rue de la Turbie* – ☎ *00 377 97 70 50 24* – *Closed Aug, Sat for lunch and Sun* – *Reservation recommended at weekends* – *11.89€ lunch* – *18.29/42.69€*. Not surprisingly, this establishment looks just like a jazz club! A modern decor with red overtones, a hushed atmosphere, deep comfortable arm-chairs and paintings illustrating New Orleans bands. Popular with locals at lunchtime. In the evening, cosier, more refined ambience with a jazzy musical accompaniment.

Polpetta – *2 Rue Paradis* – ☎ *00 377 93 50 67 84* – *Closed 10-30 Jun, Sat for lunch and Tue* – *22.87€*. A small Italian restaurant offering three different settings in which to enjoy a tasty *tagliatelle alla carbonara* or *vitello ai funghi*: the verandah giving onto the street, the rustic-style dining hall or the cosy, inti-mate room at the back.

MID-RANGE

Richart – *19 Boulevard des Moulins* – *98000 Monaco* – *Monte-Carlo* – ☎ *00 377 93 30 15 06* – *www.richart-monaco.com* – *Closed Sun except in Dec* – *24.41/34.63€*. The tiny squares of chocolate with their subtle aromas and intri-cate designs are a delight to behold... and savour! After buying a few boxes of chocolates to take back to friends, sit down in the elegant tea room decorated in white and grey and order one of the light snacks (salads, pastries, savoury tarts) while sipping a cup of delicately scented tea.

Costa à la Crémaillère – *Place de la Crémaillère* – *98000 Monaco* – *Monte-Carlo* – ☎ *00 377 93 50 66 24* – *Closed Aug, Sat for lunch and Sun* – *19.80€ lunch* – *25.99/35.50€*. The verandah of this Victorian-style restaurant has kept the original metal frame that once supported the rack-and-pinion railway sta-tion for trains heading towards La Turbie. A few photographs and frescoes recall these early days. Modern brasserie-style establishment with stalls displaying freshly caught oysters and shellfish.

La Maison du Caviar – *1 Avenue St-Charles* – ☎ *00 377 93 30 80 06* – *Closed 20 Jul-20 Aug, Sat for lunch and Sun* – *15€ lunch* – *28/43€*. This prestigious house has been serving choice caviar to Monaco residents for the past 50 years. In an unusual setting made up of bottle racks and wooden panelling, you can also purchase★ salmon, foie gras or *bœuf strogonoff*. Definitely worth a visit.

Where to stay

MODERATE

Villa Bœri – *29 Boulevard Général-Leclerc* – *06240 Beausoleil* – ☎ *04 93 78 38 10* – *30 rooms: 38.11/62.50€* – ☟ *5.34€*. A 1960s building on the French side of the border, fronted by a small garden planted with Mediterranean shrubs and flowers, offers a few rooms, some of which are lacking in modern comforts. Just cross the street and bingo... you are in Monte-Carlo!

MID-RANGE

Hôtel de France – *6 Rue de la Turbie* – *98000 Monaco* – *Near the train sta-tion* – ☎ *00 377 93 30 24 64* – *26 rooms: 63.27/80.80€*. Recent renovation work on this hotel has graced it with charming, soundproofed rooms decorated in Provençal hues and a modern breakfast lounge enhanced with metal and wood furniture.

On the town

Café de Paris – *Place du Casino* – ☎ *00 377 92 16 20 20* – *sbm.mc* – *Daily 7.30am-2am*. The terraces of this turn-of-the-century brasserie look out onto Place du Casino and the Salon Bellevue upstairs commands a superb panorama of the Franco-Italian Riviera. Each week the menus are devoted to a particular gastronomic style: traditional French food, Provençal cooking, continental cui-sine, etc. Take-away sales of shellfish and seafood (in winter) and ice-cream (in summer) on the premises.

Casino de Monte-Carlo – *Place du Casino* – ☎ *00 377 92 16 20 00* – *casino-monte-carlo.com* – *Daily from noon until the last client leaves*. This is Europe's leading casino, with over one billion francs' profit, attributed to gambling and not to slot machines and one-arm bandits as is the case in other casinos. The gambling salons and lavish dining hall Le Train Bleu, decorated in the style of the Orient-Express, are truly impressive. The terrace overlooking the sea is a haven of tranquillity, whether or not you have broken the bank!

La Terrasse (Bar du Vistamar) – *Square Beaumarchais* – ✆ *00 377 92 16 40 00* – *Daily 11.30am-1am.* This famous bar has been patronised by many celebrities, namely Onassis and Maria Callas. Its superb terrace affords beautiful views of Monaco harbour. The specialities of the house are American cocktails, notably those made with Champagne!

Sass Café – *11 Avenue Princesse-Grace* – ✆ *00 377 93 25 52 00* – *Daily 8pm-1am (restaurant), 11pm to dawn (piano-bar).* Exclusive bar-restaurant with a cosy atmosphere where members of the local jet-set drop in for a fancy vodka or Champagne cocktail before meeting up at Jimmy'z. Piano bar starting at 11pm every evening.

Le Jimmy'z – *Quai Princesse-Grace* – ✆ *00 377 92 16 22 77* – *Daily 11pm to dawn. Reservation recommended.* It would be unthinkable to leave Monte-Carlo without having paid a visit to the legendary Jimmy'z... Formal evening wear is expected in this small but select club where the rich and wealthy love to congregate, whether they come from banking, advertising, fashion, film or the entertainment world... A unique, magic experience.

Stars'N'Bars – *6 Quai Antoine-1* – ✆ *00 377 93 50 95 95* – *starsnbars.com* – *Daily 11am-midnight; 4am for the dance hall.* This is *the* great American bar of the moment, where the ambience is slightly more relaxed than in the Principality's other establishments. Stars'N'Bars caters for a younger clientele eager to drink beer, eat a hamburger or two, play billiards, surf on the Internet and dance away the night. The decoration features one of Sergei Bubka's vaulting poles, a dress worn by Sharon Stone, a handbag once belonging to Catherine Deneuve and other celebrety stuff collected throughout the world. There are supervised play areas for children. Rock concerts are organised on a regular basis. Terrace with a view of Monaco harbour.

The Living Room Club – *7 Avenue des Spélugues* – ✆ *00 377 93 50 80 31 ou 93 50 88 10* – *monte-carlo.mc/livingroom* – *Mon-Sat 11pm to dawn. Exceptionally open on Sun during the Formula 1 Grand Prix .* Select, high-class club where night owls meet up after leaving Jimmy'z. Try their special "Living Room cocktail" or one of their Champagnes. Piano bar music alternates with DJ evenings. Eclectic clientele.

Shows

Folie Russe – *12 Avenue des Spélugues* – ✆ *00 377 93 50 65 00* – *Tue-Sun, show at 10.30pm.* Cabaret attached to the Hôtel Lœss. Dance, juggling acts, magic shows.

Le Cabaret – *Place du Casino* – ✆ *00 377 92 16 36 36* – *montecarloresort.com* – *Daily except Mon: show 11pm-midnight.* This cabaret run by the Monte-Carlo Casino presents a Cuban revue. Exceptionally, it also stages concerts of jazz and contemporary pop.

Parking and public transport

Access to the Rock (Le Rocher) is permitted only to vehicles registered in Monaco and the Alpes-Maritimes. Public car parks in Monaco with more than 500 spaces are:

Sous-Sol du Stade Louis II (1 200)	**Chemin des Pêcheurs** (600)
Centre Commercial de Fontvieille (680)	**Les Boulingrins** (600)

There are large lifts providing swift vertical travel in certain districts. The main lifts are:

Place Ste-Dévote to Boulevard de Belgique (longest)
Plages du Larvotto (and Musée National) to Place des Moulins
Avenue Hector-Otto towards Boulevard de Belgique
Avenue de la Costa (Park Palace Building) towards Boulevard Princesse-Charlotte
Centre des Congrès (Boulevard Louis-II) towards Terrasses du Casino
Parking des Pêcheurs towards Musée Océanographique
Avenue de Grande-Bretagne towards Avenue des Citronniers
Centre Commercial de Fontvieille towards Place d'Armes
Port de Monaco towards Avenue de la Costa

Arriving by air – Regular daily service (6min) every 15min between Monaco and the Aéroport de Nice-Côte d'Azur provided by **Héli Air Monaco** at the Héliport de Monaco-Fontvieille. ✆ (00) 377 92 05 00 50. Daily flights also run between Monaco and Fréjus or St-Raphaël. *For details call ✆ 04 94 51 83 83 (Fréjus tourist office).*

Boat trips

Bateaux de la French Riviera – *Compagnie de Navigation et de Tourisme de Monaco* – *Quai des Etats-Unis* – ☎ *(00 377) 92 16 15 15* – *www. cntmonaco.com* – *Jul-Aug departures at 11am, 2.30pm, 4pm and 5.30pm; Jun and Sep daily except Mon departures at 11am, 2.30pm, 4pm; Apr, May, Oct daily except Mon departures at 2.30pm. 10.67€ (child 7,.2€).* Boat trips affording views of the sea depths, and marine fauna and flora.

Money, stamps and telephones

Monaco has followed in the footsteps of EU member-states by adopting the European single currency, the euro, which also applies to postage stamps. The national coins and banknotes formerly confined to the Principality have no financial value and have become collector's pieces.

To telephone a number in Monaco, dial 00 377, followed by the number required; to telephone to France dial 00 33, followed by the number required.

Shopping

All the famous trademarks have shops in Monte-Carlo and some have set up outlets in the larger hotels (Métropole, Park Palace).

Shops specialising in traditional goods are to be found in the narrow streets of the Rock (Le Rocher) opposite the palace.

The Boutique du Rocher in Avenue de la Madone is the official boutique for local arts and crafts.

D. Hée/MICHELIN

Not to be missed

The changing of the guard on Place du Palais daily at 11.55am precisely.

Picturesque procession on the Rocher and other cultural spectacles on the National Day, 18 November.

Sciaratù Carnival during the week of Shrove Tuesday when local specialities are on offer – *barbagiuàn* and *fougasse* in red and white, the colours of Monaco.

Watching the Grand Prix de Monaco from a boat moored in the middle of the port; reservations and information from the tourist office.

Before laying a bet

No one under 21 is allowed in the gaming rooms. Free admission to the fruit machine rooms in the Café de Paris (from 10am) or in the Casino de Monte-Carlo (from 2pm); the gaming rooms and American games open in the Casino at 3pm (5pm for certain games). The Sun-Casino also has some gaming rooms. During the summer season *(July to mid-September)* gambling takes place in the Salles des Palmiers of the Sporting-Club de Monte-Carlo (from 10pm). A tax of 100F is payable in most of the private room.

Around the town at the bottom of chasms between ancient buildings minuscule excavators can be seen at work: every new building must be provided with a multi-level underground car park.

There are several projects underway and due for completion at the end of 1999: an underground railway station and railway lines, the construction of a great conference and exhibition centre which will be embedded in the Larvotto shoreline. Other more long-term projects will bring into play even more daring and innovative techniques, such as the creation of artificial lagoons with a view to building districts over the shallows of Monaco's coast.

STROLLING THROUGH THE PRINCIPALITY

★★ The Rock

Tour: allow 3hr. Park in Parking des Pêcheurs and take the lift.

Monaco, capital of the Principality, is picturesquely sited on a rock jutting 800m/875yd out to sea and overlooking the bay. Crowned by the old town's ramparts, the Rocher de Monaco, as it is known, is a lovely sight to behold, especially on a fine evening, when you can admire its floodlit outlines from the Grande Corniche road or the Belvédère de La Turbie. The town is so pretty that it resembles a studio set: neat little 18C houses with their salmon-pink façades, squeezed in along quaint alleyways. This is the heart of the principality, home to the most interesting sights: the **Musée Océanographique**★★★, the museum in Chapelle de la Visitation, the Cathedral and the Palace. On the car park terraces, near the Musée Océanographique, lies the **Monte-Carlo Story** ⊘. In a large hall an audiovisual production on a wide screen retraces the history of the Grimaldi dynasty and the development of the Principality.

Facing the exotic gardens, the **Fontvieille** district, which is mainly industrial, is undergoing large-scale development with the creation of new residential and recreational areas on land reclaimed from the sea *(work in progress)*.

The changing of the guard takes place just before midday.

Terrace of the Musée Océanographique – *Go up to the second level.* The **view**★★ encompasses the Esterel range to the Italian Riviera. Towering above the modern buildings of the principality, this viewpoint affords a panorama of Tête de Chien and, beyond, Mont Agel with its relay station.

Take Avenue St-Martin on the left, leading to the cathedral.

Cathedral – The neo-Romanesque cathedral was built with white stone from La Turbie on the ruins of the church of St-Nicolas between 1875 and 1903. The high altar, the organ loft and the Bishop's chair, its canopy supported by granite columns, are of white marble inlaid with mosaic and copper motifs. In the south transept chapel stands a fine Spanish Renaissance style altar in red and gold. The Princes' tombs are located in the ambulatory.

The cathedral has a collection of **early paintings from the Nice School**★★. At the entrance to the ambulatory (left) is the **altarpiece of St Nicholas** by Louis Bréa: 18 sections in glowing colours surrounded by Renaissance carving of leaves and dolphins. In the centre St Nicholas is seated on a green throne; on most panels the names of the characters appear against a gold background: St Devota, patron of Monaco, in a small painting (bottom left); a remarkable Mary Magdalene (right); St Anne curiously cradling both the Virgin as a child and the Infant Jesus in her arms (top right). Three panels – St Roch, St Anthony and the Rosary – decorate the ambulatory. The Pietà of the White Penitents behind the high altar features a charming predella. In the south transept above the sacristy door is an altarpiece by Louis Bréa: a **Pietà** set against a Monaco landscape.

Rue Comte-Félix-Gastaldi (Renaissance doorways) leads to Rue Princesse-Marie-de-Lorraine.

Chapelle de la Miséricorde – This chapel's classic pink and white façade was built in 1646 by the Black Penitents. In a niche on the south side is a **recumbent Christ**★ by the Monégasque sculptor Bosio; on Good Friday this statue is carried through the streets of the old town.

On leaving turn right onto picturesque Rue Basse.

Historial des Princes de Monaco ⊘ – In a suite of handsome vaulted rooms the history of the Grimaldi family is set out in 24 scenes with 40 life-size wax figures.

★ **Place du Palais** – The square, ornamented with cannons given to the Prince of Monaco by Louis XIV, is bordered to the northeast by a crenellated parapet from which there is a **view** of the harbour, Monte-Carlo and the coast as far as the Bordighera headland. To the southwest is the **Promenade Ste-Barbe** ⊘ with a view of Cap d'Ail.

Rampe Major – The ramp leads down to Place d'Armes, passing through 16C, 17C and 18C gates as it descends the north face of the rock overlooking the harbour and **La Condamine**, where a lively market is held every morning.

A Host of Festivals

Everyone has heard of the Monte-Carlo Rally which has been held every year since 1911 (end January), and the Monaco Grand Prix (May) which takes place in the streets of the Principality on a winding circuit (3.145km/2mi).

There is also the Feast of Ste-Dévote (27 January); the International Television Festival (February); the Spring Arts Festival and the International Tennis Championship (April); the Flower Show (May); the Monte-Carlo Golf Open on the slopes of Mont Agel (June); the concerts in the palace courtyard and the Fireworks Festival (July-August); the National Day of Monaco (19 November); the International Circus Festival (December)...

There is no need to advertise the reputation of the Monte-Carlo Philharmonic Orchestra or that of the Opera – where the work of the worldwide famous choreographers is presented.

La Condamine *30min*

In the Middle Ages this term applied to cultivable land at the foot of a village or a castle. Nowadays La Condamine is the commercial district stretching between the Rock and Monte-Carlo.

Port – Prince Albert I commissioned the building of the harbour skirted by a broad terraced promenade and crowded with luxury yachts. The Olympic swimming pool was added by Prince Rainier. In season **boat trips** ⊘ in a glass-bottomed catamaran leave from Quai des États-Unis.

From the northwest corner of the harbour a valley separating La Condamine from Monte-Carlo runs up under a viaduct to the church of Ste-Dévote.

Église Ste-Dévote – Built in 1870 on the ruins of an old church, it contains a fine 18C marble altar.

St Devota was martyred in Corsica in the 3C when, according to tradition, the skiff carrying her body to Africa was caught in a terrific storm and was guided by a dove towards the French coast, eventually landing at Monaco.

In the Middle Ages relics of the saint were stolen and taken away by ship. But the thieves were caught and their ship razed – a legend which has given rise to the ceremony which takes place every 26 January when a ship is burned on the square in front of the church; the next day there is a procession.

Rue Grimald – The busy shopping street, lined with orange trees, leads off Place Ste-Dévote.

★★★ Monte-Carlo *1hr 15min*

Monte-Carlo is a name famous throughout the world. It brings to mind gambling and also the majestic setting of its palaces, casinos, sumptuous villas, luxurious shops and its flowered terraces, trees and exotic plants. Monte-Carlo offers visitors attractions of all kinds.

To the east of the Principality are the man-made beaches, swimming pools and ultra-modern bathing facilities of Larvotto, a luxury development partly built on land reclaimed from the sea which complements the other facilities of Monte-Carlo Beach and is linked to the Spélugues complex by Avenue Princesse-Grâce.

Monte-Carlo Opera House

Stroking the knee of the equestrian statue of Louis XIV in the entrance of the Hôtel de Paris is said to bring the gambler good luck.

The casino is surrounded by beautiful gardens and stands on a fine **terrace**★★ from which the view stretches from Monaco to the Bordighera headland. The terrace is extended by the roof-top promenades of the Spélugues complex, adorned by a composition in enamelled pumice stone by Vasarely entitled *Hexa Grace*.

SIGHTS

Casino ⊘ – The building comprises several sections: the oldest (to the west), built in 1878 by **Charles Garnier**, architect of the Paris Opera House, faces the sea; the most recent dates from 1910. As one enters the huge central hall, the theatre lies ahead and the sumptuously decorated gambling rooms on the left. First are the public rooms: the Renaissance Room, the European Grand Salon, the America Room and the Room of the Graces. A small gallery separates the America Room from the rooms of the Cercle Privé (club): the

Pierrot and Dogs by Vichy (1865),
Musée National de Monaco

two Touzet rooms and the vast and ornate François Médecin Room. A grand staircase goes down to the Ganne Room, where there is a nightclub. There is also the auditorium, designed by Charles Garnier.

★ **Palais du Prince** ⊘ – The oldest parts of the palace are 13C; the buildings on the south side, in Italian Renaissance style, 15C and 16C. The formidable perimeter is built into the vertical rock. Some battlemented towers remain standing. A monumental doorway with the Grimaldi arms adorns this robust-looking ensemble.

The tour leads first of all to the Hercules Gallery which overlooks the lovely main courtyard featuring a double staircase in white marble. The whole gallery is decorated with 16C and 17C frescoes – particularly by Ferrari. The Throne Room and the state apartments where official receptions are held are decorated with carpets and precious furniture and hung with portraits signed by Rigaud, Philippe de Champaigne and Van Loo.

★ **Musée Napoléonien et des Archives du Palais** ⊘ – The ground floor of a wing of the palace is devoted to a museum on Napoleon, of whom the Prince of Monaco is a descendant. There are numerous souvenirs and documents: lorgnette, watch, tobacco pouch, tricolour scarf, hat belonging to the "little corporal", King of Rome's clothes; also coins, medals, arms, uniforms, military insignia, flags belonging to the grenadiers on Elba; busts of Napoleon by Canova and Houdon, bust of Josephine by Bosio; on the wall is the family tree of the Bonapartes, originally from Florence, and that of the Prince of Monaco.

Apart from a portrait of Napoleon by Gérard, the upper floor is devoted to the history of Monaco: charter granted by Louis XII recognising the Principality's independence, collection of stamps, coins and medals. A piece of rock brought back from the moon by the American cosmonauts is also on display.

★ **Musée National de Monaco** ⊘ – The National Museum of Dolls and Automata, housed in a charming villa built by Charles Garnier and fronted by a rose garden dotted with sculptures – note the *Young Faun* by Carpeaux – contains a collection of 19C automata and some 400 dolls dating from the 18C to the present. The very intricate internal workings are open to view; they are set in motion several times a day. There is an 18C Neapolitan crib including 250 figures.

Musée de la Chapelle de la Visitation ⊘ – This 17C Baroque chapel houses the rich Barbara Piasecka-Johnson collection of sacred works of art. Of particular interest are works by Zurbarán, Rubens and the Italian Baroque masters.

★ **Collection des Voitures Anciennes** ⊘ – About 100 old vehicles and carriages from the royal collection are on display on the five levels of this exhibition hall. On the first level are the barouches used by Prince Charles III. Next is the De Dion Bouton (1903), the first car owned by Prince Albert I, and other famous models: a Lincoln Torpedo convertible (1928), a Packard cabriolet (1935) and the Buick Skylar (1966). The Rolls Royce Silver Cloud given by Monégasque tradesmen to Prince Rainier on his wedding day in 1956, and a 1952 Austin London taxi converted for Princess Grace bring a personal touch to this collection. The milestones of the contemporary history of the motor car are represented by a tracked vehicle, Citroën de la Croisière Jaune, a fine selection of front-wheel drives, American military equipment, a Trabant and a 1986 Lamborghini built along futuristic lines.

227

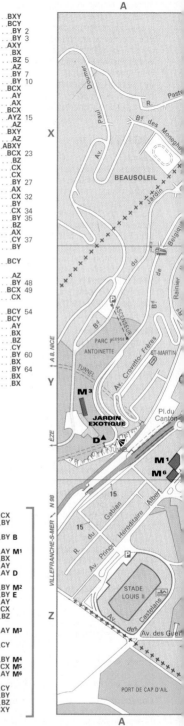

The 1929 Bugatti (winner of the 1st Grand Prix) and a 1989 Ferrari F1 (600hp) have pride of place in the hall dedicated to Formula 1. On the left, on a pedestal surrounded by flowers, is a helmet worn by the racing driver Ayrton Senna, who died during the 1994 Italian Grand Prix, a permanent reminder of the dangers of this sport.

Musée Naval ⊘ – The hundred exhibits in this museum are the cream of the royal collection of model ships covering a period from ancient times to the present day. The oldest models were built by Prince Albert I in 1874. Among the most

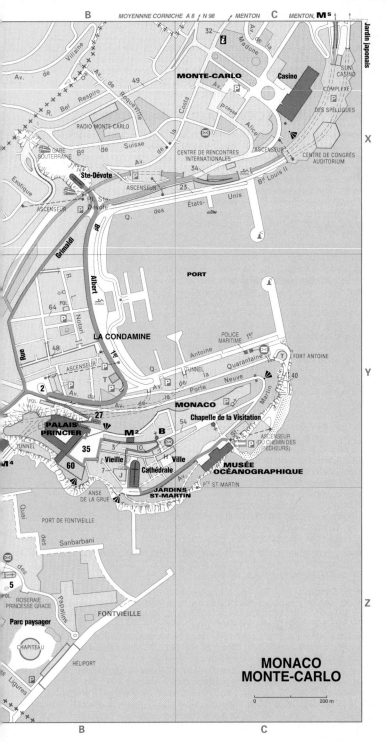

remarkable are the **gondole impériale** made in 15 days for the inspection of Napoleon I at Anvers, and the *Missouri*, depicted in the state she was in on 2nd September 1945 when the armistice was signed with Japan.

Musée des Timbres et des Monnaies ⏱ – Housed in a very modern setting, this museum contains all the stamps produced in the Principality together with a fine retrospective of the Princes' collections. The first stamp bearing the head of a Monégasque sovereign was issued in 1885 during the reign of Charles III.

Prior to that date, after the introduction of postmarks, Sardinian stamps were used for franking, and from 1860, overprinted "Monaco".

In the large gallery there is a line-engraving rotary press which was used for half a century to print Monaco's stamps. The rare stamps gallery contains several unique exhibits: letters sent from Fort Hercule (as Monaco was called under the Revolution), and the first stamps from Sardinia and Monaco printed in colour.

A set of current Monégasque stamps can be bought at the reception alongside boxes of coins, both those currently in use and collectors' items.

DISCOVERING LOCAL FAUNA AND FLORA

★★ **Musée Océanographique** ⊙ – This museum, which is also an institute for scientific research, was founded in 1910 by Prince Albert I.

The founder, who was an oceanography enthusiast, devoted the museum to marine science and housed in it the scientific collections he made during his campaigns after 1885. The large imposing freestone building occupies an exceptional site on the south face of the Rock, overlooking the Mediterranean from an impressive cliff (80m/262ft). Located in the basement, the **aquarium**★★ is one of the finest in Europe. More than 4 500 fish representing 400 different species swim in 90 pools that recreate their natural habitat. The tropical species exhibit the most astounding colours. Among the most strange, magnificent or rare specimens are the flying scorpion fish, the orange clownfish, the surgeon fish and the sunfish. In a huge pool (25 000l/5 500gal of water) a nurse shark lives happily with large green turtles and hawksbill turtles. The live coral reef from the Red Sea is an outstanding exhibit. The **Salle d'Océanographie Zoologique**★, also known as Salle de la Baleine, contains the skeletons of large marine mammals: a whale (20m/66ft), washed up on the Italian coast, a killer whale, a sperm whale, a sea-cow, a narwhal as well as stuffed specimens: giant Japanese crabs (2m/6ft wide), a giant turtle (200kg/441lb) and casts of coelacanths. An exhibition *(art de la nacre)* of mother-of-pearl contains some splendid carved shells from Prince Albert I's collection as well as recent acquisitions. In the **atrium**, opposite the entrance, are life-size models of two diving bells identical to those used on board the *Calypso*.

On the right of the atrium the former conference room has been turned into a cinema showing films made by Jacques-Yves Cousteau's team. This hall is also used as a venue for international scientific congresses.

The central oceanographic hall presents the scientific journeys of Prince Albert: models of his four research vessels, notably *Princesse Alice II*. It was on board this ship that, in 1901, the Prince collected fish from a record depth of 6 000m/19 681ft and on an expedition to Spitzberg reached a latitude of 80°N. Nearby is the reconstruction of the laboratory installed on his last vessel, *Hirondelle II*, as well as his whaling boat from which he was able to recover animals living at great depths from the stomachs of the whales he hunted.

Next is the exhibition *Découverte de l'Océan* which explains the main marine phenomena: waves, salinity of the water, the effect of the ocean on the atmosphere and more complex questions such as the rise of deep water along certain coasts (upwelling). Among the remarkable animations are a reconstruction of the sinking of the *Titanic*, a gigantic model of the Marianne trench, the deepest in the world, and one of the first submarines, *Bushnell's Turtle*.

Terrace – From the second floor terrace *(lift)*, overhanging the sea, there is a magnificent **view**★★ of the coast from the Esterel range to the Italian Riviera and of the Tête de Chien and Mont Agel inland.

★★ **Jardin Exotique** ⊙ – The tropical gardens cascade down a steep rock face which has its own microclimate favourable to cacti and other succulents, particularly arborescents: huge candelabra-like euphorbia, giant aloes, "mother-in-law cushions", Barbary figs. There are 6 000 varieties of semi-desertic flora; many of the unusual shapes and vivid colours are native to Mexico and southern Africa. The garden offers many magnificent **views**★ of the Rock of Monaco, the harbour, Monte-Carlo, Cap Martin and the Italian Riviera *(viewing table)*.

After descending 279 steps, you will reach the **Grotte de l'Observatoire** ⊙★. The grottoes, which open off the tropical gardens, have been well arranged. The tour passes through a number of chambers at different levels, adorned with stalactites, stalagmites and other delicate and varied concretions. The rock is dolomitic limestone. Excavations at the cave mouth have revealed signs of human habitation some 200 000 years ago; tools and prehistoric animal bones are on display in the museum *(see below)*.

★ **Musée d'Anthropologie Préhistorique** ⊙ – *Access through the Jardin Exotique.* The presentation and extreme diversity of the exhibits make this museum of interest even to the non-specialist. The Rainier III Gallery contains regional collections (animal bones and Stone Age tools). Owing to changes in climate not only reindeer, mammoths and cave bears but also elephants and hippopotamuses once roamed the Riviera. The skeletons of *Homo sapiens* are impressive: Grimaldi negroids, Cro-Magnon man, collective burials etc.

The Albert-I Gallery contains a retrospective exhibition on the principal milestones of the evolution of mankind. One showcase is devoted to prehistoric figurines (mammoth, horse); the other showcase to the Bronze Age.

★ **Jardin Japonais** ⊘ – *Access from Boulevard Louis-II.* In the extremely urban surroundings of the Larvotto district this garden provides a calm green oasis beside the sea. The garden (7ha/17 acres), which is designed according to Shintoist principles by a great Japanese landscape gardener, is a highly structured miniaturisation of the world of nature. The three key elements of a Japanese garden are illustrated: the line (path), the point (pool) and the surface (waterfall). The mineral constituents come from the Auvergne (granite), from Corsica (porphyry) and from the Tinée Valley (shingle in the pool). All the garden furniture and the planting are symbolic.

The **Pont Cintré "Taïko"** is a scarlet bridge (the colour of happiness) illustrating the difficult journey towards the gods, represented by the central islands: the one with two pine trees has the shape of a turtle, symbol of longevity; the small island planted with a single pine depicts a nesting crane.

Near the tea room, the **Jardin Zen** invites contemplation of the barren countryside outlined by the seven stones of Cap Corse. The ellipses traced on the gravel symbolise the perpetual movement of the universe.

The tea rooms with their spartan decoration add another oriental note to this unusual display.

★ **Jardins St-Martin** – Shaded walks offer glimpses of the sea through the tropical vegetation. Statue of Prince Albert I by François Cogné (1951). The fragments of pillars and capitals come from the church of St-Nicolas.

In high season **Azur-Express** ⊘, a small tourist train, makes two circuits leaving from Avenue St-Martin.

Princess Grace

Grace Kelly was born in Philadelphia on 12 November 1912, the third of four children. After studying at the New York Academy of Dramatic Arts, she began working as an actress for television and the theatre. Her first breakthrough in the cinema was the movie *High Noon* (1952), in which she played a young bride married to Gary Cooper. Many films were to follow but her name has remained closely associated with that of the British director Alfred Hitchcock, for whom she starred in *Dial M for Murder* (1954), *Rear Window* (1954 and *To Catch a Thief* (1955), shot entirely on location in the South of France. Grace Kelly was introduced to Prince Rainier of Monaco at the Cannes Film Festival and they were married in April 1956. She gave birth to three children, Caroline, Albert and Stéphanie.

The new princess soon won the affections of the principality's residents. She was a model mother and spent much of her time supporting charitable causes such as the Red Cross and AMADE, an organization set up to help developing countries. Her life was to end tragically in 1982 when her car veered off the Grande Corniche and crashed into the cliff face.

Parc Paysager – In this park plant species from all over the world are clustered around a charming lake. Nearby lies the **Princesse Grace Rose Garden** boasting more than 4 000 bushes belonging to 150 different rose varieties, some of which were created by celebrated gardeners. The statue of the princess was erected in 1983, the year of her death, by Kees Verkade. On the seafront is the heliport. From here there is a panoramic view inland of the foothills of the principality: the long line of high buildings of the Espace Fontvieille and behind them the sharp outline of Tête de Chien, dominated by Mont Agel. To the left is the marina of Port-Cap-d'Ail.

Coral reef with its fauna

Musée Océanographique, Monaco

The way back towards the shopping centre passes an attractive residential area rising from which can be seen a campanile with a dome covered in glazed tiles. There are three museums on the first level of the **Terrases de Fontvieille**, over the shopping centre.

Jardin Animalier ⊙ – The zoo terraces, on the southwest face of the Rock, present a large and varied collection of mammals, reptiles, exotic birds and numerous monkeys. Fine view of the sea and Cap d'Ail.

WALKING TOURS

★★Coastal Path to Cap Martin – ⌘ *3hr on foot there and back leaving from Monte-Carlo, preferably in the afternoon – local maps see MENTON and Corniches de la RIVIERA.*
Tourists wishing to take a shorter route can drive to the train station of Roquebrune-Cap-Martin and join up with the path running below.
On the left of the Monte-Carlo Beach Hotel, on the left take the steps down between two villas.

For a description of the walk in the opposite direction see ROQUEBRUNE-CAP-MARTIN: Coastal path.

★Coastal Path to Cap d'Ail – *1hr on foot there and back – local map see Corniches de la RIVIERA. Park the car near Plage Marquet, the beach to the west of Fontvieille.*
⌘ From the beach there is a path along the shore. Monaco Rock soon disappears from sight as the path rounds the headland where the sea throws up a fine spray as it crashes on the rocks. Slowly Cap Ferrat and Beaulieu come into view. On the left of La Pinède Restaurant, steps lead up to the road and Cap-d'Ail station. The path can be followed as far as the Plage Mala, then a flight of steps leads to the road back into the conurbation.

★Beausoleil; Mont des Mules – *3km/2mi then 15min on foot there and back – local map and description under Corniches de la RIVIERA.*

MONS★

Michelin map 84 fold 8, 115 fold 22 or 245 fold 36

This old village (traces of a Celto-Ligurian oppidum) is set on an isolated rock spur in the Pre-Alps of Grasse on a wild and sunny **site★** where every single type of sub-Alpine Provençal plant is known to thrive. After several plague epidemics the village was repopulated in the Middle Ages by families from the Genoa region who instigated the skilful rebuilding of the village; they also brought the land back into cultivation with olives, wheat and pastureland. The picturesque narrow streets and the tiny squares with their stone fountains make for a pleasant walk.

REGIONAL FARE

Auberge Provençale – *7 Rue du Rempart-du-Midi* – ☎ *04 94 76 38 33 – Closed mid-Nov to mid-Dec, Tue except Jul-Aug – 12.20/23.63€.* Located just off Place St-Sébastien, this restaurant has huge bay windows running the length of its terrace, commanding panoramic views of the surrounding landscape. The Provençal cooking is well worth a visit. Tea and pastries are served in the afternoon.

Calendar

Pottery market the first weekend in August.

Women's Festival on Ste-Agathe Day during the first weekend in February.

St-Pierre Festival towards the end of June.

Local festivities in honour of **Our Lady** on 15 August.

DISCOVERING MONS

Place St-Sébastien – The square is set off by an 18C fountain; the terrace looks out over the Siagne and Siagnole Valleys and provides an exceptional **view★★** which on a clear day ranges from Le Coudon (north of Toulon) via the Lérins islands and Corsica to the Alps on the Italian frontier *(viewing table).*

⌘ A ramble along Chemin de la Chapelle St-Pierre (in the village) will take you to three curious dolmens: **Riens** (400m/400yd), **La Colle** (3.5km/2mi) and **La Brainée** (7.5km/4.7mi).

Church ⊙ – The building, which was started in the Upper Provençal Romanesque style, was greatly altered in the 15C and 17C. It is fitted with unusually uniform furnishings: five Baroque altarpieces including a huge triptych dating from 1680 on the high altar dedicated to the Assumption of the Virgin and St Peter and St Paul. To the right of the high altar stands a beautiful 15C silver processional cross. The bell in the square belfry was cast in 1438.

MOUGINS

Population 16 051
Michelin map 84 fold 9, 115 south of fold 24 or 245 fold 37

On an extraordinary hilltop site★, carpeted with flowers and bushes, the old village with its narrow lanes and restored houses is contained within the boundaries of the earlier ramparts; the 12C fortified entrance is known as the "Saracen Gate".

A festive atmosphere reigns over Place de la Mairie, where the solitary elm and fountain are surrounded by the bustling village life. The town hall used to be a chapel for the White Penitents.

From the village there is a wide view of the Grasse countryside as far as the sea. The terrace of the church bell-tower ⓥclocher (bell-tower) commands a superb panorama★ over the surrounding countryside and the coast.

As early as 1935 Pablo Picasso discovered Mougins in the company of Dora Marr and the photographer Man Ray. He and his wife Jacqueline settled in Mougins in 1961 and remained there until his death in 1973. They lived in the Notre-Dame-de-Vie district in the *mas* called L'Antre du Minotaure (The Minotaur's Lair), which became a creative workshop for artists.

SIGHTS

Musée Municipal ⓥ – This museum is located on the first floor of the Mairie (town hall), which was built on the foundations of a former chapel dedicated to St Bernardin. It presents an interesting retrospective of the history of Mougins. The display includes Roman funerary stelae, a 16C reliquary and numerous exhibits of local handcrafts and agricultural implements no longer in use. Part of the display is given over to **Commandant Lamy**, born in Mougins in 1858, who explored Africa and founded the capital of Chad (once called Fort-Lamy).

Musée de la Photographie ⓥ – The Photography Museum is to be found behind the church bell-tower, beside the Saracen Gate, once part of the town's ramparts. The display occupies three floors and includes a lovely collection of old cameras, such as the **cidoscope**, an ancestor of animated cartoons, and numerous photographs of Picasso and his family by his friend André Villers. There are also works by famous photographers such as Clergue, Doisneau, Duncan, Lartigue, Roth, Otero, Denise Colomb and the press photographer Ralph Gatti.

Some rooms are given over to temporary exhibitions displaying the work of contemporary photographers.

Eating out

MID-RANGE

La Broche de Fer – *In St-Basile, Route de Valbonne* – ☎ *04 92 92 08 08* – *Closed 5-16 Mar, 5-16 Nov, Thu for lunch and Wed* – *18.29/28.20€*. Tucked away from Mougins, this roomy restaurant laid out on four levels has been charmingly decorated in the true Provençal spirit. The main speciality is meat, either grilled or cooked on a spit.

L'Amandier de Mougins – *In the village* – ☎ *04 93 90 00 91* – *25.15/30.49€*. A 14C press has been converted into a ravishing inn with a vaulted dining area and a tiny terrace that is invariably booked for both lunch and dinner. It has earned a well-deserved reputation thanks to its attractive setting, its homely cooking and its warm, congenial welcome.

Brasserie de la Méditerranée – *In the village* – ☎ *04 93 90 03 47* – *Closed 10 Jan-3 Feb and Tue 15 Oct-1 Apr* – *26.22/34.61€*. This bistro on the village square has a fine terrace giving onto the main street. Inside, the ambience is warm and intimate despite the popularity of the place. The menu presents Provençal specialities made with fresh local produce.

EXCURSIONS

Ermitage Notre-Dame-de-Vie ⓥ – *6km/3.5mi – about 45min – east of Mougins by D 235 going northwest and D 35 east; after 2km/1mi turn right.*

The site★ is strikingly beautiful; the hermitage of Notre-Dame-de-Vie stands at the top of a long meadow bordered by two rows of giant cypresses (on the right beneath the trees stands a 15C stone cross). The view★ towards Mougins is reminiscent of a Tuscan landscape. It is here that Picasso chose to spend his last years; his house, well screened by trees and bushes, is just opposite.

The chapel is 17C; the bell-tower is roofed in colourful tiles. There are three Gallo-Roman funeral inscriptions. On the high altar is a fine altarpiece of the Assumption in blue and gold; on the left-hand wall a collection of votive offerings.

Notre-Dame-de-Vie (Our Lady of Life) was known throughout the area as a "Sanctuary of Grace"; stillborn babies were brought here, sometimes from great distances. During Mass the child was thought to resuscitate for a few moments, long enough for it to be christened.

A track suitable for motor vehicles leads to D 3, which takes you back to Mougins.

Étang de Fontmerle – *3km by D 35 towards the golf course, then at the round-about take avenue de Grasse, and then turn right on the Promenade de l'Étang.* This large pond was neglected for many years until it became a protected site for the cultivation of the lotus flower. It is now the largest group of lotus plants in Europe. The pond is popular with both migrating birds and those who come to watch them from the observation tower.

★ **Musée de l'Automobiliste** ⓥ – *5km/3mi southeast. 772 Chemin de Font-de-Cur-rault. The Car Museum is located next to the Aire Nord des Bréguières (service area on the north side) of motorway A 8; it can also be reached via the footbridge from the service area on the south side.*
The museum can also be approached from Vallauris (see VALLAURIS).
From Mougins take D 234 northwest; turn right onto D 3 towards Cannes. Just before the motorway turn left onto Chemin du Belvédère, which becomes Chemin des Collines. At the second junction turn left onto Chemin de Ferrandou, then left again to cross over the motorway. Turn right onto Chemin de Font-de-Currault, which leads to the museum car park.
The façade of the futuristic building beside the motorway consists of concrete and glass to resemble a radiator. Two motoring enthusiasts, Adrien Maeght and Antoine Raffaelli, assisted by ESCOTA, the company running the French Riviera's motor-ways, have gathered a collection of vintage cars and more recent models, which are shown in rotation (about 90 at a time). Each vehicle in the gleaming display is in perfect working order; all the famous makes are represented: Benz (first serial model 1894), Bugatti (57, 1938), Ferrari, Hispano-Suiza, Delage, Rolls Royce etc. The section devoted to racing cars, some of which have won Grand Prix competitions, contains a series of Matras from the years 1967 to 1974. Every year two thematic exhibitions are held, focusing on one particular aspect of motoring. The museum cinema shows films on the history of the automobile and the part played in it by each make.

Various activities and competitions are held throughout the year in the entrance court: exchange mart, public auction, best turned-out vehicle etc.

Route NAPOLÉON

Michelin maps 77, 81, 84, 115, 244 and 245

The Route Napoléon – Napoleon's Road – follows the route taken by the emperor on his return from Elba, from the point where he landed in Golfe-Juan to his arrival in Grenoble. The new road was opened in 1932. The commemorative plaques and mon-uments bear the flying eagle symbol inspired by Napoleon's remark: "The eagle will fly from steeple to steeple until he reaches the towers of Notre-Dame".

FLIGHT OF THE EAGLE

After landing at Golfe-Juan on 1 March 1815, Napoleon and his little troop, pre-ceded by an advance guard, made a brief overnight stop at Cannes. Wishing to avoid the Rhône area, which he knew to be hostile, Napoleon headed towards Grasse so as to reach the Durance Valley by way of the Alps. Beyond Grasse the little column had a difficult time proceeding along mule tracks. It halted at St-Vallier, Escragnolles and Séranon, from which, after a night's rest, it reached Castellane on 3 March; by the afternoon it had arrived in Barrême. The next day (4 March) the party lunched at Digne. Napoleon halted that evening at Château de Malijai, impatiently awaiting news from Sisteron, where the fort commanded the narrow passage of the Durance.

Sisteron was not guarded. Napoleon lunched there (5 March) and left the town in an atmosphere of growing support for his cause. Once more on a coach road he arrived that night at Gap, where he was given an enthusiastic welcome. Next day (6 March) he slept at Corps. On 7 March he reached La Mure, only to find troops from Grenoble facing him at Laffrey. This was the site of the famous episode – commemorated today by a monument to Napoleon – which turned events in his favour. That same evening he entered Grenoble to shouts of: "Long live the Emperor!".

Office de Tourisme, Vallauris-Golfe-Juan

Re-enactment of Napoleon landing at Golfe-Juan on his return from Elba

The route as far as Col de Valferrière is described below. The continuation north of the route is described in the Michelin Green Guide to the French Alps.

GOLFE-JUAN TO COL DE VALFERRIÈRE

57km/35mi – half a day

Golfe-Juan – *See GOLFE-JUAN.*

From Golfe-Juan take N 7.

The road winds round the west face of Super-Cannes hill, facing the Lérins Islands and the Esterel Massif. The view is best at sunset.

Cannes – *See CANNES.*

From Cannes take N 85 to the north, heading for Mougins.

The road rises above the town and the sea past the perched village of Mougins.

Mougins – *See MOUGINS.*

Mouans-Sartoux – This charming village is formed from the union of two *communes*: Sartoux, a medieval village destroyed by the Saracens, and Mouans, once a stronghold protecting the road to Grasse.
In 1588, Suzanne de Villeneuve, the widow of a Huguenot, was defending her village against the troops of the Duke of Savoy. Despite an agreement reached by the two parties, the Duke razed the castle, so Suzanne pursued him as far as Cagnes, where he was forced to pay a heavy fine to recompense the inhabitants. The château, which is situated in the middle of a pleasant park, has foundations dating back to the 16C despite its late-19C external appearance. It now houses a centre of contemporary art, the **Espace de l'Art Concret** ⊘, which displays an interesting collection of works, complemented by temporary exhibitions on particular themes.
On leaving Mouans-Sartoux, the road reveals Grasse spread out across the mountain slope ahead.

★★ Grasse – *See GRASSE.*

From Grasse take N 85, going northwest.

The road skirts "Napoleon's Plateau" where he halted on 2 March outside the town. The route through the Provence Plateau and then the Pre-Alps of Grasse, Provence's limestone mountains, crosses three passes in succession: **Col du Pilon** (782m/2 566ft), **Pas de la Faye** (981m/3 218ft) and **Col de Valferrière** (1 169m/3 805ft); the view south is magnificent.

Col du Pilon – From the southern slope there is a **view★★** of La Napoule Bay with the Lérins Islands, Grasse, the Lac de St-Cassien, the Esterel and the Maures.

St-Vallier-de-Thiey – *See ST-VALLIER-DE-THIEY.*

As the road climbs to Pas de la Faye there are some very fine **views★**, particularly from the double bend.

★★ Pas de la Faye – Similar **view★★** to that seen from Col du Pilon. Those travelling south over the pass suddenly discover the Mediterranean and the Riviera coastline spread out before them.

The road runs through arid country dominated by the Audibergue and Bleine mountains to the north and the Lachens Mountain to the east, with countless **views** to the south. 1km/0.5mi before Escragnolles, by a filling station, a road to the Belvédère de Baou Mourine branches off to the left.

★ Belvédère de Baou Mourine – *1km/0.6mi plus 30min on foot there and back. Path marked with red arrows.*

🅱 Terrace **viewpoint★** over the Siagne Valley, La Napoule Bay, the Esterel and Maures Massifs.

After Escragnolles, where Napoleon made a brief halt, there are fine views to the south.

For an alternative route to Cannes via Grasse described in reverse order see GRASSE: Driving tours.

The Ascent of the Alps by Napoleon

"He disembarked at Golfe-Juan, several hours before nightfall, and established a bivouac. As the moon rose, between one and two o'clock in the morning, the bivouac was struck and they went on to Grasse. There the Emperor expected to find the road spanning the Alps that he had commissioned under the Empire but sadly it had never been built. He was therefore compelled to negotiate difficult passes in deep snow, which meant leaving his coach and two cannons in Grasse with the town guard.

... The Emperor moved like lightning. He felt that victory depended on his strength of will and that France would rally to him if he reached Grenoble. There were 100 leagues to go and we made it in five days, from 2 to 7 March, but on such roads and in such weather..."

Las Cases *(Mémorial)*

NICE★★★

Population of conurbation 342 738
Michelin map 84 folds 9, 10 and 19, 115 fold 26 or 245 fold 38
Local maps see below and also Corniches de la RIVIERA

Capital of the Côte d'Azur and Queen of the Riviera, no title is too great for this magnificent winter and summer resort, which is also a famous tourist centre. Standing at the head of the Baie des Anges, Nice is sheltered by an amphitheatre of hills. Its popularity comes from the charm of its **setting★★**, its artistic treasures, the wonderful climate and countless attractions, including the nearby skiing slopes.

The Paillon torrent, partly covered by esplanades, above which are the theatre, the Palais Acropolis and the Palais des Expositions, cuts the city in two: to the west, the modern city; to the east, the old town and port, beneath the castle hill.

Nice Carnival on Place Masséna

Festivals in Nice – The **Nice Carnival★★★** is famous. The two Saturdays and Sundays that fall within the Carnival dates are marked by processions, confetti battles, fireworks and masked balls *(veglioni)* etc. The **floral processions**, or *batailles de fleurs*, offer a picturesque spectacle and attract huge and excited crowds, drawn by the colourful fruit and flowers. The summer season now prolongs the winter festivities with popular and fashionable festivals, horse-racing (which takes place on the racetrack at Cagnes), floral processions, open-air theatrical performances and aquatic sports drawing huge crowds of visitors. The **Jazz Festival**, which attracts famous musicians to the Cimiez arena, and the International Festival of Folk Traditions are held in July *(See Calendar of events)*.

King of the Carnival – The carnival tradition dates backs a long way in Nice; it was referred to as long ago as in 1294, on the occasion of the visit of the Count of Provence, Charles II. The Nice Carnival has always been a wholesome diversion from social tensions and the problems born of the conflicts which were constantly breaking out as a result of Nice's geographical location. Until the end of the 18C, the carnival took place after the Lenten fast in the form of local festivities in the old part of the city.

After a break of several years, caused by the wars of the Revolution and the Empire, the first parade of carnival floats took place in 1830 in honour of the royal visit of King Charles Félix to Nice and the return to Sardinian sovereignty. The form of the modern carnival dates back to 1873, to the impetus given by the painter Alexis Mossa and the formal systemisation of the various stages of the festivities and the setting of a different official theme every year. Carnival-going families from Nice belong to long lines of tradition – verging on outright dynasties! – and each "stable" of carnival floats has its own characteristics. On average, about 1tonne of papier-mâché is used in the making of each float.

Famous painters from this area have played their part in enriching the carnival decorations.

The modern festivities begin with the triumphal entry of "Sa Majesté Carnaval" about three weeks before Shrove Tuesday, or Mardi Gras. An effigy of the King of the Carnival is later ceremonially burned to mark the end of the carnival season. During the intervening period celebrations are in full swing, with parades of carnival floats on Saturdays and Sundays and during some evenings, accompanied by groups of people on foot, in fancy dress and sporting huge comical heads made of papier-mâché.

FROM NIKAIA TO NISSA LA BELLA

From the Greeks to the House of Savoy – Excavations at Terra Amata *(see SIGHTS below)* reveal evidence of a human settlement in Nice 400 000 years ago. It was a Ligurian stronghold in early history and a trading-post founded about the 4C BC by the Greeks of Marseille under the name Nikaia. The Romans concentrated their colonisation efforts on Cimiez (Cemenelum), whose splendour overshadowed the little market town on the east bank of the Paillon with a port at the eastern end of what is now Quai des États-Unis.

Barbarian and Saracen invasions, however, reduced Cimiez to nothing, and it was Nice that began to develop under the Counts of Provence in the 10C.

In the 14C, the history of Nice was marked by an important event: Louis of Anjou and his cousin, Charles of Durazzo, Prince of Naples, both advanced their claims on Provence on the death of **Queen Jeanne**, Queen of Sicily and Countess of Provence, who had adopted them. Beautiful and beloved by the people of Provence, this princess was smothered to death on the orders of Durazzo (1382). **Amadeus VII**, Count of Savoy, seizing an opportune moment when troubles divided the country, moved to Provence. In 1388, working secretly with the Count of Savoy, who had been assured of the treachery of Jean Grimaldi, governor of the town, Nice and its hinterland seceded from Provence and joined Savoy. Amadeus VII entered the city amid great rejoicing. Along the route of his procession houses were decorated with colourful tapestries, and flowers covered the ground; people danced and sang round bonfires; merchants set up stalls in the streets; and everyone drank to the new sovereign. As Amadeus passed on horseback, cherubs on strings were hoisted into the air waving palm leaves. Except for a few short interruptions, Nice belonged to the House of Savoy until its restoration to France in 1860.

Catherine Ségurane – In the 16C Nice began to feel the effects of the rivalry between the Houses of France and Austria: François I and his Turkish allies launched military operations against the County of Nice, which belonged to the House of Savoy, allied to Charles V. In 1543 French and Turkish troops, under the redoubtable leader Barbarossa, besieged Nice.

It was then that, according to local tradition, Catherine Ségurane, a woman of the people, earned her fame. As she was bringing food to a soldier on the ramparts, the order for the assault was given, and some Turks appeared at the top of the wall. Catherine flung herself forward, knife in hand, hurled several attackers into the moat below, seized a standard and put fresh courage into the men of Nice. The attack was contained. From the ramparts, as a gesture of contempt, Catherine turned her back on the Turks and lifted up her skirts. Other attacks met with greater success and the town fell after more than 20 days of siege; the defenders took refuge in the castle and their resistance was such as to force the besiegers to withdraw. A statue was erected to Catherine by her fellow citizens.

Bonaparte in Nice – The County of Nice, which under the Convention became the Département of Alpes-Maritimes, had been occupied by French troops in 1792 and was re-attached to France the following year. In 1794 Bonaparte, then General of Artillery in the army fighting against the Sardinians and the Austrians in the County of Nice, lived at no 6 in the street which now bears his name, and proposed to the daughter of his landlord. It was in this house that he was arrested after the fall of Robespierre. Bonaparte had been on good terms with the Convention member whose brother was the people's representative with the army in Toulon. His detention was short as he put forward a skilful defence.

Eating out

MODERATE

Le Pain Quotidien – *3 Rue St-François-de-Paul (Cours Saleya)* – ☎ *04 93 62 94 32* – *12.20/18.29€*. Wood is the key decorative element in this restaurant, where diners are asked to sit side by side around a long banquet table, an original formula conducive to a friendly, convivial atmosphere. At weekends, there is always a wide selection of salads, open sandwiches and brunches, not to mention the tantalizing aroma of freshly baked bread!

Nissa Socca – *7 Rue Ste-Réparate* – ☎ *04 93 80 18 35* – *Closed Jan, 10 days in Jun, Mon for lunch and Sun* – ☒ – *13.70/16.70€*. Pasta, pizza and Mediterranean dishes are served here in two cosy dining areas with a Provençal touch. Simplicity and low prices guaranteed. Old-fashioned bread oven at the entrance.

La Tapenade – *6 Rue Ste-Réparate* – ☎ *04 93 80 65 63* – *Closed Nov and Mon* – *15/20€*. Curious decor recreating a typical street from the south of France, with its shutters, terracotta flower pots and strings of garlic. Do not miss the surprising fresco painted on the ceiling. The warm, friendly owners will serve you a pizza, a *tapenade* or any other local speciality.

MID-RANGE

Grand Café de Turin – *5 Place Garibaldi* – ☎ *04 93 62 29 52* – *19.82/30.49€*. This brasserie, which is over 200 years old, has become an institution in Nice. It serves seafood dishes *à la carte* at reasonable prices throughout the day. Pleasant, welcoming setting.

L'Escalinada – *22 Rue Pairolière* – ☎ *04 93 62 11 71* – ☒ – *20/30.50€*. Nestling in the old quarter, this charming restaurant offers attractively presented regional cuisine in a spruce dining room with rustic overtones. Friendly service.

Gaité-Nallino – *72 Avenue Cap de Croix, to Cimiez* – ☎ *04 93 81 91 86* – *Closed Aug, Sun and evenings* – *21.34/38.11€*. A family business that has been feeding locals since 1872... The simple setting and congenial welcome attracts a great many regular customers. Located north of the Gallo-Roman ruins of Cimiez.

La Table d'Alziari – *4 Rue François-Zannin* – ☎ *04 93 80 34 03* – *Closed Feb, Sun and Mon* – ☒ – *30€*. Unpretentious family restaurant set up in a small alley of the old district. Typical dishes from Nice and the Provence area, chalked up on a slate, are served in a homey decor, together with wine recommended by the owner.

Capeline – *06830 Gilette* – *9km/5.5mi from Gilette by D 17 Route de Roquesteron* – ☎ *04 93 08 58 06* – *Closed Mon Mar-Oct, Tue, Wed and Thu Nov-Feb* – *Reservation required* – *19.51/32.01€*. Roadside inn whose charm owes much to the lady of the house, clad in a white apron, who officiates in the kitchen and lovingly prepares tasty delicacies exuding Provençal fragrances.

Where to stay

MODERATE

Star Hôtel – *14 Rue Biscarra* – ☎ *04 93 85 19 03* – *Closed Nov* – *19 rooms: 38.11/53.36€* – ☒ *4.57€*. Small hotel away from the bustling town centre offering simple accommodation. An opportunity to discover the other facets of Nice.

MID-RANGE

Gourmet Lorrain – *7 Avenue Santa Fior* – ☎ *04 93 84 90 78* – *Closed 1-8 Jan, 15 Jul-13 Aug* – *11 rooms: 45.73/53.36€* – ☒ *6.86€* – *Restaurant 23/38€*. This "city inn" situated in a quiet residential area offers medium-sized rooms, each with its own personal touch. The charming dining hall designed as a bijou flat serves succulent dishes, illustrative of French culinary tradition, and proposes an impressive wine list.

Villa St-Hubert – *26 Rue Michel-Ange* – ☎ *04 93 84 66 51* – *Closed 15 Nov-15 Dec* – *13 rooms: 47.26/60.22€* – ☒ *4.57€*. Turn-of-the-century villa near the university campus giving onto a quiet, secluded street. Smallish but fully equipped rooms. Flowery patio where breakfast can be had in summer.

St-Gothard – *20 Rue Paganini* – ☎ *04 93 88 13 41* – *64 rooms: 53.36/62.50€* – ☒ *5.03€*. Modern, soundproofed accommodation can be found at this hotel half-way between the station and the town centre.

LUXURY

Château des Ollières – *39 Avenue des Baumettes* – ☎ *04 92 15 77 99* – *www.chateaudesollieres.com* – 🅿 – *9 rooms: 145/335€* – ☒ *14€*. This princely manor surrounded by a small park behind the Museum of Fine Arts bears witness to the presence of Russian residents in Nice during the last century. Its devastating charm derives from the luxuriously appointed salons, the precious works of art and the large, comfortable suites exuding a hushed, cosy ambience.

On the town

Casino Ruhl – *1 Promenade des Anglais* – ☎ *04 97 03 12 22* – *casinoruhl@aol.com – Daily 10am to dawn*. The casino boasts 300 slot machines and has facilities for French and English roulette, blackjack, stud poker, etc. American bar. Dinner is coupled with live performances on Fridays. Themed evenings on Thursdays.

L'Ambassade – *18 Rue du Congrès* – ☎ *04 93 88 88 87* – *www. l'ambassade.net – Wed-Sat 11pm*. Trendy nightclub near the famous Promenade des Anglais. Wide choice of musical styles including techno.

La Trappa – *Rue de la Préfecture* – ☎ *04 93 80 33 69* – *Daily 5pm-2am*. A big room with deep, comfortable settees and red walls awaits you at La Trappa, a Hispanic bar where you can nibble *tapas* and sip a Cuban cocktail while you listen to Latin American music. Friendly atmosphere and local wine list.

Le Relais – *37 Promenade des Anglais* – ☎ *04 93 16 64 00* – *direction@hotel-negresco.com – Daily 11.30am-1am, until midnight in winter*. The sumptuous decoration of this bar belonging to the legendary Negresco Hotel has remained the same since 1913: Brussels tapestry (1683), 18C paintings, replicas of the wall lamps adorning the Ballroom in Fontainebleau Château and a rug similar to that chosen by Napoleon I for the King's Bedchamber in Rome. Piano bar every evening.

Les Trois Diables – *2 Cours Saleya* – ☎ *04 93 62 47 00* – *Daily 4pm-2.30am*. Cours Saleya is at the heart of Nice and its bustling activity. This broad square is taken over by the terraces of cafés, pubs and restaurants, and notably that of Les Trois Diables. This is undoubtedly the most popular and the most enterprising bar in town. It organises rock concerts and karaoke evenings, it sponsors sporting clubs and takes part in various events such as karting competitions (Les 24 Heures du Mans). Great atmosphere. Student clientele.

Tea time

Hôtel Palais Maeterlinck – *30 Boulevard Maurice-Maeterlinck* – ☎ *04 92 00 72 00* – *palais-maeterlinck.com – Daily 11am-midnight*. Bar attached to the luxury hotel Le Mélisande, whose terrace dominates the sea and offers splendid views of the Baie des Anges. The Belgian writer Maurice Maeterlinck, 1911 Nobel Prize for Literature, once lived on the premises.

Wayne's Pub – *15 Rue de la Préfecture* – ☎ *04 93 13 46 99* – *www.waynes.fr – Daily noon-1am*. Genuine Anglo-Saxon pub, in which the owner is British, the waiters are Australian, Canadian or American, the menu is drawn up in Shakespeare's language and the rock groups who perform every evening have just hopped across the Channel! Moreover, Wayne's Pub closes at half past twelve at night, just like in Britain. Tea time is from 4pm to 6pm, and cocktail time from 6pm to 7pm.

Practical information

Aéroport Nice-Côte d'Azur – Set up on the left bank of the Var estuary, this is France's second airport in terms of traffic. To meet increasing demand the airport has been extended by 200ha/500 acres towards the sea in order to accommodate a new air terminal.

Public transport – The Sunbus network covers the city of Nice and its suburbs. The "Nice by Bus" pass provides access to public transport for 1 to 5 or 1 to 7 days. Available from 10 Avenue Félix-Faure, ☎ 04 93 16 52 10.

Guided tours – Tours of the old quarter *(1hr 30min)* Tue and Sun at 3pm. 3.05€ . Apply to the Palais Lascaris, 15 Rue Droite. ☎ 04 93 62 72 40.

Shopping

Most shops in old Nice are closed on Mondays. In Nice as a whole many shops are also closed on Shrove Tuesday afternoon.

Alziari – *14 Rue St-François-de-Paule* – ☎ *04 93 85 76 92* – *Tue-Sat. 8.15am-0.15pm, 2.15-7pm*. One of the best addresses in town for olive oil. Regional produce.

Confiserie Auer – *7 Rue St-François-de-Paule* – ☎ *04 93 85 77 98* – *Tue-Sat. 8am-0.30pm, 2.30-6pm*. Crystallized fruit from the Nice region.

Confiserie Florian – *14 Quai Papacino* – ☎ *04 93 55 43 50*. Candied fruit, lemon, orange and grapefruit preserve, chocolates and sweets, crystallized petals and delicious jams made with rose, violet and jasmine blossom. Guided tours of the factory 9am-noon, 2-6.30pm.

Maison Poilpot - Aux Parfums de Grasse – *10 Rue St-Gaétan* – ☎ 04 [...] *60 77* – *Daily except Sun afternoons 9.30am-noon, 2.30-6pm.* This trad[...] perfumery produces more than 80 different fragrances, including p[...] Mediterranean scents such as mimosa, rose, violet and lemon.

Shopping streets – The streets surrounding the Cathédrale Ste-Réparate have many shops selling typical Provençal articles: cloth *(Rue Paradis* and *Rue du Marché)*, arts and crafts *(Rue du Pont-Vieux* and *Rue de la Boucherie)* and *santons (Rue St-François-de-Paul).*

Markets

Markets in Nice are held every day of the week except Tuesday.
Fish market – the most **picturesque** – Place St-François – 6am to 1pm.
Flower market – the most **typical** – Cours Saleya – 6am to 5.30pm. According to the season, good bargains can be made in the afternoon.
Fruit and vegetable market – the most **colourful** – Cours Saleya.
Liberation market– the most **extensive** – laid out along Avenue Malausséna and on Place Charles-de-Gaulle.
Flea market – Tuesday to Saturday – Place Robilante.
Antique market – Cours Saleya – every Monday.

Leisure activities

Skiing – The nearby skiing resorts of Auron and Valberg, which are only a two-hour drive away, are undoubtedly one of the main attractions of the Nice area.

Hiking – Le CAF (Club Alpin Français) organises one-day rambling tours across the Nice hinterland leaving from Nice. ☎ 04 93 62 59 99.

Beaches – The Baie des Anges covers a 5km/3.1mi stretch of coastline with many public beaches placed under close surveillance in addition to the 15 private beaches providing a host of sporting activities.

Société de Navigation Niçoise – *24 Quai Lunel* – ☎ 04 92 04 28 30. In summer, the boats belonging to the *Gallus* network organise cruises and trips along the Riviera coastline (Monaco, St-Tropez, the islands). Île Ste-Marguerite: 13,72€; Monaco: 22,87€; St-Tropez: 27,44 €; Corniche d'Or: 18,29 € (with a stopover on the île Ste-Marguerite).

Trans Côte d'Azur – *Quai Lunel* – ☎ 04 92 00 42 30. Feb-Oct guided trips along the coast (1hr) Tue, Wed, Fri and Sun at 3pm (also Thu during school holidays). 9,15€ (child 4,57€). JJun-Sep cruises (with commentary) to the îles de Lérins, St-Tropez, San Remo, Monaco or the Corniche d'Or. 16,77€ to 32,01 € (child 12,20€ to 18,29€).

Calendar of events

★★ **Nice Carnival** – This colourful, extravagant event invariably attracts large crowds every year. Festivities take place around Shrove Tuesday and last for a fortnight. They include processions, floats, firework displays, fancy dress balls and fights involving showers of flowers and confetti!

Cougourdons Festival – *Cougourdons* are marrows that have been dried and painted. The city of Nice pays homage to these curious vegetables in April.

Nice Jazz Festival – The former Roman amphitheatre is the prestigious backdrop for the jazz festival that is held in Nice every summer, attended by leading performers from all over the world. Summer tourists may also see the International Folk Festival and several flower fights *(batailles de fleurs).*

Old town, Nice

E. Baret

241

1796 he was in Nice again on his way to take over the post of commander-in-chief of the army in Italy. The house where he lived is in Rue St-François-de-Paule, in front of the opera. He had married Josephine only a few days earlier and it was from Nice that he wrote the well-known letter: "My darling, anguish at our parting runs through my veins as swiftly as the waters flow down the Rhône... my emotion thunders in my ears like a volcano... I would like to tear out my heart with my teeth..."

At the fall of the Empire in 1814, Nice and its hinterland was handed back to the House of Savoy under the Treaty of Paris.

Two local heroes: Masséna and Garibaldi – Maréchal Masséna (1758-1817), son of a wine merchant, went to sea until he was 17 and then entered French service in the Royal Italian Regiment. As he had to wait 14 years for the gold braid befitting a 2nd lieutenant, he left the army disappointed. During the Revolution he re-entered the service at Antibes where he was then living; by 1793 he was a divisional general. Napoleon made him a Maréchal de France, Duke of Rivoli and Prince of Essling. His military genius was coupled by a ruthless ambition which sometimes caused scandal. During his career he is said to have shouted successively: "Long live the Nation! Long live the Emperor! Long live the King!" After Napoleon, he was the general most esteemed by Wellington.

Giuseppe Garibaldi (1807-82), one of the principal authors of the Italian Revolution in 1860, had an extraordinarily turbulent political and military life in Europe and South America. A great friend of France, he served in the ranks of the French Army in 1870 with his two sons, and commanded a brigade in the Vosges. In the First World War other members of the Garibaldi family fought in the Argonne at the head of Italian volunteers.

Plebiscite – As a result of the 1858 alliance between France and Sardinia (House of Savoy), Napoleon III undertook to help the Sardinians drive the Austrians out of the provinces of northern Italy, for which he would receive Nice and Savoy in return. But the *Peace of Villafranca*, signed prematurely by the Emperor, left Venice to the Austrians, thus not fully meeting the objectives of the alliance. The cession of Nice and Savoy was particularly threatened since it met with hostility on the part of Britain. In 1860 the *Treaty of Turin* between Napoleon III and the King of Sardinia, Victor Emmanuel II, stipulated that Nice be returned to France "without any constraint on the will of the people". The plebiscite was an overwhelming victory for France: 25 743 in favour, 260 against. The entry of French troops and the ceremony of annexation took place on 14 June 1860. On 12 September the Emperor and the Empress Eugénie received the silver-gilt keys to the city from the mayor of Nice in what is today Place Garibaldi. These keys are displayed in the Masséna Museum.

The regions of Tende and La Brigue were to remain Italian territory for 87 years until the treaty of 10 February 1947 allowed France, once more, to extend its natural frontiers to the Alpine chain.

"L'École de Nice" – At the beginning of the 1960s Nice became one of the most lively artistic centres in Western Europe; futuristic exhibitions and other surprising events began to take place. Unlike the painters who, during the first half of the century, worked in total seclusion, the new wave combined life and art. At the instigation of **Yves Klein** who repositioned painting within a purifying process (vacuum, monochrome paintings symbolising the sky, fire etc) and **Arman** who elevated everyday accessories to the level of art, the "New Realists" gave a distinctive impulse to modern art in Nice. Other artists then joined the Nice School: Martial Raysse, Sosno, Verdet, Chacallis, Venet and Ben. Some of these artists' works are exhibited in the **Musée d'Art Moderne et d'Art Contemporain** in Nice, and modern works can also be seen in various public places around Nice.

The present – Since 1860 the development of Nice, which then counted 40 000 inhabitants, has been remarkable; it is now the second largest town of Mediterranean France after Marseille and the fifth largest in France itself. Industry plays a key role in the local economy.

Nice is an administrative centre as well as a university town, and its Centre Universitaire Méditerranéen, École Nationale des Arts Décoratifs, Conservatoire de Musique, Centre National d'Art Contemporain and major museums make for a thriving cultural activity.

With its Palais des Expositions (an exhibition centre with 20 000 places), its new Palais Acropolis (conference and arts centre) and its many top-ranking hotels, Nice remains the most popular holiday destination in France and derives most of its income from the tourist trade.

VISITING NICE

★★ The Seafront *2hr*

★★ **Promenade des Anglais** – This magnificent, wide promenade, facing due south and flanking the sea along its entire length, provides wonderful views of the Baie des Anges that extends from the Nice Cape to Fort Carré at Antibes. Until 1820 access to the shore was difficult but the English colony, numerous since the 18C, undertook the construction of a coastal path, which gave way to the present promenade and still carries its name. The legendary promenade has retained its mythical aura although it has since been taken over by motor vehicles. The white stone and glass façades of the north side, overlooking the sea, still attract many a visitor: Ruhl Casino and Hotel Méridien (1973), Palais de la Méditerranée – fine example of 1930s architecture – the **Hôtel Ne-**

gresco, a striking Baroque structure dating from the Belle Époque (c 1900) and the Musée Masséna. Visible on the façade of the Élysée Palace, overlooking Rue Honoré-Sauvan, is the monumental bronze *Venus* (1989) by the sculptor Sacha Sosno.

The young Russian princess Maria Bashkirtseff, nicknamed Moussia, who was noted for

Baie des Anges, Nice

her eccentricity, spent ten winters in Nice, where she carried on a correspondence with Maupassant. She was dubbed *La Madone des Sleepings* (the sleeping-car madonna) by certain writers. A stone slab commemorates her stay at 63 Promenade des Anglais.

Place Masséna and Espace Masséna – Started in 1815 in the Italian style, the buildings form an architectural unit in red ochre with arcades at street level. A fountain stands in the southern section: four bronze horses rising from a basin. The north side of the square opens into Avenue Jean-Médecin (once Avenue de la Victoire) which is the main shopping street, crowded with people and traffic. To the west extends what the 18C English called Newborough. Rue Masséna and Rue de France, its continuation, form the axis of a pedestrian precinct; here are smart shops, cinemas, cafés and restaurants between the tubs of flowers; it is a pleasant place to stroll at any hour of the day.

Avenue de Verdun skirts the **Jardin Albert I**, a welcome oasis of greenery surrounding a fountain, *The Three Graces*, sculpted by Volti. It is the starting point for tours by two small **tourist trains** ⊙.

The Port – For 2 000 years ships simply tied up in the lee of the castle rock. A deep water port was excavated in 1750 under Charles-Emmanuel III, Duke of Savoy, in the marshy ground at Lympia. In the 19C it was extended and made deeper. Place Île de Beauté, a square facing the port whose houses are embellished with porticoes and pretty façades, was laid out around the same period. Today Nice harbour is a busy maritime centre catering for a wide variety of needs: it is frequented by fishing boats, yachts, car-ferries heading for Corsica, luxury liners and merchant ships (exporting cement manufactured locally).

★ Old Nice *3hr*

After enjoying a whiff of the misty sea air, turn to the old quarter of town and set off for the Baroque district of Nice, hemmed in between the Colline du Château and Rue des Ponchettes.

Cours Saleya – Once the elegant promenade of old Nice, it is now lined with shops and restaurants. The famous **flower and vegetable market** is held here in this picturesque quarter; do not miss the mouthwatering sight of black and green olives, *mesclun* lettuce and fresh ingredients for a tasty *ratatouille*. Not to mention the bunches of carnations, the most widely grown flower in the Alpes-Maritimes, cultivated on the stepped terraces extending beyond Nice.

Note the superb façade of the **Chapelle de la Miséricorde** and the yellow front of the **Caïs de Pierla Palace**, where Picasso lived in a small room facing the sea between 1921 and 1938. Left of the chapel, Place Pierre-Gautier leads to the former **Palais du Gouverneur et des Princes de Savoie** (17C). East of Cours Saleya stands the handsome, albeit forbidding, façade of the **Église St-François-de-Paule** ⊙ with its colourful bell-tower.

Turn left into Rue Droite, right into Rue Vieille and left again into Rue de la Poissonnerie.

Chapelle de l'Annonciation – Originally dedicated to St Giaume (St James the Apostle), the chapel is known locally as the **Chapelle Ste-Rita**, an Italian saint still venerated in Nice as the armfuls of flowers and pyramids of candles at her altar *(left on entering)* and in the sacristy clearly show.

The interior is a lavish illustration of local Baroque **decoration**★: altars and rails inlaid with marble, sumptuous altarpieces (in the Lady Chapel, adorned with a 16C marble statue of the Virgin), painted and coffered vaults, fine panelling.

The entrance door is handsomely carved on the outside.

★ **Église St-Jacques or Gésu** – Built as a chapel in the 17C, this church is reminiscent of the Gesù Church in Rome.

Midday Cannon

Each day at noon a short cannon shot can be heard to remind people that it is lunchtime. This custom was introduced by a visiting Englishman, Sir Thomas Coventry, who grew tired of irregular meal times. He offered to buy and maintain a cannon for the town so that each day a shot could be fired at noon from the castle hill. The tradition has been maintained, although the cannon has now been replaced by an explosive device.

Twin fluted columns support a barrel vault opening into side chapels containing loggias for the noble families. The general effect is highly ornate: there are 164 painted and 48 carved cherubs. The ceiling is painted with scenes from the life of St James and there are several paintings presented by various brotherhoods; a 16C Pietà stands on the right.

The **sacristy**, formerly the chapter-house, contains 14 huge walnut cupboards (1696), some of which display the church treasure: pyxes, monstrances and reliquaries.

Cathédrale Ste-Réparate ⊘ – The cathedral was built in 1650 by the Nice architect, J-A Guiberto, and dedicated to the patron of Nice, who was martyred in Asia Minor at the age of 15.

Colours enhance the well-proportioned façade in which the Baroque style is very evident between the ground level and the first cornice in the elegant arcading of the doorway and the decorative niches and medallions. The bell-tower is 18C and the church is roofed by a magnificent dome of glazed tiles.

Socca

The day started early in those days in the Nice bar where my uncle and I enjoyed our *socca*. The ingredients include chick-pea flour, olive oil and salt beaten into a smooth mixture in a large copper pan. It is baked in a wood fire oven, a cooking time based on exact calculation or long experience and a speedy hand in cutting the cake into pieces when it is served. *Socca* will not wait; it must be eaten piping hot – seasoned with pepper.

The recipe has never changed. This is the same *socca* that used to be delivered all over the town. It was put in a box with a zinc lid and the trays in the delivery vans were kept warm with charcoal heaters. Nothing was more satisfying to labourers, office workers, women shopping or anyone else overcome by the desire for a little something in the morning. It is the same *socca* which the dockers, who had knocked back a laced coffee at 5 o'clock, used to consume in the bars of Nice at half past six. It was their breakfast.

Louis Nucera
Chemin de la Lanterne (1981)
Published by Éditions Grasset

The **interior**★ is a riot of Baroque plasterwork and marble. The high altar and choir balustrade are of marble adorned with heraldic bearings; the frieze and cornice are particularly graphic; 17C panelling in the sacristy.

Proceed along Rue Rossetti opposite and take the third left turning into Rue Droite.

Place St-François – A fish market is held here in the mornings round the fountain. To the right is the Classical façade of the former town hall now the Labour Exchange (Bourse du Travail).

Fixed to a house on the corner of Rue Droite and Rue de la Loge is a cannon ball which dates from the siege of Nice by the Turks, allies of François I (1543).

Continue along the lively Rue Pairolière, where several establishments serve *socca*, a local speciality that must be eaten while it is still hot.

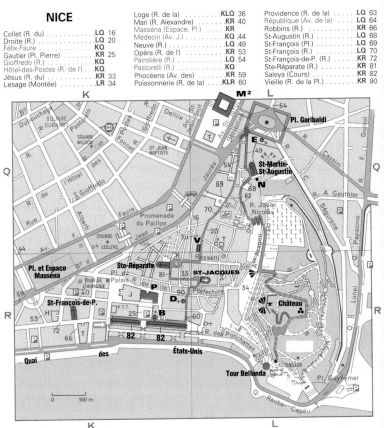

NICE

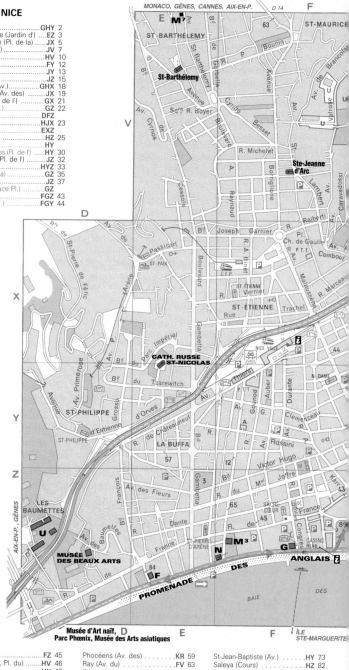

MONACO, GÊNES, CANNES, AIX-EN-P.

Place Garibaldi – The square was laid out at the end of the 18C in the Piedmont style, the buildings coloured yellow ochre. It marks the northern limit of the old town and the beginning of the new. A statue of Garibaldi stands proudly among the fountains and greenery. The **Chapelle de Saint-Sépulcre** on the south side of the square belongs to the Blue Penitents Brotherhood; it was built in the 18C and presents a blue Baroque interior.

From Place Garibaldi, take Rue Neuve until you reach the church of St-Martin-St-Augustin.

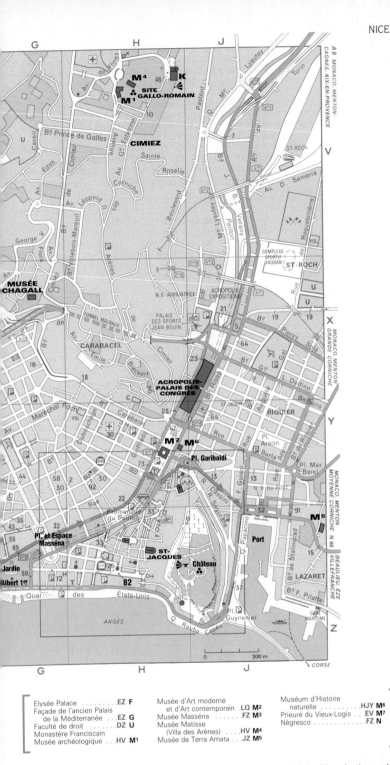

Église St-Martin-St-Augustin ⊘ – In this, the oldest parish in Nice, Luther, who was an Augustinian monk, celebrated Mass in 1510, and Garibaldi was baptised. The church has a fine Baroque **interior★** with a Pietà; the central panel of an altarpiece by Louis Bréa lies on the left in the choir.

Outside, opposite the entrance, stands a low relief sculpted in 1923, a **memorial** that pays tribute to the local heroine Catherine Ségurane *(see p 238).*

Follow the steps leading to the Château along Rue St-Augustin and Rue de la Providence.

Château – This is in fact the name given to the 92m/300ft high hill, arranged as a shaded walk, on which Nice's fortress once stood. Catinat blew up the powder magazine in 1691 and the fortress itself was destroyed in 1706 by the Duke of Berwick, Marshal of France (1670-1734), the illegitimate son of James II who served in the French army.

From the wide platform on the summit there is a sweeping **panorama★★** *(viewing table)*. Below the terrace is an artificial waterfall fed by water from the Vésubie. On the eastern side the **foundations of an 11C cathedral** (apse and apsidal chapels) have been uncovered. Below these ruins a Roman level and a Greek level have been excavated.

Walk round the ruins. From the northwest corner of castle hill *(follow the arrows to "Cimetière, Vieille Ville")* there is a path affording **bird's-eye views** of the roofs of old Nice and the Baie des Anges. Steps lead down from near a chapel on the left.

Continue towards the Tour Bellanda, which houses the Musée Naval on its lower level.

Tour Bellanda – Despite its appearance, this imposing circular bastion only dates from the 19C, when it was built as an identical replacement for one of the towers of the citadel which had been destroyed by Louis XIV's troops in 1706.

The composer Berlioz *(Roméo et Juliette, La Damnation de Faust)* lived here during the time he spent in Nice, which he wrote of with great enthusiasm: "Here I am in Nice, breathing the warm, balmy air... Here life and happiness come running swiftly to greet me, music folds me into her arms, and the future smiles on me... Here I am in Nice, strolling through orange groves..."

UNUSUAL ASPECTS OF NICE

★★ Musée des Beaux-Arts Jules-Chéret ⊘ – Since 1928 the Fine Arts Museum has been housed in a 1878 residence built in the Renaissance style of 17C Genoese palaces for the Russian princess Kotschoubey. The museum displays a rich collection of art of diverse inspiration, built up through donations and legacies around a nucleus of works sent to Nice by Napoleon III in 1860 for the creation of the very first Museum of Fine Arts.

Ground floor – On the side of the façade there are three galleries. In the first vaulted gallery, taken up by the Italian Primitives, note *Death of Cleopatra* by Francesco Cozza and *David Conqueror of Goliath* by Francesco Guarino. The second gallery displays 18C works such as *Portrait of an Old Man* by Fragonard, *Ollioules Gorges* by Hubert Robert and *Allegory of Human Life* by Donato Creti. The third gallery is given over to the important artistic dynasty, the **Van Loos**, whose most illustrious member, **Carle Van Loo**, was born in Nice in 1705. Works of his on display include *Theseus, Conqueror of the Bull at Marathon*. Jean-Baptiste Van Loo executed the famous portraits of Louis XV and Marie Leszczynska.

The great gallery branching off to the right of the entrance is decorated with large official paintings from the Third Republic, such as *Thamar* by Cabanel and some marvellous portraits of women. The patio which follows is home to *Bronze Age* by Rodin and *Triumph of Flora* by Carpeaux.

At the end of the gallery the small room on the right displays miniature 17C and 18C works.

First floor – The main staircase leads to the hall on the first floor which was used originally by musicians because of its acoustics. It is now adorned with the works of **Jules Chéret**, who died in Nice in 1932.

The first floor is mainly devoted to the art of the second half of the 19C and the start of the 20C. The first of four large galleries, all used for temporary exhibitions, concentrates on the academic tradition (Boulanger, Trachel...) and works by Orientalists such as *Rest during the Flight into Egypt* by Merson and the celebrated *Harem Servant* by Trouillebert. Among the sculptures on display is the original plaster cast of *The Kiss* by Rodin.

In the gallery, as well as a Carrière intimist, a fine series of works by the pre-Impressionist Félix Ziem evokes the romantic countryside.

The second gallery behind the façade displays paintings showing the evolution of the French countryside from the Classicism of Cordouan to Impressionism represented by Boudin *(Villefranche Anchorage)*, Monet, Sisley *(Avenue of Poplars near Moret)* and Bonnard *(Window Open on the Seine at Vernonnet)*. The third gallery is hung with pastels by Jules Chéret, the inventor of modern posters. The last room is reserved for collections by lesser-known 19C artists, grouped by subject: nudes, genre paintings, landscapes.

On the right, at the end of the gallery, two rooms display works linked to Maria Bashkirtseff, Bastien-Lepage, her spiritual mentor and to her rival Louise Breslau. The Van Dongen gallery houses the Fauvist artist's major works: *Pious Dream* and the celebrated *Dance of the Archangel*. In the display cases are ceramics by Picasso.

★★ Musée Matisse ⊘ – This museum is housed in the splendid patrician Villa des Arènes, a typical example of the development of urban architecture in Nice.

In 1670, on the site of a hut *(cabanoun)* buried in the ancient remains of Cimiez, a folly was built, with numerous symmetrical windows and façades decorated with coloured pebble-dash and *trompe-l'œil* paintings and extended by balustraded terraces. The site of the villa, facing the sea, and the characteristic Genoese architecture are explained by the thriving trade linking together the rich families of Nice and Liguria.

Its owner, the consul of Nice, named it "Palais de Gubernatis". In the 19C successive additions were made by the new owners to adapt it to a large town house. In 1950, when it was *in extremis*, the town of Nice saved it from being divided up and rechristened it Villa des Arènes. Since its redevelopment in 1993, it has housed the collections and administrative offices of the Musée Matisse on its two levels.

A large composition of cut-out gouaches, *Flowers and Fruit*, which is Henri Matisse's last work (1953), greets visitors at the entrance.

About 30 canvases illustrate the progression of the artist from the timid attempts of his early works in 1890, *Still Life: Books*, to his blossoming in 1946, *Rococo Armchair*. He went from a dark Realistic style to the discovery of the bright Mediterranean light, passing through the influence of Cézanne with *Still Life: A Harmonium* and Signac, *Young Woman with an Umbrella*, and culminating from 1916 onwards, *Portrait of Laurette*, with an explosion of pure and brilliant colour: *Odalisque with Red Case* 1926, *Window in Tahiti* 1935, *Nude in an Armchair* 1937, *Reader at the Yellow Table* 1944, *Still Life: Pomegranates* 1947 as well as the "pure blue" of *Blue Nude IV* (1952).

Drawings from his many different periods are also on display. Among the 235 works, which make up the museum's collection, the most significant one of the artist's work, are 30 sketches for the mural *The Dance* (1933). There are also many examples of book illustrations.

Matisse's activity as a sculptor is also well represented by 54 of the total of 62 **bronze sculptures** he produced during his lifetime. Note in particular *The Serf* (c 1900) and *The Serpentine* (1909). The development of more abstract form shows in the series of *Jeannette* (1910-13), *The Nudes, Henriette* (1925-29) and culminates in the monumental work *Nudes from Behind*. Two rooms contain sketches and models for the chapel in Vence (*See VENCE*), which Matisse worked on from 1948 to 1951. There are also the silkscreen prints: *The Sea, The Sky* (1947) and a huge **Beauvais tapestry**: *Polynesia*.

Dotted around the museum are his personal belongings, his furniture and his private art collection, all of which are often depicted in his paintings. The museum is also equipped with an auditorium and an information centre on Matisse.

** **Musée Marc-Chagall** ⊘ – The result of Chagall's donation to France, this museum built in 1972 by A Hermant houses the most important permanent collection of the painter's works. It is built partly in glass and hidden among the trees on a hilltop in Cimiez. The setting was designed especially bearing Chagall's "Biblical Message" in mind. The canvases are shown to their best advantage owing to the recessed walls and the large windows opening onto the bright Mediterranean light.

Welcoming the visitor into a world of lyrical, almost sacred fantasy is a multi-coloured tapestry (1971) showing Chagall's personal feeling for the Holy Scriptures brought from his past – born (1887) to a poor Jewish family in Vitebsk in Russia. He died in St-Paul in 1985.

This poetical lyricism is visible in all **17 canvases** which make up the "Biblical Message", an uninterrupted endeavour lasting 13 years (1954-67). In a large gallery are displayed 12 paintings evoking the Creation of Man, the Garden of Eden, the Story of Noah, Abraham, Jacob and Moses; among Chagall's world of rich translucent colours lies a magic spell of poetic enchantment which yet does not detract from the seriousness of the subject matter. In a nearby gallery are five paintings illustrating the Song of Songs: dreamlike figures drift among glowing colours above the rooftops of sleepy villages.

There are also several sculptures by the artist; from the

Musée Chagall, Nice - ©ADAGP, Paris 2001

Jacob and the Angel by Marc Chagall

library door look outside and admire the large **mosaic** (1970), which is reflected in the pool: it represents the Prophet Elijah, transported to Heaven in a chariot of fire, surrounded by the signs of the Zodiac.

The circular gallery (used for concerts and conferences) is immersed in a bluish light emanating from the three large windows depicting the Creation of the World.

The other rooms are used as a backdrop to temporary exhibitions or are devoted to the development of the "Biblical Message". Note the series of 39 gouaches painted by the artist in 1931 after his return from Palestine. Some of the themes were taken up again and appear in his larger canvases, 105 etchings and copper-plate engravings for the Bible edited by Tériade in 1956; 200 sketches (oils, pastels, gouaches, drawings) showing the artist's preliminary study and a series of lithographs.

★★ **Musée d'Art Moderne et d'Art Contemporain** ⊘ – Designed by Yves Bayard and Henri Vidal, the Museum of Modern and Contemporary Art is made up of four square towers with roof-top terraces, linked by glass passageways. On the parvis, between the museum and the theatre, stands a monumental stabile by Alexander Calder.

The collections, exhibited in rotation on the two upper floors (first floor is devoted to temporary exhibits), presents French and American avant-garde art movements from the 1960s to the present. Both these countries were developing parallel art movements based on similar experiences; in France these ideas were often nurtured by artists living on the Riviera. In the 1960s the American **Pop Art** movement and the French **Nouveau Réalisme** *(see Klein below)* attempted to express the reality of daily life in a modern society of consumerism and popular culture. Whereas Pop artists Andy Warhol, Roy Lichtenstein, Tom Wesselmann, James Rosenquist, George Segal, Robert Rauschenberg etc appropriated objects belonging to mass culture, the New Realists, more derisive, sought inspiration from those same objects as symbols of modern life, by collecting or breaking them (Arman), compressing them (César), capturing them under glass (Spoerri), or wrapping them (Christo)...

A section of the museum is devoted to the French painter **Yves Klein** (1928-62), whose monumental work, *Wall of Fire*, is located on the roof-top terrace. Putting aside his association with the French movement (he was the founder of Nouveau Réalisme, a term which means new realism and was coined in 1960 by the art critic Pierre Restany), Klein attempted by monochrome paintings, where gold and especially IKB (International Klein Blue) were used, to capture and express space, energy or the universal essence of things.

Musée d'Art moderne, Nice,©/ADAGP Paris,2001

Nissa Bella by Martial Rayssew

Fluxus, an off-shoot of the neo-Dadaist movement, closely linked to music (John Cage), and similar in ideology to the Happenings, was formed by a group of artists centred in Germany in the early 1960s. These artists were opposed to the rift between art and daily life. Their theory was illustrated by Beuys, prompted to question, while holding some lard, why something so essential to daily life could not be used in art? The Nice artists Ben, Serge III, Robert Filliou and Brecht explored this theory in more depth.

During this same decade abstraction in the United States was progressing in several directions: questioning the colour matter with artists Morris Louis and Larry Poons or reflecting on the medium itself with artists Frank Stella and Kenneth Noland. This influenced two movements in France, the **Support-Surface** (Viallat, Pagès, Dezeuze, Dolla, Alocco, Cane, Arnal...) and their Nice counterparts who were assembled under the Groupe 70 (Charvolen, Chacallis, Isnard, Maccaferri, Miguel); these two movements sought to reduce painting to its materialistic reality playing with the frame or medium and sought ways to apply colour to the surface. They followed Simon Hantaï's (b 1922 of Hungarian origin) experimenting with canvas, out of its stretcher, which is cut, suspended, folded... The American **Minimalists** (Sol Le Witt, Richard Serra) toned down the artist's intervention by going back to elementary forms, at times using repeated identical units and industrial materials; this idea was not foreign to the French BMPT; a group of artists (Buren, Mosset, Parmentier, Toroni) who in 1966-67 were experimenting with the idea that the work could be reduced to its bare essentials – medium, colour, texture.

The 1980s saw the return of figurative art, already announced by such artists as the Dutchman Karel Appel (b 1921; a member of **COBRA**, a European movement 1948-51). Different methods were used: traditional references for Gérard Garouste (mythological scenes) and Jean-Claude Blais, while rock culture and comics inspired the artists of Figuration Libre (Robert Combas, Hervé Di Rosa, Blanchard...), who sought simply to create without being preoccupied by realism. The museum also holds works by artists belonging to the Nice School, who were closely in tune with the movements flourishing in USA at that time but for the past 30 years have followed their own vision, such as Bernar Venet, Sacha Sosno, Gilli, Jean-Claude Fahri, Robert Malaval, Chubac...

★ CIMIEZ *3hr 30min*

Cimiez hill is the sophisticated part of Nice with many large houses. At the top of Boulevard de Cimiez is a statue of Queen Victoria, who used to stay in Cimiez.

Starting from Place Jean-Moulin, behind the Acropolis, drive west along Boulevard Carabacel and follow the route marked on the plan.

Arènes ⓥ – The ellipse-shaped amphitheatre, which is only 67m/220ft x 56m/184ft, could hold 4 000 spectators.

Traces remain of the gangways and of the sockets on the external façade, which held the posts supporting a huge adjustable awning *(velum)* used to shelter spectators from the sun and rain. The amphitheatre was designed for spear contests and gladiatorial bouts but not for animal fights. Traditional festivals take place here all year round *(Fêtes des Mai, Fêtes des Cougourdons)* and there are live performances during the summer season *(see Calendar of events)*.

Musée Archéologique ⓥ – Finds excavated at Cimiez (the ancient site of Cemenelum) and around Nice, as well as donations, make up the Archeological Museum's collections.

The ground floor is divided into two sections. The right side exhibits ceramics and bronzes from the great Mediterranean civilizations (Greece, Etruria, Roman Africa); some of the artefacts, such as the superb **mask of Silenus★**, were salvaged from shipwrecks.

The left side concentrates on the Ligurian and Roman civilizations from the region which became the Alpes-Maritimes in 14 BC: Bronze Age (statue of a warrior from Mont Bégo), Iron Age (items excavated from perched strongholds – *oppida*), milestones (1C) from the Via Julia Augusta.

Roman civilization is represented by examples of daily life (pottery, glassware, statues, jewellery...), and public life (inscriptions), a display of imperial coins in an interactive glass case, as well as models and maps of Cimiez, statues of the Imperial family (Antonia, Augustus's niece), and Roman cults.

The ground floor presents the funerary customs found at Cimiez: incineration in the 1C and 2C *(stelae)* and inhumation beginning in the 3C *(sarcophagi)*.

The tour ends with aspects of the paleo-Christian civilization (4C and 5C): pottery, coins, inscriptions etc.

★ Site Archéologique Gallo-Romain ⓥ – *Plan of site below.* **Cemenelum**, the seat of the Roman Procurator of the Alpes-Maritimes province, is estimated to have had a population of 20 000 by the end of 2C BC.

Roman Baths – Steps lead down into the *decumanus maximus* (the main east-west street of a Roman town) with its central drain and shops. On the left are the **North Baths**, probably reserved for the Procurator and other worthies. The summer bath consists of a marble basin surrounded by a peristyle embellished with Corinthian capitals.

On the eastern side are the latrines. The northern building contains the cold bath **(frigidarium)** – it was vaulted and its dimensions (10m/33ft high by 9m/30ft wide) give an idea of the huge scale of the northern baths – the warm room and the hot rooms, built above the **hypocaust** (underground stove), and the public rooms, partially excavated.

On the other side of the main street are the less elaborate but fully equipped **East Baths** for the general public, which can be viewed from a walkway.

To the south of these baths runs a parallel street lined with houses and shops; some of the paving stones have survived.

The western end of this street opens into the *cardo maximus* (main street running north-south) which returns to the Matisse Museum. On the left-hand side are the **West Baths** for women only. The fabric is quite well preserved, although it was used as a cathedral in the 5C; the choir, in the *frigidarium*, contains traces of an altar and a semicircular stone seat.

The neighbouring room to the north was used as the **baptistery**.

Place du Monastère – A twisted column of white marble, rising in the square in front of the church, bears a **calvary** dating from 1477. On one side is the crucified seraph who appeared before St Francis and imprinted the stigmata of the Passion on his body; on the other, St Clare and St Francis of Assisi stand on either side of the Virgin.

Nearby in the Cimiez **cemetery** are buried the painters Raoul Dufy and Henri Matisse who were leading exponents of Fauvism. The latter's tomb lies in an olive grove to the north of the surrounding wall.

★ **Monastère Franciscain** – The Franciscans, who in the 16C took over the buildings of a former Benedictine monastery founded in the 9C, have restored and considerably enlarged the abbey church.

Église Notre-Dame-de-l'Assomption – The church possesses three **masterpieces**★★ by the local artist Louis Bréa, illustrating the Nice School.

To the right of the entrance stands a **Pietà** (1475): although it is an early work, it is undoubtedly one of his most perfect creations. The arms of the cross and the stiff body of Christ emphasize the horizontal perspective; the gold background reveals glimpses of a landscape. Weeping cherubs cluster round the Cross while the lonely figure of Mary holds her son on her knees. One of the two side panels represents St Martin sharing his scarlet cloak; the slight inflection of the figures gives a rare elegance to the composition.

Quite different but of equal beauty is the **Crucifixion** by the same artist which is on the left in the choir. It is a later work (1512): the gold background has been replaced by an elaborate landscape showing perspective. The predella is masterly, the lances reinforcing Jesus' arrest, in contrast to the oblique treatment of Christ bearing the Cross.

In the second chapel to the left lies a recumbent figure of Christ in wood (18C).

The **Deposition** in the third chapel, which is also attributed to Louis Bréa, complements the Cruxifixion and adheres to Renaissance principles: the figures obliquely aligned on the body of Christ are counterbalanced by the vertical lines of the landscape.

A huge half Renaissance-half Baroque altarpiece carved in wood and decorated with gold leaf screens off the monks' choir.

Musée Franciscain ⊘ – The **museum** recalls the work of the Franciscans in Nice from the 13C to the present day. The social and spiritual message of the Franciscans is proclaimed through documents and works of art (frescoes, engravings, sculptures) in a restored section of the old monastery. There are also a fine illuminated antiphonary (17C), the novices' chapel and a restored 17C cell.

Monastery Gardens – On the south side of the monastery there are attractive terraced gardens with flower beds and lemon trees which look down on the Paillon Valley from a **viewpoint** over Nice, the castle and the sea, Mont Boron and the observatory to the east. A copse of cypress and holm oak marks the site of the former Ligurian oppidum.

Russian Heritage

Around the middle of the 19C, after Empress Alexandra Fedorovna, the widow of Tsar Nicolas I, had settled in Nice, many wealthy Russian aristocrats chose this city as their favourite place of residence. These "excentrics", as the locals would call them, applied themselves to recreating the atmosphere of their native country on the Riviera, hiring the services of architects who combined the Slav spirit with Mediterranean influences. Baron Von Dewies, who designed the Russian railway system, commissioned the building of the Gothic **Château de Valrose** (Science Faculty of Nice University) and set up an isba from Kiev on his huge estate. At the west entrance to Nice, not far from the railway, the **Château des Ollières** (currently a hotel) features an impressive keep flanked by four turrets. The nearby **Palais Kotschoubey** houses the Musée Chéret. Two other notable examples of Russian architecture are the **Palais Impérial** and the **Résidence Palladium** on Boulevard Tsarévitch, which was originally built for a Russian banker.

★ **Cathédrale Orthodoxe Russe St-Nicolas** ⊘ – With its six gilded onion domes and its façade of ochre brick, the **Russian Orthodox cathedral** lends an exotic touch to the Nice skyline and symbolises the importance of the Russian colony on the Riviera. It is the largest Russian religious building outside Russia itself. The frequent visits to Nice of the Russian nobility, who were regularly joined by the Imperial Court, gave rise to the erection of an immense Orthodox place of worship. The Villa Bermond was donated by the dowager Empress in 1900 for the construction of the new cathedral. The Russian architect Préobrajensky drew the plans and oversaw the work. The choice of materials was enhanced by the generosity of Czar Nicolas II: the bricks came from England, the glazed tiles on the domes and the six crosses surmounting them from Italy, the domes are coated with fine gold leaf and the mosaic icons on the façades were handmade by Russian artists. The inauguration took place in December 1912 in the presence of the Imperial Russian family. Other icons and devotional articles found a home in the cathedral after 1917.

The interior, in the form of a Greek cross, is richly decorated with frescoes, panelling and icons. At the entrance to the choir is a sumptuous **iconostasis**★ bringing together the finest examples of Russian religious art, taken from the church of Jaroslav and the church of St Basil the Blessed in Moscow. On the right of the choir is an icon of **Our Lady of Kazan**, painted on wood and decorated with chased silver and precious stones. At the end of the park on the left a **Byzantine chapel** is dedicated to Tsarevich Nicolas, the son of Czar Alexander II, who died of an illness here in 1866. His funeral was an imposing ceremony held locally at the Russian Church in Rue Longchamp.

SIGHTS

★★ Musée des Arts Asiatiques ⊙ – *From Promenade des Anglais, head towards Nice-Côte-d'Azur airport and turn right into the side road signposted "Parc Phœnix" that leads into the new Arenas complex. There is an underground car park (fee).*

Delicately poised on the lake in Phœnix Park, this dazzling construction in white marble presents sacred and traditional objects coming from several Asian countries. The building was designed by the Japanese architect **Kenzo Tange** in 1998: it is a faithful representation of the Far-East principles of cosmogony that associate the circle (sky) with the square (earth) and its four cardinal points. You can also discover these fascinating civilisations on your own with the help of earphones.

On the first floor visitors are enlightened on the history of Buddhism thanks to an informative but also highly attractive exhibition featuring a series of stone Buddhas conducive to meditation, illustrating 4C Gandhara and 12C Khmer art.

On the ground floor, each gallery is devoted to a specific civilisation: China, Japan, Cambodia and India. Set against a sparsely decorated background that invites inner comtemplation, the various sculptures, ceramics and paintings are all of considerable beauty and they reflect the religious spirit of their country.

The basement has a more contemporary touch and is devoted to temporary art shows. Interactive terminals linked to the Asian continent present a wide selection of museums devoted to Oriental art throughout the world.

Treat yourself to a Japanese **tea ceremony** in the blissfully minimalist tea room set up next to the bookshop.

★ Parc Phœnix ⊙ – This vast botanical garden (over 7ha/17 acres) inaugurated in 1991 is organised by theme and contains over 2 000 plant species from all over the world, grouped together with their corresponding animal life. Visitors can wander in this popular park around five large zones, each reflecting a particular period or climate.

The "Île des Temps Révolus" (Island of Bygone Times), in the middle of a big lake, takes visitors back into the past with a display of living plant fossils: cycads, ginkgo biloba, tree ferns etc. The crater of scents and colours next to it displays a selection of colours that blend in with the perfumes of each plant.

Throughout the park, discreetly positioned loudspeakers give out the calls and songs of the animals and birds that inhabit the particular zone of plant life the visitor is in.

In the second zone, an aviary houses a colourful collection of parrots and other tropical birds. The wadi-oasis reconstitutes part of an oasis in the Sahara.

The **giant greenhouse★**, known as the "Green Diamond", is a huge tropical hothouse covering 7 000m²/75 300sq ft beneath a 25m/82ft high roof in which seven climates of varying temperatures and hygrometry are housed: an orchid garden; a greenhouse containing plants from the southern hemisphere; an underground vivarium-insectarium; a lovely garden of ferns from various places; and in the centre, a large tropical garden containing palm trees and Madagscan traveller's trees as well as trees cultivated for food (banana, breadfruit, coffee, papaya etc). Carry on from the giant greenhouse to see the carnivorous plants and the butterfly house.

Nearby, the information centre or **infothèque** provides visitors with telematic data bases to consult for general and detailed information on tropical plants.

Outside, to the right, a garden of tropical plants and a beautiful rose garden flourish side by side.

The "Great Aztec Pyramid" is an original way of displaying what goes on beneath our feetl, regarding both plants and animals that live underground.

A large circular fountain and various musical fountains add the finishing touches to the visitor's voyage of discovery.

Faculté de Droit ⊙ – On the first floor landing of the **Law Faculty** a large-scale **mosaic★** by Chagall covers the whole of one wall: *Ulysses returning to Penelope in Ithaca.*

★ Musée d'Art Naïf Jakovsky ⊙ – *Avenue du Val-Marie. Leave the town centre by Promenade des Anglais.* The Anatole Jakovsky Bequest comprises 600 canvases *(about half are on show)* illustrating the amateur talents of many countries.

The Croatian artists *(mostly on the 1st floor)* include Generalic, Rabuzin, Kovacic and Petrovic. Among the French are Bauchant, Vivin, Vieillard, Restivo and Crociani *(Night Festival in Nice)* and more dreamlike paintings by Vercruyce and Lefranc *(Clock).* There are also works by Italians, Swiss, Belgians and Americans, from both the north and the south (particularly Brazil).

One section has been set aside for a series of unusual portraits of Jakovsky.

★ Musée Masséna ⊙ – This museum surrounded by gardens was built in 1898. It was modelled on Italian residences of the First Empire and was made after plans by Georg Tersling and the Niçois A Messian for Victor Masséna, great-grandson of the Marshal. In 1919 his son André gave it to the town.

★ Acropolis-Palais des Congrès ⊙ – The building (55 000m²/592 000 sq ft), which runs from Avenue Gallieni to Boulevard Risso over 338m/369yd, resembles a majestic vessel anchored to the five robust vaults spanning the River Paillon. It was designed by a group of local architects and the names of its various parts were taken from Greek antiquity.

It comprises five floors articulated by the agora, a vast reception hall lit by immense windows and crowned by a retracting metal roof; the vast auditorium (2 500 seats), which is located on the south side and called Apollo, has exceptionally good acoustics;

the north side comprises the conference centre and Athena auditorium (750 seats), the Mediterranean Room, lecture and meeting rooms, radio and television studios etc. Contemporary works of art perfectly suited to the architecture are displayed both inside and outside the building, along both sides and on the Esplanade Kennedy in front. These sculptures, paintings and tapestries are signed by Volti *(Nikaia)*, Vasarely, Arman *(Music Power)*, César *(Thumb)*, Paul Belmondo, Moretti *(Louis Armstrong)*, Cyril de la Patellière *(Mediterranean Tribute)* etc.

Palais Lascaris ⊘ – The palace built in the Genoese style, influenced by local tradition, from 1648 by J-B Lascaris, a descendant of the counts of Ventimiglia whose family was related to the Lascaris, emperors of Nicaea in Asia Minor in the 13C. The façade is decorated with balustraded balconies resting on consoles of carved marble and columns with flowered capitals; scrollwork ornaments the doorway.

On the ground floor a pharmacy from Besançon (1738) has been reconstructed to display a fine collection of flasks and tripods.

A grandiose balustraded **staircase**★, decorated with 17C paintings hanging in rockwork niches and 18C statues of Mars and Venus, leads to the second floor. The salon is hung with Flemish tapestries; the *trompe-l'œil* ceiling is the work of Italian artists from Genoa: the *Fall of Phaeton*, similar to one in Cagnes. In the next room hang two Flemish tapestries based on sketches by Rubens. The state bedchamber is separated from the antichamber by a stucco screen supported by atlantes and caryatids.

On the other side of the staircase are the private apartments displaying 18C ceilings, painted medallions framed in stuccowork and Louis XV woodwork inlaid with silver beneath landscaped piers.

Ground floor – The group of **salons** in Empire style, directly inspired by the Piedmontese château at Govone, has bay windows looking out on to the promenade des Anglais. The gallery contains statues and paintings (a marble bust of Marshal Masséna by Canova, a full-length portrait of Empress Joséphine by Baron Gros, a full-length marble statue of Napoleon as Roman Emperor by Chaudet) and Thomire vases. On the staircase, two remounted canvases by François Flameng are dedicated to the Masséna family.

First floor – Exhibited in the right wing is a collection of Nice primitives *(see Introduction)*: a reredos of St John the Baptist by Jacques Durandi is remarkable for the intense expression of John the Baptist and the meticulous painted detail on the predella, and the predella of an altarpiece of St Marguerite by Louis Bréa. All these pictures come from the church at Lucéram *(see Lucéram)*. In the centre of the room is a magnificent reliquary, in silver plate and enamel, known as "Baiser de Paix", from the Italian Renaissance. There is also a Virgin in multi-coloured stone, a 14C Burgundian piece and a 13C reliquary of St Commode from Limoges. Primitive Italian, Flemish and Spanish works hang on the walls, as well as a fine 16C French Crucifixion.

There are two rooms devoted to liturgical ornaments (15C-17C) and to church silver plate as well as Germanic sculpture (16C).

Among a fine collection of arms and armour (14C-18C) are a head guard belonging to Charles V, a bourguignotte (helmet) belonging to Philip II of Spain and a knight protected by German armour said to be "Maximilienne Cannelée" (16C).

Second floor – Jewels from all over the world are displayed here as well as watercolours by Niçois painters (Trachel, Costa, A Mossa). The exhibition of weights and measures contains a curious clock with 15 faces. The era of great Niçois (Masséna and Garibaldi) is evoked by documents from the period and sculptures and paintings (by Garacci and Detaille). The Revolution and the Empire are represented by a precious sketch of Bonaparte by David, coronation robes of Joséphine and Napoleon's first death mask. The history of Nice is illustrated by watercolours, a fine model of the town in 1890 and models of three superb ships as well as an interesting collection of aristocratic and bourgeois costumes (19C).

★ **Chapelle de la Miséricorde** ⊘ – The chapel, which belongs to the Black Penitents, is a masterpiece of Nice Baroque (1740) and was designed by the 17C Italian architect **Guarino Guarini**. A bowed façade, garlands and oval windows accentuate the rounded motif of the exterior design.

The architect's virtuosity is clearly demonstrated in the chapel's interior: the complex interlacing of vaulting in the bays and the sumptuous combination of gold and imitation marble enhanced by winged cherubs.

In the sacristy there are two early Nice **altarpieces**★ of Our Lady of Pity. Jean Mirailhet's work is in the Gothic tradition but the panel painted some 80 years later by Louis Bréa betrays the influence of the Italian Renaissance and shows the Virgin against a Nice landscape.

To the north is the elegant 18C façade of the old **Palais du Gouvernement**, decorated with alternate Corinthian and Doric columns and crowned by a balustrade.

The clock tower on the left is 18C.

Musée Naval ⊘ – The Naval Museum is at the top of the Tour Bellanda. At the entrance are two 17C Portuguese bronze cannons. Inside are models of ships, arms and navigational instruments. The walls are decorated with views of old Nice and there is a model of the port at different periods in its history. A section is devoted to competitive sailing and pleasure boating.

Muséum d'Histoire Naturelle ⊘ – The Natural History Museum, which is linked to a laboratory, houses a curious collection of 7 000 casts of fungi, alongside an exhibition of minerals. There is also a stratigraphy section that explains the formation of the earth's crust: fossils, geological phenomena.

Prieuré du Vieux-Logis ⊘ – The museum consists of a priory converted into a 16C farm and richly supplied with works of art, 14C to 17C furniture and items from everyday life (note the outstanding kitchen). There are numerous statues including a 15C Pietà from Franche-Comté.

Église Ste-Jeanne-d'Arc – This is a modern concrete church designed by Jacques Droz with three segmented cupolas and an ellipsoidal porch as its main doorway. The belfry wreathed in flames rises to a height of 65m/215ft.
Inside, the soaring vaulting is striking. The Stations of the Cross are frescoes by Klementief (1934).

Musée de Terra Amata ⊘ – A model of a sand dune on a fossil beach, which has been uncovered 26m/85ft above the present sea-level on the western slopes of Mont Boron, is reproduced on the ground floor of the museum, built on the site of the excavation. An open hearth and a human footprint with a calcified surface were found in the hardened limestone.
Bones, stone tools and traces of fire mark one of the earliest human settlements known in Europe. Articles, drawings, maps and a full-scale reconstruction of a shelter made of branches illustrate the life of the Acheulean hunters some 400 000 years ago (early Paleolithic).

DRIVING TOURS

★★ **① Les Deux Monts**

Round trip of 11km/6mi – about 45min – local map see overleaf. Leave Nice from Place Max-Barel on N 7, Moyenne Corniche, going east. After 2.5km/1.5mi turn sharp right onto a forest road. 1km/0.5mi further on turn sharp left onto a signposted path leading to the fort on Mont Alban.

★★ **Mont Alban** – Alt 222m/728ft. A footpath circles the height from which there is a splendid **view**★★ of the coastline: to the east lie Cap Ferrat, Cap d'Ail, the Bordighera Point and the limestone heights of Tête de Chien; to the west lie the Baie des Anges and the Garoupe Plateau. The fort, a massive 16C construction with bastions and watchtowers, can be explored on foot *(exterior only)*.
Return to the fork and proceed straight ahead to Mont Boron.

★ **Mont Boron** – Alt 178m/584ft. From the mountains there are **views**★ extending over the Villefranche anchorage and along the coast to Cap d'Antibes. On the horizon can be seen the mountains around Grasse and, further to the left, the Esterel range.
Return to Nice along the Corniche Inférieure (N 98).

Studios de la Victorine – the Story of Film-Making in Nice

With the dawning of cinema, Nice provided film-makers with the ideal ingredients for their future success: almost permanent light and sunshine, the sea and the presence of magnificent hotels as natural backdrops.
Louis Feuillade, who made *Fantômas*, was one of the first to spot the potential of the area; the roofs of the Hôtel Négresco passed into cinematic posterity in the Fantômas-Judex chase.
The "azure cinema" really took off in 1920, however, when a large unoccupied estate west of the town centre, La Victorine, was acquired by the fabulously rich Hollywood producer Rex Ingram, who had launched Rudolf Valentino and Roman Navarro. He produced the epic *Mare Nostrum*, to promote his new studios.
From that time, La Victorine studios saw both French and European film-makers prosper for the following 10 years. Then changes in public tastes brought another decade of inactivity.
The Armistice of 1940 caused French cinema to seek refuge in Nice (Abel Gance, Prévert, Carné).
The filming of *Les Visiteurs du Soir* in 1943 revived the production of large-scale films.
In 1944 came *Les Enfants du Paradis*, co-produced by Marcel Carné and Jacques Prévert with Arletty and Jean-Louis Barrault, which was the greatest production at La Victorine.
The reconstruction of "Boulevard du Crime" in the middle of the war required more than 30t of scaffolding and nearly 3 500m^2 of fencing for the sets, as well as 2 000 extras who were recruited in Nice.
The worsening of the general situation and lack of money temporarily brought a halt to this creativity.
The 15 post-war years were good ones; they were followed by a lull.
Nowadays, after several abortive projects, a revival of filming seems to be under way.

★★ 2 Plateau St-Michel

Round tour of 19km/12mi – about 1hr – local map see overleaf. Leave Nice going east along Avenue des Diables-Bleus and the Grande Corniche (D 2564).

Look back to enjoy views of Nice and the Baie des Anges and beyond Cap d'Antibes and the Paillon Basin. Ahead lie the fort of La Drète in the foreground and Mont Agel further back.

Observatoire du Mont-Gros ⊘ – *The private road to the Nice observatory leads off to the right of the Grande Corniche.*
This famous international centre for astronomical research was founded in 1881 by the scientific patron Bischoffheim. Charles Garnier oversaw the construction of the buildings, while Gustave Eiffel built the metal frame supporting the great dome (26m/85ft in diameter). This houses an astronomical telescope called the "great equatorial". It is 18m/59ft long with an optical diameter of 76cm/30in and was for a long time the largest instrument of its kind in the world. Note the neo-Classical pediment at the entrance to the dome, typical of its period.
Beyond the Quatre-Chemins Pass, Cap Ferrat Peninsula and Villefranche-sur-Mer anchorage come into view.
Bear right onto D 34 and after 500m/547yd leave the car in the car park.

★★ **Plateau St-Michel Viewpoint** – A viewing table points out all the main features of the coast from Cap d'Ail to the Esterel.
Continue along D 34 and then bear left onto the Moyenne Corniche (N 7). After a long tunnel there is a marvellous **view**★ of Beaulieu, Cap Ferrat, Villefranche-sur-Mer, Nice and Cap d'Antibes. The road winds round above Villefranche anchorage. After Col de Villefranche, Nice with its castle hill, the harbour and the Baie des Anges comes into sight; on the horizon the outline of the Esterel and the limestone hills of Grasse.
Return to Nice via Place Max-Barel.

★ 3 Tour of Mont Chauve

Round tour of 53km/33mi – about 2hr 30min – see local map overleaf. From Nice take Avenue du Ray north; turn sharp right on Avenue de Gairaut, D 14, towards Aspremont and after passing under the motorway (2km/1.2mi) bear right following D 14 and then turn left following the signs.

Cascade de Gairaut – In two great steps the waters of the Vésubie Canal, which supplies the Nice area, tumble down into a basin. From the chapel terrace there is a beautiful **view** of the town.
Return to D 14.

Soon afterwards there are fine views to the left of Nice, Mont Boron and Cap d'Antibes. As the road climbs towards Aspremont, the **view** extends to include the Baous, the Var Valley and the mountains.

Aspremont – The village, built to a concentric plan, perches prettily on its hilltop site. The **church** ⊘ has a Gothic nave decorated with frescoes and supported on solid cubic capitals; on the left there is a painted wooden Virgin and Child.
Above and behind the church once stood the castle, now destroyed. From the terrace that overlooks the town is a **panorama**★ comprising several hill villages, Vence, Cap d'Antibes, the hills beyond Nice, Mont Chauve and Mont Cima.
On leaving the village, take D 719 over a little pass, Col d'Aspremont, between Mont Chauve and Mont Cima to the rich basin of Tourrette-Levens.

Tourrette-Levens – The village clings to a knife-edged rock. The 18C **church** ⊘ presents a fine carved wooden altarpiece, also 18C, of the Virgin between St Sylvester and St Antony (behind the high altar). A short walk through the village to the **château** ⊘ (partially restored) reveals **views** of the neighbouring mountains – Chauve and Ferion – and the Gabre and Rio Sec Valleys. Your efforts will be rewarded by a charming **natural history exhibition** on tropical butterflies, including a diorama on creatures from all over the world.
Return to D 19 turning left down into the Gabre Valley.

Gorges du Gabre – The gorges have been hollowed out of limestone walls.
Bear right onto D 114 towards Falicon.

Falicon – Typical Nice village huddled on a rocky outcrop among the olive groves. The Bellevue inn *(panoramic view from the terrace)* displays mementoes belonging to the French author **Jules Romains** (1885-1972) who set one of his novels in Falicon.
Other illustrious guests were attracted to the village on account of its delightful surroundings. Queen Victoria came from Cimiez and drank tea here; the restaurant has commemorated this visit with a sign: *Au Thé de la Reine.*
The **church** ⊘, which was founded by the Benedictines of St-Pons, has a square belfry and a façade in *trompe-l'œil*. In the nave is a beautiful 17C Nativity framed in gold. Climb up the stairway to the left of the church and turn right onto a path leading to a terrace for a **view**★ of Nice, the sea, the hills and Mont Agel.
Return to D 114; turn left.

At the chapel of St-Sébastien turn right onto D 214, a narrow and dangerous road, to Mont Chauve.

Leave the car at the end of the road.

Mont Chauve d'Aspremont – *30min on foot there and back.*
🔺 Alt 854m/2 802ft. "Chauve" means bald, and the mountain lives up to its name. A disued fort stands on the naked summit offering a magnificent **panorama★★**: the snow-clad Alps and the Nice hills and the coast from Menton to Cap Ferrat. On a very fine day Corsica is visible.

Return to D 114 turning left; 2km/1.2mi further on turn sharp right onto D 19. Go under the motorway; 1km/0.5mi later there is a right-hand turning up to St-Pons.

★ **Église St-Pons** – The Benedictine abbey of St Pontius was founded during Charlemagne's reign and played an important part in local affairs for 1 000 years. The church ⊙, which was rebuilt early in the 18C, stands on a headland above the Paillon Valley, its graceful silhouette and Genoese campanile visible from all sides. The elegant curves and counter-curves of the tall Baroque façade are echoed in the peristyle. The interior forms an ellipse, preceded by a vestibule, prolonged by a semi-circular choir, ringed by side chapels opening out between powerful columns. Rich plasterwork decoration.

★④ The Two Paillons

Round tour of 90km/56mi – allow one day – see local map overleaf.

The Paillon de l'Escarène, the main river, rises to the northeast of Col St-Roch, whereas the Paillon de Contes springs from the upper slopes of Rocca Seira to the northwest of the pass; they meet at Pont de Peille and flow into the sea at Nice. The suggested route goes up one valley and down the other with detours to La Turbie and Peille.

Leave Nice by Boulevard J.-B.-Verany and Route de Turin, D 2204 going north. In La Trinité bear right to Laghet.

The road goes up the verdant Laghet Valley. The Roman road from La Turbie to Cimiez was on the opposite bank.

Sanctuaire Notre-Dame de Laghet – The sanctuary, founded in 1656, is a pilgrimage centre; its influence is felt on both sides of the border with Italy. Innumerable votive offerings, touching and amusing in their naivety, cover the church and cloisters. The best of them are displayed in the little **museum** ⊙ on Place du Sanctuaire. The interior decor is heavy Baroque. The statue of Our Lady of Laghet on the high altar is carved in wood.

The road winds steeply up through olive groves to the Grande Corniche; turn left.

★ **La Turbie** – *See La TURBIE.*

Leave La Turbie on D 53 with its views of the sea and the Paillon Basin. On the left of the road is the Chapelle St-Martin.

Église St-Martin-de-Peille ⊙ – *Currently closed for restoration.* The church stands in a secluded but beautiful setting of olive-clad mountains. It is a modern structure of very simple design, with plastic windows; the base of the altar is made from the trunk of a giant olive tree. Wide bays on either side of the altar look out onto the mountains.
The road winds round the lower slopes of Mont Agel before descending to Peille. Near the last tunnel there is a fine **view** of Peille village.

★ **Peille** – *See PEILLE.*

Join Paillon Valley at La Grave. After 2.5km/1.5mi turn left onto D 121 which climbs to the eagle's nest of Peillon.

★★ **Peillon** – *See PEILLON.*

Return to D 21 and turn right.

The village of Peille comes into view on the slopes of Mont Castellet *(right)*.

★ **Gorges du Paillon** – Beautiful green wooded ravine.

L'Escarène – Built at the junction of the road to the resort of Peïra-Cava and the beginning of the hairpin bends leading up to Col de Braus, this large town stretches along the bottom of the Paillon Valley. It was an important staging post on the old road from Nice to Turin, called the Salt Road *(Route du Sel – see SOSPEL)*. The old bridge with its single arch and Place de la Gabelle remain from that period. From the Armée des Alpes bridge crossing the Paillon, there is a good view of the old village.

★ **Église St-Pierre** – This 17C church, flanked by two chapels of the Black and White Penitents, is the work of the Niçois architect Guibert, who designed Nice Cathedral. It has a very ornate Baroque façade, and the sizeable interior dates from the same period. The font on the right is hollowed out of an ancient Gallo-Roman altar topped by a gilded 17C statuette. The organ (1791) is by the Grinda brothers.

ARRIÈRE-PAYS NIÇOIS

0   5 km

On the road to Col de Turini, the imposing mausoleum dedicated to the Ist Division France Libre, inaugurated in 1964 by General de Gaulle, commemorates the sacrifices and battles of the Liberation at the end of the Second World War.

Take D 2204 south to Col de Nice and turn right onto D 215.

Glimpses of Berre-les-Alpes can be had on the drive up.

Berre-les-Alpes – The village boasts a charming **site** at 675m/2 215ft. From the cemetery there is a **panorama★** of the Pre-Alps of Nice and the sea.

Return downhill on the same road bearing right onto D 615.

The drive from Berre-les-Alpes to Contes is enchanting. The road winds its way through a typical inland Nice landscape of chestnut and olive groves interspersed with cypress and pine trees and clumps of mimosa on the terraced land.

Contes – Originally a Roman settlement, the village is built on a rocky promontory that dominates the River Paillon de Contes like a ship's prow; modern constructions extend into the valley. A tale tells of a plague of caterpillars in the 16C. The intruders were solemnly tried and sentenced to exile. The villagers organised a procession, and the caterpillars obediently left the village forever.

The south chapel of the church contains a remarkable altarpiece by an artist belonging to the Nice School (1525). The central panel representing St Madeleine has disappeared but the **predella★** illustrates her life in five scenes. The woodwork (doorway, gallery, pulpit) is 17C. An elegant Renaissance fountain plays in front of the church. From the terrace there is a fine view of the valley.

Take D 715 to La Grave; cross the Paillon and take D 815.

The road winds uphill beneath the shade of pines and olives above the Paillon, until one can look down on Contes, on its rocky spit and on Berre-des-Alpes.

Châteauneuf-Villevieille – The village nestles against the hillside among olive groves on the site of a Ligurian settlement, later a Roman camp, overlooking the Paillon de Contes Valley. The 11C Romanesque church, **"Madone de Villevieille"** ○, is decorated with festoons and Lombard bands. A Roman inscription has been incorporated into the façade. The east end with its massive buttresses has been cleared.

The interior was restored in the 17C and frescoes painted on the ceiling; behind the high altar, a fine plaster altarpiece frames a 15C wooden statue of the Virgin and Child. The deserted ruins of medieval walls and towers *(2km/1mi further on, 30min on foot there and back)* make a strange spectacle against the rocky landscape. The people of Châteauneuf-de-Contes retreated up here in the Middle Ages to be safe from attack. From the top of the bluff there is a sweeping **panorama★** taking in Mont Chauve, Mont Férion (west) and the Alps (northeast).

Go back to D 15, which leads to Nice via the Paillon Valley.

⑤ Vallée du Var and Vallée de l'Esteron

66km/41mi – allow half a day – see local map overleaf

Leave Nice by Promenade des Anglais, which becomes Promenade Corniglion-Molinier, a pleasant drive along the Baie des Anges. Return to N 98, then turn right towards Plan-du-Var.

N 202 hugs the east bank of the Var. In a landscape composed of flower beds and vegetable plots, of vineyards and olive groves, the hill villages of Vence and the Nice hinterland stand out one by one: on the west bank Gattières, Carros and Le Broc; on the east bank Aspremont and Castagniers at the foot of Mont Chauve, followed by St-Martin-du-Var and La Roquette-sur-Var.

The **view★** includes the snow-capped Alps on the horizon. At St-Martin-du-Var the river is joined by one of its western tributaries, the Esteron.

Cross the river over Pont Charles-Albert and take D 17 to Gilette.

The site of the village of Bonson on an impressive rock spur high above the river on the west bank comes into view, followed by Gilette, in its unusual site nestling in a cleft.

Gilette – From Place de la Mairie follow the arrows up to the castle ruins for an impressive **view★** of the *corniche* roads, the Var Valley, its confluence with the Esteron and the Pre-Alps of Nice. There is a pleasant walk, bordered by acacias and plane trees, below the castle with fine views of the hill villages – Bonson and Tourette-du-Château – and of the Alps to the north.

From Gilette take D 17 north up the Esteron Valley; 2km/1mi beyond Vescous turn right onto a narrow road which climbs to Vieux-Pierrefeu.

Vieux-Pierrefeu – Alt 618m/2 028ft. This village, high above the Esteron Valley, was a Roman signalling post (Petra Igniaria), a link in the chain that ran from Hadrian's Wall on the border between England and Scotland to Rome and was used to transmit optical messages.

🚶 *The village is reserved for pedestrians.*

The church just down the road in Pierrefeu has been converted into a picture gallery called the **Musée "Hors du Temps"** ○: this small museum houses a unique collection of

paintings on the theme of the Genesis; it contains the work of 40 contemporary artists including Brayer, Carzou, Folon, Erni, Vicari, Villemont and Moretti.
The drive provides views of the Var Valley, Bonson and La Roquette, perched on its rock.

Bonson – It is built on a remarkable **site★** on a rocky spur high above the Var Valley. From the church terrace there is an exceptional **view★★** of the Vésubie springing from its gorges to mingle with the waters of the Var, the Défilé de Chaudan *(see below)*. This famous wooded area was razed by a terrible fire in 1994 which destroyed everything up to the edge of the village.
The **church** contains three beautiful Primitive paintings from the Nice School. On the back wall there is a **retable of St Antony**; the figure of St Gertrude, who was invoked against the plague, is identified by the great rats climbing up her shoulders; the painting shows some similarity with the work of Durandi. In the south aisle is a **retable of John the Baptist**, attributed to Antoine Bréa (the centre panel has been spoiled by overpainting). At the high altar, in a Renaissance frame, is a **retable of St Benedict★**, including the figure of St Agatha clutching her wounded breasts.

★**Mont Vial** – *20 km/12mi from Bonson. Take D 27 west towards Puget-Théniers.* The picturesque road twists and turns along the flank of the hill with attractive glimpses of Gilette. After Tourette-du-Château take the road going sharply down to the right which winds to Le Vial ridge before reaching the summit (1 549m/5 082ft) *(U-turns possible)*. An impressive **panorama★★** will reward those who have made the effort of climbing up. In fine weather the view extends over the course of the Var from Puget-Théniers to the mouth of the river.
Return to Bonson by the same route.

The road loops down to Pont Charles-Albert, giving beautiful **views★** of the Var Valley. Cross the bridge and turn left onto N 202. North of Plan-du-Var cross the River Vésubie where it joins the Var. The road to the right climbs up the Gorges de la Vésubie.

★★**Défilé du Chaudan** – The defile, which is named after the little village of Chaudan at its southern end, has been created by the Var, which has worn a deep, narrow and winding channel through the rocks. The road follows the course of the river in and out of every bend and through four tunnels.
At the northern end, at **Pont de la Mescla**, the River Tinée flows into the Var.
Go back to Nice on N 202.

⑥ **Vésubie Valley** – *See Vallée de la VÉSUBIE*
Plan-du-Var to the Madone d'Utelle
St-Jean-la-Rivière to St-Martin-Vésubie

⑦ **Turini Forest** – *See Forêt de TURINI*
The Authion
Vallon Ste-Élisabeth
Col de Braus road

⑧ **Col de Castillon Road** – *See MENTON: Pass Road*
Menton to Sospel

⑨ **Col de Brouis Road** – *See SOSPEL: Outings*
Sospel to La Giandola

⑩ **Saorge and Bergue Gorges** – *See SAORGE: Driving Tours*

⑪ **Route de Valdeblore** – *See SAINT-MARTIN-VÉSUBIE: Outings*

PEILLE★

Population 2 045
Michelin map 84 fold 19, 115 north of fold 27 or 245 fold 38
Local map see NICE

The village, which has maintained its medieval appearance, stands near the ruins of a castle, once the property of the counts of Provence: three mountains tower over the wild **site** above the Faquin ravine: Pic de Baudon, Mont Agel and Cime de Rastel.

Park the car on the north side of the village by the church, which is approached up a steep slope behind the hospice.

A TYPICAL PERCHED VILLAGE

★**The town** – Go down the steps leading from D 53 to Rue de la Sauterie, a cobbled alleyway punctuated by covered passageways, sloping down towards Place A.-Laugier. Rue Centrale on the right takes you to a domed 13C building, which used to be the chapel of St-Sébastian. It has been restored and now houses the town hall. Turn left and left again into Rue St-Sébastien; on the left of the crossroads stands the former salt tax office (Hôtel de la Gabelle).

The street opens out onto Place A.-Laugier, which borders what was once the consuls' residence. At the far end of the square, beyond the Gothic fountain, two arches beneath a house rest on a central Romanesque pillar: pass beneath the right arch and turn right into Rue Lascaris, then left into Avenue Mary-Garden ending in the war memorial.

Church ⊙ – The church, dating from the 12C and 13C and with an elegant Romanesque belfry, is formed from two adjoining chapels; the one on the right features rounded vaulting, the one on the left crossed pointed arching. As you enter, an altar against the wall on the left is adorned with a fine altarpiece (16C), divided into 15 panels, by Honoré Bertone. The central panel depicting a Virgin of the Rosary has been removed and replaced by a statue. A picture on the right shows Peille as it was in the Middle Ages. A 14C mural represents St Anne and the Virgin and Child.

★ **Viewpoint** – From the memorial there is a view to the north of the gardens of Peille, the Faquin ravine, the church and Pic de Baudon in the distance; to the south the Cime de Rastel and a glimpse of Nice and the Baie des Anges down the Paillon Valley.

Via Ferrata ⊙ – *Park the car in the municipal car park at the entrance to the village and follow directions. Total length 600m/1969ft. Allow 2hr 30min.* This challenging itinerary is an hair-raising experience that combines physical stamina and courage. Make your way along the narrow gangway (35m/115ft long, 50m/164ft above ground level), rope bridges and wire cables... with all the necessary safety measures!

PEILLON★★

Population 1 227
Michelin map 84 fold 19, 115 fold 27 or 245 fold 38
Local map see NICE

Set back on a narrow spur overlooking the Paillon Valley, Peillon is undoubtedly one of the most spectacular villages on the Riviera. The strict architectural unity of the village was imposed by its site and the need for a highly strategic defensive system.

Christ's Passion by Giovanni Canavesio, Peillon

E. Baret/MICHELIN

A MAZE OF VAULTED PASSAGEWAYS

★ **Village** – Untouched since the Middle Ages, the village has few streets but many steep steps and covered alleys between the flower-decked houses huddled against each other. The 18C church with its octagonal lantern crowns the village; inside are 17C and 18C canvases and an 18C wooden statue of Christ.

Chapelle des Pénitents-Blancs ⊙ – The chapel's most interesting feature are the **frescoes**★ by Giovanni Canavesio: at the far end the Crucifixion with St Antony and St Petronella; on the walls and ceiling scenes from the Passion, in particular the Flagellation and Judas' Kiss, vividly portrayed.

The similarity of style with the chapel of Notre-Dame-des-Fontaines is striking. On the altar stands a Pietà in painted wood.

▚ You can still walk along the old Roman road (now a footpath) which links Peillon to Peille – a 2h walk from one town to the other.

Le PRADET★★

Population 10 975
Michelin map 84 fold 19, 115 fold 27 or 245 fold 38
Local map see NICE

This charming resort nestling below the Massif de la Colle Noire has a good selection of small, easily accessible beaches. There is a footpath designed especially for botanical discoveries in Courbebaisse Wood.

A CHARMING SEASIDE RESORT

Beaches – La Garonne Bay is punctuated by several attractive creeks. The best way to explore them is to take the coastal path which can be followed between each beach accessible by road.

★**Coastal footpath** – 7km/4.2mi. Allow at least 3hr because of the winding path that is very steep in places. Access to the beaches is often by steep steps cut out of the rock. The route signposted in yellow runs from the car park at the lovely Crique du Pin de Galle to Bau Rouge (It is possible to continue from Bau Rouge to Carqueiranne).

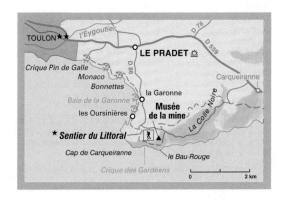

The steep slope above **Pin de Galle beach** offers magnificent views over Toulon harbour. The numerous cabins in the pine wood add to the bucolic charm of the setting. The shaded path joins the road through the park before descending steeply to **Monaco beach**. At the end of this beach, part of which is used by nudists, the path begins beyond a low wall and climbs a cliff covered by superb *maquis* vegetation. After a headland, a little further on, there is a lovely view of the indentations along the coast. A well-marked path goes down to **Les Bonnettes beach** at the foot of a remarkable rocky inlet. In season there is a lifeguards' post and an open-air café here. It was from this beach that Murat set out for Corsica.

The path then links **La Garonne beach** with **Les Oursinières beach**. Beyond Oursinières Port a footpath to the right leaves the road to Le Pradet. It leads past panoramic viewpoints on the cliffs to Bau Rouge with fine views over the coast eastwards towards Carqueiranne and of the Les Gardéens creek.

Situated at the heart of the town, the **Bois de Courbebaisse** (5ha/124 acres) is a pleasant way of discovering local botanical species.

OUTING

Musée de la Mine de Cap-Garonne ⊙ – *In Le Pradet take D 86 southwards towards Plage de la Garonne. After the beach, take the road which climbs to the left, signposted "La Mine", and continues to Carqueiranne.*

Copper ore was mined here for centuries. The first traces of workings go back to the 16C, but it was only with the concession granted in 1862 that commercial mining began. It went on until 1917, when the reduction in copper content of the ore meant that mining was no longer a profitable activity.

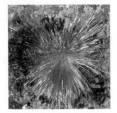

Musée de la Mine
de Cap-Garonne

The tour focuses on the redeveloped part of the galleries and, through several reconstructions and presentations, illustrates the long-standing evolution of working methods and the daily lives of miners at Cap Garonne as well as events during its lifetime such as loading ore for transport to England.

At the end of the tour, in a **great hall**★, there are tables equipped with magnifying glasses with which the many and various colours of copper ore extracted at Cap Garonne can be examined. Particularly notable are the magical blue needles of crystals of **cyanotrichite**, the principal ore of the mine. Two categories of copper ore can be recognised: the oxides (cuprite, malachite, azurite...) which are now mined in Africa and the Far East and the **sulphurated ore**, more widespread, represented above all by the iron-based chalcopyrites. There are also fine green stalagtites characteristic of the oxidation of this ore.

⚑ A **botanical footpath** *(1.2km/0.7mi, explanatory panels, viewing table)* circles the mine area and affords fine views of the Massif de la Colle Noire and Giens Peninsula.

RAMATUELLE★

Population 2 131
Michelin map 84 fold 17, 114 fold 37 or 245 fold 49
Local map under Massif des MAURES

The village, which is set among vineyards halfway up a slope, possesses all the features of an old Provençal town: narrow winding streets with arches and vaults; old houses, now restored, huddled against the old town wall near the church.

In spite of its isolated location, the village fell under the occupation of the Saracens who had otherwise made their lair in La Garde-Freinet. The old prisons are a rare example of their architecture. In 1592, having opted to side with the Catholic League, Ramatuelle was destroyed after a siege.

The cemetery contains, to the right of the entrance, the ivy-covered tomb of the actor **Gérard Philipe**, born in Cannes (1922-59), and since 1990 that of the writer Anne Philipe, his wife.

Every year, during the first fortnight in August, Ramatuelle hosts a Theatre Festival that showcases a wide selection of excellent contemporary plays, interspersed with live concerts.

Colourful markets are held on Thursdays and Sundays.

A CLUSTER OF PINK ROOFS

Church – The Romanesque church with its flat east end opens through a serpentine door (1620). Inside are two 17C Baroque altarpieces of magnificent gilded wood. Many door lintels, including that on the entrance to the church, mention the year in which the village was rebuilt: 1620.

Monument to the Resistance – Opposite the cemetery stands a memorial to the members of the Special Services who died in the Second World War; the submarines that stayed in contact with the members of the Resistance used to wait offshore by the Escudelier rock.

Ramatuelle village seen from above

Eating out

MID-RANGE

Key West Beach – *Plage de Pampelonne – 4km/2.5mi E of Ramatuelle, towards St-Tropez –* ☎ *04 94 79 86 58 – key-west-beach@com – 27.74/45.73€.* The famous Pampelonne beach provides the backdrop to this restaurant, embellished with photographs and models of sailing boats, reproductions of multicoloured fish, deep-sea diving suits and miscellaneous maritime curiosities. Have a dip in the sea or relax on a mattress in the sun... before tucking in to a delicious *truite aux amandes*!

La Forge – *Rue Victor-Léon –* ☎ *04 94 79 25 56 – Closed 16 Nov-14 Mar, for lunch in Jul-Aug and Wed – 28.20€.* The imposing bellows remind visitors that this restaurant was once the local smithy. Today flames still crackle in the fireplace but they serve to grill the meat and freshly caught fish for diners. Provençal fare in a rustic, homely setting.

LUXURY

Chez Camille – *In La Bonne Terrasse – 5km/3mi E of Ramatuelle by D 93 and Route de Camarat –* ☎ *04 94 79 80 38 – Closed 11 Oct-31 Mar, Tue (except evenings in Jul-Aug) and Mon for lunch – Reservation required in summer and on weekends – 35.06/50.31€.* Congenial restaurant where locals flock to order the owner's specialities - *bouillabaisse* and grilled fish. This former refreshments stand is strategically located at the water's edge.

Where to stay

MID-RANGE

Chambre d'Hôte Leï Souco – *3,5km/2mi from Ramatuelle on D 93, Route de St-Tropez –* ☎ *04 94 79 80 22 – www.leisouco.com – Closed 15 Oct-31 Mar* – ☑ *– 6 rooms: 61/96€.* Surrounded by vineyards, olive and mulberry trees, this *mas* is a true haven of peace. You will love the rooms with their wood panelling, red hexagonal tiling and Salernes faience. Scrumptious breakfasts are served on the terrace overgrown with wisteria. Tennis court.

LUXURY

Ferme d'Hermès – *2,5km/1.5mi SE of Ramatuelle by Route de l'Escalet and a private road –* ☎ *04 94 79 27 80 – Closed 11 Jan-31 Mar and 2 Nov-26 Dec* – *8 rooms: 121.96/140.25€ –* ☑ *12.20€.* Provençal house lost amid the vines that offers pretty, luminous rooms appointed with light wooden furniture polished in the old-fashioned style. All the rooms give onto the garden planted with olive trees and pink oleander. Outdoor pool. Peaceful atmosphere guaranteed.

Splashing out

Team Water Sports – *Route de l'Épi / Baie de Pampelonne –* ☎ *04 94 79 82 41 – May-Sep daily 10am-5pm.* Facilities for water-skiing, parascending, dodgem games with rubber rings, jet-skiing and sea scooters.

Domaine du RAYOL★★

Michelin map 114 folds 49 and 50, 84 fold 17 or 245 folds 48 and 49

The domaine du Rayol, evidence of a period of luxury, was created at the beginning of the century when European industrial and banking families built holiday resorts on previously undeveloped sites overlooking the sea, surrounded by lush vegetation. Rayol itself enjoys an exceptional **site★**, rising in a semicircle on wooded slopes among cork-oaks, mimosa and pines, in one of the most beautiful positions on the Var coast.

A HAVEN OF MEDITERRANEAN FLORA

In 1910 a Parisian banker, Courmes, after travelling extensively, had a house built here surrounded by exotic gardens. The stock market crash in 1929 put an abrupt end to the development of the estate.

The aeronautics engineer Potez, who was forced to take refuge on the coast in 1940, renovated the property and the garden. The belvedere by Patek, with its circular pergola, is linked to the coast by a magnificent flight of steps, and the garden is now glorious. In 1989 the Conservatoire du Littoral acquired the whole **estate** ⊙ (20ha/49.5 acres) after several decades of neglect, in order to preserve some of the last wild shores of the Corniche des Maures.

Domaine du RAYOL

The landscape gardener Clément created a patchwork of gardens planted with vegetation found growing in Mediterranean climates all over the world. There are dragon trees in the Jardin des Canaries, agaves from central America, extremely rare honey palms and Andean araucarias from Chile, eucalyptus, bottle brush and blue gum trees from Australia, strelitzia from South Africa and bamboos from China.

Cactus in bloom, Jardin du Rayol

Between each continent the winding paths offer glimpses of the turquoise sea and a headland carpeted with pines. During the summer season, there are evening concerts of classical music here, with the opportunity to stroll through the floodlit gardens during the interval.

★**Sentier Marin** ⓥ – A trip from the little beach at Rayol offers an unusual view of underwater life in the Mediterranean. This tour, accompanied by wardens from the Conservatoire, is preceded by an introduction to the species most likely to be seen, their description and the best place to look for them among the posidonia. Among the discoveries to be made are the amazing lifestyle of the sea cucumber, the relentless activity of the gobies, whose inquisitive nature may surprise visitors, and the curious sexual habits of the rainbow wrasse. Other finds might include sea slugs (a local species), the distracting ballet of a shoal of bream, the sparkling colours of a solitary wrasse or a conger eel lying in wait in a crevice in the rocks which are scattered around the bay.

The beach at Rayol-Canadel-sur-Mer *(2km/1mi W via D 599)* is a sheltered cove bordered by pines, one of the nicest on the Maures coast, at the foot of the Pradels moutnains.

Posidonia, the Lungs of the Mediterranean

This flowering plant, which looks like bunches of long green leaves, is an essential element of marine life in the Mediterranean. It grows on sandy seabeds on the narrow coastal fringes.

Posidonia plays the same role as forests: it provides a habitat for animal and plant species, a source of oxygen and stabilises the seabed.

It is threatened with damage and extinction by man's intervention: unpurified sewage discharge, uprooting by boats mooring, building on the coast and by the invasion of another species *(Caulerpa taxifolia)*.

Corniches de la RIVIERA★★★

Michelin map 84 folds 19 and 20, 115 folds 26-28 or 245 folds 38 and 39

The mountains plunge sharply down into the sea between Nice and Menton; the beaches are directly overlooked by the heights along which run the three famous highways known as the Grande Corniche, the Moyenne Corniche and the Corniche Inférieure. The first, which climbs to 450m/1 476ft, affords the most spectacular views; the second, beautiful vistas along the shore; and the third, access to all the coastal resorts.

In 1986 the region was devastated by fire; it will be some time yet before it regains its usual appearance.

★★★ 1 GRANDE CORNICHE

From Menton to Nice – *31km/19mi – about 3hr – see local map below*
The time given for making the tours described below does not allow for visiting Nice or Menton.

The Grande Corniche, built by Napoleon along the route of the ancient Via Julia Augusta is the highest of the three roads, passing through La Turbie from which it looks down from 450m/1 400ft onto the Principality of Monaco. It provides breathtaking views and access to the perched village of Roquebrune.

★★ **Menton** – *See MENTON. Allow 3hr.*
From Menton take Avenue Carnot and Avenue de la Madone (N 7) going west. Either bear left onto D 52 to Cap Martin or continue uphill (N 7) bearing right onto D 2564 to Roquebrune.

★ **Roquebrune-Cap-Martin** – *See ROQUEBRUNE-CAP-MARTIN.*
From Roquebrune take D 2564 westwards.

★★ **Le Vistaëro** – From nearly 300m/1 000ft above the sea where the Vistaëro Hotel stands, there is a marvellous **view**★★ extending out over Bordighera Point, Cap Mortola, Menton, Cap Martin, Roquebrune and, immediately below, Monte-Carlo Beach. To the right lie Monaco and Beausoleil, with Tête de Chien rising above them. Further inland, in a pass, can be seen La Turbie and the Alpine Trophy.

★ **La Turbie** – *See La TURBIE.*

The Grande Corniche discloses distant **views** of Cap Ferrat and then of Èze village as the road reaches its highest point at 550m/1 804ft. In Pical a stone cross on the left commemorates Pope Pius VII's return from exile in 1814.

Col d'Èze – Alt 512m/1 680ft. Extended **view** to the north over the mountains and valleys of the upper Vésubie and Var. Owing to its strategic position, Mont Bastide on the left has been a Celto-Ligurian oppidum and a Roman camp.

Astrorama ⊙ – *On leaving Col d'Èze towards Nice, turn right on the road going up signed "Parc Départemental de la Grande Corniche-Astrorama".*
After a series of hairpin bends, the road finally reaches a shelf which is home to an old gun battery belonging to the system of defence of Séré de Rivières, positioned between the forts of Drete and Revère, called the Batterie des Feuillerins. This now houses an astronomical study and observation centre designed especially for members of the public with no previous knowledge of the subject: the **Astrorama**.
Visitors may learn about the different theoretical and practical aspects of the discovery and observation of space. The site is relatively shielded from the interference of the intense artificial light that reigns all along the densely populated coast, and so various sophisticated viewing devices are put at the public's disposal, under the guidance of a member of staff.
It is possible to drive up the road as far as the car park at Fort de la Revère *(No access to the fort)*. From the base of the fort there is a superb **panorama**★★ over the whole Var coast as far as Italy and, in winter, on very clear mornings it is possible to see the outline of Corsica to the southeast.

Belvédère d'Èze – 1 200m/1 312yd beyond the pass, opposite a small café named the "Belvédère" in a right bend, there is a wide panoramic **view**★★ in which one can distinguish Tête de Chien, Èze and the sea below, the Cap Ferrat Peninsula, Mont Boron, the Cap d'Antibes, the Lérins islands, the Esterel range with the summit of Cap Roux, and the French and Italian Alps.

Col des Quatre-Chemins – A short way beyond the pass (alt 327m/1 037ft) one can see the Alps through an opening made by the Paillon Valley.
Soon afterwards, the road descends steeply offering a wide **view**★ of the Pre-Alps, and then of Nice and castle hill, the harbour, the Baie des Anges, Cap d'Antibes and the Esterel.

Enter Nice from the east by Avenue des Diables-Bleus.

★★★ **Nice** – *See NICE. One day.*

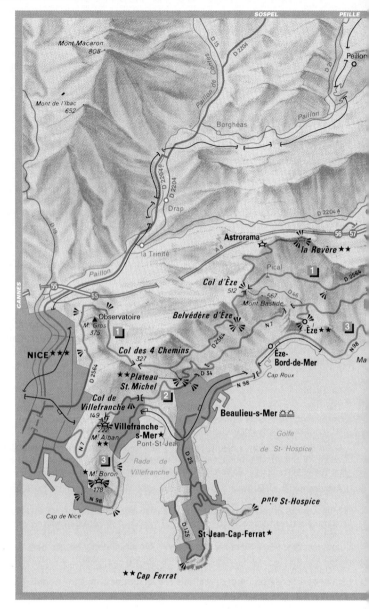

★★② MOYENNE CORNICHE

From Nice to Menton

31km/19mi – about 2hr – see local map below

Shorter and less winding than the Grande Corniche, the Moyenne Corniche is a broad modern road built between 1910 and 1928, well sited along the mountainside; it tunnels through the larger mountain chains and takes large sweeping curves into the delightful Mediterranean countryside; it offers good views of the coast and the coastal resorts and provides the only access by road to the amazing village of Èze.

As a parapet along a great part of the road obscures the view of the sea and the coast, lay-bys have been provided at all the best viewpoints.

★★★ Nice – See NICE. One day.

From Nice leaving Place Max-Barel take N 7 east.

Initially the view comprises the town, the hill with the old château, the harbour and the Baie des Anges; the Esterel chain and the limestone mountains of Grasse stand out on the horizon to the southwest.

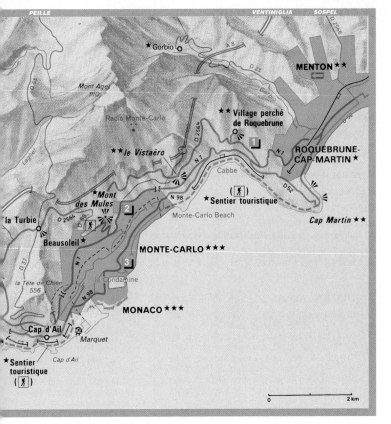

Col de Villefranche – Alt 149m/489ft. From a bend in the road soon after the pass, Villefranche-sur-Mer anchorage and Cap Ferrat come into sight.

Just before entering a 180m/200yd long tunnel, there is a very good **view★★** of Beaulieu, Cap Ferrat, Villefranche-sur-Mer, Nice and Cap d'Antibes. After the tunnel the old village of Èze comes into view, perched high on its rock against the backdrop of Tête de Chien (alt 556m/1 880ft), the mountain promontory dominating Cap d'Ail and Monaco.

★★ Plateau St-Michel – *2km/1.2mi from N 7. After the tunnel turn right onto the narrow D 34 which climbs back over the tunnel for 2km/1.2mi to a terrace car park.* Walk up to the viewing table on the edge of the plateau (371m/1 217ft). The **panorama★★** extends from the tip of Cap d'Ail to the Esterel.

★★ Èze – *See Èze.*

Beyond Èze the Moyenne Corniche circles the rocky escarpments of Tête de Chien and brings into sight new panoramic views overlooking Cap Martin and the long Bordighera headland in Italy. Below, in the foreground, lies the Principality of Monaco.

At the entrance to Monaco bear left onto N 7 which skirts the Principality and offers remarkable **views★** of Monte-Carlo, Cap Martin, the Italian coast and the coastal ranges.

★ Beausoleil – This resort forms part of the Monte-Carlo conurbation although it is officially on French territory. Its houses, reached by stepped streets, project from the slopes of Mont des Mules like balconies over the sea.

★ Mont des Mules – *Bear left onto D 53 – 1km/0.6mi plus 30min there and back on foot along a marked path.*
🔼 From the top there is a fine **panorama★** *(viewing table).*
Return to N 7 which passes below the Vistaëro before joining the Corniche Inférieure at Cabbé.

★★ Cap Martin – *See ROQUEBRUNE-CAP-MARTIN.*

★★ Menton – *See MENTON. 3hr.*

Corniches de la RIVIERA

★★③ CORNICHE INFÉRIEURE

From Nice to Menton

33km/21mi – about 6hr – see local map below

The Corniche Inférieure was conceived as long ago as the 18C by a prince of Monaco. Work was undertaken by the Empress of Russia in 1857 and completed in 1881. The road, running at the foot of the mountain slopes and following the contours of the coast, serves all the Riviera resorts.

★★★ **Nice** – *See NICE. Allow a whole day.*
From Nice take Boulevard Carnot, N 98, heading southeast.

The road skirts the base of Mont Boron with **views**★ of the Baie des Anges, Cap Ferrat, Villefranche-sur-Mer anchorage, Èze and Tête de Chien in succession.

★ **Villefranche-sur-Mer** – *See VILLEFRANCHE-SUR-MER.*

Start from Pont St-Jean for a tour of the Cap Ferrat Peninsula.

★★ **Cap Ferrat** – *Round tour of 10km/6mi – about 2hr 30min. See CAP FERRAT.*

⌂⌂ **Beaulieu** – *See BEAULIEU.*
As the road skirts Cap Roux, there is a view across the water to Cap d'Ail.

Èze-Bord-de-Mer – The resort lies beneath the cliffs below Èze-Village.
As the road hugs the rocky coast, Cap d'Ail is in full view.

Cap d'Ail – Sheltered by pine, palm and cypress trees, the elegant properties of Cap d'Ail cover the lower slopes of the Tête de Chien down to the sea.

★ **Coastal Path of Cap d'Ail** – *1hr on foot there and back. To the east side of the station go down the steps into a tunnel which comes out on a road. Turn left and at Restaurant La Pinède take another flight of steps on the right down to the sea.*

TROPICAL NIGHTS

La Réserve de la Mala – *Plage Mala – 06320 Cap-Ail – Take Avenue des Combattants d'Afrique du Nord (to "Spar" store) – ☎ 04 93 78 21 56 – plagemala@monte.carlo.mc – Closed 4 Nov-24 Mar – 28/47€.* This small, heavenly beach can be reached by the coastal path in Cap d'Ail or by a long flight of steps starting from the town centre. The restaurant has several terraces and a landing-stage. Paradise on earth.

🚶 A coastal footpath running eastwards skirts the rocks at the foot of Cap d'Ail, which are pounded furiously by the sea in high winds. To the west lie Beaulieu and Cap Ferrat; gradually Monaco Rock looms into view. The footpath ends on Marquet beach. One can take the road into Monaco or return via the footpath.

★★★ **Monaco** – *See MONACO.*
The road joins the Moyenne Corniche at Cabbé.

★★ **Cap Martin** – *See ROQUEBRUNE-CAP-MARTIN.*

★★ **Menton** – *See MENTON.*

ROQUEBRUNE-CAP-MARTIN★

Population 11692
Michelin map 84 fold 10 and 20, 115 fold 28 or 245 fold 39
Local maps see MENTON: Excursions and Corniches de la RIVIERA

This pretty resort covering the whole of Cap Martin and extending along the coast between Menton and Monte-Carlo, is watched over by the perched medieval village of Roquebrune and its castle keep.
The Roquebrune enclave is the only example in France today of a Carolingian castle, forerunner of the castles built 200 years later, when the feudal system was dominant.

HISTORICAL NOTES

The castle was built at the end of the 10C by Conrad I, Count of Ventimiglia, to stop the Saracens from establishing themselves once again in the area. For several centuries it belonged to the Grimaldis *(see MONACO)*, who remodelled part of it and introduced artillery in its defences. Originally, the castle was a fortress enclosing the keep and the village within its battlements, which were pierced by six fortified gateways. In the 15C, the keep became known as the castle and the rest of the fortress became the village, which up to the present has preserved its medieval character.

Eating out

MID-RANGE

La Roquebrunoise – *12 av. Raymond-Poincaré (in the old town)* – ☎ *04 93 35 02 19 – Closed Nov and Dec, Mon except Mon evening in Jul and Aug, Tue noon and Thu noon – 18,32€.* This pretty pink house on the edge of the village is a nice place to rest from your wanderings. The country-style dining room is hung with paintings. The food is unpretentious and tasty, and the tables on the terrace have a view of the sea and the château.

Au Grand Inquisiteur – *18 r. du Château, (in the old town, access on foot only)* – ☎ *04 93 35 05 37 – Closed 2-8 Jul, 5 Nov-25 Dec, Tue except in Jul and Aug, and Mon. – Reservation required – 22,87/34,15€.* "The Great Inquisitor" is a strange name for a restaurant indeed! Nonetheless, the welcome is warm. In the heart of the village, in a pedestrian zone, this 14C building has a small dining room with a vaulted ceiling, furnished in a pleasing style.

Where to stay

MID-RANGE

Hôtel Westminster – *14 av. L.-Laurens, by N 98, rte de Monaco by the lower corniche road* – ☎ *04 92 41 41 40 – Closed 24 Nov-10 Feb – 32 rooms.: 51,83/76,99€ – ☑ 4,88€.* In a residential street, this pleasant little hotel has a terraced garden which rises above the sea. Enjoy your breakfast with a view on the balcony of your room. There is a train that runs behind the hotel, but it passes slowly.

Hôtel Diodato – *Pointe de Cabbé (via av. Vilaren and av. Le Corbusier)* – ☎ *04 92 10 52 52 – Closed 12 Nov-20 Dec – 32 rooms: 76,22/175,32€ – ☑ 9,15€.* This hotel was once the summer residence of an aristocratic Russian family. It sits above the sea on a rocky promontory. Although it is quite close to the train station, the rooms themselves look out on the pines and palm trees in the garden. Nice swimming pool and direct access to the sea.

Traditional processions – For the past 500 years a procession, representing the principal scenes of the Passion in six tableaux, is held on the afternoon of 5 August. Unchanged since it was first performed by those who made a vow in 1467 during an epidemic of the plague, the ceremony is known to last for two hours.

At 9pm on Good Friday, a **Procession of the Entombment of Christ** is held. This procession was instituted by the Brotherhood of the White Penitents, which has now been disbanded.

A train of some 60 people – representing Roman centurions and legionaries, disciples carrying the statue of Christ and holy women – walk through the streets of the village, which are decorated with lighted motifs recalling the symbols of the Passion and illuminated with hundreds of tiny lights formed by snail and sea shells filled with olive oil, in which a small cotton wick burns.

★★A TYPICAL PERCHED VILLAGE *1hr*

The town's enviable situation and the medieval keep are not Roquebrune's sole attractions. To savour its charm, one should stroll through the maze of steep covered alleys and quaint stairways that have preserved their ancient appearance despite the art galleries and craft and souvenir shops which have edged their way between the local tradesmen.

Park on Place de la République.

The square was once the barbican – the keep's advanced defence.

★ **Rue Moncollet** – Make for Place des Deux-Frères and then turn left into Rue Grimaldi. Bear left again into the unusual and picturesque Rue Moncollet with its long and narrow, covered and stepped passageways. Medieval houses with barred windows, where those invited to join the seigneurial court once lived, give on to the road in front, while at the back they lie against or are cut into the living rock. Rue Moncollet, bending slightly to the right, leads into Rue du Château on the left.

★ **Donjon** ⊘ – After crossing the "flowered enclosure", you enter the ancient keep of the oldest feudal castle in France. It overlooks by some 26m/80ft the façades of the houses opposite in Rue Moncollet. The 2-4m/6-12ft thick walls have been fitted with a great many defensive features: cannon embrasures, machicolations, battlements, loopholes etc.

A flight of 20 steps leads up to the first floor and the Hall of Feudal Ceremonies. Note particularly: the cell recessed into the wall; in the centre, a cube-shaped water tank; and the 15C mullioned window, replacing the oblique slots 20cm/8in which once provided light. Below this hall is the storeroom, carved out of the rock. On the second floor is the small guard-room, on the right a comfortable prison and further on the archers' dormitory. On the third floor are the baronial apartments complete with furnishings; dining room, primitive kitchen with bread oven, and a bedroom containing ancient weapons.

The fourth floor includes the upper artillery platform affording a circular **panorama**★★ over the picturesque roofs of the village, the sea, Cap Martin, the Principality of Monaco, and Mont Agel (military air base).

Go down by the parapet walk and the so-called English Tower which has been badly restored. You can also visit the light artillery platform and the look-out post.

Olivier Millénaire – *Cross Place William-Ingram and turn right into Rue du Château.*

Opposite a souvenir shop, before reaching the post office, turn left into Rue de la Fontaine and the Menton road, which 200m/219yd beyond the end of the village passes a **1 000-year-old olive tree**, said to be one of the oldest trees in the world.

Return to Rue du Château (left) which leads to the church.

Église Ste-Marguerite ⊘ – The fairly plain Baroque façade masks the original 12C church, which has undergone many alterations over the years. Against the polychrome plasterwork of the interior hang two paintings by a local painter, Marc-Antoine Otto (17C): a Crucifixion (2nd altar) and a Pietà (above the door).

Turn right into Rue Grimaldi which leads, via Place des Deux-Frères, to Place de la République.

★★Cap Martin

Cap Martin with its magnificent estates is the wealthy residential suburb of Menton. It is served by roads which cut through olive groves and clumps of cypresses, perfumed by pine woods and banks of mimosa.

A massive tower of feudal appearance rises at the centre; it was the old beacon, now converted to a relay station for telecommunications. At its foot lie the ruins of the basilica of St-Martin, part of a priory built by the Lérins island monks in the 11C and destroyed by pirates about 1400.

Local legend gives the following account. One night the Prior, wishing to test the vigilance of the inhabitants who were obliged to protect the monks, sounded the alarm. His parishioners all came running, discovered it was a false alarm and returned to bed swearing not to be duped again. Some time later the pirates launched an attack; the monks sounded the alarm but nobody came to their rescue; they were massacred and the monastery burned down.

East Coast – From the road along the eastern shore there is a marvellous **view**★★ of Menton in its mountain setting and of the Italian coast as far as Bordighera. There are several beaches dominated by the old village: two at Cabbé facing southwest and one at Carnolès on the east side next to Menton.

Roquebrune-Cap-Martin

Le Cabanon de Le Corbusier ⊙ – This cabin, tucked in below promenade Le Corbusier which runs along the coast from Cabbé to Cap Martin, has a deceptively plain exterior. It is, in fact, a unique construction, whose dimensions were calculated by Le Corbusier using the **Modulor**, a measuring tool on a human scale invented by the architect for use in his projects. The Cabanon consists of a corridor decorated with a fresco painted by the architect and a room ($10m^2$/108sq ft). Each piece of furniture has several functions; even the windows, some of which are jointed, allow the passage of light and also ventilation from the sides. This building, where the architect lived on several occasions, and near where he ended his days, is still an object of curiosity for the layman and a point of reference for schools of architecture. "I have a château on the Riviera which measures 3.66m by 3.66m/12ft by 12ft. It is wonderfully comfortable and pleasant" confided Le Corbusier.

Le Corbusier's tomb, which he designed himself and where he has lain with his wife since 1965, can be seen in Roquebrune graveyard.

★Coastal Path

🔟 *A coastal footpath runs from Cap Martin to Monte-Carlo beach: 4hr on foot there and back (preferably in the afternoon). Park in Avenue Winston-Churchill car park at the seaward end of Cap Martin. A sign "Promenade Le Corbusier" near a restaurant indicates the beginning of the footpath.*

The footpath leads westwards round the headland over the rocks. After several minutes a series of steps and inclines skirts the grounds of private properties through wild and abundant vegetation. Gradually the view takes in Monaco in its natural amphitheatre, Cap Ferrat, Tête de Chien, La Turbie and Mont Agel behind Monaco, and the old village of Roquebrune with its castle.

A flight of steps on the right crossing the railway line provides a shortcut back to Carnolès beach via the town hall.

The coastal footpath continues beside the railway line to Cap Martin-Roquebrune Station above a sheer drop into the sea. Skirting the Cabbé beaches and the Bon Voyage rocks, the path goes on towards Monte-Carlo (rear view to Cap Martin), ending in a flight of steps near the Monte-Carlo Beach Hotel.

There are frequent trains to Carnolès from Monaco or Cap Martin-Roquebrune. There is also a bus which leaves from the St-Roman district of Monte-Carlo.

ROQUEBRUNE-SUR-ARGENS

Population 11 349
Michelin map 84 south of fold 7, 114 fold 24 or 245 fold 36

The small town of Roquebrune, perched on a rocky peak at the foot of the Rocher de Roquebrune, was most likely founded in the early 11C, after the land had been reconquered from the Saracens *(See La GARDE-FREINET)*. Originally a stronghold, the castrum located near the church was enlarged and surrounded by a curtain wall (destroyed in 1592 during the Wars of Religion). Traces of these ramparts are visible, particularly in Boulevard de la Liberté (below the church); houses have been built on their foundations, encompassing the clock tower. At the foot of this tower stands the old fountain (known as the Fontaine Vieille), and opposite is the picturesque Rue des Portiques, lined with houses, some of which go back to the 16C. Inside the fortifications, the narrow, winding streets and two old doorways recall Roquebrune's medieval legacy.

Lively local markets are held on Tuesday and Friday mornings. The delicious Honey Fair takes place in late October.

SIGHTS

Eglise St-Pierre-St-Paul ⊙ – The church was built in the 16C in the Gothic style and features an unusual façade, which was added in the 18C.

Inside, on the left, two chapels – remnants of the 11C building modified in the 14C – have

> **Busy as a bee**
>
> **L'Amie Ailée** – *36 Rue St-Éloi* – ☎ *04 94 45 30 20* – *Wed and Sat, 10am-noon.* Sale of honey, pollen and produce coming from local beehives.

thick quadripartite vaulting with rectangular-shaped diagonal and transverse arches. The first of these two chapels contains a wooden altarpiece (1557) of John the Baptist in high relief flanked by St Claudius and St Bridget of Sweden; while the second chapel houses an altarpiece from the same period depicting the Last Judgement. In the nave, on the right on entering, is a 16C altarpiece composed of six carved panels depicting the Passion around a large crucifix. There are two other 16C painted panels in the gallery; large canvases added in the 19C adorn the chancel and side chapels.

Musée du Patrimoine ⊙ – *Rue de l'Hospice, the continuation of Rue des Portiques.* Located in the old St-Jacques Chapel, the museum houses, for the most part, prehistoric and Roman finds; most of them were excavated in the Bouverie caves (located not far from Roquebrune) which were inhabited continuously from 30 000 to 8 000 BC; this settlement has been identified as **Bouverian** (c 15 000 to 10 000 BC), a culture unique to southeastern France, which corresponds to the Magdalenian culture elsewhere.

Also displayed are fine objects from the Neolithic Era, and remarkable Roman remains, in a reconstruction of a tomb under **tegulae**. In the sacristy there is a collection of ex-votos and historic documents.

A film *(30min)* on flint-cutting and its industry completes the exhibit.

Chapelle St-Pierre – *From Roquebrune take D7 southeast.* The chapel has preserved a Carolingian apse but was rebuilt in the Romanesque style in the 11C, after the Saracen invasion. A recessed tomb has been placed on the façade. The east end is surrounded by an ancient cemetery, the tombs of which were carved into the rock.

DRIVING TOURS

★Rocher de Roquebrune

Round tour of 14km/8.5mi – about 1hr excluding the climb.

Partially covered with cork-oaks, tree ferns and conifers, the proud silhouette of Roquebrune rock forms a small, solitary massif between the Maures and Esterel. Composed of red sandstone compacted and subsequently eroded, the rock forms a jagged silhouette which dominates the lower Argens Valley in a spectacular fashion.

From Roquebrune-sur-Argens take the small road to the south opposite the graveyard.

Chapelle Notre-Dame-de-Pitié – The chapel stands on rising ground amid pine and eucalyptus trees at the foot of a majestic red cliff, one of the first heights of the Maures Massif. Beyond the screen on the high altar stands a 17C retable framing a Pietà similar to a work by Annibale Carracci (in the Louvre in Paris). From the chapel precincts there is a **view**★ of the Argens Plain, Fréjus, St-Raphaël and the Esterel heights.

Return to Roquebrune and turn left onto D 7. After 500m/547yd bear left; 1km/0.5mi further on turn left again onto a forest road. After 2km/1.5mi leave the car where a path branches off to the right.

★ **Roquebrune Summit** – *2hr on foot there and back; a hard walk; keep to the path.* 🚶 From the summit (alt 372m/1 073ft), there is an extended **view**★ of the Maures, the lower Argens Plain, Fréjus Bay, the Esterel and the Alps on the horizon.

At the rock's summit stand three crosses of different shapes, which are the work of the sculptor Vernet. They were placed there in memory of three famous Crucifixions painted by Giotto, Grünewald and El Greco, using the summit of the rock to symbolise Golgotha.

Drive down the south face of Roquebrune rock and turn right onto D 25. After 1km/0.6mi (view of the River Argens) turn right along the north face. The road runs parallel to the motorway. Drive through the hamlet of La Roquette.

Chapelle Notre-Dame-de-la-Roquette – *30min on foot there and back. Leave the car in the car park beside the road and take the path on the right.* 🚶 The ruined chapel, an ancient place of pilgrimage and meeting place for ramblers is located in an attractive **setting**★ of lotus, chestnut and holly trees beside a great rock chaos of red sandstone.

From the terrace (alt 143m/470ft) the **view** includes the lower Argens Valley and the Provençal tableland.

Return to the road; turn right to reach D 7 and Roquebrune-sur-Argens.

SAINT-CYR-SUR-MER 🌣🌣

Population 8 898
Michelin map 84 folds 17 and 18, 114 fold 37 or 245 fold 49
Local map see Massif des MAURES

This seaside resort to which families come in both winter and summer has a sheltered harbour at the far end of a tranquil bay. The lovely beach of fine sand bordering the fertile plain planted with vines and olives and linking Les Lecque with La Madrague, is built at the foot of wooded hills where the coast abruptly changes to rocks and escarpments.

A miniature gilded replica of the Statue of Liberty was erected on Place Portalis in 1901. Those interested in sampling the country's gastronomic riches (fruit, vegetables, charcuterie, cheese etc) may visit the traditional market held on Sunday mornings or the markets offering regional produce that spread out their colourful stalls at La Madrague Port *(Monday and Thursday mornings)*, on Place Gabriel-Péri *(Tuesday and Friday mornings)* and at Les Lecques *(Wednesday and Saturday mornings)*.

Eating out

MODERATE

La Bergerie – *Rue de la Chapelle* – *83270 St-Cyr-sur-Mer* – ☎ *04 94 26 24 69* – *Closed Sun evening and Mon off season.* – *13.42/21.34€*. A rustic note prevails at La Bergerie with its pretty Provençal floor tiles, wooden beams and old-fashioned farming implements adorning whitewashed walls. This friendly restaurant provides unambitious but good food and service.

MID-RANGE

Restaurant La Calanque – *Calanque du Port Alon* – *83270 St-Cyr-sur-Mer* – *5km/3mi S of St-Cyr, towards Bandol and Port Alon* – ☎ *04 94 26 20 08* – *Closed 1 Nov-1 Feb, evenings and Tue Feb-Oct* – *24.23€ lunch* – *24.09/31.86€*. A rocky inlet is the heavenly backcloth to this restaurant serving grilled fish and other Mediterranean delicacies. Relax at the water's edge and have a paddle between courses...

Where to stay

MID-RANGE

Grand Hôtel des Lecques – *Aux Lecques* – *83270 St-Cyr-sur-Mer* – ☎ *04 94 26 23 01* – *Closed 28 Oct-30 Mar* – *58 rooms: half-board 79.15/114.92€* – ☖ *12.20€* – *Restaurant 29/46€*. The paths cutting across the luxuriant park surrounding this hotel are bordered with palms, pine trees and morning glory. A most appealing setting for the formidable 19C mansion. Smiling rooms appointed in Provençal tradition. Outdoor pool.

Chanteplage – *Aux Lecques* – *83270 St-Cyr-sur-Mer* – ☎ *04 94 26 16 55* – *Closed 16 Nov-14 Feb* – *20 rooms: 57.93/73.18€* – ☖ *6.10€* – *Restaurant 15/20€*. This homely establishment facing Les Lecques Bay is also within walking distance of the town. Its rooms enjoy balconies and pretty views all around. The two larger rooms on the third floor have a terrace.

Taking it easy

Beaches – 2 km/1.2mi of sandy beaches line the semi-circular bay running from Les Lecques to La Madrague. Initially narrow and dominated by the seafront promenade, the beach widens out on reaching La Madrague. Further west, *(10min by car)*, the **Calanque de Port-d'Alon**, nestling in a pine forest, affords greater privacy.

Nouveau Port des Lecques – *Port authority* – ☎ *04 94 26 21 98*. 431 moorings.

Port de la Madrague – *Port authority* – ☎ *04 94 26 39 81*. 400 moorings including 37 set aside for tourist traffic.

Golf de Frégate – *D 559* – ☎ *04 94 32 50 50*. Beautiful 18-hole World Class Court and 9-hole model court enjoying pretty views of the sea.

Aqualand – *ZAC des Pradeaux* – ☎ *08 92 68 66 13* – *Jun-Sep daily*. Water park.

Lecques Aquanaut Center – *Nouveau Port des Lecques* – ☎ *04 94 26 42 18*. Diving club.

Musée de Tauroentum ⏱ – *Drive along the coast towards La Madrague.* The museum is built on the foundations of a Roman villa; on display are some wreathed columns with Corinthian capitals from the villa's peristyle and a granite column from a pergola 80m/262ft long which adorned the seafront. The museum also contains three black and white 1C mosaics, fragments of frescoes and amphoras. In the showcases are many Greek and Roman objects: coins, pottery, glass, jewellery and figurines.

Behind the museum a path leads to a pottery tile kiln and remains of houses (walls bearing traces of frescoes). **View** over Les Lecques Bay.

Set up in a nearby former factory in 1993, the **Centre d'Art Sébastien** hosts temporary exhibitions and houses a permanent collection of works painted by the artist Sébastien (1909-1990), who was friends with Picasso, Matisse, Jean Cocteau and André Gide.

EXCURSION

The Coastal Path – *Take D 87 from St-Cyr. Drive along the coast as far as la Madrague. The path begins at Pointe Grenier. It is blazed with yellow trail marks as far as port d'Alon (4.5km/2.7mi) and Bandol (6km/6.6mi farther on).*

🚶 This path from la Madrague to Bandol offers ramblers a chance to enjoy a view of the sea from on high. On the inland side, you can look out over vineyards and if you are a fan of flora, you may sight a local species of violet or mushroom. The walk is not a difficult one, but do wear sturdy shoes and bring along drinking water. Be careful with children as there are some dangerous drop-offs.

ST-MARTIN-VÉSUBIE★

Population 1 098
Michelin map 84 fold 19, 115 fold 6 or 245 fold 25
Local map see NICE

St-Martin-Vésubie, stretched out along a spiny rock between the Boréon and Madone-de-Fenestre streams, and encircled by tall summits, has become an important summer **mountaineering centre** (centre d'alpinisme) ⏱ and, because it is so cool, a highly popular resort. Place du Marché is the setting for local markets held on Tuesdays, Saturdays and Sundays.

DISCOVERING THE VILLAGE

Start from the plane trees in the beautiful square Place Félix-Faure, half way along Allées de Verdun.

Rue du Docteur-Cagnoli – A narrow street bordered by Gothic houses with handsome porches and lintels runs north-south through the town with a gutter down the middle.

Chapelle des Pénitents-Blancs ⏱ – A carved façade, a bulb-shaped bell-tower and, below the altar, a recumbent figure of Christ with cherubs at the four corners holding the instruments of the Passion.

> ### RAMBLERS' DELIGHT
>
> **La Châtaigneraie** – ☎ 04 93 03 21 22 – *Closed Oct-May – 38 rooms: 63.27/69.36€ – ☞ 3.81€ – Restaurant 14/18€.* Pleasant accommodation nestling in a peaceful park, ideal for nature lovers who wish to go climbing or hiking in the Parc du Mercantour, or who simply need a taste of the countryside. Set menu for residents.

Maison des Gubernatis – No 25 at the bottom of the street, the house built over an arcade, once belonged to the Count of Gubernatis.

Place de la Frairie – Turn left into Rue du Plan which leads to Place de la Frairie marked by a fountain.

From the terrace overlooking the Madone de Fenestre Torrent, there is a **view** of the gushing river and the neighbouring mountains, Cime de la Palu and Cime du Piagu.

Go to the church behind the square.

Church – The beautiful decoration dates from the 17C. To the right of the choir is a richly dressed statue of Our Lady of Fenestre – the Madone de Fenestre *(see EXCURSIONS below)*, a 12C seated figure of polychrome wood. On the last Saturday in June it is carried in procession to her mountain sanctuary where it stays until mid-September.

The second chapel in the left-hand aisle houses two panels from an altarpiece attributed to Louis Bréa: St Peter and St Martin on the left, St John and St Petronella on the right. In the third chapel, a beautiful altar to the Rosary in carved and gilded wood: Virgin and Child surrounded by scenes from the life of Christ (17C).

From the terrace a partial **view** of the Boréon Valley and Venanson village below the round wooded Tête du Siruol.

EXCURSIONS

★ **Venanson** – *4.5km/3mi. Leave St-Martin-Vésubie via the bridge over the Boréon and take D 31 south.*
The village square standing on a triangular rocky outcrop 1 164m/3 819ft high commands a good **view**★ of St-Martin, the Vésubie Valley and its mountain setting.

Chapelle St-Sébastien ⏱ – The interior of the chapel is decorated with **frescoes**★ by Baleison. At the far end beneath a Crucifixion, St Sebastian pierced by arrows; on

Parc National du Mercantour

Le Boréon waterfall, St-Martin-Vésubie

the side walls and the ceiling, scenes from the saint's life inspired by the Golden Legend. Another panel takes prayer as its theme. The thoughts of the two figures are revealed by the direction of the lines from their faces; the one on the left sees only the wounds of Christ whom he adores while the one on the right concentrates on his house and his wealth which appear behind him.

Parish church – On the left of the entrance is a triptych of the Virgin and Child, flanked by St John and St Petronella. At the high altar is a Baroque altarpiece (1645) of the Coronation of the Virgin featuring the donor. On the right stands an altarpiece of the Rosary.

★★ **Le Boréon** – *8km/5mi. From St-Martin-Vésubie take D 2565 north up the west bank of Le Boréon.*
The resort stands on a superb site (1 500m/4 201ft) on the southern edge of the Parc National du Mercantour *(see Introduction)* by the **Cascade du Boréon**★ where the river drops 40m/130ft down a narrow gorge; above the waterfall a small lake adds its calm beauty to the green landscape of pasture and woodland.
Le Boréon is the starting place for walks in the forest, up to the high peaks and mountain lakes. One can drive by car to the Vacherie du Boréon *(2.5km/1.5mi to the east)* beneath the distinctive silhouette of La Cougourde. There is also a road running west along the southern edge of the park for 4km/2.5mi up Salèse Valley.

Vallon de la Madone de Fenestre – *12km/7.5mi east – about 30min. From St-Martin take Avenue de Saravalle (northeast on the plan). Turn right onto D 94.*
The road climbs rapidly up the Madone Valley between Cime du Piagu and Cime de la Palu, crossing and re-crossing the river. A fine forest of pines and larches rises out of heavy undergrowth before giving way to high mountain pastures.

Madone de Fenestre – The road ends in a rugged rock **cirque**★★ much appreciated by mountaineers. Caïre de la Madone, huge and pointed, rises nearby; the slopes of **Cime du Gélas** (3 143m/10 312ft), covered with frozen snow, dominate the northern horizon on the Italian border.
There are pilgrimages to the chapel ⏱ on the last Saturday in June, 26 July, 15 August and 8 September. During the summer it houses the statue of Our Lady of Fenestre which returns to St-Martin-Vésubie in solemn procession around mid-September.

VALLÉE DE LA VÉSUBIE AND VALLÉE DE LA TINÉE

★★ **The Road to Valdeblore** – *29km/18mi – about 2hr 15min – local map see NICE*

The road linking the valleys of the Tinée and the upper Vésubie passes through the Valdeblore district, a region of green pastures and wooded slopes high in the mountains.
A memory of one of the lords of Valdeblore, a sort of Bluebeard character, survives in the place names of the region. The sufferings of the monster's wives, who were incarcerated and left to die of hunger, have given rise to Valdeblore (*Val de Pleurs* = vale of tears) and Bramafan (*Crie la Faim* = cry of hunger).
From St-Martin Vésubie take D 2565.

A Mountaineering Pioneer on the Riviera

The Chevalier Victor de Cessole (1859-1940), a member of an old Nice family, took to climbing late in life and in an unusual manner. When his doctor recommended exercise and fresh air, he enrolled in the new Club Alpin Français when he was already in his thirties. His first contact with the high mountains at Madone de Fenestre awakened a passion for walking in the Alps.
He became a compulsive mountaineer, climbing successively the highest peaks in the Alpes-Maritimes (Mont Clapier, Mont Gélas) and setting several records in the Massif de l'Argentera. His recommended walks, described in illustrated brochures, are forerunners of the guide books of today. His activities earned him the presidency of the Club Alpin Français, a position which he held for 40 years, and enabled him to inaugurate and organise the chain of mountain refuges. In 1901 he opened the Nice refuge above Madone de Fenestre. He initiated the first skiing competitions and is considered to be the founder, in spirit at least, of Beuil, the oldest resort in the area. His interest in nature led him to establish the first measures for the protection of wildlife in the region – the banning of the picking of *Saxifraga florulenta*, now the emblem of the Parc du Mercantour. His extensive collection of books and papers, acquired during his research, and his interest in the local heritage are now contained in the De Cessole library, bequeathed to the Musée Masséna in Nice.

D. Faure/SCOPE

Via Ferrata du Baus de la Frema, La Colmiane

The road climbs north up the valley and overlooks the villages of St-Martin and Venanson. Just before the tunnel, there is a fine **view★** back down to the Vésubie Valley and St-Martin, up the Madone Valley and north to the Boréon.

La Colmiane – A ski resort in the Col St-Martin (alt 1 500m/4 921ft) consisting of chalets and hotels dotted among the larches and pines.

At Col St-Martin turn left onto a narrow road which leads to the chair-lift.

★★Pic de La Colmiane – *Chair-lift to the summit* ⊘ *.* From the top there is an immense **panorama★★**: south over Mont Tournairet, the Vésubie Valley and Turini Forest; east over the Mercantour chain; north and west over the Baus de la Frema to Mont Mounier with Valdeblore in the foreground.

★Via Ferrata du Baus de la Frema – *At the col turn right opposite the mini-golf (sign "Via Ferrata"). There is plenty of space to park on the way up*

the slope. The Via Ferrata begins at the end of the car park, after the information sign.

Equipment can be hired at the sports shop "Igloo Sport" at the pass. A guide to the facilities is available from the tourist office in Valdeblore.

This new development, directly accessible by car, offers ideal facilities for learning rock-climbing and overcoming vertigo. There are three routes graded blue, red and black according to their difficulty. The first course takes at least 1hr 30min. Those looking for big thrills will particularly enjoy crossing the footbridge (35m/115ft long; 50m/164ft above ground level) which links the two rocky peaks of the Aiguillettes.

Beyond the pass the road enters a green gulley, the highest part of the Valdeblore

St-Dalmas-de-Valdeblore – The Romanesque **church** ⊘ is striking with its pyramidal Alpine-style bell-tower, its stout buttresses and Lombard bands on the chevet. The church is built on the basilica plan over a pre-Romanesque groin-vaulted crypt. The interior was vaulted in the 17C to hide the original roof.

The Return of the Bearded Vulture

The bearded vulture, a magnificent bird with a huge wingspan (2.8m/9.6ft) is an example of a European endangered species. Its numbers were greatly reduced in the 19C in the Alps, although it survives in the Pyrenees and Corsica. The bearded vulture, which is the largest Alpine bird, has a curious way of life; alternating between soaring flight and perilous aerobatics, it flies over the steep, sloping pastures looking for the carcasses of chamois and sheep from which it takes the large bones (up to 3kg/6.6lb). It then drops the bones from a great height onto rocks in order to shatter them, hence their nickname of "bone-breaker" *(casseur d'os)*. It used to be looked on as the natural assistant of the shepherd.

The reintroduction of bearded vultures as chicks into the Parc du Mercantour (at Roubion) in 1993 was crowned with success. It takes eight years for the birds to reach maturity after which they can live for 40 years.

In 1996 five birds were released in the southern Alps and 60 throughout the Alps in an extensive international reintroduction programme, the only one of its kind.

Above the high altar there is a polyptych by Guillaume Planeta of St Dalmas, St Roch and the Evangelists; on the predella the Adoration of the Shepherds and the Wise Men. In the north aisle is an altarpiece of St Francis attributed to André de Cella. Behind an altarpiece of the Rosary (17C) in the south apsidal chapel are the partial remains of some very old frescoes: the history of John the Baptist and Christ in Majesty on the vault.

The road looks down on the Bramafan Valley and passes through La Roche at the foot of a grey rock spur.

La Bolline – The town, which is the administrative centre of the Valdeblore district, makes a pleasant summer resort surrounded by chestnut woods which contrast with the Bois Noir (Black Forest) on the opposite slope.

West of La Bolline turn right onto D 66.

Rimplas – The curious **site**★ of the village on a rib of rock (1 000m/3 281ft high) is very striking. From the chapel, dedicated to Mary Magdalene, at the edge of the ridge below the fort, there is an extensive **view**★ of the Tinée Valley, Bramafan Valley and the Valdeblore villages.

For an easy route back to St-Sauveur-sur-Tinée, take the path (GR 5) down to the northwest of the village.

To reach the confluence of the Valdeblore and the Tinée return to D 2565, turn right; after 7km/4mi turn right onto D 2205.

ST-PAUL★★

Population 2 847
Michelin map 84 fold 9 and 18, 115 fold 25 or 245 fold 37

The tapering outline of St-Paul stands out from afar above the rolling hills and rich valleys of the Vence countryside in a charming **setting**★. It is typical of the fortified towns which once guarded the Var frontier. Set on a spur, behind ramparts which have remained more or less intact (it continued its defensive military activities until 1870), it has kept much of its medieval appearance, while becoming one of the most popular holiday destinations in France.
After a period of prosperity in the Middle Ages, the village declined in the last century to the benefit of Vence and Cagnes. It was "rediscovered" in the 1920s by painters such as Signac, Modigliani, Bonnard and Soutine who used to meet in a café which has since become the sumptuous Auberge de la Colombe d'Or, its walls covered with paintings as in a gallery. Other artists were to follow suit – sculptors, illustrators, writers and entertainers – making St-Paul a famous Riviera landmark. The village is also a great favourite among celebrities from the silver screen, namely the famous and sadly missed couple Simone Signoret and Yves Montand.

TREADING THE MEDIEVAL ALLEYS

Park the car in one of the car parks provided at the entrance to the village, before passing through the north gate; the protruding muzzle belongs to a cannon captured at the Battle of Cérisoles (1544). A square machicolated tower houses the Tourist Information Centre *(Syndicat d'Initiative)* together with a permanent exhibition of modern paintings.

Rue Grande – Rue Grande is the main street (closed to traffic) running the full length of the village. Many of the arcaded 16C and 17C houses bearing coats of arms are now artists' studios, antique shops and art and craft galleries. The urn-shaped **fountain** with its vaulted washing place in the square is of particular interest.

Climb up the stepped street above the fountain. Take the first right and then the first left to the church.

Church – Gothic building constructed from the 12C to the 13C; the vaulting was rebuilt in the 17C and the bell-tower in the 18C. The nave and two aisles are divided by massive pillars and contain several works of art. At the end of the north aisle hangs a painting attributed to Tintoretto of St Catherine of Alexandria in a magnificent red cloak, sword in hand.

E. Baret/MICHELIN

Fountain in Rue Grande, St Paul-de-Vence

Eating out

MODERATE

Chez Andréas – *Western ramparts* – ☎ *04 93 32 98 32* – *17/20€*. Settle on the delightful terrace of this restaurant and sip a *pastis* as you admire the setting rays of the sun... The tastefully decorated dining room serves salads, the day's special and a choice of local wines.

MID-RANGE

La Cocarde de Saint Paul – *23 Rue Grande* – ☎ *04 93 32 86 17* – *22/30€*. In the main street at the heart of St-Paul, this restaurant-tea shop will seduce you by its artful blend of Mediterranean colours. Excellent cuisine and home-made pastries.

La Ferme de St-Paul – *1334 Route de la Colle* – ☎ *04 93 32 82 48* – *26.68/45.73€*. Tastefully restored old farmhouse boasting a superb decor: Provençal overtones, wooden beams, mahogany furniture, wrought-iron accessories and fine crockery. Quality cooking and interesting menu, where fish has pride of place. Charming terrace and antique shop set up in the outbuildings.

Where to stay

MODERATE

Hostellerie Les Remparts – *72 Rue Grande* – ☎ *04 93 32 09 88* – *h.remparts@wanadoo.fr* – ▯ – *9 rooms: 38.11/79.27€* – ☕ *6.86€* – *Restaurant 24€*. Handsome hostelry restored with great taste, featuring stone walls, period furniture, hexagonal floor tiling and warm colours. Each room is named after a flower; the larger ones offers pretty views of the surrounding countryside.

MID-RANGE

Chambre d'Hôte La Bastide de St-Donat – *Route du Pont de Pierre, Parc St-Donat* – *06480 La Colle-sur-Loup* – *2km/1.2mi S of St-Ptol by D 6* – ☎ *04 93 32 93 41* – ✉ – *5 rooms: 60.98/91.47€*. The 1850 stone façade of this old sheep barn is deceptive.. Step inside and you will be astonished by the lavish decoration. The handsomely restored rooms boast visible beams, antique furniture and low-key colours. You will succumb to the charm of the terrace, lulled by the gentle babbling of the nearby stream.

LUXURY

Hostellerie des Messugues – *Quartier des Gardettes, by Route de la Fondation Maeght: 2km/1.2mi* – ☎ *04 93 32 53 32* – *Closed Oct-Mar* – *15 rooms: 76.22/106.71€* – ☕ *8.38€*. Just below the Maeght Foundation, in a lush and peaceful garden, lies this big Provençal villa surrounded by vines. The upstairs rooms are larger and slightly more comfortable. Do not miss the pool and its small island planted with banana trees.

Tennis

Tennis Club des Serres – *56 Chemin de Rome* – ☎ *04 93 32 85 09* – *Daily*. Exclusive clay court tennis court offering nice views of the nearby valley and sea. Highly reasonable rates.

The best café in town

Café de la Place – *Place du Général-de-Gaulle* – ☎ *04 93 32 80 03* – *Jul-Aug: daily 8am-1am; rest of the year: daily 8am-8pm*. This café, set up on the main square where villagers like to congregate and play *pétanque*, is at the heart of life in Saint-Paul. It belongs to the legendary Colombe d'Or Hotel (located opposite), once the property of the actor Yves Montand, and has welcomed many a celebrity in its time, notably Picasso and Prévert.

The choir stalls are 17C carved walnut.

The south transept chapel is particularly noteworthy for its ornate stucco decoration; before the altar a low relief depicting the martyrdom of St Clement; above the altar a 17C Italian canvas of St Charles Borromeo; on the left, an Assumption from the Murillo School.

The next chapel is adorned with a Madonna of the Rosary (1588) with Catherine de' Medici featured among the crowd. The Stations of the Cross are modern although painted in tempera, a 16C technique.

The **treasury** in the side aisle is rich in 12C to 15C pieces – statuettes, ciborium, processional cross, reliquaries and, in particular, a 13C enamel Virgin and Child – all of which testify to the skill of Provençal craftsmen. There is also a parchment signed by King Henri III.

Donjon – The **keep** opposite the church currently houses the town hall.

Return to Rue Grande and continue down to the south gate.

★ **Ramparts** – From the bastion of the south gate, overlooking the cemetery, there is a superb **view** of the Alps, the sea (Cap d'Antibes) and the Esterel.
The ramparts remain much as they were when built (1537-47) by François I in response to the challenge of the Citadel of Nice. Follow them round anti-clockwise using the parapet walk where possible; it commands good views both of the orange trees and flower fields in the valley and the hills and mountains inland.

SIGHTS

★★ **Fondation Maeght** ⊙ – This modern art museum is located northwest of St-Paul in a pine wood on a hill, the Colline des Gardettes.
Using white concrete and rose-coloured bricks the architect **José Luis Sert** has created an architectural complex in the true Mediterranean style.
Incorporated into the enclosure wall is a mosaic by Tal-Coat; in the park the visitor is greeted by a Calder stabile, as well as mobiles, sculpture, a bronze by Zadkine, Arp's *Giant Pip* and a fountain by Pol Bury. In another garden stands the Labyrinth with sculpture and ceramics by Miró and in the chapel of St-Bernard are stained-glass windows by Ubac and Braque; the Stations of the Cross are the work of Ubac. A Braque mosaic forms the backdrop to a pond while another by Chagall decorates the external wall of the bookshop.
The **museum** consists of two buildings divided by a court peopled with sculptures by Giacometti. The collection of modern art is exhibited in rotation in specially designed rooms: canvases, sculpture, ceramics and drawings by Braque, Chagall, Léger, Kandinsky, Miró, Giacometti, Bonnard, Bazaine, Hartung, Tapiès, Alechinsky etc as well as works by several artists belonging to the younger generation (Adami, Garache, Messagier, Viallat).
The Foundation organises annual exhibitions. In summer, during the temporary exhibitions, the permanent collection is not displayed.

Musée d'Histoire Locale ⊙ – *Place de la Castre*. This museum offers an interesting account of the village's history. Eight illustrated scenes with life-size figures depict the stages marking its development, which often mirror those of Provence itself.
The tour begins with a scene illustrating the arrival of the Count of Provence, Raimond Bérenger V, in St-Paul in 1224. Subsequent scenes include the visit of Queen Jeanne, then that of François I during the "Truce of Nice" *(see VILLEFRANCHE)*. A visit by Vauban was instrumental in integrating the village into the defensive system guarding the border. Finally, there are local scenes of the war between the French republicans and the Austro-Sardinian alliance.
An exhibition of photographs of famous people who have stayed in St-Paul adds a contemporary note to this historical display.

ST-RAPHAËL★

Population 30 671
Michelin map 84 fold 8, 114 fold 25, 115 fold 33 or 245 fold 36
Local map see Massif de l'ESTEREL

St-Raphaël, a fashionable summer and winter resort situated on Fréjus Bay, has a well-sheltered beach at the foot of the Esterel. The anchorage is deep enough for warships; the old harbour is used by fishing boats and trading vessels; a double marina, including **Santa Lucia**, southeast of the town can accommodate up to 1 800 pleasure craft.
Markets are held every day on Place de la République and Place Victor-Hugo. The old port serves as a picturesque backdrop to the local fish market.

HISTORICAL NOTES

Origins – St-Raphaël, like Fréjus, is a daughter of Rome. A Gallo-Roman holiday resort stood on the site now occupied by the large Casino. It was built in terraces decorated with mosaics, and included thermal baths and a vivarium (fish reserve). At that period rich Romans came here to take the sea air.
In the Middle Ages the villas were plundered by Saracen pirates. After their expulsion (end of the 10C), the Count of Provence left these deserted lands to the abbeys of Lérins and St-Victor in Marseille. The monks built a village round the church. In the 12C its defence was entrusted to the Templars. In the 18C the

ST-RAPHAËL

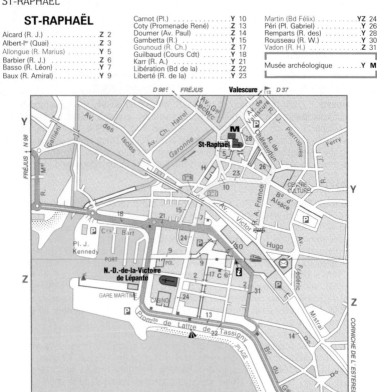

fishermen and peasants who lived in St-Raphaël occupied what are now the old quarters; marsh fever so weakened the inhabitants that they became known in the region as "pale faces".

After Corsica was united with France in 1768, the port of St-Raphaël became the terminus for a short-lived sea link with the island, also known as the Île de Beauté.

Bonaparte in St-Raphaël – On 9 October 1799 the small village was suddenly brought into the limelight when Bonaparte, returning from Egypt, landed there after a voyage of 48 days (a pyramid standing in Avenue Commandant-Guilbaud commemorates this event).

In 1814 St-Raphaël received Napoleon once again, this time as a defeated man leaving for Elba, his new and minute kingdom.

Two Men who Developed the Resort: Alphonse Karr and Félix Martin – Alphonse Karr (1808-90) was an extravagant personality who used his talents as journalist and pamphleteer to oppose Napoleon III from Nice where he was in exile. His horticultural interests led him to settle in St-Raphaël in 1864 in a villa named "Maison Close". Writing to one of his Parisian friends, he said: "Leave Paris and plant your stick in my garden: the next morning, when you awake, you will see that it has grown roses." Writers and artists responded to his invitation: Alexandre Dumas, Maupassant, Berlioz, Gounod.

Félix Martin, local mayor and civil engineer, followed Karr's lead and transformed the village into a smart resort, encouraging building and linking St-Raphaël with Hyères (then an expanding resort) by means of a small railway along the coast. Martin engaged the architect Pierre Audlé, who left his mark on the design of the resort.

Illustrious guests marked their stay in St-Raphaël with works of art: Gounod composed *Roméo et Juliette* there in 1869, Scott Fitzgerald wrote *Tender is the Night* in Saint-Raphaël and Félix Ziem painted some of his pictures there.

THE RESORT

The original town centre consists of an important and quite rare collection of sea-side architecture dating from the beginning of the Third Republic.

Seafront – There is bustling activity on the waterfront by the old harbour stimulated by the cafés and shops which line the broad pavement of Cours Jean-Bart and Quai Albert-Ier.

Eating out

MODERATE

La Sarriette – *45 Rue de la République – ☏ 04 94 19 28 13 – Closed 22-30 Dec, Sun evening and Wed – 10.52/13.42€.* Away from the crowded beaches, a stone's throw from Marché de la République, the pretty terrace of this colourful house is sheltered by a large plane tree. Inexpensive, unsophisticated cooking with a Provençal touch served in two homely dining rooms.

MID-RANGE

Pastorel – *54 Rue de la Liberté – ☏ 04 94 95 02 36 – Closed 14-21 May, Nov, for lunch in Aug, Sun evening and Mon – 25.92/32.01€.* If you are looking for a quiet and friendly restaurant away from the lively town centre, this place is definitely for you. Tuck into Provençal specialities, seated in the shade of an arbour on a pretty terrace.

Where to stay

MODERATE

Hôtel Bellevue – *22 Boulevard Félix-Martin – ☏ 04 94 19 90 10 – 🅿 – 20 rooms: 44.97€ – ⚏ 3.81€.* Homey, unpretentious establishment ideally situated between the beach and the casino. The air-conditioned, soundproofed rooms are decorated simply. Comparatively low prices for the area.

LUXURY

Sol e Mar – *Route de la Corniche-d'Or – 83530 Agay – 6km/3.6mi from St-Raphël by N 98 – ☏ 04 94 95 25 60 – Closed 16 Oct-6 Apr – 46 rooms: 83.85/117.39€ – ⚏ 7.62€ – Restaurant 23/35€.* This 1960 hotel facing the sea arranges its beach mattresses in its solarium or around one of the outdoor pools filled with seawater. Almost all the rooms give onto the îles d'Or and Cap Dramont.

On the town

There are numerous activities for all ages in St-Raphaël and its neighbouring city Fréjus: casino, golf, water sports... Nightlife too offers interesting prospects thanks to the many bars, restaurants, discotheques and ice-cream parlours!

Casino de St-Raphaël – *Square Gand – ☏ 04 98 11 17 77 – Jul-Aug: daily 10am-5am; rest of the year: 10am-4am.* The casino was built on the site of a Roman villa in 1881. It has over 100 fruit machines and offers tradition gambling facilities. Piano bar music every evening.

Theatre and concert hall

Palais des Congrès – *Port de Plaisance de Santa-Lucia – ☏ 04 98 11 89 00 – Check the programme of events.* This conference centre hosts a variety of activities including a wide selection of theatrical plays, ballets and classical music concerts.

Golf

Golf de Valescure – *Avenue des Golfs – ☏ 04 94 82 40 46 – Jul-Aug: daily 8am-8pm; May-Jun and Sep-Oct: 8am-7pm; Nov-Apr: 8am-5pm.* Fine 18-hole golf course complemented by a hotel, a bar and a restaurant set up in a delightful house.

Circus school

École de Cirque – *Cap Esterel Village – ☏ 04 94 82 58 12 – capesterel.com – Mon-Sun 9am-noon, 4-6pm.* Professional circus performers will share the secrets of their juggling acts or will introduce you to the perilous art of the trapeze, the tightrope and the trampoline. Lessons by the hour or intensive courses available.

Under Scottish influence

The Lock Ness – *15 Avenue de Valescure – ☏ 04 94 95 99 49 – Daily 7am-1am; school holidays: 7am-4am.* This tastefully decorated pub with a strong Scottish touch is one of the finest in the area. Impressive choice of draught beers.

Transport

Boat rides to St-Tropez *(50min there and back)* leaving from the old port are available for 16.77€. 5 departures in high season and 2 departures in low season (except Fri). For details apply to the boat harbour at ☏ 04 94 95 17 46. You can also take part in excursions to the Esterel Massif or the îles de Lérins.

From beneath the palms and plane trees of Promenade René-Coty and Avenue du Général-de-Gaulle, there is a fine **view** of the sea and the twin rocks known as the Land Lion and the Sea Lion. The road follows the coast eastwards to the marina with its terraces, shops and restaurants.

Villas – During the redevelopment of the residential area between Promenade René-Coty and Rue Alphonse-Karr many of the exotically decorated villa façades were lost. Among those remaining in Promenade René-Coty is the Villa Roquerousse (1900) with its lavish ornamentation; there are also several characteristic façades still standing in Boulevard Félix-Martin: the charming oriental Villa Sémiramis, Villa Paquerettes decorated with ceramics; a little further on the shadow of Gounod still haunts *"l'Oustelet dou Capelan"* ("The Priest's House" in Provençal).
Both Plateau Notre-Dame and St-Sébastien hill are full of remarkable villas and the Palladian inspiration of their designers is evident in the arrangement of the gardens and the flights of stairs.

Notre-Dame-de-la-Victoire-de-Lépante – This original **church**, in neo-Byzantine style, was built in 1883 by Pierre Aublé, the architect of many of the villas in St-Raphaël. The church was named by its creator who came from Greece.

Quartier de Valescure – This district, on the right bank of the Garonne, was once much patronised by foreign visitors. The director of the Paris Opera in 1880, Carvalho, laid out, with advice from Charles Garnier, a park decorated with vestiges from the Palais des Tuileries in Paris. At the crossroads of Rue Allongue and Rue Maréchal-Leclerc there is a fountain, a remnant of the extravagances of the period, which also came from the Tuileries.

Église St-Pierre-des-Templiers – This church, built in the 12C in the Romanesque-Provençal style, served as a fortress and a refuge for the population in the event of attack by pirates. The watchtower, which tops one of the apsidal chapels, brings to mind the military constructions of the Templars.
In one of the side chapels a red sandstone monolith, once a pagan altar, now supports the altar table. The gilded wooden bust of St Peter is carried by the fishermen in procession to the Sea Lion in August.
Near the church are fragments of a Roman aqueduct which brought water to St-Raphaël.

SIGHT

North of the railway station, the old town, once surrounded by ramparts, extends beyond the Hôtel de Ville. There are still ramparts to be seen in Rue Allongue and in the gardens of the Musée Archéologique; Rue des Remparts follows their original course.

Musée Archéologique ⊙ – This Archeology Museum profits from the fact that St-Raphaël was situated at a crossroads for major land (Via Aurelia) and sea routes (between Massalia and the western Mediterranean) and is thus endowed with a rich heritage of archeological remains dating from Antiquity.
The rooms on the ground floor display a remarkable collection of **amphorae★**, dating from the 5C BC to the 5C AD. There is also an interesting reconstruction of the loading of a Roman galley. In the garden, there is a milestone dating from 3 BC which was found on Cap Roux. A gallery of technology contains a display on the evolution of scuba diving equipment and underwater photography, as well as on the process of preserving wood under water.
On the second floor, two rooms are given over to the finds from the excavation of prehistoric sites in the Esterel which date from the Paleolithic Era to the Bronze Age.

ST-TROPEZ★★

Population 5 444
Michelin map 84 fold 17, 114 fold 37 or 245 fold 49
Local map see Massif des MAURES

On the southern shore of one of the most beautiful bays of the Riviera, facing Ste-Maxime and separated on the east from the elegant bay of Cannébiers by a promontory topped by a citadel, the little port of St-Tropez has become one of the best-known resorts in Europe, a crossroads where journalists and photographers, writers, artists and celebrities all meet.

HISTORICAL NOTES

The Legend of St Tropez – Tropez (Torpes), a Christian centurion beheaded in his native Pisa by order of Emperor Nero, was placed in a boat with his head beside him and cast adrift with a cock and a dog who were meant to devour his remains, which however they left intact. The boat is supposed to have drifted ashore where St-Tropez now stands.

Republic of St-Tropez (15C-17C) – In 1470 the Grand Seneschal of Provence accepted the offer of a Genoese gentleman, Raffaele de Garezzio, to settle in St-Tropez together with 60 Genoese families, which had been destroyed by war at the end of the 14C. De Garezzio undertook to rebuild and defend the town provided it was freed of all taxes. The town was quick to prosper.
St-Tropez became a sort of small republic administered by the heads of the families and, later, by two consuls and 12 councillors who were elected.

Judge Suffren (18C) – Pierre André de Suffren was born in 1729 in St-Cannat in Provence. He first served in the Order of Malta, where he earned his title of judge (*bailli*), and then in the French Navy. His career advanced slowly; at 55 he was still only a captain. Appointed in 1781 to command five ships being sent as a reinforcement to the Indies, Suffren sailed from Brest with his fellow Provençal, Count de Grasse (*see Le BAR-SUR-LOUP*), with whom he parted company at the Azores.
Then he embarked on an amazing campaign, which went on for two years from the Cape Verde Islands to the Cape of Good Hope, from La Réunion to Ceylon, from Sumatra to Madras. When the Treaty of Versailles was signed in 1783, Suffren, by then an Admiral, had to return. He died in 1788 at the age of 59 from an unfortunate bloodletting. A statue has been raised in his honour on the quay in St-Tropez.

The "Bravades" – Two *bravades* or "acts of defiance" take place every year.
The first of these acts, a simple religious procession in honour of St Tropez, has maintained its local importance since the end of the 15C. On 16 and 17 May the gilded wooden statue of St Tropez is carried through the town escorted by the town captain, elected by the municipal council, and the corps of *bravadeurs*. Strangers flock to witness this colourful tradition.
The second act has a page of local history as its origin. On 15 June 1637, 22 Spanish galleys, attempting to take the town by surprise and to make off with four of the king's ships anchored in the port, were forced to flee in the face of the energetic defence offered by the St-Tropez militia.

St-Tropez

S. Sauvignier/MICHELIN

A Popular Resort among Intellectuals – At the turn of the century St-Tropez was a charming little village unknown to tourists and poorly served by a narrow-gauge branch line. In the harbour tartans (single-masted sailing vessels) laden with sand and wine were moored beside the fishing boats. It was then that Maupassant discovered it. The painters who followed Signac's example were the ones to make it more widely known *(see below)*. Between the two World Wars Colette, who used to spend the winter here, contributed to its fame. Other famous residents included politicians, the couturier Paul Poiret and later Jean Cocteau.
From the 1950s St-Tropez became the fashion with the literary set from St-Germain-des-Prés in Paris and then with the cinema people, together with their fans, and so became internationally famous.

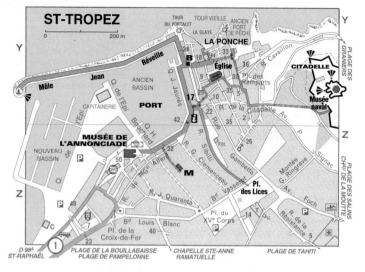

In season, pedestrian area in the old town

ENJOYING YOUR STAY

★★ Harbour – The harbour teems with life. The fishing boats, commercial vessels and excursion craft share the mooring with a crowd of yachts – from the most humble to the most luxurious. On the waterfront and in the neighbouring streets the old pink and yellow houses have been converted into cafés and pastry shops, cabarets and restaurants, luxury boutiques, galleries and antique shops. In season a picturesque and cosmopolitan crowd strolls beneath the bronze effigy of Suffren.

Beaches – The beaches around Saint-Tropez are truly heavenly, with their fine sand and charming rocky creeks. The nearest is Bouillabaisse beach *(1km/0.6mi by D 98ᴬ, ① on the plan)*. To the east of the town lies **Graniers beach** *(access from Rue Cavaillon)*. Further east round the headland is **Les Salins beach** *(4.5km/2.8mi on Avenue Foch)*. But by far the most appealing and also the most fashionable are the **Pampelonne beaches**, well-sheltered from the *mistral* winds. Cannebiers Bay affords glimpses of the superb villas belonging to the rich and the famous: La Hune (Paul Signac), La Treille Muscate (Colette) and La Madrague (Brigitte Bardot).

STROLLING THROUGH ST-TROPEZ

★★ Môle Jean-Réveille – The attractive **panorama★** from the top of the jetty includes all of St-Tropez – Portalet tower, the harbour, the town and its commanding citadel; the head of the bay, Grimaud and its castle ruins; Beauvallon; Ste-Maxime; Cap des Sardinaux; Issambres Point; Dramont headland; Cap Roux summit and, in the distance, the Esterel and in fine weather, the Alps.

La Ponche Quarter – Turn right at the seaward end of Quai Jean-Jaurès onto Place de l'Hôtel-de-Ville; on the left stands the massive **Château de Suffren des Seigneurs de St-Tropez**. Turn left beyond the Hôtel de Ville to reach the bay of La Glayel; Rue de la Ponche leads through the old gateway to a beach overlooked by the Vieille Tour (old tower) where the fishing boats ride at anchor: two typical districts which have attracted painters.

Retrace your steps, turning left into Rue du Commandant-Guichard.

Church – The 19C edifice is in the Italian-Baroque style; the bell-tower is crowned with wrought-iron work. The interior contains some finely carved woodwork and to the left of the high altar, a bust of St Tropez, and, laid around it like a tribute of votive offerings, several old blunderbusses which exploded without hurting anyone during a *bravade*. At Christmas a beautiful 19C Provençal crib with figures in traditional costume adorns the church.

MID-RANGE

Régis Restaurant – *19 Rue de la Citadelle* – ☎ *04 94 97 15 53 – Closed 10 Oct-1 Apr* – 🍴 – *19/30€*. Pasta in all shapes and sizes, cooked in various ways, attract a regular clientele to this restaurant located on a steep, narrow street in St-Tropez. The food is served on the terrace or inside one of the small dining areas decorated in white.

La Cantina el Mexicano – *16 Rue des Remparts* – ☎ *04 94 97 40 96 – Closed Nov to Mar and for lunch* – *24/34€*. After sipping your tequila, savour generous helpings of Mexican cuisine in this typical setting characterised by religious statues, painted wood furnishings and vases. Even the bathroom warrants a visit! Youngish clientele. Friendly, relaxed ambience.

Leï Salins – *Plage des Salins* – ☎ *04 94 97 04 40 – www.lei-salins.com – Closed 15 Oct-31 Mar* – *30/50€*. Open-air beach restaurant offering a tasty bill of fare consisting of salads and grilled, freshly caught fish. Charming seaside location coupled with attractive surroundings.

LUXURY

La Table du Marché – *38 Rue Georges-Clemenceau* – ☎ *04 94 97 85 20 – www.christophe-leroy.com – Closed 15 Nov-6 Apr* – *38.11/53.36€*. Gourmets will love this temple of gastronomy located near Place des Lices, open at all hours of the day. In addition to the restaurant offering traditional French cuisine, there is a Japanese restaurant upstairs and a tea room for mid-afternoon snacks. La Table du Marché is also known for its homemade pastries that can be purchased on the premises: croissants, cakes and the legendary *gendarme de St-Tropez* – mouthwatering chocolate mousse in the shape of a policeman's cap filled with vanilla crème brûlée. Who can resist?

Leï Mouscardins – *Port (Tour du Portalet)* – ☎ *04 94 97 29 00 – Closed Nov to Feb, for lunch in Jul-Aug and Wed Sep-May* – *57.93€*. Tucked away behind the harbour, near Tour du Portalet, this restaurant pays homage to Mediterranean tradition. It has a faithful following of gourmets, lured by its creative and lovingly prepared cuisine, presented to you in two dining rooms opening out onto St-Tropez Bay.

Where to stay

MID-RANGE

Hôtel Lou Cagnard – *Avenue P.-Roussel* – ☎ *04 94 97 04 24 – Closed 6 Nov-27 Dec* – *19 rooms: 47.26/89.94€* – ☕ *6.86€*. Enjoy breakfast seated in the shade of a mulberry tree, in a tiny garden just off Place des Lices, in a pretty Provençal house, lulled by the chirping of cicadas... Highly reasonable prices for St-Tropez.

LUXURY

Hôtel Sube – *15 Quai Suffren* – ☎ *04 94 97 30 04 – Closed Jan* – *28 rooms: 90/230€* – ☕ *9.91€*. Conveniently located near the trendy night spots, this is the only hotel facing the boats in the former harbour. Homely rooms decorated in Provençal tradition. The big English-style bar upstairs is appointed with a fireplace and leather armchairs and is adorned with a great many photographs of yachts.

Bastide des Salins – *4km/ 2.4mi SE of St-Tropez* – ☎ *04 94 97 24 57 – Closed 11 Oct-31 Mar* – *14 rooms: 213.43/335.39€* – ☕ *10.67€*. You will be greeted like friends of the family at this old Provençal house surrounded by extensive leafy grounds. Barely 5 minutes from Place des Lices and yet totally isolated, this hotel offers large rooms decorated in the Provençal spirit, appointed with great simplicity.

Hôtel Ponche – *Place Révelin* – ☎ *04 94 97 02 53 – Closed 5 Nov-31 Mar* – *18 rooms: 213.43/304.90€* – ☕ *15.24€ – Restaurant 30/38€*. The rooms of this cosy hotel occupy four village houses formerly belonging to fishermen; the blue one was a favourite of Romy Scneider's. You will be under the charm of the rooftop terraces nestling between the citadel and the bell-tower. The warm, generous hues and considerate service make the Hôtel Ponche an absolute must.

Hôtel Byblos – *Avenue Paul-Signac* – ☎ *04 94 56 68 00 – Closed mid-Oct to mid-Apr* – *76 rooms: 320.14/762.25€* – ☕ *21.34€*. This hotel, which caters for the needs of millionnaires, stars and trend-setters, is designed like a village, offering a kaleidoscope of colours, patios and small courtyards. This is the place to be: relaxing by the pool, chatting with friends in the restaurant or dancing the night away at the famous discotheque "Les Caves du Roy" *(see below)*.

On the town

Saint-Tropez has two facets. In summer, it is a town for the rich and wealthy and is given over to sailing, bathing, entertainment and nightlife. However, in winter, it looks more like a ghost town. Indeed, most business close down between November and April and the swinging bars, restaurants and hotels that have made the reputation of St-Tropez are completely deserted.

Bar du Château de la Messardière – *Route de Tahiti* – ☎ *04 94 56 76 00* – *hotel@messardiere.com* – *Apr-Oct*. This bar belongs to one of the Riviera's most prestigious hotels. Hushed, cosy ambience in the piano bar of this former 18C private residence. The terrace commands nice views of St-Tropez Bay.

Chez Nano – *2 Rue Sibille* – ☎ *04 94 97 72 59* – *Daily 7pm-3am*. A must for any visitor to St-Tropez. Frequented by wealthy yacht owners and foreign patrons, Chez Nano exudes a cosy atmosphere and is often used as a venue for painting exhibitions.

Les Caves du Roy – *Avenue du Maréchal-Foch* – ☎ *04 95 56 68 00* – *byblos.com* – *Apr-May, mid-Sep to mid-Oct Fri-Sat 11pm-5am, Jun-mid-Sep daily 11pm-5am*. This is undoubtedly one of the Riviera's most exclusive nightclubs and the opportunity to end up on the dance floor... beside a Hollywood star, a leading top model or some other high society celebrity!

Working out

Artemis – *Route des Plages* – ☎ *04 94 97 86 69* – *artemis-stk@wanadoo.fr* – *Jul-Aug Mon-Sat 9am-9pm; Sep-Jun Mon-Fri 9am-8pm, Sat 9am-2pm*. This gym club features an unusual method unique in France, aimed at establishing a personalised programme for members: all the relevant information about their state of health is fed into a computer that decides on the number and nature of the fitness sessions. Artemis also dispenses beauty care sessions.

Cocktail time

Bar Sube – *15 Quai de Suffren* – ☎ *04 94 97 30 04* – *Open daily 6pm-11pm, until 3am Jul-Aug* This is one of the most attractive bars in town. The cosy interior, complete with fireplace and leather armchairs, is adorned with models of ships. Settle on the terrace with its coffee tables, offering beautiful views of the harbour

Café de Paris – *15 Quai de Suffren* – ☎ *04 94 97 00 56* – *May-Sep: daily 7am-2am; Oct-Apr: daily 7am-11pm*. This is definitely the most fashionable bar in St-Tropez, patronised by yuppies and the gilded youth. Its new decor features lamps and red plush armchairs. In the summer, the annexe "Le Living Room" offers cocktails and Japanese specialities.

Chez Fuchs – *7 Rue des Commerçants* – ☎ *04 94 97 01 25* – *Open daily Sep-Jun 7am-10pm, Jul-Aug 7am-midnight*. Small, unprepossessing restaurant with a noisy, homey ambience. Regulars meet up here after work to sip a *pastis*, smoke a cigar or sample the tasty Provençal dishes made by Madame Fuchs.

Kelly's Traditional Irish Pub – *Quai Frédéric-Mistral* – ☎ *04 94 54 89 11* – *Daily 10.30am until dawn*. Small pub housed in a charming basement offering drinks at unbeatable prices. Wide choice of beers.

For your sweet tooth

La Tarte Tropézienne – *36 Rue Georges-Clemenceto* – ☎ *04 94 97 71 42* – *Daily 7am-8pm*. It was in this *pâtisserie* that the famous **tarte tropézienne** saw the light of day, invented by Polish baker Alexandre Micka: a round delightfully moist, brioche cake flavoured with orange blossom, filled with custard and sprinkled with crystallised suger.

Sénéquier – *Quai Jean-Jaurès* – ☎ *04 94 97 00 90* – *Daily 8am-7pm; Jul-Aug: 8am-3am*. The pavement terrace and crimson chairs of this tea room are famous throughout the world... or so say the locals! Renowned personalities such as Jean Marais, Errol Flynn or Colette would come here for a cup of delicately fragrant tea, an iced coffee, a delicious ice-cream or a few squares of homemade nougat.

Domaine du Bourrian et Domaine de Pin Pinon – *2496 Chemin du Bourrian* – *83580 Gassin* – ☎ *04 94 56 16 28* – *domainedubourrian.com / domainedepinpinon.com* – *Jan-Feb: 8am-noon, 2-6pm; Mar-Oct: 8am-noon, 2.30-7pm; Nov-Dec: 8am-noon, 1-5pm*. Domaine du Bourrian is one of the area's oldest vineyards. On the site of a former Gallo-Roman settlement, and in conjunction with the Domaine de Pin-Pinon, three generations of growers have applied themselves to producing country wines from Maures area as well as the popular AOC Côtes-de-Provence.

Transport

MMG boat trips – ☎ *04 94 96 51 00*. Regular services to Ste-Maxime leaving from St-Tropez operate Apr to end of Oct, 10,21€ there and back; to Les Issambres Jul to end of Aug, 10,67€ there and back; to Port-Grimaud Jul to mid-Sep, 8,84€ there and back; to Les Cannebiers Bay at 3.30pm leaving from St-Tropez, 8,38€ there and back and at 3pm leaving from Ste-Maxime, 11,43 there and back.

Shopping

Markets – Tuesdays and Saturdays on Place des Lices.

Shopping streets – The most lively shopping streets are Rue Clemenceau, Rue Gambetta and Rue Allard, offering an impressive selection of local arts and crafts: pottery, glassware etc.

Les Sandales Tropéziennes – *16 Rue Georges-Clemenceto* – ☎ *04 94 97 19 55 – nova.fr – Oct-Mar, Tue-Sat 9.30am-noon and 2.30-6.30pm; Apr-Sep daily until 8pm.* The Rondini house has been crafting St-Tropez sandals since 1927. The distinctive, namesake model in natural leather is the most popular, but the snakeskin version sells well, too!

Leisure activities

Maison du Tourisme du Golfe de St-Tropez – *83580 Gassin* – ☎ *04 94 55 22 00.* This tourist office issues the list of all the companies based in St-Tropez Bay that are specialised in deep-sea diving.

The charming **Place aux Herbes**, traditionally bathed in light and skilfully rendered by Marquet in his paintings, is the backcloth to a small market open in the mornings. Walk past the animated fish stalls, underneath Porte de la Poissonnerie and proceed to Quai Jean-Jaurès and the tourist office.

Place des Lices – Leaving the port, take Rue Laugier, then Rue Gambetta, two lively shopping streets lined with boutiques of international renown, and walk on to Place des Lices, a busy square and popular meeting-place among locals and visitors alike: its convivial cafés and restaurants, colourful market, venerable plane trees and sandy areas for playing *boules* attract huge crowds in both summer and winter.

SIGHTS

★★ L'Annonciade, Musée de St-Tropez ○ – The chapel of Our Lady of Annonciade, built in 1510 and deconsecrated during the Revolution, was split onto two levels in the early 19C and set up as a museum in 1937.

Georges Grammont (patron of the arts) donated some 10 sculptures and about 50 paintings covering 1890-1940. The collection confirms the important role St-Tropez played in the Post-Impressionist movement.

In 1892 **Paul Signac** (1863-1935) landed at St-Tropez. Enthralled by the site, he stopped to paint and ended up living there. Around him gathered other painters – Matisse, Bonnard, Marquet, Camoin, Dunoyer de Segonzac – some residing longer than others. Fascinated by the exceptional light in the region, these artists sought different methods of expressing colour, contributing to, or instigating the great movements of the late 19C and 20C, such as Pointillism *(see Introduction)*, Fauvism, The Nabis and Expressionism.

Tour – Displayed amid the Pointillists, Signac is represented by his oils and watercolours (exhibited in rotation). He is surrounded by his followers H-E Cross *(St-Clair Beach)*, Théo van Rysselberghe, Maximilien Luce and several artists, like Derain (London scenes) and Picabia, who were momentarily part of the movement before taking a different direction.

The Fauves, delighting in small touches of pure colour, are represented by Matisse *(The Gypsy)*, Braque *(Estaque Landscape)*, Manguin, Vlaminck, Kees Van Dongen and Dufy.

The Nabis group reacted against Impressionism, painting in primary colours on an essentially flat surface. They are represented by Bonnard, Vuillard *(Women Under a Lamp)*, Félix Vallotton *(Misia at Her Desk)*...

The Expressionists, who used painting as a means to convey the intensity of their emotions, via exaggerated facial expressions for example, are represented by Rouault, Chabaud *(Hôtel-Hôtel)*, Utrillo and his mother Suzanne Valadon.

The Rower, a Cubist work by Roger de La Fresnaye, landscapes and harbour scenes (Camoin, Bonnard, Marquet) complete this prestigious collection where the various artistic movements all tend to use the human figure as their central theme, regardless of how different their theories may be.

The sculpture, complementing the collection and of the same period, is by Maillol (*Nymph*) and Despiau; note also the sandstone vases by E Decœur.

Maison des Papillons (Musée Dany-Lartigue) ⊘ – *9 Rue Étienne-Berny*. This charming Provençal house, tucked into an alleyway away from the crowded port, is the former home of the photographer JH Lartigue and his son, Dany, a painter and entomologist. It houses a collection of nearly 5 000 butterflies, comprising all the diurnal species existing in France, caught by the artist in person, as well as a donation of 20 000 exotic specimens. The staircase wall is hung with JH Lartigue's photos and family souvenirs of the composer A Messager, the painter's grandfather. Artistic arrangements show the capacities for mimicry of insects in their natural environment. A pleasant patio with a fountain leads out from this room and contains two paintings illustrating local festivals. Upstairs rare and exotic species (such as the famous black Apollon of Mercantour and numerous Zerynthis and Parnassus) are grouped in display cases.

In Rue du Clocher turn right towards Place de l'Ormeau and right again towards Rue de la Citadelle.

★**Citadelle** – The citadel stands on a hillock at the east end of town. A fine hexagonal **keep** with three round towers was built in the 16C. In the 17C a fortified wall was added.

La Nioulargue, a Sailing Festival

This great event at the end of the season in St-Tropez brings together real lovers of the sea and the most aristocratic traditional sailing boats (swans, ketches and schooners built during the 1920s for film stars or famous owners). Since its first meeting in 1981, more than 250 competitors (most of whom have previously taken part in the America's Cup) rush here every year in early October to take part in this race which has become the great European meeting for old boats.

The course starts at the Tour du Portalet, goes round the shallows marked by the Nioulargue (sea nest, in Provençal) buoy and returns to the harbour. A spectator who has managed to find himself a good viewing point will be rewarded with the unforgettable sight of these large sailing boats in action. The skilful dances performed by ketches (recognisable by the small mast at the stern) and schooners (with the small mast in the bows) call for miraculous feats in anticipating manœuvres and great strength to move the enormous sails (the stress at the foot of the main mast can be as much as 500t!).

The best way to follow the race – This can be achieved by boarding the launches run by MMG who operate a shuttle service in the gulf (boarding opposite the restaurant l'Escale in the old port). A more peaceful view of the scene is possible from the buttresses of the citadelle, with a good pair of binoculars. Lastly, share the hire of a small boat so as to appreciate the skills of the skippers at close quarters.

The ramparts command a fine **panorama**★ of St-Tropez, the bay, Ste-Maxime and the Maures.

Musée Naval ⊘ – This Maritime Museum in the citadel keep is an annexe of the Musée de la Marine in the Palais de Chaillot in Paris. In the courtyard are two handsome 16C Spanish bronze cannons. Within the keep are displayed models of ships (including a reconstruction of a Greek galley), engravings and seascapes illustrating the history and local activities of St-Tropez with an explanation of the 1944 Allied landing. Note the full-scale cross-section of a torpedo from the local naval shipyard. The exhibition room illustrates a different theme each year.

There is a magnificent **view**★★ from the keep terrace of the town, St-Tropez Bay, the Maures and the Esterel; on a clear day the Alps can be spotted in the far distance.

DRIVING TOURS

★**Moulins de Paillas and Gassin** – *Round tour of 28km/18mi*

This tour into the countryside around St-Tropez offers extensive views over the coast and the Maures hinterland and includes villages which have retained their original character.

Chapelle Ste-Anne – *1km/0.7mi. From St-Tropez take Avenue Paul-Roussel and Route de Ste-Anne.*

Standing on a volcanic rock spike in the shelter of huge trees, this attractive Provençal chapel is a place of pilgrimage for seafarers and *"bravadeurs" (see above)* with a **view★** of the sea in all directions, particularly of St-Tropez and the bay.

The road passes through the vineyards above Pampelonne Bay.

Turn right onto D 61 towards Ramatuelle.

★ **Ramatuelle** – See RAMATUELLE.

Turn right onto D 89 towards Col de Paillas.

★★ **Moulins de Paillas** – Beyond three ruined olive mills, there is a radio beacon on a circular platform. *Follow the signposted path.* On walking round the enclosure, there are glimpses through the trees of a fine **panoramic view★★** – *(seawards from north to south)* over Cap Roux and the rough peaks of the Esterel, the coast of the Maures Massif, Ste-Maxime, St-Tropez Bay, the long stretch of Pampelonne beach, Cap Camarat lighthouse rising white above the pine woods, and, out to sea, the Île du Levant and Île de Port-Cros; *(inland)* Gassin *(below)*, the Pradels range *(southwest)* and the Sauvette chain *(northwest)*, as well as Cogolin and Grimaud in the valley *(north-northwest)*.

Return to the junction and turn right to Gassin.

★ **Gassin** – Alt 201m/659ft. In contrast to modern resorts this village has proudly retained its Provençal character, with its network of alleyways sometimes linked by flights of steps.
The **Terrasse des Barri**, planted with lotus trees and exuding delightful Mediterranean fragrances, provides a **view★** over St-Tropez Bay, Cavalaire Bay and the Îles d'Hyères; when the mistral blows, the Alps are visible *(east)*.
Around the town, there are several vineyards producing local AOC Côtes de Provence wines. The festival of St Laurent, the patron saint of the village, is celebrated on the second Sunday in August with a special meal including generous helpings of garlic mayonnaise *(aïoli)*.

Take D 559, then D 98 to return to St-Tropez.

RAMBLING TOURS

★★ Headlands by Coastal Path

Although in high season tourism takes over the town of St-Tropez, the surrounding country presents a traditional landscape of rectangular vineyards alternating with rows of cypress trees and immaculate farms *(mas)* in the shade of rustling umbrella pines. The coastline consists of the rocky headlands – Cap Camarat, Cap Taillat and Cap Lardier – and the long ribbon of fine sand in Pampelonne Bay, which has been preserved from concrete invasion by the active intervention of the Coastal Conservatory.
◪ This path, signposted in yellow, links St-Tropez with Cavalaire beach via Cap Camarat and Cap Lardier *(about 40km/24mi)* but this is not a walk which can be completed in a single day as the time required exceeds 11hr.

St-Tropez to Tahiti beach – *Allow 3hr.*
◪ The path leaves from Graniers beach at the western edge of the harbour. It follows the contours of the coast and provides superb views of the foothills of the Maures and the overhanging red rocks of the Esterel. Via Rabiou Point and Cap de St-Tropez, the path reaches Les Salins beach, the first stopping point where refreshment is available in the open-air cafés *(guingettes)* during the summer season. The path then rounds Cap Pinet and comes out on Tahiti beach at the north end of Pampelonne Bay.

Tahiti beach to Cap Camarat – *Mid-June to end of September. 2-5pm.*
◪ The path follows a track parallel with the long sandy stretch of Pampelonne beach *(5km/3mi)* to Bonne-Terrasse Point. On reaching Bonne-Terrasse Bay, the path climbs the first rocks through thicker vegetation. Near Rocher des Portes there is a footpath *(right)* towards Camarat lighthouse which is visible through a forest of arbutus and tree ferns.

The Customs Officers' Footpath

This footpath, which follows the whole of the Var coastline, hugging to the shore, dates from the First Empire (early 19C). It was commissioned by Fouché when he was Minister and was originally intended to facilitate the patrolling of armed customs officers, who enjoyed powers as wide-ranging as those granted to the police. They were ordered to crack down on smugglers of salt and, subsequently, of tobacco and arms. Since 1976 the path has been restored and all private properties adjoining the shore are obliged to allow a passage (at least 3m/10ft wide) across their land. Walls and solid fences erected prior to that date are, however, exempt. Nearly 200km/124mi of Varois coastline are subject to these provisions.

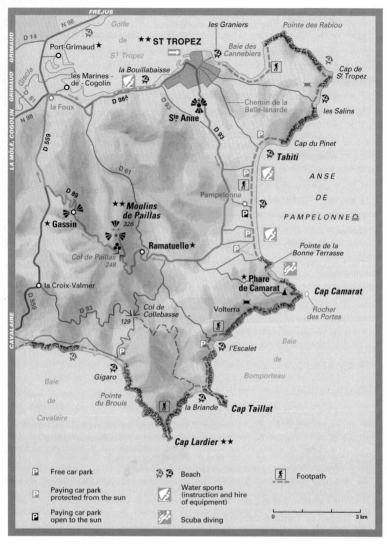

Legend:

- **P** Free car park
- **P** Paying car park protected from the sun
- **P** Paying car park open to the sun
- 🏖 Beach
- 🏄 Water sports (instruction and hire of equipment)
- 🤿 Scuba diving
- 🚶 Footpath

0   3 km

★ **Phare de Camarat** – *From Ramatuelle take D93 east; turn right on the road sign-posted "Route du Phare" running along the promontory beyond Les Tournels camp site; park outside the lighthouse enclosure which is a pedestrian area.*

This magnificent **lighthouse** ⊙commissioned in 1831 was electrified after the Second World War. It is one of the tallest in France (129.8m/426ft above sea-level) and has a range of 60km/37mi. Since 1977 it has been operated electrically. From the summit there are superb **views★★** over Pampelonne Bay, the whole of the peninsula and St-Tropez Bay.

Cap Camarat to Cap Taillat – *About 2hr. No refreshments available except in L'Escalet.*

Tips for Ramblers

It is advisable to wear stout walking shoes to cross the steep rocky points where the path has collapsed and to bring plenty to drink. Avoid the hottest hours of the day when visibility is reduced by a heat haze. The sandy beaches are small at Gigaro, Briande and l'Escalet; however the path wends its way along many creeks that are an invitation to wander through unspoilt contryside.

🚶 After skirting Rocher des Portes, the path leads to the beach at L'Escalet passing a succession of creeks which are easily accessible and isolated by great rock slabs ideal for sunbathing. This walk offers the unexpected sight of the imposing **Château de Volterra** *(closed to the public)* overlooking the bay. The path then reaches Cap Taillat.

E. Baret/MICHELIN

La Briande beach, Ramatuelle

It is possible to join the route from the customs shed at the entrance to the car park at l'Escalet.

The path cuts across the base of the headland and disappears into scrub vegetation dominated by ilex until l'Escalet beach. The area boasts a wide range of forest species. Beyond these woods the countryside is carpeted with vineyards. **Cap Taillat** is in fact a growing sand bar connecting the rocky reef to the coast, turning it into a peninsula. At the very end stands a semaphore signal.

Cap Taillat to Gigaro via Cap Lardier – Most of the route falls within the **protected site**★★ of Cap Lardier run by the Conservatoire du Littoral, a state body in charge of preserving France's coastal heritage. The coastal path runs along an uninterrupted succession of steep cliffs from which there is a view of Briande Bay ending in the east in the characteristic silhouette of Cap Taillat.

It is possible to return to Gigaro from Briande beach by the inland path (route DFCI) through dense pinewoods, ending at the information booth in Gigaro.

There is a car park on the sea front or on the left just before the pinewood. In season there is an information booth near the sign at the edge of the Gigaro pinewoods. You can return to St-Tropez by bus, leaving from La Croix-Valmer.

History of the Cap Lardier Estate

In Edwardian times a remarkable vineyard occupied the site of the present development and Mas de Gigaro; these date from the 1950s when the estate was sold and made into a camp site. At the beginning of the 1970s, a banking institution purchased the estate, together with a few plots of land around Brouis beach, with a view to building a marina. The residents rallied against this plan, and when the Conservatoire du Littoral bought the estate in 1976, the conservation of this unspoilt part of the coastline was guaranteed.

ST-VALLIER-DE-THIEY

Population 2 261
Michelin map 114 folds 12 and 13, 115 fold 24 or 245 folds 36 and 37

This medieval village, once a Roman stronghold, is situated in the middle of a fertile plateau and is a popular holiday destination for the inhabitants of Grasse. The Romanesque church, which dates from the early 12C and was restored in the 17C, has a lovely 13C nave with pointed barrel vaulting and houses two Baroque altarpieces. The bell-tower is decorated with arcading, a remnant from the original construction, and surmounted by an elegant 19C campanile. The old seigneurial château beside the church now houses the town hall. The line of the neighbouring houses marks the position of the old fortified wall, of which only a fine gateway with loopholes remains.
In the square, a column bearing a bust of Napoleon commemorates the Emperor's passage on 2 March 1814.

R. Delon/CASTELET

Souterroscope de la Baume Obscure, St Vallier-de-Thiey

A CURIOUS GROTTO

★**Souterroscope de la Baume Obscure** ☉ – *From St-Vallier-de-Thiey drive south towards St-Cézaire; turn right onto the road to the cemetery (signposted "Grotte Baume Obscure"). Continue beyond the cemetery (unsurfaced track) for 2km/1.2mi to a large car park opposite a shelter built over the ticket office. Audio guide tour 1hr. Shoes with non-slip soles advised. Narrow passages.*

The cave consists of an underground network of galleries that were not brought to light until 1958 because of the long, narrow tunnels leading to them, which tended to put off early explorers.

The detailed exploration of those galleries currently open to the public was eventually completed in 1980, as was the introduction of facilities suitable for guided tours.

Experts have explored 1 200m/1 312yd of the underground network; the tour of the cave actually covers 500m/547yd and takes visitors down 50m/164ft to the **Galerie du Pas de Course**. There is a constant temperature of 14°C/57°F.

At the end of a long corridor, once filled in with clay, visitors will discover a series of nine galleries containing features such as vast domes, natural dams forming cascades and a profusion of thread-like stalactites, resembling thin, straight spaghetti hanging down, an absolute forest of needle-shaped concretions scattered all over the roofs. In the gallery with the *gours*, note the unusual colour of the water brought out by the lighting, and the ground which is formed from an enormous petrified flow of calcite at the base of a stalagmite. This whole network of caves is also widely renowned for the variety of strange formations it has generated.

EXCURSIONS

★Plateau de Caussols

From St-Vallier-de-Thiey to Gourdon – 30km/19mi – allow 2hr, not including the tour of the observatory. On leaving the village, take N 85 towards the Pas de la Faye, then D 5 to the right, which twists and turns along the side of the mountain, affording lovely views over the St-Vallier Basin. After going through a pass, Col de Ferrier, the road overlooks the wooded valley of Nans. Leave the main road which skirts the Audiberghe Mountain, taking D 12 which leads off to the right (sign "Caussols").

The **Plateau de Caussols**, lying at an average altitude of 1 000m/3 281ft, is itself enclosed by higher land. It is one of the rare examples of karst relief in France. The north of the plateau features a landscape of cultivated land and meadows thanks to its fertile soil; the south, on the other hand, reflects a less orderly setting, with *dolines*, swallowholes and chasms forming a landscape typical of limestone relief eroded by rainwater. Walkers should take care when near these pits and chasms, especially in rainy weather. There is a particularly spectacular example of this feature to be seen by taking the small road to the right, leaving the centre of the sprawling village of **Caussols** to the east. The narrow road crosses the plateau diagonally to reach **Les Claps★** (Provençal for "rocks"). These are in fact a remarkable rock chaos. The mineral nature of this feature is all the more striking for the absence of any plantlife nearby. Some stone dwellings *(bories)* indicate that man was once resident here. Turning round to face the plateau gives a view of the domes of the CERGA Observatory.

Return to D 12 and follow it for 2km/1.2mi towards Gourdon.

Observatoire du CERGA ⊘ – *2km/1.2mi after Caussols on D 12, a road leads off to the left signposted "St-Maurice – Observatoire du CERGA". After passing the houses, carry on past the sign "Route Privée" which indicates the entrance to the CERGA property.* The road winds its way round a series of hairpin bends, giving lovely views of Caussols in its dip.

The **Plateau de Calern**, at an altitude of 1 300m/4265ft, is home to the various installations and equipment of the CERGA Observatory, specialised in geodynamic and astronomical research. The site is unique from a geological point of view. The observatory, inaugurated in 1974, is aimed at developing modern instrumentation for astronomy and monitoring the movements of the Earth. It is associated with the Observatoire de la Côte d'Azur, which includes the observatory at Nice.

The tour of the observatory brings visitors into contact with the teams who work with interferometers (for measuring diameters of stars), the Schmidt telescope (for observing the sky), laser telemeters (for measuring the distance from the Earth to the Moon and to the satellites) and astrolabes (for calculating the position of the stars).

Return to D 12 and follow it towards Gourdon.

The road carries straight to the eastern edge of the plateau and then begins its descent onto Gourdon. There is a lovely **view★** of the Loup Valley from the first big bend.

★ **Gourdon** – *See GOURDON.*

SAINTE-MAXIME ⌂⌂

Population 11 785
Michelin map 84 folds 17 and 18, 114 fold 37 or 245 fold 49
Local map see Massif des MAURES

The fashionable resort of Ste-Maxime lies along the north shore of St-Tropez Bay. It faces due south in a pretty setting protected from the *mistral* by wooded hills. Alongside the fishing harbour there is a well-appointed marina and a beautiful beach of fine sand. In summer the town centre is a pedestrian precinct.

DISCOVERING STE-MAXIME

Seafront – Running along the beach, then the port, the pleasantly shaded Promenade Simon-Lorière commands fine views of St-Tropez. It is accessible to road traffic under the name Avenue Charles-de-Gaulle. Here stands the first marker on the route taken by the Allied forces in 1944 from Ste-Maxime to Langres in the north of France.

D. Pazery/MICHELIN

Eating out

MODERATE

Chez Sophie – *4 Place des Sarrasins* – ☎ *04 94 96 71 00* – *Closed 15 Nov-15 Dec and Wed off season.* – *14.94€*. Charming restaurant that epitomises the Provençal spirit: colourful decoration, wooden furnishings, terrace shaded by a plane tree, menu inspired by regional cuisine...The dishes and tasty homemade desserts are served by charming locals with a genuine Mediterranean drawl...

La Maison Bleue – *48 Rue Paul-Bert* – ☎ *04 94 96 51 92* – *Maisonbl@aol.com* – *Closed 6 Jan-9 Feb, 23 Feb-30 Mar and 20 Oct-27 Dec* – *15.09/21.34€*. A Provençal house entirely dedicated to pasta and its history: early advertising posters, enamelled plaques and old wrappers adorn the ochre walls of this restaurant, whose terrace is pleasantly shaded by plane trees. Naturally, the menu too pays tribute to pasta by offering a wide choice of spaghetti dishes.

Where to stay

MODERATE

L'Auberge Provençale – *19 Boulevard Aristide-Briand* – ☎ *04 94 55 76 90* – *Closed 20 Dec-10 Jan* – *15 rooms: 53.36€* – *Restaurant 33€*. Despite its unprepossessing façade, this inn offers charming accommodation in keeping with Provençal tradition. The renovated bedrooms and bathrooms have been given warm, earthy hues and the southern cuisine relies on fresh market produce.

MID-RANGE

Le Chardon Bleu – *29 Rue de Verdun* – ☎ *04 94 55 52 22* – *www.auberge-duchardonbleu.fr* – *Closed Jan* – *25 rooms: 62.50/76.22€* – ☞ *5.95€*. Conveniently situated at the heart of the resort, barely 150 yards from the sea, this hotel offers air-conditioned rooms with small balconies. Two rooms have a big terrace, ideal for late-morning breakfasts in the sun!

On the town

Unlike those in Saint-Tropez on the opposite side of the bay, the cafés and pubs in Sainte-Maxime are open all year round, making it a lively seaside resort both in summer and winter.

Golf Plaza – *Avenue Célestin – BP 29* – ☎ *04 94 56 66 66* – *golf-plaza.fr* – *Mar-Jan from 6.30pm*. Prestigious hotel bar set against a backdrop of cork oaks and Mediterranean scrubland, overlooking Sainte-Maxime and Saint-Tropez Bay. Additional facilities include a golf course, a fitness club and a large-scale game of chess.

Outdoor performances

Théâtre de la Mer – *Promenade Simon Lorière* – ☎ *04 94 49 18 86 / 06 03 69 32 23: Jun-Sep: Check the programme (45 shows, many of them free of charge)*. Every summer this open-air theatre stages concerts of classical music and contemporary pop, folk dance, and firework displays. Apply to Sainte-Maxime Animation for details.

Golf

Golf de Sainte-Maxime – *Route du Débarquement – BP 1* – ☎ *04 94 55 02 02* – *ste.maxime@bluegreen.com* – *Daily*. Superb, undulating golf course laid out over the heights of Sainte-Maxime, dominating St-Tropez Bay. Bar with terrace facing the sea.

Water sports

Club Nautique de Sainte Maxime – *Boulevard Jean-Moulin* – ☎ *04 94 96 07 80* – *School holidays: Mon-Sat 8.30am-6.30pm, Sun 1.30-6.30pm*. This water sports club organises sailing courses during the school holidays. Equipment available for hire in July and August.

Time for refreshments

Big Pierrot's Café – *24 Rue d'Alsace* – ☎ *04 94 49 16 65* – *Sun-Thu 5pm-1am, Fri-Sat 5pm-3am*. Small pub set up in a 300-year-old building, one of the oldest in town. The fireplace on the first floor is a recent acquisition... barely 150 years old! Needless to say, the house speciality here is beer.

Café de France – *Place Victor-Hugo* – ☎ *04 94 96 18 16* – *Jul-Aug: daily 7am-3am Oct-Mar: 7am-8pm; Sep and Apr-Jun: 7am-midnight.* A whiff of the past is perceptible in this brasserie originally opened in 1852, when Ste-Maxime was but a modest fishing village. Old-fashioned photographs and an ancient mirror evoke this bygone era. The big terrace sheltered by venerable plane trees faces the marina.

L'Esquinade – *112 Avenue Charles-de-Gaulle* – ☎ *04 94 49 23 72* – *Daily 6pm-2am.* Newly opened nightclub whose attractive decoration recalls a ship's hold. A congenial meeting-place where the barman will serve you one of his special cocktails or whiskies...

Shopping

Markets – There are fairs on Fridays and lively markets held in a covered venue near Place du Marché every morning.

Up in the air

Héli Sécurité – *Quartier Perrat - ZA Grimaud* – *83316 Grimaud* – ☎ *04 94 43 39 30. Daily 9am-7pm.* This flying club organises recreational flights in helicopters but also ensures shuttle services between airports or stations.

Tour Carrée des Dames – *Opposite the church, facing the port.* A square defensive tower, built in the 16C by the Lérins monks and later used as law courts, has been transformed into a **Museum of Local Tradition** (Musée des Traditions Locales) ⊘. Ste-Maxime and its surrounding area are presented with exhibits on nature (sea), history and regional customs (arts and crafts, Provençal dress).

Church – Modern ceramic tympanum above the doorway. Inside, fine Baroque (17C) green and ochre marble altar from the Chartreuse de la Verne; note the 15C choir stalls.

Parc St-Donat – *10km/6mi – about 1hr. From Ste-Maxime take Boulevard Georges-Clemenceau, D 25 north.*
A leisure park has been laid out in the woods between Col de Gratteloup and St-Donat Chapel. The main attraction is the Museum of Mechanical Musical Instruments.

Musée du Phonographe et de la Musique Mécanique ⊘ – The building, which recalls a turn-of-the century barrel organ, houses an astonishing collection of 350 musical instruments and sound recording machines; among the rare and bizarre exhibits are a melophone (1780, forerunner of the accordion), musical boxes from all periods, barrel organs and pianolas, phonographs from 1878 (Edison) to the present day, a 1903 dictaphone, a Pathegraphe for the study of foreign languages (first audiovisual machine) and even a singing bird (Bontemps, 1860).

SANARY-SUR-MER ⌂

Population 16 995
Michelin map 84 fold 14, 114 fold 44 or 245 fold 46
Local map see Excursions below

The name Sanary derives from St Nazaire, who is venerated in the local church. The charming resort, all pink and white, is popular at all seasons.
Sanary boasts a smart little harbour bordered by palm trees. The bay is fairly well protected from the *mistral* winds by wooded hills, dominated to the north by the Gros Cerveau, and has fine beaches.
Local markets are held in the port on Wednesday mornings.

"Capital of German Literature" before the Second World War – The little port of Sanary, known to German painters in the 1920s, became a refuge for many intellectuals who had fled from Hitler's regime in the 1930s. A German refugee journalist christened Sanary "Capital of German Literature". Famous residents featured Thomas Mann and his brother Heinrich, who stayed at Villa "La Tranquille", the writer Feuchtwanger, as well as Alma Mahler and Franz Werfel. Zwieg visited the resort on his way to the United States.
After the armistice in 1940, many were able to seek refuge in the USA thanks to the intervention of President Roosevelt. However, some of the lesser-known figures were interned at Camp des Milles near Aix-en-Provence. In the port, above the bowling area, a plaque commemorates the names of these refugees and a leaflet detailing the villas that were used is available from the bookshop.
The former mayor and architect **Marius Michel** (1819-1907), nicknamed Michel Pacha on account of his love of Ottoman civilisation, added a whiff of Eastern promise by designing several houses in the Oriental style.

297

Eating out

MODERATE

Restaurant du Théâtre – *Impasse de l'Enclos – Near the theatre –* ☎ *04 94 88 04 16 – Closed Jul-Aug, Sun evening and Mon – 12.20/18.29€.* Take a few steps down and enter this U-shaped restaurant appointed with rustic furnishings. Your attention will soon be caught by the mouthwatering sight of salmon, meat, prawns and skewered dice of game roasting in the open fireplace!

MID-RANGE

Cour des Arts – *Rue Barthélémy-de-Don –* ☎ *04 94 88 08 05 – Closed Nov, Sun and Mon except Jul-Aug and for lunch Sep-Jun – 28.20/33.54€.* Discreetly situated in an alley of the town centre, this restaurant opens up its patio as soon as the first rays of sun appear. The bill of fare focuses on regional cuisine, which can be enjoyed in the shade of cream-coloured umbrellas or in the small dining room painted in pastel hues. Special lunchtime formula.

Where to stay

MID-RANGE

Chambre d'Hôte Villa Lou Gardian – *646 Route de Bandol –* ☎ *04 94 88 05 73 – 🖂 – 4 rooms: 60.98/68.60€ – Meal 45.73€.* Despite its location near a main road, the colourful, sparsely decorated rooms of this recently renovated hotel are comparatively quiet. It is advisable to choose one nearer the pool. A large garden, a tennis court and a table d'hôte set up in the summer patio await your arrival.

On the town

La Mezzanote – *1370 Route de Bandol –* ☎ *04 94 88 16 00 – Thu-Sun 9pm-4am.* A highly successful bar-restaurant that organises karaoke and themed evenings every week and acts as an "antechamber" for the adjoining Mai Taï nightclub. If you tend to shy away from crowds, it is best to avoid weekends.

Seeing the sea

Aquascope – *Quai d'Honneur (opposite the town hall) –* & *Boat trips (30min) daily Jul-Aug 9am-6.30pm; Apr-Jun and Sep 2-5pm; Jan and Mar Sat-Sun and public holidays. 11.43€ (child 7.62€).* Try this unusual approach to the discovery of marine flora and fauna by boarding a semi-submersible boat affording close-up views of the sea depths.

VISITING SANARY

Chapelle Notre-Dame-de-Pitié – *Access via Boulevard Courbet.* The chapel was built in 1560 on a hillock west of the town and it is decorated with votive offerings, mostly naive paintings. From the stepped approach bordered by oratories there is **view★** of Sanary Bay with the Toulon hills rising in the background, and the coast as far as the Embiez Archipelago beyond which loom the heights of Cap Sicié.

Sanary port

E. Baret/MICHELIN

EXCURSIONS

★★ **1** Gros Cerveau *13km/8mi – about 1hr 15min. From Sanary take Avenue de l'Europe-Unie D 11 east, ② on the town plan.*

Flowers, vines and fruit trees are cultivated on the fertile land.
At the entrance to Ollioules turn left onto D 20.

At the start of the drive through terraced gardens and vineyards, the view extends both over the hillock on which the Six-Fours Fort stands and over the inner anchorage of Toulon at the foot of Mont Faron. Gradually the panorama extends southeast over Toulon and Cap Sicié Peninsula from an impressive *corniche* road.

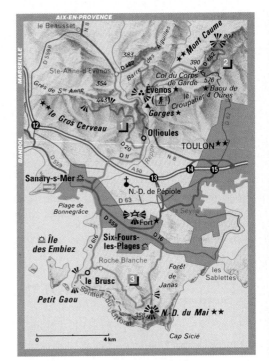

Further on the **view★** is magnificent: to the right, the Grès de Ste-Anne (enormous rocks riddled with caves), Beausset Plain, the Ste-Baume Massif, the Évenos hills and the Ollioules Gorges; on the left, a view of the coast.

8km/5mi after Ollioules (sign) make a U-turn to a platform.

A short walk will reveal a marvellous **view★★** of the coast stretching from the Giens Peninsula to Île Verte off La Ciotat.

★★ **2** Mont Caume

23km/14.3mi northeast – allow 2hr. Leave Sanary on Avenue de l'Europe-Unie going east and follow D 11 to Ollioules.

Ollioules – Old arcaded houses and a Provençal Romanesque church stand at the foot of the 13C castle. A cut-flower market (exporting to countries all over Europe) is held here.

Théâtre National de la Danse et de l'Image de Châteauvallon – This centre was designed by Komatis and Gérard Paquet from 1965 and was developed around a 17C walled town, with a large open-air amphitheatre as well as an indoor theatre. Theatre and jazz festivals are staged here throughout the year.

Beyond Ollioules turn left onto N 8 which immediately enters the gorges.

★ **Gorges d'Ollioules** – The arid and sinuous gorges were formed by the Reppe which tumbles into the sea in Sanary Bay. As the road emerges at the northern end there is a view on the left of the Grès de Ste-Anne, a curious mass of sandstone rocks, hollowed and pitted by erosion.

In Ste-Anne-d'Évenos, turn right onto D 462.

The road climbs a ravine dominated by the abrupt Barre des Aiguilles on the left.
Turn right towards Évenos and park the car near a cross set in a rock.

★ **Évenos** – *15min on foot there and back.*
🔲 The village is a jumble of half-ruined and abandoned houses, built of grey basaltic stone, clinging to the steep rock slopes. The 13C church has a bell-tower with two bays. Over all brood the ruins of a 16C castle; the keep, also made of basalt, stands on the edge of a volcano from which the lava slag is still visible. The platform commands a **view** of Destel Gorges, Croupatier hill, Ollioules Gorges and Gros Cerveau in the foreground, with Cap Sicié and the Ste-Baume Massif on the horizon.

Continue east along D 62 turning left at Col du Corps de Garde onto D 662.

Mont Caume – Mont Caume rises to 801m/2 628ft. The steep approach road offers fine viewpoints; from the top *(climb the mound)* there is a magnificent **panorama**★★ of the coast, from Cap Bénat to La Ciotat Bay and inland towards the Ste-Baume Massif.

★③ Cap Sicié Peninsula

Round tour of 25km/15.5mi – about 2hr (not including Île des Embiez). From Sanary take Avenue d'Estienne-d'Orves.

The road skirts Bonnegrâce beach and Pointe Nègre: views of Sanary Bay and Bandol.

Le Brusc – Fishing village and resort; ferries to Île des Embiez leave from the port.

⌂ **Ile des Embiez** – *See Île des EMBIEZ.*

Petit Gaou – The rocky promontory pounded by the sea, once an island, resembles a Breton seascape. There is an extensive **view** of the coast and the neighbouring islands.

Return to Le Brusc and take D 16 towards Six-Fours; in Roche-Blanche bear right.

The road runs parallel to the coast about 1km/0.6mi inland but gives glimpses of La Ciotat, Bandol and Sanary. At the crossroads there is a **view**★★ of the Toulon anchorage, Cap Cépet, the Giens Peninsula and the Îles d'Hyères.

Turn right and park next to the radio station.

★★ **Chapelle Notre-Dame-du-Mai** ⊘ – *Walk round the radio station to the chapel.* The chapel is a place of pilgrimage (14 September) dedicated to Our Lady of the May Tree, also known as Our Lady of Good Protection, and contains many votive offerings. From the top of Cap Sicié there is a dizzying drop to the sea and a splendid **panorama**★★ of the coast from the Îles d'Hyères to the *calanques* lying east of Marseille.

Return to the crossroads continuing straight ahead.

The narrow road cuts through **Forêt de Janas**, a fine plantation of conifers, before rejoining D 16; turn left.

⌂ **Six-Fours-les-Plages** – *See SIX-FOURS-LES-PLAGES.*
Return to Sanary on D 559.

SAORGE★★

Population 323
Michelin map 84 fold 20, 115 fold 18 or 245 fold 26
Local map see NICE

In a rugged **setting**★★ the stone-covered houses and the proud belfries of the church and chapels cling to the steep slopes of a natural amphitheatre where the Roya Valley temporarily broadens out. Saorge was originally a Ligurian settlement and then a Roman colony. In the Middle Ages the town was said to be impregnable but it has yielded twice: in 1794, to the French under Masséna, and in April 1945.

STROLLING THROUGH SAORGE

★ **Old town** – *Park the car at the north entrance.* The stepped and twisting streets, sometimes arched, make an interesting walk past 15C houses with decorative doorways and carved lintels. On the far side of the square, go straight, then right and right again to reach a terrace offering a beautiful **view**★ into the bottom of the Gorges de la Roya.

TABLE WITH A VIEW

Le Bellevue – *5 Rue L.-Périssol – ☎ 04 93 04 51 37 – Closed 1-15 Jun, 1-8 Sep, 18 Nov-8 Dec, Tue evening and Wed except Jul-Aug – 15.25/22.50€.* Interrupt your tour of the covered alleys and settle in the yellow dining room with its ceiling enhanced by wainscoting. Attractive menu. Panoramic views of the village and the Roya Gorges.

Église St-Sauveur – Built in the 16C and revaulted in the 18C, the church comprises three naves supported by columns with gilded Corinthian capitals and is decorated with altarpieces. The **organ**, which was built in 1847 by the Lingiardi of Pavia, was shipped by sea from Genoa to Nice and thence to Saorge on muleback. The south nave presents an 18C canvas depicting Elijah with the Virgin and Child; a fine Renaissance tabernacle; a 15C font beneath a painting by a local artist (1532); a Virgin in gilded wood beneath a canopy (1708). To the left is a 16C Primitive over the altar of the Annunciation.

Leave from the southern end of the village, bearing right at the road fork.

Madonna del Poggio – *Private property.* The early Romanesque building boasts a soaring **belfry** with six rows of Lombard bands and a fine chevet. The three naves rest on columns crowned by capitals decorated with a stylised leaf motif. This is the oldest religious building in the Roya Valley. The return to the village offers a fine **view** of Saorge and terraced olive groves.

Take a sharp right at the road fork towards the monastery.

Couvent des Franciscains ⊙ – Overlooking the village from the south, the 17C buildings of the Franciscan convent, to which the monks returned in 1969 after a long absence, are prettily set among olive trees. The church, which is in the Baroque style, has a porch surmounted by a balustrade; the belltower is capped by a bulbous roof of coloured tiles. Small **cloisters** are decorated with unrefined but nonetheless pretty paintings on pious themes. From the terrace, a splendid **view★★** of Saorge, the Roya Valley and the gorge.

Saorge

DRIVING TOUR

Saorge Gorges and Bergue Gorges

39km/24mi – allow 4hr – local map see NICE

Breil-sur-Roya – *See BREIL-SUR-ROYA.*

Leave Breil-sur-Roya to the north by N 204.

The road to Col de Brouis (see SOSPEL) forks off to the left.

La Giandola – *See SOSPEL.*

★★ **Gorges de Saorge** – The road follows the river's every curve in narrow *corniche* style beneath overhanging rocks. The Nice-Cuneo railway also passes through these gorges by way of tunnels and other engineering feats.
At the end of the gorges, there is a view between two rock cliffs of the extraordinary **setting★★** of Saorge built in curved tiers, on a hillside clad in olive trees.

★ **Gorges de Bergue** – Beyond Fontan, the road ascends gorges cut through red schist where the rock appears deeply coloured and foliated.
The valley widens out into the St-Dalmas-de-Tende Basin *(see TENDE)*.

SEILLANS★

Population 2 115
Michelin map 84 fold 7, 114 fold 11 or 245 fold 36

The village was often visited by Gounod and Alphonse Karr, and the illustrator **Max Ernst** (1891-1976) chose to live here towards the end of his life. The artist, known as an active member of the Dada movement, settled in Seillans with his wife, the painter Dorothée Tanning, in 1964. A small **museum** ⊙ displays several of his lithographs, remarkable for their strong imaginative streak and sense of humour. The ivory and pink houses cascade down the steep slope of the Canjuers Plateau. Quaint cobbled lanes lead up to the church and the old castle with its ramparts and fountain. The main local activity is the production of honey and aromatic herbs, exported to countries all over the world.
A faience fair is held here on 15 August. Other local festivities feature an Olive Fair on the first weekend in February and tributes paid to Notre-Dame-des-Selves (first weekend in July), St-Cyr and St-Léger (last weekend in July).

A STROLL THROUGH SEILLANS

Church – The rebuilding of the church in 1477 incorporated a few sections dating from the 11C. The interior is decorated (right) with two beautiful triptychs: a 15C Coronation of the Virgin painted on wood and a marble stoup (1491). From the church there is a fine view over Fayence in the plain to the Tanneron Massif.

Shepherds' adoration in the chapel
N.-D. de l'Ormeau

301

Chapelle Notre-Dame-de-l'Ormeau ⊘ – *1km/0.6mi southeast on the Fayence road.*
The Romanesque chapel, which is dedicated to Our Lady of the Elm Tree, is flanked by a bell-tower of dressed stone but marred by the subsequent addition of an open porch.

The interior contains a remarkable 16C **altarpiece★★**. In the centre, a crowd of people is climbing the Tree of Jesse; the Adoration of the Shepherds (left) and the Adoration of the Magi (right) are both strikingly expressive. The predella, beneath a wooden peristyle, illustrates (left to right) the life of St Anne, the birth and marriage of the Virgin and the Annunciation.

To the left of the altarpiece is a fine low-relief sculpture of the Assumption (17C); to the right, in a recess, an early statue of Our Lady of the Elm Tree.

To the left of the entrance there is a Roman tombstone with an inscription. The walls are adorned with numerous votive offerings dating from around 1800.

A PICTURESQUE HOTEL

Les Deux Rocs – *Place Font-d'Amont* – ☎ *04 94 76 87 32 – Closed Nov-Mar, Tue and Thu except evenings – 14 rooms: 48.78/91.47€ – ☑ 7.62€ – Restaurant 40€.* Imposing inn housed in an old village building. The original staircase leads to the rooms, appointed with colourful wall hangings and antique furniture. Enjoy your meal by the fireplace or in the welcome shade of plane trees on the summer terrace near the village fountain.

SIX-FOURS-LES-PLAGES⌂

Population 32 742
Michelin map 84 fold 14, 114 folds 44 and 45 or 245 fold 46
Local map see SANARY-SUR-MER: Excursions

This widespread *commune* encompasses no fewer than 125 hamlets and districts; there are several beaches – the nearest and largest (2km/1.5mi of sand) is Bonnegrâce near Sanary.

The name comes from the Latin *sex furni*, a fortified post which was the first sign of settlement left by the Phocaeans from Massilia. During the Middle Ages the village was clustered around the summit of a hill and protected by three rows of ramparts. The Collégiale St-Pierre remains from this highly fortified site.

A REFUGE FOR EARLY CHRISTIANS

Old Six-Fours

Access via Avenue du Maréchal-Juin; turn left onto a narrow road.

The steep climb offers alternating views of Sanary Bay and the Toulon anchorage.

★ **Fort de Six-Fours** – Alt 210m/689ft. From the platform at the entrance to the fort a **panorama★** extends from east to west over Toulon anchorage, St-Mandrier Peninsula, Cap Sicié, Sanary Bay, Le Brusc and the Île des Embiez.

Collégiale St-Pierre ⊘ – At the foot of the fortress stands the church of the now abandoned village of old Six-Fours. Early Christians persecuted for their religious views fled and sought refuge in this collegiate church. Subsequently, it was occupied in the 5C, as evidenced by the altar, the baptistry and various sections of the apsidal chapel. The monks of Montmajour, then those of St-Victor, built a priory and a chapel in the 11C. The church features two naves set at right angles; in the 17C a Gothic-style nave was built. The Romanesque nave contains a polyptych attributed to Louis Bréa. In the Gothic chapels are a late-16C Flemish Descent from the Cross and a Virgin attributed to Pierre Puget.

Coastal Path

▣ *Start from Bonnegrâce beach (on the edge of Sanary).* The path runs along the beaches through low thorny vegetation. It leads to the little fishing port of Le Brusc with its busy small boats *(pointus)*. This stretch of the path also crosses the rocky promontory of **Petit Gaou**. There is a fine **view★** over the southern tip of Cap Sicié Peninsula.

Experienced hikers may choose to tackle the continuation of the coastal path up to Notre-Dame-de-Mai, where it is possible to be met by car *(car park at the TDF radio station)*.

Eating out

MODERATE

Le Ligure – *60 Avenue John-Kennedy, Route de Playes* – ☎ *04 94 25 63 87* – *Closed 15 Nov-15 Dec, Sun evening and Mon off season.* – *10.37/20.89€*. Outstanding views can be had of Sanary Bay from the panoramic terrace of this restaurant painted in Provençal colours. The bill of fare concentrates on fish, seafood and freshly cooked pizzas.

La Marmite – *Quai St-Pierre,–Port du Brusc* – ☎ *04 94 34 04 81* – *lamarmite@infonie.fr* – *Closed Jan, Sun evening and Mon except Jul-Aug* – *9.90€ lunch* – *14.50/22.59€*. Sober setting with wide bay windows offering glimpses of the nearby harbour. The attractive prices are another asset.

Where to stay

MID-RANGE

L'Île Rose – *242 Promenade du Général-de-Gaulle* – ☎ *04 94 07 10 56* – *www.hotelilerose.com* – *Closed Nov* – ▣ – *21 rooms: 45.73/54.88€* – ⌸ *5.49€* – *Restaurant 18€*. This small hotel is popular on account of its choice location barely 20 yards from Bonnegrâce beach. Every morning, on opening your shutters, you will be rewarded by views of Sanary Bay and the Embiez Islands.

EXCURSIONS

★★ **Chapelle Notre-Dame-du-Mai** – *Closed to traffic mid-June to mid-September. You may reach the chapel by walking round the radio station.* The chapel is a place of pilgrimage (14 September) dedicated to Our Lady of the May Tree, also known as Our Lady of Good Protection, and contains a great many votive offerings. From the top of Cap Sicié there is a dizzying drop to the sea and a splendid **panorama**★★ of the coast from the Îles d'Hyères to the *calanques* lying east of Marseille.

Notre-Dame-de-Pépiole – *3km/2mi – about 1hr. From Six-Fours drive north. After a short distance turn left at the roundabout onto a narrow road (signposted "Monuments Historiques"). Park on the terrace, 100m/110yd from the chapel.*
This chapel of yellow, rose and grey stone, surmounted by two charming campaniles, stands in a most attractive **setting**★ of pines, cypress trees, olive trees, vines and broom, against the mountainous backdrop of Toulon.
The **Chapelle Notre-Dame-de-Pépiole** ⊙ (5C-6C) is one of the oldest early Christian buildings in France; for centuries it was hidden under heavy layers of plaster which helped to preserve it. It originally consisted of three separate chapels; in the 12C great lateral arcades of blue stone were added to create a unique place of worship. The chapel on the left contains a 17C statue of Notre-Dame-de Pépiole.

Mediterranean Caviar

Edible sea urchins, known as sea chestnuts, have been appreciated since ancient times for their fine "eggs"; they are therefore intensively harvested, leading to great scarcity on the shores of the Mediterranean. This echinoderm lives on algae, tiny animals and bacteria caught by its spines. It attaches itself to the sea by means of the suckered feet around its mouth. It moves very slowly (about 1cm/less than 0.5in a minute) by moving its spines. At certain times of the year bacterial infection can cause it to lose its spines. The edible part of the sea urchin consists of its sexual organs, divided into five branches, which are orange in the female and off-white in the male. Fishing for sea urchins is prohibited between May and August (when there is no 'r' in the month); during this period the creatures are empty. Professional fishermen, who use diving equipment, carry a gauge to check that the sea urchins are more than 5cm/2in in diameter and catch them in large nets which contain up to 20 dozen creatures.
Information campaigns designed to bring about more active conservation of sea urchins are led by the Institut Océanographique Paul-Ricard at Les Embiez and other similar institutes.

SOSPEL★

Population 2 885
Michelin map 84 fold 20, 115 west of fold 18 or 245 folds 25, 26
Local map see NICE

The old houses of Sospel, a cool mountain resort, line both banks of the Bévéra, composing a highly picturesque scene. The village lies in a cultivated basin (olive groves) surrounded by high mountains and is a good excursion centre owing to its position at the confluence of the River Merlanson and River Bévéra, where the road from Menton to the upper Vésubie meets the road from Nice to Turin via Col de Tende. Sospel was the capital of the stewardship under the County of Ventimiglia in the 13C, then bishopric during the Great Schism and one of the places travellers had to pass through on the **Salt Road** *(Route du Sel)* linking Turin, capital of the Kingdom of Sardinia, to the coast.

★A TOWN STEEPED IN HISTORY

South bank – The church and arcaded houses on Place St-Michel make a charming sight. The oldest house (Palais Ricci) to the right of the church bears a plaque recording Pope Pius VII's stay in 1809, when Napoleon had him brought to France away from the Papal States.

Église St-Michel – At the time of the Great Schism this church was a cathedral. The Romanesque bell-tower with Lombard bands flanks an imposing Baroque façade. The interior decor is pure Baroque: altar with baldaquin, huge altarpieces, *trompe-l'œil* frescoes, gilding. A denticulated cornice runs the length of the nave walls.

In the north apsidal chapel the Virgin of Mercy does not seem to belong to the Nice School but the **Immaculate Virgin★** is one of François Bréa's most accomplished works: a retable of the Virgin against a charming landscape thronged with angels. To the right of the parvis, large stairways lead to the ruins of a Carmelite convent, now almost hidden by vegetation. Carry on to reach the remains of some fortifications, including a huge 15C corner tower and, further on, a semicircular arched gateway in the curtain wall. Go through this gateway and follow a stairway to **Rue St-Pierre**, which runs on from the cathedral parvis. The road, which is lined by arcades, leads to the little square behind the *mairie* (town hall) in which there is a pretty wall fountain.

Old bridge, Sospel

THE OLD BRIDGE INN

L'Auberge du Pont Vieux – *3 Avenue Jean-Médecin – ☎ 04 93 04 00 73 – Closed for school holidays in Feb and Nov, Jun-7 Jul, and Sun evening off season. – 10.52€ lunch – 13.42/19.82€.* Homely inn set up on the premises of a former 14C monastery, providing generous meals that pay homage to Provençal cooking. The dining area is enhanced by wood panelling and brightly coloured tablecloths. All the bedrooms have been renovated.

Shopping

Markets on Place Gianotti on Thursdays and on Place de la Cabraïa on Sunday mornings: honey and goat's cheese. There is a market selling regional produce on St Michel's fête day.
The village is known for its production of honey and its handcrafted objects made with olive wood.

Leisure activities

ABC d'Air – ☎ 04 93 21 11 39. The summit of Mont Agaisen overlooking the village is a perfect starting-point for paragliding, affording fine views of the valley below. Maiden paragliding flights.

Jérôme Béretti – *3 Place Auguste-Cotta – ☎ 08 00 59 83 25.* Mountain guide available to accompany you on a canoeing excursion or to the Via Ferrata development (La Colmiane, Tende and Peille), and to recommend the hire of suitable equipment.

Hiking – A list of all the signposted hiking paths starting from the village is available from the tourist office. There are also facilities for exploring the neighbouring countryside on horseback.

In Rue St-Pierre note the emblazoned door lintels (nos 3, 20 and 29). Most of these carved stones are surmounted by a grill covering the semicircular archway and providing natural air-conditioning. There is an interesting façade (no 30) endowed with two Renaissance windows. The ground floor, in Gothic style, features a diagonal rib window and door.

Fountains – The economic supremacy of the town in past times is recalled by numerous sculpted fountains scattered around the village. On Place de la Cabraïa, the most imposing fountain has two levels and was used as a drinking trough. This place is in fact named after the flocks of goats that were once seen here. There are other fountains on Place St-Nicolas (the oldest), at the end of Rue de la République and on Place St-Pierre, behind the town hall.

★ **Old bridge** – The toll tower on the 11C bridge was destroyed during the Second World War. It has been rebuilt and now houses the Syndicat d'Initiative (tourist office) and, in season, an information centre about the Parc National du Mercantour.

North bank – Cross the old bridge, paved with cobblestones, to visit Place St-Nicolas with its old houses and pretty paving. Beneath the arcades of the erstwhile community centre, decorated with a paschal lamb in bas-relief, there is a lovely 15C fountain. Rue de la République to the right once housed a host of small businesses and enormous cellars used as warehouses by passing merchants before they settled their toll at the bridge. The houses along this road feature beautifully carved stone lintels (nos 14, 15, 23 and 51). In a recess (right, after no 51) there is an elegant Provençal fountain. The picturesque and narrow Rue des Tisserands leads to the 17C Ste-Croix Chapel.

EXCURSION

★ **Fort St-Roch** ⊘ – *1km/0.6mi south of the village, on D 2204 to Nice. After the cemetery, take an old army road to the right (signed).*
This military construction was designed to block the Bévéra Valley and cover the Col de Brouis and the exit of the railway tunnel coming from Breil. Completed in 1932, it amounts essentially to an underground town, 50m/164ft deep, which was able to survive for up to three months without contact with the outside world. The fort was part of the Alpine Maginot Line of fortifications built in the region during the 1930s. The tour covers over 2km/2.6mi of underground galleries, including the kitchens, an electricity generating station, an operations block, ventilation chambers, the firing stations – up a 45° slope served by a funicular which was used for ammunition, a small cinema and the artillery rooms (81mm mortar and 75mm gun), as well as the periscopes which enabled the inhabitants of the fort to view their surroundings. This interesting visit is completed by a museum containing a retrospective on the Alpine Army between 1939 and 1945.

HIKING TOURS

Botanic path – *1hr 30 min on foot there and back. This delightful footpath, sign-posted and marked with boards detailing the plants to be seen, is below D 93 to the right towards the Olivetta frontier post. Go down the slope from the road towards the railway, then turn left under the bridge. A signpost near a ruin marks the start of the botanic footpath.*

▶ The path goes through a wood of young oak trees, alders growing in a damp area, and then scrubland which was once cultivated in terraces, and a holm oak wood.

Mont Agaisen – *7km/4.3mi by car and then 2hr on foot there and back. From Sospel take the road that runs alongside the post office and then climbs up the north bank of the Bévéra. After 1.5km/1mi, turn right and follow a road uphill towards Serres des Bérins.*

▶ The road winds its way up the hillside between orchards, offering pretty glimpses of the valley. On entering the Bérins district, take the surfaced road on the right, heading south. After a short stretch through some woods, the old army road reaches the first small forts of the fortified complex of Mont-Agaisen *(not open to the public)*.

It is possible to leave the car at any one of the many lay-bys along the climb. Follow the path that leads to the summit (alt 745m/2 444ft) on foot. Here and there you will come across a casemate or a firing turret. Heading due south will bring you to the edge of the summit, near a large metal cross. There is a good view of the village, the Bévéra Valley and Mont Barbonnet, recognisable by its fortified glacis. There are many other viewpoints on the summit, towards Col de Brouis, for example, or north towards the sunken valley dominated by the bare peak of Mont Mangiabo (alt 1 801m/5 909ft).

The more experienced ramblers can opt for a variation on this excursion, leaving from the village and undertaking it entirely on foot. In this case, they should leave from the Groupe Scolaire overlooking the village and follow the path leading off to the right, marked "GR 52 – Mont Agaisen" *(allow 3hr)*.

The track merges with that of GR 52; follow the red and white blazes along this for about 1km/0.6mi. At the junction with a surfaced road, turn left onto this and follow it uphill for another half a mile or so until you reach the first ruins of military buildings and rejoin the car itinerary described above.

DRIVING TOURS

★Piène-Haute via Col de Vescavo

9km/5.6mi – allow half a day. From Sospel take D 2204 east. After 2km/1.2mi turn right onto a road signed "Piène-Olivetta". After 4km/2.5mi D 93 reaches Col de Vescavo (alt 478m/1 568ft) which overlooks the bank on the Italian side of the Bévéra. The road then meanders through pine trees and olive groves to the border checkpoint before the Italian village of Olivetta. Follow D 193 to the left.

The road continues to climb up to the charming little village of **Piène-Haute**, in solitary splendour on an outcrop 613m/2 011ft in altitude. The best place to park is on the esplanade at the entrance to the village. Before setting off downhill on foot, admire the **view**★ of the old houses huddled side by side, overlooked by the castle ruins. Tiny streets crammed with flowers and bursting with colour lead to the pretty square fronting the *mairie* (town hall). The church, on a rise, has a beautiful carved bell-tower and houses an unusual red marble altarpiece. Above the village, by the castle ruins, there are splendid views of the valley of the Roya and the hamlet of Piène-Basse on the border.

The Salt Road

Owing to its essential role in the preservation of meat and the tanning of hides, salt has always been of considerable interest to tradesmen. Provençal salt-works have supplied Piedmont since the Middle Ages. The salt was unloaded from sailing barges in Nice and transported by mule to Turin. Among the routes used at the time, the one favoured by the princes of Savoy crossed Col de Braus, Col de Brouis and Col de Tende and passed through Sospel and Saorge. This strategic highway became known as the Salt Road *(Route du Sel)*. The returning caravans carried rice from Piedmont, as well as hemp and cloth. The heavy traffic (more than 5 000t of salt a year), which by the end of the 18C was using close to 15 000 mules, obliged the authorities to improve the road and make it suitable for carts and carriages; they also drew up plans for a tunnel under Col de Tende but it was not completed until 1883.

The road, which is now embellished with works of modern art, is still the main highway between the Riviera and the cities of Piedmont.

 Experienced hikers may wish to extend the excursion from here to Col de Brouis or as far as the Arpette peak (alt 1 610m/5 282ft) via the hamlet of Libre, following the line of the crest along the border, overlooking the village *(half a day to Brouis, a whole day as far as Arpette)*.

★Col de Brouis Road

21km/13mi – about 1hr – local map see NICE.

This road is an extension of the Col de Braus Road *(see Forêt de TURINI)* towards Turin, formerly known as the "Salt Road", linking the Bévéra Valley to the Roya Valley.

From Sospel take D 2204 east.

There is a view to the rear over Sospel guarded by the Fort du Barbonnet.

Col du Pérus – Alt 654m/2 146ft. The road runs above the Bassera ravine.

★**Col de Brouis** – Alt 879m/2 884ft. This pass takes its name from the particular type of heather-like shrub that thrives in the area, known locally as *brouis*. The monument above the car park on the right commemorates the last French attack of April 1945 against the German forces, who had been driven back into the valleys. A broad **view**★ opens up of the peaks on the far bank of the Roya.
The road descends two steep slopes before winding down to La Giandola.

La Giandola – Attractive mountain hamlet with a Renaissance church tower.
Beyond La Giandola the road climbs the Roya Valley which becomes ever more enclosed.

Massif du TANNERON

Michelin map 84 folds 8 and 9, 115 north of folds 33 and 34 or 245 folds 36 and 37

The Tanneron is a northern extension of the Esterel, from which it is separated by a shallow depression through which N 7 and the Provençal motorway run.
However, its rounded contours and the nature of its rocks (gneiss) suggest that it is more closely related to the Maures.

A bouquet of mimosa – The Tanneron is well known for its winter display of brilliant yellow mimosa contrasting with the clear winter sky. The snowfalls and hard frosts in 1985 and 1986 have unfortunately caused considerable damage to this plant.
Once the massif was covered with sea pines and chestnut trees, but the forest has been much reduced under the triple assault of man (cultivation rights have existed since the Middle Ages), the cochineal (a parasitic insect which kills pine trees) and fire.

DRIVING TOURS

From Cannes to Mandelieu

56km/35mi – allow half a day

Cannes – *See CANNES.*
From Cannes take N 7. For a description of the route as far as the Logis-de-Paris crossroads see Massif de l'ESTEREL 2.

Then turn right onto D 237 which offers **fleeting views** of La Napoule Bay and Mont Vinaigre. Beyond Les Adrets de l'Esterel the view extends to the Pre-Alps of Grasse. The road crosses over the Provençal motorway on the edge of the Montauroux woods before skirting St-Cassien Lake.

Mimosa blossom

N. Thibaut/EXPLORER

Lac de St-Cassien – *Before Pré-Claou bridge turn right onto D 38.*

The road rises through a pine wood with pleasant **glimpses** of the lake, the dam and the mountain peaks on the horizon. Near the hamlet of Les Marjoris the road winds over mimosa-clad slopes down to the River Verrerie.

Mellow Yellow

Mimosa was introduced into the Mediterranean region from Australia in 1839 and is first mentioned near Cannes in 1864. Since then it has invaded the slopes of the Tanneron Massif and brought financial success to the region. Mimosa belongs to the acacia family of plants. There are three main varieties of mimosa tree. Silver wattle *(mimosa argenté)*, has bluish-green bushes that blossom in winter and can be seen thriving on the terraces west of Cannes. The small trees are cultivated and the bright yellow flowers sold both in France and abroad. Blue-leaved wattle *(mimosa glauque)* is characterised by its greyish pendent twigs and is used for decorative purposes. Thirdly, the most common variety in Provence is four-seasons wattle *(mimosa des quatre saisons)*, which grows in huge swathes and flowers all year round. The leaves are light green and the delicately fragrant pale yellow balls are a familiar sight in many parks and gardens of the Riviera. Flowering can be induced or improved by forcing techniques. Fronds are cut prematurely and shut up in a dark room for two or three days at a temperature of 22-25°C/71-77°F with very high humidity. Mimosa can also be cut when the flowers are still in bud; a special powder mixed with hot water will cause the flowers to open. Tonnes of cut flowers from the Tanneron are sold in France and abroad each year.

Before reaching Tanneron village, turn right onto a steep narrow road.

★**Chapelle Notre-Dame-de-Peygros** ⊘ – Alt 412m/1 352ft. From the terrace of the Romanesque chapel, there is a fine **panorama★** of the Lac de St-Cassien, the Siagne Valley and Grasse; Mont Agel on the coast and the Alps on the Italian border stand out to the east; the Esterel and the Maures Massifs dominate the southern horizon.
Follow signs to the small outlet where locally produced honey *(miel)* can be sampled and purchased.

Pass through Tanneron to the Val-Cros crossroads.

The drive down reveals fine **views** of Auribeau, Grasse and the broad Siagne Valley.

★**Auribeau-sur-Siagne** – *7km/4.3mi – leaving from the Val-Cros crossroads (alt 296m/971ft).* A narrow twisting road sunk between banks of mimosa leads up to the charming village, which dates from the 12C, on a hill beside the Siagne. It was rebuilt in 1490 by settlers from Genoa. Pass under the 16C Porte Soubran, the Upper Gateway, and stroll through the stepped and, at times, narrow streets. The old houses (restored) huddle around the **church** ⊘, which contains a 15C silver-gilt and enamelled reliquary and a 16C chalice.

From the church square the **view** encompasses the wooded hills of the Siagne Valley, Grasse and its ring of mountains, Pic de Courmettes and the Valbonne Plateau.

Starting from the church's west façade, take the stepped streets (Degrés de l'Église and Degrés Soubran) leading to Porte Soutran, the Lower Gateway, which is set in a bend of a street. It is fortified and has a rounded arch.

Return to the Val-Cros crossroads and go straight across towards Mandelieu-la-Napoule on D 109.

COUNTRY LIFE

Champfagou – *Place du Village – 83440 Tanneron* – ☎ *04 93 60 68 30 – Closed Oct, Nov, evenings 15 Oct-15 Dec – 19.06/25.92€.* A pink façade, clumps of hydrangeas, a tidy garden and a shaded terrace are the undeniable assets of this village inn. The menu pays tribute to Mediterranean cooking. Small, homey rooms appointed with bamboo furniture.

Auberge de Nossi-Bé – *06810 Auribeau-sur-Siagne –Village Centre –* ☎ *04 93 42 20 20 – Closed 1 Nov-15 Dec and Wed – 6 rooms: 45.73/50.31€ –* ⌷ *7.62€ – Restaurant 28€.* Appealing stone house with a terrace commanding superbs views of the valley and wooded heights near La Siagne. Smallish but well kept rooms in the rustic tradition. French cuisine.

★★**Road to Mandelieu** – The slopes of the massif are covered by scrub. The drive through the mimosa down a steep hill to Mandelieu-la-Napoule is marvellous, with many **views★★** of the Esterel, the town and its aerodrome, La Napoule Bay, Cannes and the Îles de Lérins, the Siagne Valley, Grasse and the Pre-Alps. On the horizon loom the majestic Alps.

Mandelieu-la-Napoule – *See MANDELIEU-LA-NAPOULE. Return to Cannes by D 92 and N 98 along the seafront.*

TENDE★

Population 1 844
Michelin map 84 fold 10, 115 fold 8 or 245 fold 26
Local map see NICE

Tende (alt 816m/2 677ft) has a breathtaking **setting**★, in an Alpine landscape on the banks of the Roya beneath the steep rock face of the Riba de Bernou. The tall austere houses beneath their shingled roofs seem to be stacked on top of one another. A jagged tooth of wall sticking 20m/65ft into the air is all that remains of the former splendour of the Lascaris family, whose castle was pulled down by the French during the War of the League of Augsburg in 1692. A curious terraced cemetery near the walls adds a bizarre touch. Tende commands access to the road over the pass into Italy and, together with St-Dalmas, it is the starting point for organised excursions to the Vallée des Merveilles.

Old town, Tende

AN ALPINE SETTING

★**Old town** — Most of the houses, some dating from the 15C, are built with the local stone, green and purple schist. The maze of narrow streets boasts several carved lintels bearing escutcheons, huge overhanging eaves and balconies on all floors. Note the Renaissance bell-towers on the chapels of the Black and White Penitents. From above the town on the site of the old castle, the **view**★ looks down onto the village, its shingled-roofed houses and bell-towers.

Collégiale Notre-Dame-de-l'Assomption — This collegiate church was built in the early 15C with green schist, except for the Lombard tower capped with a pretty little dome. The Renaissance-style **doorway** is flanked by two Doric columns resting on two lions, inspired by Romanesque art; the entablature is decorated with statues of Christ and the Apostles. The tympanum illustrates the Assumption. The inside is divided equally into three aisles by thick, green-schist (from the Roya) columns. The lords of Lascaris are buried here. The sacristy ceiling is decorated with 17C frescoes and stuccowork.

SIGHT

Musée des Merveilles ⊙ – *Avenue du 16-Septembre-1947, opposite the Customs Office.* A visit to this museum, with its modern façade consisting of 12 parallelepiped columns and a square green stone from the Roya depicting rock art motifs, is recommended as the ideal complement to a walk around the sites of Mont Bégo. The history of the Vallée des Merveilles and its inhabitants is illustrated in the museum, centring on three themes: relief models and animations show the regional geology; archeology forms a major exhibit with dioramas reconstructing daily life in the Bronze Age, many casts of the carvings, the original stela known as *chef de tribu* (moved because of erosion damage) and objects discovered during excavations; modern popular and pastoral traditions are brought to life in an exhibition of objects and dioramas which show a continuity with prehistoric life.
The museum also houses a university training centre and facilities for research into rock art of the period.

309

EXCURSIONS

St-Dalmas-de-Tende – Attractive resort surrounded by chestnut forests. It is a good excursion centre, particularly for the Vallée des Merveilles, and offers numerous facilities for cycling, riding, skiing and hiking. The station with its vast and luxurious façade reminds visitors that, back in the 1930s, it used to be the frontier post on the road linking Nice to Cuneo.

La Brigue – *2.5km/1.5mi east of St-Dalmas-de-Tende along the charming Levense Valley. See La BRIGUE.*

★★ **Notre-Dame-des-Fontaines** – *4km/2.5mi east of La Brigue on D 43 and D 143. For a description of the chapel, see La BRIGUE.*

Return to St-Dalmas-de-Tende and after 1km/0.6mi take D 91 to the Lac des Mesches then turn left in the direction of Granile.

A LOCAL RESTAURANT ...

Auberge Tendasque – *65 Avenue du 16-Septembre-1947 – ☎ 04 93 04 62 26 – Closed Tue Jun-Oct and evenings Oct-Jun except Sat – 12.96/19.82€.* This modest restaurant is within walking distance of the fascinating Musée des Merveilles, which presents the archeological and geological heritage of the region. Good provençal cuisine. Reasonable prices.

... AND A LOVELY HOTEL

Prieuré – *06430 St-Dalmas-de-Tende – 4km/2.4mi S of Tende by N 204 – ☎ 04 93 04 75 70 – Closed between Christmas and 1 Jan – 24 rooms: 40.40/57.17€ – ☑ 5.64€ – Restaurant 14/21€.* Tastefully restored former priory containing large, well kept rooms with a modern decor and fine furniture. The vaulted dining hall opens out onto a pleasant patio. The menu offers Mediterranean cuisine. Sit down under the arbour on the terrace and admire the sight of Mont Bego in the distance.

Granile – The road twists for 5km/3mi through chestnut woods and Scots pine before finishing in a cul-de-sac at Granile. This charming village, seemingly isolated on the side of a mountain, has an unusual appearance with its mountain houses decorated with wooden balconies and roofs covered with stone slabs. There is an impressive view of the Gorges de la Roya and *(east)* of the ridge of peaks on the frontier.

To the south of the village, a path leads either to N 204 at the foot of the valley or to the village of Bergue (or Berghe) further south.

Return to St-Dalmas-de-Tende and continue up the valley.

The apple trees in the meadows contrast with the rock-strewn olive groves in the regions round Sospel and Breil. At a bend, Tende comes into view.

Abbaye du THORONET★★

Michelin map 84 fold 6, 114 fold 21 or 245 fold 34
9km/6mi southwest of Lorgues

Le Thoronet, the oldest of the three Cistercian abbeys in Provence *(see Michelin Green Guide PROVENCE: Sénanque and Silvacane)* is surrounded by wooded hills in an isolated spot, in keeping with the strict rules of the Cistercian Order.

From foundation to the present – In 1136 monks from the abbey of Mazan (Haut-Vivarais) settled in the valley of the River Florège near Tourtour, but later they moved to Le Thoronet near Lorgues and finally established themselves on land presented to them by Raymond Bérenger, Count of Barcelona and Marquis of Provence. The abbey soon became prosperous from the many donations it received, particularly from the lords of Castellane. The church, the cloisters and the monastic buildings were built between 1160 and 1190.

A few years later the abbey's most famous abbot was appointed – **Folquet de Marseille**. His family came from Genoa but he gave up a career in trade to devote himself to poetry. He became a famous troubadour, quoted by Dante, and then in 1196 decided to become a Cistercian monk. In 1201 he was appointed Abbot of Le Thoronet and then Bishop of Toulouse in 1205.

Like many other Cistercian abbeys in the 14C, Le Thoronet sank into decline. First internal dissension and later the Wars of Religion caused the monks to desert the premises. In 1787 it was attached to the See of Digne. During the Revolution it was sold and yet again abandoned. In 1854 it was bought by the State and saved from ruin at the instigation of Prosper Mérimée.

Chapterhouse

The restoration and consolidation work which has been carried out since then has been made even more necessary by the bauxite extraction site nearby and the subsidence caused by the weather.

TOUR ⏱ *1hr*

Thanks to the quality of the surviving buildings (church and cloisters), and their simple but rigorous style, the abbey of Le Thoronet is widely considered one of the jewels of Cistercian architecture.

★ **Church** – This was built in the style of the Provençal-Romanesque School.

Exterior – The building is squat, austere and rigorously geometric. It is extraordinarily similar in plan to the abbey church at Sénanque. The stonework is remarkable; the blocks have been accurately cut and assembled without mortar. The square bell-tower of stone is an exception to the architectural rules of the order, which allowed only simple wooden structures. It was permitted here because of the violent winds and the risk of fire.

In the west front there are four small windows and an oculus but no central door; instead there are two side doors opening into the aisles, both surmounted by a small window which is slightly off-centre. The door on the left was for the lay brothers. In the south wall, on the opposite side to the cloisters, is a round-arched niche, one of the rare external funerary repositories in Provence.

Interior – The nave is covered with barrel vaulting, slightly pointed, supported on tranverse arches. It consists of three bays, prolonged by a fourth of the same height at right angles to the transept: only the raised arches indicate the presence of two arms of the transept which are vaulted like the nave. As at Sénanque, the eastern wall of each transept opens into two semicircular chapels which, on the outside, are rectangular in shape.

The chancel ends in an oven-vaulted apse, as at Sénanque, and is lit through three windows. It is preceded by a shallow bay, featuring a triumphal arch surmounted by an oculus. The aisles are lower than the nave and covered with rampant pointed vaulting resting on transverse arches.

There is hardly any sculpture or carved decoration in the church to detract from its majestic proportions and purity of line. There is, however, a gentle curve on the imposts on the pillars and the half-columns supporting the transverse arches and rise to only 2.90m/9.5ft above the ground according to Cistercian tradition.

★ **Cloisters** – The cloisters on the north side of the church are austere and solidly built in the form of a trapezium. The south gallery is at about the same level as the church, but the west (exhibition of manuscripts and illuminated texts) and the north and east (which once supported another storey beneath a pitched roof) are lower because of the uneven ground; in all, seven steps were needed to compensate for the change of level. The galleries have transverse arches and barrel vaulting. The solid, round-headed arches which open onto the cloisters' garth (now a garden) are each divided in two by a stout column; the tympanum is pierced by an oculus.

Opposite the refectory door, projecting into the garth, is the **lavabo** where the monks washed their hands before meals. The hexagonal structure has been restored; the water container is provided with holes and spouts through which the water ran into the basin below.

Conventional buildings – These stand on the north side of the church round the cloisters. The door of the library **(armarium)**, which is on the ground floor, is surmounted by a triangular lintel.

The **chapter-house**★ dates from the early Gothic period; the ogival vaulting, in which the ribs fan out like palm trees, is supported by two columns with roughly sculpted capitals, ornamented with leaves, pine cones, palm fronds and a hand gripping a staff. These are the only carvings in the abbey. The stone benches have been partially reconstructed. Next to the chapter-house is the **parlour** which also serves as a passage between the cloisters and the outer garden. The **dormitory** over the chapter-house is reached by a vaulted stairway; it is roofed with pointed vaulting supported on transverse arches; the 18 windows with double embrasures have been reglazed. At the southern end, jutting out above the cloisters, is the Abbot's chamber. The doors in the north gallery opened into the monks' room, the warming room, the refectory and the kitchen, which have all disappeared.

The **store room**, on the west side of the cloisters, has pointed vaulting and contains 18C vats for wine and olive oil as well as the remains of a press.

The lay-brother building, at the northwest corner of the store room, provided separate housing for the lay-brothers, who carried out manual labour for the monks and who lived a less restrained monastic life. It has been partially restored and comprises a refectory on the ground floor and a dormitory above.

Outbuildings – Beside the stream, the foundations of the **guesthouse** have been excavated. The **tithe barn** on the south side of the church was later converted into an oil mill and contains some mill stones and a mortar.

THE SUNFLOWER

Le Tournesol – *9 Rue des Trois-Ormetox – 83340 Le Thoronet – 4km/2.4mi from the Abbey –* ☎ *04 94 73 89 81 – Closed Jan – ☑ – 15€.* This tiny 17C house in a village alley will surprise you by its colourful walls and furniture, its homely cooking and its charming terrace giving onto the street.

TOULON★★

Population of conurbation 519 640
Michelin map 84 fold 15, 114 fold 45 or 245 fold 46
Local map see Excursions below
Plan of conurbation in the current Michelin Red Guide France

France's second naval port lies behind its **anchorage**★★, one of the most secure and most beautiful harbours of the Mediterranean, surrounded by tall hills crowned by forts. The suburbs lie along the shore and form terraces on the sunny slopes of the surrounding hills.

HISTORICAL NOTES

Toulon purple – In Roman times Toulon was celebrated for the manufacture of the imperial purple. The dye was obtained by steeping the colour glands of the pointed conches (genus *Murex*) which proliferate along the coast in salt solution previously brought to boiling point for 10 days in lead vats. The purple obtained was used to dye silk and woollen materials. This sumptuous colour was initially reserved for emperors but later its use spread, though the imperial treasury maintained a monopoly over its manufacture. The foundations of the old Toulon dye-works were uncovered during reconstruction work in the arsenal.

The age of the galleys (17C and 18C) – One of the attractions for travellers of the 17C and 18C was to visit the galleys moored in the old port (Vieille Darse). Each ship had only one bank of oars – 25 or 26 oars per side, each about 16m/52ft long and manned by four men; the sails were triangular; artillery had begun to be used. Thousands of galley slaves were needed. Criminals and poachers not being numerous enough, political and religious prisoners were added; Turks were bought and there were even some volunteers! All these men were bare-foot, wore a red cloak and a red or green bonnet; faces and heads were clean shaven but the Turks were allowed to retain a tuft of hair and the volunteers their moustaches. On board, the galley slaves rowed with one foot bound to the deck and one wrist chained to the oar, eating and sleeping without leaving their places. The slave-master stimulated their efforts with cuts from a rawhide whip.

The slaves were allowed to go ashore but were chained together in pairs. In 1748 galleys were abolished and replaced by naval prisons. In 1854 these too disappeared and the system of transportation overseas followed.

One of the Painted Walls of Toulon

Bonaparte's first feat of arms – On 27 August 1793, Royalists handed Toulon over to an Anglo-Spanish fleet. A Republican army was sent to Toulon; the artillery was under the command of an obscure junior captain called Bonaparte. Between La Seyne and Tamaris, where Fort Carré or Fort Napoléon stands today, the British had built a fortification so strong that it was called "little Gibraltar".

A battery was installed facing the British fort, but was subjected to such terrible fire that the gunners faltered. Bonaparte set the example; he laid the guns and manned the sponge-rod. It was in this engagement that Sergeant Junot distinguished himself. As he was writing down an order dictated by Bonaparte, a shell burst nearby covering them both with flying earth: "Good!" said Junot, brushing himself down, "now I shall not need any sand to dry the ink". "Little Gibraltar" fell on 17 December. The foreign fleet withdrew after burning the French ships, the arsenal, and the provision depots, as well as taking part of the population with them. While Napoleon was being made a brigadier-general, Toulon came within a hair's breadth of being destroyed; 12 000 workers were requisitioned to raze "the infamous city", but at the last moment the Convention cancelled the order.

Second World War – In November 1942, in response to the Allied landings in North Africa, Hitler decided to invade the French free zone. The decision was therefore taken to scupper the French fleet *(see below)*.

On 19 August 1944, four days after the Allied landing on the Maures beaches, French troops attacked the Toulon defences, a plan of which had been smuggled out in 1942 by sailors in the Resistance. The city was liberated on 26 August. On 13 September the French fleet, which had taken part in the liberation, sailed into the anchorage, where the scuttled ships still lay on the bottom.

Post-war – Up to 1939 Toulon had been too dependent on the naval dockyard and very isolated by its geographic position. After the war efforts were made to diversify: the Arsenal broadened the scope of its production, commercial trade in the port was developed and new industries were introduced. The construction of holiday homes in the region sustained the building trade in the period after the post-war reconstruction boom. Improvements in the road network made the town more easily accessible. Tourism, the founding of a university and of the **Centre Culturel de Châteauvallon** all underpin hopes for the city's successful future.

Bagne de Toulon

The only remains of this terrible penal colony, described in detail by Victor Hugo in his novel *Les Misérables*, is a wall in the arsenal. The withdrawal of the galleys in 1748 turned the galley slaves into convicts *(see above)*. At its peak the colony held nearly 4 000 convicts, employed in shipbuilding and harbour maintenance. They formed a marginal but highly structured society, with a common feature – the chain weighing 7kg/15lb to which they were permanently attached. In 1854 the government introduced transportation to penal settlements in the French colonies, such as Guyana and New Caledonia. The penal colony in Toulon was finally closed on 1 January 1874 when the last 300 inmates were shipped to Cayenne on board the frigate *La Guerrière*.

Eating out

MODERATE

Al Dente – *30 Rue Gimelli* – ☎ *04 94 93 02 50* – *Closed Sun for lunch* – *9.15€ lunch* – *16.16/22.87€*. The main reason for coming here is the remarkable choice of pasta dishes and Italian specialities, with additional menus at highly affordable prices. Regular customers also appreciate the modern decor bursting with colour.

MID-RANGE

Chez Mimi – *83 Avenue de la République* – ☎ *04 94 92 79 60* – *Closed Jul and Mon* – *19.82/25.92€*. No need to hop across the Mediterranean to sample a delicious *couscous* in a homey setting enhanced by traditional Tunisian artwork. The friendly welcome and thoughtful service come straight from the heart.

Lido – *Avenue Frédéric-Mistral. Morillon* – ☎ *04 94 03 38 18* – *Closed Sun evening and Mon 30 Sep-30 May* – *21.34/28.97€*. The terrace of this restaurant draws tourists and locals alike in the first days of spring. The dining room is a tribute to fishermen with its marine decoration consisting of seascapes and hulls of ships. It will come as no surprise to discover that the menu proposes... fish, seafood and shellfish.

LUXURY

Chez Daniel "Restaurant du Rivage" – *83500 La Seyne-sur-Mer* – *4km/2.4mi S of La Seyne by Route de St-Mandrier and country lane* – ☎ *04 94 94 85 13* – *Closed Nov, Sun evening and Mon Sep-Jun* – *35.06/57.93€*. A small rocky inlet is the choice setting for this seafood restaurant that knows the true meaning of Provençal life. The freshly caught fish offered to diners may come from the sea or from the big fish tank set up on the premises. One of the dining rooms proudly displays a collection of old barouches and farming tools.

Where to stay

MODERATE

Grand Hôtel Dauphiné – *10 Rue Berthelot* – ☎ *04 94 92 20 28* – *grandhotel-dudauphine@wanadoo.fr* – *55 rooms: 36.59/45.73€* – ☖ *5.64€*. This centrally located hotel is the perfect starting-point for a tour of the old city and its intricate maze of streets. The lively rooms hung with printed fabric are above all functional.

Les 3 Dauphins – *9 Place des 3 Dauphins* – ☎ *04 94 92 65 79* – *14 rooms: 38.11/42.69€* – ☖ *4.12€*. The windows of this recently renovated hotel give onto a tiny square dominated by a bust of Raimu. The smallish rooms have been tastefully appointed and decorated in smiling shades. Charming welcome and service.

MID-RANGE

New Hôtel de l'Amirauté – *4 Rue A.-Guiol* – ☎ *04 94 22 19 67* – *58 rooms: 60.98/65.55€*. In the centre of town, this hotel is a good opportunity to reconcile a business trip with the delights of tourism. The decor is reminiscent of the large luxury liners of bygone times. Functional, efficiently soundproofed rooms.

Val'Hôtel – *Avenue René-Cassin, ZA Paul Madon* – *83160 La Valette* – *Take exit 5 off the A 57, behind the "Leroy-Merlin" store, follow signs to ZI de Toulon-la-Valette* – ☎ *04 94 08 38 08* – *www.val-hotel.com* – 🅿 – *42 rooms: 48.78€* – ☖ *5.34€*. The lush setting, the large, colourful rooms with balcony or terrace, and the inexpensive weekend rates will soon make you forget the motorway exit nearby.

On the town

Like many big cities, Toulon is swarming with people. Its anchorage (one of the finest in Europe), its concert halls and its many leisure activities have made it a leading centre for tourism, culture and sport. The city also lives by night, thanks to the many bars, cafés and restaurants.

La Lampa – *117 Quai de Sinse* – ☎ *04 94 03 06 09* – *Daily 10am-1am*. This small bar taken up by a long counter attracts an extremely varied clientele. All year round, La Lampa organises evenings devoted to specific themes.

Shows

Café-Théâtre – *Place Armand-Vallée* – ☎ *04 94 92 99 75* – *Check the programme of events*. All year round, this *café-théâtre* organises clarinet and jazz concerts, pantomime shows and stand-up comedy.

Opéra de Toulon – *Boulevard de Strasbourg –* ☎ *04 94 92 70 78 / 04 94 93 03 76 – Mon-Fri 9am-12.30pm, 2.30-6pm30, and evenings of performances.* Built in 1862, the Opéra de Toulon is ranked 2nd in France on account of its seating capacity and remarkable acoustics. The 2001-2002 season focuses on opera *(Norma, Manon, La Traviata, Don Giovanni...)*, operetta *(The Viennese Waltzes, The Merry Widow)*, ballet *(Sleeping Beauty, Don Quichotte...)* and theatrical plays.

Zénith-Oméga – *Place des Lices –* ☎ *08 36 68 06 86 – Check programme of events.* This concert hall organises various events such as stage productions, classical concerts, pop music, alongside international fairs and exhibitions.

Sit back and relax

Bar à Thym – *32 Boulevard de Cunéo –* ☎ *04 94 41 90 11 / 04 94 41 90 10 – barathym.com – Mon-Tue: 6pm-1am; Wed-Sat: 6pm-3am; May-Sep; 6pm-5am.* Popular watering hole for the younger generation. The impressive choice of beers (over 100, including 12 draught beers) is a definite asset. Choose between the live concerts *(Tue-Wed-Thu)* or the evenings run by a disc jockey. Special evenings on a particular theme are also organised *(Fri-Sat)*

Le Panoramique – *Sommet du Mont Faron –* ☎ *04 94 88 08 00 – Jun-Sep: daily 9.30am-10pm; Oct-May: daily 10am-6pm.* This café-restaurant perched atop Mont Faron commands outstanding views of Toulon anchorage. The Souza family, who own the nearby zoo, settled here in April 2000 and will be delighted to explain the local sights to you *(binoculars available)*. Warm welcome.

Market in Cours Lafayette, Toulon

Transport

Pedestrian area – The district in the old part of town bordered by Rue Anatole-France, Avenue de la République, Avenue de Besagne and Boulevard de Strasbourg is closed to traffic. The largest car parks are located on Place d'Armes, Place de la Liberté and in the Mayol shopping mall.

Buses – The RMTT provides an efficient bus service covering Toulon and its outskirts. Plans, timetables and tickets can be obtained from the newsstand on Place de la Liberté.

Boat shuttle service – *SITCAT/RMTT on Quai Cronstadt or 720 Avenue du Colonel-Picot –* ☎ *04 94 03 87 03.* There are several daily services to and from **La Seyne-sur-Mer, Les Sablettes, Tamaris** and **St-Mandrier-sur-Mer**.
These lines are part and parcel of the local transport system and they charge similar rates to those requested on buses.

Guided tours

Guided tours of the city – Guided tours *(1hr 30min)* starting out from the tourist office are a great opportunity to discover the old quarter of Toulon: Jul-Aug Wed-Fri at 10am; Sep-Jun Wed and Fri at 2pm. 3.5€.

Culinary specialities

The café terraces on Quai Cronstadt provide a good view of the life of the old port – *Bar du Soleil, La Gourmandise* and *Le France.* The natives of Toulon *(moccots)* particularly enjoy *l'escabèche de sardine, la cade* (a flat cake made from chickpeas, similar to *socca* in Nice), *la pompe à l'huile* (a hard cake, oiled and flavoured with orange water) and the famous sweet doughnut *(chichifregi)* which can be bought from the stalls in the Lafayette market. Several restaurants specialise in fish dishes (Place du Théâtre and Rue Jean-Jaurès).

In **Mourillon** many restaurants have terraces which are ideal places to sit and try the seafood dishes (Corniche Henri-Fabre, Port St-Louis).

Shopping

The best place to go shopping is the area around Rue Jean-Jaurès, Rue Hoche, Place Victor-Hugo and Rue d'Alger.

Côté Tissus – *8 Rue de la Fraternité* – ☎ *04 94 46 37 92* – *Tue-Sat 9am-noon, 2.30-7pm.* Delightful boutique with stone walls that sells Provençal fabric. The arch on the right reminds visitors that a river flowed through the premises over one hundred years ago.

Les Navires de la Royale – *30 Rue des Riaux* – ☎ *06 14 45 19 38* – *Mon-Sat 9am-noon, 2-6pm.* Amateurs sailors should make a point of visiting this shop, owned by Jean-Michel Delcourte, an enthusiastic lover of all things maritime! His days are spent making and restoring all sorts of boats, ranging from yachts to schooners to catamarans!

Centre Mayol – Supermarket, FNAC (books, records, photographic equipment), trendy fashion labels.

La Santonnerie – *92 Rue Alphonse-Daudet - 83220 Le Pradet* – ☎ *04 94 75 04 35* – *9am-noon, 3-7pm.* Traditional clay figures.

Moulin de St-Côme – *St-Côme district* – *83740 La Cadière-d'Azur* – ☎ *04 94 90 11 51.* Olive oil, regional produce, high-quality fabric. Free visit of olive press and tastings of olive oil.

Having a dip

☙ **Mourillon beach** – *To the east, along Littoral Frédéric-Mistral, between Fort St-Louis and the water sports centre. First-aid posts. Restaurants, bathroom facilities.* To avoid paying the fee charged by the Mourillon car park, go there by bus ! Lines 3, 13 and 23 (Mourillon) or 7 and 23 (Magaud and Méjean coves) will drop you at the beach.

The long Toulon beach, separated from the road by a large park, consists of four curved stretches of coastline covered with fine sand or gravel, or a combination of both, depending on their location. The lands descends into the sea on a gradual slope and bathers are sheltered by the piers.

Méjean and Magaud beaches – *From Le Mourillon, follow directions to La Garde-Le Pradet.* At the entrance to La Garde, Chemin de la Mer leads to two natural sandy beaches, the twin coves of Magaud *(on the left)* and Méjean *(on the right).*

DISCOVERING TOULON

☐ From Square to Square

Place de la Liberté – This square is the heart of the modern town. The monumental fountain, Fontaine de la Fédération, erected in 1889 to celebrate the centenary of the Republic, is the work of André Allar. The superb Grand Hôtel (1870) in the background, with its charming old-fashioned façade, is the last remaining example of the buildings of the Edwardian era.

On either side of the square, Boulevard Strasbourg and Avenue du Général-Leclerc (built on the site of the former fortifications) form the main axis of the town, separating the old town to the south from the new town to the north. The Opéra Municipal (1862), formerly the largest auditorium outside Paris, was the centre of attraction in the evenings until just before the Second World War. The many local cafés and cabarets helped to give this district a festive atmosphere.

Place Victor-Hugo – Further on you will discover one of the façades belonging to the Théâtre de Toulon, one of France's finest regional theatres. Go round the building to admire the other façade and to enjoy Place Victor-Hugo and its lively pavement cafés.

Place d'Armes – Its building was commissioned by Colbert as a venue for him to review his troops. It was then called Champ de Bataille. It soon became a highly popular meeting-place among local nobility and officers leaving on overseas assignments, featuring many restaurants and cafés, bandstands etc. It was also home to the headquarters of leading daily newspapers such as *Le Petit Marseillais*.

Corderie – *To the south of Place d'Armes. Military property, not open to the public.* This building (320m/1 050ft long), designed by Vauban to house the naval rope factory, now houses the navy's administrative offices. The fine **door**★ (1689) came from the former Jesuit college and was added to the façade in 1976. Magnificent allegories of Law *(Loi)* and Might *(Force)* frame the top floor.

Arsenal Maritime – The naval arsenal covers some 240ha/593 acres overall and employs in the region of 6 300 civilians. Its main activity is the maintenance of the French Mediterranean fleet: frigates, aircraft carriers, sloops, submarines and minesweepers. Some of the dry docks date from the 17C.

★ ② **Old Town** *2hr 30min*

The ancient heart of Toulon, with its characteristic confusion of streets, is bounded to the east by Cours Lafayette, to the west by Rue Anatole-France and to the north by Rue Landrin, a perimeter which follows the line of the fortifications in the reign of Henri IV. A programme of renovation is planned for the whole town centre.

Église St-Louis – This church is a fine example of neo-Classical architecture, built in the late 18C in the form of a Greek temple. It comprises three naves separated by a double Doric colonnade supporting a coffered vault. Ten Corinthian columns in the choir support a windowed cupola decorated with a foliage frieze. The pulpit is elaborately carved.

Fontaine des Trois-Dauphins – The character of Place Puget is embell-

---

Painted Walls of Toulon

The high points of life in Toulon are illustrated by enormous wall frescoes to be found throughout the town:
Place Victor-Hugo – The card game from *César*
Rue du Noyer *(corner of Place Raimu)* – The glory of the merchant navy
Avenue Franklin-Roosevelt – Félix Mayol
Corner of Rue Micholet – Typical activities in 19C Toulon, on three levels

---

ished by this curious fountain sculpted in 1780 by two local artists; its distinction is due to the plants which have grown in its basins. The three intertwined dolphins are covered in moss and calcium deposits, on which grow ferns, a fig tree, a medlar and an oleander. Place Puget is pleasantly shaded and the cafés surrounding it are ideal places for sitting and enjoying the coolness.
Northwest of Place Puget is **Place des Trois-Dauphins** containing a bust of Raimu.

Rue d'Alger – This pedestrian precinct is the main commercial street leading to the old port.

Église St-François-de-Paule ⊙ – This small church was built in 1744 by the Recollects; its double-arched façade and Genoan bell-tower identify it with the Nice Baroque style. It has a nave and two aisles separated by coupled columns and galleries with balustrades; the chancel opens into a dome. In the south aisle is a statue of Our Lady of Peace carved in wood by one of Puget's pupils.
Rue Méridienne and Place à l'Huile lead to Place de la Poissonnerie which for several centuries accommodated the covered Fish Market (Halles aux Poissons), one of the livelier spots in Toulon. The last market building was demolished in 1898.

Cathédrale Ste-Marie – The cathedral was constructed in the 11C and restored in the 12C. In the 17C it was enlarged and the classical façade was erected; the bell-tower dates from 1740. The fairly dark interior is a mixture of Romanesque and Gothic, since the 17C architects retained the plan of the earlier building.
There are several interesting works of art: in the north aisle, an Annunciation by Pierre Puget; in the south aisle, a canvas by J-B Van Loo, the *Triumph of the Eucharist*, and one by Pierre Puget, *The Vision of St Felix of Cantalice*. The elaborately carved pulpit dates from 1824; the Baroque altar in marble and plasterwork was designed by a pupil of Puget.

Porte d'Italie – This bastioned gate, built in 1790 on the site of ancient fortifications, is the only remnant of the defences which surrounded Toulon. Honoré de Balzac used it as a backdrop when Vidocq made use of a funeral cortège to help him escape from the town.

Atlantes by Puget on the old town hall, Toulon

AMONG THE MADDING CROWD

Cours Lafayette – The vegetable and flower market held here every morning is a noisy, bustling, highly coloured occasion.

Quai Cronstadt – Attracted by the shops and cafés, an animated crowd throngs the waterfront. The tall modern buildings with their many-coloured windows form a screen between the old port and the old town. The only reminders of the past are the famous **atlantes★** by Pierre Puget, which support the main balcony of the old town hall.

SIGHTS

Musée du Vieux Toulon ⊘ – This museum, located in the headquarters of the old bishopric, is currently undergoing restoration. The two galleries display maps, engravings and paintings recalling great moments in the history of the city since the Middle Ages. The display cases contain ceramics, statuettes, costumes and exhibits of Provençal traditions. In the second gallery, there is a lovely relief map of the city, made in 1880.

Muséum ⊘ – Two galleries in the right side of the building on the ground floor house the zoological collection (birds, mammals, primates etc; note the two large sperm whales' jaws).

Musée d'Art ⊘ – In the left side of the building. The Flemish, Dutch, Italian and French Schools (16C-18C) are all represented in the museum's collections, which also feature works by 19C artists, including a large number of Provençal painters, such as the Toulon landscapist Vincent Courdouan.
The museum also possesses a very eclectic collection of contemporary painting and sculpture, exhibited in rotation.

Musée de la Figurine – Three thousand figurines are on display in the former public bath house. The lead soldiers are set out to illustrate Bonaparte's campagne in Egypt.

Jardin Alexandre-Ier – This garden is home to some attractive trees, including magnolias, palms and cedars. The bust of Puget is by Injalbert and the 1914-18 War Memorial is by Honoré Sausse.

A MILITARY PAST

★The Port ⊘

Construction of the old port (Vieille Darse or Darse Henri-IV) began in 1589 on the orders of the Duke of Épernon, Governor of Provence. Expenses were borne by the town of Toulon which imposed a 25% tax on olive oil. The two breakwaters, closing the harbour on the south side, except for a 30m/100ft wide passage across which a chain was slung, were completed in 1610.
At that time there was no royal fleet; when the king required ships, he leased them from lords and captains who had them built, armed and equipped. It was Richelieu who created a military arsenal to build and repair warships. Under Louis XIV the port proved too small and Vauban had the new port (Darse Neuve) excavated between 1680 and 1700. This became the naval port while the old port was turned

over entirely to merchant shipping. In the 19C the navy needed yet more space, and in 1836 an annexe, which is still in use, was built at Mourillon. In 1852 Prince Louis-Napoléon established the harbour at Castigneau but 10 years later the port was again declared too small and Napoleon III created the Missiessy Harbour.

While retaining its position as a naval port, Toulon is increasing its commercial role. Merchant shipping is directed to the new facilities in Brégaillon Bay on the west side of the inner anchorage, while the east side is used by the passenger ferries plying to the Îles d'Hyères, Corsica and Sardinia and by pleasure boats and cruise liners throughout the year.

Arsenal Maritime – The naval arsenal covers some 240ha/593 acres overall and employs in the region of 6 300 civilians. Its main activity is the maintenance of the French Mediterranean fleet: frigates, aircraft carriers, sloops, submarines and minesweepers. Some of the dry docks date from the 17C.

Tour Royale ⊙ – Known also as the Grosse Tour or Mitre Tower, this was built by Louis XII in the early 16C for defensive purposes (its walls are 7m/23ft thick at the base). It then served as a prison. From the watchpath there is a lovely **panorama★** of Toulon, with Mont Faron looming beyond it, the anchorages and the coast from the Gien Peninsula to Cap Sicié.

Toulon naval harbour

D. Pazery/MICHELIN

★ Tour by boat of the Petite Rade and the Grande Rade ⊙ – The tour of the inner and outer harbours leaves from Quai Cronstadt in the old port. The Toulon Roads are home to the Force d'Action Navale which includes two aircraft carriers, *Foch* and *Clemenceau*, the largest vessels in the French navy. They alternate between time in port and time on duty patrolling the Mediterranean. The military port is lined with naval vessels – minesweepers, anti-submarine or missile-launcher frigates and, sometimes, the slender, dark contours of a nuclear submarine.

The tour then passes the naval graveyard, where ships at the end of their useful life wait to be broken up, and approaches La Seyne Port with its lifting bridge and the large area once occupied by the shipyards.

The Tamaris coast road leads to Balaguier Bay, where there are two forts – Balaguier and l'Ayguillette. The structures on piles in the centre of the bay mark the position of mussel beds. The tour returns via Lazaret Bay, along the St-Mandrier Peninsula and the long sea wall, which protects the eastern end of the outer harbour.

★ Musée de la Marine ⊙ –Entrance to the Naval Museum is through an impressive 18C doorway; four marble columns support a pediment, flanked by statues of Mars (left) and Bellona (right). On entering, the visitor might be plunging straight into the Quai de l'Artillerie and the old arsenal – the subject of this large, likelife fresco was taken from a painting (18C) by Joseph Vernet. Note the sky painted in gold leaf. On the ground floor there are large-scale models of a frigate, *La Sultane*, and of an 18C vessel, the *Duquesne*. The room is decorated with statues of great 17C admirals carved in wood by Puget's pupils and an impressive figurehead of Neptune. Fine paintings by Vernet's pupils, drawings and other exhibits recall Toulon's seafaring history and its prison. Note in the stairwell another figurehead, Bellona in gilded and painted wood (1807). On the first floor there is an interesting collection of model ships and submarines from the 19C to the present.

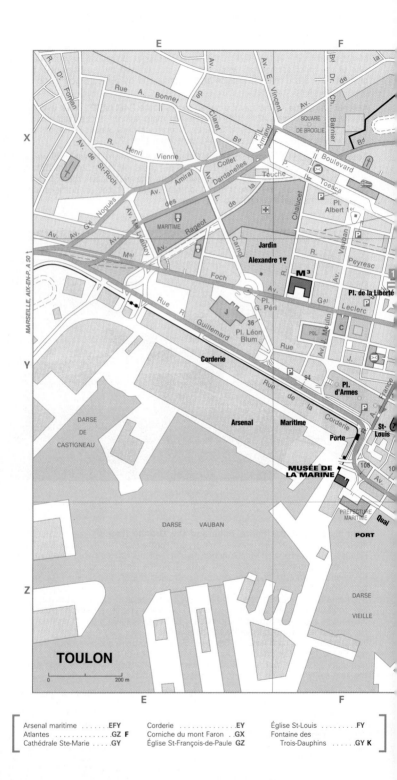

TOULON

0   200 m

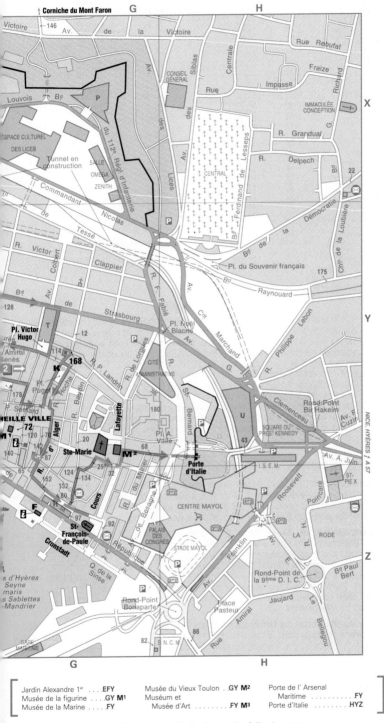

Index of street names for Toulon on the following page

index of street names for Toulon

Félix Mayol

The Mayol Centre and Stadium perpetuate the memory of the comedian who was the first of a long line of performers from Toulon. Félix Mayol (1872-1941) was 20 when he started the fashion for the quiff of hair that characterised his silhouette as well as for the bunch of lily of the valley that he always wore in his buttonhole. In 1910, when he was the comedian at a café-concert in Paris, he bought the hall where he was appearing and rechristened it *Concert Mayol*. From his home town he hired comedians whose fame had not yet spread beyond the Toulon district – including Raimu, Sardou, Tramel and the singer Turcy – who were ironically named *Des Comiques à l'Huile* by Parisians at their first performances. During his career Mayol produced more than 500 works and light comedies.

EXCURSIONS

Mont Faron – Alt 584m/1 916ft. Small limestone massif, bordered by deep valleys, that immediately overlooks Toulon. It is a pleasant drive in summer over pine-clad slopes providing good **views**★ of Toulon, the inner and outer anchorages, the St-Mandrier and Cap Sicié Peninsulas and Bandol.

Téléphérique du Mont Faron ⊘ – *Take Boulevard Ste-Anne and follow signs ("Téléphérique du Mont Faron") to the cable-car station in Avenue Perrichi. At busy periods it is possible to park below the station on the left.*
The cable-car ride *(6min)* offers fine **views**★ over the town, the harbour and the limestone cliffs circling Toulon. To the left the remains of many small forts can be seen. The view from the terrace of the upper station is for customers only. A pleasant view can also be had by walking about 10m/33ft to the left along the access road to Mont Faron.

★ **Musée-Mémorial du Débarquement en Provence** ⊘ – Installed in the Beaumont Tower left of the road is the memorial to commemorate the liberation of the southeast of France by the Allies in August 1944. The first section is devoted to the memory of the English, American, Canadian and French who took part. In the second part there is a diorama *(12min)* of the liberation of Toulon and Marseille and a cinema (documentaries – *15min* – filmed during the landing).
From the terrace *(accessible during a tour of the museum)* there is a magnificent **sweeping panorama**★★★ *(three viewing tables)* of Toulon, the anchorages, the Mediterranean, and the islands and mountains all around Toulon.

Zoo ⊘ – Animals include lions, tigers, jaguars and monkeys.

The road crosses a wooded plateau, which ends abruptly at the foot of a steep slope, and then climbs up to Fort Croix-Faron from where there is a beautiful **view**★ of the coast from the Giens Peninsula to Bandol. Walk 100m/110yd north of the fort to enjoy a view of the Provençal Alps.

Solliès-Ville

15km/9.3mi northeast – 1hr 30min. From Toulon take A 97 motorway. At the La Farlède junction follow directions to La Farlède and then D 67 to Solliès-Ville.

The old town of Solliès-Ville clings to the side of a hill overlooking the rich Gapeau Plain; below lies Solliès-Pont, a busy market town in a region famous for its cherry orchards and its fig trees. Solliès-Ville markets more than three-quarters of the French production of figs.

The **church** ⓥ with two naves combines Romanesque traits with Gothic arches. The monolith at the high altar is thought to be a 15C ciborium. The walnut organ case dates from 1499. There is a 17C altarpiece (left) and another from the 16C near the pulpit. The crucifix on the pillar is 13C. The lords of Solliès are buried in the crypt.

The **Maison Jean-Aicard** ⓥ is the house of the poet, novelist and dramatist Jean Aicard (1848-1921) which has been converted into a small museum. He became a member of the Académie Française in 1909.

On **Esplanade de la Montjoie**, the ruined castle of the Forbins, lords of Solliès, commands a beautiful **view★** of the Gapeau Valley and the Maures Massif.

DRIVING TOURS

The roads used in these excursions, although serving military installations, are classified as part of the civilian network. Traffic is permitted up to the entrance of these installations without formality but the military authorities categorically forbid anyone to enter certain places indicated by notices and signposts, particularly at the immediate approaches to the forts of Croix-Faron, Lieutenant-Girardon and Cap Brun.

★★① Tour of the Anchorage

17km/10.5mi south. Allow 1hr 30min. Leave Toulon by highway A 50, then D 559 and turn left towards La Seyne.

La Seyne-sur-Mer – La Seyne, built beside the bay which bears its name, looks eastwards towards the inner anchorage. It has a harbour for fishing boats and pleasure craft but is basically an industrial town that depended for its livelihood upon the naval shipyards. These were founded in 1856, when they built ships for the merchant navy, as well as producing some of the most outstanding vessels of the war fleets. The site is being modified; it will be rebuilt round the sea while preserving the environment. The old overhead crane at the entrance to the dockyards is still in place.

Fort Balaguier – The fort was recaptured from the English in 1793 by the young Napoleon. Set up in the fort's rooms, with walls 4m/13ft thick, is the **Musée Naval** ⓥ, containing an interesting collection of model ships and memorabilia from the Napoleonic era. On the walls hang seascapes and paintings of the Toulon region. The 17C chapel contains objects relevant to the Toulon galleys and naval prisons: registers, chains and works of art made by the prisoners.

From the terrace overlooking the fort's garden and its aviary, there is a remarkable **view★** of the coastline from Toulon to the Île du Levant.

Tamaris – In the shaded resort on the hillside, George Sand wrote several of her novels. Fine view of St-Mandrier Peninsula.

Villa Tamaris-Pacha ⓥ – The history of this magnificent residence, still unfinished, is worthy of the *Arabian Nights*. Towards the middle of the 19C, the Frenchman Marius Michel, a native of Sanary-sur-Mer, became by a series of happy coincidences the concessionnaire of the lighthouses, quays and warehouses of Constantinople. He was thus the creator of the modern port of Istanbul and of reconnaissance of the coasts under the Ottoman administration. As the Var coast closely resembled the Golden Horn and the Bosphorus, he chose to build his wife a palace inspired by the Florentine villas in Tamaris. After three years of hard work, when his wife was stabbed by a mentally ill person in 1893, Michel Pacha, as he was nicknamed, stopped all work on the villa and the palace remained unoccupied for a century. Now redeveloped, the villa houses a cultural institution and organises exhibitions.

The Unusual Military Career of the St-Mandrier Peninsula

The hill of La Croix aux Signaux, a secret German naval base, was from September 1943 to August 1944 an assembly base for midget submarines which left via an access tunnel ending up on Cavalas beach. In 1929, however, the Marine Nationale Française had buried there (14m/46ft deep) two enormous gun turrets each holding two 340 guns, 17m/56ft long, covering a sector from Le Lavandou to La Ciotat! Shelling preparatory to the landing in Provence in 1944 brought an end to development of this base.

It was from the rifle range at St-Mandrier that the first French liquid-powered rocket was launched in March 1945, inaugurating the European space race.

Beside the bay, a luxurious house, the work of Michel Pacha, displays the ornately carved Mauresque style.

All along Le Lazaret Bay are small cabins perched on stilts above the mussel beds.

Les Sablettes – Long wide beach of fine sand open to the sea. The houses were rebuilt after the last war in the neo-Provençal style, designed by the architect F Pouillon.

Take the road along the narrow sandy isthmus, which links the peninsula to the land mass. Fine view of Toulon surrounded by mountains.

★**Presqu'île de St-Mandrier** – The road round the peninsula offers a **view**★ of the whole anchorage and of Toulon and its setting before skirting the bight of St-Georges, which harbours an aeronaval base and training centre for marine engineers as well as the fishing and leisure port of **St-Mandrier-sur-Mer**. A right-hand turning at the entrance to the town climbs steeply to a small cemetery with a **panoramic view**★★ of Toulon, Cap Sicié and the Îles d'Hyères.

★★ ② Corniche du Mont Faron

The Corniche du Mont Faron provides the best view of the whole of Toulon harbour. The best time is late afternoon, when the light is ideal.

To reach the Corniche du Mont Faron take Pont de Ste-Anne, Avenue de la Victoire and Boulevard Ste-Anne (left).

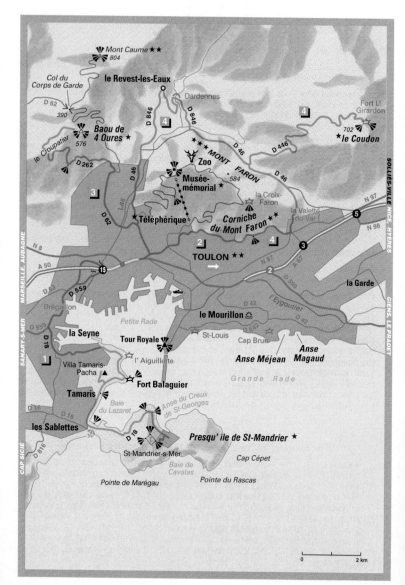

Mont Faron cable-car

The drive along the magnificent Corniche Marius-Escartefigue and the slopes of Mont Faron provides views of Toulon and its surroundings – the old town clustered round the port and the suburbs set against the surrounding mountains.

The **view**★ of the anchorage is very fine – the Petite Rade between Le Mourillon and La Seyne backed by the cliffs of Cap Sicié; the Grande Rade, partially enclosed *(south)* by the St-Mandrier Peninsula and its low narrow isthmus and *(east)* by Cap Carqueiranne, Giens Bay and Giens Peninsula.

★ 3 Baou de Quatre Oures

11km/6.8mi northwest – 1hr – see local map below

From Toulon take Avenue St-Roch, Rue Dr-Fontan, Avenue Général-Gouraud and then turn left onto Avenue des Routes; on Place Macé turn right onto D 62 (Avenue Clovis). After 4km/2.5mi turn left onto D 262.

3km/2mi further on is a platform offering a magnificent **view**★★ of Toulon, the anchorages and the coast.

The narrow road to the top (4km/2.5mi) crosses a firing range (open to traffic).

At the top there is a fine **panorama**★★ of the coast from Cap Bénat to La Ciotat and inland from Ste-Baume to the Maures.

The road skirts the small bay between forts Aiguillette and Balaguier, which were built in the 17C opposite the Tour Royale *(see 6 below)* to seal off the harbour entrance. Close inshore are mussel beds and some old ships at anchor. There is a good view inland across the inner anchorage beyond Toulon to Mont Faron and Le Coudon.

★ 4 Le Coudon

Round tour of 36km/22mi – about 1hr 30min – see local map below

From Toulon take Pont de Ste-Anne and Avenue de la Victoire; turn left onto Boulevard Ste-Anne and right onto Boulevard Escartefigue. At the end of Boulevard Escartefigue turn left onto Avenue de la Canaillette, which leads to D 46. Turn right and right again onto D 446, a steep and narrow road.

★ **Le Coudon** – Alt 702m/2 303ft. At the start of the climb you can see Mont Coudon in its entirety and also La Crau and the surrounding plain. The road, which narrows after going through pine woods and then olive groves, finally comes out onto a wasteland scattered with evergreen oaks; the **view**★ widens continuously until at the entrance to Fort Lieutenant-Girardon the entire coast from the Giens Peninsula to the former island of Gaou near Le Brusc is visible.

Return to D 46 and turn right. After 2.5km/1.5mi – D 846 crosses a dam to Le Revest-les-Eaux.

Le Revest-les-Eaux – This is a delightful old village with a 17C church at the foot of Mont Caume overlooked by a Saracen tower. Its 17C château is now an inn.

Return to Toulon through the Las Valley (D 846) between the mountains of Faron and Croupatier.

TOURRETTES-SUR-LOUP★

Population 3 870

Michelin map 84 fold 9 and 18, 115 fold 25 (west of Vence) or 245 fold 37

This is violet country; the flowers are cultivated under the olive trees. The unusual fortified village, its outer houses forming a rampart, stands on a rock plateau above a sheer drop; Route des Quenières, the continuation of Route St-Jean, provides the best **view★**. The weavers, potters, sculptors, engravers and painters who have come to live in Tourrettes have made it an arts and crafts centre.

THE LAND OF VIOLETS

★**Old Village** – To see this apparently untouched medieval village, pass under the belfry gate in the south corner of the main square and follow the Grande Rue in a semicircle through the village. This steep, paved street lined with shops where craftsmen can be seen plying their trade, will take you down to the old walls, where there is a superb view of the surrounding landscape. Walk up the other side and re-enter the square through another gate.

Church ⊘ – In the 15C nave (south) is a triptych by the Bréa School: St Antony flanked by St Pancras and St Claude. In the chancel (south) a handsome altarpiece in carved wood depicts scenes from the life of the Virgin. There are other altarpieces in the transepts as well as reliquaries and busts from the 15C, 16C and 17C. Behind the high altar stands a Gallo-Roman altar originally dedicated to Mercury.

Chapelle St-Jean ⊘ – This chapel was decorated in 1959 with naive **frescoes** by Ralph Souplaut. On the far wall are John the Baptist and St John the Divine on either side of the cross, symbolising the link between the Old and New Testaments.

Eating out

MID-RANGE

Chez Grand-Mère – *4 Place Maximin Escalier – ☎ and fax 04 93 59 33 34 – Closed Nov, Wed, and Sat lunchtime. Menus 15.3/19.5€. À la carte dishes 7.7/17€.* Stone walls decorated with old-fashioned farming tools provide the rustic setting for this charming restaurant that serves one of best *couscous* in town. The tasty grilled scampi, *merguez* sausages and steaks are prepared before you in the blazing fireplace at the back of the dining room. For starters, try their "*coupe exotique*", a mixed diced salad served in a large round glass. The warm, friendly welcome and excellent service make this an absolute must.

Auberge de Tourrettes – *11 Route de Grasse – ☎ 04 93 59 30 05 – Closed 10 Jan-18 Feb, Mon and Tue Oct-May – 34.30/57.17€.* A pink façade with green shutters, a fine dining room streaming with light and a terrace commanding pretty views of the valley are three good reasons to end up at this charming inn. Not to mention the tasty meals made with fresh local ingredients. Extend your stay by checking into one of the charming bedrooms.

Where to stay

MID-RANGE

Chambre d'Hôte Mas des Cigales – *1673 Route des Quenières – 2km/1.2mi from Tourrettes, Route de St-Jean – ☎ 04 93 59 25 73 – http://mascigale.online.fr – Closed 30 Oct-1 Mar – ⊠ – 6 rooms: 69/77€.* Handsome villa surrounded by a leafy garden. From the terrace running alongside the pool, you can look down onto a small waterfall, a tennis court and, in the far distance, the sea. The rooms are comfortable and tastefully appointed. Attentive welcome.

The art of weaving

Hélène Chenard – *10 Grande Rue – ☎ 04 93 59 36 36 – Open 10am-1pm and 3-7pm. Closed Nov and 2 weeks in Jan.* One of the distinguishing features of this shop are the fine hand-woven ties made with merino wool that have become collector's pieces over the years. In their charming boutique with stone walls, dominated by a huge loom, Hélène Chenard and her daughter Nathalie perpetuate the long-standing tradition of weaving, producing a wide range of garments, running from bright, colours to subtle shades of mauve, pink and almond green. The long stoles *(étoles)* are particularly elegant and the shawls, cloaks and three-quarter coats are perfect for a cool winter's night. The shop also stocks a fine collection of women's summer wear: diaphanous blouses, stylish dresses etc.

Shopping

Confiserie des Gorges du Loup (Florian) – *Pont-du-Loup – ☎ 04 93 59 32 91.* Candied fruit, lemon, orange and grapefruit preserve, chocolates and sweets, crystallized petals and delicious homemade jams concocted with rose, violet and jasmine blossom. Guided tours of the factory 9am-noon, 2-6.30pm.

TOURTOUR★

Population 472
Michelin maps 84 fold 6, 114 fold 21 or 245 fold 34

This village, set in a cool and wooded region, flanked on each side by an old castle, occupies a dominant position (alt 625m/2 050ft) on a ridge backing onto the last foothills of the Pre-Alps, facing the Varois Plain.

Here in the 12C Cistercian monks founded the Abbaye de Florielle, before moving to Thoronet. Remains of this abbey can still be seen near the Chapelle de Florielle *(southeast)*.

There is a lively local market on Place des Ormeaux Wednesday and Saturday mornings.

★OLD VILLAGE

The village has retained its medieval character with the remains of fortifications, attractively restored houses and narrow, sloping streets, linked by vaulted passages, which converge on the central square.

The two large olive trees growing in this square replaced the elms planted at the time of the visit of Anne of Austria in 1638. A vaulted passageway leads from the square beside the **Tour de l'Horloge** (Clock Tower) to an old mill, which now houses the Fossil Museum.

Beside the museum building *(left)* are the ruins of a 12C castle.

Further on *(1km/0.6mi)* is a two-storey medieval tower, **Tour Grimaldi**.

Beside the approach road on the way up is a charming wash-house.

Église St-Denis – This 11C church, standing on its own at the southeastern edge of the ridge, was extensively modified in the last century.

★**Viewpoint** – From the grassy esplanade in front of the church there is a wide **panorama**★★ *(viewing table)* over the Argens and Nartuby valleys, extending *(east)* to the Maures and *(west)* to Ste-Baume, Mont Ste-Victoire and the Luberon. A few miles further on *(east)* is the residential village of St-Pierre-de-Tourtour, in a lovely forest setting, designed in its entirety by Beaumont who was responsible for Les Issambres.

SIGHTS

Musée des Fossiles ⓥ – This museum contains an interesting exhibition of local fossils – dinosaur eggs, large ammonites and fossil impressions.

Go down below the old castle to the oil mill.

Regional produce

Ferme de Tourtour – *Route de Villecroze* – ☏ *04 94 70 56 18*. Mouthwatering delicacies can be purchased here, namely pâtés, foie gras, *tapenades* (seasoning made of capers, olives, anchovies, olive oil, lemon and aromatics), *anchoïades* (mashed anchovies with crushed garlic), jams and preserves, fruit purée.

Moulin à Huile ⓥ – This communal oil mill has been in service since the 17C and has three presses. During the autumn, when production takes place, 5 000l/1 100gal of oil are produced here, showing the continuing importance of the industry in this region. During the summer, the mill houses exhibitions of paintings. The town hall occupies the former Château des Raphelis, a solid 16C building with pepper-pot towers.

The church and its cemetery

D. Pazery/MICHELIN

La TURBIE★

Population 3 021
Michelin map 84 folds 10 and 19, 115 fold 27 or 245 fold 38
Local maps see NICE and Corniches de la RIVIERA

The village of La Turbie was built on the Grande Corniche at an altitude of 480m/1 575ft, in a pass at the base of the massive Tête de Chien promontory over-looking Monaco, and on either side of the Roman Via Julia Augusta which ran from Genoa to Cimiez. In addition to the Alpine Trophy, a masterpiece of Roman art for which the village is famous, La Turbie boasts splendid panoramas of the coast and Monaco. At night, the lights of Monte-Carlo and Monaco are a magnificent spectacle.

HISTORICAL NOTES

When Caesar died, the greater part of the Alps was occupied by several unconquered tribes who posed a constant threat to communications between Rome and her pos-sessions in Gaul and Spain.

Augustus decided to put an end to this situation and extend Roman rule into the Alps. Several campaigns were mounted between 25 BC and 14 BC; Augustus probably took part in some of them in person and was assisted by Drusus and Tiberius. New provinces were established linking Italy, Gaul and Germania; one of them was the "Maritime Alps" with Cimiez as its capital. In 6 BC the Senate and the Roman people decreed that these important victories should be commemorated by the erection of a trophy. The posi-tion chosen was on the Via Julia Augusta, which had been built during the campaigns, at the foot of Mont Agel, where the Mediterranean coast is visible in both directions for several miles. There is only one other Roman trophy still standing (at Adam-Klissi in Romania, 150km/93mi from Bucharest). During the years of peace under the Romans a settlement grew up round the monument; its Latin name, *Tropea Augusti*, gradually evolved into La Turbie.

A ROMAN LEGACY

Start from Avenue Général-de-Gaulle and follow the route marked on the town plan.

Fountain – It was built in the 19C at the end of the Roman aqueduct brought back into service at around the same time.

Place Neuve – From the southwest corner of the square there is a fine **view**★ of the coast as far as the Maures Massif.

Rue Comte-de-Cessole – This street, part of the former Via Julia Augusta, built by the Romans, now goes through the West Gate, climbing between medieval houses to the Trophy. A house on the right bears a plaque with the verses Dante dedicated to La Turbie. Another plaque shows that the town appeared in the Antonine Itin-erary (a reference list of the staging posts on the main roads of the Roman Empire with the distances between them). Fine view of the Trophy at the top of the street.

Église St-Michel-Archange – The church, set back from the street, is a fine exam-ple of the Nice Baroque style. Built in the 18C on an ellipsoidal plan, it has a shal-low concave façade – two storeys beneath a triangular pediment – and a bell-tower surmounted by a cupola of coloured tiles.

★ **Interior** – *Walk round clockwise.* The decoration of the nave and chapels is Baroque; the cradle vaulting, supported by tall pillars, is adorned with frescoes and mouldings. There are two paintings by J-B Van Loo: *St Charles Borromeo* and *Mary Magdalene*;

a copy of Raphaël's *St Michael* which is in the Louvre. The chapel on the left of the choir contains a Pietà from the Bréa School and a *St Mark Writing his Gospel* attributed to Veronese. The 17C communion table is in onyx and agate. The high altar in multicoloured marble comes from the abbey of St-Pons in Nice and was used for the cult of Reason during the Revolution; above it is an 18C Christ in painted wood. Also 18C are the two triptychs in the choir; the one on the right shows Christ together with the Church, represented as a queen in a white robe, and the Synagogue, turn-ing away so as not to see the truth.

In the first chapel on the right is a canvas attributed to Ribera and a 15C Virgin and Child. In the second chapel a painting of Mary by the Murillo School and a *Flagellation* in Rembrandt's style; also *St Catherine of Siena* by a pupil of Raphael.

Trophée des Alpes, La Turbie

E. Baret/MICHELIN

SIGHT

★**Trophée des Alpes** – The **Alpine Trophy**, (originally 50m/164ft high and 38m/125ft wide) comprised: a square podium bearing a lengthy inscription to Augustus and a list of the 44 conquered peoples; a large circular Doric colonnade with niches containing statues of the leaders who took part in the campaigns; a stepped cone serving as a base for a huge statue of Augustus, flanked by two captives. Stairways gave access to all levels.

Most of the monument is built with beautiful white stone produced in local quarries. After the Romans had left, it was damaged and despoiled; in the Middle Ages it was converted into a defensive structure (the blind arcading at the top dates from this period) and so was preserved from further deterioration; it survived Louis XIV's order for it to be blown up; later it served as a source of building stone, particularly for the construction of the church of St-Michel-Archange. At the beginning of the modern era all that remained was a ruined tower emerging from a cone of rubble.

Skilful and patient restoration has been carried out through the generous help of Edward Tuck, an American, and directed by Jules Formigé. The trophy has been rebuilt up to about 35m/115ft high but a large part of it has been left untouched. The inscription has been restored – Pliny had quoted it – and replaced in its original position; it is the longest left to us from Roman times. Its elevated position means that the Trophy is visible from a long way off.

Museum – Plans, drawings and photographs recount the story of the Trophy and its restoration (model reconstruction). The display includes milestones, inscriptions, fragments of the Trophy, pieces of sculpture and documents on the other Roman monuments in Europe.

Terraces – From the raised terraces there is a splendid **panorama★★★** of the coast from the Italian border, via Cap Martin, the Principality of Monaco 450m/1 350ft below, Èze and Cap Ferrat to the Esterel; inland is the Laghet Valley with Mont Agel behind.

Return along Avenue Prince-Albert-Ier-de-Monaco turning left onto Rue Droite which passes through the east gate; it follows part of the ancient Via Julia Augusta towards Italy then turns left and becomes Rue Incalat.

Forêt de TURINI★★

Michelin map 84 folds 19 and 20, 115 folds 17 and 18 or 245 fold 25

For people living on the coast between Nice and Menton the forest of Turini evokes another world of cool green shade. The huge forest, only 25km/15.5mi from the Mediterranean coast, is unusual, for its trees are generally found in more northerly latitudes. The lower slopes are covered with maritime sea pines and young oaks but higher up there are maple, beech, chestnut, spruce and superb pine trees, some of which reach 35m/115ft on the northern slopes. Between 1 500-2 000m/5 000-6 500ft the larch predominates. The forest covers a total of 3 500ha/1 350sq mi between the Vésubie and Bévéra valleys.

Several roads meet at **Col de Turini**, which is a good starting point for visiting this beautiful district.

★DRIVING TOUR

★★The Authion

Round tour of 18km/11mi from Col de Turini – allow 45min – local map see NICE
The roads are usually blocked by snow in winter and sometimes late into spring. A nature trail explains the flora and fauna of the forest.

From Col de Turini the Authion road (D 68) passes through pine and larch woods. As the road climbs, the mountain scenery becomes more magnificent. 4km/2.5mi from the pass stands a war memorial to those who perished in 1793 and 1945.

Monument aux Morts – The Authion Massif has twice been a backdrop to military action. In 1793 the Convention's troops fought here against the Austrians and Sardinians, and in 1945 there was a bitter struggle before the Germans were driven out. Panoramic **view★** from the memorial.

Continue along D 68 bearing right at the fork to Cabanes Vieilles, an old military camp which was damaged in the fighting in 1945. The road runs through Alpine pastures and offers marvellous **views★** of the Roya Valley.

Turn right by another monument onto a track which leads (500m/547yd) to a platform where it is possible to turn the car round.

★★**Pointe des Trois-Communes** – At this altitude (2 082m/6 830ft) there is a marvellous **panorama★★** of the peaks in the Mercantour National Park and the Pre-Alps of Nice.

Return to D 68; at the war memorial take the road back to Col de Turini.

Monte-Carlo Rally

EXCURSIONS

★Vallon de Ste-Élisabeth

Round tour of 15km/10mi leaving from Col de Turini – 1hr – local map see NICE

The road (D 70) winds northwest cutting its way between the mountain peaks (Cime de la Calmette and Tête du Scoubayoun) overlooking the small Vésubie tributary which flows down the Ste-Élisabeth Valley.

Gorges de Ste-Élisabeth – This rugged gorge cuts a savage gash between the deep, concertina-like folds in the rock strata.

Soon after the tunnel, at a bend in the road, stop by the Chapelle St-Honorat.

★**St-Honorat Viewpoint** – The view extends from the terrace by the chapel over the perched village of Bollène – the **site** of the village can be seen particularly clearly from this angle; up the Vésubie from Lantosque to Roquebillière; north to the Mercantour peaks.

La Bollène-Vésubie – This pleasant village stands on a hill in a chestnut wood at the foot of a mountain peak, Cime des Vallières. The streets are laid out concentrically, climbing between the 18C houses to the church.

The road winds its serpentine course down into the Vésubie Valley, giving breathtaking views at it goes.

★★Col de Braus Road

Round tour of 76km/47mi leaving from Col de Turini – allow one day – local map see NICE

The drive to Peïra-Cava passes through the thickest part of Turini Forest. There are fine **views** west into the valley of the Vésubie and the surrounding mountains.

★★**Cime de Peïra-Cava** – *1.5km/1mi – plus 30min on foot there and back. On entering the village of Peïra-Cava turn left up a steep hill by the post office; bear right at the fork and leave the car in the car park.*

🅱 It is an easy climb to the top (follow the lift) for a panoramic **view**★★ of the Vésubie Valley and mountains on one side and of the Bévéra Valley, Le Mercantour and the high peaks on the Franco-Italian frontier on the other. South beyond the Pre-Alps of Nice lies the sea and, in fine weather, a glimpse of Corsica.

★**Peïra-Cava** – Alt 1 450m/4 757ft. The village is a winter sports centre and a summer resort. It stands on a narrow ridge between the Vésubie and Bévéra valleys with an almost aerial view of the district.

Beyond the village a sharp right turn leads to a car park: a walk of 50m/55yd leads to some steps on the left.

★★**Pierre Plate** – This peak provides a **panoramic view**★★ similar to the view from Cime de Peïra-Cava *(viewing table)*.

Return downhill to D 2566 and continue south through the forest. In La Cabanette turn left onto D 21 to Lucéram. The road descends through a succession of steep bends with magnificent **views**★ on all sides. On the edge of the forest a left-hand turn takes a picturesque route over Col de l'Orme to Col de Braus; D 21 continues to Lucéram.

★ Lucéram –
See LUCÉRAM.

South of Lucéram D 2566 descends the Paillon Valley to L'Escarène.

L'Escarène – *See NICE* 4 : *Les Deux Paillons.*

From L'Escarène D 2204 climbs northeast up the Braus Valley to Sospel through a series of astonishing bends scaling the Pre-Alps of Nice. The road over Col de Braus, which links the Paillon and Bévéra valleys, is a section of the old Piedmont road from Nice to Turin.

Touët-de-l'Escarène –
Charming little village with a Baroque church.
The olive groves give way to a landscape of Spanish broom.

Clue de Braus – This rift that opens up beyond Touët village is short but impressive. From St-Laurent (hamlet) one can reach the Braus waterfall (◪ *15min there and back*) leaving the car by the restaurant.
Over the next 3km/2mi, D 2204 negotiates 16 bends. As the road climbs the **view★** extends from the white dome of the Nice observatory on top of Mont Gros to Cap d'Antibes and the Esterel Massif outlined against the sea.

Col de Braus – Alt 1 002m/3 287ft. It is interesting to look back down over the series of hairpin bends which carry the road up to the pass.
Beyond the pass the road descends through 18 bends offering extensive **views★★** of the mountains of the Bévéra Valley, particularly the Authion and Cime du Diable ("Devil's Peak").
The road runs round Mont Barbonnet crowned with the fortifications of Fort Suchet.

Col St-Jean – At Col St-Jean, between the dwellings on the left, an old army road leads off to the entrance porch of **Fort Suchet**, built 1883-86 and then modernised in the 1930s. Note in particular the two striking 155mm turrets on top.
After the Col St-Jean, the road draws near the Merlanson Valley, and then reaches Sospel. On a level with the casemates of Fort St-Roch, there is a good view of the village.

★ Sospel – *See SOSPEL.*

Olive groves reappear in the wide depression at Sospel. D 2566 climbs northwest through the forest up the **Bévéra Valley★**. The river has created a very deep, narrow and winding channel lined by rocky and wooded heights. There is a beautiful **waterfall** on the right.

★★ Gorges du Piaon – The *corniche* road runs beneath an overhang of rock high above the bed of the stream, which is strewn with huge boulders.

Chapelle Notre-Dame-de-la-Menour – An oratory marks the beginning of a path (right) which provides a good view of the valley and the gorge. A great flight of steps leads up to the chapel, which has a two-storey Renaissance façade.

Moulinet– Charming village in a fresh green hollow.
The road returns through the forest to Col de Turini.

UTELLE★

Population 488
Michelin map 84 fold 19, 115 fold 16 or 245 fold 25
Local map see NICE

At 800m/2 625ft the village projects like a balcony over the Vésubie Valley facing Turini Forest and the Gordolasque mountains to the north. In the past it was the most important town between the Tinée and the Vésubie. The isolated village has retained its original character: fountain in the square, old houses with sundials, ruined fortifications.

A TRIBUTE TO THE MADONNA

Église St-Véran – Built in the 14C on the basilica plan and altered in the 17C, the church has an elegant Gothic porch with carved panels illustrating the legend of St Veranus in 12 tableaux.

The architecture of the interior – groin and barrel vaulting supported ted by archaistic Romanesque columns and capitals – contrasts surprisingly with the generous Classical decoration verging on Baroque. At the high altar a **carved wooden altarpiece★** depicting scenes from the Passion is dominated by a statue of St Veranus. There is an altarpiece of the Annunciation (Nice School) above the first altar in the north aisle and a 13C recumbent Christ below the altar in the south aisle. Fine 17C woodwork (choir, pulpit) and 16C carved font. The sacristy contains some handsome vestments in silk and Genoan velvet.

> **FAR FROM THE CROWDS**
>
> **L'Aubergerie Del Campo** – *Route d'Utelle – 06450 St-Jean-la-Rivière – 5km/3mi E of Utelle by D 132 –* ☎ *04 93 03 13 12 –* ✉ *– Reservation recommended for evenings – 16.77/28.97€.* Small inn built on the ruins of a former sheep barn offering Provençal cooking in a homely, slightly bohemian ambience. Unpretentious dining room lit by tiny windows and charming terrace overlooking the Vésubie Gorges.

Chapelle des Pénitents-Blancs – The chapel, which is near the church, contains a carved wooden altarpiece of the Descent from the Cross by Rubens and six large 18C paintings.

EXCURSION

★★★ **Madone d'Utelle Panorama** – The sanctuary of the Madonna of Utelle, founded in 850 by Spanish sailors who had survived a storm, was rebuilt in 1806. It is a place of pilgrimage where faithful disciples can pay tribute to the Holy Virgin on 15 August and 8 September.

A short distance from the chapel stands a viewing table (1 174m/3 852ft) covered by a dome. Breathtaking **panorama** over a wide expanse of the Alpes-Maritimes *département* and the Mediterranean.

VALBONNE

Population 10 746
Michelin map 84 fold 9, 115 south of folds 24 and 25 or 245 fold 37

This hospitable spot (*vallis bona* in Latin, meaning Happy Valley) has been occupied since Antiquity. The Plateau de Valbonne slopes gently from the Grasse Pre-Alps to the coast with an average altitude of 200m/650ft. It comprises some 2 000ha/4 940 acres of pines and holm oaks and is drained by the Brague and its tributaries, the Bouillide and the Bruguet.

A STROLL THROUGH VALBONNE

Old Village – The village is a curious example of ribbon development, with its houses with ramparts and chequerboard districts, having been rebuilt in the 16C by the Lérins monks. The **main square** with its 15C-17C arcading and old elm trees is an attractive backdrop to the lively cafés and restaurants. Every year around St Blaise's Day (3 February) the Feast of the "Servan grape" (which ripens late) is celebrated.

Church – In 1199 the Chalais Order founded an abbey, which came under the control of Lérins before becoming the parish church. The building, in the form of a Latin cross with a square chevet, has been badly restored on several occasions but has retained the austere character typical of Chalais buildings.

The abbey houses an interesting **Musée du Patrimoine** ⊘, that enlightens visitors on the area's heritage.

Sophia-Antipolis (Parc international d'Activités) – *Southeast of Valbonne.* A wooded plateau (2 300ha/ 5 683 acres) has been chosen to house the premises of an **International Science Park**. About two-thirds of the area has been carefully landscaped to provide a pleasant, natural setting for the third or so that is occupied by offices, housing and leisure facilities. The project completed so far has centred on four main sectors of activity: information technology, electronics and telecommunications; health and biotechnology; teaching and research; science and the environment. These businesses have been incorporated into the housing, cultural and sporting facilities so as to preserve the environment, creating an "international forum for knowledge, science and technology".

The park is ideally located near Nice International Airport and the A8 motorway; the buildings are resolutely modern. French and foreign enterprises, 900 in total, have settled in; among them are the Air France worldwide reservations centre, certain departments of the Centre National de la Recherche Scientifique (National Research Centre), the École des Mines, France Télécom and foreign companies specialising in high technology. Further development is planned, particularly to the north of the park, which will double the surface area of the development and the number of businesses it can accommodate.

This complex is the latest stage in the **Route des Hautes-Technologies** linking together a number of centres involved in developing high technology between Aix-en-Provence and Valbonne.

Auberge Fleurie – *Route de Cannes – 1,5km by D 3 –* ☎ *04 93 12 02 80 – Closed Dec, Sun evening except Jun-Sep and Mon – 19.82/25.61€.* Choose between the dining room or the outdoor verandah to enjoy the generous helpings of imaginative and carefully prepared cuisine with dishes such as duck pâté with aubergines...

... AND RELAXATION

Château de la Bégude – *06650 Opio – 2km/1.2mi NE of Valbonne by Route de Biot –* ☎ *04 93 12 37 00 – Closed mid-Nov to mid-Dec – 36 rooms: 70.13/144.83€ –* ☕ *10.67€ – Restaurant 20/25€.* If you wish to indulge in the farniente way of life, come to this 17C manor and dip into the pool or try your hand at golf... The château is set up on the site of the Opio-Valbonne golf course: it successfully combines the pleasures of old stone with the modern conveniences of the 21st century. The restaurant is also used as a club-house and bar available to golfers.

East end and bell tower's Valbonne church

VALLAURIS

Population 25 773 with Golfe-Juan
Michelin map 84 fold 9, 115 fold 39 or 245 fold 37
For plan of conurbation see CANNES

Vallauris lies close to the sea among rounded hills fragrant with orange blossom and mimosa. The centre is laid out on a grid plan; the town was razed to the ground in 1390 and rebuilt and repopulated in the 16C by immigrants from neighbouring regions. The town's traditional craft of pottery was in decline when Picasso gave it a new breath of life. In the town centre, on the marketplace fronting the church, stands a bronze statue presented by the artist to the town of which he became an honorary citizen. Vallauris is now an important French centre for ceramics: its Biennial International Festival of Ceramic Art (July to mid-October) enjoys a worldwide reputation. Local activities also include the production of cut flowers and aromatic plants.

Provençal dragon flask (1952).
ceramic by Pablo Picasso

SIGHTS

Château – Originally a priory attached to Lérins, it was rebuilt in the 16C and is a rare example of Renaissance archi-tecture in Provence. It is a rectangular two-storey building with a round pep-per-pot tower at each corner. It houses two museums.

Musée Magnelli - Musée de la Céramique ○ – The ceramics which won awards at the Biennial Festival are displayed in the vaulted rooms.

A fine Renaissance staircase leads to two rooms on the second floor displaying ceramics by Picasso (plates, dishes, humorously decorated vases).

Six rooms are devoted to the **Magnelli bequest**: works in oil, collage and gouache together with a large mural. Alberto Magnelli (1888-1971) was born in Florence but spent the greater part of his life in France. The rooms are arranged from left to right to trace the evolution of the artist's style; from large washes of pure colour he turned to Abstract art, which he temporarily abandoned in the 1920s. Finally, there are some lovely collections of Art Deco, Art Nouveau and 1950s ceramics.

★ **Musée National "La Guerre et la Paix"** ○ – Only the Romanesque chapel of the priory has survived. Deconsecrated, it was decorated in 1952 by Picasso with a huge com-position: *War and Peace*. This work evokes the horrors of war; black invaders, tram-pling the symbols of civilization underfoot, attack a knight in shining armour who is just (his spear forms the arm of a balance) and peaceful (his shield bears the device of a dove). The figures on the opposite wall are depicted indulging in honest labour and the innocent virtues of peace. The end panel symbolises fraternity between races.

Musée de la Poterie ○ – *Rue Sicard*. Located in a pottery workshop that is still operational, the Pot-tery Museum shows how clay was worked in the first half of the 20C. Dis-plays illustrate the tech-niques used for extracting clay from the earth, its preparation, shaping, glaz-ing and baking in the wood-fired kiln. Old pot-tery is also on view.

A visit to the present work-shop helps one to appreci-ate the evolution of the potter's techniques.

Browsing and shopping

Tour of traditional pottery workshops – *Rue du Plan. Daily (except Sat-Sun) at 10.30am and 3.30pm. No charge.* Apply to the tourist office.

Galerie Madoura – *Rue Suzanne-et-Georges-Ramié* – ☎ *04 93 64 66 39* – *www.madoura.com – closed Sat-Sun*. Exhibi-tion and sale of ceramics made on the premises as well as reproductions of pieces crafted by Picasso.

Here and in the neighbouring streets are the pottery shops and workshops **(ateliers de céramique)** ○, their displays of ceramics spilling out onto the pavement. High-quality work vies for attention with second-rate wares.

VENCE★

Population 16 982
Michelin map 84 fold 9 and 18, 115 fold 25 or 245 fold 37

Vence is a delightful winter and summer resort, 10km/6mi from the sea between Nice and Antibes, in a countryside where mimosa, roses and carnations are cultivated and where olive and orange trees thrive. It is a picturesque old market town, favoured by artists and art galleries, standing on a rock promontory bordered by two ravines and sheltered from the cold north winds by the last foothills of the Alps. The wines from the surrounding stony hillsides (La Gaude, St-Jeannet) are highly regarded.

HISTORICAL NOTES

An episcopal town – Vence, founded by the Ligurians, was an important Roman town. With the coming of Christianity, it acquired greater influence, that of an episcopal seat. Among the bishops from 374 to 1790 were St Veranus (5C) and St Lambert (12C), Alessandro Farnese, an Italian prince who became Pope Paul II (16C), Antoine Godeau (see below) and Surian, a great preacher.
During the Wars of Religion Vence was besieged by the Huguenot Lesdiguières in 1592, but held out; the victory is commemorated each year at Easter.

The Lords of Vence (13C) – The bishops of Vence were in continual conflict with the barons of Villeneuve, lords of the town. This family drew its fame from **Romée de Villeneuve**, an able Catalan who in the 13C reorganised the affairs of the Count of Provence, Bérenger V. The count had four marriageable daughters and an empty treasury.
Romée induced Blanche of Castille to ask for the eldest, Marguerite, for the future St Louis. Eleanor married Henry II and became Queen of England and another became Empress of Austria. The last daughter, Beatrix, heiress of Provence, married Charles of Anjou, brother of St Louis in 1246, and became Queen of the Two Sicilies.

Bishop Godeau (17C) – The memory of Antoine Godeau has remained vivid throughout the region. His beginnings did not seem likely to lead him to a bishopric: he was the oracle of the House of Rambouillet. Small, skinny, swarthy – in short uncommonly ugly – he was, nevertheless, in great demand among some cultured society ladies (les précieuses) because of his wit, his fluency and his rich and ready poetical vein: they called him Julie's dwarf (Julie d'Angennes was the daughter of the Marquise de Rambouillet) and also, tongue-in-cheek, the "Jewel of the Graces". His reputation was unprecedented. Richelieu made him the first member of the French Academy. At the age of 30, Godeau, no doubt weary of verse-making, took holy orders and, the following year, was made Bishop of Grasse and Vence. The towns would not accept a joint bishop and so for several years he remained between the two dioceses, finally opting for Vence. The former wit and ladies' confidant took his new role seriously; he repaired his cathedral, which was falling in ruins, introduced various industries – perfumery, tanning and pottery – and introduced a number of measures aimed at bringing prosperity to his poor and primitive diocese. He died in 1672 at the age of 67.

A MEDIEVAL VILLAGE

Start from Place du Grand-Jardin but before entering the old town stop to look at Place du Frêne and the enormous ash tree which gives the square its name and which, according to legend, was planted in memory of the visit of François I and Pope Paul III in 1538.

Old town – The old town was enclosed within elliptical walls, parts of which can still be seen, pierced by five gateways.
Skirt the 15C square tower adjoining the château to reach and pass beneath the Peyra Gateway (1441). This part of town is bustling with artists, craftsmen and boutiques.

★ **Place du Peyra** – The square is picturesque with a striking square tower and gushing fountain in the form of an urn (1822). It was the forum of the Roman town.

From the south side of the square take Rue du Marché and turn left to reach Place Clemenceau.

Chapelle du Rosaire (chapelle Matisse)

S. Sauvignier/MICHELIN

335

Eating out

MODERATE

Crêperie Bretonne Hervé – *6 Place Surian – ☎ 04 93 24 08 20 – Closed 2-28 Nov, Wed evening and Thu Sep-May – 7.62/15.24€.* In the heart of the old quarter, a spruce creperie combines Breton tradition with a touch of Provence. The big terrace giving onto the square is an invitation to sit down and sample one of the tasty pancakes on the menu.

Le Pêcheur de Soleil – *1 Place Godeau – ☎ 04 93 58 32 56 – Closed Nov, Dec, Sun and Mon 15 Oct-15 Mar – 10.67/22.87€.* Fancy a pizza? This restaurant in the medieval quarter of Vence is definitely the right place to choose. An astounding choice of homemade pizzas, freshly baked in an open oven, are served in a rustic dining room whose beams are decorated with old-fashioned kitchen utensils. In summer, eat out on the terrace at the foot of the cathedral.

MID-RANGE

Chez Jordi – *8 Rue de Hôtel-de-Ville – ☎ 04 93 58 83 45 – Closed 15 Jul-15 Aug, 20 Dec-14 Jan, Sun and Mon – Reservation required – 18.29/22.87€.* This modest restaurant in a secluded alley serves generous helpings and will prepare Spanish specialities at your request: *paella, zarzuella.*

Auberge des Seigneurs – *Place du Frêne – ☎ 04 93 58 04 24 – Closed 16 Nov-14 Mar, Tue for lunch, Wed for lunch and Mon – 25.92/37.35€.* Handsome 17C mansion standing at the entrance to the old medieval district. The rustic setting with its thick wooden tables is alleviated by the refined silverware. A few rooms are available for weary travellers.

Where to stay

MODERATE

Hôtel La Victoire – *Place du Grand-Jardin – ☎ 04 93 58 61 30 – Closed mid-Nov to mid-Dec – 15 rooms: 25.92/35.06€ – ☞ 5.34€.* The main asset of this hotel located on Vence's main square is the excellent quality/price ratio. The well kept rooms are pleasantly furnished in the 1970s style; the ones on the third floor are slightly darker. Homely welcome.

Parc Hôtel – *50 Avenue Foch – ☎ 04 93 58 27 27 – Closed late Sep to Easter-13 rooms: 39.64/56.41€ – ☞ 6.10€.* Turn-of-the-century residential mansion giving onto a courtyard lined with palm trees. The smallish rooms are all identical.

MID-RANGE

Villa Roseraie – *Route de Coursegoules – ☎ 04 93 58 02 20 – 14 rooms: 74.70/114.34€ – ☞ 10.67€.* A 1900 villa is the setting for this tastefully appointed hotel in which the small rooms are cool and attractive. Tempting outdoor pool. Pretty terrace adorned with sculptures.

LUXURY

La Bastide aux Oliviers – *1260 Chemin de la Sine – Route de Tourrettes-sur-Loup – ☎ 04 93 24 20 33 – bastidoliv@netcourrier.com – Closed 15 Nov to late Jan except between Christmas and 1 Jan – ✉ – 4 rooms: 99.09/114.34€.* Three beautiful bedrooms and a suite done up in Provençal tones await you in this country house built in light stone lost among pines and olive trees. The terrace affords a lovely view of the Loup Valley.

La Tour de Vence – *310 Chemin du Baou des Noirs – NE of Vence towards St-Jeannet – ☎ 04 93 24 59 00 – latourdevence@wanadoo.fr – Closed 15 Nov-15 Dec – ✉ – 4 rooms: 137.20/274.41€.* Who can resist the charm of this superb mansion built with stones taken from a former Burgundy monastery? Cosy, comfortable rooms decorated with great taste. Breathtaking views of the Mediterranean coastline and surrounding mountains.

Markets

Flowers and regional produce: daily (except Monday) on Place du Grand-Jardin and Place Surian.

Second-hand books and furniture: Wednesdays on Place du Grand-Jardin.

Other markets: Tuesdays and Fridays on Place Clemenceau, Place Godeau, Rue de l'Évêché, Impasse Cahours.

Calendar

Easter celebrations, end of March to early April.

"Les Nuits du Sud" Festival, mid-July to early August.

Village fête on Ste-Elizabeth Day, end of July to early August.

Traditional Folk Festival, end of September.

Ramparts – Leave the church through the east door which opens onto Place Godeau, overlooked by the square tower with its parapet and surrounded by old houses. At the centre stands a Roman column erected to the god Mars. Take Rue St-Lambert and then Rue de l'Hôtel-de-Ville to reach the 13C Signadour Gateway and turn left.

The next gate on the left is the Orient (east) gateway, opened in the 18C; the date 1592 carved on a stone (top left) refers to the siege of the Protestant Duke François de Lesdiguières during the Wars of Religion. Boulevard Paul-André follows the line of the ramparts; several narrow stepped streets open into it; there are fine **views** of the high peaks *(baous)* and the foothills of the Alps. Re-enter the old town through the Gothic Lévis Gateway (13C) and walk up Rue du Portail-Lévis between handsome old houses to Place du Peyra.

SIGHTS

Cathedral ⓥ – The Roman temple of Mars built on this site was replaced in the 5C by a Merovingian church incorporated into subsequent structures. The present church, the old cathedral, was begun in the Romanesque style but was later altered and enlarged several times. Some Roman inscriptions have been included in the Baroque façade; those on either side of the door are dedicated to the emperors Elagabalus and Gordian.

The interior consists of a nave and four aisles. The tomb of St Lambert and his epitaph are to be found in the second chapel on the right; a 5C Roman sarcophagus, said to be the tomb of St Veranus, is in the third chapel on the right. The north aisle contains a handsome carved doorway with Flamboyant Gothic rose windows; on the same side is a 16C retable of angels. Some fine pieces of Carolingian carving have been incorporated in certain of the pillars. The baptistery contains a mosaic by Chagall, *Moses in the Bulrushes*. The most unusual feature is the **organ loft**; the singing desk and the **choir stalls**★ are admirable: the risers, elbow rests and misericords are the work of Jacques Bellot, a sculptor from Grasse (15C) whose lively imagination sometimes borders on the irreverent.

★ **Chapelle du Rosaire or Chapelle Matisse** ⓥ – "Despite its imperfections I think it is my masterpiece... the result of a lifetime devoted to the quest for truth." This was Henri Matisse's opinion of the chapel which he had designed and decorated between 1947 and 1951. The fame of this artist and the daring of his design, a contemporary echo of the genius of the medieval masters, aroused enormous interest in the building.

From the outside it resembles an ordinary Provençal house with a roof of coloured tiles surmounted by a huge wrought-iron cross with gilt tips.

Inside, the community nave and the parish nave meet at the altar, which is set at an angle.

Everything is white – floor, ceiling, tiled walls – except for the small high stained-glass windows which make a floral pattern in lemon, bottle green and ultra-marine. The decoration, furnishings and vestments are strikingly plain and simple. The mural compositions, the Stations of the Cross and St Dominic have been reduced to a play of black lines on a white background. Although not in sequence, the Stations of the Cross provide a visual progression towards the Calvary at the climax of the composition. The gallery, containing studies made by Matisse for his finished designs, is well worth a visit.

Château de Villeneuve – Fondation Émile Hugues ⓥ – The old castle of the Barons of Villeneuve, built in the 17C, incorporates the 13C watchtower. The foundation was set up to forge a link between local heritage and artistic creativity

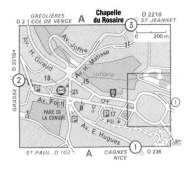

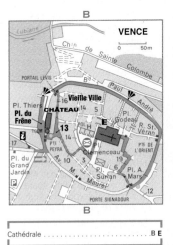

inspired by the region. Note the lovely interior decoration on each floor. Thematic exhibitions show to full advantage works by the great masters of the 20C, such as Matisse, Dubuffet, Dufy and Chagall, inspired by the time they spent in Vence. Alternating with these are exhibitions on modern and contemporary art.

EXCURSION

Galerie Beaubourg-Château Notre-Dame-des-Fleurs ⌚–
3km/2mi northwest along D 2210A

The castle was built in the 19C on the site of an 11C Benedictine abbey, Notre-Dame-des-Crottons (Our Lady of the Caves), which housed the bishops of Vence from 1638 to 1728. Its name was changed to Notre-Dame-des-Fleurs (Our Lady of the Flowers) by its owner, a Grasse perfumer.

A gallery of contemporary art displays the works of many artists in the rooms and gardens.

From the terrace, decorated with aromatic plants, the **view★** extends from Cap Ferrat to the Esterel. The pre-10C Romanesque chapel was restored in 1988; its chancel is adorned with a stained-glass window by Bernard Dhonneur.

Nearby, the bishop's private chapel contains a 6C Virgin.

DRIVING TOUR

★★Routes des Crêtes

Round trip of 59km/37mi – half a day

Leave Vence by D 2210, going northeast towards St-Jeannet.

The road skirts three peaks – Baou des Blancs, Baou des Noirs and Baou de St-Jeannet – and provides a long leisurely view of the **site★** of St-Jeannet.

Gattières – This perched village looks out over vineyards and olive groves to the Var Valley and the neighbouring hamlets. The charming Romanesque-Gothic **church** ⌚ contains a naïve painted sculpture of St Nicholas and the three children he revived *(right of chancel)* and a beautiful modern Christ in the choir.

Leave Gattières by D 2209 going west and north.

The *corniche* road skirts the edge of the Grasse Pre-Alps overlooking the Var and provides an attractive glimpse of Gattières to the south.

Carros – The old village occupies a remarkable **position★** huddled round the castle (13C-16C). Just below the village a rock, which bears traces of an old mill, has been made into a terrace: **panorama★★** *(viewing table).*

The road from Carros to Le Broc provides magnificent **views★** of numerous hill villages, of the Var, flowing in its several channels round the banks of flat white pebbles which lie in its broad bed, and of its confluence with the Esteron.

Le Broc – This hill village has a fountain (1812) in the square, which is surrounded by arcades. The 16C **church** ⌚was decorated by the modern painter Guillonet. From the village there is a fine view of the Var Valley.

The road overlooks the confluence of the Esteron and the Var before turning west into the Bouyon ravine.

Bouyon – Every part of the village offers a **view★** of Mont Cheiron, the Var and Esteron valleys and the Alps of the Franco-Italian border.

South of Bouyon the road (D 8) skirts the northern flank of Mont Chiers passing through Bézaudun-les-Alpes to Coursegoules.

Coursegoules – Perched on a rocky spit at the foot of the south face of Mont Cheiron, the tall houses rise above the ravine of the nascent River Cagne. The **church** ⌚ contains a **retable** by Louis Bréa of John the Baptist between St Petronilla and St Gothard; the detail on the latter figure is remarkable.

The Jaboulet workshops established in this tiny village are famous for their santons, said to be the most beautifully crafted in the region.

Take D 2 southeast to Vence.

The road runs through barren countryside beside the River Cagne which turns into a waterfall when it rains. There is always something interesting to look at along this stretch.

★★Col de Vence – Alt 970m/3 182ft. Just south of the pass a fine **panorama★★** opens up: the high peaks east of the Var as far as Mont Agel; along the coast from Cap Ferrat, past the Baie des Anges, Cap d'Antibes and the Lérins islands to the Esterel. To the north the white slopes of Mont Cheiron stand out dramatically against the sky. The road descends through the barren limestone *garrigue* on the southern edge of the Pre-Alps of Grasse.

⚑ Ramble – After you pass the Col de Vence, there is a trail to the left which leads to St-Jeannet via the GR 51 footpath, stretching alongside the Cagne. Beautiful views! *4h from the pass to St-Jeannet. Local map P 258.*

Vallée de la VÉSUBIE★★

Michelin map 84 folds 9 and 19, 115 folds 6, 16 and 17 or 245 fold 25
Local map see NICE

The Vésubie, an eastern tributary of the Var, is formed by two torrents – the Madone de Fenestre and the Boréon – which rise near the Italian border. Drawing its source amid mountains of 2 500m/8 000ft, the Vesubie is fed by the snows of the last high Alpine ranges. The valley, one of the most beautiful above Nice, presents a number of characteristics: the upper valley has Alpine green pastures, pine forests, cascades and peaks while the middle valley, between Lantosque and St-Jean-la-Rivière, shows signs of Mediterranean climate – the slopes are less steep and are partially cultivated in terraces or planted with vines and olive trees. In its lower reaches below St-Jean-la-Rivière, the torrent has created a gorge with vertical walls through which it passes to join the Var as it emerges from the Défilé du Chaudan.

DRIVING TOURS

Plan-du-Var to La Madone d'Utelle

25km/15mi – about 1hr

D 2565 follows the bed of the narrow, winding **Gorges de la Vésubie★★★**: the steep rock walls are layered in many colours.
In St-Jean-la-Rivière turn left onto the road (D 32) which climbs towards Utelle, giving **views** of the Vésubie Gorges.

★**La Madone d'Utelle** – *See UTELLE.*

St-Jean-la-Rivière to St-Martin-Vésubie

85km/53mi – about 4hr

Beyond St-Jean-la-Rivière, the valley squeezes between bluffs of rock, widening slightly at Le Suquet to skirt the eastern foothills of the Brec d'Utelle.

Lantosque – It is sited on a limestone ridge which crosses the valley.

Roquebillière – This little town has been rebuilt six times since the 6C owing to rock falls and floods. The last landslide in 1926 left some of the austere old houses, but it was necessary to re-build on the west bank of the Vésubie where the 15C church already stood.

> **THE GOOD WELL INN**
>
> **Auberge du Bon Puits** – *06450 Le Suquet – 5,5km3.4mi S of Lantosque towards Nice – ☎ 04 93 03 17 65 – Closed 1 Dec to Easter and Tue except Jul-Aug – ⌷ – 16.77/25.15€.* This roadside inn made with local stone stands on the banks of the Vésubie. The dining hall features visible beams and an open fireplace. There are a few rooms as well as an ornamental park with ponies and a playing area for children.

Located in the new town, the **Église St-Michel-du-Gast** ⓥ is one of many examples in Provence of the Romanesque and Gothic styles combined. Sadly, the Romanesque spire is disfigured by a clock. Three Gothic naves are supported by squat Romanesque columns. An **altarpiece** from the Nice School is dedicated to St Antony; the predella represents scenes from his legend. The Maltese Cross carved on the volcanic stone of the font shows that the church was originally owned by the Knights of St John. Fine collection of 17C and 18C priestly vestments in the sacristy.

On leaving Roquebillière-Vieux turn right onto a narrow road to Belvédère.

It is a picturesque road up the **Vallon de la Gordolasque★★** between Cime du Diable (Devil's Peak) and Cime de la Valette.

Vallon de Gordolasque

E. Baret/MICHELIN

The Return of the Wolf

The presence of wolves *(canis lupus)* in the Parc du Mercantour, detected by tracks found in 1989, was verified during the winter of 1992. Observations made in spring 1995 confirmed the presence of a pack of eight wolves, and also probably an isolated couple.

Arriving in one of the successive migrations from the Abruzzi (Central Italy) where the wolf population is estimated at more than 500, the wolf is constantly seeking new territories where its capacity for adaptation is astounding. The pack is the basic family unit, consisting of the parents and their offspring from the last two years, about six to eight members.

The return of the wolf is a sign of ecological health in the area. The Parc du Mercantour conducts a campaign of awareness and education with shepherds who are directly involved in the new problems of living with wolves. Measures have been taken: penning of flocks at night and the introduction of a sheepdog (the Pyrenean Patou) with a great deterrent effect on the wolves' attacks. The creation of a Maison du Loup in the Parc has helped to inform the public.

Belvédère – The **site★** of this charming village overlooks both the Gordolasque and the Vésubie. From the terrace behind the *mairie* (town hall) there is a fine **view★** of Roquebillière-Vieux immediately below backed by Tournairet Mountain, of the Vésubie downstream to Mont Férion and Turini Forest.

The road (D 171) continues up the valley past massive rocks and tumbling waterfalls.

★Cascade du Ray – The river divides into two gushing waterfalls.

The road follows the valley due north divided from the eastern parallel valley, Vallée des Merveilles, by Cime du Diable.

Further north are the indented rocks of the Grand Capelet.

★Cascade de l'Estrech – The road ends near the beautiful Estrech waterfall *(1km/0.6mi of mountain track)* which flows down from a **cirque★★** of snow-capped mountains dominated by Cime du Gélas and Mont Clapier, both of which reach 3 000m/4 828ft.

Return to D 2565.

Berthemont-les-Bains – *4km/2.5mi from D 2565.* This spa is in a shaded setting. The sulphurous, radioactive waters at 30°C were used as long ago as in Roman times. The complaints treated include respiratory diseases, rheumatism and diseases of the joints.

As the road climbs, the valley changes to a landscape of chestnuts, pines and green pastures which has earned the region round St-Martin-Vésubie the title of "Suisse Niçoise" (Nice's Switzerland). Venanson overlooks the valley from the west bank.

VILLECROZE

Population 1 087
Michelin map 84 fold 6 (northeast of Salernes),
114 fold 21 or 245 fold 34

The village has developed around a group of caves, partly converted into dwellings. It lies in the wooded foothills of the Provençal tableland. The surrounding landscape is a charming stretch of land combining vineyards, orchards and olive groves.

A QUAINT VILLAGE

Medieval origins – The flavour of the Middle Ages lingers in the clock tower, Rue des Arcades and the Romanesque church with its wall belfry.

Parc Municipal – *Entrance via Route d'Aups, then a right-hand turning leading to a car park.* A beautiful waterfall cascades 40m/130ft down the cliff face and forms a stream in an oasis of greenery beside a lovely rose garden. A marked path leads to the caves *(grottes)*.

Caves – In the 16C the caves were partially converted into dwellings by the lords of Villecroze; some mullioned windows set into the rock remain. The tour includes several little chambers with attractive concretions.

Viewpoint – 1km/0.5mi from the village on the Tourtour road, there is a look-out point *(viewing table)*. The **panorama**★ extends from the Provençal tableland over Tourtour, Villecroze and Salernes to the Bessillon peaks, the Maures and Ste-Baume.

★ **Belvédère de Villecroze** – *From Tourtour take D 51 towards Villecroze.*
The little road winds through woods which soon give way to strangely shaped rocks and caves. About 1km/0.6mi before Villecroze, a belvedere can be seen beside the road. The circular **panorama**★ from the viewing table takes in Tourtour, the Plans de Provence, Villecroze, Salernes, Gros Bessillon and *(further east)* the Maures and Ste-Baume.

VILLEFRANCHE-SUR-MER★

Population 6 833
Michelin map 84 fold 10 and 19, 115 fold 27 or 245 fold 38
Local map see Corniches de la RIVIERA

Villefranche, a fishing port and holiday resort, is built on the wooded slopes encircling one of the most beautiful **harbours**★★ in the Mediterranean. The deep bay of 25-60m/13-33 fathoms, where cruise liners and warships can lie at anchor, lies between the Cap Ferrat Peninsula and the Mont Boron heights.
Villefranche has preserved its 17C character in its ports, citadel and old streets.

The Origins of Villefranche – The town owes its name to the Count of Provence, Charles II of Anjou, nephew of St Louis, who founded it at the start of the 14C and granted it commercial independence. Between its cession to Savoy in the late 17C and the excavation of the Lympia harbour in Nice in the mid-18C, Villefranche was the major port of the Savoyard and then the Sardinian states.

The Congress of Nice – In 1538, the Congress of Nice was convened by Pope Paul III, former Bishop of Vence, to bring peace between François I and Charles V. During the Congress, Charles V stayed in Villefranche, François I in Villeneuve-Loubet and the Pope, acting as mediator, in Nice.
The Queen of France, sister of Charles V, went to see her brother, whose ship was moored at Villefranche. Charles, giving his hand to the Queen and followed by the Duke of Savoy and lords and ladies of his suite, advanced majestically along the wooden gangway between the jetty and the ship. With a cracking noise the gangway collapsed, and the Emperor, the Queen and the Duke could only splash about helplessly in the water until, soaked and dishevelled, they were pulled ashore by onlookers.
The peace of Nice lasted for barely five years.

From Naval Base to Zoological Station – The Russian presence in Villefranche increased at the end of the 18C and has been remarkably consistent ever since. The strategic potential of the harbour did not escape the notice of the Russian naval authorities of the period. Each conflict between the Russian Empire and Turkey brought about

Villefranche-sur-Mer Bay

B. Kaufmann/MICHELIN

341

the temporary anchorage of Russian naval units at Villefranche. It was, however, just after the Crimean War, in 1856, that Villefranche harbour became even more useful to the Russian military fleet deprived of access to the Mediterranean via the Bosphorus. In 1857 an agreement was reached with the king of Sardinia for the transfer of storehouses and the harbour at Villefranche to Russia, who would use it as a depot for fuel and provisions as well as a home base for the Imperial nobility on holiday on the coast. Uniting with the Comté de Nice maintained these arrangements but interest in the site developed at the end of the century.

In 1893 a team of Russian scientists and academics from Kiev replaced the soldiers to carry out oceanographic research, taking advantage of the upcurrent in the harbour. These studies, in spite of political ups and downs between the two nations, were continued until the 1930s, when the premises were reclaimed by the Université de Paris, who established a marine zoology station of international repute there.

A CHARMING ANCHORAGE

★**Old town** – A row of brightly painted houses lines the waterfront of this delightful fishing harbour.
Rue du Poilu is the main street in a network of narrow alleys, some of which are stepped or vaulted, such as the strange **Rue Obscure** where the population took refuge during bombings.

Église St-Michel – This Italian Baroque church contains 18C altarpieces. In the north transept is a crucifix carved with impressive realism from the trunk of a fig tree by an unknown convict in the 17C, and a 16C polychrome wood statue of St Roch and his dog stands against a pillar (left). The typically French organ, dated 1790 and recently restored, was built by the well-known Grinda brothers of Nice.

Harbour (Darse) – Once a military port where galleys were built and manned, this is now an anchorage for yachts and pleasure boats.

SIGHTS

★**Chapelle St-Pierre** ⊘ – This chapel was decorated in 1957 by **Jean Cocteau**. The staring eyes on either side of the door – the flames of the Apocalypse – were painted later to resemble ceramics.
The frescoes are typical of Cocteau's style of drawing, in precise but ample lines. His theme, the life of St Peter, is illustrated by simple realistic scenes; there are also some secular scenes celebrating the young women of Villefranche and gypsies. They are linked together by geometric motifs.

Eating out

MODERATE

La Caravelle – *3 Rue de l'Église, in the old town* – ☎ *04 93 01 81 10 – Closed Nov-Dec, for lunch and Wed off season. – 12.96/16.77€.* Small restaurant with a terrace that pays homage to the sea, whose decor is painted in shaded tones of blue. Homely cooking, unpretentious service and a friendly welcome are the hallmarks of La Caravelle, whose owner offers invaluable advice about the Villefranche area.

MID-RANGE

La Grignotière – *3 Rue du Poilu* – ☎ *04 93 76 79 83 – Closed for lunch except Sun, and Wed evening off season. – 16.62/27.29€. Nouvelle cuisine* is an unknown expression in this restaurant, which makes a point of serving hearty meals made with fresh ingredients of excellent quality. Follow the example of the local population and tuck into a gargantuan dinner unashamedly!

Where to stay

MID-RANGE

Le Riviera – *2 Avenue Albert-1er* – ☎ *04 93 76 62 76 – contact@hotel-riviera-hrv.com – Closed Jan – 24 rooms: 45.73/60.98€* – ☑ *7.32€.* Unpretentious, prettily restored hotel lying on the Corniche Inférieure. The rooms, of different sizes, are gradually being refurbished; some afford views of the sea. Agreable rooftop terrace for summer breakfasts.

Visiting Villefranche

Guided tours – Guided tours of the town *(1hr 45min)* are organised by the tourist office on Wednesdays at 10am. 4.57€. Treat yourself to breakfast and a guided tour of the Volti gardens (with commentary) on Fridays between May and October. 7.62€.

VILLEFRANCHE-SUR-MER

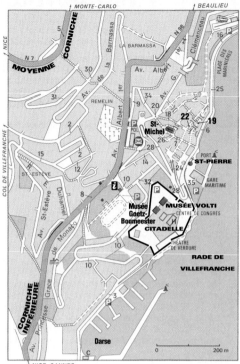

Citadelle – The stronghold was constructed in 1560 by the Duke of Savoy to guard the port. It was much admired by Vauban and spared by Louis XIV together with Fort du Mont Alban, when the defences of the County of Nice were destroyed.

The building was restored in 1981 and comprises the town hall, the former chapel of St Elmo used for temporary exhibitions, an auditorium and an open-air theatre. The casemates of the citadel house a **collection of submarine archeology** ⊙. The exhibits come from the wreck of a Genoese ship that sank in the Villefranche anchorage in the 16C and was excavated in the 1980s.

They are also home to the **Collection Roux** ⊙, an exhibition of ceramic figurines displayed in small tableaux evoking everyday life in the Middle Ages and during the Renaissance. These scenes are based on treaties and other documents dating from these periods.

★ **Musée Volti** ⊙ – The main courtyard of the citadel and the surrounding vaulted casemates provide an admirable setting for a collection of sculptures by Antoniucci Volti, a citizen of Villefranche of Italian origin.

His work is strictly representational; he concentrates exclusively on the human body, not without humour, as in the group in beaten copper exhibited in the courtyard. He excels in countless representations of the female figure: supremely elegant *(Parisiennes)*, gracefully reclining *(Nikaïa)*, seated with dignity *(Cachan Maternity)*, crouching or curled up *(Lotus)*.

Some of his most recent works verge on the monumental *(Queen, Minerva...)*. The sculptures are complemented by several very fine drawings in red chalk.

Musée Goetz-Boumeester ⊙ – The main collection was given to the town of Villefranche by the painter-engraver **Henri Goetz**, born in 1909, and his wife Christine Boumeester (1904-71); there are about 100 works, representing 50 years of pictorial research ranging from the figurative to the Abstract. There are also some souvenir works signed by Picasso, Miró, Hartung, Picabia etc.

VILLENEUVE-LOUBET

Population 12 935
Michelin map 84 fold 9, 115 fold 25 or 245 fold 37
Town plan see CAGNES-SUR-MER

The district of Villeneuve-Loubet on the banks of the River Loup is bordered on the coast by a vast beach. The old village is dominated by a medieval **castle**, the property of the Villeneuve family, which was restored in the 19C and is well preserved.

The tall pentagonal keep was begun in the 9C. François I stayed in the castle during his negotiations with Charles V, leading to the Treaty of Nice which was signed in the castle in 1538.

The village preserves the traditional form of the Provençal sport *pelota*, which is played without a glove.

SIGHTS

★**Musée de l'Art Culinaire** ⊘ – The Culinary Museum occupies the house where **Auguste Escoffier** (1846-1935) was born and contains souvenirs of his career as head chef at the Savoy and the Carlton in London (he was the creator of the mouthwatering **Peach Melba**). There are many documents on the art of cooking; also, amazing show-pieces made of icing sugar or almond paste. The room which has been arranged as a Provençal kitchen leads to an upstairs room displaying a collection of 5 000 menus; some date back to 1820.

Marina Baie des Anges – *In Villeneuve-Loubet-Plage. Take D 2 south and turn right onto N 7 (towards Antibes); after crossing the motorway, turn left.*
The shallow S-bends of the four pyramidal blocks of luxury seafront flats are the brainchild of André Minangoy and one of the most amazing property developments on the Riviera. Each floor diminishes in surface area towards the top storey providing terraces at every level. Their distinctive silhouettes dominate the Baie des Anges from Cap Martin to Cap d'Antibes. The beach is complemented by a swimming pool, marina, cafés, shops and restaurants to form an impressive residential complex.

Marina Baie des Anges, Villeneuve-Loubet

344

Admission times and charges

The information given below applies to individual adults. Reduced rates may be available for families, children, students, senior citizens (old-age pensioners) and the unemployed. In some cases there is no admission charge on certain days. Special rates and admission times are generally available for group bookings. As admission times and charges are liable to alteration, the information printed below is for guidance only. Prices are given in euros (€). During the introduction of the euro, prices given may be conversions of the prices reported to our services in francs. In some cases, no price was indicated to our services, but the attraction may not necessarily be free of charge. Religious buildings are closed during services. Some churches and most chapels are often closed and admission times and charges are given if the interior is of special interest. Where visitors must be accompanied by the keyholder, a fee may be payable or a donation expected. In some places, guided tours of the whole town or historical districts only are available throughout the tourist season. These are mentioned at the start of the admission times and charges for the towns concerned. The symbol ▲ refers to towns, rich in art and history (Villes d'Art et d'Histoire), with tours conducted by lecturers from the Historic Monuments Association (Caisse Nationale des Monuments Historiques et des Sites).

Where there are facilities for the disabled, Tthe symbol ⅍ indicates that the site is accessible to disabled personsis shown after the place-name.

Museum lovers take note: The French Riviera Museum Pass provides direct, unlimited access to 62 museums, monuments and gardens in the area, for a period of 3 days (12.20€). It is available at the larger museums and monuments, and from tourist offices in Nice, Antibes, Cagnes-sur-Mer, Eze, Grasse, Vallauris, Vence. For up-to-the-minute information, travellers should contact the CMCA: Carte Musées Côte d'Azur, Le Consul - 37/41 Boulevard Dubouchage, 06000 Nice, ☎ 04 93 13 17 51 – Fax: 04 93 13 17 52. Internet www.cmca.net

A

ANTIBES

🖸 11, Place du Général-de-Gaulle – 06200 – ☎ 04 92 90 53 00

Fort Carré – Guided tours (45min) 10am-6pm (Oct-May: 430pm). 3,05€ ☎ 06 14 89 17 45.

Musée Archéologique – ⅍ Open daily (except Mon) 10am-noon, 2-6pm; Jun-Sep open daily (except Mon) 10am-6pm, Fri open late until 10pm. Closed 1 Jan, 1 May, 1 Nov, 25 Dec. 3,05€. ☎ 04 92 90 54 35.

Musée Peynet et de la Caricature – ⅍ Open daily (except Mon) 10am-noon, 2-6pm; Jun-Sep open daily (except Mon) 10am-6pm, Fri open late until 10pm. Closed 1 Jan, 1 May, 1 Nov, 25 Dec. 3,05€. ☎ 04 92 90 54 30.

Musée de la Tour des Arts and Traditions Populaires – Open Wed, Thu, Sat 4-7pm (winter: 3-5pm). Closed public holidays. 3,05€. ☎ 04 93 34 50 91 or ☎ 04 93 34 66 07.

Musée Picasso – Open daily (except Mon) 10am-noon, 2-6pm; Jun-Sep 10am-6pm, Fri open late until 10pm. Closed 1 Jan, 1 May, 1 Nov and 25 Dec. 4,57€. ☎ 04 92 90 54 20.

Excursions

Marineland – ⅍ Open Jul-Aug 10am-midnight; spring and autumn 10am-7pm; winter 10am-5pm. 22,71€ (adult), 15,09€ (child). ☎ 04 93 33 49 49.

Parc Aqua-Splash – Open mid-Jun to early Sep 10am-7pm. 15,09€ (adult), 12,65€ (child). ☎ 04 93 33 49 49.

Jungle des Papillons – ⅍ Open 10am to dusk. 7,01€ (adult), 4,73€ (child). ☎ 04 93 33 49 49.

Cap d'ANTIBES

Sanctuaire de la Garoupe – ⅍ 9.30am-noon, 2.30-7pm (winter 10am-noon, 2.30-5pm). ☎ 04 93 67 36 01.

Phare de la Garoupe – Guided tours (30min) 3-6pm (Oct-Apr 3-5pm). ☎ 04 93 61 57 63.

Cap d'Antibes

Jardin Thuret – Open daily (except Sat-Sun) 8am-6pm; winter open daily (except Sat-Sun) 8.30am-5.30pm. Closed between 24 Dec and 2 Jan, public holidays. No charge. ☎ 04 93 67 88 66.

Musée Napoléonien – Open daily (except Sun) 9.30am-noon, 2.15-6pm, Sat 9.30am-noon. Closed in Oct and public holidays. 3,05€. ☎ 04 93 61 45 32.

Les ARCS
🖪 Place du Général-de-Gaulle – 83460 – ☎ 04 94 73 37 30

Excursion

Chapelle Ste-Roseline – Open daily (except Mon) 3-7pm; Mar-May open daily (except Mon) 2-6pm; Oct-Feb open daily (except Mon) 2.30-5pm. No charge. ☎ 04 94 73 37 30.

ASPREMONT

Church – Closed between services.

AUPS
🖪 Place F.-Mistral – 83630 – ☎ 04 94 70 00 80

Collégiale St-Pancrace – Open on request only. Apply to ☎ 04 94 70 00 80.

Musée Simon-Ségal – Open mid-Jun to mid-Sep 10am-noon, 3-7pm. 2,29€. ☎ 04 94 70 01 95.

AURIBEAU-SUR-SIAGNE

Église – Open Sun 10am-6pm. Apply to Mme Vacance, ☎ 04 93 42 25 46.

B

BANDOL
🖪 Allée Alfred-Vivien – 83150 – ☎ 04 94 29 41 35

Jardin Exotique et Zoo de Sanary-Bandol – ♿ Open 8am-noon, 2-6pm, Sun and public holidays 2-6pm (Jun-Sep 7pm); Sun and public holidays 10am-noon, 2-7pm. 6,10€ (child 4,57€). ☎ 04 94 29 40 38.

Driving tours

Chapelle Notre-Dame du Beausset-Vieux – Open 2-5pm.

BARGEMON

Church – Open on request. Apply to the priest. ☎ 04 94 39 13 30.

Le BAR-SUR-LOUP
🖪 Place F.-Paulet – 06600 – ☎ 04 93 42 72 21

Église St-Jacques – Guided tours available on request. Apply to the tourist office.

BEAULIEU-SUR-MER
🖪 Place Georges-Clemenceau – 06310 – ☎ 04 93 01 02 21

Villa Grecque Kerylos – Open mid-Feb to 11 Nov 10.30am-6pm; Jul-Aug 10.30am-7pm; mid-Dec to mid-Feb 2-6pm, Sat-Sun, public holidays, school holidays 10.30am-6pm. Closed mid-Nov to mid-Dec, 1 Jan, 25 Dec. € (adult), 25F (child). ☎ 04 93 01 61 70.

Île de BENDOR
🖪 Allées Vivien in Bandol – 83150 – ☎ 04 94 29 41 35

Access – Departures every 30min leaving from Bandol (7min). 4,27€ there and back. ☎ 04 94 29 44 34.

Exposition des Vins and Spiritueux – Open Easter to end of Sep daily (except Wed) 10am-noon, 2-6pm (Jul-Aug 7am). No charge. ☎04 94 29 44 34.

BIOT
🖪 46 r.St-Sébastien – 06410 – ☎ 04 93 65 78 00

Musée National Fernand-Léger – ♿ Open daily (except Tue) 10am-0.30pm, 2-5.30pm (Jul-Sep closed at 6pm). Closed 1 Jan, 1 May and 25 Dec. 4,57€. No charge 1st Sun of each month. ☎ 04 92 91 50 20.

Bonsaï Arboretum – Open daily (except Tue) 10am-noon, 2-5.30pm; Apr-Sep open daily (except Tue) 10am-noon, 3-6.30pm. Closed 1 Jan, 1 May. 3,81€. ☎ 04 93 65 63 99.

Musée de Biot – Jul-Sep open daily (except Mon and Tue) 10am-6pm; Oct-Jun open daily (except Mon and Tue) 2-6pm. Closed public holidays. 1,52€. No charge 1st Sun of each month. ☎ 04 93 65 54 54.

BORMES-LES-MIMOSAS

🏛 Place Gambetta – 83230 – ☎ 04 94 01 38 38

Église St-Trophyme – Summer: Guided tours Thu 6pm30; winter: Sat 4pm30. S'adresser to la Mayrie.

Musée "Arts et Histoire" – Open daily (except Tue 10am-noon, 2pm30-5pm30, Sun and public holidays 10am-noon (Jun-Aug: Open daily 10am-noon, 3pm30-19am). No charge. ☎ 04 94 71 56 60.

BREIL-SUR-ROYA

🏛 Place Bianchéri – 06540 – ☎ 04 93 04 99 76sep
🏛 Office du tourisme de la Vallée de la Roya – ☎ 04 93 04 99 90

Écomusée du Haut Pays – Open Jul-Sep Thu and Sun 10.30am-5.30pm. 2,29€. ☎ 04 93 04 46 91.

BRIGNOLES

🏛 10 Rue Palais – 83170 – ☎ 04 94 69 27 51

Église St-Sauveur – Open on request. Apply to the presbytery. ☎ 04 94 69 10 69.

Musée du Pays Brignolais – Open Apr-Sep daily (except Mon and Tue) 9am-noon, 2.30-6pm, Sun 9am-noon, 3-6pm; Oct-Mar open daily (except Mon and Tue) 10am-noon, 2.30-5pm, Sun 10am-noon, 3-5pm. Closed public holidays. 4€. ☎ 04 94 69 45 18.

La BRIGUE

Chapelle de l'Assomption – Guided tours only, available on request. Apply to the tourist office.

Chapelle de l'Annonciation- Church treasure – Guided tours available on request. Apply to the tourist office.

Collégiale St-Martin – Guided tours available on request. Apply to the tourist office.

Le BROC

Church – Guided tours 9am-noon, 2-5pm.

C

CABASSE

Église St-Pons – Apply to the café on the church square.

CABRIS

🏛 9 Rue Frédéric-Mistral – 06530 – ☎ 04 93 60 55 63

Grottes des Audides – Guided tours (45min) mid-Feb to end of Oct daily (except Mon and Tue) 2-5pm; Jul-Aug daily 10am-6pm; Nov to mid-Feb on request only. Closed 1 and 8 May, Ascension. 4,57€ caves, 3,05€ parc (child 3,05€/2,29€). ☎ 04 93 42 64 15.

CAGNES-SUR-MER

🏛 6, Boulevard Maréchal-Juin – 06800 – ☎ 04 93 20 61 64
🏛 20 Avenue des Oliviers – ☎ 04 93 07 67 08

Église St-Pierre – Open 2-7pm. Closed on rainy days. ☎ 04 93 20 67 14.

Chapelle Notre-Dame-de-Protection – Open Mon, Sat, Sun 3-5pm. Closed 1 Jan, 1 May, 25 Dec. No charge. ☎ 04 93 20 61 64

Château-Musée – Open daily (except Tue) 10am-noon, 2-5pm; May-Sep 2-6pm. Closed in Nov, 1 Jan, 1 May, 25 Dec. 3,05€. ☎ 04 93 20 87 29.

Musée Renoir – Open daily (except Tue) 10am-noon, 2-5pm (May-Sep 6pm). Closed in Nov, 1 Jan, 1 May, 25 Dec. 3,05€. ☎ 04 93 20 87 29.

CALLAS

Église – Open early Jul to end of Aug. Guided tours Sat 10am.

CANNES

🏛 Palais des Festivals, 1, La Croisette – 06400 – ☎ 04 93 39 24 53
🏛 Aile Est de la Gare SNCF – ☎ 04 93 99 19 77

La Malmaison – Open during temporary exhibitions. 1,52€. ☎ 04 93 38 55 26.

Musée de la Castre – Open daily (except Tue) 10am-noon, 2-5pm (Apr-Jun 6pm; Jul-Sep open daily (except Tue) 10am-noon, 3-7pm. Closed in Jan and public holidays. 1,52€. ☎ 04 93 38 55 26.

Chapelle Bellini – ♿ Open 2-5pm, Sat-Sun on request. Closed public holidays. No charge. ☎ 04 93 38 61 80.

Église Orthodoxe St-Michel-Archange – Guided tours on request. Apply to M. Wsevolojsky. ☎ 04 93 43 35 35.

Le CANNET
🖻 Avenue du Campon – 06110 – ☎ 04 93 45 34 27

Chapelle St-Sauveur – ♿ 9am-noon, 2-5.30pm, Fri 9am-noon, 2-4.30pm on request. Apply to the Point d'Information Tourisme. No charge. ☎ 04 93 46 74 00 or ☎ 04 93 45 34 27.

CAP FERRAT

Musée Île-de-France – Open 10am-6pm; Nov-Jan 2-6pm, Sat-Sun and public holidays 10am-6pm; Jul-Aug 10am-7pm. 7,62€. ☎ 04 93 01 33 09.

Parc d'Acclimatation – ♿ 9.30am-7pm (winter 9.30am-5.30pm). 9,15€ (child 6,40€). ☎ 04 93 76 07 60.

La CELLE

Abbaye de La Celle – Guided tours (30min) Apr-Oct daily 9.30am-noon, 2-6pm, Sat-Sun and public holidays 10am-noon, 2-6pm; Nov-Mar apply to the town hall (Mairie). Closed 1 Jan, 1 May, 1 and 11 Nov, 25 Dec. 3,05€. ☎ 04 94 59 19 05.

CHATEAUNEUF-VILLEVIEILLE

Église "Madone de Villevieille" – 9am-6pm. ☎ 04 93 79 23 76 or ☎ 04 93 79 00 58.

COARAZE
🖻 Place Ste-Catherine – 06390 – ☎ 04 93 79 37 47

Chapelle Saint Sebastien – Guided tours available on request. Apply to the tourist office.

Notre-Dame-de-la-Pitié – Guided tours available on request. Apply to the tourist office.

COGOLIN
🖻 Place de la République – 83310 – ☎ 04 94 55 01 10

Espace Raimu – ♿ Open Jul to mid-Sep 10am-noon, 4-7pm, Sun 4-7pm; mid-Sep to end of Jun 10am-noon, 3-6pm, Sun 3-6pm. Closed 1 Jan, mid-Nov to end of Nov, 25 Dec. Prices not communicated. ☎ 04 94 54 18 00.

Cogolin pipes – ♿ Workshop open 9am-noon, 2-6pm, Sat 9am-noon, 12-5pm, Sun and public holidays by appointment. Boutique open 9am-7pm. ☎ 04 94 54 63 82.

Manufacture de Tapis de Cogolin – The exhibition gallery is open daily except Sat-Sun 8am-noon, 2-6pm, (Fri 5pm). Closed 15 days in Aug and 24 Dec to 2 Jan. ☎ 04 94 55 70 65.

La COLMIANE

Via Ferrata du Baus de la Frema – Open daily 8.30am-7pm. Access 3,05€. Equipment can be hired from the shop "Igloo Sport" at the pass. Closed in winter. ☎ 04 93 23 25 90 or 04 93 02 83 54.

COURSEGOULES

Church – 9-11.30am.

D

DRAGUIGNAN
🖻 Avenue Carnot – 83300 – ☎04 98 10 51 05

Guided tours of the city – Jul-Aug Wed and Sat at 10am. 3,05€. Apply to the tourist office.

Buses and coaches – The city is served by the bus network Draguibus (4 lines). Single tickets available from bus drivers, books of tickets from the bus station on Place Claude-Gay (Mon-Sat 8am-noon, 2-6pm). Coaches will take you to St-Raphaël and to the train station of Les Arcs-Draguignan (allow 25min). ☎ 04 94 68 15 34.

Tour de l'Horloge – Guided tours available on request. Apply to the tourist office.

Musée Municipal – ♿ Open daily (except Sun) 9am-noon, 2-6pm, Mon 2-6pm. Closed public holidays. No charge. ☎ 04 94 47 28 80.

Musée des Arts and Traditions Populaires de Moyenne Provence – Open daily (except Mon) 9am-noon, 2-6pm, Sun and public holidays 2-6pm. Closed 1 Jan, 1 May, Easter and 25 Dec. 3,05€. ☎ 04 94 47 05 72.

Cimetière Américain and Mémorial du Rhône – ♿ 9am-5pm. No charge. ☎ 04 94 68 03 62.

Musée de l'Artillerie – Open daily (except Sat-Sun) 8.30am-noon, 2.30-6pm, Fri 8.30am-noon, 2.30-5pm. Closed mid-Dec to mid-Jan and public holidays. No charge. ☎ 04 98 10 83 86.

E

Île des EMBIEZ

Access – Le Brusc landing-stage to Six-Fours; 20 to 24 crossings a day. (10min), both ways depending on the season. 5,64€ there and back (child 4,12€ there and back).

Institut Océanographique Paul-Ricard – Guided tours (30min) 10am-0.30pm, 1.30-5pm30; Jun, Sep to Mar Wed, Sat, Sun and public holidays 2-5.30pm. 3,81€ (child 1,83€). ☎ 04 94 34 02 49.

ENTRECASTEAUX   🚹 Cours Gabriel-Péri – 83570 – ☎ 04 94 04 40 50

Château – Guided tours. The times are displayed at the entrance to the château. 5,34€. ☎ 04 94 04 43 95.

ÈZE   🚹 Place du Général-de-Gaulle – 06360 – ☎ 04 93 41 26 00

Guided tours of the village – Guided tours (1hr 15min) available on request. Apply to the tourist office. 4,57€.

Église – Summer 9am-7pm (winter 9.30am-6.30pm). Apply to the tourist office. ☎ 04 93 41 26 00.

Chapelle des Pénitents Blancs – Closed to the public but you can see the chapel through the railings.

Jardin Exotique – 9am-6pm; Jul-Aug 9am-8pm; Sep 9am-7pm; Oct-Jan 9am-5pm. Closed 1 Jan and 25 Dec. 2,28€. ☎ 04 93 41 26 00.

Astrorama – Last admission 1hr before closing time. Fri, Sat 6-10pm; Jul-Aug open daily (except Sun) 6-11pm. Closed 1 Jan and 25 Dec. 6€ (9€ including lecture). ☎ 04 93 85 85 58.

F

FALICON

Church – Thu 3-5.30pm. ☎ 04 93 84 14 56.

FAYENCE   🚹 Place Léon-Roux – 83440 – ☎ 04 94 76 20 08

Driving tours

Notre-Dame-des-Cyprès – Apply to M. Rebuffel, in the wine cellar at the east end of the church 8am-noon and after 6pm.

FRÉJUS   🚹 325 Rue Jean-Jaurès – 83600 – ☎ 04 94 51 83 83
1 Boulevard de la Libération – ☎ 04 94 51 48 42

Guided tours of the city 🅰 – To showcase its precious cultural and architectural heritage, the city of Fréjus has laid out 4 itineraries (2hr) covering the old city and the Roman ruins, and provides qualified tour guides. Apply to the tourist office.

Cathedral Close – ♿ Open Apr-Sep daily 9am-7pm; Oct-Mar open daily (except Mon) 9am-noon, 2-5pm. Closed 1 Jan, 1 May, 1 and 11 Nov, 25 Dec. 4€. ☎ 04 94 51 26 30.

Arènes – ♿ Open Apr-Oct 10am-1pm, 2.30-6.30pm; Nov-Mar 10am-noon, 1.30-5.30pm. Closed 1 Jan, 1 May, 1 and 11 Nov, 25 Dec. No charge. ☎ 04 94 53 58 75.

Pagode Bouddhique Hông Hiên – Open Nov-Oct 9am-noon, 2-6pm; Nov-Tue 9am-noon, 2-5pm. 0,80€. ☎04 94 53 25 29.

FRÉJUS

Mémorial des Guerres en Indochine – Open daily (except Tue) 10am-5.30pm. Closed 1 Jan, 1 May, 25 Dec. No charge. ☎ 04 94 44 42 90.

Musée des Troupes de Marine – Open mid-Jun to mid-Sep daily (except Tue and Sat) 10am-noon, 3-7pm; mid-Sep to mid-Jun open daily (except Tue and Sat) 2-6pm (mid-Nov to mid-Feb 5pm). Closed 24 Dec to 2 Jan. No charge. ☎ 04 94 17 86 55.

Parc Zoologique – Open Mar-Sep daily 10am-6pm; Oct-Feb 10am-6pm. 9,70€ (child 6,05€). ☎ 04 94 40 70 65.

Chapelle Notre-Dame-de-Jérusalem – Open Apr-Oct daily (except Tue and Sun) 2.30-6.30pm, Sat 10am-1pm, 2.30-6.30pm; Nov-Mar 1.30-5.30pm, Sat 9.30am-0.30pm, 1.30-5.30pm.

G

La GARDE-FREINET

Chapelle St-Éloi – Closed for restoration work.

GATTIÈRES

Church – Closed for restoration work.

GONFARON

Écomusée du Liège – Open on request Jan to end of Dec daily (except Sat-Sun) 2-6pm. Closed public holidays. 3,81€. Apply to the Écomusée du Liège ☎ 04 94 78 25 65.

Village de Tortues de Gonfaron – ♿ Open Mar to end of Nov 9am-7pm. 7€ (child 4,5€). ☎ 04 94 78 26 41.

GOURDON

Château – Guided tours (15min) Jun-Sep 11am-1pm, 2-7pm; Oct-May daily (except Tue) 2-6pm. 3,81€. ☎ 04 93 09 68 02.

GRASSE

Musée Provençal du Costume et du Bijou – Open Feb-Oct daily 10am-6pm; Nov-Jan 10am-noon, 2-6pm. No charge. ☎ 04 93 36 44 65.

Musée de la Marine – Open Jun-Sep 10am-7pm; Oct-May open daily (except Sun) 10am-5pm. Closed in Nov and public holidays. 3,05€. ☎ 04 93 40 11 11.

Musée d'Art et d'Histoire de Provence – Open Jun-Sep 10am-7pm; Oct-May open daily (except Tue) 10am-0.30pm, 2-5.30pm. Closed in Nov and public holidays. 3,05€, 3,81€ (including exhibitions). ☎ 04 93 36 01 61.

Cathédrale Notre-Dame-du-Puy – Open daily (except Sun afternoons).

Musée International de la Parfumerie – Open Jun-Sep 10am-7pm; Oct-May open daily (except Tue) 10am-0.30pm, 2-5.30pm. Closed in Nov and public holidays. 3,05€ standing exhibitions, 3,81€ temporary exhibitions. No charge 1st Sun of each month. ☎ 04 93 36 80 20.

Villa-Musée Fragonard —— Same times and charges as for the Musée d'Art et d'Histoire de Provence.

H

HYÈRES

Ancienne Collégiale St-Paul – Open Wed-Sat 10am-noon, 3-6pm, Mon 3-6pm, Sun 10am-0.30pm. ☎ 04 94 00 55 50 (Église St Louis).

Jardins Olbius-Riquier – Open daily 8am-7pm.

Tropical hothouse – 8.30-11.30am, 2.30-5pm, Sat 8.30-11.30am. No charge.

Villa de Noailles – Guided tours (1hr 30min) mid-Jun to mid-Sep Fri at 4pm. 4,57€ (free for children). Apply to the tourist office. ☎ 04 94 01 84 40.

Musée Municipal – ♿ Open daily (except Tue and Sat-Sun) 10am-noon, 2.30-5.30pm. Closed 24 Dec to 2 Jan and public holidays. No charge. ☎ 04 94 00 78 42.

Parc du Château Ste-Claire – Open in summer 8am-7pm; in winter 8am-5pm. No charge.

I

Île de Porquerolles

Information Office – Open Jun to end of Sep. ☎ 04 94 58 33 76.

Fort Ste-Agathe – Open May to end of Sep 10am-noon, 2-5.30pm. 3,81€. ☎ 04 94 12 30 40.

Lighthouse – Guided tours 10am-noon, 2-4pm. No charge. The lighthouse may be closed for safety or technical reasons.

Île de Port-Cros

Parc National – Details from Castel Ste Claire 83400 Hyères (☎ 04 94 12 82 30 or Centre d'Information de Port-Cros, in the port, 1st building on the left of the landing-stages. ☎ 04 94 05 90 17 (open in summer).

Fort de l'Estissac – Open May to end of Sep. No charge. ☎ 04 94 01 40 72.

Underwater path – Open mid-Jun to end of Sep. Guided tours by one of the park attendants (except in the event of bad weather). No charge.

Île Ste-Marguerite

Botanical nature trail – Guided tours year-round of the island's flora, fauna and natural heritage. Prices not communicated. For details apply to the Office National des Forêts. ☎ 04 93 43 49 24.

Fort Royal: Musée de la Mer – Open daily (except Tue) 10.30am-0.15pm, 2.15-4.30pm ; Jul-Sep 6.30pm; Apr-Jun 5pm30. Closed in Jan and public holidays. 1,52€. ☎ 04 93 38 55 26.

Île St-Honorat

Monastère Moderne: Abbey Church – Open daily 8.45-11.15am, 2-5.30pm, Sun 8.45-9.40am, 11.30am-0.25pm, 2-5.30pm. No charge. ☎ 04 92 99 54 00.

Ancien Monastère Fortifié – Open Jul to mid-Sep 10.30am-0.30pm, 2.30-5pm, Sun 2.30-5pm; mid-Sep to end of Jun 9am-5pm. 2,29€. ☎ 04 92 99 54 00.

Church – Open to the public during Mass. Open daily at 11.25am, Sun at 9.50am.

L

LEVENS
🚹 12 Rue du Docteur Faraut – 06670 – ☎ 04 93 79 71 00

Mairie – To see the frescoes, apply to the secretariat. Open daily (except Sun) 8.30am-noon, 1.30-4pm, Tue 1.30-4pm, Sat 9am-noon. ☎ 04 93 91 61 16.

La LONDE-les-MAURES

Jardin des Oiseaux Exotiques – ♿ Open Jun-Sep 9am-7pm; Feb-May and Oct 2-6pm. Closed Nov to end of Jan 6,86€ (child 4,57€). ☎ 04 94 35 02 15.

LORGUES
🚹 Place d'Antrechaux – 83510 – ☎ 04 94 73 92 37

Chapelle Notre-Dame-de-Benva – Guided tours on request. Apply to the tourist office. ☎ 04 94 73 92 37.

Saut du LOUP

Open Jun to end of Sep 10am-7pm. 0,46€. ☎ 04 93 09 68 88.

Le LUC
🚹 Château des Vintimille, Place de la Liberté – 83340 – ☎ 04 94 60 74 51

Musée Historique du Centre-Var – ♿ Open mid-Jun to mid-Oct daily (except Sun) 2.30-5.30pm; Jul to mid-Sep open daily (except Sun) 3-6pm; mid-Oct to mid-Jun on request. Closed public holidays. No charge. ☎ 04 94 60 70 12.

Musée Régional du Timbre – ♿ Open daily (except Mon and Tue) 2.30-6pm, Fri, Sat-Sun 10am-noon, 2.30-6pm (Oct-May 5pm30). Closed in Sep, 1 Jan, 1 May, 25 Dec 1,5€. ☎ 04 94 47 96 16.

LUCÉRAM
🚹 Mairie – 06440 – ☎ 04 93 91 60 50

Église Ste-Marguerite – Open daily (except Mon and Tue) 10am-noon, 2-6pm. For guided tours, apply to the Centre d'Interprétation du Patrimoine at ☎ 04 93 91 60 50.

Chapelle St-Grat – Ask for the key at ☎ 04 93 79 46 50.

Chapelle Notre-Dame-de-Bon-Coeur – Ask for the key at ☎ 04 93 79 46 50.

M

MAGAGNOSC

Église St-Laurent – ☎ For opening times call ☎ 04 93 77 28 33.

Massif des MAURES

Driving tours

Arboretum de Gratteloup – Open daily. No charge. ☎ 04 97 71 06 07.

Monastère de la Verne – Open daily (except Tue) 11am-5pm (Apr-Oct 6pm). Closed in Jan, Easter, Ascension, Pentecost, 15 Aug, 1 Nov, 25 Dec. 4,57€ (child 2,29€). ☎ 04 94 43 48 28.

MENTON   🄻 Palais de l'Europe, 8 Avenue Boyer – 06500 – ☎ 04 92 41 76 76

Guided tours of the city 🄰 – To showcase its precious cultural and architectural heritage, the city of Menton has laid out several itineraries (2hr) covering the old city, and provides qualified tour guides. Tues at 2.30pm. Apply to the Maison du Patrimoine, 5 Rue Ciapetta ☎ 04 92 10 33 66.

Basilique St-Michel – Guided tours Tue at 2.30pm. ☎ 04 92 10 97 10.

Musée Jean-Cocteau – Open daily (except Tue) 10am-noon, 2-6pm. Closed public holidays. 3,05€. ☎ 04 93 35 49 71.

Basilique St-Michel-Archange – Open daily (except Sat mornings and public holidays) 10am-noon, 3-5.15pm.

Musée des Beaux-Arts – Open daily (except Tue) 10am-noon, 2-6pm. Closed public holidays. No charge. ☎ 04 93 35 49 71.

Hôtel de Ville – The hall decorated by Jean Cocteau is open daily (except Sat-Sun) 8.30am-0.30pm, 1.30-5pm. Closed public holidays. 1,53€. Apply to the tourist office. ☎ 04 92 10 50 00.

Musée de Préhistoire Régionale – Open daily (except Tue) 10am-noon, 2-6pm. Closed public holidays. No charge. ☎ 04 93 35 49 71.

Église Orthodoxe Russe – Guided tours 4th Sat of each month at 4.30pm. Apply to the Maison du Patrimoine. 5€.

Garavan :

Jardin du Val Rameh – Open May-Sep 10am-0.30pm, 3-6pm; Oct-Apr 10am-0.30pm, 2-5pm. 3,05€. ☎ 04 93 35 86 72.

Jardin des Colombières – Open Jul to early Aug. Guided tours on request. Apply to the Service du Patrimoine, Hôtel d'Adhémar de Lantagnac, 24 Rue St-Michel, ☎ 04 92 10 97 10. 7,62€.

Jardin des Romanciers (Villa Fontana Rosa) – Guided tours (2hr) Fri at 10am. 5€. ☎ 04 92 10 97 10.

Serre de la Madone – Open mid-Feb to end of Mar and Oct to end of Nov. Guided tours (2hr) at 2.30pm; Apr-May at 2.30pm, 4.30pm; Jun-Sep at 9am and 5.30pm. Closed Mon 7,62€. ☎ 04 93 57 73 90.

Jardin de Maria Serena – Guided tours (2hr) Tue at 10am. 5€. ☎ 04 92 10 97 10.

Excursion

Fort Maginot de Ste-Agnès – Guided tours (1hr) Jul-Sep 3-6pm; Oct-Jun Sat-Sun 2.30-5.30pm. 3€. ☎ 04 93 35 84 58.

Vallée des MERVEILLES

Guided tours of the engravings – **Vallée des Merveilles**: departures from the CAF des Merveilles refuge. Jul-Aug departures at 8am, 11am, 1pm and 3pm; Jun and Sep departures Mon, Fri and Sat-Sun at 8am and 1pm. **Vallée de Fontanalbe**: departures from the Fontanalbe refuge. Jun-Sep departures at 8am, 11am and 2pm. 7,62€ (child 3,81€). Apply to the Association Merveilles, Gravures et Découvertes, 13 Rue Antoine-Opperto, 06430 Tende, ☎ 06 86 03 90 13, or to the information office in the national park in Castérino.

Les Merveilles refuge – ☎ 04 93 04 64 64 or 04 93 04 69 22 (low season) – Open Jun to mid-Oct daily. In low season open Sat-Sun and public holidays.

Fontanalbe refuge – ☎ 04 93 04 89 19 or 04 93 04 69 22 (low season) – Open Jun to end of Sep

Principauté de MONACO

2a, Boulevard des Moulins – 98030
☎ 00 377 92 16 61 66

To telephone Monaco from France, dial 00 followed by 377 (code for Monaco) and then the 8-digit telephone number.

Azur-Express – Operates 10.30-6pm (5pm in winter). Closed Jan. 6,10€. ☎ 00 377 92 05 64 38.

Jardin Exotique – Open mid-May to mid-Sep 9am-7pm; mid-Sep to mid-May 9am-6pm or dusk depending on the season. Closed 19 Nov and 25 Dec. 6,25€ (combined ticket with Grotte de l'Observatoire and Musée d'Anthropologie Préhistorique). ☎ 00 377 93 15 29 80.

Grotte de l'Observatoire – Same times and charges as for the Jardin Exotique.

Musée d'Anthropologie Préhistorique – Open Apr-Sep 9am-6.30pm (mid-May to mid-Sep 7pm); Feb-Mar and Oct:9am-6pm; Jan and Nov 9am-5.30pm; Dec 9am-5pm. Closed 19 Nov and 25 Dec 6,25€ (including tour of the Jardin Exotique). ☎ 00 377 93 15 80 06.

Église St-Martin – Closed Ascension Thu and the following Sun.

Collection des Voitures Anciennes – & Open 10am-6pm. Closed 25 Dec 4,57€ (child 2,29€).☎00 377 92 05 28 56.

Musée Naval – & Open 10am-6pm. 3,81€. ☎ 00 377 92 05 28 48.

Musée des Timbres and des Monnaies – & Open 10am-5pm (Jul-Sep 6pm). 3,04€. ☎ 00 377 93 15 41 50.

Musée Océanographique – & Open Apr-Sep 9am-7pm; Oct-Mar 10am-6pm. Closed Sun during Grand Prix Automobile de Monaco. 11€. ☎ 00 377 92 16 77 93.

Musée de la Chapelle de la Visitation – & Open daily (except Mon) 10am-4pm. Closed 1 Jan, 1 May, 1-4 Jun, 19 Nov, 25 Dec. 3,05€. ☎ 00 377 93 500 700.

Monte-Carlo Story – & Open Mar-Oct 11am-5pm (Jul-Aug 6pm); Nov-Feb 2-5pm. Closed in Dec. 4,57€ (child 2,45€). ☎ 00 377 93 25 32 33.

Historial des Princes de Monaco – & Open Feb-Mar 11am-5pm; Apr-Nov and end Dec to early Jan 10am-6pm. 3,50€ (child 2€). ☎ 00 377 93 30 39 05.

Palais du Prince – Open Jun-Sep 9.30am-6.30pm; Oct 10am-5pm. 4,57€. ☎ 00 377 93 25 18 31.

Musée Napoléonien and des Archives du Palais – Open Jun-Sep 9.30am-6.30pm; Oct to 11 Nov 10am-5pm; mid-Dec to end of May daily (except Mon) 10.30am-0.30pm, 2-5pm. Closed mid-Nov to mid-Dec, 1 Jan, 25 Dec 3,05€. ☎ 00 377 93 25 18 31.

Jardin Animalier – & Open Jun-Sep 9am-noon, 2-7pm; Mar-May 10am-noon, 2-6pm; Oct-Feb 10am-noon, 2-5pm. 3,05€. ☎ 00 377 93 25 18 31.

Casino – Forbidden to people under 21 years of age. Open from noon. 7,62€. Identity papers required. ☎ 00 377 92 16 20 00.

Jardin Japonais – & Open 9am to dusk. No charge. ☎ 00 377 93 15 22 77.

Musée National de Monaco (des Poupées et Automates) – Open Easter to Sep 10am-6.30pm (last admission 1hr before closing time); Oct to Easter 10am-0.15pm, 2.30-6.30pm. Closed 1 Jan, 1 May, 19 Nov, 25 Dec and during the 4 days of the Grand Prix Automobile de Monaco. 4,57€. ☎ 00 377 93 30 91 26.

MONS

Place St-Sébastien – 83440 – ☎ 04 94 76 39 54

Church – Guided tours 2-6pm on request. Apply to the tourist office. ☎ 04 94 76 39 54.

MOUANS-SARTOUX

Espace de l'Art Concret – Open Jun-Sep 11am-7pm; Oct-May 11am-6pm. 2,29€. ☎ 04 93 75 71 50.

MOUGINS

15 Avenue Ch-Malet – 06250 – ☎ 04 93 75 87 67

Church bell-tower – Open Jul-Sep daily (except Mon and Tue) 2-8pm; Oct-Jun open daily (except Mon) 10am-noon, 2-6pm (Sun and public holidays 2-6pm). Closed in Nov. Apply to the Musée de la Photographie to get the key. No charge. ☎ 04 93 75 85 67.

Musée Municipal – Open Jan to mid-Apr daily (except Sat-Sun) 10am-5pm; mid-Apr to end of Oct 10am-noon, 2-6pm. Closed in Nov and public holidays. No charge. ☎ 04 92 92 50 42.

Musée de la Photographie – Open Jul-Sep daily (except Mon and Tue) 2-8pm; Oct-Jun daily (except Mon and Tue) 10am-noon, 2-6pm (Sun and public holidays 2-6pm). Closed in Nov. 0,76€. ☎ 04 93 75 85 67.

Ermitage Notre-Dame-de-Vie – Open during Mass Sun mornings.

Musée de l'Automobiliste – Open Apr-Sep 10am-7pm; Oct-Mar 10am-6pm. Closed mid-Nov to mid-Dec. 6,1€ (child 3,81€). ☎ 04 93 69 27 80.

N

Ermitage NOTRE-DAME-DES-ANGES

Ermitage Notre-Dame-des-Anges – Chapel open year-round. Accommodation available Apr-Oct. For reservations, apply to the Ermitage. ☎ 04 94 59 00 69.

La NAPOULE

Château-Musée – Guided tours (1hr) Mar to end of Oct daily (except Tue) 2.30-5.30pm; Jul-Aug daily (except Tue) 2.30-6.30pm. Closed 1 May. 3,80€. ☎ 04 93 49 95 05.

NICE

🅱 Avenue Thiers – 06000 – ☎ 04 93 87 07 07
🅱 2 Rue Massenet – 06000 – ☎ 04 93 87 60 60

Chapelle de l'Annonciation: Chapelle Ste-Rita – Open daily (except Sun mornings).

Musée des Arts Asiatiques: Tea Ceremony – Sun (except in Aug) 3pm and 4pm. 7,62€. Book one week in advance. ☎ 04 92 29 37 02.

Palais Masséna: Musée d'Art et d'Histoire – Closed for restoration work. Reopening scheduled for spring 2004.

Galerie de la Marine – ♿ Open daily (except Mon) 10am-noon, 2-6pm, Sun 2-6pm. Closed 1 Jan, Easter Mon, 1 May, 25 Dec. No charge. ☎ 04 93 62 37 11.

Galerie des Ponchettes – ♿ Open daily (except Mon) 10am-noon, 2-6pm, Sun 2-6pm. Closed 1 Jan, Easter Mon, 1 May, 25 Dec. No charge. ☎ 04 93 62 31 24.

Château: Lift – ♿ Operates Apr-Sep 9am-7pm; Jun-Aug 9am-8pm; Oct-Mar 10am-6pm, last ascent 30min before closing time. 0,58€ to the top, 0,84€ there and back. ☎ 04 93 85 62 33.

Musée Naval – Open Jun-Sep daily (except Mon and Tue) 10am-noon, 2-7pm; Oct-May 10am-noon, 2-5pm. Closed mid-Nov to mid-Dec. 2,29€ (child 1,37€). ☎ 04 93 80 47 61.

Église St-Martin-St-Augustin – Open daily (except Mon and Sun afternoons) 8.30am-noon, 2-4pm. ☎ 04 93 92 60 45.

Palais Lascaris – Open daily (except Mon) 10am-noon, 2-6pm. Closed in Nov. No charge. ☎ 04 93 62 72 40.

Chapelle de la Miséricorde – Open Tue 2.30-5.30pm; the other days on request. Apply to M. Dunan, 2 Place Pierre Gautier 06300 Nice.

Musée Marc-Chagall – ♿ Open daily (except Tue) 10am-5pm (Jul-Sep 6pm), last admission 30min before closing time. Closed 1 Jan, 1 May, 25 Dec. 4,57€ (exhibition 5,79€. ☎ 04 93 53 87 20.

Musée Matisse (Villa des Arènes) – ♿ Open daily (except Tue) 10am-5pm (Apr-Sep 6pm). Closed 1 Jan, 1 May, 25 Dec 3,81€. ☎ 04 93 81 08 08.

Musée Archéologique – ♿ Open daily (except Mon) 10am-1pm, 2-5pm; Apr-Sep daily (except Mon) 10am-noon, 2-6pm. Closed mid-Nov to early Dec, 1 Jan, 1 May, 25 Dec. 3,81€, including access to the archeological site. No charge 1st Sun of each month. ☎ 04 93 81 59 57.

Site Archéologique Gallo-Romain – Same times and charges as for the Musée Archéologique.

Musée Franciscain – Open daily (except Sun) 10am-noon, 3-6pm. Closed public holidays. No charge. ☎ 04 93 81 00 04.

Musée des Beaux-Arts Jules-Chéret – Open daily (except Mon) 10am-noon, 2-6pm. Closed 1 Jan, 1 May, 25 Dec. 3,80€. No charge 1st Sun of each month. ☎ 04 92 15 28 28.

Musée d'Art Naïf A.-Jakovsky – Open daily (except Tue) 10am-noon, 2-6pm. Closed 1 Jan, Easter, 1 May, 25 Dec. 3,81€. No charge 1st Sun of each month. ☎ 04 93 71 78 33.

Parc Phoenix – ও Open mid-Mar to mid-Oct 9am-7pm; mid-Oct to mid-Mar 9am-5pm. 6,40€ (child 3,81€). ☎ 04 93 18 03 33.

Law Faculty: Chagall's mosaic – Open daily (except Sat-Sun) 9-11.30am, 2-5pm during the academic year. ☎ 04 92 15 70 01.

Musée d'Art Moderne et d'Art Contemporain – Open daily (except Tue) 10am-6pm. Closed 1 Jan, 1 May, Sun de Pâques, 25 Dec 3,81€, No charge 1st Sun of each month. ☎ 04 93 62 61 62.

Acropolis-Palais des Congrès – Guided tours on request. ☎ 04 93 92 82 35.

Museum d'Histoire Naturelle – Open daily (except Tue) 9am-noon, 2-6pm. Closed mid-Aug to mid-Sep, 1 Jan, Easter, 1st May, 25 Dec. 25F. ☎ 04 93 55 15 24.

Cathédrale Orthodoxe Russe – Closed Sun mornings and on the mornings of Russian Orthodox holidays. 2,29€. ☎ 04 93 96 88 02.

Église Ste-Jeanne-d'Arc – Open daily 8.30-11.30am, 3.30-6pm. Apply to ☎ 04 93 84 54 60.

Prieuré du Vieux-Logis – Guided tours (45min) Wed, Thu, Sat, 1st Sun of each month. 3-6pm. No charge. ☎ 04 93 88 11 34.

Musée de Terra Amata – Open daily (except Mon) 9am-noon, 2-6pm. Closed 1 Jan, Easter, 1 May, 25 Dec. 3,81€ (no charge for children). No charge 1st Sun of each month. Audiovisual tour with commentary in French, English, Italian and German. ☎ 04 93 55 59 93.

Musée des Arts Asiatiques – ও Open daily (except Tue) 10am-5pm; May to mid-Oct daily (except Tue) 10am-6pm. Closed 1 Jan, 1 May, 25 Dec. 5,34€. No charge 1st Sun of each month. ☎ 04 92 29 37 00.

Observatoire du Mont-Gros – Guided tours (2hr) Sat at 3pm. 4,5€. ☎ 04 93 85 85 58.

Église St-François-de-Paule – Open daily (except Sun).

NOTRE-DAME-DE-LAGHET

Sanctuaire Notre-Dame-de Laghet: Museum – Sanctuaire: Open daily (except Tue) 7.30am-9.30pm. Museum: open in summer daily (except Tue) 3.30-5.30pm; open in winter daily (except Tue) 3-5pm. Closed 1st fortnight in Jan. No charge. ☎ 04 93 41 50 50.

Chapelle NOTRE-DAME-DES-FONTAINES

Guided tours 3-5pm. Apply to the tourist office in La Brigue.

P

PEILLE
🚹 Mairie – 06440 – ☎ 04 93 91 71 71

Église – Tours on request. Apply to the Mairie. ☎ 04 93 91 71 71.

Musée du Terroir – Open Sun 2-5pm. No charge.

Via Ferrata – Access 3,05€. Equipment can be hired from the bar l'Absinthe. If you wish to be accompanied, apply to mountain guides in Sospel or Tende. ☎ 04 93 91 71 71.

PEILLON
🚹 Mairie – 06440 – ☎ 04 93 79 91 04

Chapelle des Pénitents-Blancs – Tours of the interior on request one week in advance. Apply to the Mairie at ☎ 04 93 79 91 04.

Île de PORQUEROLLES

Conservatoire Botanique National Méditerranéen – Open May-Sep 9.30am-0.30pm, 1.30-5pm. ☎ 04 94 12 30 32.

Le PRADET
🚹 Place du Général-de-Gaulle – 83220 – ☎ 04 94 21 71 69

Musée de la Mine de Cap-Garonne – Guided tours (1hr 15min) during school holidays 2-5pm (Jul-Aug: last admission at 5.30pm);outside school holidays Wed, Sat-Sun and public holidays 2-5pm. Closed 1 Jan and 25 Dec. 6,10€. ☎ 04 94 08 32 46

R

RAYOL-CANADEL-SUR-MER 🄸 Place du Rayol – 83240 – ☎ 04 94 05 65 69

Estate – Open end of Jan to end of Nov (last admission 45min before closing time) 9.30am-0.30pm, 2.30-6.30pm; Jul-Aug 9.30am-0.30pm, 3-7pm; the rest of the year by appointment only. 6,10€ (child 3,05€). ☎ 04 98 04 44 00.

Sentier marin – Open early Jul to end of Aug only. Guided underwater tours of Mediterranean flora and fauna (1hr 30min) Open daily (except Sat). Reservation and payment required in advance. 12,20€ (child 9,15€). All equipment is supplied on the premises (diver's suit, mask, flippers and tuba).

ROQUEBILLIÈRE

Église St-Michel-du-Gast – ♿ Guided tours 10am-noon, 2-6pm. No charge. ☎ 04 93 03 45 62.

ROQUEBRUNE-CAP-MARTIN 🄸 214 Avenue Aristide-Briand – 06190 ☎ 04 93 35 62 87

Donjon – Apr-Sep: 10am-noon30, 2-6pm30 (Jul-Aug: 10am-noon30, 3-7pm30); Feb-Mar and Oct: 10am-noon30, 2-6pm; Nov-Jan: 10am-noon30, 2-5pm. 3,04€. ☎ 04 93 35 07 22.

Église Ste-Marguerite – 3-5pm30.

Le Cabanon de Le Corbusier – Guided tours Tue at 10am and Fri at 10am; Jul-Aug Tue at 10am, Fri at 4pm by appointment. Apply to the tourist office. 7,62€. ☎ 04 93 35 62 87, fax 04 93 28 57 00.

ROQUEBRUNE-SUR-ARGENS 🄸 1 Rue Jean-Aicard – 83520 – ☎ 04 94 19 89 89

Église St-Pierre and St-Paul – Open afternoons daily. ☎ 04 94 45 72 70.

Chapelle St-Pierre – Apply to the tourist office. ☎ 04 94 45 72 70.

Musée du Patrimoine Roquebrunois – ♿ Open Jun-Sep daily (except Sun and Mon) 10-11.30am, 2-5.30pm; Oct-May open Thu and Sat 10am-noon, 2-6pm. Closed public holidays. 1,52€. ☎ 04 94 45 34 28.

Notre-Dame-de-Pitié – Apply to the tourist office. ☎ 04 94 45 75 51.

S

ST-CYR-SUR-MER

Musée de Tauroentum – Open daily (except Tue) 3-6pm. 2,29€. ☎ 04 94 26 30 46.

SAINT-DALMAS-VALDEBLORE

Church – Apply to M. Alcoy. ☎ 04 93 02 82 29.

ST-MARTIN-DE-PEILLE

Church – Closed for restoration work. ☎ 04 93 91 71 71.

ST- MARTIN -VÉSUBIE

Madone de Fenestre – Open Open daily de mid-Jun to mid-Sep

ST-MARTIN-VÉSUBIE 🄸 Place Félix-Faure – 06450 – ☎ 04 93 03 21 28

Chapelle des Pénitents-Blancs – Guided tours by appointment. Apply to the tourist Office.

ST-PAUL 🄸 Maison de la Tour, Rue Grande – 06570 – ☎ 04 93 32 86 95

Musée d'Histoire Locale – Open 10am-0.30pm, 1.30-5.30pm. Closed 1 Jan, 25 Dec. 3,05€. ☎ 04 93 32 41 13.

Fondation Maeght – Open 10am-0.30pm, 2.30-6pm; Jul-Sep: 10am-7pm. 7,62€. No charge for children under 10 years of age. ☎ 04 93 32 81 63.

ST-PONS

Church – Open in the afternoons by appointment. ☎ 04 93 55 07 94 (before 11am).

ST-RAPHAËL
🅱 Rue Waldeck-Rousseau – 83700 – ☎ 04 94 19 52 52

Musée Archéologique – Open Jun-Sep daily (except Sun and Mo 10am-noon, 2-5.30pm; Oct-May daily (except Sun and Mon) 10am-noon, 3-6.30pm. Closed public holidays. 1,52€. ☎ 04 94 19 25 75.

ST-TROPEZ
🅱 Quai Jean-Jaurès – 83990 – ☎ 04 94 97 45 21

L'Annonciade, Musée de St-Tropez – Open daily (except Tue) 10am-noon, 2-6pm; Jun-Sep 10am-noon, 3-7pm. Closed in Nov, 1 Jan, 1 May, Ascension, 25 Dec. 4,57€. ☎ 04 94 97 04 01.

Maison des Papillons – Open Avr-Oct and mid-Dec to early Jan daily (except Tue) 10am-noon, 2-6pm; Jun-Oct daily (except Tue) 10am-noon, 3-7pm. Closed 1, 16-18 May, 14 Jul 3,05€. ☎ 04 94 97 63 45.

Musée Naval – Open Apr-Sep daily (except Tue) 11am-6pm (last admission 30min before closing time); Oct-Mar daily (except Tue) 10am-noon, 1-5pm. Closed in Nov, 1 Jan, 1 May, Ascension, 25 Dec. 3,81€. ☎ 04 94 97 59 43.

Presqu'île de ST TROPEZ

Phare de Camarat: Lighthouse – Open mid-Jun to end of Sep 2-5pm.

ST-VALLIER-DE-THIEY
🅱 10 Place de la Tour – 06460 – ☎ 04 93 42 78 00

Souterroscope de la Baume Obscure – Open May-Sep 10am-5pm, Sun and public holidays 10am-7pm; Jul-Aug 10am-7pm; Oct-Apr daily (except Mon) 10am-5pm. Closed mid-Dec to end of Jan. 7,62€ (child 3,81€). ☎ 04 93 42 61 63.

Observatoire du CERGA – Guided tours (2hr) May to end of Sep Sun at 3pm30. 4,5€. ☎ 04 93 85 85 58.

STE-MAXIME
🅱 Promenade Simon-Loriere – 83120 – ☎ 04 94 55 75 55

Musée des Traditions Locales – Open daily (except Tue) 10am-noon, 3-6pm, Mon 3-6pm. 2,29€. ☎ 04 94 96 70 30.

Musée du Phonographe et de la Musique Mécanique – ♿ Open Easter to end of Sep daily (except Mon and Tue) 10am-noon, 3-6pm. 3,05€. ☎ 04 94 96 50 52.

SAORGE

Couvent des Franciscains – Open Apr-Oct daily (except Tue) 2-6pm; Nov-Mar Sat-Sun 2-5pm. 3,96€. ☎ 04 93 04 55 55.

SEILLANS
🅱 Rue du Valat – 83440 – ☎ 04 94 76 85 91

Dorothy Tanning Bequest: Museum – Open mid-Jun to mid-Sep daily (except Mon and Sun) 10am-noon, 3-7pm; mid-Sep to mid-Jun 2-6pm. Closed 1 Jan, 1 May, 14 Jul, 25 Dec. 1,52€. ☎ 04 94 76 85 91.

Notre-Dame-de-l'Ormeau – Open Jul-Aug Tue, Thu 11am-noon, Sun 10.30am-0.30pm, 2-6pm. ☎ 04 94 76 97 65; Sep-Jun Thu 11am-noon, Sun 10.30am-0.30pm by appointment. Apply to the tourist office at ☎ 04 94 76 85 91.

La SEYNE-SUR-MER
🅱 Place Ledru-Rollin – 83500 – ☎ 04 94 94 73 09

Fort Balaguier: Musée Naval – Open mid-Jun to mid-Sep daily (except Mon) 10am-noon, 3-7pm; mid-Sep to mid-Jun daily (except Mon) 10am-noon, 2-6pm. Closed in Jan, 1 May, 25 Dec. 1,52€. ☎ 04 94 94 84 72.

SIX-FOURS-LES-PLAGES
🅱 Promenade Charles-de-Gaulle – 83140 – ☎ 04 94 07 02 01

Collégiale St Pierre – Summer: 3-7pm, Sun 9am-noon, 3-7pm. Winter: 2-6pm, Sun 10am-noon, 2-6pm. ☎ 04 94 34 24 75.

Chapelle de Notre-Dame-du-Mai – Open by appointment only. Apply to M. Peyrat. ☎ 04 94 25 50 39.

Chapelle Notre-Dame-de-Pépiole – Guided tours 3-6pm.

SILLANS-LA-CASCADE

Tourist office – ☎ 04 94 04 78 05.

SOLLIÈS-VILLE

Église – Apply to the Maison Jean-Aicard.

Maison Jean-Aicard – Guided tours (15min) May-Oct daily (except Tue and Sun) at 10am, Mon 2.30-4.30pm; Nov-Apr (except Sun-Mon mornings and Tue) the 2nd and 3rd Sat-Sun of each month at 10am, 2-4pm. Closed Pentecost, Easter, 1 Nov, 25 Dec, 1 Jan. No charge. ☎ 04 94 33 72 02.

SOSPEL   🖪 Le Pont-Vieux – 06380 – ☎ 04 93 04 15 80

Fort St-Roch – Guided tours (1hr 30min) Apr to end of Oct Sat-Sun and public holidays 2-6pm; Jun-Sep daily (except Mon). 3,81€ (child 2,29€). ☎ 04 93 04 14 41 or ☎ 04 93 04 00 70.

T

TAMARIS-SUR-MER

Villa Tamaris-Pacha – Open daily (except Mon) 2-6pm. Closed 1 Jan, 1 May and 25 Dec. No charge. ☎ 04 94 06 84 00.

Le Massif du TANNERON

Chapelle Notre-Dame-de-Peygros – Closed. Apply to the Mairie. ☎ 04 93 60 68 13.

TENDE   🖪 Avenue du 16-Septembre-1947 – 06430 – ☎ 04 93 04 73 71

Musée des Merveilles – ♿ Open May to mid-Oct daily (except Tue) 10am-6.30pm; mid-Oct to end of Apr daily (except Tue) 10am-5pm. Closed mid-Mar to end of Mar and mid-Nov to end of Nov, 1 Jan, 25 Dec. 4,57€. No charge 1st Sun of each month. ☎ 04 93 04 32 50.

Abbaye du THORONET

Open Apr-Sep 9am-7pm, Sun 9am-noon, 2-7pm; Oct-Mar 10am-1pm, 2-5pm. Closed 1 Jan, 1 May, 1 and 11 Nov, 25 Dec. 5,49€. ☎ 04 94 60 43 90.

TOULON   🖪 Place Raimu – 83000 – ☎ 04 94 18 53 00

Musée de la Marine – Open Apr-Sep 10am-6.30pm; Oct-Mar daily (except Tue) 10am-noon, 2-6pm. Closed 1 Jan, 1 May, Nov, 25 Dec. 4,57€. ☎ 04 94 02 02 01.

Église St-François-de-Paule – Open daily (except Sun) 10am-noon, 3-6pm.

Cathédrale Ste Marie – Open daily 9am-noon, 3-5.30pm (closed during Mass). ☎ 04 94 92 28 91.

Musée du Vieux Toulon – Open daily (except Sun) 2-5.45pm. Closed public holidays. No charge. ☎ 04 94 62 11 07 or ☎ 04 94 92 29 29.

Muséum – Open 9.30am-noon, 2-6pm, Sat-Sun 1-6pm. Closed public holidays. No charge. ☎ 04 94 36 81 10.

Musée d'Art – Open daily (except Sun) 2-5.45pm. Closed public holidays. No charge. ☎ 04 94 93 15 54.

Musée de la Figurine – Tues-Sat 10am-12.30pm, 1.30-6pm. No charge. ☎ 04 94 93 07 59.

Boat Tour of Toulon Harbour – Tour of Toulon harbour with commentary (1hr) from landing-stage on Quai Cronstad, beside the Préfecture Maritime, mid-Apr to end of Oct mornings and afternoons. 8,38€. Reservations from SNRTM, 1247 Route du Faron, ☎ 04 94 62 41 14.

Téléphérique du Mont Faron – Operates Jun-Sep daily (except Mon) 9.30am-noon, 2-6.30pm; mid-Jun to mid-Sep daily (except Mon) 9.30am-7pm (Jul-Aug 7.45pm); Oct-May daily (except Mon) 9.30am-noon, 2-5.30pm (Apr-May and Oct 6pm). Closed Dec-Jan, public holidays (except 14 Jul and 15 Aug). 5,79€ AR (child 3,96€). 8,54€ for a combined ticket with the zoo (child 5,49€). ☎ 04 94 92 68 25.

Mont Faron: Zoo – ♿ Open May-Sep 10am-6.30pm; Oct-Apr 2-5.30pm. 6,10€ (child 4,60€). ☎ 04 94 88 07 89.

Tour Royale – Open Apr-Sep 10am-6.30pm; Oct-Mar by appointment. Closed in Nov, 1 Jan, 1 May and 25 Dec. 4,57€. ☎ 04 94 02 02 01.

Musée-Mémorial du Débarquement de Provence – ♿ Open Jul-Sep 9.45am-0.45pm, 1.45-6.30pm (last admission 1hr before closing time); May-Jun daily (except Mon) 9.45am-0.45pm, 2-6pm; Oct-Apr daily (except Mon) 9.45-11.45am, 2-5.30pm. 3,65€. ☎ 04 94 88 08 09.

TOURRETTE-LEVENS

Église – Open daily (except Fri 5-6.30pm).

Château: Natural History Exhibition – Open Apr-Oct 2-6pm; Nov-Mar 2-5.30pm. No charge. Closed 1 Jan. ☎ 04 93 91 03 20.

TOURRETTES-SUR-LOUP   🖪 5 Route de Vence – 06140 – ☎ 04 93 24 18 93

Chapelle St Jean – By appointment only. Apply to the Mairie. ☎ 04 93 59 30 11.

TOURTOUR   🖪 Avenue des Ormeaux – 83690 – ☎ 04 94 70 54 36

Musée des Fossiles – Open mid-Jun to mid-Sep daily (except Tue) 2-6pm; school holidays daily (except Tue) 3-5pm; the rest of the year open Tue by appointment. No charge. ☎ 04 94 70 57 20 or ☎ 04 94 70 56 06.

Moulin à Huile – Open mid-Jun to mid-Sep, depending on temporary exhibitions. Closed mid-Sep to mid-Jun. No charge. ☎ 04 94 70 57 20 or ☎ 04 94 70 56 06.

La TURBIE

Le Trophée des Alpes – Open mid-Jun to mid-Sep 9.30am-7pm; Apr to mid-Jun 9.30am-6pm; mid-Sep to end of Mar daily (except Mon) 10am-5pm. Closed 1 Jan, 1 May, 1 and 11 Nov, 25 Dec. 3,96€. ☎ 04 93 41 20 84.

Forêt de TURINI

Col St-Jean: Fort Suchet – Open Jul to end of Aug. Apply to the tourist office in Sospel. ☎ 04 93 04 15 80.

V

Le VAL

Musée du Santon – ♿ Summer: 10am-0.30pm, 3-5.30pm. Winter: 9.30am-noon, 2-5.30pm. Closed 1 Jan, 25 Dec. 1,52€. ☎ 04 94 37 02 22.

Musée d'Art Sacré – ♿ Same times and charges as for the Musée du Santon.

Musée de la Figurine Historique – ♿ Same times and charges as for the Musée du Santon.

VALBONNE   🖪 Espace de la Vignasse – 06560 – ☎ 04 93 12 34 50

Musée du Patrimoine – Open May-Sep daily (except Mon) 3-7pm; Oct-May Open daily (except Mon) 2-6pm. Closed end of Dec to end of Jan. 3,75€. ☎ 04 93 12 96 54.

VALDEBLORE   🖪 06000 – ☎ 04 93 02 88 59

Pic de la Colmiane – Chair-lift reserved for skiers Sep-Jun Sat-Sun 10am-6pm; Jul-Aug daily. 3,51€ (season ticket available). ☎ 04 93 02 83 54.

VALLAURIS   🖪 Square du 8-Mai-1945 – 06227 – ☎ 04 93 63 82 58

Musée National "La Guerre and la Paix" – Same times and charges as for the Musée Magnelli - Musée de la Céramique.

Musée Magnelli - Musée de la Céramique – Open daily (except Tue) 10am-noon, 2-6pm ; Jun-Sep daily (except Tue) 10am-6.30pm. Closed 1 Jan, 1 May, 1 Nov, 25 Dec. 2,59€, No charge 1st Sun of each month. ☎ 04 93 64 98 05.

Musée de la Poterie – ♿ Open May-Oct 9am-6pm, Sun and public holidays 2-6pm; Feb-Apr 2-6pm. Closed Nov-Jan. 2,29€. ☎ 04 93 64 66 51.

VARAGES

Church – Guided tours by appointment. Apply to Mme Mione. ☎ 04 94 77 66 36.

Musée des Faïences – Open end of Jun to mid-Sep 3-7pm. 2,29€. ☎ 04 94 77 60 39.

Atelier de Faïence – ♿ Open daily (except Thu) 9am-noon, 3-6pm. Prices not communicated. ☎ 04 94 77 64 10.

VENANSON

Chapelle St-Sébastien – Open by appointment. Apply to the priest or the restaurant "La Bella Vista". ☎ 04 93 03 23 24 or ☎ 04 93 03 25 11.

VENCE

Chapelle du Rosaire (Chapelle Matisse) – Open Mon, Wed and Sat 2-5.30pm; Tue and Thu 10-11.30am, 2-5.30pm, Sun 10.45-11.45am. Also open Fri during school holidays 2-5.30pm. ☎ 04 93 58 03 26, fax 04 98 58 21 10.

Château de Villeneuve-Fondation Émile-Hugues – Open daily (except Mon) 10am-0.30pm, 2-6pm; Jul-Sep daily (except Mon) 10am-6pm. Closed 1 Jan, 1 May, 25 Dec. 4,57€. ☎ 04 93 24 24 23 or ☎ 04 93 58 15 78.

Cathédrale – Guided tours of the choir stalls by appointment in summer. ☎ 04 93 58 42 00.

Galerie Beaubourg-Château Notre-Dame-des-Fleurs – Open daily (except Sun) 11am-7pm. ☎ 04 93 24 52 00.

VIEUX-PIERREFEU

Musée "Hors du temps" – Open Jul-Aug 10am-noon, 3-7pm; the rest of the year by appointment only. Apply to the Mairie. 1,52€. ☎ 04 93 08 58 18.

VILLECROZE

Caves – Guided tours (15min) Jul to mid-Sep 10am-noon, 2.30-7pm; May-Jun 2-6pm; winter school holidays 2-6pm; Mar and mid-Sep to mid-Oct Sat-Sun 2-6pm. Closed mid-Oct to winter school holidays. 1,52€. ☎ 04 94 70 63 06.

VILLEFRANCHE-SUR-MER🖪 Jardin François-Binon – 06230 – ☎ 04 93 01 73 68

Chapelle St-Pierre – Open mid-Jun to mid-Sep daily (except Mon) 10am-noon, 4-8.30pm; mid-Sep to mid-Dec daily (except Mon) 9.30am-noon, 2-6pm; mid-Dec to mid-Mar daily (except Mon) 9.30am-noon, 2-5pm; mid-Mar to mid-Jun Open daily (except Mon) 9.30am-noon, 3-7pm. Closed mid-Nov to mid-Dec, 25 Dec. 1,83€. ☎ 04 93 76 90 70.

Collection Roux – Open Jun-Sep daily (except Tue) 9am-noon, 3-6pm, Sun 3-6pm; Jul-Aug daily (except Tue) 10am-noon, 3-7pm, Sun 3-7pm; Oct-May daily (except Tue) 10am-noon, 2-5pm, Sun 2-5pm. Closed public holidays. No charge. ☎ 04 93 76 33 27.

Musée Volti – Open Jul-Aug daily (except Tue) 10am-noon, 3-7pm, Sun 3-7pm; Jun and Sep daily (except Tue) 9am-noon, 3-6pm, Sun 3-6pm; Oct-May daily (except Tue) 10am-noon, 2-5pm, Sun 2-5pm. Closed in Nov, 1 Jan, 1 May, 25 Dec. No charge. ☎ 04 93 76 33 33.

Musée Goetz-Boumeester – Open Jun-Sep daily (except Tue) 9am-noon, 3-6pm, Sun 3-6pm; Jul-Aug daily (except Tue) 10am-noon, 3-7pm, Sun 3-7pm; Oct-May daily (except Tue) 10am-noon, 2-5pm, Sun 2-5pm. Closed 1 Jan, 1 May, in Nov and 25 Dec. No charge. ☎ 04 93 76 33 27.

VILLENEUVE-LOUBET

Musée de l'Art Culinaire – Open daily (except Mon) 2-6pm (end of Jun to end of Sep 7pm). Closed in Nov and public holidays. 3,80€. ☎ 04 93 20 80 51.

Musée d'Histoire et d'Art – Open 9am-noon, 2-6pm, Sat 9.30am-0.30pm, Sun 10am-noon. Closed 1 Jan, 1 May and Christmas. No charge. ☎ 04 92 02 60 56.

Index

O

P

Q — R

S

W

Z

Notes

Please write to us !
Your input will help us to improve our guides.

Please send this questionnaire to the following address:
**MICHELIN TRAVEL PUBLICATIONS, The Edward Hyde Building
38 Clarendon Road Watford Herts WD1 1SX**

1. Is this the first time you have purchased THE GREEN GUIDE? yes   no

2. Which title did you buy?:

3. What influenced your decision to purchase this guide?

	Not important at all	Somewhat important	Important	Very important
Cover				
Clear, attractive layout				
Structure				
Cultural information				
Practical information				
Maps and plans				
Michelin quality				
Loyalty to THE GREEN GUIDE collection				

Your comments :

4. How would you rate the following aspects of THE GREEN GUIDE?

	Poor	Average	Good	Excellent
Maps at the beginning of the guide				
Maps and plans throughout the guide				
Description of the sites (style, detail...)				
Depth of cultural information				
Amount of practical information				
Format				

Please comment if you have responded poor or average on any of the above:

5. What do you think about the establishments provided in the guide?

HOTELS:	Not Enough	Sufficient	Too many
All categories			
"Budget"			
"Moderate"			
"Expensive"			

RESTAURANTS:	Not Enough	Sufficient	Too many
All categories			
"Budget"			
"Moderate"			
"Expensive"			

Your comments:

6. On a scale of 1-20, please rate THE GREEN GUIDE (1 being the lowest, 20 being the highest):

How would you suggest we improve these guides?

1. Maps and Plans:

2. Sights:

3. Establishments:

4. Practical Information:

5. Other:

Demographic information: (optional)

Male   Female   Age

Name:

Address: